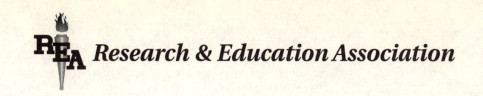

Research & Education Association

The Best Teachers' Test Preparation for the

OGET™/OSAT™

Oklahoma General Education Test™
(Field 74)

Oklahoma Subject Area Tests™
(Fields 50 & 51)

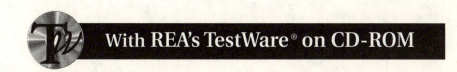

With REA's TestWare® on CD-ROM

Staff of
Research & Education Association

Foreword by
David Rosen, M.A.

Former Program Director
Oklahoma Teacher's Recruitment Program

For updates to the test or this book visit:
www.rea.com/state/oget.htm

Research & Education Association
61 Ethel Road West
Piscataway, New Jersey 08854
E-mail: info@rea.com

The Best Teachers' Test Preparation for the OGET™/OSAT™ (Oklahoma General Education Test™ and Oklahoma Subject Area Tests™)
With TestWare® on CD-ROM

Published 2010

Copyright © 2006 by Research & Education Association, Inc.
All rights reserved. No part of this book may be reproduced in any form without permission of the publisher.

Printed in the United States of America

Library of Congress Control Number 2006923800

ISBN-13: 978-0-7386-0154-0
ISBN-10: 0-7386-0154-3

Windows® is a registered trademark of Microsoft Corporation.

The OGET/OSAT Test Objectives presented in this book were created and implemented by the Oklahoma Commission for Teacher Preparation and Pearson Education, Inc. For further information visit the OCTP website at *www.octp.org*.

For all references in this book, Oklahoma General Education Test™, Oklahoma Subject Area Tests™, OGET™, and OSAT™ are trademarks of the Oklahoma Commission for Teacher Preparation and Pearson Education, Inc.

REA® and TestWare® are registered trademarks of Research & Education Association, Inc.

CONTENTS

OGET

——————————————— OSAT ———————————————

Contents

Foreword

It is my pleasure to welcome you to the extraordinary, extra-ordinary, world of education. As a tenured English Instructor and former Program Director for the Oklahoma Teacher's Recruitment Program, I can assure you that the key to success in academia, as in any field of endeavor, lies in your preparation and practice. Whether it is in the preparation of your daily lesson plans, or in your preparation to enter the discipline, becoming familiar with the appropriate materials will greatly enhance your chances for success. Preparation and practice are what REA's *The Best Teachers' Test Preparation for the OGET/OSAT* is all about.

This comprehensive guidebook will familiarize you with everything you will need to successfully complete the Oklahoma General Education/Subject Area Test. From how to prepare for the actual exam, to detailed explanations of how the test's questions and answers sections are scored, as well as the criteria that will be used when scoring them, this is your opportunity to "take the test," before you actually do. Once you're acquainted with the style, structure, and overall concepts of the *OGET/OSAT*, the stress of the unknown will be eliminated and the more you'll relax on test day. Preparation will help you to answer the questions with more confidence, and this confidence will translate into higher test scores and greater academic opportunities down the road.

A key factor in preparation for the *OGET/OSAT* is practice. Face it, the more you practice at something, whether it's playing the piano, throwing a football, or taking a certification exam, the better you get. So, it goes without saying that the more time you spend with this book, the better prepared you'll be and the better prepared you are, the higher your test scores will be.

Since REA's study guides contain a wealth of information, I suggest that rather than trying to cram it all into your brain at once, you review small sections at a time. Spend a few minutes at various times during the day with the guide, thumbing through the various sections not only for the information, but also for practice. You can answer several questions, then check yourself with the accompanying details section. Working back and forth like this will allow you to monitor your progress while you take note of subject areas where you need to improve. After a few practice sections, you'll know your strengths and weaknesses. Then, of course, you can devote additional study time and energy to the areas of the test that give you the most headaches. By the time you take the actual test, you'll have a clear understanding of what is required and how to deal with each section.

Oklahoma is a wonderful place to live and teach. It is a combination of agrarian beauty and high academic standards. Combine the information in this guidebook with your own dedication to practice and preparation, and you'll never find a place or an occupation more rewarding. Good luck, and again to all my new colleagues, welcome to the extra-ordinary world of education.

—Prof. David M. Rosen

About Research & Education Association

Founded in 1959, Research & Education Association is dedicated to publishing the finest and most effective educational materials—including software, study guides, and test preps—for students in middle school, high school, college, graduate school, and beyond.

REA's Test Preparation series includes books and software for all academic levels in almost all disciplines. Research & Education Association publishes test preps for students who have not yet completed high school, as well as for high school students preparing to enter college. Students from countries around the world seeking to attend college in the United States will find the assistance they need in REA's publications. For college students seeking advanced degrees, REA publishes test preps for many major graduate school admission examinations in a wide variety of disciplines, including engineering, law, and medicine. Students at every level, in every field, with every ambition can find what they are looking for among REA's publications.

REA's practice tests are always based upon the most recently administered exams and include every type of question that you can expect on the actual exams.

REA's publications and educational materials are highly regarded and continually receive an unprecedented amount of praise from professionals, instructors, librarians, parents, and students. Our authors are as diverse as the fields represented in the books we publish. They are well-known in their respective disciplines and serve on the faculties of prestigious high schools, colleges, and universities throughout the United States and Canada.

Today, REA's wide-ranging catalog is a leading resource for teachers, students, and professionals.

We invite you to visit us at *www.rea.com* to find out how "REA is making the world smarter."

Acknowledgments

We would like to thank REA's Larry B. Kling, Vice President, Editorial, for supervising development; Pam Weston, Vice President, Publishing, for setting the quality standards for production integrity and managing the publication to completion; John Paul Cording, Vice President, Technology, for coordinating the design, development, and testing of REA's TEST*ware*® software; Christine Reilley, Senior Editor, for project management and preflight editorial review; Diane Goldschmidt, Associate Editor, for post-production quality assurance; Michelle Boykins, Heena Patel, and Amy Jamison, software project managers, for their tireless software testing efforts; Jeremy Rech, Graphic Artist, for interior page design; Christine Saul, Senior Graphic Artist, for cover design; and Jeff LoBalbo, Senior Graphic Artist, for post-production file mapping.

We gratefully acknowledge David M. Myton, Ph.D., Renay M. Scott, Ph.D., Karen Bondarchuk, M.F.A., John A. Lychner, Ph.D., Janet E. Rubin, Ph.D., Ellen R. Van't Hof, M.A., Nelson Maylone, Ph.D., and Ginny Mullen, Ph.D., for providing foundational material for this book. We also thank Al Davis, M.A, M.S., for editing this book in accordance with Oklahoma's OGET/OSAT standards.

We also gratefully acknowledge the team at Publication Services for editing, proofreading, and page composition.

Teach...
Lead...
Inspire...

INTRODUCTION

With this book in hand, you've taken an important step toward becoming a certified teacher in the state of Oklahoma. REA's all-new **OGET/OSAT** teacher certification test prep is designed to help you get into an Oklahoma classroom. The instructive chapters in this book provide complete coverage of the **Oklahoma OGET** and **OSAT** tests with in-depth reviews of every topic and area appearing on the exam. Full-length practice tests carefully derived from actual OGET (Field 74) and OSAT (Fields 50 and 51) exams will hone your test-taking skills. All practice test answers are explained in thorough detail to provide you with a greater understanding of the exam's content and difficulty. When you finish preparing with this book, you will be well-equipped with all the knowledge, practice, and strategies needed to succeed on these important exams.

ABOUT THE TESTS

What are the OGET and OSAT used for?

The Oklahoma General Education Test (OGET) is designed to assess state core general education knowledge and skills, including critical thinking, computation, and communication. The Oklahoma Subject Area Tests (OSAT) are designed to assess subject-matter knowledge and skills. The OSAT Elementary Education test consists of two subtests: One is for reading, language arts, and social studies, while the second covers math, science, health, and fine arts.

Am I required to take these tests if I hold a teaching certificate from another state?

Comparable test evaluation is now available for out-of-state candidates. Contact the State Director of Assessment at the Oklahoma Commission for Teacher Preparation, (405) 525-2612, for more information.

How is the test content determined?

The Oklahoma Commission for Teacher Preparation (OCTP) has the responsibility of developing a competency-based testing program for teacher candidates. The assessment was designed to examine competency in the following areas: general education, subject area, and professional teaching knowledge. Candidates for teacher licensure/certification are required to successfully complete the Oklahoma General Education Test (OGET), the Oklahoma Subject Area Test (OSAT), and the Oklahoma Professional Teaching Examination (OPTE).

Who administers the OGET and OSAT?

OCTP has contracted with National Evaluation Systems (NES) and the Buros Center for Testing to assist in the development, validation, and administration of the assessments included in the Certification Examinations for Oklahoma Educators (CEOE) program.

When are the OGET and OSAT tests offered? How long is the testing time?

The OGET and OSAT tests are offered five times a year. Test sessions are determined by the type of test you are taking. The OGET is only given in the morning. OSATs are given in both the morning and the afternoon. Additional information is available from the Oklahoma Commission for Teacher Preparation. The department can be contacted as follows:

Oklahoma Commission for Teacher Preparation
4545 N. Lincoln Blvd., Suite 275
Oklahoma City, OK 73105-3418
Phone: 405-525-2612
Fax: 405-525-0373
E-mail: octp@octp.org
Website: *www.octp.org*

Is there a registration fee?

Yes. Only cashiers' checks, money orders, or credit cards (Visa and MasterCard) are accepted for test fee payment. Information on testing fees and registration can be found in the CEOE Registration Bulletin available online at *www.ceoe.nesinc.com*.

HOW TO USE THIS BOOK

What do I study first?

We recommend beginning your study with the comprehensive chapter reviews. It is important to read over each review, noting crucial test-taking suggestions and insights. By studying each review thoroughly, you will reinforce basic skills that are vital to performing well on the OGET and OSAT. After reviewing, take the practice tests. This will familiarize you with the actual exam's format, procedures, and level of difficulty. An added bonus to taking these practice tests is knowing what to expect on exam day.

Apart from the book itself, we give you a CD-ROM with full-length practice tests. **We strongly recommend that you begin your preparation with the TEST*ware*® tests.** The software provides the added benefits of instantaneous, accurate scoring and enforced time conditions.

Wisely scheduling your study time is also a key component to your success on the OGET/OSAT. To best utilize your study time, follow our flexible study schedule at the end of this chapter. The schedule is based ideally on a seven-week program, but can be condensed if needed.

When should I start studying for the OGET/OSAT tests?

It is never too early to start studying for your test. Time is your ally here. The earlier you begin, the more time you will have to sharpen your skills and focus your efforts. Do not procrastinate! Cramming is not an effective way to study, since it does not allow you enough time to learn what will be required of you. It takes time to learn the tested areas and test format. Make the most of your time while you have it. Use it well to master the essentials necessary to pass.

FORMAT OF THE OGET/OSAT TESTS

What is the basic format of the OGET/OSAT?

The OGET includes both selected-response questions and a single constructed-response (writing assignment) question. There are approximately 80–100 selected-response (multiple-choice) questions that account for approximately 80% of the test's scaled score. Each constructed-response question offers four possible answer choices. The writing assignment accounts for 20% of the total scaled test score.

The OSAT Elementary Education subtest 1 focuses on reading, language arts, and social studies. Subtest 1 contains approximately 40 selected-responses that account for 85% of your score. As with the OGET, the OSAT's selected-response questions offer four possible answers. Subtest 1's single constructed-response assignment accounts for 15% of your total scaled test score. The OSAT Elementary Education subtest 2 focuses on mathematics, science, health and fitness, and fine arts. Subtest 2 contains approximately 40 selected-response questions.

The constructed-response assignment is intended to assess subject knowledge and skills, not writing ability. However, your response must be communicated clearly enough to be scored. Your response to the constructed-response assignment will be evaluated on the basis of the following criteria:

- The extent to which your response answers the question

- The accuracy and appropriateness of subject matter knowledge

- The quality and relevance of your supporting details

- The soundness of your argument and your understanding of the subject matter

About the Subject Reviews

The subject reviews in this book are designed purposefully to provide you critical insight into the content and form of the OGET and OSAT. For smarter study, we break down this part of test preparation into more manageable "chunks." Before you begin reviewing, it is important to note that your own schooling experience has taught you most of what is needed to answer the questions on the actual tests. Our review is written to help you fit and shape information acquired over the years into a context ideally suited for taking the OGET and OSAT.

You may also be taking test preparation classes for the OGET and OSAT, or have purchased other study guides and textbooks. Reviewing class notes and textbooks along with our subject reviews will provide you with an even better foundation for passing the OGET and OSAT.

SCORING THE OGET/OSAT

Your test score report will be mailed to you and to the Oklahoma Commission for Teacher Preparation approximately four weeks after you take the test. Unofficial scores will be available for online access by 5 p.m. CT on the official score report mailing date for each test administration. To access your unofficial scores, go to *www.ceoe.nesinc.com* and follow the score retrieval instructions.

Total test scores are reported as scaled scores. For the OGET and OSAT, scaled scores are reported using a range from 100 to 300, with 240 as the minimum passing scaled score. Your score report will indicate whether you have passed the test and will include your total test score and a description of your performance on the major content subareas of the test. These scores will provide you with valuable information for identifying the strengths and weaknesses in your content preparation.

And finally, if you do not do well on test day, don't panic! Each test can be taken again, so you can work on improving your score on your next test. A score on the OGET or OSAT that does not match your expectations does not mean you should change your plans about teaching.

Test-Taking Strategies

Although you may not be familiar with tests like the OGET/OSAT, this book will help acquaint you with this type of exam and help alleviate test-taking anxieties. Here are the key ways you can more easily get into an OGET/OSAT state of mind:

Become comfortable with the format of the OGET/OSAT. Practice tests are the best way to learn the format of the OGET/OSAT. When you take a practice test, try to simulate the environmental conditions of the actual testing facility. Remember, you are in training for the OGET/OSAT, and simulated testing conditions will only help you perform better. Stay calm and pace yourself. After simulating a test even once, you boost your chances of doing well, and you will be able to sit down for the actual OGET/OSAT with much more confidence.

Read all the possible answers. Examine each answer choice to ensure that you are not making a mistake. Jumping to conclusions without considering all the answers is a common test-taking error.

Use the process of elimination. GUESS if you do not know. If you do not know the answer immediately after reading the answer choices, try to eliminate as many of the answers as possible. Eliminating just one or two answer choices gives you a far better chance of selecting the right answer.

Do not leave an answer blank. There is no penalty for wrong answers, and you might even get it right if you had to guess at the answer.

Familiarize yourself with the test's directions and content. Familiarizing yourself with the directions and content of the OGET/OSAT not only saves you valuable time, but can also aid in reducing anxiety before the test. Many mistakes are caused by anxiety. It's simply better to go in knowing what you will face.

Mark it right! Be sure that the answer oval you mark corresponds to the appropriate number in the test booklet. The test is multiple-choice and is graded by machine. Marking just one answer in the wrong place can throw off the rest of the test. Correcting an error like this will deprive you of precious test time.

The Day of the Test

Your admission ticket lists your test site, test date, and reporting time. Report to the test site no later than 7:30 a.m. for the morning session or 12:30 p.m. for the afternoon session. Testing is scheduled to begin approximately one half hour after the reporting time. If you arrive late to a test session, you may not be admitted. If you are admitted late, you will not be given any additional time beyond the scheduled ending time for the test session, and you will be required to sign a statement acknowledging this.

You **must** bring the following with you to the test site on test day:

- Your official admission ticket or a printout of your e-mail admission information (I-Ticket).

- Several sharpened No. 2 pencils with erasers (no pens); pencils will not be supplied at the test site.

- Two pieces of personal identification; one must contain a recent photograph.

After the Test

When you finish your test, hand in your materials and you will be dismissed. Then, you are free. Go home and relax. Meet with friends. Go out to dinner. Or go shopping. Whatever you do, make it a great day! After all you have done to get this far, you deserve it!

OGET/OSAT Study Schedule

The following study schedule allows for thorough preparation to pass the OGET/OSAT. This is a suggested seven-week course of study. This schedule can, however, be condensed if you have less time available to study, or expanded if you have more time. Whatever the length of your available study time, be sure to keep a structured schedule by setting aside ample time each day to study. Depending on your schedule, you may find it easier to study throughout the weekend. No matter which schedule works best for you, the more time you devote to studying for the OGET/OSAT, the more prepared and confident you will be on the day of the test.

Week	Activity
1	Take the practice tests on CD-ROM as a diagnostic tool. Your score will indicate where your strengths and weaknesses lie. Try to take the test under simulated exam conditions, and review the explanations for the questions you answered incorrectly.
2	Study the OGET/OSAT test objectives to get a better idea of the content on which you will be tested. You should make a list of the objectives that you know you will have the most trouble mastering so that you can concentrate your study on those areas.
3	Study *The Best Teachers' Test Preparation for the OGET/OSAT*. Take notes on the sections as you work through them, as writing will aid in your retention of information. Keep a list of the subject areas for which you may need additional aid.
4	Identify and review references and sources. Textbooks for college composition, science, social studies, arts, and mathematics courses will help in your preparation. You may also want to consult the Oklahoma curriculum website at *www.sde.state.ok.us.*
5	Condense your notes and findings. You should develop a structured outline detailing specific facts. You may want to use index cards to aid you in memorizing important facts and concepts.
6	Test yourself using the index cards. You may want to have a friend or colleague quiz you on key facts and items. Then, retake the tests on CD-ROM. Review the explanations for the questions you answered incorrectly.
7	Study any areas you consider to be your weaknesses by using your study materials, references, and notes. You may want to retake some tests on CD-ROM.

OGET

Oklahoma General Education Test

Review

Critical Thinking Skills: Reading and Communications

The reading portion of the OGET asks you to utilize critical reading and reading comprehension skills. The objectives for this section of the test are to understand the main ideas of the passage based on the supporting evidence or details and to understand the author's purpose, point of view, and/or intended meaning.

You will be asked to read a passage and answer questions about the material included in that passage. The reading section is entirely multiple choice. It will be to your benefit to read the questions about the particular passage first. This will give you an idea of what to look for and focus on as you are reading. It is also crucial that you understand the passage as a whole and comprehend the overall intention, meaning, or main idea of the material you have read.

This review was developed to prepare you for the reading section of the OGET. You will be guided through a step-by-step approach to attacking reading passages and questions. Also included are tips to help you quickly and accurately answer the questions that will appear in this section. By studying this review, you will greatly increase your chances of achieving a good score on the reading section of the OGET.

Fast Facts

The more you know about the skills tested, the better you will perform on the test.

Remember, the more you know about the skills tested, the better you will perform on the test. In this section, the objectives you will be tested on are contained in the following list:

SUBAREA I—CRITICAL THINKING SKILLS: READING AND COMMUNICATIONS

Competency 0001

Identify a writer's point of view and intended meaning.

The following topics are examples of content that may be covered under this competency.
- Identify the statement that best expresses the main idea of a paragraph or passage.
- Recognize ideas that support, illustrate, or elaborate the main idea of a paragraph or passage.
- Use the content, word choice, and phrasing of a passage to determine a writer's opinions or point of view (e.g., belief, position on an issue).

Competency 0002

Analyze the relationship among ideas in written material.

The following topics are examples of content that may be covered under this competency.
- Identify the sequence of events or steps presented in technical, scientific, or research material.
- Identify cause-effect relationships from information in a passage.
- Analyze relationships between ideas in opposition (e.g., pro and con).
- Identify a solution to a problem presented in a passage.
- Draw conclusions inductively and deductively from information stated or implied in a passage.

Competency 0003

Use critical reasoning skills to evaluate written material.

The following topics are examples of content that may be covered under this competency.
- Draw valid conclusions using information from written communications.
- Recognize the stated or implied assumptions on which the validity of an argument depends.
- Determine the relevance or importance of particular facts, examples, or graphic data to a writer's argument.
- Use inductive and deductive reasoning to recognize fallacies in the logic of a writer's argument.
- Evaluate the validity of analogies used in written material.
- Distinguish between fact and opinion in written material.
- Assess the credibility, objectivity, or bias of the writer or source of written material.

Competency 0004

Recognize the roles of purpose and audience in written communication.

The following topics are examples of content that may be covered under this competency.

- Recognize a writer's stated or implied purpose for writing (e.g., to persuade, to describe).
- Evaluate the appropriateness of written material for a specific purpose or audience.
- Recognize the likely effect on an audience of a writer's choice of a particular word or words (e.g., to evoke sympathy, to undermine an opposing point of view).

Competency 0005

Recognize unity, focus, and development in writing.

The following topics are examples of content that may be covered under this competency.

- Recognize unnecessary shifts in point of view (e.g., shifts from first to third person) or distracting details that impair the development of the main idea in a piece of writing.
- Recognize revisions that improve the unity and focus of a piece of writing.
- Recognize examples of well-developed writing.

To help you master these skills, we present examples of the types of questions you will encounter and explanations of how to answer them.

The Passages

The reading passages in the reading section are designed to be on the level of the type of material encountered in college textbooks. They will present you with very diverse subjects. Although you will not be expected to have prior knowledge of the information presented in the passages, you will be expected to know the fundamental reading comprehension techniques presented in this chapter. Only your ability to read and comprehend material will be tested.

The Questions

Each passage will be followed by a number of questions. The questions will ask you to make determinations based on what you have read. You will commonly encounter questions that will ask you to:

- Determine which of the given answer choices best expresses the main idea of the passage.

- Determine the author's purpose in writing the passage.

- Determine which fact best supports the writer's main idea.

- Know the difference between fact and opinion in a statement.

- Organize the information in the passage.

- Determine which of the answer choices best summarizes the information presented in the passage.

- Recall information from the passage.

- Analyze cause-and-effect relationships based on information in the passage.

- Determine the definition of a word as it is used in the passage.

- Answer a question based on information presented in graphic form.

- Answer a question based on an excerpt from a table of contents or an index.

Strategies for the Reading Section

The following is a recommended plan of attack to follow when answering the questions in the reading section.

When reading the passage,

Step 1: Read quickly while keeping in mind that questions will follow.

Step 2: Uncover the main idea or theme of the passage. Many times it is contained within the first few lines of the passage.

Step 3: Uncover the main idea of each paragraph. Usually it is contained in either the first or last sentence of the paragraph.

Step 4: Skim over the detailed points of the passage while circling key words or phrases. These are words or phrases such as *but, on the other hand, although, however, yet,* and *except.*

When answering the questions,

Step 1: Approach each question one at a time. Read it carefully.

Step 2: Uncover the main idea or theme of the passage. Many times it is contained within the first few lines of the passage.

Step 3: If the question is asking for an answer that can only be found in a specific place in the passage, save it for last since this type of question requires you to go back to the passage and therefore takes more of your time.

Additional Tips

- Read over the questions before reading the passage. This will give you an idea of what you are reading for.

- Look over all the passages first and then attack the passages that seem easiest and most interesting.

- Identify and underline what sentences are the main ideas of each paragraph.

- If a question asks you to draw inferences, your answer should reflect what is implied in the passage, rather than what is directly stated.

- Use the context of the sentence to find the meaning of an unfamiliar word.

- Identify which sentences are example sentences and label them with an "E." Determine whether or not the writer is using facts or opinions.

- Circle key transitions and identify dominant patterns of organization.

- Make your final response and move on. Don't dawdle or get frustrated by the really troubling passages. If you haven't gotten answers after two attempts, answer as best you can and move on.

- If you have time at the end, go back to the passages that were difficult and review them.

A Four-Step Approach

When you take the reading section of the OGET, you will have two tasks: to read the passage, and to answer the questions.

Of the two, carefully reading the passage is the more important; answering the questions is based on an understanding of the passage. What follows is a four-step approach to reading:

Step 1:   preview
Step 2:   read actively
Step 3:   review the passage
Step 4:   answer the questions

You should study the following exercises and use these four steps when you complete the reading section of the OGET.

Step 1: Preview

A preview of the reading passage will give you a purpose and a reason for reading; previewing is a good strategy to use when taking a test. Before beginning to read the passage (usually a four-minute activity if you preview and review), you should take about thirty seconds to look over the passage and questions. An effective way to preview the passage is to quickly read the first sentence of each paragraph, the concluding sentence of the passage, and the questions—but not the answers—following the passage. A passage follows; practice previewing the passage by reading the first sentence of each paragraph and the last line of the passage.

> **A preview of the reading passage will give you a purpose and a reason for reading.**

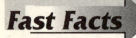
Fast Facts

Passage

That the area of obscenity and pornography is a difficult one for the Supreme Court is well documented. The Court's numerous attempts to define obscenity have proven unworkable and left the decision to the subjective preferences of the justices. Perhaps Justice Stewart put it best when, after refusing to define obscenity, he declared, but "I know it when I see it." Does the Court literally have to see it to know it? Specifically, what role does the fact-pattern, including the materials' medium, play in the Court's decision?

Several recent studies employ fact-pattern analysis in modeling the Court's decision making. These studies examine the fact-pattern or case characteristics, often with ideological and attitudinal factors, as a determinant of the decision reached by the Court. In broad terms, these studies owe their theoretical underpinnings to attitude theory. As the name suggests, attitude theory views the Court's attitudes as an explanation of its decisions.

These attitudes, however, do not operate in a vacuum. As Spaeth explains, "the activation of an attitude involves both an object and the situation in which that object is encountered." The objects to which the court directs its attitudes are litigants. The situation—the subject matter of the case—can be defined in broad or narrow terms. One may define the situation as an entire area of the law (e.g., civil liberties issues). On an even broader scale, the situation may be defined as the decision to grant certiorari or whether to defect from a minimum-winning coalition.

Defining the situation with such broad strokes, however, does not allow one to control for case content. In many specific issue areas, the cases present strikingly similar patterns. In examining the Court's search and seizure decisions, Segal found that a relatively small number of situational and case characteristic variables explain a high proportion of the Court's decisions.

Despite Segal's success, efforts to verify the applicability of fact-pattern analysis in other issue areas and using broad-based factors have been slow in forthcoming. Renewed interest in obscenity and pornography by federal and state governments as a result of lobbying campaigns by fundamentalist groups, the academic community, and other antipornography interest groups pro and con indicate the Court's decisions in this area deserve closer examination.

The Court's obscenity and pornography decisions also present an opportunity to study the Court's behavior in an area where the Court has granted significant decision-making authority to the states. In *Miller v. California* (1973) the Court announced the importance of local community standards in obscenity determinations. The Court's subsequent behavior may suggest how the Court will react in other areas where it has chosen to defer to the states (e.g., abortion).

Questions

1. The main idea of the passage is best stated in which of the following?

    A. The Supreme Court has difficulty convicting those who violate obscenity laws.

    B. The current definitions for obscenity and pornography provided by the Supreme Court are unworkable.

    C. Fact-pattern analysis is insufficient for determining the attitude of the Court toward the issues of obscenity and pornography.

    D. Despite the difficulties presented by fact-pattern analysis, Justice Segal found the solution in the patterns of search and seizure decisions.

2. The main purpose of the writer in this passage is to

    A. convince the reader that the Supreme Court is making decisions about obscenity based on their subjective views alone.

    B. explain to the reader how fact-pattern analysis works with respect to cases of obscenity and pornography.

    C. define obscenity and pornography for the layperson.

    D. demonstrate the role fact-pattern analysis plays in determining the Supreme Court's attitude about cases in obscenity and pornography.

3. Of the following, which fact best supports the writer's contention that the Court's decisions in the areas of obscenity and pornography deserve closer scrutiny?

    A. The fact that a Supreme Court Justice said, "I know it when I see it."

    B. Recent studies that employ fact-pattern analysis in modeling the Court's decision-making process.

    C. The fact that attitudes do not operate in a vacuum.

    D. The fact that federal and state governments, interested groups, and the academic community show renewed interest in the obscenity and pornography decisions by the Supreme Court.

4. Among the following statements, which states an opinion expressed by the writer rather than a fact?

    A. It is well documented that the area of obscenity and pornography is a difficult one for the Supreme Court.

    B. The objects to which a court directs its attitudes are the litigants.

    C. In many specific issue areas, the cases present strikingly similar fact-patterns.

    D. The Court's subsequent behavior may suggest how the Court will react in other legal areas.

5. The group of topics in the list that follows that best reflects the organization of the topics of the passage is

    A. I.   The difficulties of the Supreme Court
        II. Several recent studies
        III. Spaeth's definition of *attitude*
        IV. The similar patterns of cases
        V.   Other issue areas
        VI. The case of *Miller v. California*

    B. I.   The Supreme Court, obscenity, and fact-pattern analysis
        II. Fact-pattern analyses and attitude theory
        III. The definition of *attitude* for the Court
        IV. The definition of *situation*
        V.   The breakdown in fact-pattern analysis
        VI. Studying Court behavior

    C. I.   Justice Stewart's view of pornography
        II. Theoretical underpinnings
        III. A minimum-winning coalition
        IV. Search and seizure decisions
        V.   Renewed interest in obscenity and pornography
        VI. The importance of local community standards

    D. I.   The Court's numerous attempts to define obscenity
        II. Case characteristics
        III. The subject matter of cases
        IV. The Court's proportion of decisions
        V.   Broad-based factors
        VI. Obscenity determination

6. Which paragraph among those that follow is the best summary of the passage?

    A. The Supreme Court's decision-making process with respect to obscenity and pornography has become too subjective. Fact-pattern analyses used to determine the overall attitude of the Court reveal only broad-based attitudes on the part of the Court toward the situations of obscenity cases. But these patterns cannot fully account for the Court's attitudes toward case content. Research is not conclusive on whether fact-pattern analyses work when applied to legal areas. Renewed public and local interest suggests continued study and close examination of how the Court makes decisions. Delegating authority to the states may reflect patterns for Court decisions in other socially sensitive areas.

    B. Though subjective, the Supreme Court decisions are well documented. Fact-pattern analyses reveal the attitude of the Supreme Court toward its decisions in cases. Spaeth explains that an attitude involves both an object and a situation. For the Court, the situation may be defined as the decision to grant certiorari. Cases present strikingly similar patterns, and a small number of variables explain a high proportion of the Court's decisions. Segal has made an effort to verify the applicability of fact-pattern analysis with some success. The Court's decisions on obscenity and pornography suggest weak Court behavior, such as in *Miller v. California*.

    C. To determine what obscenity and pornography mean to the Supreme Court, we must use fact-pattern analysis. Fact-pattern analysis reveals the ideas that the Court uses to operate in a vacuum. The litigants and the subject matter of cases are defined in broad terms (such as an entire area of law) to reveal the Court's decision-making process. Search and seizure cases reveal strikingly similar patterns, leaving the Court open to grant certiorari effectively. Renewed public interest in the Court's decisions proves how the Court will react in the future.

    D. Supreme Court decisions about pornography and obscenity are under examination and are out of control. The Court has to see the case to know it. Fact-pattern analyses reveal that the Court can only define cases in narrow terms, thus revealing individual egotism on the part of the Justices. As a result of strikingly similar patterns in search and seizure cases, the Court should be studied further for its weakness in delegating authority to state courts, as in the case of *Miller v. California*.

7. Based on the passage, the rationale for fact-pattern analyses arises out of what theoretical groundwork?

    A. Subjectivity theory

    B. The study of cultural norms

    C. Attitude theory

    D. Cybernetics

8. Based on data in the passage, what would most likely be the major cause for the difficulty in pinning down the Supreme Court's attitude toward cases of obscenity and pornography?

    A. The personal opinions of the Court Justices

    B. The broad nature of the situations of the cases

    C. The ineffective logistics of certiorari

    D. The inability of the Court to resolve the variables presented by individual case content

9.   In the context of the passage, *subjective* might be most nearly defined as

A.   personal.

B.   wrong.

C.   focused.

D.   objective.

By previewing the passage, you should have read the following:

- It is well documented that the areas of obscenity and pornography are difficult ones for the Supreme Court.

- Several recent studies employ fact-pattern analysis in modeling the Court's decision making.

- These attitudes, however, do not operate in a vacuum.

- Defining the situation with such broad strokes, however, does not allow one to control for case content.

- Despite Segal's success, efforts to verify the applicability of fact-pattern analysis in other issue areas and using broad-based factors have been slow in coming.

- The Court's obscenity and pornography decisions also present an opportunity to study the Court's behavior in an area where the Court has granted significant decision-making authority to the states.

- The Court's subsequent behavior may suggest how the Court will react in other areas where it has chosen to defer to the states (e.g., abortion).

These few sentences tell you much about the entire passage. As you begin to examine the passage, you should first determine the main idea of the passage and underline it so you can easily refer to it if a question requires you to do so (see question 1). The main idea should be found in the first paragraph of the passage, and may even be the first sentence. From what you have read thus far, you now know that the main idea of this passage is that the Supreme Court has difficulty in making static decisions about obscenity and pornography.

In addition, you also know that recent studies have used fact-pattern analysis in modeling the Court's decision. You have learned that attitudes do not operate independently and that case content is important. The feasibility of using fact-pattern analysis in other areas and broad-based factors have not been quickly verified. To study the behavior of the Court in an area in which they have granted significant decision-making authority to the states, one has only to consider the obscenity and pornography decisions. In summary, the author suggests that the Court's subsequent behavior may suggest how the Court will react in those other areas in which decision-making authority has previously been ceded to the states. As you can see, having this information will make the reading of the passage much easier.

You should have also looked at the stem of the question in your preview. You do not necessarily need to spend time reading the answers to each question in your preview. The stem alone can help to guide you as you read.

The stems in this case are

1.   The main idea of the passage is best stated in which of the following?

2.   The main purpose of the writer in this passage is to _____?

3.   Of the following, which fact best supports the writer's contention that the Court's decisions in the areas of obscenity and pornography deserve closer scrutiny?

4.   Among the following statements, which states an opinion expressed by the writer rather than a fact?

5.   The group of topics in the list that follows that best reflects the organization of the topics of the passage is _____.

6.   Which paragraph among those that follow is the best summary of the passage?

7.   Based on the passage, the rationale for fact-pattern analyses arises out of what theoretical groundwork?

8.   Based on data in the passage, what would most likely be the major cause for the difficulty in pinning down the Supreme Court's attitude toward cases of obscenity and pornography?

9.   In the context of the passage, *subjective* might be most nearly defined as _____.

Step 2: Read Actively

After your preview, you are now ready to read actively. This means that, as you read, you will be engaged in such things as underlining important words, topic sentences, main ideas, and words denoting the tone of a passage. If you think underlining can help you save time and help you remember the main ideas, feel free to use your pencil.

Read the first sentence of each paragraph carefully, since this often contains the topic of the paragraph. You may wish to underline each topic sentence.

During this stage, you should also determine the writer's purpose in writing the passage (see question 2), as this will help you focus on the main points and the writer's key points in the organization of a passage.

You can determine the author's purpose by asking yourself whether the relationship between the writer's main idea and evidence the writer uses answer one of the following four questions:

- What is the writer's primary goal or overall objective?

- Is the writer trying to persuade you by proving or using facts to make a case for an idea?

- Is the writer trying only to inform and enlighten you about an idea, object, or event?

- Is the writer attempting to amuse you? To keep you fascinated or laughing?

Read these examples and see whether you can decide what the primary purpose of the statements that follow might be.

(A) Jogging too late in life can cause more health problems than it solves. I will allow that the benefits of jogging are many: lowered blood pressure, increased vitality, better cardiovascular health, and better muscle tone. However, an older person may have a history of injury or chronic ailments that makes jogging counterproductive. For example, the elderly jogger may have hardening of the arteries, emphysema, or undiscovered aneurysms just waiting to burst and cause stroke or death. Chronic arthritis in the joints will only be aggravated by persistent irritation and use. Moreover, for those of us with injuries sustained in our youth—such as torn Achilles tendons or knee cartilage— jogging might just make a painful life more painful, cancelling out the benefits the exercise is intended to produce.

(B) Jogging is a sporting activity that exercises all the main muscle groups of the body. That the arms, legs, buttocks, and torso voluntary muscles are engaged goes without question. Running down a path makes you move your upper body as well as your lower body muscles. People do not often take into account, however, how the involuntary muscle system is also put through its paces. The heart, diaphragm, and even the eye and facial muscles take part as we hurl our bodies through space at speeds up to five miles per hour over distances as long as twenty-six miles and more for some.

(C) It seems to me that jogging styles are as identifying as fingerprints! People seem to be as individual in the way they run as they are in personality. Here comes the Duck, waddling down the track, little wings going twice as fast as the feet in an effort to stay upright. At about the quarter-mile mark, I see the Penguin, quite natty in the latest jogging suit, body stiff as a board from neck to ankles and the ankles flexing a mile a minute to cover the yards. And down there at the half-mile post—there goes the Giraffe—a tall fellow in a spotted electric yellow outfit, whose long strides cover about a dozen yards each, and whose neck waves around under some old army camouflage hat that may have served its time in a surplus store in the Bronx or in the Arabian desert. If you see the animals in the jogger woods once, you can identify them from miles away just by seeing their gait. And, by the way, be careful whose hoof you're stepping on, it may be mine!

In (A) the writer makes a statement that a number of people would debate and which isn't clearly demonstrated by science or considered common knowledge. In fact, common wisdom usually maintains the opposite thesis. Many would say that jogging improves the health of the aging—even to the point of slowing the aging process. As soon as you see a writer point to or identify *an issue open to debate* that stands in need of proof, he or she is setting out to persuade you that one side or the other is the more justified position. You'll notice, too, that the writer in this case takes a stand here. It's almost as if he or she is saying, "I have concluded that . . ." But a thesis or arguable idea is only a *hypothesis* until evidence is summoned by the writer to prove it. Effective arguments are based on serious, factual, or demonstrable evidence, not merely opinion.

In (B) the writer is just stating a fact. This is not a matter for debate. From here, the writer's evidence is to *explain* and *describe* what is meant by the fact. This is accomplished by *analyzing* (breaking down into its constituent elements) the way the different muscle groups come into play or do work when jogging, thus explaining the fact stated as a main point in the opening sentence. The assertion that jogging exercises all the muscle groups is not in question or a matter of debate. Besides taking the form of explaining how something works or what parts it comprises (for example, the basic parts of a bicycle are . . .), writers may show how the idea, object, or event functions. A writer may use this information to prove something. But if the writer doesn't argue to prove a debatable point one way or the other, then the purpose must be either to inform (as here) or to entertain.

In (C) the writer is taking a stand yet not attempting to prove anything; a lighthearted observation is made instead and nothing more. In addition, all of the examples used to support the statement are fanciful, funny, odd, or peculiar to the writer's particular vision. Joggers aren't *really* animals, after all.

Make sure to examine all the facts that the author uses to support the main idea. This will allow you to decide whether or not the writer has made a case, and what sort of purpose it supports. Look for supporting details—facts, examples, illustrations, the testimony or research of experts—that are relevant to the topic in question and show what the writer says is so. In fact, paragraphs and theses consist of *show* and *tell*. The writer *tells* you something is so or not so and then *shows* you facts, illustrations, expert testimony, or experiences to back up whatever is assertedly the case or is not the case. As you determine where the author's supporting details are, you may want to label them with an "S" so that you can refer back to them easily when answering questions (see question 3).

It is also important for you to be able to recognize the difference between the statements of fact presented versus statements of the author's opinion. You will be tested on this skill in this section of the test (see question 4). Look at the following examples. In each case ask yourself whether you are reading a fact or an opinion.

1.   Some roses are red.

2.   Roses are the most beautiful flower on Earth.

3.   After humans smell roses, they fall in love.

4.   Roses are the worst plants to grow in your backyard.

Item 1 is a fact. All you have to do is look at the evidence. Go to a florist. You will see that item 1 is true. A fact is anything that can be demonstrated to be objectively true in reality or which has been demonstrated to be true in reality and is documented by others. For example, the moon is orbiting about 250,000 miles from the Earth.

Item 2 is an opinion. The writer claims this as truth, but since it is a subjective quality (beauty), it remains to be seen. Others may hold different opinions. This is a matter of taste, not fact.

Item 3 is an opinion. There is probably some time-related coincidence between these two, but there is no verifiable, repeatable, or observable evidence that this is always true—at least not the way it is true that if you throw a ball into the air, it will come back down to Earth if left on its own without interference. Opinions have a way of sounding absolute; they are held by the writer with confidence, but are not facts that provide evidence.

Item 4, though perhaps sometimes true, is nevertheless a matter of opinion. Many variables contribute to the health of a plant in a garden: soil, temperature range, amount of moisture, and number and kinds of bugs. This is a debatable point for which the writer would have to provide evidence.

As you read, you should note the structure of the passage. There are several common structures for the passages. Some of these structures are described below.

Main Types of Paragraph Structures

1. The structure is a main idea plus supporting arguments.

2. The structure is a main idea plus examples.

3. The structure includes comparisons or contrasts.

4. There is a pro and a con structure.

5. The structure is chronological.

6. The structure has several different aspects of one idea.

For example, a passage on education in the United States in the 1600s and 1700s might first define education, then describe colonial education, then give information about separation of church and state, and then outline the opposing and supporting arguments regarding taxation as a source of educational funding. Being able to recognize these structures will help you recognize how the author has organized the passage.

Examining the structure of the passage will help you answer questions that ask you to organize (see question 5) the information in the passage or to summarize (see question 6) the information presented in that passage.

For example, if you see a writer using a transitional pattern that reflects a sequence moving forward in time, such as "In 1982 . . . Then, in the next five years . . . A decade later, in 1997, the . . .," chances are the writer is telling a story, history, or the like. Writers often use transitions of classification to analyze an idea, object, or event. They may say something like, "The first part . . . Secondly . . . Thirdly . . . Finally . . ." You may then ask yourself what the analysis is for. Is it to explain or to persuade you of something? These transitional patterns may also help reveal the relationship of one part of a passage to another. For example, a writer may be writing, "On the one hand . . . On the other hand . . ." This should alert you to the fact that the writer is comparing two things or contrasting them. What for? Is one better than the other? Worse?

By understanding the *relationship* among the main point, transitions, and supporting information, you may more readily determine the pattern of organization as well as the writer's purpose in a given piece of writing.

As with the paragraph examples above showing the difference among possible purposes, you must look at the relationship between the facts or information presented (that's the show part) and what the writer is trying to point out to you (that's the tell part) with that data. For example, a discussion presented about education in the 1600s might be used

- to prove that it was a failure (a form of argument).

- to show that it consisted of these elements (an analysis of the status of education during that time).

- to show that education during that time was silly.

To understand the author's purpose, the main point and the evidence that supports it must be considered together to be understood. To be meaningful, a controlling or main point is needed. You need to know if that main point is missing. You need to be able to distinguish between the writer showing data and the writer making a point.

In the two paragraphs that follow, consider the different relationship between the same data above and the controlling statement, and how that controlling statement changes the discussion from explanation to argument.

(A) Colonial education was different than today's education and consisted of several elements. Education in those days meant primarily studying the three "R's" (Reading, 'Riting, and 'Rithmetic) and the Bible. The church and state were more closely aligned with one another—education was, after all, for the purpose of serving God better, not to make more money.

(B) Colonial "education" was really just a way to create a captive audience for churches. Education in those days meant studying the three "R's" in order to learn God's word— the Bible—not commerce. The churches and the state were closely aligned with one another, and what was good for the church was good for the state—or else you were excommunicated, which kept you out of Heaven for sure.

The same informational areas are brought up in both cases, but in choice A the writer treats it more analytically ("consisted of several elements"), not taking as debatable a stand on the issue. However, the controlling statement in choice B puts forth a more volatile hypothesis, and then uses the same information to support that hypothesis.

Step 3: Review the Passage

After you finish reading actively, take ten or twenty seconds to look over the main idea and the topic sentences that you have underlined, and the key words and phrases you have marked. Now you are ready to enter Step 4 and answer the questions.

Step 4: Answer the Questions

In Step 2, you gathered enough information from the passage to answer questions dealing with main idea, purpose, support, fact vs. opinion, organization, and summarization. Let's look again at these questions.

Main Idea Questions

Looking back at the questions that follow the passage, you should see that question 1 is a *main idea* question.

1.   The main idea of the passage is best stated in which of the following?

    A.   The Supreme Court has difficulty convicting those who violate obscenity laws.

    B.   The current definitions for obscenity and pornography provided by the Supreme Court are unworkable.

    C.   Fact-pattern analysis is insufficient for determining the attitude of the Court toward the issues of obscenity and pornography.

    D.   Despite the difficulties presented by fact-pattern analysis, Justice Segal found the solution in the patterns of search and seizure decisions.

In answering the question, you see that answer choice C is correct. The writer uses the second, third, fourth, and fifth paragraphs to show how fact-pattern analysis is an ineffective determinant of the Supreme Court's attitudes toward obscenity and pornography.

Choice A is incorrect. Nothing is ever said directly about *convicting* persons accused of obscenity, only that the Court has difficulty defining it.

Choice B is also incorrect. Though the writer states it as a fact, it is only used as an effect that leads the writer to examine how fact-pattern analysis does or does not work to reveal the "cause" or attitude of the Court toward obscenity and pornography.

Also, answer choice D is incorrect. The statement is contrary to what Segal found when he examined search and seizure cases.

Purpose Questions

In examining question 2, you see that you must determine the author's purpose in writing the passage:

2.   The main purpose of the writer in this passage is to

   A.   convince the reader that the Supreme Court is making decisions about obscenity based on their subjective views alone.

   B.   explain to the reader how fact-pattern analysis works with respect to cases of obscenity and pornography.

   C.   define obscenity and pornography for the layperson.

   D.   demonstrate the role fact-pattern analysis plays in determining the Supreme Court's attitude about cases in obscenity and pornography.

Looking at the answer choices, you should see that choice D is correct. Though the writer never states it directly, the data is consistently summoned to show that fact-pattern analysis only gives us part of the picture, or "broad strokes" about the Court's attitude, but cannot account for the attitude toward individual cases.

Choice A is incorrect. The writer doesn't try to convince us of this fact, but merely states it as an opinion resulting from the evidence derived from the "well-documented" background of the problem.

B is also incorrect. The writer not only explains the role of fact-pattern analysis but also rather shows how it cannot fully apply.

The passage is about the Court's difficulty in defining these terms, not the man or woman in the street. Nowhere do definitions for these terms appear. Therefore, choice C is incorrect.

Support Questions

Question 3 requires you to analyze the author's supporting details.

3.   Of the following, which fact best supports the writer's contention that the Court's decisions in the areas of obscenity and pornography deserve closer scrutiny?

   A.   The fact that a Supreme Court Justice said, "I know it when I see it."

   B.   Recent studies that employ fact-pattern analysis in modeling the Court's decision-making process.

   C.   The fact that attitudes do not operate in a vacuum.

   D.   The fact that federal and state governments, interested groups, and the academic community show renewed interest in the obscenity and pornography decisions by the Supreme Court.

Look at the answer choices to answer this question. Choice D must be correct. In the fifth paragraph, the writer states that the "renewed interest"—a real and observable fact—from these groups "indicates the Court's decisions . . . deserve closer examination," another way of saying scrutiny.

Choice A is incorrect. The writer uses this remark to show how the Court cannot effectively define obscenity and pornography, relying on "subjective preferences" to resolve issues.

In addition, choice B is incorrect because the writer points to the data in D, not fact-pattern analyses, to prove this. C, too, is incorrect. Although it is true, the writer makes this point to show how fact-pattern analysis doesn't help clear up the real-world situations in which the Court must make its decisions.

Fact vs. Opinion Questions

By examining question 4, you can see that you are required to know the difference between fact and opinion.

4.   Among the following statements, which states an opinion expressed by the writer rather than a fact?

   A.   It is well documented that the area of obscenity and pornography is a difficult one for the Supreme Court.

   B.   The objects to which a court directs its attitudes are the litigants.

   C.   In many specific issue areas, the cases present strikingly similar fact-patterns.

   D.   The Court's subsequent behavior may suggest how the Court will react in other legal areas.

Keeping in mind that an opinion is something that is yet to be proven to be the case, you can determine that choice D is correct. It is the only statement among the four for which evidence is yet to be gathered. It is the writer's opinion that this may be a way to predict the Court's attitudes.

A, B, and C are all derived from verifiable data or documentation, and are therefore incorrect.

Organization Questions

Question 5 asks you to organize given topics to reflect the organization of the passage.

5.   The group of topics in the list that follows that best reflects the organization of the topics of the passage is

A.   I. The difficulties of the Supreme Court
II. Several recent studies
III. Spaeth's definition of *attitude*
IV. The similar patterns of cases
V. Other issue areas
VI. The case of *Miller v. California*

B.   I. The Supreme Court, obscenity, and fact-pattern analysis
II. Fact-pattern analyses and attitude theory
III. The definition of *attitude* for the Court
IV. The definition of *situation*
V. The breakdown in fact-pattern analysis
VI. Studying Court behavior

C.   I. Justice Stewart's view of pornography
II. Theoretical underpinnings
III. A minimum-winning coalition
IV. Search and seizure decisions
V. Renewed interest in obscenity and pornography
VI. The importance of local community standards

D.   I. The Court's numerous attempts to define obscenity
II. Case characteristics
III. The subject matter of cases
IV. The Court's proportion of decisions
V. Broad-based factors
VI. Obscenity determination

After examining all of the choices, you will determine that choice B is the correct response. These topical areas lead directly to the implied thesis that the "role" of fact-pattern analysis is insufficient to determine the attitude of the Supreme Court in the areas of obscenity and pornography.

Choice A is incorrect because the first topic stated in the list is not the topic of the first paragraph. It is too global. The first paragraph is about the difficulties the Court has with defining obscenity and how fact-pattern analysis might be used to determine the Court's attitude and clear up the problem.

C is incorrect because each of the items listed in this topic list represents supporting evidence or data for the real topic of each paragraph. (See the list in B for correct topics.) For example, Justice Stewart's statement about pornography is only cited to indicate the nature of the problem the Court has with obscenity. It is not the focus of the paragraph itself.

Finally, D is incorrect. As with choice C, these are all incidental pieces of information or data used to support broader points.

Summarization Questions

To answer question 6, you must be able to summarize the passage.

6.   Which paragraph among those that follow is the best summary of the passage?

   A.   The Supreme Court's decision-making process with respect to obscenity and pornography has become too subjective. Fact-pattern analyses used to determine the overall attitude of the Court reveal only broad-based attitudes on the part of the Court toward the situations of obscenity cases. But these patterns cannot fully account for the Court's attitudes toward case content. Research is not conclusive on whether fact-pattern analyses work when applied to legal areas. Renewed public and local interest suggests continued study and close examination of how the Court makes decisions. Delegating authority to the states may reflect patterns for Court decisions in other socially sensitive areas.

   B.   Though subjective, the Supreme Court decisions are well documented. Fact-pattern analyses reveal the attitude of the Supreme Court toward its decisions in cases. Spaeth explains that an attitude involves both an object and a situation. For the Court, the situation may be defined as the decision to grant certiorari. Cases present strikingly similar patterns, and a small number of variables explain a high proportion of the Court's decisions. Segal has made an effort to verify the applicability of fact-pattern analysis with some success. The Court's decisions on obscenity and pornography suggest weak Court behavior, such as in *Miller v. California*.

   C.   To determine what obscenity and pornography mean to the Supreme Court, we must use fact-pattern analysis. Fact-pattern analysis reveals the ideas that the Court uses to operate in a vacuum. The litigants and the subject matter of cases are defined in broad terms (such as an entire area of law) to reveal the Court's decision-making process. Search and seizure cases reveal strikingly similar patterns, leaving the Court open to grant certiorari effectively. Renewed public interest in the Court's decisions proves how the Court will react in the future.

   D.   Supreme Court decisions about pornography and obscenity are under examination and are out of control. The Court has to see the case to know it. Fact-pattern analyses reveal that the Court can only define cases in narrow terms, thus revealing individual egotism on the part of the Justices. As a result of strikingly similar patterns in search and seizure cases, the Court should be studied further for its weakness in delegating authority to state courts, as in the case of *Miller v. California*.

The paragraph that best and most accurately reports what the writer demonstrated based on the implied thesis is answer choice C, which is correct.

Choice A is incorrect because, while it reflects some of the evidence presented in the passage, the passage does not imply that all Court decisions are subjective, just the ones about pornography and obscenity. Similarly, the writer does not suggest that ceding authority to the states (as in *Miller v. California*) is a sign of some weakness, but merely that it is worthy of study as a tool for predicting or identifying the Court attitudes.

Response B is also incorrect. The writer summons information over and over to show how fact-pattern analysis cannot pin down the Court's attitude toward case content.

D is incorrect. Nowhere does the writer say or suggest that the justice system is "out of control" or that the justices are "egotists," only that they are liable to be reduced to being "subjective" rather than having a cogent and identifiable shared standard.

At this point, the three remaining question types must be discussed: recall questions (see question 7), cause/effect questions (see question 8), and definition questions (question 9). They are as follows.

Recall Questions

To answer question 7, you must be able to recall information from the passage.

7.   Based on the passage, the rationale for fact-pattern analyses arises out of what theoretical groundwork?

    A.   Subjectivity theory

    B.   The study of cultural norms

    C.   Attitude theory

    D.   Cybernetics

The easiest way to answer this question is to refer back to the passage. In the second paragraph, the writer states that recent studies using fact-pattern analyses "owe their theoretical underpinnings to attitude theory." Therefore, we can conclude that response C is correct.

Answer choices A, B, and D are incorrect, as they are never discussed or mentioned by the writer.

Cause/Effect Questions

Question 8 requires you to analyze a cause-and-effect relationship.

8. Based on data in the passage, what would most likely be the major cause for the difficulty in pinning down the Supreme Court's attitude toward cases of obscenity and pornography?

    A. The personal opinions of the Court Justices

    B. The broad nature of the situations of the cases

    C. The ineffective logistics of certiorari

    D. The inability of the Court to resolve the variables presented by individual case content

Choice D is correct, as it is precisely what fact-pattern analyses cannot resolve.

Response A is incorrect because no evidence is presented for it; all that is mentioned is that they do make personal decisions. Answer choice B is incorrect because it is one way in which fact-pattern analysis can be helpful. Finally, C is only a statement about certiorari being difficult to administer, and this was never claimed about them by the writer in the first place.

Definition Questions

Returning to question 9, we can now determine an answer.

9. In the context of the passage, *subjective* might be most nearly defined as

    A. personal.

    B. wrong.

    C. focused.

    D. objective.

Choice A is best. By taking in and noting the example of Justice Stewart provided by the writer, we can see that Justice Stewart's comment is not an example of right or wrong. Most of the time, if we are talking about people's "preferences," they are usually about taste or quality, and they are usually not a result of scientific study or clear reasoning, but arise out of personal taste, idiosyncratic intuitions, et cetera. Thus, A is the most likely choice.

C is incorrect because the Court's focus is already in place: on obscenity and pornography. Choice B is incorrect. Nothing is implied or stated about the tightness or wrongness of the decisions themselves. Rather it is the definition of obscenity that seems "unworkable." D is also incorrect. Objective is an antonym of subjective in this context. To reason based on the object of study is the opposite of reasoning based upon the beliefs, opinions, or ideas of the one viewing the object, rather than the evidence presented by the object itself, independent of the observer.

You may not have been familiar with the word subjective, but from your understanding of the writer's intent, you should have been able to figure out what was being sought. Surrounding words and phrases almost always offer you some clues in determining the meaning of a word. In addition, any examples that appear in the text may also provide some hints.

Interpretation of Graphic Information Questions

Graphs, charts, and tables may play a large part on the OGET, and you should be familiar with them. More than likely, you will encounter at least one passage that is accompanied by some form of graphic information. You will then be required to answer any question(s) based on the interpretation of the information presented in the graph, chart, or table.

Graphs are used to produce visual aids for sets of information. Often, the impact of numbers and statistics is diminished by an overabundance of tedious numbers. A graph helps a reader rapidly visualize or organize irregular information, as well as trace long periods of decline or increase. The following is a guide to reading the three principal graphic forms that you will encounter when taking the OGET.

Line Graphs

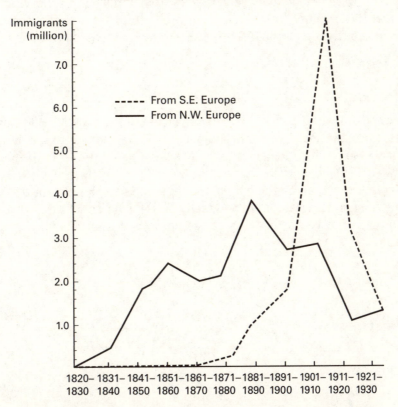

IMMIGRATION TO THE UNITED STATES, 1820–1930

Source: Immigration and Naturalization Service of the U.S. Dept. of Justice

Line graphs are used to track multiple elements of one or more subjects. One element is usually a time factor, over whose span the other element increases, decreases, or remains static. The lines that compose such graphs are connected points that are displayed on the chart through each integral stage. For example, look at the preceding immigration graph.

The average number of immigrants from 1820 to 1830 is represented at one point; the average number of immigrants from 1831 to 1840 is represented at the next. The line that connects these points is used only to ease the visual gradation between the points. It is not meant to give a strictly accurate representation for every year between the two decades. If this were so, the line would hardly be straight, even progression from year to year. The sharp directness of the lines reveals otherwise. The purpose of the graph is to plot the average increases or decreases from point to point. When dealing with more than one subject, a line graph must use either differently colored lines or different types of lines if the graph is black-and-white. In the graph, the dark bold line represents immigration from Northwestern Europe; the broken line represents immigration from Southeastern Europe.

To read a line graph, find the point of change that interests you. For example, if you want to trace immigration from Northwestern Europe from 1861 to 1870, you would find the position of the dark line on that point. Next, trace the position to the vertical information on the chart. In this instance, one would discover that approximately 2 million immigrants arrived from Northwestern Europe in the period of time from 1861 to 1870. If wishing to discover when the number of immigrants reached 4 million you would read across from 4 million on the vertical side of the graph, and see that this number was reached in 1881–1890 from Northwestern Europe, and somewhere over the two decades from 1891 to 1910 from Southeastern Europe.

Bar Graphs

Bar graphs are also used to plot two dynamic elements of a subject. However, unlike a line graph, the bar graph usually deals with only one subject. The exception to this is when the graph is three-dimensional, and the bars take on the dimension of depth. However, because we will only be dealing with two-dimensional graphs, we will be working with only a single subject. The other difference between a line and a bar graph is that a bar graph usually calls for a single element to be traced in terms of another, whereas a line graph usually plots either of the two elements with equal interest. For example, in the following bar graph, inflation and deflation are being marked over a span of years.

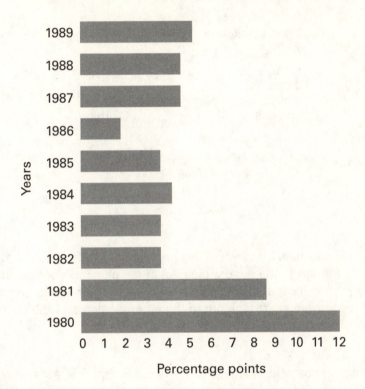

INFLATION
Inflation is a rise in the general level of prices.
Deflation is a decline in the general level of prices.

Percentage points are assigned to each year's level of prices, and that percentage decreases (deflation) from 1980 to 1981, and from 1981 to 1982. The price level is static from 1982 to 1983. The price level then increases (inflation) from 1983 to 1984. Therefore, it is obvious that the bar graph is read strictly in terms of the changes exhibited over a period of time or against some other element. Conversely, a line graph is used to plot two dynamic elements of equal interest to the reader (e.g., either number of immigrants or the particular decade in question).

To read a bar graph, simply begin with the element at the base of a bar and trace the bar to its full length. Once reaching its length, cross-reference the other element of information that matches the length of the bar.

Pie Charts

Pie charts differ greatly from line or bar graphs. Pie charts are used to help a reader visualize percentages of information with many elements to the subject. An entire "pie" represents 100 percent of a given quantity of information. The pie is then sliced into measurements that correspond to their respective shares of the 100 percent. For example, in the pie chart that follows, Myrna's rent occupies a slice greater than any other in the pie, because no other element equals or exceeds 25 percent of Myrna's monthly budget.

MYRNA'S MONTHLY BUDGET

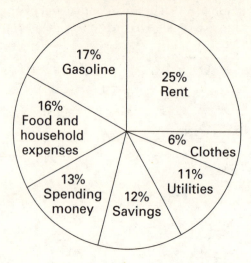

Another aspect of pie charts is that the smaller percentage elements are moved consecutively to the larger elements. Therefore, the largest element in the chart will necessarily be adjacent to the smallest element in the chart, and the line that separates them is the beginning or endpoint of the chart. From this point the chart fans out to the other elements of the chart, going from the smallest percentages to the largest.

To read a pie chart, choose the element of the subject that interests you and compare its size to those of the other elements. In cases where the elements are similar in size, do not assume that they are equal. The exact percentage of the element will be listed within that slice of the chart. For example, Myrna's utilities, savings, and spending money are all similar in size, but it is clear when reading the chart that each possesses a different value.

Reading Tables

Tables are useful because they relate to large bodies of information within a confined area. To read a table, cross-reference the column headings that run horizontally across the top of the table with the row headings that run vertically down the left side of the table. Scanning the table for the overall information within is usually done by reading line by line, as if reading regular text, while referring to the appropriate headings of the table to interpret the information listed. Note that some tables possess horizontal subheadings, which further ease the separation of different areas of information.

Effects of Common Drugs

Drug	Psychological Dependence	Physical Dependence	Physical Withdrawal Effects	Development of Tolerance
Depressants				
Alcohol	Mild to very strong	Very strong	Severe/dangerous	Minimal
Barbiturates	Develops slowly	Develops slowly	Death possible	Minimal
Narcotics				
Opiates (heroin, morphine)	Very strong; develops rapidly	Rapid/increases with dosage	Frightening symptoms but not dangerous	Very high; Goes down quickly after withdrawal (Danger if user returns to original dose)
Stimulants				
Amphetamines	Strong	Not in formal sense, but body seeks "rush"	Mild	Extremely high
Cocaine	Very strong	None	None (can cause heart spasms and instant death even if healthy)	None
Crack	Strong	Strong	Mild	High
Psychedelics				
LSD	Unpredictable	None	None	Extremely high
Marijuana	Mild to strong	Some, in high doses	None	None (Some to high doses)

To use the preceding table, one should simply choose a particular drug, and then find the appropriate information needed about that drug through the headings listed at the top of the table. For example, the physical withdrawal effects of amphetamines, a stimulant drug, are mild in effect.

Helpful Hints

You should approach any graphic information you encounter as a key to a larger body of information in abbreviated form. Be sure to use the visual aids of the graphics (e.g., the size of slices on pie charts) as aids only; do not ignore the written information listed on the graph, table, et cetera.

Note especially the title and headings so that you know exactly what it is at which you are looking. Also, be aware of the source of the information, where applicable. Know what each element of the graphic information represents; this will help you compare how drastic or subtle any changes are, and over what span of time they take place. Be sure you realize what the actual numbers represent, whether it is dollars, so many thousands of people, millions of shares, and so forth. Finally, note the way in which the graphic information relates to the text it seeks to illustrate; know in what ways the graphic information supports the arguments of the author of the given passage.

Communication Skills

The communication skills portion of the OGET asks the test taker to use skills in the areas of grammar and composition. The objectives for this section of the test are to recognize correct and incorrect grammar and usage and to recognize good and bad features of various kinds of writing.

Test takers will be asked to read a passage and answer questions about the words or punctuation included in that passage. You may also be asked to fill in a blank with a sentence or phrase that makes the passage more effective. When taking the test, you should skip ahead to read the questions about the particular passage first. This will give you an idea of what to look for and focus on as you are reading. It is also important that you understand the passage as a whole and comprehend its overall intention, meaning, or main idea.

This review was developed to prepare you for the communication skills section of the OGET. You will be guided through a step-by-step approach to attacking reading passages and questions. Also included are tips to help you quickly and accurately answer the questions. By studying this review, you will greatly increase your chances of achieving a good score on the communication skills section of the OGET.

SUBAREA II—COMMUNICATION SKILLS

Competency 0006

Recognize effective organization in writing.

The following topics are examples of content that may be covered under this competency.
* Recognize methods of paragraph organization.
* Reorganize sentences to improve cohesion and the effective sequence of ideas.
* Recognize the appropriate use of transitional words or phrases to convey text structure (e.g., however, therefore).

Competency 0007

Recognize sentences that effectively communicate intended messages.

The following topics are examples of content that may be covered under this competency.
* Recognize ineffective repetition and inefficiency in sentence construction.
* Identify effective placement of modifiers, parallel structure, and use of negatives in sentence formation.
* Recognize imprecise and inappropriate word choices.

Competency 0008

Recognize standard conventions of formal written English usage in the United States.

The following topics are examples of content that may be covered under this competency.
* Recognize the standard use of verb forms.
* Recognize the standard use of pronouns.
* Recognize the standard formation and use of adverbs, adjectives, comparatives and superlatives, and plural and possessive forms of nouns.
* Recognize standard punctuation.
* Identify sentence fragments and run-on sentences (e.g., fused sentences, comma splices).
* Identify standard subject-verb agreement.

To help you master these skills, we present examples of the types of questions you will encounter and explanations of how to answer them. A drill section is also provided for further practice. Even if you are sure you will perform well on this section, be sure to complete the drills, as they will help sharpen your skills.

The Reading Passages

The reading passages in this section are designed for several different audiences. The readings will present you with very diverse subjects. Although you will not be expected to have prior knowledge of the information presented in the passages, you will be expected to know the fundamental writing techniques needed to convey the passage's message to its intended audience. Only your ability to write standard English for a specific audience will be tested. For example, you may get a passage like this one, written for a high-school history textbook:

[1]After the Civil War, raw cotton regained its traditional role as America's largest export good. [2]From 1803 to 1937, the Civil War and two other years excluded, unprocessed cotton was America's largest merchandise export. [3]The United States was also an important exporter of grain and mineral products. [4]What most characterized the growth of American exports in the late nineteenth century, _____, was the rise of manufactured goods exports: refined petroleum, machinery, and other manufactured goods. [5]Most of these goods were mass-produced products made by methods that were not used abroad, such as sewing machines, harvesters, and, later, automobiles). [6]Exports, increased rapidly, as American goods became highly competitive in world markets.

[7]Exports rose even faster than imports, with the consequence that exports always exceeded imports until 1971. [8]When the balance of trade remained consistently positive, Americans gradually recognized that a high tariff policy was no longer necessary or even desirable. [9]In 1913, with traditionally low-tariff Democrats in control of Congress, the Underwood Tariff lowered duties substantially. [10]International commerce expanded faster in the late nineteenth and early twentieth centuries than did worldwide output, with the gold standard aiding in this growth.

The Questions

Each passage will be followed by a number of questions. Some questions may ask you to find mistakes in standard English usage; others may ask you to supply appropriate words or phrases in blanks. You will commonly encounter questions that will ask you to:

- Identify the incorrect use of words.

- Identify the incorrect use of punctuation.

- Determine which sentence best makes the transition from one thought to another.

- Determine which word or phrase would be best for a specific audience.

- Determine the type of organization the author of the passage is using.

For example, questions for the passage above might be like these:

1. Which of the following parts does not use standard punctuation?

    A. Part 2

    B. Part 6

    C. Part 8

    D. Part 9

2. Which of the following words used in the blank in Part 4 would make a good transition from the previous sentence?

    A. consequently

    B. moreover

    C. nevertheless

    D. however

(Note that superscripted numbers in the passage are referred to in the answers as "Part X.")

Sentence Structure

Parallelism

Sentences should use the same kind of grammatical construction for all items in a series—those usually joined by a coordinating conjunction (*and, but, or,* and *nor*). "No smoking, eating, or drinking" is parallel; "No smoking, food, or drinking" is not, because *food* is not a verb form. Making elements parallel also requires knowledge of parallel correlative pairs, that is, the use of appropriate pairs together: *neither* and *nor, either* and *or, both* with *and, whether* with *or,* and *not only* with *but also.*

Parallel structure is used to express matching ideas. It refers to the grammatical balance of a series of any of the following:

> **Phrases.** The squirrel ran *along the fence, up the tree,* and *into his hole* with a mouthful of acorns.

> **Adjectives.** The job market is flooded with *very talented, highly motivated,* and *well-educated* young people.

Nouns. You will need a *notebook, pencil,* and *dictionary* for the test.

Clauses. The children were told to decide *which toy they would keep* and *which toy they would give away.*

Verbs. The farmer *plowed, planted,* and *harvested* his corn in record time.

Verbals. *Reading, writing,* and *calculating* are fundamental skills we should all possess.

Correlative Conjunctions. *Either* you will do your homework *or* you will fail. *Note:* Correlative conjunctions must be used as pairs and not mixed with other conjunctions, such as *neither* with *or* or *not only* with *also.*

Near-parallelisms. Sometimes a string of seemingly parallel thoughts are not in fact parallel. Consider this sentence: "I *have quit* my job, *enrolled* in school, and *am looking* for a reliable babysitter." In this sentence the writer has already *quit* and *enrolled* but is still looking for a babysitter; therefore she cannot include all three in a parallel structure. A good revision of this sentence is, "I have quit my job and enrolled in school, and I am looking for a babysitter."

Misplaced and Dangling Modifiers

Many people, probably including at least some parents of your students, consider misplaced and dangling modifiers to be a sure sign of ignorance about the English language. Although this belief on their part may be unfair, teachers need to be aware that it is firmly held. As the name suggests, a misplaced modifier is one that is in the wrong place in the sentence. Misplaced modifiers come in all forms—words, phrases, and clauses. Sentences containing misplaced modifiers are often very comical: *Mom made me eat the spinach instead of my brother.* Misplaced modifiers, like the one in this sentence, are usually too far away from the word or words they modify. This sentence should read *Mom made me, instead of my brother, eat the spinach.*

Such modifiers as *only, nearly,* and *almost* should be placed next to the word they modify and not in front of some other word, especially a verb, that they are not intended to modify. For example, *I only sang for one reason* is wrong if the writer means to say that there was *only one* reason for singing.

A modifier is misplaced if it appears to modify the wrong part of the sentence or if the reader cannot be certain what part of the sentence the writer intended it to modify. To correct a misplaced modifier, move the modifier next to the word it describes.

UNREVISED: She served hamburgers to the men on paper plates.

REVISED: She served hamburgers on paper plates to the men.

A **squinting modifier** is one that may refer to either a preceding or a following word, leaving the reader uncertain about what it is intended to modify. Correct a squinting modifier by moving it next to the word it is intended to modify.

UNREVISED: Snipers who fired on the soldiers often escaped capture.

REVISED: Snipers who often fired on the soldiers escaped capture. OR
Snipers who fired on the soldiers escaped capture often.

A **dangling modifier** is a modifier or verb in search of a subject: the modifying phrase (usually a participle phrase—an *-ing* word group or an *-ed* or an *-en* word group—or an infinitive phrase—a *to + verb* word group) has nothing to modify. It is figuratively *dangling* at the beginning or the end of a sentence. The sentences often look and sound correct at first glance: *To be a student government officer, your grades must be above average.* However, the verbal modifier has nothing to describe. You are supposed *to be a student government officer; your grades* cannot become an officer.

To correct a dangling modifier, reword the sentence by either (1) changing the modifying phrase to a clause with a subject, or (2) changing the subject of the sentence to the word that should be modified. Here are some other examples of correct revision of dangling modifiers:

UNREVISED: Shortly after leaving home, the accident occurred.

REVISED: Shortly after we left home, the accident occurred.

UNREVISED: To get up on time, a great effort was needed.

REVISED: To get up on time, I made a great effort.

Sentence Fragments

A fragment is an incomplete construction that either (1) lacks a subject or a verb or (2) is preceded by a subordinating conjunction (e.g., *because, which, when, although*). A complete construction, such as a sentence or an independent clause, expresses a complete thought.

UNREVISED: Traffic was stalled for ten miles on the freeway. Because repairs were being made on potholes. (The second "sentence" is a dependent, or subordinate, clause.)

REVISED: Traffic was stalled for ten miles on the freeway because repairs were being made on potholes.

UNREVISED: It was a funny story. One that I had never heard before. (The second "sentence" has no verb for its subject, "One.")

REVISED: It was a funny story, one that I had never heard.

Run-On/Fused Sentences

A run-on, or fused, sentence is not necessarily a long sentence or a sentence that the reader considers too long; in fact, a run-on might consist of two short sentences: *Dry ice does not melt it evaporates.* A run-on results when the writer fuses, or runs together, two separate sentences without any correct mark of punctuation separating them.

UNREVISED: Knowing how to use a dictionary is no problem each dictionary has a section in the front of the book that tells you how.

REVISED: Knowing how to use a dictionary is no problem. Each dictionary has a section in the front of the book that tells you how.

The most common type of run-on sentence is characterized by a comma splice—the incorrect use of only a comma to separate what are really two separate sentences. There are three quick ways to fix a comma splice: (1) replace the comma with a period and start a new sentence; (2) replace the comma with a semicolon; and (3) add a coordinating conjunction, such as *and* or *but,* after the comma.

UNREVISED: Bob bought dress shoes, a suit, and a nice shirt, he needed them for his sister's wedding.

REVISED: Bob bought dress shoes, a suit, and a nice shirt. He needed them for his sister's wedding.

UNREVISED: One common error in writing is incorrect spelling, the other is the occasional use of faulty diction.

REVISED: One common error in writing is incorrect spelling; the other is the occasional use of faulty diction.

UNREVISED: We have never won the track championship, we have won the cross-country title.

REVISED: We have never won the track championship, but we have won the cross-country title.

If one of the complete thoughts is subordinate to the other, you may also use a subordinate conjunction to connect the two:

UNREVISED: Neal won the award, he had the highest score.

REVISED: Neal won the award because he had the highest score.

Subordination, Coordination, and Predication

Suppose that you wanted to combine the information in these two sentences to create one statement: *I studied a foreign language. I found English quite easy.* How you decide to combine this information should be determined by the relationship you'd like to show between the two facts. *I studied a foreign language, and I found English quite easy* adds little or nothing to the original meaning. The **coordination** of the two ideas (connecting them with the coordinating conjunction *and*) is therefore ineffective. Using **subordination** instead (connecting the sentences with a subordinating conjunction) clearly shows the relationship between the expressed ideas:

After I studied a foreign language, I found English quite easy. OR

Because I studied a foreign language, I found English quite easy.

When using any conjunction—coordinating or subordinating—be sure that the sentence parts you are joining are in agreement:

UNREVISED: She loved him dearly but not his dog.

REVISED: She loved him dearly, but she did not love his dog. OR She loved him, but not his dog, dearly.

Another common mistake is to forget that each member of the pair must be followed by the same kind of construction.

UNREVISED: She complimented her friends both for their bravery and thanked them for their kindness.

REVISED: She both complimented her friends for their bravery and thanked them for their kindness.

While refers to time and should not be used as a substitute for *though, and,* or *but.*

UNREVISED: While I'm usually interested in Fellini movies, I'd rather not go tonight.

REVISED: Although I'm usually interested in Fellini movies, I'd rather not go tonight.

Where refers to a place and should not be used as a substitute for *that.*

UNREVISED: We read in the paper where they are making strides in DNA research.

REVISED: We read in the paper that they are making great strides in DNA research.

After words such as *reason* and *explanation,* use *that,* not *because.*

UNREVISED: His explanation for his tardiness was because his alarm did not go off.

REVISED: His explanation for his tardiness was that his alarm did not go off.

Punctuation and Capitalization

Commas

Commas should be placed according to standard rules of punctuation for purpose, clarity, and effect. On the test, you will be given choices that require your knowledge of such rules. The proper use of commas is explained in the following rules and examples.

In **a series**:

> When more than one adjective describes a noun, use a comma to separate and emphasize each adjective. The comma takes the place of the word **and** in the series.

> > the long, dark passageway

> > another confusing, sleepless night

> > an elaborate, complex, brilliant plan

> Some adjective-noun combinations are thought of as one word. In these cases, the adjective in front of the adjective-noun combination needs no comma. (If you inserted **and** between the adjective-noun combination, it would not make sense.)

> > a stately oak tree

> > a superior elementary school

> The comma is also used to separate words, phrases, and whole ideas (clauses); it still takes the place of **and** when used this way.

> > a lovely lady, an elegant dress, and many admirers

> > She lowered the shade, closed the curtain, turned off the light, and went to bed.

> One question that exists about the use of commas in a series is whether one should be used before the final item. It is standard usage to do so, although newspapers and many magazines do not use the final comma. Occasionally, the omission of the comma can be confusing.

With a **long introductory phrase**:

Usually if a phrase of more than five or six words or if a dependent clause precedes the subject at the beginning of a sentence, a comma is used to set it off:

After last night's fiasco at the disco, she couldn't bear the thought of looking at him again.

Whenever I try to talk about politics, my wife leaves the room.

If an introductory phrase includes a verb form that is being used as another part of speech (a **verbal**), it must be followed by a comma:

UNREVISED: When eating Mary never looked up from her plate.

REVISED: When eating, Mary never looked up from her plate.

UNREVISED: Having decided to leave Mary James wrote her a long email.

REVISED: Having decided to leave Mary, James wrote her a long email.

To separate sentences with **two main ideas**:

To understand this use of the comma, you need to be able to recognize compound sentences. When a sentence contains more than two subjects and verbs (clauses), and the two clauses are joined by a coordinating conjunction (**and, but, or, nor, for, yet**), use a comma before the conjunction to show that another independent clause is coming.

I thought I knew the poem by heart, but he showed me some lines I had forgotten.

He is supposed to leave tomorrow, but he is not ready to go.

Jim knows you are disappointed, and he has known it for a long time.

If the two parts of the sentence are short and closely related, it is not necessary to use a comma.

He threw the ball and the dog ran after it.

Be careful not to confuse a sentence that has a compound verb and a single subject with a compound sentence. If the subject is the same for both verbs, there is no need for a comma.

UNREVISED: Charles sent some flowers, and wrote a long note explaining why he had not been able to attend.

REVISED: Charles sent some flowers and wrote a long note explaining why he had not been able to attend.

UNREVISED: Last Thursday we went to the concert with Julia, and afterwards dined at an old Italian restaurant.

REVISED: Last Thursday we went to the concert with Julia and afterwards dined at an old Italian restaurant.

In general, words and phrases that stop the flow of the sentence or are unnecessary for the main idea are set off by commas.

Abbreviations after names

Martha Harris, Ph.D., will be the speaker tonight.

Interjections (An exclamation without added grammatical connection)

Oh, I'm so glad to see you!

Hey, let us out of here!

Direct address

Roy, won't you open the door for the dog?

Hey, lady, watch out for that car!

Tag questions

Jerry looks like his father, doesn't he?

Geographical names and addresses

The concert will be held in Chicago, Illinois, on August 12. [**Note:** Punctuation must always follow a state name when that name follows a city—except in postal addresses, as illustrated in the next item.]

The letter was addressed to Mrs. Marion Heartwell, 1881 Pine Lane, Palo Alto, California 95824.

Transitional words and phrases

On the other hand, I hope he gets better.

I've always found, however, that the climate is better in the mountains.

Parenthetical words and phrases

In fact, I planted corn last summer.

The Mannes affair was, to put it mildly, a surprise.

With **nonrestrictive elements**:

Parts of a sentence that modify other parts are sometimes essential to the meaning of the sentence and sometimes not. When a modifying word or phrase is not vital to the meaning of the sentence, it is set off by commas. Because it does not restrict the meaning of the words it modifies, it is called **nonrestrictive**. Modifiers that are essential to the meaning of the sentence are **restrictive**; they are not set off by commas.

ESSENTIAL: The girl *who wrote the story* is my sister.

NONESSENTIAL: My sister, *the girl who wrote the story,* has always loved to write.

ESSENTIAL: The man who is wearing the red sweater is the best-dressed person in the class.

NONESSENTIAL: Jorge, who is wearing the red sweater, is the best-dressed person in the class.

To set off **direct quotations**:

Most direct quotes or quoted materials are set off from rest of the sentence by commas.

"Please read your part more loudly," the director insisted.

"I won't know what to do," said Michael, "if you ever leave me alone."

Who was it who said, "Do not ask for whom the bell tolls; it tolls for thee"?

Note: In American English, commas always go inside the closing quotation mark, even if the comma is not part of the material being quoted.

To set off **contrasting elements**:

Her intelligence, not her beauty, got her the job.

It was a reasonable, though not appealing, idea.

In **dates**:

In the month-day-year form, commas follow the day and year.

She will arrive April 6, 2006, on the *Queen Elizabeth*.

If only the month and year are given, no commas are necessary.

The minister's January 1967 resignation was unexpected.

The day-month-year form requires no punctuation.

The events of 14 April 1865 were unprecedented.

Because a specific date makes a descriptive phrase following it nonessential, that phrase will be nonrestrictive and therefore set off by a comma.

He was married on 7 October 1988, which fell five days after his forty-third birthday.

When a subordinate clause is at the end of a sentence, a comma preceding the clause is optional. However, when a subordinate clause introduces a sentence, a comma should be used after the clause. Here are some common subordinating conjunctions:

after	even though	till
although	if	unless
as	inasmuch as	until
as if	since	when
because	so that	whenever
before	though	while

Semicolons

This review section covers the basic uses of the semicolon: to separate independent clauses not joined by a coordinating conjunction, to separate independent clauses separated by a conjunctive adverb, and to separate items in a series with internal commas.

Use the **semicolon** in the following cases:

To separate independent clauses that are not joined by a coordinating conjunction.

I understand how to use commas; the semicolon I have yet to master.

To separate two independent clauses connected by a conjunctive adverb.

He took great care with his work; therefore, he was very successful.

Usually a comma follows the conjunctive adverb. Note also that a period can be used to separate two sentences joined by a conjunctive adverb. Here are some common conjunctive adverbs:

accordingly	indeed	now
besides	in fact	on the other hand
consequently	moreover	otherwise
finally	nevertheless	perhaps
furthermore	next	still
however	nonetheless	therefore

Then is also used as a conjunctive adverb, but it is not usually followed by a comma.

To combine two independent clauses connected by a coordinating conjunction if either or both of the clauses contain other internal punctuation:

> Success in college, some maintain, requires intelligence, industry, and perseverance; *but* others, fewer in number, assert that only geniality is important.

To separate items in a series when each item has internal punctuation. It is important to be consistent; if you use a semicolon between *any* of the items in the series, you must use semicolons to separate *all* of the items in the series.

> I bought an old, dilapidated chair; an antique table that was in beautiful condition; and a new, ugly, blue and white rug.

Do *not* use the semicolon in any other cases, especially as a substitute for a comma. Here are some examples of nonstandard semicolon use; all of them should be replaced with a comma:

> You should never make such statements; even though they are correct.

> My roommate also likes sports; particularly football, basketball, and baseball.

> Being of a cynical mind; I should ask for a recount of the ballots.

Note: The semicolon is not a terminal mark of punctuation; therefore, it should not be followed by a capital letter unless the first word in the second clause ordinarily requires capitalization.

Colons

The difference between the colon and the semicolon and between the colon and the period is that the colon is an introductory mark, not a terminal mark. The colon signals the reader that a list, explanation, or restatement of the preceding thought will follow. It is like an arrow, indicating that something is to follow.

Here are some examples of colons used to introduce lists. Note that some lists may have only one item.

> I hate just one course: English.

Three plays by William Shakespeare will be presented in repertory this summer at Illinois State: *Hamlet*, *Macbeth*, and *Othello*.

The reasons he cited for his success are as follows: honesty, industry, and a pleasant disposition.

A colon should also be used to separate two independent clauses when the second clause is a restatement or explanation of the first:

All of my high school teachers said one thing in particular: college would be difficult.

You should also use a colon to introduce a word or word group that is a restatement, explanation, or summary of the first sentence:

The first week of camping was wonderful: we lived in cabins instead of tents.

In standard English the colon should only be used after statements that are grammatically complete. Do *not*, for example, use a colon after a verb or a preposition.

UNREVISED: My favorite holidays are: Christmas, New Year's Eve, and Halloween.

REVISED: My favorite holidays are Christmas, New Year's Eve, and Halloween.

UNREVISED: I enjoy different ethnic dishes, such as those from: Greece, China, Provence, and Italy.

REVISED: I enjoy different ethnic dishes, such as those from Greece, China, Provence, and Italy.

However, the use of a colon to set off a *displayed* list is becoming more common and may now be considered standard.

Apostrophes

Apostrophes are used to make a noun possessive, not plural. Remember the following rules when considering how to show possession:

Add **'s** to singular nouns and indefinite pronouns:

Tiffany's flowers

at the owner's expense

a dog's bark

Add **'s** to singular nouns ending in *s,* unless this distorts the pronunciation:

Delores's paper

the boss's pen

Dr. Yots' class or Dr. Yots's class (depending on pronunciation)

for righteousness' sake

Add **an apostrophe** to plural nouns ending in *s* or *es*:

two cents' worth

three weeks' pay

ladies' night

Add **'s** to plural nouns not ending in *s*:

men's room

children's toys

Add **'s** to the last word in compound words or groups:

> brother-in-law's car

> someone else's paper

Add **'s** to the last name when indicating joint ownership:

> Joe and Edna's home

> Ted and Jane's marriage

Add **'s** to both names if you intend to show ownership by each person:

> Joe's and Edna's trucks

> Ted's and Jane's marriage vows

Possessive pronouns change their forms *without* the addition of an apostrophe:

> hers, his, its, yours, theirs

Quotation Marks and Italics

The most common use of double quotation marks (") is to set off quoted words, phrases, and sentences.

> "If everybody minded their own business," said Mrs. O'Leary in a huff, "the world would be a much nicer place."

Single quotation marks are used to set off quoted material within a quote.

> "Shall I bring 'Rhyme of the Ancient Mariner' along with us?" asked her brother.

> "If she said that to me," Katherine insisted, "I would tell her, 'I never intend to speak to you again! Goodbye, Susan!'"

To set off titles of poems, stories, and book chapters, use quotation marks. Book, motion picture, newspaper, and magazine titles are italicized when printed.

> The article "Moving South in the Southern Rain," by Jergen Smith, appeared in the *Southern News.*

> The assignment is "Childhood Development," which is Chapter 18 of *Abnormal Behavior.*

Remember that commas and periods at the end of quotations are *always* placed inside the quotation marks even if they are not actually part of the quote. Semicolons and colons are always placed outside. Question marks are placed inside or outside, depending on whether the quotation is a question.

> UNREVISED: "If my dog could talk", Mary mused, "I'll bet he'd say, 'Take me for a walk right this minute'".

> REVISED: "If my dog could talk," Mary mused, "I'll bet he'd say, 'Take me for a walk right this minute.'"

> UNREVISED: She called down the stairs, "When are you going"?

> REVISED: She called down the stairs, "When are you going?"

> UNREVISED: We have to "pull ourselves up by our bootstraps;" we can't just talk about our plans.

> REVISED: We have to "pull ourselves up by our bootstraps"; we can't just talk about our plans.

Remember to use only one mark of punctuation at the end of sentence ending with a quotation mark.

> UNREVISED: She thought out loud, "Will I ever finish this project in time for that class?".

> REVISED: She thought out loud, "Will I ever finish this project in time for that class?"

Capitalization

There are many conventions for beginning words with capital letters; this section will review just a few of the more common ones. In general, capitalize (1) all proper nouns and adjectives, (2) the first word of a sentence, and (3) the first word of a direct quotation. Points (2) and (3) are easy to figure out, but knowing which nouns and adjectives are "proper" is sometimes difficult. Here is a brief list that will help you remember what words to capitalize.

Names of persons, geographical places, and organizations:

Kelvim Escobar is a pitcher for the Anaheim Angels, who play in the American League.

Titles of books, poems, songs, TV shows, newspapers, and the like:

The *Washington Post* ran an interesting review of Frost's *Collected Poems*; its opinions about "Mending Wall" were especially interesting.

Geographical regions, but not compass directions:

Many movies are set in the West.

The Northern Hemisphere is the part of the earth that lies north of the equator.

The cultural division between East and West has persisted throughout modern times.

Titles of persons, if they appear immediately before the person's name:

President George W. Bush held a press conference last week.

George W. Bush, president of the United States, visited our town twice during his first term.

Political parties and philosophy, but not systems of government or individual adherents to a political philosophy:

The problems within the Communist Party foreshadowed the difficulties that communism would have in establishing itself.

The Republicans and Democrats often argue about how best to spread democracy to other countries.

Pronouns

Pronoun Case

One of the most embarrassing mistakes you can make in written English is confusing the spelling of common pronouns: "its" and "it's" and "your" and "you're." The words "its" and "your" are possessive pronouns, meaning "belonging to it" and "belonging to you," respectively. "It's" and "you're" are contractions for "it is" and "you are."

Watch *your* step; if you don't, you might break *your* neck.

It's not likely that the company will give back *its* windfall profits.

Other commonly asked questions regarding the use of pronouns are about the confusion of nominative case pronouns with objective case pronouns.

Nominative Case	Objective Case
I	me
he	him
she	her
we	us
they	them
who	whom

Use the nominative case (subject of pronouns) in the following:

Subject of a sentence:

We students studied until early morning.

Alan and *I* "burned the midnight oil" too.

Pronouns in apposition to the subject:

Only two students, Alex and *I*, were asked to comment.

Predicate nominative/subject complement:

The cast members nominated for the award were *she* and *I*.

The subject of a subordinate clause:

Robert is the driver *who* reported the accident.

The only pronouns that are acceptable in standard English after prepositions are the objective case pronouns. When deciding between *who* and *whom* in the sentence "We're having difficulty deciding *who* we can trust," try substituting *he* for *who* and *him* for *whom*; then follow these transformation steps:

1. Isolate the *who* or *whom* clause: who we can trust.

2. Invert the natural word order if necessary, to the normal English subject–verb order: we can trust who

3. Read the final form with the *he* or *him* inserted: we can trust ~~who~~ *him*. The correct pronoun is thus *whom*.

Use the objective case (subject of pronouns) for the following:

Direct object of a verb:

Mary invited *us* to her party.

Object of a preposition:

The torn books belonged to *her*.

Just between you and *me*, I'm bored.

Indirect object of a verb:

Soren gave *her* a dozen roses.

Appositive of an object:

The committee selected two delegates, Barbara and *me*.

Object of an infinitive:

The young boy wanted to help *us* paint the fence.

Subject of an infinitive:

The boss told *him* to work late.

Object of a gerund:

Enlisting *him* was surprisingly easy.

When a conjunction connects two pronouns or a pronoun and a noun, one good way to determine the case of a pronoun is to remove the "and" and the noun or other pronoun:

Mom gave ~~Tom and~~ myself a piece of cake.

Mom gave ~~Tom and~~ I a piece of cake.

Mom gave ~~Tom and~~ me a piece of cake.

Removal of the crossed-out words reveals that the correct pronoun should be *me*.

Pronoun-Antecedent Agreement

Some questions might ask you about *pronoun-antecedent agreement*. These kinds of questions test your knowledge of using an appropriate pronoun to agree with its antecedent in number (singular or plural form) and gender (masculine, feminine, or neuter). An *antecedent* is a noun or pronoun to which another noun or pronoun refers.

Here are the two basic rules for pronoun reference-antecedent agreement:

1.   Every pronoun must have a conspicuous antecedent.

2.   Every pronoun must agree with its antecedent in number, gender, and person.

When an antecedent is one of dual gender—such as *student, singer, person,* or *citizen*—use **his** or **her.** Some careful writers change the antecedent to a plural noun to avoid using the sexist, singular masculine pronoun.

UNREVISED: Everyone hopes that they will win the lottery.

CORRECT BUT AMBIGUOUS: Everyone hopes that he will win the lottery.

CORRECT BUT AWKWARD: Everyone hopes that he or she will win the lottery.

REVISED: Most people hope that they will win the lottery.

Ordinarily, the relative pronoun **who** is used to refer to people, **which** to refer to things and places, **where** to refer to places, and **that** to refer to places or things. The distinction between **that** and **which** is a grammatical distinction (see the section on Word Choice Skills). Many writers prefer to use **that** to refer to collective nouns, even for people: A family that traces its lineage is usually proud of its roots.

Many writers, especially students, are not sure when to use the *reflexive case* pronoun and when to use the *possessive case* pronoun. The rules governing the usage of the reflexive case and the possessive case are simple.

Use the **possessive case**:

Before a noun in a sentence:

My dog has fleas, but *her* dog doesn't.

Before a gerund in a sentence:

Her running helps to relieve stress.

As a noun in a sentence:

Mine was the last test graded that day.

To indicate possession:

Brad thought the book was *his*, but it was someone else's.

Use the **reflexive** case:

As a direct object to rename the subject:

I kicked *myself*.

As an indirect object to rename the subject:

Henry bought *himself* a tie.

As an object of a prepositional phrase:

Tom and Lillie baked the pie for *themselves.*

As a predicate pronoun:

She hasn't been *herself lately.*

Do not use the reflexive in place of the nominative pronoun:

UNREVISED: Both Randy and *myself* plan to go.

REVISED: Both Randy and *I* plan to go.

UNREVISED: *Yourself* will take on the challenges of college.

REVISED: *You* will take on the challenges of college *yourself.*

Watch out for careless use of the pronoun form:

UNREVISED: George *hisself* told me it was true.

REVISED: George *himself* told me it was true.

UNREVISED: They washed the car *theirselves.*

REVISED: They washed the car *themselves.*

Notice that reflexive pronouns are not set off by commas:

UNREVISED: Mary, *herself*, gave him the diploma.

REVISED: Mary *herself* gave him the diploma.

Pronoun Reference

Pronoun reference questions require you to determine whether the antecedent is conspicuously written in the sentence or whether it is remote, implied, ambiguous, or vague, none of which results in clear writing. In the following, make sure that every italicized pronoun has a conspicuous antecedent and that one pronoun substitutes only for another noun or pronoun, not for an idea or a sentence.

Pronoun reference problems occur in the following instances:

1. When a pronoun refers to either of two antecedents.

    UNREVISED: Joanna told Tina that *she* was getting fat.

    REVISED: Joanna told Tina, "I'm getting fat." OR Joanna told Tina, "You're getting fat."

2. When a pronoun refers to a nonexistent antecedent.

    UNREVISED: A strange car followed us closely, and *he* kept blinking his lights at us.

    REVISED: A strange car followed us closely, and its driver kept blinking his lights at us.

3. When **this, that,** and **which** refer to the general idea of the preceding clause or sentence rather than the preceding word.

    UNREVISED: The students could not understand the pronoun reference handout, *which* annoyed them very much.

    REVISED: The students could not understand the pronoun reference handout, *a fact that* annoyed them very much. OR The students were annoyed because they could not understand the pronoun reference handout.

4. When a pronoun refers to an unexpressed but implied noun.

   UNREVISED: My husband wants me to knit a blanket, but I'm not interested in *it*.

   REVISED: My husband wants me to knit a blanket, but I'm not interested in *knitting*.

5. When **it** is used as something other than an expletive to postpone a subject.

   UNREVISED: The football game was canceled because it was bad weather.

   REVISED: The football game was canceled because the weather was bad.

6. When **they** or **it** is used to refer to something or someone indefinitely, and there is no definite antecedent.

   UNREVISED: At the job placement office, *they* told me to stop wearing ripped jeans to my interviews.

   REVISED: At the job placement office, I was told to stop wearing ripped jeans to my interviews.

7. When the pronoun does not agree with its antecedent in number, gender, or person.

   UNREVISED: Any graduate student, if *they* are interested, may tend the lecture.

   REVISED: Any graduate student, if *he or she* is interested, may attend the lecture.

   REVISED: All graduate *students*, if *they* are interested, may tend the lecture.

Verbs

This section covers the principal parts of some irregular verbs, including such troublesome verbs as *lie* and *lay.* The use of regular verbs, such as *look* and *receive*, poses little problem for most writers, because the past and past participle forms end in *-ed*; it is the irregular forms that pose the most serious problems—for example, *seen, written,* and *begun.*

Verb Tenses

Tense sequence indicates a logical time sequence.

Use **present tense**:

In statements of universal truth:

I learned that the sun *is* ninety-million miles from the earth.

In statements about the contents of literature and other published work:

In this book, Sandy *becomes* a nun and *writes* a book about psychology.

Use **past tense**:

In statements or questions about action that happened in the past and is now finished:

I *fell* over the limb and *broke* my arm.

How *did* you break your arm?

In statements concerning writing or publication of a book:

He *wrote* his first book in 1949, and it *was published* in 1956.

Use **present perfect tense**:

For an action that began in the past but continues into the future:

I *have lived* here all my life.

Use **past perfect tense**:

For an earlier action that is mentioned in relation to a later action:

Cindy ate the apple that she *had picked*.

(First she picked it; then she ate it.)

Use **future perfect tense**:

For an action that will have been completed at a specific future time:

You *will have graduated* by the time we next meet.

Use **a present participle**:

For action that occurs at the same time as the verb:

Speeding down the interstate, I saw a cop's flashing lights.

Use **a perfect participle**:

For action that occurred before the main verb:

Having read the directions, I started the test.

Use the **subjunctive mood**:

To express a wish or state a condition contrary to fact:

If it were not raining, we could have a picnic.

In "that" clauses after such verbs as **request, recommend, suggest, ask, require,** and **insist**; and after such expressions as **it is important** and **it is necessary**:

It is necessary that all papers *be* submitted on time.

Subject-Verb Agreement

Agreement is the grammatical correspondence between the subject and the verb of a sentence or clause: *I do; you do; we do; they do; he, she, it does.* One source of confusion for many students is which verb form is singular and which forms are plural, so this section begins by focusing on making that distinction and then tackles the task of identifying the real subject of a sentence. Finally, this section deals with subjects that are commonly construed as singular and those that are construed as plural.

Every English verb has five forms, two of which are the bare form (plural) and the **-s** form (singular). Simply put, singular verb forms end in **–s**; plural forms do not.

Study these rules governing subject-verb agreement:

A verb must agree with its subject, not with any additional phrase in the sentence such as a prepositional or verbal phrase.

Your *copy* of the rules *is* on the desk.

Ms. Craig's *record* of community service and outstanding teaching *qualifies* her for a promotion.

In an inverted sentence beginning with a prepositional phrase, the verb must still agree with its subject.

At the end of the summer *come* the best *sales.* Under the house *are* some old Mason *jars.*

Prepositional phrases beginning with compound prepositions such as **along with, together with, in addition to, and as well as** should be ignored, for they do not affect subject-verb agreement.

Gladys Knight, along with the Pips, *is* riding the midnight train to Georgia.

A verb must agree with its subject, not its subject complement.

Taxes are a problem.

One *problem is* taxes.

His main *source* of pleasure *is* food and women.

Food and women are his main source of pleasure.

When a sentence begins with an expletive such as **there**, **here**, or **it**, the verb agrees with the subject, not the expletive.

Surely there *are* several *alumni* who would be interested in starting a group.

There *are* 50 *students* in my English class.

There *is* a horrifying *study* on child abuse in *Psychology Today*.

Indefinite pronouns such as **each**, **either**, **one**, **everyone**, **everybody**, and **everything** are singular.

Somebody in Detroit *loves* me.

Does either [one] of you have a pencil?

Neither of my brothers *has* a car.

Indefinite pronouns such as **several**, **few**, **both**, and **many** are considered plural.

Both of my sorority sisters *have* decided to live off campus.

Few seek the enlightenment of transcendental meditation.

Indefinite pronouns such as **all**, **some**, **most**, and **none** may be singular or plural, depending on their referents.

Some of the food *is* cold.

Some of the vegetables *are* cold.

I can think of some retorts, but *none seem* appropriate.

None of the children *is* as sweet as Sally.

Fractions such as **one-half** and **one-third** may be singular or plural, depending on the referent.

> *Half of the* mail *has* been delivered.

> *Half of* the letters *have* been read.

Subjects joined by **and** take a plural verb unless the subjects are commonly thought of as one item or unit.

> *Jim* and *Tammy were* televangelists.

> *Guns and Roses is* my favorite group.

In cases when the subjects are joined by **or, nor, either . . . or**, or **neither . . . nor**, the verb must agree with the subject closer to it.

> Either the teacher or the *students are* responsible.

> Neither the students nor the *teacher is* responsible.

Relative pronouns—such as **who, which**, or **that**—require plural verbs if they refer to plural antecedents. However, when the relative pronoun refers to a singular subject, the pronoun takes a singular verb.

> She is one of the best *cheerleaders who have* ever attended our school.

> She is the only *cheerleader who has* a broken leg.

Subjects preceded by **every** and **each** are singular.

> *Every* man, woman, and child *was* given a life preserver.

> *Each* undergraduate *is* required to pass a proficiency exam.

A collective noun, such as **audience, faculty**, and **jury**, requires a singular verb when the group is regarded as a whole, and a plural when the members of the group are regarded as individuals.

> The *jury has* made its decision.

> *The faculty are* preparing their grade rosters.

Subjects preceded by **the number of** or **the percentage of** are singular; subjects preceded by **a number of** or **a percentage of** are plural.

The number of vacationers in Florida *increases* every year.

A number of vacationers *are* young couples.

Certain nouns of Latin and Greek origin have unusual plural forms.

Singular	**Plural**
criterion	criteria
alumnus	alumni
datum	data
medium	media

The *data are* available for inspection.

The only *criterion* for membership *is* a high GPA.

Some nouns, such as *deer*, *shrimp*, and *sheep*, have the same spelling for both their singular and plural forms. In these cases, the meaning of the sentence will determine whether they are singular or plural.

Deer are beautiful animals.

The spotted *deer is* licking the salt block.

Some nouns ending in *-ics*, such as *economics* and *ethics*, take singular verbs when they refer to principles or a field of study; however, when they refer to individual practices, they usually take plural verbs.

Ethics is being taught in the spring.

His unusual business *ethics are* what got him into trouble.

Some nouns that end in **-s** may appear to be plural but are not; examples are *measles* and *news*.

Measles is a very contagious disease.

News of her arrival *was* not welcome.

A verbal noun (infinitive or gerund) serving as a subject is treated as singular, even if the object of the verbal phrase is plural.

Hiding your mistakes *does* not make them go away.

A plural subject followed by a singular appositive requires a plural verb; similarly, a singular subject followed by a plural appositive requires a singular verb.

When the girls throw a party, *they* each bring a *gift.*

The *board*, all ten members, *is* meeting today.

Adjectives and Adverbs

Correct Usage

Be careful and *Drive carefully* are sentences that illustrate the differences that this section discusses: the proper use of an adjective or an adverb, including distinctions between *bad* and *badly* and *good* and *well.*

Adjectives are words that modify nouns or pronouns by defining, describing, limiting, or qualifying those nouns or pronouns.

Adverbs are words that modify verbs, adjectives, or other adverbs and that express such ideas as time, place, manner, cause, and degree. In general, use adjectives as subject complements with linking verbs; use adverbs with action verbs.

The old man's speech was *eloquent*.	ADJECTIVE
Mr. Brown speaks *eloquently*.	ADVERB
Please be *careful*.	ADJECTIVE
Please drive *carefully*.	ADVERB

Good and Well

Good is an adjective; its use as an adverb is colloquial and nonstandard.

NONSTANDARD: He plays *good.*

STANDARD: He plays *well.*

STANDARD: He looks *good* to be an octogenarian.

Well may be either an adverb or an adjective. As an adjective it means "in good health."

He plays *well.*	ADVERB
My mother is not *well.*	ADJECTIVE

Do not confuse *good* and *well* when used with *feel.* If you say "*I feel good,*" you're referring to your general health or mood, whereas "*I feel well*" refers only to your sense of touch.

Bad or Badly

Bad is an adjective used after sense verbs, such as *look, smell, taste, feel,* or *sound,* or after linking verbs (is, am, are, was, were).

UNREVISED: I feel *badly* about the delay.

REVISED: I feel *bad* about the delay.

Badly is an adverb used after all other verbs.

UNREVISED: It doesn't hurt very *bad.*

REVISED: It doesn't hurt very *badly.*

Real or Really

Real is an adjective; its use as an adverb is colloquial and nonstandard. It means "genuine."

NONSTANDARD: He writes *real* well.

STANDARD: This is *real* leather.

Really is an adverb meaning "very."

    NONSTANDARD: This is *really* diamond.

    STANDARD: Have a *really* nice day.

This is *real* amethyst.	ADJECTIVE
This is *really* difficult.	ADVERB
This is a *real* crisis	ADJECTIVE
This is *really* important.	ADVERB

Faulty Comparisons

This section covers comparisons that use adjectives and adverbs with certain conjunctions, such as *than* and *as,* to indicate a greater or lesser degree of what is specified in the main part of the sentence. Errors occur when the comparison being made is illogical, redundant, or incomplete. Watch for **-er** and **-est** forms of words meaning *more* and *most,* and correlative pairs like *as . . . as.* Other clues are *than* and *other.* Often, sentences containing a faulty comparison sound correct because their problem is not one of grammar but of logic. Read such sentences closely to make sure that like things are being compared, that the comparisons are complete, and that the comparisons are logical.

When comparing two persons or things, use the comparative (**-er**), not the superlative (**-est**) form, of an adjective or an adverb. Use the superlative form for comparison of more than two persons or things. Use *any*, *other*, or *else* when comparing one thing or person with a group of which it, he, or she is a part.

Most one- and two-syllable words form their comparative and superlative forms with **-er** and **-est** suffixes. Adjectives and adverbs of more than two syllables form their comparatives and superlatives with the addition of *more* and *most.*

Word	Comparative	Superlative
good	better	best
old	older	oldest
friendly	friendlier	friendliest
lonely	lonelier	loneliest
talented	more talented	most talented
beautiful	more beautiful	most beautiful

When in doubt, consult a dictionary; most of them give the comparative and superlative forms.

Here are examples of some common types of faulty comparison:

Double comparison

UNREVISED: He is the *most nicest* brother.

REVISED: He is the *nicest* brother.

UNREVISED: She is the *more meaner* of the sisters.

REVISED: She is the *meaner* sister.

Illogical comparison

UNREVISED: The interest at a loan company is higher *than* a bank.

CORRECT: The interest at a loan company is higher *than at* a bank.

Ambiguous comparison

UNREVISED: I like Mary *better than* you. (than you *what*?)

REVISED: I like Mary *better than* I like you. OR I like Mary *better than* you do.

Incomplete comparison

UNREVISED: Skywriting is *more* spectacular.

REVISED: Skywriting is *more* spectacular *than* billboard advertising.

Omission of words **other**, **any**, or **else** when comparing one thing or person with a group of which it, he, or she is a part

UNREVISED: Joan writes better *than any* student in her class.

REVISED: Joan writes better *than any other* student in her class.

Omission of the second *as* in an **as . . . as** construction

> UNREVISED: The University of West Florida is *as large* or larger than the University of North Florida.

> REVISED: The University of West Florida is *as large as* or larger than the University of Northern Florida.

Word Choice

Usage

Consider this sentence: The high school *principal* resigned for two *principal* reasons. If you think that the second *principal* is the wrong word (that it should be *principle*), think again. This usage is correct. You may be asked about words that are commonly confused and misused, as well as the use of words based on their grammatical appropriateness in a sentence, such as the distinction between *principal* and *principle*, *fewer* and *less*, and *lie* and *lay*. Here are some commonly confused pairs:

> *principal*—as an adjective, most important; as a noun, the chief authority.

> *principle*—always a noun: a fundamental law. "We hold these principles to be self-evident."

> *affect*—usually a verb, meaning to *influence*; sometimes a noun, with a specific meaning in psychology. "Her performance was adversely affected by the heat."

> *effect*—usually a noun, meaning something that results from something else; occasionally a verb, meaning *to cause to come into being*. "The heat had no effect on his performance." "Her persistence helped to effect the new zoning ordinance."

Connotative and Denotative Meanings

The denotative meaning of a word is its *literal,* dictionary definition: what the word denotes, or "means." The connotative meaning of a word is what the word connotes, or "suggests"; it is a meaning apart from what the word literally means. A writer should choose a word based on the tone and context of the sentence; this ensures that a word bears the appropriate connotation while still conveying some exactness in denotation. For example, a gift might be described as "cheap," but the directness of the word has a negative connotation—something cheap is something of little or no value. The word "inexpensive" has a more positive connotation, although "cheap" is a synonym for "inexpensive." You may very well have to make a decision regarding the appropriateness of words and phrases within the context of a sentence.

Wordiness and Conciseness

Some questions will test your ability to detect redundancies (unnecessary repetitions), circumlocution (failure to get to the point), and padding with loose synonyms. These questions require you to select sentences that use as few words as possible to convey a message clearly, economically, and effectively.

Effective writing is concise. Wordiness, on the other hand, decreases the clarity of expression by cluttering sentences with unnecessary words. Of course, not all short sentences are better than long ones simply because they are brief. As long as a word serves a function, it should remain in the sentence. However, repetition of words, sounds, and phrases should be used only for emphasis or other stylistic reasons. Editing your writing will make a difference in its impact. Notice what revision does here:

UNREVISED: The medical exam that he gave me was entirely complete.

REVISED: The medical exam he gave me was complete.

UNREVISED: Larry asked his friend John, who was a good, old friend, if he would join him and go along with him to see the foreign film made in Japan.

REVISED: Larry asked his good, old friend John if he would join him in seeing the Japanese film.

UNREVISED: I was absolutely, totally happy with the present that my parents gave to me at 7 AM on the morning of my birthday.

REVISED: I was happy with the present my parents gave me on the morning of my birthday.

UNREVISED: It seems perfectly clear to me that although he went and got permission from the professor, he still should not have played that awful, terrible joke on the dean.

REVISED: It seems clear that, although he got permission from the professor, he should not have played that terrible joke on the dean.

Drill: Editing Skills

DIRECTIONS: Select the sentence that clearly and effectively states the idea and has no structural errors.

(A)   South of Richmond, the two roads converge together to form a single highway.

(B)   South of Richmond, the two roads converge together to form an interstate highway.

(C)   South of Richmond, the two roads converge to form an interstate highway.

(D)   South of Richmond, the two roads converge to form a single interstate highway.

The correct answer is (C); *together* is not needed after *converge*, and *single* is not needed to modify *highway*.

(A)   Vincent van Gogh and Paul Gauguin were close personal friends and companions who enjoyed each other's company and frequently worked together on their artwork.

(B)   Vincent van Gogh and Paul Gauguin were friends who frequently painted together.

(C)   Vincent van Gogh was a close personal friend of Paul Gauguin, and the two of them often worked together on their artwork because they enjoyed each other's company.

(D)   Vincent van Gogh, a close personal friend of Paul Gauguin, often worked with him on their artwork.

The correct answer is (B). Choices (A) and (C) pad the sentences with loose synonyms that are redundant. Choice (D), although a short sentence, does not convey the meaning as clearly as choice (B).

Transitions and Coherence

On the Communication Skills portion of the OGET, you will be asked tell whether a particular passage develops its ideas well. You will also be asked to supply missing words, phrases, or sentences that would make a particular passage develop more logically. Let's look at the following passage, which is adapted from a similar passage that appeared in Chapter 1.

Passage

[1]That the area of obscenity and pornography is a difficult one for the Supreme Court is well documented. [2]The Court's numerous attempts to define obscenity have proven unworkable and left the decision to the

subjective preferences of the justices. [3]Perhaps Justice Stewart put it best when, after refusing to define obscenity, he declared, but "I know it when I see it." [4]Does the Court literally have to see it to know it? [5]Specifically, what role does the fact-pattern, including the materials' medium, play in the Court's decision?

[6]Several recent studies employ fact-pattern analysis in modeling the Court's decision making. [7]These studies examine the fact-pattern or case characteristics, often with ideological and attitudinal factors, as a determinant of the decision reached by the Court. [8]In broad terms, these studies owe their theoretical underpinnings to attitude theory. [9]As the name suggests, attitude theory views the Court's attitudes as an explanation of its decisions.

[10]These attitudes, however, do not operate in a vacuum. [11]As Spaeth explains, "the activation of an attitude involves both an object and the situation in which that object is encountered." [12]The objects to which the court directs its attitudes are litigants. [13]The situation—the subject matter of the case—can be defined in broad or narrow terms. [14]One may define the situation as an entire area of the law (e.g., civil liberties issues). [15]On an even broader scale, the situation may be defined as the decision to grant certiorari or whether to defect from a minimum-winning coalition.

[16]Defining the situation with such broad strokes, _____, does not allow one to control for case content. [17]In many specific issue areas, the cases present strikingly similar patterns. [18]In examining the Court's search and seizure decisions, Segal found that a relatively small number of situational and case characteristic variables explain a high proportion of the Court's decisions.

[19]Despite Segal's success, efforts to verify the applicability of fact-pattern analysis in other issue areas and using broad-based factors have been slow in forthcoming. [20]Renewed interest in obscenity and pornography by federal and state governments as a result of lobbying campaigns by fundamentalist groups, the academic community, and other antipornography interest groups pro and con indicate the Court's decisions in this area will get closer examination.

[21]The Court's obscenity and pornography decisions _____ present an opportunity to study the Court's behavior in an area where the Court has granted significant decision-making authority to the states. [22]In *Miller v. California* (1973) the Court announced the importance of local community standards in obscenity determinations. [23]The Court's _____ behavior may suggest how the Court will react in other areas where it has chosen to defer to the states (e.g., abortion).

Questions

1. This passage would be most appropriate in which type of publication?

    A. A popular magazine such as *Time* or *Newsweek*

    B. An editorial about pornography in a newspaper

    C. A chapter on pornography in a sociology textbook

    D. An article in a law journal

2. Which of the following phrases, if inserted in the blank in Part 16, would best help the reader under the author's progression of ideas.

    A. consequently

    B. however

    C. nevertheless

    D. furthermore

3. In the final paragraph, which words or phrases, if inserted in order in the blanks, help the reader understand the author's logical sequence?

    A. in fact; foolish

    B. will; later

    C. also; subsequent

    D. theoretically; firm

4. Which of the following best describes the method of organization used by the author of this passage?

    A. problem and solution

    B. chronological order

    C. order of importance

    D. comparison and contrast

5. Which of the following sentences, if added between Parts 10 and 11, would be most consistent with the writer's purpose and intended audience?

    A. Situations with which the Court is faced are often quite complex.

    B. Supreme Court justices have been known to read newspapers as well as law journals.

    C. Pornography has been a point of public dispute for many decades now.

    D. If they did operate in a vacuum, predicting a justice's vote on a particular issue from his record before his appointment would be somewhat straightforward.

6. Which word would best replace the underlined words in Part 20?

   A. deserve

   B. are garnering

   C. will continue to elude

   D. have avoided

Answers

Keep in mind that the first step to answering these types of questions involves applying the Four-Step Approach discussed in Chapter 1. You cannot answer questions about the purpose, audience, or organization of a passage without first having analyzed it through the four-step approach. You will see that, in the practice test in this book and in the actual examination, passages are generally shorter than this passage; this one has been included so that you can review the Four-Step Approach while answering these questions.

The answer to Question 1 is **D**. The quotes from scholars eliminate A and B from consideration, because newspapers and magazines for general readers do not usually quote experts without identifying why they are worthy of being experts. Choice B is further eliminated by the fact that the passage takes no position that the average newspaper reader might act upon. The tone of the passage might conceivably be appropriate to choice C, but the passage focuses on law rather than pornography.

The correct answer to Question 2 is **B**. The previous paragraph ended with a statement about a "broad scale," and the new paragraph begins by saying that looking at the broad scale is inadequate. This sentence, then, must convey that contrast, so choices A and D are immediately eliminated. Choice C conveys the correct general meaning, but the use of *nevertheless* directly before a negative—*does not*—would be confusing to a reader.

The correct answer to Question 3 is **C**. To find this answer, you will first have to notice that the author is switching topics from obscenity to states' rights; therefore, the choice A is eliminated, because *in fact* is a transition that signals an example of what has just been discussed. (In addition, nothing in the passage indicates that the author regards the Court's behavior as "foolish.") Choice B is wrong simply because the word "will" is not accurate: the decisions *already do* present an opportunity for further analysis. Choice D's "theoretically" is plausible, but "firm" is definitely wrong because it does not describe the author's opinion of the Court's 1973 decision, which just announces the importance of local standards rather than making firm law regarding them.

Question 4's answer is **D**. Although a problem and solution are implied in the passage, there is no direct statement of the problem followed by a solution. Chronological order and order of importance are clearly not present here, but the writer does compare and contrast analytical methods and attempts to explicate their strengths and weaknesses.

The best answer to Question 5 is **D**. Choices A and C are far from the point of the paragraph, which concerns how justices reach decisions. The choice of D over B depends on the tone of the two sentences as well as the specific content. The content of the two sentences is similar, although the content of D is somewhat more on message. The tone of choice B, however, is a bit flippant and would undoubtedly be out of place in most articles aimed at law scholars.

The best answer to Question 6 is **A**. Choice D contradicts the facts as presented in the paragraph, and choice C is out of line with the entire passage, which does give close examination to the subject. Choice B is technically correct (although not very informative for a final thought in a paragraph), but the word *garner* would be more at home in a newspaper article ("Duncan Garners Another Award") than in an article like this one.

Chapter

3

Critical Thinking Skills: Mathematics

Questions from this sub-area of the OGET will ask you to analyze situations and to find solutions to problems that require some mathematical knowledge. This chapter will help you review data representation and analysis, and it will go over some basic ways to solve problems. The chapter will close with a review of how to set up solutions to problems that involve one or two variables.

Data Interpretation and Analysis

Competency 0009

Solve problems involving data interpretation and analysis.

The following topics are examples of content that may be covered under this competency:

- Interpret information from line graphs, bar graphs, histograms, pictographs, and pie charts.
- Interpret data from tables.
- Recognize appropriate representations of various data in graphic form.

Interpret Information from Graphs, Tables, or Charts

Graphs, tables, and charts come in many different forms; most simply represent numerical data in neat visual formats. A bar graph, like the one below, typically shows "how much" for each of many categories (or persons, or time periods, or whatever).

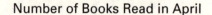
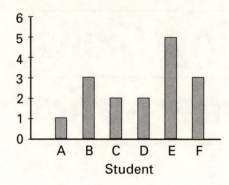

Number of Books Read in April

Broken line graphs, like the one below, are reserved for indicating *change over time*. Do not use broken line graphs unless one of the axes (usually the bottom or horizontal axis) indicates time. *Trends* are often revealed by broken line graphs.

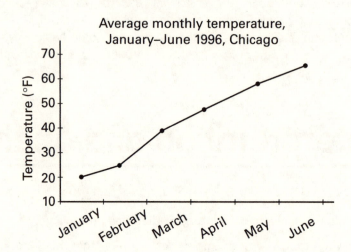

Average monthly temperature, January–June 1996, Chicago

Pie graphs (also known as circle graphs or pie charts) often show how finite quantities are "split up." As with the example below, pie graphs may not necessarily be accompanied by specific numeric values. They are especially good for showing relative amounts or allotments at a glance.

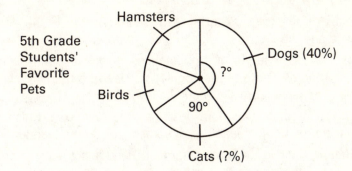

Because pie graphs are circles, the angle formed at the center by the boundaries of each catagory can be determined from the fact that the circle contains 360°. For example, if dogs are the favorite pets of 40% of fifth graders, what is the central angle? (**Answer:** 40% × 360° = .4 × 360° = 144°.) If the central angle of the "Cats" portion of the graph is 90°, what percentage of fifth graders prefer cats? (**Answer:** 90/360 = 1/4 = 25%.)

A key to interpretation of graphs, tables, and charts is to pay close attention to labels. Specific axis labels are also important. Don't assume anything about what a graph, table, or chart might be saying without carefully reading all labeled elements.

Statistical Concepts

The term *data* refers to numerical information acquired by counting or measuring. The number of students in a class, their test scores on a test, and their individual heights are all examples of data.

Data can be represented in *discrete* or *continuous* form, depending on what they represent. If data are discrete, they have gaps between them. The bar graph is a common way to depict discrete data. For example, the bar graph on page 80 represents the number of books read by each of six separate students. Discrete data are generally obtained from counting rather than measuring. Continuous data are usually represented by an unbroken line on a graph, and they are usually obtained by measuring rather than counting. The data shown in the graph at the bottom of 80 are continuous because there are no gaps between the months.

Here is a list of other statistical concepts that you might have to know for the test:

mean   The mean is the sum of a set of numbers divided by the quantity of numbers *n* in the set. It gives the *average value* of a data set.

range   The range is the measure of spread (*variation*) that is the difference between the largest value and the smallest value in a set of data.

sample survey   This is a survey of a population, usually human, made by taking a sample judged to be representative of the population. Use of a random mechanism for choosing the sample is essential for validity and believability.

spread of data   Spread, or **variation**, describes the degree to which data are spread out around their center. Useful measures of spread include the standard deviation and range.

standard deviation   This is the most commonly used expression of spread, or variation, of data. The higher the standard deviation, the higher is the degree of spread around the center of the data (that is, the data are more inconsistent with each other).

median   The median is the center value in a set of numbers: there are an equal number of values above and below it.

percentiles   These are the measures of where a piece of data stands in relation to the other data in its set. Perhaps best known from standardized tests, percentiles tell how many other data are lower in value. For instance, a test taker might have a raw score of 82% (that is, 82% of the answers correct) but rank in the 91st percentile, meaning that 90% of all test takers received lower raw scores. The median occurs at the 50th percentile.

frequency distributions   These represent the probability that a statistic of interest will fall in a certain interval; for example, the height of a person chosen at random may follow the *normal distribution*. Following are some samples of kinds of distributions, with location of the means and medians indicated:

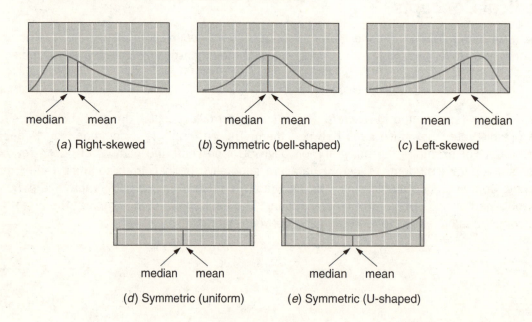

(*a*) Right-skewed   (*b*) Symmetric (bell-shaped)   (*c*) Left-skewed

(*d*) Symmetric (uniform)   (*e*) Symmetric (U-shaped)

Distribution (*b*) in the figure is the famous normal, or bell-shaped, curve on which tests are often said to be graded. Notice that more scores fall in the middle here than on the high or low ends. In the right-skewed distribution, shown in (*a*), more of the scores are low, and in (*c*) more of the scores are high (assuming that all of these graphs represent test scores). The distribution in (*d*) shows that all scores are distributed equally from high to low, and (*e*) shows a distribution in which most scores were either high or low, with very few being average. Notice that in (*a*), the right-skewed distribution, the mean is higher than the median, and in (*c*) the median is higher than the mean.

correlation Correlation is the relationship between two variables. For example, a graph of tar and nicotine in cigarettes might look like this:

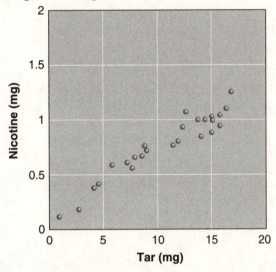

Each dot represents a particular cigarette, and the placement of the dot depends on the amounts of its tar (*x*-axis) and nicotine (*y*-axis). Drawings like this are called *scatterplots*. You could draw a straight line through this scatterplot, and it would go up and to the right, because, in general, the higher the amount of tar, the higher the amount of nicotine. The amounts of tar and nicotine are thus *positively correlated*. Some variables are *negatively correlated*; for instance, the weight of a vehicle would be negatively correlated with gas mileage if several models of vehicle were plotted in a scatterplot.

Here are some other scatterplots with varying kinds of correlation:

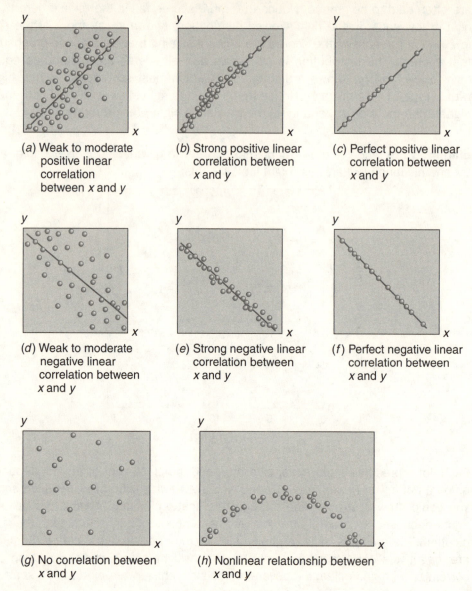

(a) Weak to moderate positive linear correlation between x and y

(b) Strong positive linear correlation between x and y

(c) Perfect positive linear correlation between x and y

(d) Weak to moderate negative linear correlation between x and y

(e) Strong negative linear correlation between x and y

(f) Perfect negative linear correlation between x and y

(g) No correlation between x and y

(h) Nonlinear relationship between x and y

When a correlation is linear or almost linear, you can use the graph to make predictions. For example, in the graph of tar and nicotine above, you could predict with a fair amount of certainty that a cigarette with 10 mg of tar would have between 0.7 and 0.8 mg of nicotine. In scatterplots without a linear correlation [(g) and (h) above], it's much harder to predict what y would be given x; in fact, in graph (g) it's nearly impossible.

Mathematical Reasoning

Competency 0010

Apply mathematical reasoning skills to analyze patterns and solve problems.

The following topics are examples of content that may be covered under this competency.
• Draw conclusions using inductive reasoning.
• Draw conclusions using deductive reasoning.

When presented with math or logic problems, including geometry problems, *deductive reasoning* may be helpful. Deductive reasoning is reasoning from the general to the specific, and is supported by deductive logic. Here is an example of deductive reasoning:

All humans who have walked on the moon are males (a general proposition). Neil Armstrong walked on the moon, therefore he is a male (a specific proposition.)

Note that conclusions reached via deductive reasoning are sound only if the original assumptions are actually true.

With *inductive* reasoning, a general rule is inferred from specific observations (which may be limited). Moving from the statement "All fish I have ever seen have fins" (specific but limited observations) to "All fish have fins" (a general proposition) is an example of inductive reasoning. Conclusions arrived at via inductive reasoning are not necessarily true.

An example of how logical reasoning can be used to solve a geometry problem is given hereafter. (In this case *deductive* reasoning is used to find the measure of ∠J.)

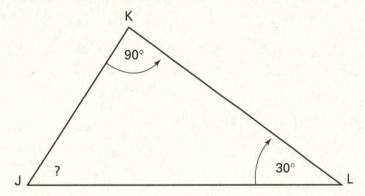

The sum of the measures of the three angles of any triangle is 180° (a general proposition). The sum of the measures of ∠K and ∠L is 120°, therefore the measure of ∠L is 60° (a specific proposition).

Mathematical Induction

A special case of inductive reasoning is *mathematical induction*. With mathematical induction, we can actually prove mathematical propositions about positive integers (i.e., all *n* natural numbers) that we derive from specific observations. In order to prove something by mathematical induction, we need to do the following:

1. Show that the proposition holds when $n = 0$.
2. Show that if the proposition is true when $n = m$, then it is also true when $n = m + 1$.

For example, you might notice that the sum of consecutive integers $1 + 2 + 3 = 6$, and that $1 + 2 + 3 + 4 + 5 = 15$. From these facts, you might conclude (after a bit of algebraic wrangling, which we won't go into here) that the sum of the first *n* positive integers in $n(n + 1)/2$—which does fit our two examples, and which we could easily show fits $1 + 2 + 3 + 4 = 10$ and $1 + 2 + 3 + 4 + 5 + 6 + 7 = 28$. But would it also work for $n = 952$? We can prove that it does by mathematical induction.

First we have to demonstrate that if n = 0, the proposition holds. Clearly it does, since $0 = 0(0 + 1)/2$. Then we can prove the validity of the proposition by proving that if *m* works, then so does *m* +1. Thus, we assume that $1 + 2 + 3 + ... + m = m(m + 1)/2$. Adding $m + 1$ to the sum, we get

$$1 + 2 + 3 + ... + m + m + 1 = m(m + 1)/2 + m + 1$$
$$= m(m + 1)/2 + 2(m + 1)/2$$
$$= (m^2 + m + 2m + 2)/2$$

By factoring the numerator on the right side of the equation, we get $(m + 1)(m + 2)/2$, or $(m + 1)((m + 1) + 1)/2$, which shows that, starting at zero, we can go up one by one to prove that each succeeding sum follows the same pattern. Thus, the sum of natural numbers 1 through 952 is truly $(952)(953)/2$.

Using Algebra in Deductive Reasoning

On the OGET, you may have to answer a question that gives you general statements that are known to be true. From those you must deduce which of four other statements is also true. For example, consider the following question:

Ghita grows daffodils, crocuses, and tulips in her garden. When asked about how many daffodils she has, she replies that she has at least as many daffodils as she has tulips, and she also says that she has at least as many tulips as crocuses. Assuming her statements are true, which of the following statements is also true?

A.   She has exactly as many crocuses as daffodils.

B.   She has at least as many crocuses as daffodils.

C.   She has at least as many daffodils as crocuses.

D.   She has more daffodils than crocuses.

To answer this question, let d equal the number of daffodils, t be the number of tulips, and c be the number of crocuses. Thus we know that $d \geq t$ and that $t \geq c$. Thus $d \geq t \geq c$, which means that she has *at least* as many daffodils as crocuses (choice C). She may have more daffodils than crocuses (choice D), but we can't be sure of that. The inequalities comparing c to d would be reversed, and neither choice A nor choice B would be true.

Word Problems and Algebraic Methods

Competency 0011

Solve applied problems using a combination of mathematical skills (including word problems involving one and two variables).

The following topics are examples of content that may be covered under this competency.
*   Apply combinations of algebraic skills to solve problems.
*   Apply combinations of mathematical skills to solve a series of related problems.
*   Identify the algebraic equivalent of a stated relationship.
*   Identify the proper equation or expression to solve word problems involving one and two variables.

Word Problems

The key to converting word problems into mathematical problems is attention to *reasonableness*, with the choice of operations most crucial to success. Often, individual words and phrases translate into numbers and operations symbols, and making sure that the translations are reasonable is important. Consider this word problem:

> Roberto babysat for the Yagers one evening. They paid him $5 just for coming over to their house, plus $7 for every hour of sitting. How much was he paid if he babysat for 4 hours?

"Plus" indicates addition, and "for every hour" suggests multiplication. Thus, the computational work can be set up like this: 5 + (7 × 4) = Roberto's earnings. It would have been unreasonable to use a multiplication symbol in place of the addition sign. He earned $5 *plus* $7 for each of 4 hours.

Each word problem requires an individual approach, but keeping in mind the reasonableness of the computational setup should be helpful. (See more on this topic further in this review, "Solving word problems involving one and two variables.")

Solving One- and Two-Variable Equations

When attempting to solve one-variable equations, it is helpful to think of the task as that of producing a series of equivalent equations until, in the last equation, the variable has been *isolated* on one side. There are several ways to produce equivalent equations, but chiefly they are produced by performing identical operations on the two expressions making up the sides of equations. The equation $2x = 12$, for instance, can be solved by dividing both sides of the equation by 2, as follows:

$$\frac{2x}{2} = \frac{12}{2}$$

This then gives an equivalent equation of $x = 6$. Therefore, 6 is the solution to the original equation.

There are several caveats to observe when solving one-variable equations in that manner. One is that care must be taken to perform operations on *entire* expressions, and not simply on "parts" of expressions. In the example below, the last equation fails to give a solution to the original equation because, in the second step, only *part* of the expression $2x + 8$ has been divided by 2.

$$2x + 8 = 14$$
$$\frac{2x}{2} + \frac{8}{2} = \frac{14}{2}$$
$$x + 4 = 7$$
$$x = 3$$

Avoid dividing by zero. That operation is considered meaningless and will not provide a solution. Also, not all single-variable equations have solutions. $0x + 3 = 9$, for instance, has no real number solutions. If the variable carries an exponent, as in $x^2 = 16$, taking the square root of each side of the equation produces the solutions. (Note that *both* 4 and –4 work.)

"Solving one variable in terms of a second" simply means rewriting multivariable equations such that the desired variable is isolated on one side of the equation. For instance, the equation $x - 3y = 5$ can be rewritten as $x = 3y + 5$. The variable x has been solved in terms of the second variable y.

Solving a *system* of two-variable linear equations (such as $y = x + 6$ and $2y = 4x$) means finding the ordered pair (or pairs) of numbers that solves both equations simultaneously. Using trial and error, we can see that (6, 12) works in both of the equations above. There are also more formal methods for solving systems of two-variable equations. If we graph each equation on the coordinate plane, the point of intersection (if any) will give the solution to the system. Another method is to literally add or subtract one equation from the other, with the intention of eliminating one variable in the process, enabling us to solve for one variable, then the other. (One or both equations may first require multiplication in order to "line up" variables with opposite coefficients.) In the example that follows, the system of $y = x + 6$ and $2y = 4x$ has been solved using multiplication and addition.

$$y = x + 6$$
$$2y = 4x$$
$$-2y = -2x - 12$$
$$2y = 4x$$
$$0 = 2x - 12$$
$$x = 6$$

If $x = 6$, y must equal 12, so the solution to the system is (6, 12).

Solving Word Problems Involving One and Two Variables

One helpful approach when attempting to solve algebraic word problems is to *translate* the word problem into an equation (or, sometimes, an inequality), then solve the equation. Consider the word problem: "The Acme Taxicab Company charges riders 3 dollars just for getting into the cab, plus 2 dollars for every mile or fraction of a mile driven. What would be the fare for a 10-mile ride?" "Translating into math" we get $x = 3 + (2 \times 10)$. The equation can be read as "the unknown fare (x) is equal to 3 dollars *plus* 2 dollars for each of the 10 miles driven." Solving the equation gives 23 for x, so $23 is the solution to the word problem.

There are several common translations to keep in mind: The word *is* often suggests an equal sign; *of* may suggest multiplication, as does *product*. *Sum* refers to addition; *difference* suggests subtraction; and a *quotient* is obtained after dividing. The key when translating is to make sure that the equation accurately matches the information and relationships given in the word problem.

Understanding Operations with Algebraic Expressions

Only like (or similar) algebraic terms can be added or subtracted to produce simpler expressions. For instance, $3x^2$ and $5x^2$ can be added together to get $8x^2$, because the terms are like terms; they both have a base of x^2. We *cannot* add $8m^3$ and $6m^2$; m^3 and m^2 are unlike bases.

When multiplying exponential terms together, the constant terms are multiplied, but the exponents of terms with the same variable bases are *added* together, which is somewhat counterintuitive. For example, $5w^2$ times $2w^3$ gives $10w^5$ (*not* $10w^6$, as one might guess).

When like algebraic terms are divided, exponents are subtracted. For example,

$$\frac{7w^5}{2w^2}$$

becomes

$$\frac{7w^3}{2}$$

In algebra, we frequently need to multiply two binomials together. (*Binomials* are algebraic expressions of two terms.) The FOIL method is one way to multiply binomials. FOIL stands for "first, outer, inner, last." Multiply the first terms in the parentheses, then the "outermost" terms, followed by the "innermost terms," and finally the last terms, then add the products together. For example, to multiply ($x + 2$) and ($3x - 1$), we multiply x by $3x$ (the "firsts"), x by -1 ("outers"), 2 by $3x$ ("inners"), and 2 by -1 ("lasts"). The four products ($3x^2$, $-x$, $6x$ and -2) add up to $3x^2 + 5x - 2$. If the polynomials to be multiplied have more than two terms (*trinomials*, for instance), make sure that *each* term of the first polynomial is multiplied by *each* term of the second.

The opposite of polynomial multiplication is factoring. Factoring a polynomial means rewriting it as the product of factors (often two binomials). The trinomial $x^2 - 4x - 21$, for instance, can be factored into ($x + 3$)($x - 7$). (You can check this by "FOILing" the binomials.)

When attempting to factor polynomials, it is sometimes necessary to first "factor out" any factor that might be common to all terms. The two terms in $3x^2 - 12$, for example, both contain the factor 3. This means that the expression can be rewritten as $3(x^2 - 4)$, and then, $3(x - 2)(x + 2)$.

The task of factoring a polynomial is often aided by first setting up a pair of "empty" parentheses, like this: $2x^2 - 9x - 5 = ($ $)($ $)$. The task is then to fill in the four spaces with values which, when multiplied (FOILed), will "give back" $2x^2 - 9x - 5$.

Factoring is useful when solving some equations, especially if one side of the equation is set equal to zero. Consider $x^2 + 3x - 8 = 2$. It can be rewritten as $x^2 + 3x - 10 = 0$. This allows the left side to be factored into $(x - 2)(x + 5)$, giving equation solutions of 2 and –5.

Computation Skills

Chapter 4

Basic Number Skills

Competency 0012

Solve word problems involving integers, fractions, decimals, and units of measurement.

The following topics are examples of content that may be covered under this competency.
- Solve word problems involving integers, fractions, and decimals (including percentages).
- Solve word problems involving ratio and proportions.
- Solve word problems involving units of measurement and conversions (including scientific notation).

Fractions need to have common denominators before adding. Thus, to add, say, $\frac{1}{2}$ and $\frac{2}{3}$, change both fractions to equivalent fractions. These new equivalent fractions will have the same *value* as $\frac{1}{2}$ and $\frac{2}{3}$ and will have common (same) denominators, but will look different from the original fractions. The lowest common denominator is 6, because both of the original denominators can be changed into 6; $\frac{1}{2}$ can be written as $\frac{3}{6}$, and $\frac{2}{3}$ can be written as $\frac{4}{6}$.

After changing the "appearance" of $\frac{1}{2} + \frac{2}{3}$ to $\frac{3}{6} + \frac{4}{6}$, we can then simply add the numerators together, giving $\frac{7}{6}$, or $1\frac{1}{6}$.

When adding mixed fractions (those made up of a whole number and a fraction), add the fractions first, then—separately—the whole numbers. If the fractions add up to more than 1, add 1 to the whole number sum. For example, if after adding we have 3 and $1\frac{3}{4}$, the final sum is $4\frac{3}{4}$.

The algorithm for subtracting fractions is generally the same as that for adding. Common denominators are required. A problem, however, may be encountered when attempting to subtract mixed fractions such as $3\frac{2}{5}$ and $1\frac{4}{5}$. Note that $\frac{4}{5}$ can't be subtracted from $\frac{2}{5}$ (without involving negative numbers.) The solution is to rename $3\frac{2}{5}$ as $2\frac{7}{5}$. (This is accomplished by "borrowing" 1, or $\frac{5}{5}$, from the 3.) The new problem—still equivalent to the original—is $2\frac{7}{5}$ minus $1\frac{4}{5}$, or $1\frac{3}{5}$.

One approach to multiplying fractions is to multiply the numerators together and the denominators together, then simplify the resulting product. $\frac{2}{3} \times \frac{3}{4}$, for instance, equals $\frac{6}{12}$, or $\frac{1}{2}$. There is no need to use common denominators (as with fraction addition and subtraction.)

If the numbers to be multiplied are mixed fractions, first rewrite them as "improper" fractions, such as $\frac{14}{3}$, then use the procedure described earlier.

To divide fractions, invert the divisor (or the "second" number; the one "doing the dividing") and multiply instead. In the case of $\frac{1}{5}$ divided by $\frac{3}{8}$, change the original problem to the equivalent problem $\frac{1}{5} \times \frac{8}{3}$. Using the algorithm for multiplying fractions, we get $\frac{8}{15}$ as the quotient.

Decimal notation provides a different way of representing fractions whose denominators are powers of 10. $\frac{13}{100}$, for instance, is written as 0.13, $\frac{1}{1000}$ as 0.001, and so forth.

To add or subtract decimal numbers, arrange them vertically, aligning decimal points, then add or subtract as one would whole numbers. (A whole number can be written as a decimal numeral by placing a decimal point to its right, with as many zeros added as needed. Thus, 7 becomes 7.0, or 7.00, etc.) The decimal point then "drops down" directly into the sum or difference; its position is not shifted.

Using the traditional algorithm for multiplying decimal numbers does *not* require aligning decimal points; the numbers to be multiplied can simply be arranged vertically, with right "justification." The numbers can then be multiplied as if they were whole numbers. The number of digits to the right of the decimal point in the product should equal the total number of digits to the right of the two factors. Here is an example:

$$
\begin{array}{r}
1.64 \\
\times\ 0.3 \\
\hline
= 0.492
\end{array}
$$

One method for dividing decimal numbers is to use the traditional whole number division algorithm, placing the decimal point properly in the answer. The number of digits to the right of the decimal point in the divisor is how far the decimal point in the quotient (the answer) should be moved to the right, with the decimal point in the dividend as our starting position. Here is an example:

$$0.3\overline{)1.44} = 4.8$$

Note that careful placement of digits when writing both the problem and the quotient helps ensure a correct answer.

The rules for performing operations on integers (whole numbers and their negative counterparts) and on fractions and decimal numbers where at least one is negative are generally the same as the rules for performing operations on non-negative numbers. The trick is to pay attention to the sign (the positive or negative value) of each answer. The rules for multiplication and division when at least one negative number is involved are the same: two positives or two negatives give a positive, whereas "mixing" a positive and a negative gives a negative ($-5 \times 3 = -15$, for instance). When at least one negative number is involved in addition and subtraction, it may be useful to think of the values as money, with "adding" being thought of as "gaining," "subtracting" being thought of as "losing," positive numbers being seen as "credits" and negative numbers, "debts." (Careful: Adding or "gaining" -8 is like *losing* 8.)

Sometimes, mathematical expressions indicate several operations. When simplifying such expressions, there is a universally agreed-upon order for "doing" each operation. First we compute any multiplication or division, left to right. Then, compute any addition or subtraction, also left to right. (If an expression contains any parentheses, all computation within the parentheses must be completed first.) Treat exponential expressions ("powers") as multiplication. Thus, the expression $3 + 7 \times 4 - 2$ equals 29. (Multiply 7 by 4 *before* doing the addition and subtraction.)

Exponential notation is a way to show repeated multiplication more simply. $2 \times 2 \times 2$, for instance, can be shown as 2^3, and is equal to 8. (Note: 2^3 does *not* mean 2×3.)

Scientific notation provides a method for showing any numbers using exponents (although it is most useful for very large and very small numbers.) A number is in scientific notation when it is shown as a number between 1 and 10 times a power of 10. Thus, the number 75,000 in scientific notation is shown as 7.5×10^4.

Other common mathematical notation symbols include the following:

$<$ means "less than"
$>$ means "greater than"
$\neq$ means "not equal to"

Graphing and Solving Equations

Competency 0013

Graph and solve algebraic equations with one and two variables.

The following topics are examples of content that may be covered under this competency.
*   Graph numbers or number relationships.
*   Find the value of the unknown in a given one-variable equation.
*   Express one variable in terms of a second variable in two-variable equations.

Two-Dimensional Graphing

The coordinate plane is useful for graphing individual ordered pairs and relationships. The coordinate plane is divided into four quadrants by an *x*-axis (horizontal) and a *y*-axis (vertical). The upper right quadrant is quadrant I, and the others (moving counterclockwise from quadrant I) are II, III, and IV.

Ordered pairs indicate the locations of points on the plane. For instance, (–3, 4) describes a point that's three units *left* from the center of the plane (the "origin") and four units *up*, as shown below.

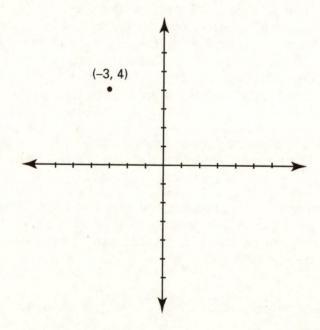

Sets of data can be paired to form many ordered pairs, which in turn can be graphed on the coordinate plane. Consider the following sets of data, which have been paired:

x	y
3	5
4	6
5	7
6	8

Considering each pairing individually, the following ordered pairs are produced: (3, 5), (4, 6), (5, 7), (6, 8). *Plotting* each pair on the coordinate plane produces the following graph:

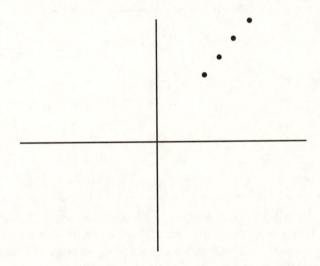

If the sets represent continuous change, the resulting graph may be a line (straight or curved in various ways). Often, relationships between sets of data can be shown as two variable equations or inequalities. Consider the following ordered pairs: (–4, –2), (–2, –1), (0, 0), (2, 1), (4, 2).

Note that the first value in each (the *x* value) is twice as big as the second (the *y* value). Assuming that the ordered pairs represent continuous change, the equation $x = 2y$ can be used to describe the relationship of the *x* values and the *y* values. It is helpful to think of the equation as stating that "*x* is always twice as big as *y*." We can show the equation on the coordinate plane by graphing at least two of the points, then connecting them as shown below.

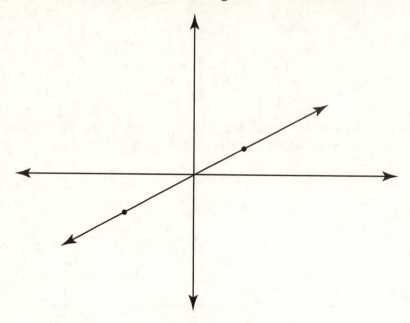

The generic equation $y = mx + b$ is a template for graphs on the plane that are straight lines. That form (sometimes called the "*y*-intercept form" of an equation) is especially useful because it tells two important characteristics of lines at a glance. The coefficient of *x* in the equation (or *m*) indicates the steepness, or *slope* of the line on the plane. The larger the absolute value of *m*, the steeper the slope of the line. (A number's absolute value is its distance from zero, giving no regard to negative signs.) Consider the two equations that follow and their accompanying graphs.

$y = 1/4x + 2$ $y = 5x - 1$

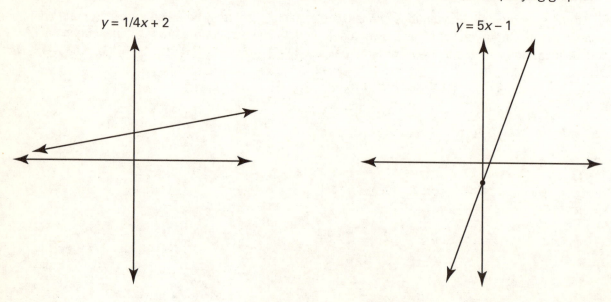

Note that the equation on the left has a small slope ($\frac{1}{4}$), so its graph is nearly horizontal. The other equation has a comparatively large slope (5), so it is steep.

If the coordinates of any two points of a straight line are known, the numerical slope of that line can easily be computed by finding the difference between the points' *y* values and dividing by the difference of the points' *x* values. For example, if (2, 5) and (4, 10) are points on a line, the slope of the line is $\frac{5}{2}$ [(5 − 10) ÷ (2 − 4)]. Note that slopes are generally shown as fractions or whole numbers, but not as mixed fractions.

The equation of a straight line in the form *y* = *mx* + *b* tells something else about the line at a glance. The *b* value indicates where the line will cross or *intercept* the *y* (vertical) axis. Consider the graph of *y* = 2*x* + 3 that follows.

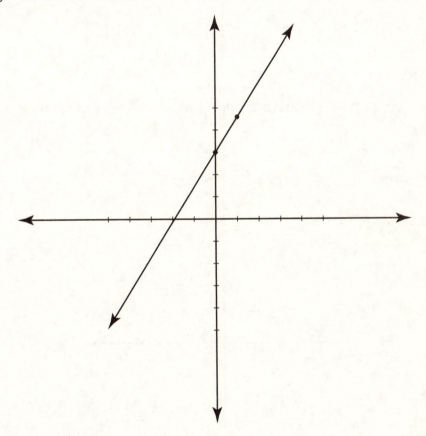

Note that the graph crosses the *y*-axis at a point that is 3 units above the origin. As long as the equation of a straight line is in the form *y* = *mx* + *b*, *m* gives the slope and *b* gives the *y*-intercept. (Note: If *b* = 0, the graph will pass through the origin. In that case, both the equation and the graph are referred to as *direct variations*.)

Other equations may produce curved graphs. For instance, $y = x^2$ produces the following graph, known as a *parabola*.

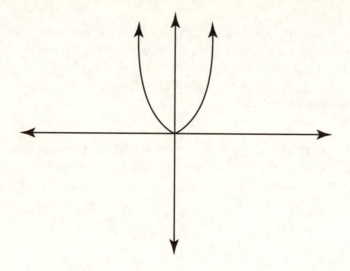

The equation $y = \frac{1}{x}$ is an *inverse variation*; it produces a graph known as a *hyperbola*, as shown below.

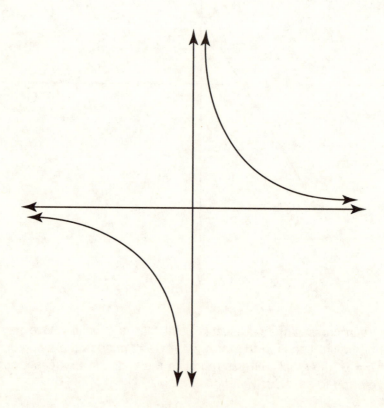

The graphs of *functions* can be shown on the coordinate plane. Such graphs always indicate a continuous (although not necessarily consistent) "movement" from left to right. Below left is the graph of a function; the graph on the right is *not* a function.

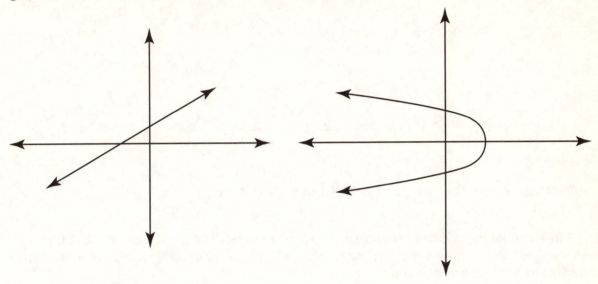

Geometry

Competency 0014

Solve problems involving geometric figures.

The following topics are examples of content that may be covered under this competency.
- Solve problems involving two-dimensional geometric figures (e.g., perimeter and area problems).
- Solve problems involving three-dimensional geometric figures (e.g., volume and surface area problems).

Solving Problems Involving Geometric Figures

The following are formulas for finding the areas of basic polygons (informally defined as closed, coplanar geometric figures with three or more straight sides). Abbreviations used are as follows: *A* stands for *area*, *l* stands for *length*, *w* stands for *width*, *h* stands for *height*, and *b* stands for *length of the base*.

Triangle (a three-sided polygon): $A = \frac{b \times h}{2}$. (Note that, as shown in the figure that follows, the height of a triangle is not necessarily the same as the length of any of its sides.)

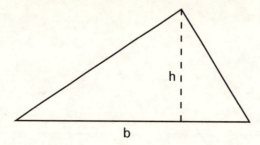

Rectangle (a four-sided polygon with four right angles): $A = l \times w$

Parallelogram (a four-sided polygon with two pairs of parallel sides): $A = b \times h$. (Note that, as with triangles, and as shown in the figure below, the height of a parallelogram is not necessarily the same as the length of its sides.)

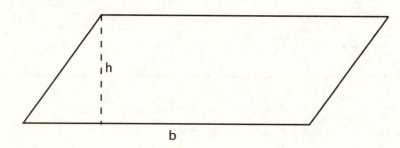

The area of a circle can be found by squaring the length of its radius, then multiplying that product by π. The formula is given as $A = \pi r^2$. (π, or pi, is the ratio of a circle's circumference to its diameter. The value of π is the same for all circles; approximately 3.14159. The approximation 3.14 is adequate for many calculations.) The approximate area of the circle shown below can be found by squaring 6 (giving 36), then multiplying 36 by 3.14, giving an area of about 113 square units.

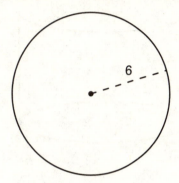

Here are several commonly used volume formulas:

The volume of a rectangular solid is equal to the product of its length, width, and height; $A = l \times w \times h$. (A rectangular solid can be thought of as a box, wherein all intersecting edges form right angles.)

A prism is a polyhedron with two congruent, parallel faces (called bases) and whose lateral (side) faces are parallelograms. The volume of a prism can be found by multiplying the area of the prism's base by its height. The volume of the triangular prism shown hereafter is 60 cubic units. (The area of the triangular base is 10 square units, and the height is 6 units.)

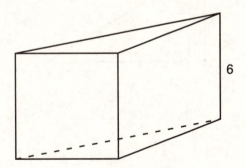

A cylinder is like a prism in that it has parallel faces, but its rounded "side" is smooth. The formula for finding the volume of a cylinder is the same as the formula for finding the volume of a prism: The area of the cylinder's base is multiplied by the height. The volume of the cylinder in the following figure is approximately 628 cubic units. ($5 \times 5 \times \pi \times 8$).

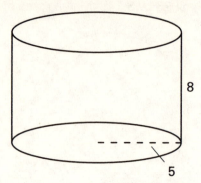

A property of all triangles is that the sum of the measures of the three angles is 180°. If, therefore, the measures of two angles are known, the third can be deduced using addition, then subtraction.

Right triangles (those with a right angle) have several special properties. A chief property is described by the Pythagorean Theorem, which states that in any right triangle with legs (shorter sides) a and b, and hypotenuse (the longest side) c, the sum of the squares of the sides will be equal to the square of the hypotenuse ($a^2 + b^2 = c^2$). Note that in the right triangle shown hereafter, $3^2 + 4^2 = 5^2$.

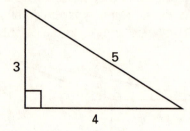

Applying Reasoning Skills

Geometric figures are *similar* if they have the exact same shapes, even if they do not have the same sizes. In transformational geometry, two figures are said to be similar if and only if a similarity transformation maps one figure onto the other. In the figure that follows, triangles A and B are similar.

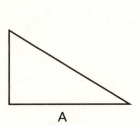 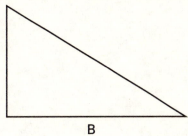

A   B

Corresponding angles of similar figures have the same measure, and the lengths of corresponding sides are proportional. In the similar triangles below, $\angle A \cong \angle D$ (meaning "angle A is congruent to angle D"), $\angle B \cong \angle E$, and $\angle C \cong \angle F$. The corresponding sides of the triangles below are proportional, meaning that:

$$\frac{AB}{DE} = \frac{BC}{EF} = \frac{CA}{FD}$$

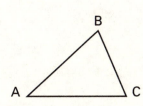 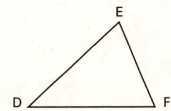

Figures are *congruent* if they have the same shape *and* size. (Congruent figures are also similar.) In the figure below, rectangles A and B are congruent.

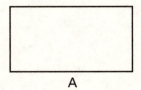 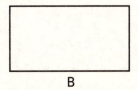

A   B

Straight lines within the same plane that have no points in common (that is, they never cross) are parallel lines. Note that the term *parallel* is used to describe the relationship between two coplanar lines that do not intersect. Lines that are not coplanar—although they never cross—are not considered to be parallel. Coplanar lines crossing at right angles (90°) are perpendicular.

Liberal Studies: Science, Art, Literature, and Social Sciences

Scientific Principles

Competency 0015

Understand and analyze major scientific principles, concepts, and theories, and apply skills, principles, and procedures associated with scientific inquiry.

The following topics are examples of content that may be covered under this competency.
- Analyze the nature of scientific thought and inquiry.
- Use an appropriate illustration or physical model to represent a scientific theory or concept.
- Relate major scientific principles, concepts, or theories to everyday phenomena.
- Apply scientific principles to assess real-world questions or problems.

What Is Science?

The modern word "science" is derived from the Latin *sciencia*, or "knowledge," and refers both to the process of gathering knowledge about the physical world and to the accumulated body of knowledge which is its result. The nature and goals of "science" can be understood in more than one way. Science is often categorized as either "pure," in which scientific knowledge is pursued as its own end, or as "applied," which designates fields such as medicine or engineering that use scientific knowledge to address human needs. Furthermore, the process through which such knowledge is achieved can be classified in two ways. Scientific practice can be divided into **experiment**, which seeks to gather first-hand information, and **theory**, or the development of models to explain these observations. The **empirical** school of thought emphasizes inductive reasoning and reliance on the senses and on individual observation and experience. It holds that scientific theories are objective and can be tested and contradicted. **Scientific realism**, on the other hand, is based on the idea that scientific claims build on one another to become progressively more accurate, and aims to discover an "ideal scientific theory" which accounts for unobservable as well as observable phenomena.

All science relies on the **scientific method** for the collection of reliable data. Although the scientific method is not a specific and uniform set of procedures, it can usefully be broken down into four broad components:

- **Characterization**, or preliminary observations and measurements

- **Hypotheses**, or theoretical explanations for these observations and measurements

- **Predictions**, or logical deductions based on the hypotheses

- **Experiments**, or strategically designed testing of all of the above

The final three steps are frequently repeated until a hypothesis that stands up to testing is achieved. If the conclusions drawn from a hypothesis are not disproved, that hypothesis becomes an accepted scientific **theory** or **law**. It is critical to note that no scientific theory or law is ever definitively proven to be true. If subsequent experimentation disproves it entirely or in part, even a long-standing theory or law must be discarded or modified. The best known recent example of this process is of course the advent of quantum mechanics when, after over two hundred years, Newtonian mechanics were found to be inaccurate for speeds approaching that of light.

Measurement is also central to the scientific method. For a hypothesis to be accepted, the results of an experiment must be **reproducible**; that is, another scientist following the same procedure should be able to duplicate them. Scientific experiments should be carefully designed and controlled, as far as possible, to yield quantitative rather than qualitative results. Thus, science relies heavily on the related discipline of **mathematics**, which scientists use as a tool to evaluate the results of their observations and to organize large quantities of data into averages, ranges, and statistical probabilities. All measurements are limited by the fundamental uncertainty of the measuring device, which necessitates the use of **significant figures**. This concept is based on the fact that calculations on measurements cannot generate results that are more precise than the measurements themselves. When scientists read the results of measurements made by others, therefore, they presume that the recorded values involve a final digit that is an estimate based on the inherent accuracy of the instrument or device.

Science can be roughly divided into three main areas: the **physical sciences**, the **earth sciences**, and the **life or biological sciences**. The physical sciences include physics, chemistry, and astronomy; the earth sciences include geology, paleontology, oceanography, and meteorology, and the life sciences include all the branches of botany, zoology, and cell or microbiology. These areas of specialization can be divided into further sub-sections. Physics, for example, has given rise to disciplines that include mechanics, thermodynamics, and optics. In addition, there are numerous scientific fields that combine the three main branches of science, such as geophysics or biochemistry.

Teaching Science

The sheer bulk and variety of scientific knowledge both provides ample opportunities for students to apply scientific principles and methods to real-world questions and phenomena, and raises questions about how to teach these skills. Models and illustrations can often help to make scientific concepts accessible by helping students to visualize a relevant system—for example, a volcano, a cell wall, or a virus. All models share some important features and limitations. In general and abstract terms, models have an information input, an information processor, and an output of expected results. It is important to emphasize the artificiality of any given model, its status as a simplified replica of the system it illustrates. For models to be effective as teaching tools, certain guiding parameters must be in place: simplifying assumptions must be acknowledged, boundary conditions or initial conditions must be identified, and the range of applicability of the model should be understood. The following are varieties of models frequently employed in the classroom:

Conceptual Models are qualitative, often schematic, models that make sense of real world systems and processes. They are used as a first step in the development of more complex models. Conceptual models should be familiar to students, as human beings are constantly, if unconsciously, employing them. Everyone receives information, processes it, and responds accordingly on a daily basis. This sort of processing of information results in a sort of mental model teachers can use deliberately to explain how things in our surrounding environment work.

Interactive Demonstrations replicate part of a system of interest and are often constructed from materials or objects familiar to students from everyday life. Interactive demonstrations are accessible physical models of systems that share key characteristics with their extant counterparts. These models often provide a link between conceptual models and models of more complex real-world systems.

Mathematical and Statistical Models involve solving equations relevant to a system or characterizing it based on statistical values such as mean, mode, or variance. Mathematical models can be further divided into *Analytical Models* and *Numerical Models*. Statistical models are useful in identifying patterns and underlying relationships between data sets.

Visual Models are models, including illustrations, charts, graphs, and diagrams, that help students "see" how a system operates. A visual model such as a graph can stand alone as a direct rendering of data, or it can be applied to one or more other types of model in order to present its output in a visually accessible format.

In practice, most models combine more than one of the above functions.

In recent decades, many science educators have become concerned that, despite access to models and to hands-on experimentation, traditional science programs emphasize memorized facts and formulas over critical thinking and application of the scientific method, thus making it difficult for students to apply scientific knowledge to the real world. They advocate programs which foster **conceptual change**, or the process of identifying students' incorrect assumptions and replacing them through experimentation, thus enabling them to construct their own models of scientific principles. Science education, according to proponents of conceptual change, should:

- *Stress relevance*. Unless students appreciate the relevance of their experiments to their everyday life, they may dismiss surprising results as applicable only to the classroom or laboratory setting.

- *Encourage students to make predictions*. Students asked to predict the results of their experiments are more willing to change their minds than those who observe passively. This aspect of science instruction is essential because it asks students to link their new and existing knowledge in order to form hypotheses.

- *Stress consistency*. Teachers should make students aware of inconsistencies in their thinking and ask them to consider how two contradictory statements could be true. Ideally, students will confront inconsistencies and change their thinking as a result.

The goal of these science programs is the development of logical, consistent thought and of an orderly view of the world which prevents the compartmentalization of knowledge.

The Development and Social Contexts of Science

Competency 0016

Understand and analyze the historical development and cultural contexts of science and technology and the impact of science on society.

The following topics are examples of content that may be covered under this competency.
- Analyze the historical development and impact of key scientific ideas and discoveries.
- Evaluate factors that have promoted or hindered developments in science and technology.
- Assess the implications of recent developments in science and technology.

The Origins of Science

The combination of theory and practice that we know as modern science is a relatively recent development which had separate beginnings in the technology of early tool-making and other crafts, and in philosophy and religion. In the early civilizations of the Tigris-Euphrates and Nile valleys, for example, artisans and craft-workers were responsible for practical advances in metallurgy, agriculture, transportation, and navigation, and priests and scribes developed written language and early mathematics for the purposes of record keeping, land division, and calendar determination.

Science in Western Antiquity

What we think of as "pure science," or scientific theory devised simply for the expansion of knowledge or understanding of the physical world, has its roots in early Greek, or Hellenic, culture and its attempts to order the world according to philosophical principles. Notable among these is the theory, which persisted into the Middle Ages and Renaissance, that the universe is composed of the four basic elements earth, air, fire, and water. Early Greece produced such scientific figures as Hippocrates of Cos (4th century BCE), who formulated the science of diagnosis based on accurate descriptions of the symptoms of various diseases, and the philosophers Plato (427–347 BCE) and Aristotle (384–322 BCE).

Early Eastern Contributions to Science

Although a great deal of Eastern thought was devoted to theological and political rather than "scientific" concerns, prevailing religious and philosophical doctrines gave rise to multiple theories of metallurgy, alchemy, and medicine. Eastern societies were also the first to adopt many advanced technologies, making several accomplishments in science parallel to early developments in the West. Important early discoveries made by Asian scientists include paper, in the 2nd century CE, block printing in the 7th, movable clay type by the 11th, and cast-metal type in Korea by the beginning of the 15th. Gunpowder was invented in the 3rd century and firearms were in use by the 13th, as was the magnetic compass during the 11th and 12th. Indian mathematicians developed a numeral system based on place value and including a zero, and important Hindu scientists flourished in the 6th and 7th centuries, making contributions to astronomy and mathematics. During the 7th and 8th centuries, Muslim scholars introduced and preserved the scientific works both of these Hindu and other Asian scholars and of the Greeks, modifying them and adding valuable commentary. This body of learning first began to be discovered by Europeans in the 11th century.

The European Renaissance and the Scientific Revolution

The commonplace description of the Middle Ages as "Dark Ages" is a misnomer. The Middle Ages saw the establishment of many of Europe's great universities, as well as the development of several important labor-saving technologies and, in the 15th century, of the printing press. Nevertheless, science, in the modern sense of the term, is a 16th or 17th century development made possible by the union of the technologically motivated craft tradition with philosophically based scientific theory. A pervasive feeling of dissatisfaction with extant modes of understanding, which dated back to the later Middle Ages and was both the product and the stimulus of events such as the Protestant Reformation and the widespread growth of literacy in Europe, also gave rise to the revolution in science embodied in the work of Copernicus, Paracelsus, Vesalius, and others. The development of practical tools of observation such as the telescope, microscope, and mechanical clock were also of course central to the rise of empiricism and the scientific method.

Another important factor in the scientific revolution was improved communication and general societal interest, made manifest in the 17th and 18th centuries, in the establishment of learned societies and academies throughout Europe. The Royal Society in England (est. 1660) and the Academy of Sciences in France (est. 1666) were two of the most important early societies, to be joined later by royal academies established at Berlin (1700) and at St. Petersburg (1724). The societies and academies provided early opportunities for the widespread dissemination and consideration of scientific methodologies and results. The best-known figure associated with the scientific societies is Sir Isaac Newton, whose work on mechanics and astronomy dominated those fields for over two centuries.

Technological Advancement and the Industrial Revolution

It was during the 18th and 19th centuries that the individual branches of science developed into the traditional forms by which they are recognized today. The major 19th-century technological impetus was the Industrial Revolution. The need to supply power to factories, mines, ships, and railroads led to the invention of the steam engine. The development of the internal combustion engine led to the growth of petroleum technology. The 19th century also saw new agricultural machinery and a drastic accompanying increase in productivity as well as the invention of the electric generator, electric motor, and numerous other electric devices central to contemporary life.

New Directions: The Rise of Modern Science

In addition to rapid technological development, the 18th and early 19th centuries were characterized by a feeling of certainty that most important scientific discoveries had been made and that remaining areas of the unknown could be addressed by resolving minor details within the existing corpus of knowledge. Subsequent discoveries in all areas of science, however, have forced scientists to reevaluate some of their most fundamental assumptions. In physics, the early 20th century explanation of atomic structure necessitated the rejection of classical notions of space, time, matter, and energy in favor of the quantum theory and the theory of relativity. Related developments, such as Werner Heisenberg's Uncertainty Principle—which states that accurate measurement of one quality, such as momentum, makes the precise measurement of another, such as position, impossible—have cast doubt on the fundamental possibility of understanding the physical world. These theories, particularly the quantum theory, have revolutionized chemistry, biology, physics, and every other scientific field.

In biology, the modern revolution began in the 19th century with the publication of Charles Darwin's theory of evolution (1859) and Gregor Mendel's theory of genetics. The development of biochemistry and the field of molecular biology have enabled such monumental results as the discovery of the structure of deoxyribonucleic acid (DNA), the molecule carrying the genetic code. In medicine, modern biology and biochemistry have made possible drugs such as penicillin and insulin, mechanical devices such as pacemakers, and procedures for implantation of artificial or donated organs.

Practical and Ethical Implications of Scientific Development

Modern science has had an immeasurable impact on everyday life. The recent proliferation of electronic computers has revolutionized not only medicine but also communication, education, and business. Also instrumental in the development of these areas has been a dramatic improvement in transportation capacity, from the advent of the automobile and the early airplane to the modern supersonic jet, and finally, the realization of space travel. Prevention or cure seems on the horizon for an unprecedented number of diseases, and science is also working toward increased control over the environment and new sources of energy.

Modern science also faces a number of challenges. Some of these are practical, such as the production and distribution of enough food and energy to meet the demands of a population which is both rapidly growing and increasingly dependent on technology and the elimination or reduction of pollutants in the environment. Science must also, however, address a myriad of political and sociological questions. Recent issues have included the proliferation of nuclear, biological, and chemical weapons, and questions regarding the use of computers and other electronic devices that may seriously infringe on individual privacy and freedom. Many recent developments in medicine and biology, such as gene manipulation, organ transplantation, and the increasing capacity to artificially sustain life, have important and complex ethical implications. Science is a self-consciously "rational" discipline, but can never really exist in cerebral isolation. Scientific research and development is, rather, in constant interaction with political and social events, developments in the arts, philosophy, and religion, and the life experience of the individual scientist.

The Fine Arts

Competency 0017

Understand, interpret, and compare representations from the visual and performing arts from different periods and cultures, and understand the relationship of works of art to their social and historical contexts.

The following topics are examples of content that may be covered under this competency.
- Identify and evaluate major historical and contemporary developments and movements in the arts.
- Interpret and compare representations of works of art from different periods and cultures in terms of form, theme, mood, or technique.
- Analyze ways in which the content of a given work of art reflects or influences a specific social or historical context.

Visual Arts in the Western World

The earliest Western works of painting and sculpture were generally religious in nature. In Egypt and Mesopotamia, as well as Europe and the Americas, very early artists created representations of deities or other pieces with religious or ritual significance or use. Classical and Hellenic Greek art was more strictly representational, and took as its most common subject the human form: the Greeks' naturalistic rendering of the human body would influence European sculpture for centuries to come. Roman adaptations of the Greek style were less concentrated on idealizing the body than on reproducing its particularities, and ushered in the craft of portraiture.

European art during the Middle Ages, however, was almost entirely religious in subject matter and was unconcerned with realism. Medieval artists strove to express theological truths, rather than to reproduce reality, and the media they most commonly employed were part of Christian practice—stained glass, wall paintings, and statuary in cathedrals, and illuminated manuscripts of devotional texts. Late medieval, or Gothic, architecture was popularly revived in the late 18th and early 19th centuries.

The Renaissance brought a return to classical models and a renewed interest in realism, along with a broader variety of subject matter. Renaissance artwork was still generally large scale and for public consumption. The most famous example is perhaps Michelangelo's Sistine Chapel. Painting and sculpting, in the 17th and 18th century, were to become increasingly detailed and ornate, elaborate and rich in texture and—for painting—color.

The late 18th and early 19th century saw diverse reactions against this trend, producing a great number of smaller and more intimate paintings suitable for private homes and allowing the expression of emotion to take precedence over the extreme realism that characterized the preceding centuries.

Art produced during the 19th and 20th centuries took many directions, but generally, painters began to revolt against the classic codes of composition, careful execution, harmonious coloring, and heroic subject matter. Patronage by the church and state sharply declined at this time, and artists' views became more independent and subjective.

Major Movements in Western Painting and Sculpture

Style	Historical Period	Defining Aesthetic	Major Artists
Gothic	12th – 16th C.	Religious themes, schematic rather than realistic composition,	Generally anonymous. Martini, Pisano
Renaissance	14th – 17th C.	Realism, interest in anatomy, perspective. Large-scale works.	Botticelli, Da Vinci, Ghirlandio, Michelangelo
Baroque/Rococo	17th – 18th C.	Less complex. Realistic, emotional, increasingly ornate.	Caravaggio, Bernini, Caracci, Boucher
Neoclassicism	mid 18th – early 19th C.	Borrows heavily from ancient Greeks. Less emotional, rigid.	Canova, Antoine, Ingres
Romanticism	late 18th – mid-19th C.	Reaction to Neoclassicism. Emotional, individual.	Constable, Turner, Blake
Impressionism	1860s – 1880s	Reproduces the subjective impression of light.	Monet, Sisley, Renoir
Post-Impressionism	1880s – 1900s	Various. Generally emotionally charged, often dystopic.	Gauguin, Cezanne, Van Gogh, Rousseau, Toulouse-Lautrec
Expressionism/ Abstract Expressionism	1910s – 1940s	Subjective. Without object, or does not represent accurately.	Kandinsky, Rothko, Pollock
Surrealism	1924 – 1950s	Fantastic visuals from subconscious. No logical composition.	Dalí, Arp, Magritte, Modigliani
Contemporary art	~1960 – present	Various. Often multi-media and political.	Quinn, Mapplethorpe, Cathal, Haring, Basquiat

Performing Arts in the Western World

Western performing arts have their beginnings in the Greek tragedies written by such playwrights as Seneca and Euripides. These performances were shaped by the large outdoor arenas in which they were performed, and the actors, all of whom were male, employed exaggerated facial expressions and costuming in order to make themselves understood by the audience. Medieval drama also tended to privilege expressiveness over realism. It took the form of mystery and morality plays in which guilds of amateurs—also all men—enacted Biblical or other religious pieces in the spirit of broad comedy, interacting freely with the audience.

Modern professional acting began in the 16th century, a period perhaps best known for the works of playwrights such as William Shakespeare and Christopher Marlowe. Although actors in the early Renaissance remained exclusively male, the period saw the beginnings of psychological realism and of efforts to sustain the illusion of naturalism. Theater in the late 17th and early 18th centuries tended to be more comedic and irreverent, and women were beginning to appear on the stage. Despite the contemporary theater's interest in naturalism, though, actors still declaimed their lines in the deliberate style that, innovations by actors such as David Garrick and Charles Macklin notwithstanding, would hold sway until the beginning of the 20th century.

The best known figure behind the shift to a more natural style of acting is Constantin Stanislavsky, whose intensely psychological Method was made famous by actors such as Marlon Brando. Contemporary performance art merges the visual and the performing arts, blending acting with film, video, sound, and static visual imagery. Although the drama of every period has commented—some times more explicitly than others—on the social and political realities of the regime which produced it, modern drama is often overtly political, addressing issues including the experience of women, minorities, and gay and lesbian artists, foreign policy, and crises such as the AIDS epidemic.

Literature

Competency 0018

Understand, interpret, and compare examples of literature from different periods and cultures, and understand the relationship of works of literature to their social and historical contexts.

The following topics are examples of content that may be covered under this competency.

- Identify and evaluate major historical and contemporary developments and movements in world literature.
- Interpret and compare works of literature from different periods and cultures in terms of form, subject, theme, mood, or technique.
- Analyze ways in which the content of a given work of literature reflects or influences a specific social or historical context.

While it is impossible to be an expert in all areas of literature, one would do well to have at least a passing familiarity with the works of the following authors. Keep in mind that this list is not meant in any way to be exhaustive or comprehensive; rather, it is meant to serve as a catalyst to begin thinking about literature in its historical context.

Important Authors

Edward Abbey

Chinua Achebe

Richard Adams

Edward Albee

Louisa May Alcott

Sherman Alexie

Nelson Algren

Maya Angelou

Aristophanes

Jane Austen

Paul Auster

James Baldwin

Amiri Baraka (LeRoi Jones)

Donald Barthleme

Baudelaire

Samuel Beckett

Saul Bellow

Ray Bradbury

Bertolt Brecht

Joseph Bruchac

Jorge Luis Borges

Charlotte and Emily Bronte

Pearl S. Buck

Charles Bukowski

William S. Burroughs

Albert Camus

Truman Capote

Lewis Carroll

Raymond Carver

Willa Cather

Louis-Ferdinand Celine

F. Scott Fitzgerald

Gustave Flaubert

Robert Frost

Gabriel García Márquez

William Gass

Nikolai Gogol

Gunter Grass

Graham Greene

Thomas Hardy

Nathaniel Hawthorne

Joseph Heller

Ernest Hemingway

Herman Hesse

Abbie Hoffman

Homer

Nick Hornby

Langston Hughes

Victor Hugo

Zora Neale Hurston

Aldous Huxley

Henrik Ibsen

John Irving

Henry James

Stephen Graham Jones

James Joyce

Franz Kafka

John Keats

Jack Kerouac

Ken Kesey

Jamaica Kincaid

Maxine Hong Kingston

George Orwell

Ovid

Walker Percy

Sylvia Plath

Plato

Edgar Allan Poe

Ezra Pound

Richard Powers

Marcel Proust

Alexander Pushkin

Thomas Pynchon

Ishmael Reed

John (Jack) Reed

Carter Revard

Adrienne Rich

Philip Roth

Arundati Roy

Salman Rushdie

J.D. Salinger

David Sedaris

William Shakespeare

George Bernard Shaw

Mary Shelley

Sam Sheppard

Leslie Marmon Silko

Upton Sinclair

Susan Sontag

Gertrude Stein

John Steinbeck

Wallace Stevens

Robert Louis Stevenson

Miguel de Cervantes

Paddy Chayefsky

Raymond Chandler

Geoffrey Chaucer

Anton Chekhov

Sandra Cisneros

J.M. Coetzee

Joseph Conrad

James Fenimore Cooper

Quentin Crisp

e.e.cummings

Dante Alighieri

Daniel Defoe

Don DeLillo

Charles Dickens

Emily Dickinson

Joan Didion

Isak Dinesen

Stephen Dixon

John Dos Passos

Fyodor Dostoevsky

Frederick Douglass

W.E.B. DuBois

Alexander Dumas

Umberto Eco

Dave Eggers

George Eliot

T.S. Eliot

Ralph Ellison

Ralph Waldo Emerson

Louise Erdrich

William Faulkner

Lawrence Ferlinghetti

Rudyard Kipling

Milan Kundera

Jerzy Kosinsky

Nella Larsen

D.H. Lawrence

Harper Lee

Ursula K. LeGuin

Sinclair Lewis

Jack London

Federico Garcia Lorca

Norman Mailer

Thomas Mann

William Maxwell

D'Arcy McNickle

Herman Melville

Arthur Miller

Henry Miller

N. Scott Momaday

Irvin Morris

Toni Morrison

Alice Munro

Robert Musil

Vladimir Nabokov

Howard Nemerov

Pablo Neruda

Frederick Nietzsche

Frank Norris

Joyce Carol Oates

Flannery O'Connor

Clifford Odets

Kole Omotoso

Ayn Rand

Bram Stoker

Jonathan Swift

Luci Tapahonso

Dylan Thomas

Hunter S. Thompson

Henry David Thoreau

Laura Tohe

Leo Tolstoy

John Kennedy Toole

Dalton Trumbo

Mark Twain

John Updike

Edgardo Vega Yunque

Jules Verne

Gore Vidal

Voltaire

Kurt Vonnegut, Jr.

David Foster Wallace

H.G. Wells

Nathaniel West

Edith Wharton

Walt Whitman

Oscar Wilde

Tennessee Williams

William Carlos Williams

Sloan Wilson

Virginia Woolf

Richard Wright

Howard Zinn

Emile Zola

Some Important Literary Movements

Victorian

British Realism

American Colonial Literature

Post-Modern Meta-Fiction

Harlem Renaissance

German Expressionism

The Beat Poets

Existentialism

Southern Gothic

Transcendentalism

History and Its Influences

Competency 0019

Understand and analyze the major political, social, economic, scientific, and cultural developments that shaped the course of history.

The following topics are examples of content that may be covered under this competency.

- Demonstrate an understanding of the principal characteristics and important cultural values of the major civilizations of Asia, Africa, Europe, and the Americas.
- Evaluate the influence of varied ideas, movements, and historical developments on Western religious, artistic, scientific, and political ideas and beliefs (e.g., the Renaissance, the Reformation, the French Revolution).
- Analyze the major causes of varied historical developments (e.g., the Industrial Revolution, Colonialism) and evaluate their impact on the politics and culture of the modern world.
- Demonstrate knowledge of the major political movements of the twentieth century and analyze their influence on contemporary societies.
- Demonstrate an understanding of significant individuals, movements, ideas, and conflicts that have shaped U.S. history and culture (e.g., the Civil War, the New Deal).

World History

From earliest times, humans lived in hunter-gatherer societies, often nomadic and heavily dependent on local natural resources such as edible plants and game animals. Over time, other forms of social organization have developed, such as semi-nomadic livestock herding and subsistence farming, village-based subsistence farming, city-states, kingdoms, and empires. Societies have been classified according to their level of technological development based on whether their tools were made of stone, bronze, iron, or more advanced materials. This has led to the designations Stone Age, Bronze Age, Iron Age, etc.

These designations have also applied to historical periods in Western civilization based on the level of technology in use at the time. During these periods, civilizations arose in the ancient Middle East to which modern Western civilization can trace its roots. These civilizations include Sumeria, Israel, Egypt, Assyria, Babylonia, and Medo-Persia. In these empires, writing systems and codes of laws were developed that represent the earliest origins of modern Western writing systems and law codes.

Of pivotal importance in Western history is the rise of the ancient Greek civilization, beginning with the conquest by Alexander the Great in the 4th century B.C.E. of much of the former territory of the previous Middle Eastern empires. This led to the spread of the Greek culture and language throughout the region. The presence of many words with Greek roots in modern European languages, including English, testifies to the lasting impact of ancient Greek civilization. Even after the fall of the political structures founded by Alexander the Great, ancient Greek learning in the arts, the sciences, philosophy, and political thought formed part of the basis of Western learning for centuries to come.

The civilization of Rome was strongly influenced by ancient Greece, but in time achieved greater dominance in the Middle East and the Mediterranean region. By conquering the Greek dynasty ruling over Egypt in 31 B.C.E., Rome became the undisputed regional power and in time went on to conquer much of the known world. Rome was the first empire to extend the ancient Middle Eastern and Greek cultures northward into Europe. In the first and second centuries C.E., the period known as *Pax Romana* (Roman Peace) saw the development of an extensive system of roads, as well as a postal system, that facilitated transportation and thus favored the expansion of trade. This was also favored by a relative absence of internal conflicts, enforced by Roman troops. The peace of this period led to a flourishing of the arts and higher learning, still heavily influenced by classical Greek models.

Beginning in the 3rd century, Rome began a long decline as the succession of emperors grew unstable and the army began to encounter problems maintaining control over outlying provinces. In the 5th century, Rome was conquered by invading Germanic tribes. Remnants of imperial power survived, however, in the Eastern Empire with its capital in Constantinople and the Roman Catholic Church. The Germanic invaders also preserved and adopted much of what was left of the Roman Empire.

Even after Rome's power was broken, its impact was still felt in its former territories in Europe. The vacuum of power resulting from Rome's fall was filled by the Church and the feudal system. In this system of social organization, the peasants, who worked the land, were ruled by nobles. Among the nobles, the less powerful swore oaths of loyalty to the more powerful, who promised them military protection in exchange for their loyal support. This system, with many variations, was the dominant system in Europe throughout the Middle Ages. The Holy Roman Empire was the foremost political organization of the feudal system in Europe.

The Middle Ages were also known as the Dark Ages because of political instability in the early centuries after Rome's fall. The sharp decrease in the spread of knowledge, widespread illiteracy and disasters such as the Black Plague of the 14th century contributed to the problems of the era. Stability was highly valued in the midst of such problems, and medieval world views emphasized finding security by accepting one's status in the great scheme of things. In time, however, the increase of political stability and the growth of trade and commerce set the stage for the early modern era of Western history.

The modern era began with the period known as the Renaissance, meaning "rebirth," beginning around 1450. In this period, an increased interest in classical Roman and Greek learning led to advances in the arts. The growth of commerce, banking, and industry in this period favored the spread of knowledge among the rising middle class. Around the time of the Renaissance, the Reformation also challenged the dominance of the Roman Catholic Church and led to the development of Protestantism, which more closely reflected the values of Northern European cultures and the middle class. The interest in discovering new knowledge, and the attitude of challenging traditional views, have continued until today. At this time England, Spain, and Portugal also began exploring the globe and founding overseas colonies.

The renewed interest in classical learning of the Renaissance spurred a great increase of scientific knowledge in the 17th century, which further challenged traditional views of humanity, earth, and the universe. This period was also marked by political change as the feudal system slowly gave way to the development of monarchies in Western Europe. In this form of government, power was centralized in the hands of the king rather than shared among the nobles. Advances continued in the fields of science, politics, education, and commerce; these advances further removed Europe from its medieval past and favored the growth of the middle class.

The 18th century saw the development of such ideals as rationality, reason, logic, and the application of scientific knowledge for the good of society. This period, known as the Enlightenment, further challenged medieval ideals of stability and order by championing progress and planned change. The growing pressures for progress caused strained relations between the ruling class and the middle class; the conflict eventually exploded in the French Revolution of 1792. This event highlighted the need for the rule of law in order to restrain the excesses of nobles and monarchs, and favored the development of representative forms of government.

Meanwhile, the Industrial Revolution and colonialism were transforming the face of Europe and many other regions of the world. In the 19th century, the pressures for progress unleashed in the Enlightenment found expression in the unprecedented growth of industry and technology, and Western civilization expanded its power throughout the rest of the world. While Spain and Portugal were losing their colonies in the Americas, England, France, the Netherlands, and Germany expanded into Africa, Asia, and the Pacific, including areas that had never been colonized by Western nations before. The colonies were intended to serve as sources of cheap raw materials for Western industry, and markets for the manufactured goods it produced.

Patterns of Historical Development in Recent Times

The competition for the resources from overseas colonies was one of the major reasons for World War I, which, despite its name, was mainly a European war. Sparked by the assassination of the heir to the throne of Austria-Hungary, it soon claimed the lives of many more soldiers than any previous war. In addition, in countries such as Great Britain and Germany, the scale of the war meant for the first time that people from all walks of life—not just professional soldiers—became casualties of the war. In France, about half the men of an entire generation were killed, and in one battle (the battle of Sommes) the British suffered over 60,000 casualties on the first day alone.

Germany, the major instigator of World War I, fell far short in its attempt to expand its empire. At the end of World War I, the few colonies that Germany controlled fell into the hands of Great Britain and France, and Germany was a much poorer country than it had been before losing the war. Even though most of the world, especially Europe, was horrified over the carnage of World War I, Germany turned to a dictator who promised to restore the country's military might less than 20 years after the end of the first war. Adolf Hitler eventually failed in that mission, but he did temporarily make Germany a feared military power, killing 12 million people in concentration camps, including 6 million Jews, and 20 million Soviets while trying to conquer Europe. During World War II, which began in 1939 when Hitler invaded Poland, Germany was joined by Japan and Italy to form the Axis, which fought against the Allies—mainly Great Britain, the United States, and the Soviet Union. (France, perhaps remembering the dead of World War I, surrendered to Germany early in the war.) Although Great Britain was supposedly among the winners of the war, it expended so many resources in winning that it was no longer the dominant power in the world.

The Soviet Union was formed from Russia and other countries under Russian rule during World War I, by way of a Communist revolution. Communism had arisen during the nineteenth century, partly in response to the Industrial Revolution and the spread of capitalism. Its main theorist, Karl Marx, had expected revolution to come in one of the more industrially advanced countries, such as Britain or his native Germany, but the unpopularity of World War I helped create a power vacuum in Russia, where there had been plenty of misery among the poor along with relatively organized protest against the rich. The Communist Party under Vladimir Lenin took advantage of this to create a promised "worker's paradise." The Soviet Union was, however, beset by many problems from the beginning, and the Communist system was not well equipped to handle them. After Lenin's death in 1927, Josef Stalin took over the political machinery, and through disastrous policies and legal executions, Stalin was responsible for a tremendous amount of death and suffering. After Hitler invaded Poland in 1939, Stalin signed a non-aggression treaty with Germany, but Hitler nevertheless invaded the Soviet Union soon thereafter. The Soviets suffered far greater devastation than any other country during World War II, but they persevered and eventually drove the German armies all the way back to Germany and became one of the two main beneficiaries of the war.

Almost immediately after World War II, the Cold War began. The British Empire began to crumble. Its most important colony, India, broke away in 1948 under the famously nonviolent leadership of Mohandas Gandhi, and it was unable to prevent the establishment of the Jewish state of Israel in formerly British Palestine in the same year. Most of Britain's African colonies became independent in the 1950s and 1960s. In the meantime, Europe was divided by a figurative Iron Curtain between U.S.-dominated Western Europe and Soviet-dominated Eastern Europe.

In most of the rest of the world—what came to be known as the Third World—the two Cold War antagonists used both military might and peacefully persuasive means to gather as many countries as possible into their sphere. China, in which a Communist revolution under Mao Ze-Dong succeeded following the great devastation of Japanese occupation during World War II, was solidly in the Soviet camp for many years but was also rather independent during much of the Cold War. Japan, though not allowed to have a military as a condition of its defeat in World War II, became a U.S. ally and a dominant Asian economic power. The United States and the Soviet Union waged war through their allies in Korea (each side got half the country) and Vietnam (the Soviets got the whole country, but the United States succeeded in stopping the expansion of Soviet influence beyond Southeast Asia). The Cold War came to an end in 1989, when the Soviet Union essentially surrendered. It had never been a war between equals; the United States had emerged much stronger than had its rival, but the Soviet Union was able to keep up the appearance of equality by mimicking the U.S. development of weapon systems centered around nuclear devices. Even in that arena, however, the United States eventually wore down the Soviet Union, and the post–Cold War government soon gave independence to most of the non-Russian countries under its control and withdrew its troops from Eastern Europe.

The end of the Cold War did not, however, bring peace to the world. In the formerly Soviet-dominated state of Yugoslavia, long-buried ethnic rivalries (of which most Yugoslav citizens were barely aware) led to civil war, genocide, and an eventual split into three countries. In Africa, many of the countries that France and Britain had set up during the Colonial Period started to break apart along old tribal lines, occasionally leading to terrible bloodbaths, such as the Rwandan slaughter of the Tutsis. Although the South African revolution, led by Nelson Mandela, was a relatively peaceful victory for the people of that country, most of Africa is still subject to poverty, disease, and war. In the Middle East, the presence of Israel, along with the failure of the governments of the mostly Muslim countries of the region to defeat Israel or establish wealth for most of their citizens, has led to a spread of fundamentalist Islam. These extremist groups have wreaked much havoc in the world, most notably in the attacks on the World Trade Center and the Pentagon in 2001. Although extreme wings of all the major religions have dealt death and destruction throughout history, the fundamentalist Muslim extremists are perhaps the most feared threat to peace in the early twenty-first century.

Critical Thinking Skills: Writing

SUBAREA VI—CRITICAL THINKING SKILLS: WRITING

Competency 0021

Prepare an organized, developed composition in edited English in response to instructions regarding content, purpose, and audience.

The following topics are examples of content that may be covered under this competency.

- Demonstrate the ability to prepare a unified and focused piece of writing on a given topic using language and style appropriate to a specified audience, purpose, and occasion.
- Demonstrate the ability to take a position on a contemporary social or political issue and defend that position with reasoned arguments and supporting examples.
- Demonstrate the ability to use effective sentence structure and apply the standards of edited English.
- Demonstrate the ability to spell, capitalize, and punctuate according to the standards of edited English.

This portion of the OGET contains a writing assignment. The written assignment asks test-takers to compose a composition, or written response, on a given subject. You will be evaluated on your ability to communicate the written message to a specified audience. The compositions are graded on the following criteria: appropriateness (how the writer uses language and style in relation to the given audience and purpose), unity and focus (the clarity of the main idea), development (supporting details are specific and clearly understood), organization (logical sequence of thoughts and ideas, and overall clarity of the work), sentence structure, usage, and mechanical conventions (the extent to which the response has no errors in usage, spelling, capitalization, punctuation, and the precision of word choice). The responses are graded on a scale from "4" to "U," or "Unscorable," or "B", "Blank."

In an essay earning a score of 4, ideas are presented clearly, arguments are well organized, and there is extensive and specific supporting detail. The writer communicates through effective sentence structure and uses proper spelling, grammar, and punctuation.

In an essay scoring 3, ideas are well communicated, but supporting details might not be as precise or extensive as in a paper scoring 4. The ideas might be incomplete or generally ineffective. Minor errors in areas such as punctuation, spelling, word choice, or general usage are present.

A score of 2 is given to essays that do not support the main idea with specific details, and in which the overall organization of the work is unclear. The purpose of the essay might need to be inferred because it is vaguely stated. Errors are found in word choice, usage, sentence structure, spelling, and punctuation.

The response score 1 would be given to an essay that does not communicate the overall message and is lacking logical sequence of ideas. Often the main idea is not clearly stated, and supporting details are confusing. Common errors include incorrect use of language and sentence structure. Spelling and punctuation errors are found throughout the response.

A response given a U is deemed unscorable. A U score would be given if the essay is not on the given topic, is illegible, too short, or not written in English.

A response given a B is self-explanatory (i.e., a blank sheet that contains no answer).

Sample essays from different scoring levels appear at the end of the Practice Test, accompanied by critical commentary.

Carefully read the assignment before you begin to write. Think about your ideas and what you would like to communicate to the reader. You may wish to make an outline for the topic to help organize your thoughts, but be sure to write the final draft of your response in the test booklet. Your score will be based on what is written in the response booklet. When you have finished writing, be sure to review your work and make any changes you believe would enhance your score.

This review will guide you through a step-by-step process of how to write an essay, from writing strategies to budgeting time during the exam. Even if you feel that you are a good writer, you should still study this review, as it will help you become familiar with essay writing. The strategies included are provided to help you write an essay that is to the point, easily understood, properly structured, well supported, and correct according to the rules of grammar. You will not be expected to write a best-selling book in order to pass this test. Remember, the more you practice the strategies provided in this review, the easier it will be for you to write a good essay.

Strategies for the Essay

To give yourself the best chance of writing a good essay, you should follow these steps.

Before the test, this is your plan:

Step 1: Study the following review to enhance your ability to write an essay. Remember, the sharper your skills, the more likely you are to receive a passing grade on your writing sample.

Step 2: Practice writing an essay. The best way to do this is to complete the Practice Test.

Step 3: Learn and understand the directions, so that you don't waste valuable time reading them on the test day. This will allow you to quickly review them before writing your essay.

Step 4: Develop your essay from the notes you have made. Present your position clearly and logically, making sure to provide adequate examples and/or support. Write your draft on scratch paper.

Step 5: Proofread your essay! Check every word for errors in spelling. Be sure that your sentences are concise and grammatically correct. Make any necessary revisions.

Step 6: Copy the final version of your essay into the response booklet.

Additional Tips

- Be sure that you have not strayed from your topic or introduced points that you have not explained.

- Vary your types of sentences so that your essay flows smoothly and is easy to read.

- Use vocabulary that suits your audience. Make sure not to insult your audience by using simple vocabulary, or by explaining things they already know. Likewise, do not alienate your audience by using complicated jargon, or by assuming that they are already familiar with the subject on which you are writing.

Use vocabulary that suits your audience.

Fast Facts

Recognizing Effective Writing

Why Essays Exist

People write essays for purposes other than testing. Some of our best thinkers have written essays that we continue to read from generation to generation. Essays offer the reader a logical, coherent, and imaginative written composition showing the nature or consequences of a single controlling idea when considered from the writer's unique point of view. Writers use essays to communicate their opinion or position on a topic to readers who cannot be present during their live conversation. Writers use essays to help readers understand or learn about something that readers should or may want to know or do. Essays always express more or less directly the author's opinion, belief, position, or knowledge (backed by evidence) about the idea or object in question.

Organization and Purposeful Development

For this test you will need to recognize and generate the elements of an excellent essay. In essence, you will be taking the principles covered in this review and utilizing them to create your own original essay. With that in mind, read carefully the standards and explanations below to prepare you for what to look for in your own essay response.

Essay Writing

In academic writing, two purposes dominate essays:

1. Persuasion through argumentation using one, some, or all of the logical patterns described here.

2. Informing and educating through analysis and using one, some, or all of the logical patterns described here.

All of an essay's organizational strategies may be used to argue in writing. The author offers reasons and/or evidence so an audience will be inclined to believe the position that the author presents about the idea under discussion. Writers use seven basic strategies to organize information and ideas in essays to help prove their point (thesis). All of these strategies might be useful in arguing for an idea and persuading a reader to see the issue the writer's way. Your job is to use strategies that are appropriate to demonstrate your thesis. For example, you may wish to use comparison and contrast to demonstrate that one thing or idea is better or worse than another.

The following seven steps can be used to prove a thesis.

Seven Steps to Prove a Thesis

1.   Show how a *process* or procedure does or should work, step by step, in time.

2.   *Compare or contrast* two or more things or ideas to show important differences or similarities.

3.   *Identify a problem* and then explain how to solve it.

4.   *Analyze* into its components, or *classify* by its types or categories an idea or thing to show how it is put together, how it works, or how it is designed.

5.   *Explain* why something happens to produce a particular result or set of results.

6.   *Describe* the particular individual characteristics, beauty and features of a place, person(s), time, or idea.

7.   *Define* what a thing is or what an idea means.

Depending upon the purpose of the essay, one pattern tends to dominate the discussion question. (For example, the writer might use *description* and *explanation* to define the varied meanings of "love.")

During this test you will be called upon to exercise control over your writing by using the writing process and by knowing the pitfalls of weak writing and correcting them. Using the steps outlined below, compose your essay in the order suggested and note the elements and qualities to correct during each stage of the process of composing your essay test response. Make any corrections you need during the appropriate stage of the writing process; to correct errors at the wrong stage may waste time and interfere with your producing the best essay response.

Composing Your Essay: Using the Writing Process

Some people (erroneously) think that writers just sit down and churn out a wonderful essay or poem in one sitting in a flash of genius and inspiration. This is not true. Writers use the writing process from start to finish to help them to write a clear document. If you do not reflect on your composition in stages and make changes as you develop it, you will not see all the problems or errors in it. Don't try to write an essay just once and leave the room. Stay and look through it. Reflect upon it using the writing process.

The writing process has five steps: (1) Prewriting, or planning time; (2) The rough draft; (3) Organizing and revising the ideas (not the words or sentences themselves); (4) Polishing, or editing (making sure sentences themselves are sentences, that the words you use are the right words, and that the spelling and punctuation are correct); and (5) Proofreading, to make sure no mistakes are left.

Using this process does not mean that you have to write five drafts. Write one draft (stages 1 and 2), leaving space for corrections (e.g., writing on every other line) and then working on the existing draft through the rest of the stages (3 through 5). If time allows, you may want to do the whole process on scrap paper and then copy the finished product onto the allotted test paper. But if you do copy it, make sure you proofread your copy to see whether, while transcribing it, you left anything out or said a word twice or made any other errors.

Writing Your Essay

Prewriting/Planning Time

Read the essay question and decide on your purpose. Do you want to persuade your reader? Would you rather explain something?

Sample: "Television is bad for people."

Do you agree or disagree with this statement? Decide. Take a stand. Don't be noncommittal. Write down the statement of your position.

Sample: "I agree that television is bad for people."

or

"Television is an excellent learning tool and is good for most people."

This is your thesis.

Consider Your Audience

The writer's responsibility is to write clearly, honestly, and cleanly for the reader's sake. Essays would be pointless without an audience. Why write an essay if no one wants or needs to read it? Why add evidence, organize your ideas, or correct bad grammar? The reason to do any of these things is that someone out there needs to understand what you mean to say. What would the audience need to know in order to believe you or to come over to your position? Imagine someone you know (visualize her or him) listening to you declare your position or opinion and then saying, "Oh yeah? Prove it!"

Fast Facts

The writer's responsibility is to write clearly, honestly, and cleanly for the reader's sake.

In writing your essay, make sure to answer the following questions: What evidence do you need to prove your idea to this skeptic? What would she disagree with you about? What does she share with you as common knowledge? What does she need to be told by you?

Control Your Point of View

We may write essays from one of three points of view, depending upon the essay's audience. The points of view below are discussed from informal to formal.

1. Subjective/Personal Point of View:
   "I think/believe/feel cars are more trouble than they are worth."

2. Second-Person:
   "If you own a car, you soon find out that it is more trouble than it is worth."

3. Third-Person Point of View (focuses on the idea, not what "I" think of it):
   "Cars are more trouble than they are worth."

For now, stick with one or another; don't switch your "point of view" in the middle. Any one is acceptable.

Consider Your Support

Next, during prewriting, jot down a few phrases that show ideas and examples that support your point of view. Do this quickly on a separate piece of paper for about five minutes. Don't try to outline, simply list things that you think might be important to discuss. After you have listed several, pick at least three to five things you want or need to discuss, and number them in the order of importance that is relevant to proving your point.

Write Your Rough Draft

Spend about ten to twenty minutes writing your rough draft. Looking over your prewriting list, write down what you think is useful to prove your point in the order you think best to convince the reader. Be sure to use real evidence from your life experience or knowledge to support what you say. You do not have to draw evidence from books; your own life is equally appropriate.

For example, don't write, "Cars are more trouble to fix than bicycles," and then fail to show evidence for your idea. Give examples of what you mean: "For example, my father's Buick needs 200 parts to make one brake work, but my bicycle only has four pieces that make up the brakes, and I can replace those myself." Write naturally and quickly. Don't worry too much at this point about paragraphing, spelling, or punctuation—just write down what you think or want to say in the order determined on your list.

Transitions

To help the reader follow the flow of your ideas and to help unify the essay, use transitions to show the connections among your ideas. You may use transitions at the beginnings of paragraphs, or you may use them to show the connections among ideas within a single paragraph.

Here are some typical transitional words and phrases that you should use when writing your essay.

To link similar ideas, use the words:

again	equally important	in addition	of course
also	for example	in like manner	similarly
and	for instance	likewise	too
another	further	moreover	
besides	furthermore	or	

To link dissimilar or contradictory ideas, use words such as:

although	and yet	as if	but
conversely	even if	however	in spite of
instead	nevertheless	on the contrary	on the other hand
otherwise	provided that	still	yet

To indicate cause, purpose, or result, use:

as	consequently	hence	then
as a result	for	since	therefore
because	for this reason	so	thus

To indicate time or position, use words like:

above	at the present time	first	second
across	before	here	thereafter
afterward	beyond	meanwhile	thereupon
around	eventually	next	
at once	finally	presently	

To indicate an example or summary, use phrases such as:

as a result	in any case	in conclusion	in short
as I have said	in any event	in fact	on the whole
for example	in brief	in other words	to sum up
for instance			

Providing Evidence in Your Essay

You may employ any one of the seven steps previously listed to prove any thesis that you maintain is true. You may also call on evidence from one or all of the four following kinds of evidence to support the thesis of your essay. Identify which kind(s) of evidence you can use to prove the points of your essay. In test situations, most essayists use anecdotal evidence or analogy to explain, describe, or prove a thesis. But if you know salient facts or statistics, don't hesitate to call upon them.

1.   **Hard data** (facts, statistics, scientific evidence, research)—documented evidence that has been verified to be true.

2.   **Anecdotal evidence**—stories from the writer's own experience and knowledge that illustrate a particular point or idea.

3.   **Expert opinions**—assertions or conclusions, usually by authorities, about the matter under discussion.

4.   **Analogies**—show a resemblance between one phenomenon and another.

Organizing and Reviewing the Paragraphs

The unit of work for revising is the paragraph. After you have written what you wanted to say based on your prewriting list, spend about twenty minutes revising your draft by looking to see whether you need to indent for paragraphs anywhere. If you do, make a proofreader's mark to indicate to the reader that you think a paragraph should start here. Check to see whether you want to add anything that would make your point of view more convincing. Be sure to supply useful transitions to keep up the flow and maintain the focus of your ideas. If you don't have room on the paper, or if your new paragraph shows up out of order, add that paragraph and indicate with a number or some other mark where you want it to go. Check to make sure that you gave examples or illustrations for your statements. In the examples below, two paragraphs are offered: one without concrete evidence and one with evidence for its idea. Study each. Note the topic sentence (T) and how that sentence is or is not supported with evidence.

Paragraphing with No Evidence

Television is bad for people. Programs on television are often stupid and depict crimes that people later copy. Television takes time away from loved ones, and it often becomes addictive. So, television is bad for people because it is no good.

In this example, the author has not given any concrete evidence for any of the good ideas presented. He just declares them to be so. Any one of the sentences above might make a good opening sentence for a whole paragraph. Take the second sentence, for example:

Watching television takes time away from other things. For example, all those hours people spend sitting in front of the tube, they could be working on building a chair or fixing the roof. (*Second piece of evidence*) Maybe the laundry needs to be done, but because people watch television, they may end up not having time to do it. Then Monday comes around again and they have no socks to wear to work—all because they couldn't stand to miss that episode of "Everybody Loves Raymond." (*Third piece of evidence*) Someone could be writing a letter to a friend in Boston who hasn't been heard from or written to for months. (*Fourth piece of evidence*) Or maybe someone misses the opportunity to take in a beautiful day in the park because she had to see "General Hospital." They'll repeat "General Hospital," but this beautiful day only comes around once.

Watching television definitely keeps people from getting things done.

The primary evidence the author uses here is that of probable illustrations taken from life experience that is largely anecdotal. *Always* supply evidence. Three examples or illustrations of your idea per paragraph is a useful number. Don't go on and on about a single point. You don't have time. In order for a typical test essay to be fully developed, it should have about five paragraphs. They ought to be organized in the following manner:

Introduction: A paragraph that shows your point of view (thesis) about an issue and introduces your position with three general ideas that support your thesis.

Development: Three middle paragraphs that prove your position from different angles, using evidence from real life and knowledge. Each supporting paragraph in the middle should in turn support each of the three ideas you started out with in the introductory or thesis paragraph.

Conclusion: The last paragraph, which sums up your position and adds one final reminder of what the issue was, perhaps points to a solution:

> So, television takes away from the quality of life and is therefore bad for human beings.
> We should be watching the sun, the sky, the birds, and each other, not the "boob tube."

Write a paragraph using this sentence as your focus: "Television takes valuable time away from our loved ones."

Check for Logic

Make sure that you present your argument in a logical manner. If you have not, you may not have proven your point. Your conclusion must follow from a logical set of premises, such as:

- Either/Or—The writer assumes that only two opposing possibilities may be attained: "Either _____, or this _____."

- Oversimplification—The writer simplifies the subject: "The rich only want one thing."

- Begging the question—The writer assumes she has proven something (often counterintuitive) that may need to be proven to the reader: "The death penalty actually increases, rather than deters, violent crime."

- Ignoring the issue—The writer argues against the truth of an issue due to its conclusion: "John is a good boy and, therefore, did not rob the store."

- Arguing against a person, not an idea—The writer argues that somebody's idea has no merit because he is immoral or personally stupid: "Eric will fail out of school because he is not doing well in gym class."

- Non Sequitur—The writer leaps to the wrong conclusion: "Jake is from Canada; he must play hockey."

- Drawing the wrong conclusion from a sequence—The author attributes the outcome to the wrong reasons: "Betty married at a young age to an older man and now has three children and is therefore a housewife."

Polishing and Editing Your Essay

If the unit of work for revising is the paragraph, the unit of work for editing is the sentence. Check your paper for mistakes in editing. To help you in this task, use the following checklist.

Polishing Checklist

- Are all your sentences *really* sentences, or have you written some fragments or run-on sentences?

- Are you using vocabulary correctly?

- Have you used a word that seems colloquial or too informal?

- Did you leave out punctuation anywhere? Did you capitalize, or not capitalize, correctly? Did you check for commas, periods, and quotation marks?

Proofreading

In the last three to five minutes, read your paper word for word, first forward and then backward, reading from the end to the beginning. Doing so can help you find errors that you may have missed by having read forward only.

OGET

Oklahoma General Education Test

Practice Test

This test for the OGET is also on CD-ROM in our special interactive OGET/OSAT TEST*ware*®. It is highly recommended that you first take this exam on computer. You will then have the additional study features and benefits of enforced timed conditions and instant, accurate scoring. See page xii for guidance on how to get the most out of our OGET/OSAT book and software.

TEST DIRECTIONS

A sample of the general directions for the OGET is shown in the box below. You may want to familiarize yourself with the directions, as similar versions will be used for the actual examination.

You should have in front of you:

(1) a test booklet for the test for which you registered (check the field name on the front cover);

(2) an answer document (be sure you have signed your answer document and filled in the required information on pages 1 and 3); and

(3) a No. 2 lead pencil.

IF YOU DO NOT HAVE ALL OF THESE MATERIALS, PLEASE INFORM THE TEST ADMINISTRATOR. REMOVE ALL OTHER MATERIALS FROM YOUR DESK.

GENERAL DIRECTIONS

This test booklet contains two sections: a selected-response section and a writing assignment. You may complete the sections in the order you choose, but it is suggested that you complete the selected-response section of the test first. The directions for each section appear immediately before that section.

Each selected-response question in this booklet has four answer choices. Read each question carefully and choose the ONE best answer. Record your answer on the answer sheet in the space that corresponds to the question number. Completely fill in the space having the same letter as the answer you have chosen. *Use only a No. 2 lead pencil.*

Sample Question:

1. Which of these cities is farthest north?

   A.   Oklahoma City

   B.   Muskogee

   C.   Tulsa

   D.   Lawton

The correct answer to this question is C. You would indicate that on the answer sheet as follows:

1.   Ⓐ Ⓑ ● Ⓓ

For the writing assignment, you will be asked to prepare a written response to a writing assignment. Record your written response on pages 3 to 6 of the answer document. You may use **ONLY** one answer document. You may either print or write, as long as your handwriting is legible. You must use a pencil. Make sure that you have time to plan, write, review, and revise what you have written.

You should answer all questions. Even if you are unsure of an answer, it is better to guess than not to answer a question at all. You may use the margins of the test booklet for scratch paper, but all of your answers, including your response to the writing assignment, must be recorded in your answer document. Answers that are written in the test booklet will **NOT** be scored.

The words "End of Section" indicate you have completed a section. After you have completed one section, you may go on to the other section. You may go back and review your answers and your written response to the writing assignment, but be sure you have answered all selected-response questions, completed the writing assignment, and rechecked all the information in your answer document, particularly your identification information on pages 1 and 3, before you raise your hand for dismissal. Your test materials must be returned to a test administrator when you finish the test.

FOR TEST SECURITY REASONS, YOU MAY NOT TAKE NOTES OR REMOVE ANY OF THE TEST MATERIALS FROM THE ROOM.

This session will last four hours. You may work at your own pace on the different sections of the test. If you have any questions, please ask them now before you begin the test.

STOP
DO NOT GO ON UNTIL YOU ARE TOLD TO DO SO.

Answer Sheet

1. Ⓐ Ⓑ Ⓒ Ⓓ	26. Ⓐ Ⓑ Ⓒ Ⓓ	51. Ⓐ Ⓑ Ⓒ Ⓓ	76. Ⓐ Ⓑ Ⓒ Ⓓ
2. Ⓐ Ⓑ Ⓒ Ⓓ	27. Ⓐ Ⓑ Ⓒ Ⓓ	52. Ⓐ Ⓑ Ⓒ Ⓓ	77. Ⓐ Ⓑ Ⓒ Ⓓ
3. Ⓐ Ⓑ Ⓒ Ⓓ	28. Ⓐ Ⓑ Ⓒ Ⓓ	53. Ⓐ Ⓑ Ⓒ Ⓓ	78. Ⓐ Ⓑ Ⓒ Ⓓ
4. Ⓐ Ⓑ Ⓒ Ⓓ	29. Ⓐ Ⓑ Ⓒ Ⓓ	54. Ⓐ Ⓑ Ⓒ Ⓓ	79. Ⓐ Ⓑ Ⓒ Ⓓ
5. Ⓐ Ⓑ Ⓒ Ⓓ	30. Ⓐ Ⓑ Ⓒ Ⓓ	55. Ⓐ Ⓑ Ⓒ Ⓓ	80. Ⓐ Ⓑ Ⓒ Ⓓ
6. Ⓐ Ⓑ Ⓒ Ⓓ	31. Ⓐ Ⓑ Ⓒ Ⓓ	56. Ⓐ Ⓑ Ⓒ Ⓓ	81. Ⓐ Ⓑ Ⓒ Ⓓ
7. Ⓐ Ⓑ Ⓒ Ⓓ	32. Ⓐ Ⓑ Ⓒ Ⓓ	57. Ⓐ Ⓑ Ⓒ Ⓓ	82. Ⓐ Ⓑ Ⓒ Ⓓ
8. Ⓐ Ⓑ Ⓒ Ⓓ	33. Ⓐ Ⓑ Ⓒ Ⓓ	58. Ⓐ Ⓑ Ⓒ Ⓓ	83. Ⓐ Ⓑ Ⓒ Ⓓ
9. Ⓐ Ⓑ Ⓒ Ⓓ	34. Ⓐ Ⓑ Ⓒ Ⓓ	59. Ⓐ Ⓑ Ⓒ Ⓓ	84. Ⓐ Ⓑ Ⓒ Ⓓ
10. Ⓐ Ⓑ Ⓒ Ⓓ	35. Ⓐ Ⓑ Ⓒ Ⓓ	60. Ⓐ Ⓑ Ⓒ Ⓓ	85. Ⓐ Ⓑ Ⓒ Ⓓ
11. Ⓐ Ⓑ Ⓒ Ⓓ	36. Ⓐ Ⓑ Ⓒ Ⓓ	61. Ⓐ Ⓑ Ⓒ Ⓓ	86. Ⓐ Ⓑ Ⓒ Ⓓ
12. Ⓐ Ⓑ Ⓒ Ⓓ	37. Ⓐ Ⓑ Ⓒ Ⓓ	62. Ⓐ Ⓑ Ⓒ Ⓓ	87. Ⓐ Ⓑ Ⓒ Ⓓ
13. Ⓐ Ⓑ Ⓒ Ⓓ	38. Ⓐ Ⓑ Ⓒ Ⓓ	63. Ⓐ Ⓑ Ⓒ Ⓓ	88. Ⓐ Ⓑ Ⓒ Ⓓ
14. Ⓐ Ⓑ Ⓒ Ⓓ	39. Ⓐ Ⓑ Ⓒ Ⓓ	64. Ⓐ Ⓑ Ⓒ Ⓓ	89. Ⓐ Ⓑ Ⓒ Ⓓ
15. Ⓐ Ⓑ Ⓒ Ⓓ	40. Ⓐ Ⓑ Ⓒ Ⓓ	65. Ⓐ Ⓑ Ⓒ Ⓓ	90. Ⓐ Ⓑ Ⓒ Ⓓ
16. Ⓐ Ⓑ Ⓒ Ⓓ	41. Ⓐ Ⓑ Ⓒ Ⓓ	66. Ⓐ Ⓑ Ⓒ Ⓓ	91. Ⓐ Ⓑ Ⓒ Ⓓ
17. Ⓐ Ⓑ Ⓒ Ⓓ	42. Ⓐ Ⓑ Ⓒ Ⓓ	67. Ⓐ Ⓑ Ⓒ Ⓓ	92. Ⓐ Ⓑ Ⓒ Ⓓ
18. Ⓐ Ⓑ Ⓒ Ⓓ	43. Ⓐ Ⓑ Ⓒ Ⓓ	68. Ⓐ Ⓑ Ⓒ Ⓓ	93. Ⓐ Ⓑ Ⓒ Ⓓ
19. Ⓐ Ⓑ Ⓒ Ⓓ	44. Ⓐ Ⓑ Ⓒ Ⓓ	69. Ⓐ Ⓑ Ⓒ Ⓓ	94. Ⓐ Ⓑ Ⓒ Ⓓ
20. Ⓐ Ⓑ Ⓒ Ⓓ	45. Ⓐ Ⓑ Ⓒ Ⓓ	70. Ⓐ Ⓑ Ⓒ Ⓓ	95. Ⓐ Ⓑ Ⓒ Ⓓ
21. Ⓐ Ⓑ Ⓒ Ⓓ	46. Ⓐ Ⓑ Ⓒ Ⓓ	71. Ⓐ Ⓑ Ⓒ Ⓓ	96. Ⓐ Ⓑ Ⓒ Ⓓ
22. Ⓐ Ⓑ Ⓒ Ⓓ	47. Ⓐ Ⓑ Ⓒ Ⓓ	72. Ⓐ Ⓑ Ⓒ Ⓓ	97. Ⓐ Ⓑ Ⓒ Ⓓ
23. Ⓐ Ⓑ Ⓒ Ⓓ	48. Ⓐ Ⓑ Ⓒ Ⓓ	73. Ⓐ Ⓑ Ⓒ Ⓓ	98. Ⓐ Ⓑ Ⓒ Ⓓ
24. Ⓐ Ⓑ Ⓒ Ⓓ	49. Ⓐ Ⓑ Ⓒ Ⓓ	74. Ⓐ Ⓑ Ⓒ Ⓓ	99. Ⓐ Ⓑ Ⓒ Ⓓ
25. Ⓐ Ⓑ Ⓒ Ⓓ	50. Ⓐ Ⓑ Ⓒ Ⓓ	75. Ⓐ Ⓑ Ⓒ Ⓓ	100. Ⓐ Ⓑ Ⓒ Ⓓ

Practice Test

WATER

The most important source of sediment is earth and rock material carried to the sea by rivers and streams; glaciers and winds may also have transported the same materials. Other sources are volcanic ash and lava, shells and skeletons of organisms, chemical precipitates formed in seawater, and particles from outer space.

Water is a most unusual substance because it exists on the surface of the Earth in its three physical states: ice, water, and water vapor. There are many substances that exist in a solid and liquid or gaseous state at temperatures normally found at the Earth's surface, but there are fewer substances that occur in all three states.

Water is odorless, tasteless, and colorless. It is a substance known to exist in a natural state as a solid, liquid, or gas on the surface of the Earth. It is a universal solvent. Water does not corrode, rust, burn, or separate into its components easily. It is chemically indestructible. It can corrode almost any metal and erode the most solid rock. A unique property of water is that, when frozen in its solid state, it expands and floats on water. Water has a freezing point of 0°C and a boiling point of 100°C. Water has the capacity to absorb great quantities of heat with relatively little increase in temperature. When *distilled*, water is a poor conductor of electricity but when salt is added, it is a good conductor of electricity.

Sunlight is the source of energy for temperature change, evaporation, and currents for water movement through the atmosphere. Sunlight controls the rate of photosynthesis for all marine plants, which are directly or indirectly the source of food for all marine animals. Migration, breeding, and other behaviors of marine animals are affected by light.

Water, as the ocean or sea, is blue because of the molecular scattering of the sunlight. Blue light, being of short wavelength, is scattered more effectively than light of longer wavelengths. Variations in color may be caused by particles suspended in the water, water depth, cloud cover, temperature, and other variable factors. Heavy concentrations of dissolved materials cause a yellowish hue, while algae will cause the water to look green. Heavy populations of plant and animal materials will cause the water to look brown.

1. Which of the following lists of topics best organizes the information in the selection?

   A. I. Water as vapor
      II. Water as ice
      III. Water as solid

   B. I. Properties of seawater
      II. Freezing and boiling points of water
      III. Photosynthesis
      IV. Oceans and seas

   C. I. Water as substance
      II. Water's corrosion
      III. Water and plants
      IV. Water and algae coloration

   D. I. Water's physical states
      II. Properties of water
      III. Effects of the sun on water
      IV. Reasons for color variation in water

2. According to the passage, what is the most unique property of water?

   A. Water is odorless, tasteless, and colorless.

   B. Water exists on the surface of the Earth in three physical states.

   C. Water is chemically indestructible.

   D. Water is a poor conductor of electricity.

3. Which of the following best defines the word *distilled* as it is used in the last sentence of the third paragraph?

   A. Free of salt content

   B. Free of electrical energy

   C. Dehydrated

   D. Containing wine

4. The writer's main purpose in this selection is to

   A. explain the colors of water.

   B. examine the effects of the sun on water.

   C. define the properties of water.

   D. describe the three physical states of all liquids.

5. The writer of this selection would most likely agree with which of the following statements?

   A. The properties of water are found in most other liquids on this planet.

   B. Water should not be consumed in its most natural state.

   C. Water might be used to serve many different functions.

   D. Water is too unpredictable for most scientists.

Read the passage below; then answer the five questions that follow.

¹DeMarco was asked if he had read any of the books that were on display in Mrs. W's classroom. ²He answered that he had read none of them yet, although he usually keeps one or more in his desk.

³Nevertheless, the researcher did see him respond positively to the first classroom reading experience of the year. ⁴Mrs. W was reading Louis Sachar's *Sideways Stories from Wayside School* while the children, each of whom had a copy of the book, were silently reading along. ⁵Like nearly all of the class, DeMarco was laughing in all the right places. ⁶The researcher has since noticed that he grasps and comprehends just about anything well when it is read by a competent reader, whether a teacher or an advanced fellow student.

⁷_____ ⁸The class writes almost daily in a "Small Moments Journal," in which they are to record, in a few sentences and perhaps a picture, memorable events in their lives. ⁹Mrs. W has spent considerable time prompting the students to write down topics, with the result that some students have well over 100 topics listed so far. ¹⁰DeMarco, through the last day he was observed, had seven. ¹¹He had written only two entries in his journal, both about a visit two years ago to his relatives in Mississippi. ¹²Like many of his classmate's accounts of their comings and goings, his writing lacks detail and personality, but most others have written appreciably more. ¹³Asked follow-up questions about the events he has written about, his answers were evasive.

6. Which of the following sentences, used in place of the blank labeled sentence 7, would best make a transition to the new paragraph?

   A. Another topic of interest of the study was DeMarco's writing ability.

   B. Moreover, DeMarco's writing shows no enthusiasm.

   C. DeMarco's writing, however, shows no spark at all.

   D. Consequently, it is advisable that we look at DeMarco's writing.

7. Which of the numbered sentences should be revised to reduce unnecessary repetition?

    A.   sentence 3

    B.   sentence 5

    C.   sentence 6

    D.   sentence 8

8. Which of the numbered sentences should be revised to correct an error in sentence structure?

    A.   sentence 2

    B.   sentence 9

    C.   sentence 10

    D.   sentence 13

9. Which of the following changes is needed in the passage?

    A.   Sentence 4: Change *Sideways Stories from Wayside School* to "Sideways Stories from Wayside School"

    B.   Sentence 11: Change "had" to "has"

    C.   Sentence 11: Change "journal" to "Journal"

    D.   Sentence 12: Change "classmate's" to "classmates'"

10. Which of the underlined words or phrases in the third paragraph should be replaced by more precise or appropriate words?

    A.   <u>record</u>

    B.   <u>considerable</u>

    C.   <u>comings and goings</u>

    D.   <u>appreciably</u>

11. The distance from Tami's house to Ken's house is 3 miles. The distance from Ken's house to The Soda Depot is 2 miles. Which of the following statements are true?

      I. The greatest possible distance between Tami's house and The Soda Depot is five miles.

      II. The greatest possible distance between Tami's house and The Soda Depot is six miles.

      III. The shortest possible distance between Tami's house and The Soda Depot is one mile.

      IV. The shortest possible distance between Tami's house and The Soda Depot is two miles.

    A. I and III only

    B. I and IV only

    C. II and III only

    D. II and IV only

12. Use the figure to answer the question that follows.

```
┌─────────────┐
│   75 MPH    │
│  MAXIMUM    │
│             │
│   40 MPH    │
│  MINIMUM    │
└─────────────┘
```

Which inequality describes the allowable speeds indicated by the speed limit sign?

    A. $75 \leq x \leq 40$

    B. $75 < x > 40$

    C. $40 \leq x \leq 75$

    D. $40 < x > 75$

13. Which types of graphs or charts would be appropriate for displaying the following information?

Favorite lunch foods of 40 surveyed 6th graders

Pizza	18
Chicken Nuggets	12
Macaroni and Cheese	4
Tacos	4
Hamburgers	2

    I.   bar graph
   II.   circle (pie) chart
  III.   scatter plot
  IV.   broken-line graph

A. I and II only

B. III and IV only

C. I and III only

D. II and IV only

14. Which one of the following statements is most true regarding the materials of visual art?

A. Industrial innovations in art-making materials have improved art in the past 150 years.

B. The use of uncommon materials in art making has improved art in the past 150 years.

C. The use of unusual materials in art making has changed the standards by which we view art.

D. Industrial innovations in art-making materials have had little influence on visual art.

Read the passage below; then answer the four questions that follow.

The issue of adult literacy has finally received recognition as a major social problem. Unfortunately, the issue is usually presented in the media as a "women's interest issue." Numerous governors' wives and even Laura Bush have publicly expressed concern about literacy. As well-meaning as the politicians' wives may be, it is more important that the politicians themselves recognize the seriousness of the problem and support increased funding for literacy programs.

Literacy education programs need to be directed at two different groups of people with very different needs. The first group is composed of people who have very limited reading and writing skills. These people are complete illiterates. A second group is composed of people who can read and write but whose skills are not sufficient to meet their needs. This second group is called *functionally illiterate*. Successful literacy programs must meet the needs of both groups.

Instructors in literacy programs have three main responsibilities. First, the educational needs of the illiterates and functional illiterates must be met. Second, the instructors must approach the participants in the program with empathy, not sympathy. Third, all participants must experience success in the program and must perceive their efforts as worthwhile.

15. What is the difference between illiteracy and functional illiteracy?

    A.   There is no difference.

    B.   A functional illiterate is enrolled in a literacy education program but an illiterate is not.

    C.   An illiterate cannot read or write, a functional illiterate can read and write but not at a very high skill level.

    D.   There are more illiterates than functional illiterates in the United States today.

16. What does "women's interest issue" mean in the passage?

    A.   The issue is only interesting to women.

    B.   Many politicians' wives have expressed concern over the issue.

    C.   Women illiterates outnumber male illiterates.

    D.   Politicians interested in illiteracy often have their wives give speeches on the topic.

17. According to the passage, which of the following is NOT a characteristic of successful literacy programs?

    A.   Participants should receive free transportation.

    B.   Participants should experience success in the program.

    C.   Instructors must have empathy, not sympathy.

    D.   Programs must meet the educational needs of illiterates.

18. What is the author's opinion of the funding for literacy programs?

    A.   Too much

    B.   Too little

    C.   About right

    D.   Too much for illiterates and not enough for functional illiterates

SOURCES OF IMMIGRATION, 1820–1840

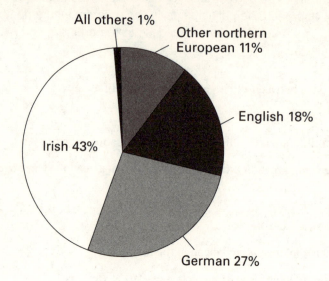

All others 1%

Other northern European 11%

English 18%

Irish 43%

German 27%

19. According to the graph, from 1820 to 1840

   A. there were more Irish immigrants than all other nationalities combined.

   B. the combined number of immigrants from England and Germany exceeded those from Ireland.

   C. one percent of American immigrants were from Italy.

   D. there were an equal number of English and German immigrants.

20. A hot-air balloon rises when propane burners in the basket are used to heat the air inside the balloon. Which of the following statements correctly identifies the explanation for this phenomenon?

   A. Heated gas molecules move faster inside the balloon, their force striking the inside causes the balloon to rise.

   B. Hot gas molecules are themselves larger than cool gas molecules, resulting in the expansion of the gas.

   C. The amount of empty space between gas molecules increases as the temperature of the gas increases, resulting in the expansion of the gas.

   D. The combustion of propane releases product gases that are lighter than air which are trapped in the balloon causing it to rise.

21. A marble and a feather are both released at the same time inside a tube that is held at very low pressure (a near vacuum). Which of the following correctly links the observation to explanation?

   A.   The marble falls faster because it is heavier.

   B.   The marble falls faster because it has less air resistance.

   C.   Both fall at the same rate because there is no air resistance in a vacuum.

   D.   Both fall at the same rate because the forces of gravity are different in a vacuum.

Read the passage below; then answer the five questions that follow.

[1]The Tuskegee Experiment's true nature had to be hidden from the subjects to ensure their cooperation. [2]The sharecroppers' grossly disadvantaged lot in life made them easy to manipulate. [3]Pleased at the prospect of free medical care—almost none of them had ever seen a doctor before—these unsophisticated and trusting men became the dupes in what James Jones, author of the excellent history on the subject, *Bad Blood,* identified as "the longest nontherapeutic experiment on human beings in medical history".

[4]The study was meant to discover how syphilis <u>effected</u> African Americans as opposed to whites—the theory being that whites experienced more neurological complications from syphilis <u>whereas</u> African Americans were more <u>susceptible</u> to cardiovascular damage. [5]_____ [6]Although the scientists touted the study as one of great scientific merit, from the <u>outset</u> its actual benefits were hazy. [7]It took almost forty years before someone involved in the study took a hard and honest look at the end results, he reported that "nothing learned will prevent, find, or cure a single case of infectious syphilis or bring us closer to our basic mission of controlling venereal disease in the United States." [8]When the media learns of the experiment in 1972, the CBS news anchor Harry Reasoner called it a project that "used human beings as laboratory animals in a long and inefficient study of how long it takes syphilis to kill someone."

22. Which of the following sentences, used in place of the blank labeled sentence 5, would be most consistent with the writer's purpose and intended audience?

   A.   If the theory had been proven, much would have changed in the clinical treatment of syphilis.

   B.   How this knowledge would have changed the clinical treatment of syphilis is uncertain.

   C.   On the other hand, neurological complications were much more important to the scientists.

   D.   We will never know what the racist scientists of the 1920s were thinking when they devised this theory.

23. Which of the underlined words or phrases in the second paragraph should be replaced by more precise or appropriate words?

   A.   <u>effected</u>

   B.   <u>whereas</u>

   C.   <u>susceptible</u>

   D.   <u>outset</u>

24. Which of the numbered sentences should be revised to correct a nonstandard use of a comma?

   A.   sentence 2

   B.   sentence 3

   C.   sentence 7

   D.   sentence 8

25. Which of the following changes is needed in the first paragraph?

   A.   Sentence 1: Change "Experiment's" to "Experiments"

   B.   Sentence 3: Change "had" to "has"

   C.   Sentence 2: Change "easy to manipulate" to "easily manipulated"

   D.   Sentence 3: Move the period at the end inside the quotation mark

26. Which of the numbered sentences contains nonstandard use of a verb form?

   A.   sentence 2

   B.   sentence 3

   C.   sentence 6

   D.   sentence 8

27. Each month the teacher kept track of the number of books as well as the genre of the books the students read during free-reading time in school. Here is the graph constructed from the data from September and May of the same year. This teacher completed a unit on fairy tales in April. What conclusions could be reached?

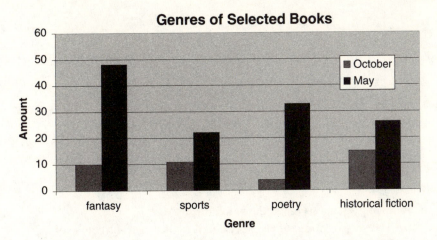

Genres of Selected Books

  I.   These children are reading more titles during free reading time.
 II.   Completing a fairy tale unit created interest in the fantasy genre.
III.   These children need to complete more worksheets.
 IV.   These children are participating in an Accelerated Reader Program.

A.   I, II, and III

B.   All of the above

C.   None of the above

D.   I and II

28. Use the figure to answer the question that follows.

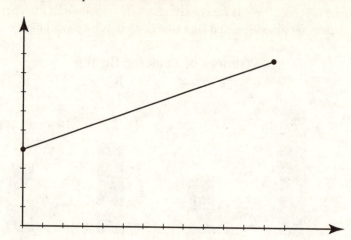

Which of the following situations might the graph illustrate?

I. The varying speed of an experienced runner over the course of a 26-mile race.

II. The number of households a census taker still has to visit over the course of a week.

III. The value of a savings account over time, assuming steady growth.

IV. The changing height of a sunflower over several months.

A. I and II only

B. III and IV only

C. II, III, and IV only

D. I, III, and IV only

29. The following graph shows the distribution of test scores in Ms. Alvarez's class.

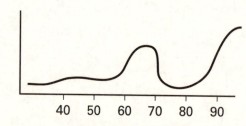

Which of the following statements do you know to be true?

I. The majority of students scored higher than 60.

II. The test was a fair measure of ability.

III. The mean score is probably higher than the median.

IV. The test divided the class into distinct groups.

A. I and II only

B. I and IV only

C. I, III, and IV only

D. IV only

30. What is the solution to this equation?

    $\frac{x}{3} - 9 = 15$

    A. 18

    B. 8

    C. 36

    D. 72

31. What are the solutions of this equation?

    $3x^2 - 11 = 1$

    A. 2 and –2

    B. 3 and –3

    C. 4 and –4

    D. 1 and –1

32. The atmospheres of the Moon and other planets were studied using telescopes and spectrophoto-meters long before the deployment of interplanetary space probes. In these studies, scientists studied the spectral patterns of sunlight that passed through the atmosphere of distant objects to learn what elements make up those atmospheres. Which of the following explains the source of the black-line spectral patterns?

    A. When an element is excited, it gives off light in a characteristic spectral pattern.

    B. When light strikes an object, some wavelengths of light are absorbed by the surface and others are reflected to give the object its color.

    C. When light passes through a gas, light is absorbed at wavelengths characteristic of the elements in the gas.

    D. The black lines are the spectra of ultraviolet light, which is called black light because it cannot be seen with human eyes.

33. We may be told to "gargle with saltwater" when we suffer from a sore throat. Which of the following phenomena would be used to explain this advice?

    A. lowering of vapor pressure

    B. increasing osmotic pressure

    C. increasing boiling point

    D. decreasing freezing point

34. In announcing the Emancipation Proclamation, Lincoln's immediate purpose was to

   A.   free black slaves in all of the slave states.

   B.   free black slaves in only the border slave states that had remained loyal to the Union.

   C.   let the Southern states know that whether or not they chose to secede from the Union, slavery would not be tolerated by his administration once he took office.

   D.   rally Northern morale by giving the war a higher moral purpose than just preserving the Union.

Read the passage below; then answer the four questions that follow.

Language not only expresses an individual's ideology, it also sets perimeters while it persuades and influences the discourse in the community that hears and interprets its meaning. Therefore, the language of failure should not be present in the learning environment (i.e., the classroom) because it will have a prohibitive impact on the students' desire to learn as well as a negative influence on the students' self-esteem. The *Oxford English Dictionary* defines *failure* as a fault, a shortcoming, a lack of success, a person who turns out unsuccessfully, becoming insolvent, etc. We as educators might well ask ourselves if this is the sort of doctrine that we want to permeate our classrooms. Perhaps our own University axiom, *mens agitat molem* (the mind can move mountains), will help us discover if, indeed, the concepts of failure are really the types of influences we wish to introduce to impressionable new students. Is the mind capable of moving a mountain when it is already convinced it cannot? One must remain aware that individuals acquire knowledge at independent rates of speed. Certainly no one would suggest that one infant "failed" the art of learning to walk because she acquired the skill two months behind her infant counterpart. Would anyone suggest that infant number one *failed* walking? Of course not. What would a mentor project to either toddler were he to suggest that a slower acquisition of walking skills implied failure? Yet we as educators feel the need to suggest student A failed due to the slower procurement of abstract concepts then student B. It is absolutely essential to shift the learning focus from failure to success.

35. Which of the following statements best conveys the meaning of the passage?

   A.   Learning is something that happens at different speeds and is, therefore, natural.

   B.   Instructors need to be sensitive to students' individual needs.

   C.   Instructors need to shift the educational focus from failure to success in learning environments.

   D.   Failure is a potential hazard in the classroom and should be avoided at all costs.

36. As stated in the context of the passage, what does University axiom mean?

    A. University Latin

    B. University motto

    C. University rhetoric

    D. University sophomore

37. According to the passage, what will have a negative effect on student self-esteem?

    A. The rhetoric of diction

    B. The slower procurement of abstract concepts

    C. The learning focus from failure to success

    D. The language of failure

38. According to the passage, what does language do besides aid individual expression?

    A. It establishes individual thought and tells of individual philosophies.

    B. It paints visual images and articulates individual declaration.

    C. It suggests individual axioms and community philosophy.

    D. It persuades and influences the discourse in the community that hears and interprets its meaning.

39. Solve for y.

    $\frac{y}{3} - \frac{x}{2} = 4$

    A. $y = \frac{x}{2} + 12$

    B. $y = \frac{3x}{2} + 12$

    C. $y = \frac{3x}{2} - 12$

    D. $y = -\frac{3x}{2} - 12$

40. Translate this problem into a one-variable equation, then solve the equation.

    "There are ten vehicles parked in a parking lot. Each is either a car with four tires or a motorcycle with two tires. (Do not count any spare tires.) There are 26 wheels in the lot. How many cars are there in the lot?"

    A. 8

    B. 6

    C. 5

    D. 3

41. Which equation could be used to solve the following problem?

"Three consecutive odd numbers add up to 117. What are they?"

A. $x + (x + 2) + (x + 4) = 117$

B. $1x + 3x + 5x = 117$

C. $x + x + x = 117$

D. $x + (x + 1) + (x + 3) = 117$

42. Which equation could be used to solve the following problem?

"Here is how the Acme Taxicab Company computes fares for riders: People are charged three dollars for just getting into the cab, then they are charged two dollars more for every mile or fraction of a mile of the ride. What would be the fare for a ride of 10.2 miles?"

A. $3 \times (2 \times 10.2) = y$

B. $3 + (2 + 11) = y$

C. $3 \times (2 + 10.2) = y$

D. $3 + (2 \times 11) = y$

43. The characteristics of fascism include all of the following EXCEPT:

A. democracy.

B. totalitarianism.

C. romanticism.

D. militarism.

44. The industrial economy of the nineteenth century was based upon all of the following EXCEPT:

A. the availability of raw materials.

B. an equitable distribution of profits among those involved in production.

C. the availability of capital.

D a distribution system to market finished products.

45. The term "Trail of Tears" refers to

A. the Mormon migration from Nauvoo, Illinois, to what is now Utah.

B. the forced migration of the Cherokee tribe from the southern Appalachians to what is now Oklahoma.

C. the westward migration along the Oregon Trail.

D. the migration into Kentucky along the Wilderness Road.

46. Thomas Paine's pamphlet *Common Sense* was significant in that it

   A.   emotionally aroused thousands of colonists to the abuses of British rule, the oppressiveness of the monarchy, and the advantages of colonial independence.

   B.   rallied American spirit during the bleak winter of 1776, when it appeared that Washington's forces, freezing and starving at Valley Forge, had no hope of surviving the winter, much less defeating the British.

   C.   called for a strong central government to rule the newly independent American states and foresaw the difficulties inherent within the Articles of Confederation.

   D.   asserted to its British readers that they could not beat the American colonists militarily unless they could isolate New England from the rest of the American colonies.

Read the passage below; then answer the six questions that follow.

¹Before the Europeans arrived, animism and spirit worship was the hallmark of Timorese belief in a superior force. ²The great Hindu, Buddhist, and Islamic kingdoms that dominated South and Southeast Asia had not taken root in Timor. ³The island's geographic location, which was far from the major ports of Asia, and its subsequent lack of commercial activity, placed it off the beaten track for traders and proselytizers. ⁴The exceptions being sandalwood and later slave trade.

⁵All that changed with the arrival of the Europeans. ⁶By the late 1500s Dominican friars from Portugal had established a mission on Timor, _____ they made only modest headway in converting the Timorese to Christianity. ⁷Although the Portuguese were in Timor for centuries they had little positive influence on Timorese culture until after World War II. ⁸For years the local people consistently resisted Portugal's attempts to take control of their island, and some of the Dominican missionaries who were posted there supported them in this effort. ⁹It was not until Portugal considered granting East Timor its independence that Catholicism began to be accepted among the people, and _____ it was not until the Indonesian invasion in 1975 that large numbers of Timorese embraced the Catholic faith. ¹⁰Indonesian law requires citizens to have a religious affiliation. ¹¹The Catholic Church was the only organization that the Indonesian government in Timor allowed relative freedom.

¹²Timorese also found the Church a source of support during the guerrilla war against the Indonesians. ¹³Timorese fled to the highlands to escape Indonesian rule, and their families were often relocated in camps far from their villages to prevent them from lending assistance to the guerrillas. ¹⁴The Church saw the abject misery of the people and provided support and comfort. ¹⁵Membership in the Catholic Church grew dramatically from 1975 to 1999 as the Timorese people came to rely on it to protect them and to help them locate missing family members. ¹⁶Today 90% of East Timor's population is Catholic, although many Timorese Catholics include some aspects of animism in their beliefs.

47. Read the following sentence:
    "The priests and nuns of the church provided health and education to the Timorese during that chaotic period."
    In which of the following locations in the third paragraph should this sentence be placed?

    A.   Before sentence 13

    B.   Before sentence 14

    C.   Before sentence 15

    D.   Before sentence 16

48. The method of organization for the second and third paragraphs, respectively, is

    A.   chronological order; problem and solution

    B.   chronological order; cause and effect

    C.   order of importance; chronological order

    D.   comparison and contrast; cause and effect

49. Which of the numbered sentences should be revised to correct a nonstandard sentence structure?

    A.   sentence 2

    B.   sentence 4

    C.   sentence 7

    D.   sentence 8

50. Which of the following changes is needed in the second paragraph?

    A.   Sentence 7: Insert comma after "centuries"

    B.   Sentence 8: Change "who" after "missionaries" to "whom"

    C.   Sentence 9: Change "its" to "their"

    D.   Sentence 11: Capitalize "government"

51. Which words or phrases would, if inserted *in order* into the blanks in the second paragraph, help the reader understand the logical sequence of the writer's ideas?

    A.   however; therefore

    B.   and so; in those circumstances

    C.   however; even then

    D.   but; even then

52. Which of the numbered sentences should be revised to correct a nonstandard verb form?

    A.   sentence 1

    B.   sentence 3

    C.   sentence 10

    D.   sentence 16

53. In the figure below, what is the perimeter of square *ABCD* if diagonal *AC* = 8?

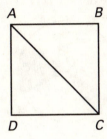

    A.   32

    B.   64

    C. $4\sqrt{2}$

    D. $16\sqrt{2}$

54. Three small circles, all the same size, lie inside a large circle as shown below. The diameter *AB* of the large circle passes through the centers of the three small circles. If each of the smaller circles has area 9π, what is the circumference of the large circle?

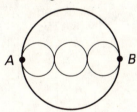

    A.   9

    B.   18

    C. 18π

    D. 27π

55. If $2x^2 + 5x - 3 = 0$ and $x > 0$, then what is the value of x?

   A. $-\frac{1}{2}$

   B. $\frac{1}{2}$

   C. 1

   D. $\frac{3}{2}$

56. The center of the following circle is the point O. What percentage of the circle is shaded if the measure of arc AB is 65° and the measure of arc CD is 21.4°?

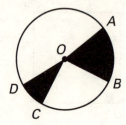

   A. 86.4%

   B. 24%

   C. 43.6%

   D. 27.4%

57. According to the chart, in what year was the total sales of Brand X televisions the greatest?

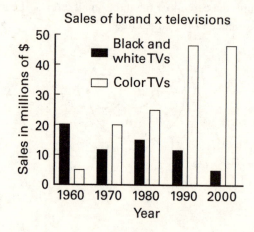

   A. 1960

   B. 1970

   C. 1980

   D. 1990

58. Dance can be a mirror of culture. Which of the following is not an illustration of this statement?

    A. Women in the Cook Islands dance with their feet together and sway while the men take a wide stance and flap their knees.

    B. Movement basics include body, space, time, and relationship.

    C. In Africa, the birth of a child is an occasion for a dance that asks for divine blessings.

    D. The court dancers of Bali study for many years to achieve the balance, beauty, and serenity of their dance.

59. Which of the following best explains why the boiling point of water is reduced and cooking times are increased at high altitudes?

    A. At high altitudes there is greater atmospheric pressure than at sea level.

    B. At high altitudes there is less oxygen than at sea level.

    C. At high altitudes the vapor pressure of water is reduced because of the reduced atmospheric pressure.

    D. At high altitudes water boils at a lower temperature because of the reduced atmospheric pressure.

Read the passage below; then answer the three questions that follow.

The teaching apprentice initiated the discussion in a clear and well-prepared manner. To _____ the lecture topic, the teaching apprentice utilized overhead transparencies of both lexicon and abstract representation to better _____ the theories behind various pedagogical concepts. The class culminated whereby students established enthymemes extrapolated from the class discussion. The class maintained integrity and continuity.

60. Which of these grouped words, if inserted *in order* into the passage's blank lines, would address the logical sequencing of the narrative?

    A. refute; criticize

    B. conflate; discern

    C. undermine; explain

    D. support; illustrate

61. The definition of the term "pedagogical" as used in the passage means

    A. academic.

    B. abstract.

    C. meaningless.

    D. obtuse.

62. The passage suggests that the author's classroom experience was

    A. a needless waste of time and energy.

    B. intelligible and pragmatic.

    C. haphazard and disorderly.

    D. too advanced and complicated.

63. What does it mean that multiplication and division are *inverse operations*?

    A. Multiplication is commutative, whereas division is not. For example: 4×2 gives the same product as 2×4, but $4 \div 2$ is not the same as $2 \div 4$.

    B. Whether multiplying or dividing a value by 1, the value remains the same. For example, 9×1 equals 9; $9 \div 1$ also equals 9.

    C. When performing complex calculations involving several operations, all multiplication must be completed before completing any division, such as in $8 \div 2 \times 4 + 7 - 1$.

    D. The operations "undo" each other. For example, multiplying 11 by 3 gives 33. Dividing 33 by 3 then takes you back to 11.

64. One day, 31 students were absent from Pierce Middle School. If that represents about 5.5% of the students, what is the population of the school?

    A. 177

    B. 517

    C. 564

    D. 171

65. Which of the following are equivalent to 0.5%?
> I. One-half of one percent
> II. 5%
> III. 1/200
> IV. 0.05

A. I and III only

B. I and IV only

C. II and III only

D. II and IV only

Read the passage below; then answer the two questions that follow.

America's national bird, the mighty bald eagle, is being threatened by a new menace. Once decimated by hunters and loss of habitat, this newest danger is suspected to be from the intentional poisoning by livestock ranchers. Authorities have found animal carcasses injected with restricted pesticides. These carcasses are suspected to have been placed to attract and kill predators such as the bald eagle in an effort to preserve young grazing animals. It appears that the eagle is being threatened again by the consummate predator, humans.

66. One can conclude from this passage that

A. the pesticides used are beneficial to the environment.

B. ranchers believe that killing the eagles will protect their ranches.

C. ranchers must obtain licenses to use illegal pesticides.

D. poisoning eagles is good for livestock.

67. The author's attitude is one of

A. uncaring observation.

B. concerned interest.

C. uninformed acceptance.

D. suspicion.

68. Use the figure to answer the question that follows.

What is the approximate area of the shaded region, given that:

    a.   the radius of the circle is 6 units

    b.   the square inscribes the circle

A.   106 square units

B.   31 square units

C.   77 square units

D.   125 square units

69. How many lines of symmetry do all non-square rectangles have?

A.   0

B.   2

C.   4

D.   8

70. Use the figure to answer the question that follows.

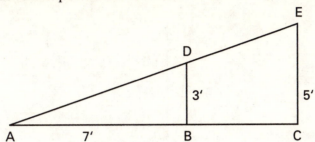

The figure above is a sketch of a ramp. Given that the two ramp supports (DB and EC) are perpendicular to the ground, and the dimensions of the various parts are as noted, what is the approximate distance from point B to point C?

A. 4.7 feet

B. 4.5 feet

C. 4.3 feet

D. 4.1 feet

71. What is the slope of a line passing through points (−2, 6) and (4, −2) on the coordinate plane?

A. $-\frac{3}{4}$

B. $\frac{3}{4}$

C. $-\frac{4}{3}$

D. $\frac{4}{3}$

72. Use the graph to answer the question.

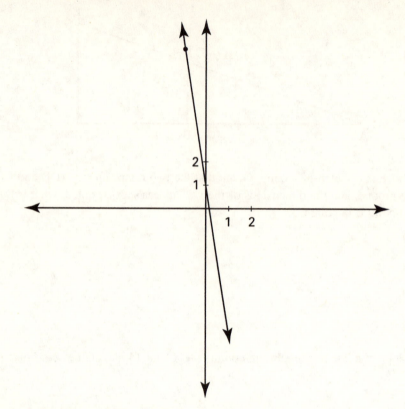

Which equation best describes the graph above?

A. $y = 0x$

B. $y = x + 0$

C. $y = -8x$

D. $y = 8x$

73. Which point represents the y-intercept of the equation $2x = 3y - 12$?

A. $(4, 0)$

B. $(0, -6)$

C. $(-6, 0)$

D. $(0, 4)$

Read the passage below; then answer the three questions that follow.

The early decades of the fifteenth century were a period in our history when English took a "great (linguistic) vowel shift" by redistributing the vowel pronunciation and configuration. Each vowel changed its sound quality, but the distinction between one vowel and the next was maintained. There was a restructuring of the sounds and patterns of communication. One has to conclude that a concurrent stress and exhilaration was also occurring within the perimeters of the literate society. Musicians, artists, poets, and authors all must have relished the new freedom and experimentation that was now possible with the new-found linguistic shifts.

74. The passage tells about

   A.   a shift in vowel pronunciation and configuration.

   B.   a fifteenth-century renaissance for musicians, artists, poets, and authors.

   C.   a new-found linguistic freedom from conventional sound and linguistic structure.

   D.   various vowel stresses and their effect on artistic expression.

75. What is the meaning of the word *linguistic* as used in the passage?

   A.   Artistic freedom

   B.   Verbal or rhetorical

   C.   Social or expressive

   D.   Vowel configuration

76. Because "each vowel changed its sound quality,"

   A.   there was a restructuring of the sounds and patterns of communication.

   B.   language could never be spoken in the same way again.

   C.   artists had to develop new means of expression.

   D.   communication went through a divergent change of status and culture.

77. Ms. Williams plans to buy carpeting for her livingroom floor. The room is a rectangle measuring 14 feet by 20 feet. She wants no carpet seams on her floor, even if that means that some carpeting will go to waste. The carpeting she wants comes in 16-foot-wide rolls. What is the minimum amount of carpeting that will have to be wasted if Ms. Williams insists upon her no-seams requirement?

A. 40 square feet

B. 60 square feet

C. 80 square feet

D. 100 square feet

78. Use the figure to answer the question that follows.

Consider this sequence of calculator keystrokes:

That sequence would be useful for finding which of the following values?

A. The total distance an automobile travels if it covers 182 miles one day, but only 1.03 and 1.04 miles over the next two days.

B. The amount of money in a savings account after the original deposit of $182 earns 3% and then 4% simple annual interest over two years.

C. The total distance an automobile travels if it covers 182 miles one day, 103 miles the next day, and 104 miles the third day.

D. The amount of money in a savings account after the original deposit of $182 grows by $1.03 and $1.04 in interest over two days.

79. The distribution of a high school chorus is depicted in the graph below. There is a total of 132 students in the chorus.

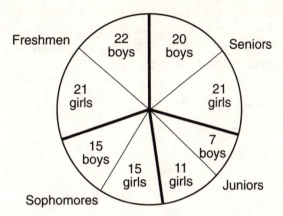

Which of the following expressions represents the percentage of freshman and sophomore girls in the chorus?

A. $\dfrac{21+15}{132} \times 100$

B. $\dfrac{21+15}{132} + 100$

C. $\dfrac{21+15}{132}$

D. $\dfrac{21+15}{100} \times 132$

Read the passage below; then answer the two questions that follow.

[1]The Dead Sea Scrolls are considered the archaeological find of the century. [2]The scrolls, about 800 different documents, are written on leather and papyrus. [3]They may be the oldest versions of the Judeo-Christian sacred texts in existence. [4]The manuscripts are believed to have been written between 200 b.c. and a.d. 50 by the Essenes, members of an ascetic Jewish sect. [5]Most of the Old Testament books (except Esther) appear in the scrolls, and some of the scrolls are multiple copies of these books written by different scribes. [6]Other scrolls are books of the Apocrypha, such as Jubilees, Tobit, and the Wisdom of Solomon, as well as hymns, prayers, prophecies, and biblical commentaries.

[7]For nearly 2,000 years this priceless cache of sacred writings lay hidden in the desert of Judah along the Dead Sea. [8]The first find was in 1947 when a Bedouin shepherd boy discovered the scrolls in a rocky cave of Qumran, ten miles from Jerusalem on the edge of the Dead Sea. [9]Shortly after, other manuscripts were uncovered nearby in different caves. [10]The larger group of scrolls was found in 1952.

¹¹Four photographic copies of the scrolls were distributed, and these photographic copies were kept under the strict supervision of a group of 40 scholars dedicated to studying the photographs and analyzing the copies. ¹²In December 1990, however, the Huntington Library in San Marino, California, began granting access to anyone who wants to view and study the photographs. ¹³This move is hailed by those who have felt left out of the elite cadre of 40 scroll scholars.

80. Which of the following changes is needed?

   A.   Sentence 4: Change "between" to "among."

   B.   Sentence 7: Change "lay" to "have lain."

   C.   Sentence 10: Change "larger" to "largest."

   D.   Sentence 12: Change "who" to "whom."

81. Which of the following requires revision for unnecessary repetition?

   A.   Sentence 5

   B.   Sentence 7

   C.   Sentence 8

   D.   Sentence 11

82. Use the graph to answer the question that follows.

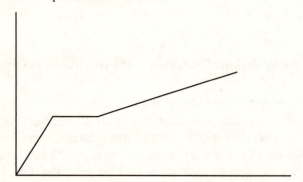

Which of the following scenarios could be represented by the graph above?

   A.   Mr. Cain mowed grass at a steady rate for a while, then took a short break, and then finished the job at a steady but slower rate.

   B.   Mr. Cain mowed grass at a steady rate for a while, and then mowed at a steady slower rate, then he took a break.

   C.   Mr. Cain mowed grass at a variable rate for a while, then took a short break, and then finished the job at a variable rate.

   D.   Mr. Cain mowed grass at a steady rate for a while, then took a short break, and then finished the job at a steady but faster pace.

83. Use the bar graph that follows to answer the question thereafter.

MS. PATTON'S EARNINGS, 1998–2002

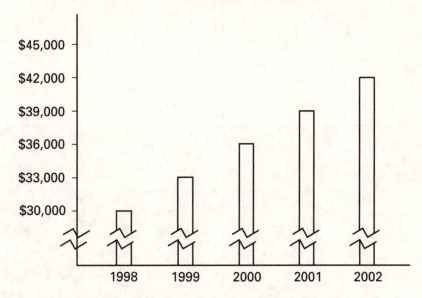

Only one of the statements below is necessarily true. Which one?

A. The range of Ms. Patton's earnings for the years shown is $15,000.

B. Ms. Patton's annual pay increases were consistent over the years shown.

C. Ms. Patton earned $45,000 in 2003.

D. Ms. Patton's average income for the years shown was $38,000.

84. A line passes through points (–6,0) and (0,4) on the coordinate plane. Which of the following statements are true?

    I. The slope of the line is negative.
    II. The slope of the line is positive.
    III. The y-intercept of the line is –6.
    IV. The y-intercept of the line is 4.

A. I and III only

B. I and IV only

C. II and III only

D. II and IV only

85.   Use the graph that follows to answer the question.

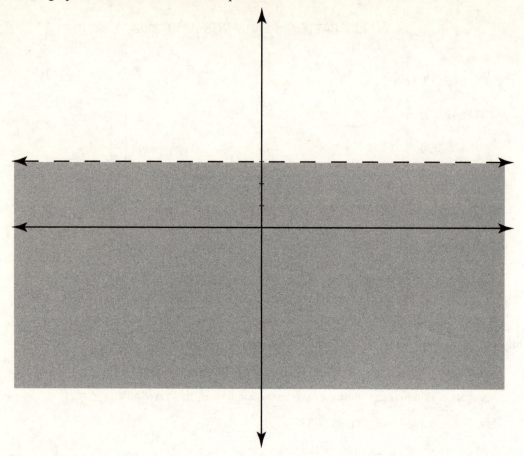

Which inequality describes the graph?

A. $y < 3$

B. $x < 3$

C. $y > 3$

D. $x > 3$

86. Use the figure to answer the question that follows.

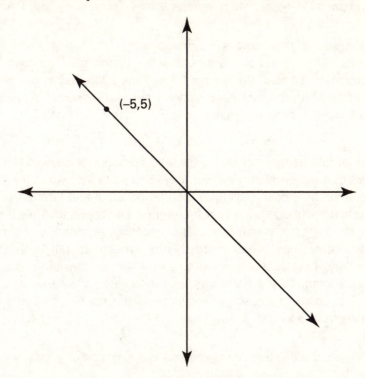

(−5,5)

Which of the following statements about the graph of a linear equation (shown) are true?

    I.   The graph shows an inverse variation.

    II. The graph shows a direct variation.

    III.   The slope of the line is −1.

    IV. The slope of the line is 1.

A.   I and III only

B.   I and IV only

C.   II and III only

D.   II and IV only

[1]Most banks require that buyers be responsible for paying hazard insurance premiums and real estate taxes on houses they are financing. [2]The reason is that if the insurance premium or taxes are not paid, the bank's interest in the property may be jeopardized. [3]Therefore, the mortgage servicer sets up a special account called an escrow account to handle these expenses.

[4]A mortgage loan is usually set up so that the homeowner pays to the bank each month an amount that will eventually pay for taxes and insurance when these expenses come due. [5]Each month's house payment, then, is principal and interest plus 1/12 of the estimated total amount due each year for interest and taxes. [6]Because the amount of taxes levied by the county may vary, and because sometimes insurance rates rise, the bank will sometimes collect more then it will actually pay out. [7]The overage is applied toward the next year's payments, so the house payment reflects a lower amount due each month. [8]If the bank has underestimated the taxes and insurance, there will be a shortage in the escrow account, so the house payments will rise in order that the bank may recoup its loss.

87. Which of the following, if added between sentences 4 and 5, is most consistent with the writer's purpose and audience?

    A.   This money is put into a special account called a mortgage escrow account.

    B.   Some folks resent the fact that the bank hangs on to a part of their money in an interest-free account.

    C.   Most mortgage servicers do not set up an escrow account.

    D.   How anybody can fail to see that banks are going out of their way to protect clients is beyond me.

88. Which of the following is needed in the second paragraph?

    A.   Sentence 4: Change "set" to "sit."

    B.   Sentence 6: Change "then" to "than."

    C.   Sentence 7: Change "so" to "but."

    D.   Sentence 8: Change "rise" to "raise."

89. Simplify the following expression.

    $\frac{2x^2}{3} + 7x + 9 + \frac{x^2}{3} - 12x + 1$

    A. $x^2 - 5x + 10$

    B. $6x^3 + 10$

    C. $6x^2 + 10$

    D. $x^4 - 5x + 10$

90. Multiply the following binomials.

    $(-2x^2 - 11)(5x^2 + 3)$

    A. $-10x^2 - 8$

    B. $-10x^2 - 14x - 8$

    C. $-10x^4 - 61x^2 - 33$

    D. $-10x^2 - 52x - 33$

91. Factor the following expression into two binomials.

    $-8x^2 + 22x - 5$

    A. $(4x - 1)(-2x + 5)$

    B. $(-4x - 1)(-2x - 5)$

    C. $(4x + 1)(-2x + 5)$

    D. $(4x + 1)(2x + 5)$

92. Use the figure below to answer the question that follows. Assume that:

Point *C* is the center of the circle.

Angles *xyz* and *xcz* intercept minor arc *xz*.

The measure of angle *xyz* is 40°.

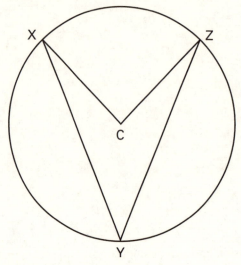

What is the measure of major arc *xyz*?

A.   140°

B.   280°

C.   160°

D.   320°

93. The novel *Huckleberry Finn*, by Mark Twain, has been a subject of controversy because:

A.   it contains graphic descriptions of violence considered unsuitable for young readers.

B.   it challenges contemporary attitudes toward race in America.

C.   it portrays a hostile relationship between a young boy and an escaping slave.

D.   it was thought to have influenced the outcome of the Civil War.

94. The Japanese form of poetry called haiku is known for its:

A.   brevity and concision.

B.   elaborate and flowery description.

C.   logic and directness of statement.

D.   humor and lifelike detail.

95. Which author wrote: "What's in a name? That which we call a rose/ By any other name would smell as sweet"?

    A. Christopher Marlowe

    B. Ben Johnson

    C. William Shakespeare

    D. Geoffrey Chaucer

96. Why did medieval artists not generally employ techniques such as portraiture or realistic perspective?

    A. These were advances in art which were unavailable to them.

    B. They were reacting against Classical artistic models.

    C. They used the composition of their works to express theological ideas.

    D. They considered excessive realism sacrilegious.

97. Which artistic movement saw an important revival in recent centuries?

    A. Classical

    B. Baroque

    C. Gothic

    D. A and C

98. Contemporary performance art often makes use of which media?

    A. photography

    B. film

    C. the spoken word

    D. all of the above

99. Contemporary writers of world literature such as Chinua Achebe have emphasized which of the following themes?

    A. imperialism and the impact of Western culture on traditional societies

    B. conflicts between traditional and modern ways of life

    C. the living conditions and problems of everyday life in developing nations

    D. all of the above

100. The novel *One Hundred Years of Solitude*, by Gabriel García Márquez, is characterized by:

    A.   an interweaving of exaggeration and straightforward narrative known as magic realism.

    B.   strict realism and historical accuracy.

    C.   an indifference toward politics.

    D.   a focus on the life course of a single outstanding protagonist.

Constructed-Response Question

**Read the passage below on studying literature of the past,
and then follow the instructions for writing your essay.**

Many scholars note the decline of interest in literature written before the twentieth century. A diminishing number of students pursue studies in Classical, Medieval, and even Renaissance literature. Some observers think this trend is acceptable, since the literature of these early periods is not particularly interesting to the general public. Others say that any lessening of study about the past, and especially its artistic expression, is a negative trend.

In this essay, argue whether you feel that the trend of studying modern versus past literature is commendable or contemptible. Reflect on modern culture and the effects of literature upon it. Discuss the advantages and/or disadvantages of a course of study that excludes or minimizes the literature of earlier periods. Finally, draw upon your own exposure to and attitude toward modern and past literatures, respectively.

Practice Test Answer Sheets

Begin your essay on this page. If necessary, continue on the next page.

_____

_____

_____

_____

_____

_____

_____

_____

_____

_____

_____

_____

_____

_____

_____

_____

_____

_____

Continue on the next page if necessary.

Continuation of your essay from previous page, if necessary.

OGET

Oklahoma General Education Test

Practice Test Answers

Answer Key

1. (D)	26. (D)	51. (D)	76. (A)
2. (B)	27. (D)	52. (A)	77. (A)
3. (A)	28. (B)	53. (D)	78. (B)
4. (C)	29. (B)	54. (C)	79. (A)
5. (C)	30. (D)	55. (B)	80. (C)
6. (C)	31. (A)	56. (B)	81. (D)
7. (C)	32. (C)	57. (D)	82. (A)
8. (D)	33. (B)	58. (B)	83. (B)
9. (D)	34. (B)	59. (D)	84. (D)
10. (C)	35. (C)	60. (D)	85. (A)
11. (A)	36. (B)	61. (A)	86. (C)
12. (C)	37. (D)	62. (B)	87. (A)
13. (A)	38. (D)	63. (D)	88. (B)
14. (C)	39. (B)	64. (C)	89. (A)
15. (C)	40. (D)	65. (A)	90. (C)
16. (B)	41. (A)	66. (B)	91. (A)
17. (A)	42. (D)	67. (B)	92. (B)
18. (B)	43. (A)	68. (B)	93. (B)
19. (B)	44. (B)	69. (B)	94. (A)
20. (C)	45. (B)	70. (A)	95. (C)
21. (C)	46. (A)	71. (C)	96. (C)
22. (B)	47. (A)	72. (C)	97. (D)
23. (A)	48. (B)	73. (D)	98. (D)
24. (C)	49. (B)	74. (A)	99. (D)
25. (D)	50. (A)	75. (B)	100. (A)

Detailed Explanations of Answers

1. **D**

    D is correct because its precepts are summations of each of the composition's main paragraphs. Choice A only mentions points made in the second paragraph; B and C only mention scattered points made throughout the passage, each of which does not represent a larger body of information within the passage.

2. **B**

    The second paragraph states that this is the reason that water is a most unusual substance. Choices A and C list unusual properties of water, but are not developed in the same manner as the property stated in B. Choice D is not correct under any circumstances.

3. **A**

    The sentence contrasts distilled water to that which contains salt, so A is correct. Choices B, C, and D are not implied by the sentence.

4. **C**

    The writer's didactic summary of water's properties is the only perspective found in the passage. Choices A and B are the subjects of individual paragraphs within the passage, but hardly represent the entire passage itself. An in-depth discussion of the physical states of liquids is not offered within the passage.

5. **C**

    The correct choice is C because of the many properties of water ascribed to it in the passage, each of which might serve one practical purpose or another. Choices A and D are contradicted within the passage, while B is not implied at all by the passage.

6. **C**

This sentence includes a remark about the "lack of spark" in DeMarco's writing, which makes a contrast with the previous sentence, where his potential reading competence is regarded as positive. The rest of the paragraph supports this observation. Choice B is also supported by the rest of the paragraph, but it contains no transition of contrast (*moreover* rather than *however*).

7. **C**

The best answer here is sentence 6, with its "grasps and comprehends." These two words mean exactly the same thing in this context, so one of them is unnecessary. The phrase "all of the class" in sentence 5 is somewhat wordy (it could be "the whole class"), but it is not redundant.

8. **D**

Sentence 13 contains a **dangling modifier**. The verbal phrase at the beginning of the sentence should modify a person ("answers" cannot be asked a question), but the only choices are "his" and "answers." Thus the phrase modifies nothing and is a dangling modifier.

9. **D**

Sentence 12 refers to journals of all classmates, so the apostrophe should follow the s. Choice A is wrong because Sideways Stories from Wayside School *is a book, not a story, a fact that prospective elementary teachers should know.*

10. **C**

The phrase "comings and goings" could possibly fit into this sentence, but it is slightly off, whereas the other choices have little or nothing wrong with them. One problem with "comings and goings" is its informal tone: a case study in a textbook usually does not use slangy terms like this one. In addition, the sentence refers to all the students' accounts, not just their travels.

11. **A**

Drawing a sketch with dots marking the possible locations of the two houses and The Soda Depot is a good idea. You can start with dots for the two houses, using inches for miles:

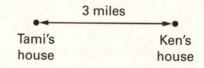

3 miles

Tami's house   Ken's house

If you then draw a dot representing The Soda Depot two miles (inches) to the right of Ken's house, as in the figure that follows, you see that the greatest possible distance between Tami's house and The Soda Depot is five miles.

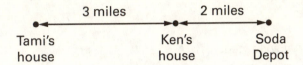

If you draw The Soda Depot dot to the left of Ken's house, as in the figure below, you see that The Soda Depot could be as close as one mile to Tami's house, but no closer. Only statements I and III, then, are true.

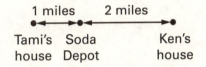

12. **C**

Each combined inequality can be seen as the combination of two single inequalities. Inequality A, for instance, can be seen as the combination of the following two single inequalities:

$75 \leq x$

and

$x \leq 40$.

The meaning of a single inequality is often made clearer if you transpose the statement, placing the variable on the left. That is:

$75 \leq x$

means the same thing as

$x \geq 75$.

So, combined inequality A says that x (the speeds that vehicles may drive at) is greater than or equal to 75 mph and less than or equal to 40 mph.

You can separate combined inequalities B and D into individual inequalities in the same way:

Combined inequality B, $75 < x > 40$, means the same as

$x > 75$

and

$x > 40$.

That means that drivers have to drive faster than 75 mph! That doesn't match what the sign says.

Combined inequality D, 40 < x > 75 means the same as

x > 40

and

x > 75.

That's the same as combined inequality B.

The correct answer is C, 40 ≤ x ≤ 75, because that combined inequality means the same as

x ≥ 40

and

x ≤ 75.

That is, vehicles can travel at or faster than 40 mph, but no faster than 75 mph.

13. **A**

A bar graph works well here. The height of each of five bars would be determined by the number of votes for each lunch food.

A circle or pie chart could also be used. The 18 votes for pizza give the fraction 18/40, so pizza would be assigned 45% of the area of a circle chart, or 162°. The same approach would tell us the appropriate size of each lunch food's slice of the pie chart.

A scatter plot illustrates the relationship between sets of data. A broken-line graph generally illustrates change over time. Neither is appropriate for illustrating the given data.

14. **C**

Choice C is the correct answer. The use of uncommon materials has dramatically changed the criteria by which one assesses visual art.

15. **C**

Choice C is correct because this is the definition of illiterate and functional illiterate stated in paragraph two. Choice A cannot be correct because the passage clearly distinguishes between illiterates and functional illiterates. Choice B is not correct because the definition stated is not related to participation in a program. Choice D is incorrect because the relative number of illiterates and functional illiterates is not discussed.

16. **B**

Choice B is correct because the passage begins by stating that many politicians' wives have expressed interest in literacy. Choice A is incorrect because the author of the passage does not suggest that only women are interested. Choice C is incorrect because the passage does not discuss the number of male or female illiterates. Choice D is incorrect because there is no discussion in the passage of politicians' wives giving speeches.

17. **A**

This question must be answered using the process of elimination. You are asked to select a statement that names a possible program component which is not characteristic of successful literacy programs. Choice A is correct because choices B, C, and D are specifically mentioned in the passage.

18. **B**

Choice B is correct because the author specifically states that politicians should support increased funding for literacy programs. Choices A and C are incorrect because the author states that funding should be increased. There is no discussion of funding for different programs, so choice D is incorrect.

19. **B**

The combined percentages of English and German immigrants equal 45 percent (Irish immigrants represent 43 percent of the graph). Choice A is incorrect because the Irish immigrants represent less than half of the graph. Choice C is incorrect because the graph nowhere implies that the "All Others" section of the graph is restricted to Italian immigrants. D is incorrect because the English and German percentages are unequal.

20. **C**

The gas molecules themselves do not expand in size when heated, but the spaces between them increases as the molecules move faster. The expanding hot air leaves the balloon body through the opening at the bottom. With less air in the balloon casing, the balloon is lighter. The combustion products of propane are carbon dioxide (molar mass 44 g/mol), which is heavier than air, and water (molar mass 18 g/mol), which is lighter.

21. **C**

The upward force of air resistance partially counteracts the force of gravity when a feather falls in air. In a vacuum, or near vacuum, this force is dramatically reduced for the feather and both objects will fall at the same rate. The effect can be modeled without a vacuum pump by comparing the falling of two papers, one crumpled to reduce air resistance and the other flat.

22. **B**

Sentence 6 begins with "Although"—used for mentioning the scientists' public statements—and refers to the "hazy" benefits derived from the study. Thus the sentence has to deal with speculation about the "uncertain" benefits. Choice D fits in with the paragraph's development fairly well, but it is not the best answer because the pejorative word "racist" would not generally be used to characterize someone in a textbook. (There is little doubt that the author considers the experiment itself to be racist, but he or she does not otherwise characterize any of the individuals involved in this passage—and should not do so without offering evidence.)

23. **A**

The word should be "affected"; see the discussion of effect and affect in Chapter 2. The other words are used in standard ways and, even though "whereas" may sound out of place, it is not as obviously wrong as "effected" and is therefore not the best answer.

24. **C**

Sentence 7 contains a comma splice. The sentence has two independent clauses, and they are not joined by a coordinating conjunction. They must therefore be separated by a semicolon, not a comma. Sentence 3, which contains several commas, is correctly punctuated (except for the period at the end), but they are all necessary to separate the two nonrestrictive phrases: (a) author of the excellent history on the subject and (b) Bad Blood.

25. **D**

By convention in American English, periods and commas are always placed inside of quotation marks.

26. **D**

The verb learn *should clearly be in past tense, not present, because it concerns something that happened in 1972. Incidentally, the word "media" is technically plural, so the verb form should be "learn" rather than "learns" even if present tense were correct.*

27. **D**

This teacher is doing a good thing by collecting data and displaying the data.

28. **B**

One way to approach the problem is to examine each scenario for reasonableness. Even though a runner's mile-by-mile pace in a marathon varies up and down, the runner continually increases the distance covered, and the graph will always move upward, so situation I doesn't go with the graph. The number of households a census taker has left to visit decreases with each visit, so situation II doesn't fit either.

Both situations III and IV are examples of steady growth, so both match the graph. Answer B is therefore correct.

29. **B**

Just from looking at the graph, it's clear that most of the space under the curve is past the 60 mark on the x-axis, so answer D is eliminated because it doesn't include statement I.

Statement II can't be answered by what the graph shows. It appears possible that certain questions were too hard for many in the class and that there weren't enough questions to differen-

tiate B students from C students, but perhaps the class performed exactly as it should have, given the students' ability and Ms. Alvarez's teaching. The distribution can give a teacher many clues about the test and the students and even herself, but by itself tells us nothing about the fairness of the test. Thus, answer A can be eliminated.

Statement III is also false; in left-skewed distributions such as this one, the median is higher than the mean. This is true because the mean is lowered by the lowest scores while the median is relatively unaffected by them.

Statement IV is true: one fairly large group has scored in the high 80s and 90s and another discernible group in the low to mid 60s, whereas few students fall outside these two groups. Thus, the answer has to be B.

30. **D**

Using the rules for solving one-variable equations, the original equation is transformed as follows:

$$\frac{x}{3} - 9 = 15$$

Adding 9 to each side of the equation gives

$$\frac{x}{3} = 24$$

Multiplying both sides by 3 gives

$x = 72$.

31. **A**

Again, using the rules for solving one-variable equations produces these transformations:

$3x^2 - 11 = 1$

Adding 11 to each side of the equation gives

$3x^2 = 12$

Dividing both sides by 3 gives

$x^2 = 4$

You next find the square roots of 4: 2 and –2.

The solutions can be checked by substituting them (one at a time) into the original equation to see if they work. In this case, both 2 and –2 indeed do work.

32. **C**

Black line spectra are formed when the continuous spectra of the Sun passes through the atmosphere. The elements in the atmosphere absorb wavelengths of light characteristic of their spectra (these are the same wavelengths given off when the element is excited; for example, the red color of a Neon light). By examining the line spectral gaps, scientists can deduce the elements that make up the distant atmosphere. Choice A is true, but it explains the source of a line spectrum. B is true, and it explains why a blue shirt is blue when placed under a white or blue light source. Recall that a blue shirt under a red light source will appear black because there are no blue wavelengths to be reflected. D is a partial truth; black lights do give off ultra-violet light that the human eye cannot see.

33. **B**

Salt is a strong electrolyte that completely dissociates in solution. When this solution is in contact with a semi-permeable membrane, like the inflamed cells in the throat, water moves across the membrane from the side with lowest solute concentration to the side of higher solute concentration. In the case of the sore throat, water from inside the inflamed cells moves out toward the higher concentration salt water and the throat cells shrink due to the loss of water. All the items listed are colligative properties that, like osmotic pressure, are a function of the number, but not the nature, of particles in solution.

34. **B**

Lincoln's immediate purpose in announcing the Emancipation Proclamation was to rally flagging Northern morale. Lincoln waited until after a major Union victory, at Antietam in 1862, so he couldn't be charged with making the announcement as an act of desperation. He recognized that the costs of the war had reached a point where preserving the Union would not be a powerful enough reason to motivate many Northerners to continue the war. Framing the war as a war against slavery would mobilize powerful abolitionist forces in the North and perhaps create an atmosphere of a "holy crusade" rather than one of using war to resolve a political conflict.

While the Emancipation Proclamation had the announced purpose of freeing the slaves, Lincoln himself indirectly stated that freeing the slaves was a means to a greater end, preserving the Union. In a statement released before the Emancipation Proclamation, Lincoln asserted, "If I could save the Union without freeing any slave I would do it, and if I could save it by freeing all the slaves I would do it. . . . What I do about slavery, and the colored race, I do because I believe it helps to save the Union."

35. **C**

The passage suggests that education is at present based primarily on failure and negative reinforcement and that, in order to create a more productive and positive learning environment, the emphasis must shift to success. While answers A and B may be correct, they are not the main ideas of the passage. D is simply a statement that is not based upon any factual evidence whatsoever. Therefore, C is the correct answer.

36. **B**

An axiom in this case is another word for motto. It can also mean an accepted truism or principle, which would also apply here. Answers A, C, and D are erroneous definitions; therefore, B, University motto, is the correct answer.

37. **D**

The passage states that "the language of failure . . . will have a prohibitive impact on the students' . . . self-esteem," so D is the correct answer. Answers A, B, and C do not apply in this case.

38. **D**

The first paragraph of the passage tells the reader that, in addition to personal expression, language also has the power to persuade and influence. While answers A, B, and C may indeed be attributes of language, they are not focused upon in the passage.

39. **B**

Solving for a particular variable in an equation means to isolate that variable on one side of the equation. In this case, use of the rules for transforming equations allows you to change the original equation into the desired one:

$$\frac{y}{3} - \frac{x}{2} = 4$$

Adding $\frac{x}{2}$ to each side gives

$$\frac{y}{3} = \frac{x}{2} + 4$$

Then, multiplying each side by 3 gives

$$y = \frac{3x}{2} + 12$$

40. **D**

One way to solve the problem is by writing a one-variable equation that matches the information given:

$4x + 2(10 - x) = 26$

The "4x" represents four tires for each car. You use x for the number of cars because you don't know how many cars there are.

(10 – x) represents the number of motorcycle tires in the lot. (If there are ten vehicles total, and x of them are cars, you subtract x from 10 to get the number of motorcycles.) Then 2(10 – x) stands for the number of motorcycle tires in the lot.

The sum of the values 4x and 2(10 – x) is 26, and that gives you your equation. Using the standard rules for solving a one-variable equation, you find that x (the number of cars in the lot) equals 3.

Another approach to the problem when given multiple answer choices is to try substituting each answer for the unknown variable in the problem to see which one makes sense.

41. **A**

The correct equation must show three consecutive odd numbers being added to give 117. Odd numbers (just like even numbers) are each two apart. Only the three values given in answer A are each two apart.

Because the numbers being sought are odd, one might be tempted to choose answer D. However, the second value in answer D (x + 1) is not two numbers apart from the first value (x); it's different by only one.

42. **D**

All riders must pay at least three dollars, so 3 will be added to something else in the correct equation. Only answers B and D meet that requirement. The additional fare of two dollars "for every mile or fraction of a mile" tells you that you will need to multiply the number of miles driven (you use 11 because of the extra fraction of a mile) by 2, leading you to answer D.

43. **A**

Democracy is the correct response because it is the antithesis of the authoritarianism of fascism. Indeed, the totalitarian, romantic, militaristic, and nationalistic characteristics were, in large part, a reaction against the perceived inadequacies of democracy.

44. **B**

The industrial economy of the nineteenth century was not based upon an equitable distribution of profits among all those who were involved in production. Marxists and other critics of capitalism condemned the creed of capitalists and the abhorrent conditions of the industrial proletariat. Raw materials, a constant labor supply, capital, and an expanding marketplace were critical elements in the development of the industrial economy.

45. **B**

The term "Trail of Tears" is used to describe the relocation of the Cherokee tribe from the southern Appalachians to what is now Oklahoma. The migration of Mormons from Nauvoo, Illinois, to the Great Salt Lake in Utah, the westward movements along the Oregon Trail, and, much earlier, the Wilderness Road, all took place and could at times be as unpleasant as the Cherokees' trek. They were, however, more voluntary than the Cherokee migration and therefore did not earn such sad titles as the "Trail of Tears."

46. **A**

Thomas Paine wrote several pamphlets before and during the American Revolution. Common Sense was the most significant because it carefully documented abuses of the British parliamentary system of government, particularly in its treatment of the American colonies. Paine portrayed a brutish monarchy interested only in itself and pointedly argued how independence would improve the colonies' long-term situation. His argument was directed at the common man, and it struck a chord unlike anything previously written in the colonies. Its publication in 1774 was perfect in reaching the public at just the moment that their questions and concerns regarding British rule were peaking. The answers provided in Paine's essays were pivotal in the subsequent behavior of many colonists who, until that time, had been unsure of what they believed regarding independence and British rule.

Answer B is incorrect. Paine wrote another essay called American Crisis during the winter of 1776. This essay, not Common Sense, helped rally American spirits during that long, demoralizing winter. Answers C and D are also incorrect. Paine wrote to an American, not a British, audience. He also wrote Common Sense well before American independence was achieved.

47. **A**

The last phrase of the sentence—"that chaotic period"—could refer to either the guerilla war mentioned in sentence 12 or the period of relocation mentioned in sentence 13, meaning that the sentence would have to be inserted after sentence 12 or 13 (choices A or B). However, the sentence about the Church's individual members providing support cannot just sit beside a sentence about the church itself providing support: the two thoughts would have to be joined in a logical way. Thus choice B is not as good as choice A. With choice A, sentence 12 would be explained by the new sentence, and then sentence 13 would describe the circumstances under which the support was provided.

48. **B**

The second paragraph proceeds from the 1500s to 1975, and the third paragraph describes the cause for the effect mentioned at the end of the second paragraph: the embrace of Catholicism by the Timorese.

49. **B**

Sentence 4 is a fragment: because "being" is a verbal rather than a standard verb form, it does not act as a verb for "exceptions." (Note: Substituting "were" for "being" would fix the fragment but would not produce an effective sentence—"the exceptions" to what?) Sentence 7 does contain a punctuation error (discussed in the answer to question 50), but the question specifically asks for nonstandard "sentence structure." Be sure to read each question thoroughly.

50. **A**

Sentence 7 begins with a subordinate clause, and a comma should separate that clause from the independent clause that follows, so the answer is A. The "who" in sentence 8 is correct even though it refers to "missionaries," which is the object of a preposition, because it is the subject of its own clause—"who were posted"—so B is incorrect. The "its" following East Timor in sentence 9 is correct because the pronoun refers to the country as a whole, not to all the people of the country, so C is incorrect. The word "government" in sentence 11 is not capitalized even though it occurs with the proper adjective "Indonesian," so D is incorrect.

51. **D**

Because the first blank must show a contrast with the previous thought, choice B is not possible. Because a comma rather than a semicolon precedes the first blank, "however" is not possible, either, eliminating A and C. If "however" were inserted, the sentence would have a comma splice, because "however" is not a coordinating conjunction ("but" is).

52. **A**

The first sentence has a plural subject—"animism and spirit worship"—so it should have a plural form of verb as well.

53. **D**

Let s be the length of each side of square ABCD. Since triangle ADC is a right triangle, we can use the Pythagorean Theorem to solve for s. We have $AD^2 + DC^2 = AC^2$ or $s^2 + s^2 = 8^2$. Simplifying the equation, we get: $2s^2 = 64$. Now divide both sides of the equation by two:

$$s^2 = 32 \quad so \quad s = \sqrt{32} = \sqrt{16} \times \sqrt{2} = 4\sqrt{2}.$$

Therefore, the perimeter of square ABCD is

$$P = 4s = 4 \times 4\sqrt{2} = 16\sqrt{2}$$

54. **C**

Let r be the length of the radius of each of the small circles and let R be the length of the radius of the large circle. Then, R = 3r. The area of each of the small circles is $\pi r^2 = 9\pi$. Now divide both sides of the equation by π:

$r^2 = 9r = 3$. *Then,*

$R = 3r = 3 \times 3 = 9$.

Therefore, the circumference of the large circle is

$C = 2\pi R = 2\pi \times 9 = 18\pi$.

55. **B**

To solve the equation $2x^2 + 5x - 3 = 0$, we can factor the left side of the equation to get $(2x - 1)(x + 3) = 0$. Then use the following rule (sometimes called the Zero Product Property): If $a \times b = 0$, then either $a = 0$ or $b = 0$. Applying this to our problem gives us

$2x - 1 = 0$ *or* $x + 3 = 0$.

Solve these two equations:

$2x - 1 = 0 \rightarrow 2x = 1 \rightarrow \dfrac{1}{2}$ *or* $x + 3 = 0 \rightarrow x = -3$.

But $x > 0$, so $x = \dfrac{1}{2}$.

56. **B**

∠AOB and ∠COD are central angles, meaning that their vertices are at the center of a circle. The measure of a central angle is equal to the measure of its intercepted arc. Hence, since arc AB and arc CD are the intercepted arcs of ∠AOB and ∠COD, respectively, the measure (m) of ∠AOB = 65° and m∠COD = 21.4°. So,

m∠AOB + m∠COD = 86.4°.

Therefore, since one revolution of a circle is 360°, the shaded portion of the circle is represented by the following:

$$\frac{86.4}{360} = 0.24 = 24\%$$

57. **D**

First find the total sales for each year by reading the graph for the sales of (i) black and white televisions and (ii) color televisions. Then combine these numbers:

1960	$20,000,000 + $5,000,000	= $25,000,000
1970	$10,000,000 + $20,000,000	= $30,000,000
1980	$15,000,000 + $25,000,000	= $40,000,000
1990	$10,000,000 + $45,000,000	= $55,000,000
2000	$5,000,000 + $45,000,000	= $50,000,000

The greatest total sales occurred in 1990.

58. **B**

The statement "Movement basics include body, space, time, and relationship" is the correct answer because this describes only the dimensions of dance movement; in no way does it speak to how dance reflects the culture of which it is part.

59. **D**

A liquid will boil when its vapor pressure, which depends on temperature, is equal to the atmospheric pressure above the liquid. At high altitudes the atmospheric pressure is lower, thus water will boil at a lower temperature. The boiling point of water is only 100°C at 1 atmosphere pressure (760 torr). In Leadville, Colorado, elevation 10,150 feet, when the atmospheric pressure may be as low as 430 torr, the boiling point of water may be 89°C. The lower temperature increases cooking times.

60. **D**

A teaching apprentice would be expected to lay the foundation for her lecture and then present greater detail by way of example, or as the passage puts it, "illustration." Someone in this position, having set this task for herself, would not be prone to refuting her own lecture notes (A), attempting to cause confusion (B), or perhaps least of all, working to subvert the lecture topic she herself had elected to teach (C).

61. **A**

The definition of the term "pedagogical" is answer A, academic. The answers B, abstract; C, meaningless; and D, obtuse, are incorrect.

62. **B**

The author's classroom experience was answer B, intelligible (understandable) and pragmatic (practical or utilitarian). The passage gives credence to this by the author's use of such words as "clear and well-prepared." Answers A and C suggest the opposite of a positive experience, and there is no evidence given that the experience was too advanced or complicated (D).

63. **D**

It's true that multiplication is commutative and division isn't, but that's not relevant to them being inverse operations. Answer A doesn't address the property of being inverse.

Answer B also contains a true statement, but again, the statement is not about inverse operations.

Answer C gives a false statement. In the example shown in answer C, the order of operations tells you to compute 8 ÷ 2 first, before any multiplication.

As noted in answer D, the inverseness of two operations indeed depends upon their ability to undo each other.

64. **C**

One way to arrive at the answer is to set up a proportion, with one corner labeled x:

$$\frac{31}{x} = \frac{5.5}{100}$$

To complete the proportion (and to find the answer), cross-multiply 31 and 100, giving 3100, then divide by 5.5, giving approximately 564.

65. **A**

The value 0.5 is equivalent to $\frac{5}{10}$ or $\frac{1}{2}$. That means that 0.5 percent (which is one way to read the original numeral) is the same as one-half of one percent, so answer I is correct.

One-half of one percent can't be the same as five percent, so answer II cannot be correct.

$\frac{1}{200}$ *is equivalent to 0.5%. Here's why: One percent is equivalent to $\frac{1}{100}$. Half of one percent, (0.5%, as noted above) is therefore $\frac{1}{200}$, so answer III is correct. Therefore A, I and III only, is correct.*

66. **B**

The ranchers believe that killing the eagles will protect their ranches. This is understood by the implication that "attract[ing] and kill[ing] predators . . . in an effort to preserve young grazing animals" will protect their ranches. Choice D is not wrong, but it is not as good a choice as B, because the passage offers no proof that the eagles do harm livestock.

67. **B**

The author's use of words such as "mighty bald eagle" and "threatened by a new menace" supports concern for the topic. For the most part, the author appears objective; thus, Choice B, concerned interest, is the correct answer.

68. **B**

First, it is helpful to view the shaded area as the area of the square minus the area of the circle. With that in mind, you simply need to find the area of each simple figure, and then subtract one from the other.

You know that the radius of the circle is 6 units in length. That tells you that the diameter of the circle is 12 units. Because the circle is inscribed in the square (meaning that the circle fits inside of the square touching in as many places as possible), you see that the sides of the square are each 12 units in length. Knowing that, you compute that the area of the square is 144 square units (12 × 12).

Using the formula for finding the area of a circle (πr^2), and using 3.14 for π, you get approximately 113 square units. (3.14 × 6 × 6). Then, you subtract 113 (the area of the circle) from 144 (the area of the square) for the answer of 31.

69. **B**

If you can fold a two-dimensional figure so that one side exactly matches or folds onto the other side, the fold line is a line of symmetry. The figure below is a non-square rectangle with its two lines of symmetry shown.

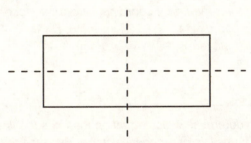

One might think that lines drawn from opposite corners are lines of symmetry, but they're not. The two halves would be the same size and shape, but wouldn't fold onto each other.

Note that the question asked about non-square rectangles. Squares (which are rectangles) have four lines of symmetry.

70. A

To answer the question, you must recognize that triangles ADB and AEC are similar triangles, meaning that they have the same shape. That means that the corresponding angles of the two triangles are the same, or congruent, and that corresponding sides of the two triangles are proportional. Given that, you can set up the following proportion, where x is the distance from point A to point C:

$$\frac{3}{7} = \frac{5}{x}$$

Solving the proportion by cross-multiplication, you see that the length of segment AC is about 11.7. Knowing that the length of segment AB is 7 feet, you subtract to find the length of BC (11.7 – 7 = 4.7).

71. C

There are several methods for finding the slope of a line if two points are known. The most straightforward method is to use the slope formula:

$$m = \frac{y_2 - y_1}{x_2 - x_1}$$

This can be read as "the slope of a line (m) is equal to the difference of the y coordinates of any two points on the line ($y_2 - y_1$) divided by the difference of the x coordinates.

$(x_2 - x_1)$.

For this problem, you subtract the first y coordinate from the second [(–2) – 6], giving –8. You then do the same for the x coordinates [4 – (–2)], giving 6. Dividing –8 by 6 is the same as showing the fraction $-\frac{8}{6}$ or, in lowest terms, $-\frac{4}{3}$.

72. C

There are several ways to determine which equation matches the line. An easy way is to decide first whether the line has a positive or a negative slope. Because the line moves from the upper left to the lower right, you would say it has a negative slope.

In a linear equation of the form y = mx + b (where y is isolated on the left side of the equation), the coefficient of x is the slope of the line. The only equation with a negative slope (–8) is response C, so that is the correct answer.

Another clue that C is correct can be found by considering the apparent slope, or steepness/ shallowness of the line. The line in this problem is fairly steep, and a slope of –8 (or 8) is considered fairly steep too, suggesting that C is correct.

73. **D**

The y-intercept *of a linear equation is the point at which its graph passes through, or intercepts, the vertical y-axis. One way to determine the y-intercept is by rewriting the equation in* y-intercept form:

$y = mx + b$

If a linear equation is in that form, b *tells you where the graph of the line intercepts the y-axis. In this case, you rewrite (or transform) the equation following these steps:*

$2x = 3y - 12$

$3y - 12 = 2x$

$3y = 2x + 12$

$y = \dfrac{2}{3}x + 4$

That final version of the equation is indeed in y-intercept form. The 4 tells you that the graph of the equation intercepts the y-axis at point (0, 4).

74. **A**

The passage tells of the "great (linguistic) vowel shift" of the early fifteenth century. While the passage speaks of B, an artistic renaissance; C, new linguistic freedoms; and D, effects on artistic expression, these are all results of the shift and not the shift itself. The shift is what the passage is about. Thus, A is the correct answer.

75. **B**

In this case, linguistic *refers to speaking, talking, verbiage, and/or the act of oration. A, C, and D are not acceptable definitions for the word* linguistic. *Consequently, Choice B, verbal or rhetorical, is the correct answer.*

76. **A**

Answers B, C, and D are generalized answers resulting from the vowel shift. Choice A is a direct result of the shift and is quoted directly from the passage.

Therefore, A is the correct answer.

77. **A**

The only way carpet from a 16-foot-wide roll will cover Ms. Williams' floor without seams is if she buys 20 feet of it. She can then trim the 16-foot width to 14 feet so that it fits her floor. Buying 20 feet of a 16-foot-wide roll means that she will have to buy 320 square feet. Her living room has an area of only 280 square feet (14 feet × 20 feet), so she'll be wasting 40 square feet (320 − 280), but no more, so A is the correct answer.

78. **B**

The keystrokes indicate multiplication, and only answer B involves multiplication. Multiplication is hidden within the concept of interest. One way to compute a new savings account balance after interest has been earned is to multiply the original balance by (1 + the rate of interest). In this case, that's first 1.03, then 1.04. The keystrokes match that multiplication.

79. **A**

In order to solve this problem we must first add the number of freshman girls to the number of sophomore girls (21 + 15). In order to find the percentage we divide this sum by the total number of students in the chorus and multiply by 100.

$$\frac{21+15}{132} \times 100 = \text{\% of freshman and sophomore girls in chorus}$$

Answer B is incorrect; in order to find the percentage we need to multiply the fraction by 100, not divide by 100. Answers C and D are incorrect because the number of freshman and sophomore girls must be divided by the total number of students in the chorus. We then multiply by 100 to get the percent.

80. **C**

Choice C is the correct answer. The comparative degree is used for comparing two things, so "larger" should be changed to the superlative degree, "largest," because more than two caves were discovered containing scrolls. Choice A correctly uses "between" to indicate something falling between two dates; "among" is used for more than two things. In choice B, the use of "lay" is correct; the past tense is required for a condition no longer in effect. In choice D "who" is correct as the subject of the subordinate clause with the verb "wants." "Whom" is the objective case and cannot be a subject.

81. **D**

Choice D should be revised to eliminate unnecessary repetition of "photographic" and "copies." Choices A, B, and C are concise sentences.

82. **A**

The somewhat steep straight line to the left tells you that Mr. Cain worked at a steady rate for a while. The completely flat line in the middle tells you he stopped for a while—the line doesn't go up because no grass was cut then. Finally, the line continues upward (after his break) less steeply (and therefore more flatly), indicating that he was working at a slower rate.

83. **B**

Because Ms. Patton's increases were consistent ($3,000 annually), and because the directions tell you that only one statement is true, answer B must be correct. To be more confident, however, you can examine the other statements:

The range of Ms. Patton's earnings is $12,000 (the jump from $30,000 to $42,000), not $15,000, so answer A cannot be correct.

Although Ms. Patton may have earned $45,000 in 2003, you don't know that, so answer C cannot be correct.

Answer D gives the incorrect earnings average; it was $36,000, not $38,000.

84. D

It is helpful to make a sketch of the line on the coordinate plane. (To do that you need to know how to plot individual points.)

The line "travels" from the lower left to the upper right, meaning that it has a positive slope. Statement II is therefore true. The y-intercept of a line is the spot at which the line crosses, or intercepts, the vertical axis. In this case, that's at point (0, 4). (You can simply say that the y-intercept is 4, without mentioning the 0). Statement IV is therefore true as well.

85. A

Consider various random points in the shaded area: (5, –2), (–1, 2), (12, 2.5) and (–9, 1). Notice that all points in the shaded area have a y-coordinate value less than 3. The inequality that states this fact is the one in A ("y is less than 3.")

86. C

Inverse variations give graphs that are curves. As equations, they take the forms $xy = k$ or $y = \frac{k}{x}$. The graph shown is simpler than that, so statement I is false.

The graphs of direct variations are straight lines that pass through the point (0,0) (the origin.) As equations, they take the form $y = mx + 0$, or simply $y = mx$. The line shown is the graph of a direct variation, so statement II is true.

Because point (–5, 5) is equally distant from both the x- and y-axes, the line "cuts" quadrant II at a 45° angle. Lines that form 45° angles with the x- and y-axes (assuming the same scales on both axes) have slopes of 1 or –1. The line here travels from upper left to lower right, meaning that its slope is negative, so statement III is also true.

87. A

Choice A contains the transition "This money," a phrase that clearly refers to "amount" in sentence 4. Also, the repetition of "mortgage" indicates the correct flow of ideas. Choice B is too casual in using "folks," and choice D changes voice, with "me," and is also too casual in phrasing. Choice C is contradicted by information in the passage.

88. B

Choice B correctly changes "then," a word indicating passage of time in a narrative, to "than," a word indicating contrast. Choice A (sentence 6) correctly uses "set" in meaning that the bank's account has been set up, or arranged deliberately. Choice C incorrectly changes the transition "so," which shows cause-and-effect, to the transition word "but," which shows contrast. Sentence 8 (choice D) correctly uses "rise" to indicate something going up.

89. **A**

The key to simplifying expressions such as these is to combine only like terms. Like terms are those with identical bases. $4x^2$ and $\frac{3}{5x^2}$, for instance, have like bases. So do $9x$ and $\frac{1}{5x}$. Real numbers without attached variables are their own like terms: 4, –21, 0.12, and $\frac{5}{8}$ are all like terms. In the given expression, $\frac{2x^2}{3}$ and $\frac{x^2}{3}$ are like terms; their sum is $\frac{3x^2}{3}$, or $1x^2$, or just x^2; $-12x$ and $7x$ are like terms; they add up to $-5x$; 9 and 1 are also like terms, with a sum of 10.

Those three terms (x^2, $-5x$, and 10) are then separated by addition symbols to give the simplified version of the original expression.

90. **C**

Each *term* of each *binomial must be multiplied by* both *terms in the other binomial. That means that four products are generated:

$(-2x^2) \times (5x^2)$ gives $-10x^4$ (and right here you see that answer C is correct).

$(-2x^2) \times (3) = -6x^2$

$(-11) \times (5x^2) = -55x^2$

$(-11) \times (3) = -33$

The two middle terms are like terms, and can be combined into $-61x^2$. The three terms (which cannot be further combined) give you the answer of $-10x^4 - 61x^2 - 33$.

91. **A**

One approach to factoring the expression is to start with a set of two empty parentheses written as follows: (__ + __) (__ + __). The task is to then fill in the four blanks with values that "multiply back" to the original expression. Educated trial and error works well here. Here's a good place to start: You know that the two blanks at the end of the parentheses must be 1 and 5, because 5 is a prime number; no other whole numbers multiply by anything to give you 5.

A bit more experimentation shows that only $(4x - 1) \times (-2x + 5)$ "multiplies back" to $-8x^2 + 22x - 5$, so A is the answer. (Be sure to pay attention to whether values are positive or negative.)

92. **B**

Angle xyz is an inscribed angle (its vertex is on the circle). Angle xcz is a central angle (its vertex is at the circle's center). When two such angles intercept (or "cut off") the same arc of the circle, there exists a specific size relationship between the two angles. The measure of the central angle will always be double the measure of the inscribed angle. In this case, that means that the measure of angle xcz must be 80°.

That means that minor arc xz also has measure 80°. Every circle (considered as an arc) has measure 360°. That means that major arc xyz has measure 280° (360 – 80), so B is correct.

93. **B**

B is correct. While the novel does contain some violent scenes, none of them are graphic enough to be considered unsuitable for young readers, so A is not correct. The relationship between Huckleberry Finn and Jim, the escaping slave, is mostly warm and trusting rather than hostile, so C is incorrect; also, the book was written after the Civil War, eliminating D. It did challenge some attitudes toward race, however, because it portrayed such close fellowship between two people of different races and showed a young white man's willingness to take risks on behalf of a black man's freedom (answer B).

94. **A**

A is correct. Haiku are by definition too short to contain much elaborate description. The haiku form does not emphasize logic or direct statements. And while some haiku are humorous and/or contain lifelike details, these qualities do not characterize all haiku poems.

95. **C**

C is correct. Those lines are spoken by Juliet in Romeo and Juliet, *by William Shakespeare.*

96. **C**

The emphasis in medieval art on theological subjects and themes was accompanied by a de-emphasis of realism.

97. **D**

During the 19th century, there was a revival of interest in Classical and Gothic styles.

98. **D**

Contemporary performance art often takes a multi-media approach, combining many different types of elements.

99. **D**

All of these themes have been emphasized in works of Chinua Achebe and Sembene Ousmane, among other writers of world literature.

100. **A**

A is correct. García Márquez is known for his use of magic realism rather than strict realism. One Hundred Years of Solitude comments indirectly on various events of Colombian political history, and it has an extensive cast of characters, none of whom dominate the novel as the main protagonist.

Constructed Response

WRITING SAMPLE WITH A SCORE OF 4

The Literature of the Past

The direction of modern literary scholarship points toward an alarming conclusion. The depreciation of the literary study of bygone periods is a sign of two disturbing trends. First, scholars are avoiding more difficult study in preference to what seems light or facile. Furthermore, the neglect of the literature of former eras is a denial of the contribution that past authors have made toward modern literature. This is not to suggest that all scholars who study modern literature do so because they are either intimidated by past literature or do not appreciate its value. However, the shrinking minority of past literary scholarship is a clear indication that intimidation and awe of past conventions are deterrents to many students of literature.

The dread associated with past literature reflects poorly upon our society. The attempts to simplify literature to accommodate simpler audiences has resulted in a form of literary deflation. The less society taxes its audience's minds, the less comprehensive those unexercised minds become. Information and ideas are now transmitted to the average man through the shallow medium of television programming. Modern students are evolving from this medium, and the gap separating them from the complexity of the classics is continuing to grow.

Once more, it is important to stress that this essay does not seek to diminish students of modern literature. The only demand this argument makes upon modern students is that they supplement their study with significant portions of the classics from which all subsequent literature has been derived, whether consciously or unconsciously. Failure to do so is an act akin to denying the importance of history itself. Like history, literature exists as an evolutionary process; modern literature can only have come into existence through the development of past literature.

Concerning the relative complexity of the classics to modern literature, the gap is not so great as one may think. Surely, one who glances at the works of Shakespeare or Milton without prior exposure will be daunted by them. However, a disciplined mind can overcome the comprehensive barriers erected over the past few centuries through persistence and perseverance.

Unfortunately, the ability to overcome the barriers to past literature may eventually become obsolete. The more frequently students select their courses of study through fear rather than interest, the wider the literary gap will become, until the pampered minds of all future readers will prove unequal to the task of reading the literature of our fathers. The more frequently students deny the usefulness of the literature antedating this century, the more frequently they deny their own literary heritage, the more probable it will become for modern literature's structure to crumble through lack of firm foundation.

FEATURES OF THE WRITING SAMPLE SCORING 4

Appropriateness

The paper's topic and the writer's viewpoint are both well laid out in the first paragraph. The two trends described by the author in the topic paragraph are explored in deeper detail throughout the essay. The language and style fit the writer's audience. The style is formal, but possesses a personalized voice.

Unity and Focus

The essay follows the course presented in the topic paragraph, reemphasizing major points such as the writer's reluctance to condemn all modern scholars. This emphasis is not straight repetition, but carries different viewpoints and evidence for the writer's argument. The digression on television in the second paragraph neatly rounds off the writer's overall concern for cultural consequences of historical literature's depreciation.

Development

The writer follows the suggestions of the writing assignment closely, structuring his essay around the reflections and discussions listed therein. Each paragraph bears an example to lend authority to the writer's argument.

The second paragraph uses the theory of television's vegetative influence. The third paragraph utilizes the evolutionary equality of history. The fourth paragraph evokes names that the reader can relate to in terms of comprehensive difficulty.

Organization

Many transitional conventions are utilized. "Once more . . ."; "Concerning the relative complexity . . ."; "Unfortunately . . ." The examples throughout the paragraphs have a pointed direction. The concluding paragraph completes the argument with a premonition of future calamity should its warning go unheeded.

Sentence Structure

The sentences are standardized and vary in form, although some passive constructions ("will be daunted," "the more probable it will become") might have been avoided. The repetition of "the more frequently" in the final paragraph is particularly effective and pointed.

Usage

Words are chosen to offer variety. "Past literature" is supplemented by "literary study of bygone days" and "the literature of former eras." Phrasing is consistent and standard, although the third sentence of the second paragraph ("The less society taxes . . . the less comprehensive") is slightly awkward, though the repetition does achieve some effect.

Mechanical Conventions

Spelling and punctuation are mostly standard throughout the essay. The sentences in the final paragraph might be divided and shortened, although this may diminish their effect.

WRITING SAMPLE WITH A SCORE OF 3
Modern Literature

It doesn't matter whether or not we read past literature. Past literature has been converted into what we now know as "modern literature". The elements of the past are therefore incorporated into the body of what we now have.

When we read a work of modern literature based upon the classics, such as Joyce's *Ulysses*, it doesn't matter whether or not we've read Homer's *Odyssey*. What matters is what Joyce made out of Homer's epic; not what Homer started out with.

When we see *West Side Story* in the movies, it doesn't matter whether or not we've read *Romeo and Juliet*: the end result is the same; therefore, we do not need to know the original source. I don't think it makes a difference whether or not we even recognize Tony and Maria as Romeo and Juliet. Tony and Maria are today's versions of Romeo and Juliet, and they match the culture that they are told in.

It has been said that all of the good plots have been used up by past ages, and that all we create now are variations of those plots. This statement is false. It is rather the case that these plots are universal variables that each age must interpret in its own unique way. I find it rather faseatious to study the interpretation of other cultures. We should be concerned only with our own.

Past literature is not necessary in a modern world that has reformed the mistakes of the past. Anything that hasn't carried over from the past is negligible: what was good for Shakespeare's audience may not be what we need. In conclusion, I would have to strongly conclude that the "trend of studying modern versus past literature" is commendable, and not contemptible.

FEATURES OF THE WRITING SAMPLE SCORING 3
Appropriateness

The main topic is not supplied directly within the work. Though the reader is aware of the conflict between modern and past literature, there is no sense of scholarly consensus as suggested by the writing assignment. The writer's somewhat informal style is unbalanced throughout the work by his uncertainty with his audience.

Unity and Focus

Though the writer knows the point he is trying to promote, his evidence is presented haphazardly and without a logical design. However, his rather abrupt conclusion is somewhat supported by his points.

Development

The essay does not follow a logical pattern; one premise does not meld fluidly into another. Though the premises loosely support the conclusion, they do not support each other.

Organization

Transitions are slight, if any. The repetition of "when we" opening two paragraphs is noticeable. Each point should have been further developed. The writer assumes his reader is quite familiar with *West Side Story* and its characters.

Sentence Structure

Most sentences follow standard sentence structure, although some are very irregular. The first sentence of paragraph three expresses two or three independent thoughts and should be separated accordingly. The final sentence of the fourth paragraph contains an unclear modifier: "own" should read either "own interpretation" or "own culture."

Usage

Most words are used in their proper context, and an attempt has been made to use some erudite words. "End result" is redundant; "end" should have been excluded. The declaration "this statement is false" in the fourth paragraph is not supported by logical evidence. In this case, the writer should have asserted that this was his own opinion. However, in other cases it is recommended that the writer be bold with assertions. A degree of proof is all that is required to make those assertions. "In conclusion" is redundant with "conclude" in the final sentence of the essay. Contractions such as "we've" and "don't" should be written out in their long forms.

Mechanical Conventions

Most words are spelled properly, although "faseatious" should be spelled "facetious." (The period in the second sentence of the first paragraph should lie within the quotation marks.) The comma after "commendable" in the final paragraph should be eliminated because it does not introduce a new clause.

WRITING SAMPLE WITH A SCORE OF 2 OR 1
Literature

Modern literature is no better than past literature, and vice-versa. It is interest that matters. If people aren't interested in the past, then so be it. A famous man once said "To each his own". I agree.

For example, you can see that books are getting easier and easier to understand. This is a good thing, because more knowledge may be comunicated this way. Comunication is what literature is all about: Some people comunicate with the past, and others with the present.

I communicate with the present. I'm not saying we all should. It's all up to your point of view. When a scholer chooses past over present, or vice-versa, that's his perogative. It doesn't make him better or worse than anybody else. We should all learn to accept each other's point of view.

When I read someone like Fitzgerald or Tolkien, I get a different feeling than Shakespeare. Shakespeare can inspire many people, but I just don't get that certain feeling from his plays. "The Hobbit," "The Great Gatsby," "Catcher in the Rye," and "Of Mice and Men." These are all great classics from this century. We should be proud of them. However, some people prefer "The Trojan War" and "Beowulf." Let them have it. Remember: 'To each his own.'

FEATURES OF THE WRITING SAMPLE SCORING 2 OR 1
Appropriateness

The writer misconstrues the topic and writes about the relative worth of modern and past literature. The topic does not call for a judgment of period literatures; it calls for a perspective on the way in which they are studied. Her personal style is too familiarized; it is unclear to whom the essay is addressed.

Unity and Focus

The writer seems to contradict her own points at times, favoring modern literature rather than treating the subject as objectively as he had proposed. It is clear that the writer's train of thought shifted during the essay. This was covered up by ending with the catch phrase, "to each his own."

Development

The writer attempts to angle her argument in different ways by presenting such concepts as "communication" and "point of view." However, her thought processes are abrupt and underdeveloped.

Organization

There is neither direction nor logical flow in the essay. One point follows the next without any transition or connection. All three persons are used to prove his argument: the writer resorts to "I," "you," and "a famous man." There is no clear overall thesis guiding the essay.

Sentence Structure

Some sentences follow standard formation. Sentence three of the final paragraph is a fragment. The sentences are short and choppy, as are the thoughts they convey. Too many sentences are merely brief remarks on the preceding statements (e.g., "I agree," "Let them have it," etc.). These are not appropriate because they do not evoke new thought. The reference to Shakespeare in the first sentence of the final paragraph implies more than the writer intended. It should read: "than when I read Shakespeare."

Usage

Many words are repeated without any attempt to supply synonyms (e.g., "communication," "past"). Colloquial expressions are widespread and should be avoided. The *Trojan War* is evidently an improper reference to Homer's *Iliad*.

Mechanical Conventions

There are many mechanical errors. Punctuation and spelling are inconsistent. "Comunication" and "comunicate" are spelled improperly in paragraph two, while "communicate" is spelled correctly in paragraph three. "Scholer" should be spelled "scholar." "Perogative" should be spelled "prerogative." In the fourth sentence of the first paragraph, the period should lie within the quotation marks, as it does in the final sentence of the essay. The book titles in sentences three and six of the final paragraph should be underlined and not quoted.

OSAT

**Oklahoma Subject Area Test
Elementary Education**

Subtest 1 Review

Chapter 7

Reading

Language is an intensely complex system that allows us to create and express meaning through socially shared conventions. What is amazing about language is that children generally master their native language within their first four years of life, well before they enter the elementary school, even though their teachers (family members) generally have no special training. Once children enter elementary school, their knowledge of language continues to grow and develop through opportunities to interact with teachers and other children, as they explore the language arts skill areas.

There are four cueing systems through which we organize language, making written language possible. The first cueing system is semantics, or the meaning system of language. Children, early on, are taught that the speech stream needs to convey meaning. Likewise, text needs to be meaningful. If some words in a passage are unknown, the child will know that some words make sense in the context of the passage and other words do not. The second cue is syntax, or the structural system of language. Again, if a child gets stuck while reading, some words are semantically appropriate but can be ruled out because of syntactic constraints. The third cue, according to this view, is phonological, or letter-sound, information. The phonological cue can confirm predictions that are made based on semantics and syntax. The fourth cueing system is the pragmatic system, or the social and cultural restraints placed on the use of language, along with differences in pronunciation.

The Reading Process

SUBAREA I—READING

Competency 0001

Understand the reading process.

The following topics are examples of content that may be covered under this competency.
- Understand reading as a process of constructing meaning through dynamic interaction among the reader, the text, and the context of the reading situation.
- Understand factors that affect reading (e.g., cultural, social, linguistic, developmental, environmental).
- Understand the oral language foundation of reading and the interrelatedness of reading, writing, listening, and speaking.

Literacy can be defined as a child's ability to read and write in order to function adequately in society. A child's literacy skills begin to develop in infancy and continue to expand throughout the school years. An infant's response to a parent's singing, a toddler's ability to choose a book and ask to have it read to her, and a preschooler's interest in attempting to write his name on a birthday card are all examples of literacy development. Research has shown that early, frequent exposure to printed words, both in the real world and through being read to on a regular basis, will likely enhance a child's literacy acquisition.

As the child enters school, formal reading instruction begins. How children should be taught to read is a subject that stirs up intense feeling. Basically, it boils down to a discussion about starting points, and how to proceed with instruction. The two approaches are the skills-based approach, and the meaning-based approach.

In 1967, Jeanne Chall, a Harvard professor, was investigating successful practices in early childhood reading instruction. She wrote a book called *Learning to Read: The Great Debate.* In the book, she stated that the programs that stressed systematic phonics instruction were better at getting young children, and especially poor young children, to read. This pronouncement sparked a great deal of conversation about how small children should be taught, what they should be taught, and where instruction should begin.

Phonological Skills

Competency 0002

Understand phonological skills and strategies related to reading.

The following topics are examples of content that may be covered under this competency.

- Understand how to foster students' phonemic awareness (i.e., ability to perceive and discriminate the sounds of the English language) through rhyming, blending, and segmenting sounds in words.
- Demonstrate knowledge of instruction in letter-sound correspondences and systematic, explicit phonics.
- Understand strategies to promote students' rapid, automatic decoding through the application of phonics skills.

Phonics is a method of teaching beginners to read and pronounce words by teaching them the phonetic value of letters, letter groups, and syllables. Because English has an alphabetical writing system, an understanding of the letter-sound relationship may prove helpful to the beginning reader. However, the suggestion of this view of initial reading instruction is that these relationships should be taught in isolation, in a highly sequenced manner, followed by reading words that represent the regularities of English in print. The children are asked to read decodable texts, by sounding out words. Typically, this approach uses reading programs that offer stories with controlled vocabulary made up of letter-sound relationships and words with which children are already familiar. Thus, children might be asked to read a passage such as, "The bug is in the pan. The bug ran and ran." Writing instruction follows in the same vein; children are asked to write decodable words, and fill in the blanks with decodable words in decodable sentences in workbooks, on the assumption that, once the children progress past this initial reading instruction timeframe, meaning will follow. This type of instruction was widely used in the late 1960s and 1970s. Today, it is still being promoted. The flaw in this kind of instruction is that many English words, including the highest frequency word of all, the, are not phonetically regular. Also, comprehension of text is limited, because there is not a great deal to comprehend if the text is, for example, "The bug is in the pan. The bug ran and ran." The assumption is that textual meaning will become apparent in time. Furthermore, it must be stressed that teaching phonics is not the same as teaching reading. Also, reading and spelling require much more than just phonics; spelling strategies and word-analysis skills are equally important. Nor does asking children to memorize phonics rules ensure application of those rules, and, even if it did, the word the child is attempting to decode is frequently an exception to the stated rule. Another point: teaching children how to use phonics is different from teaching them about phonics. In summary, the skills-based approach begins reading instruction with a study of single letters, letter sounds, blends and digraphs, blends and digraph sounds, and vowels and vowel sounds in isolation in a highly sequenced manner. The children read and write decodable words, with a great emphasis on reading each word accurately, as opposed to reading to comprehend the text as a whole.

The other side of the great reading debate is the meaning-based approach to reading. This approach grew out of the work of Dr. Kenneth Goodman, who was a leader in the development of the psycholinguistic perspective, which suggests that, to derive meaning from text, readers rely more on the structure and meaning of language than on the graphic information from text. He and other researchers demonstrated that literacy development parallels language development. One of Goodman's contributions to the field was a process called miscue analysis, which begins with a child reading a selection orally, and an examiner noting variations of the oral reading from the printed text. Each variation is called a miscue and is analyzed for type of variation. Previously, preservice teachers were urged to read and reread texts with young children until the child could read every word in the text perfectly. Goodman suggested, however, that only miscues that altered meaning needed to be corrected, while other, unimportant miscues could be ignored.

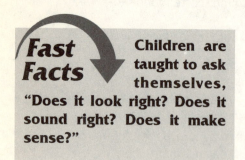

Fast Facts Children are taught to ask themselves, "Does it look right? Does it sound right? Does it make sense?"

Goodman also developed a reading model that became known as the whole-language approach. It stands in sharp contrast to the emphasis on phonics that is promoted in the skills-based approach to reading. The meaning-based approach to reading emphasizes comprehension and meaning in texts. Children focus on the wholeness of words, sentences, paragraphs, and entire books, seeking meaning through context. Whole-language advocates stress the importance of children's reading high-quality children's literature and extending the meaning of the literature through conversation, projects, and writing. Instead of fill-in-the-blank workbooks, children are encouraged to write journals, letters, and lists, and to participate in writing workshops. Word-recognition skills, including phonics, are taught in the context of reading and writing, and are taught as those things relate to the text in hand. Children are taught the four cueing systems, and are taught to ask themselves, "Does it look right? Does it sound right? Does it make sense?" The children are taught that the reason people read books is to make meaning. Thus, the focus of this approach is on both comprehension and making connections. Its flaw is that it makes heavy instructional demands on the teacher. With a skilled teacher, it's a joy to watch. Today, many classrooms are places where young children enjoy learning to read and write in a balanced reading instructional program. Research into best practice strongly suggests that the teaching of reading requires solid skill instruction, including several techniques for decoding unknown words, including, but not limited to, phonics instruction embedded in interesting and engaging reading and writing experiences with whole, authentic literature-based texts to facilitate the construction of meaning. In other words, this approach to instruction combines the best skill instruction and the whole-language approach to teach both skills and meaning and to meet the reading needs of individual children.

Vocabulary Skills

Competency 0003

Understand skills and strategies related to word identification and vocabulary development.

The following topics are examples of content that may be covered under this competency.
- Apply knowledge of word identification strategies (e.g., decoding, recognizing affixes, using context clues).
- Understand ways to help students master common irregular sight words.
- Understand strategies for increasing students' vocabulary knowledge and their ability to apply vocabulary knowledge in new contexts.

Vocabulary building is a skill that needs to be worked on daily in the classroom. One of the goals of this type of instruction is to assist children in becoming skillful in rapid word recognition.

Research suggests that fluent word identification needs to be present before a child can readily comprehend text. If a child needs to painstakingly analyze many of the words in a text, the memory and attention needed for comprehension are absorbed by word analysis, and the pleasure of a good story is lost.

Vocabulary building is a skill that needs to be addressed daily in the classroom. *Fast Facts*

Typically, children who are just beginning to read decode each word as they read it. Through repeated exposure to the same words, instant-recognition vocabulary grows. It is particularly important that developing readers learn to recognize those words that occur very frequently in print. A computer analysis of books in print revealed that 100 words make up approximately 50 percent of the words read. This percentage was for all books, not just children's literature. Although game-like activities and writing seem to have some impact on developing word recognition, the single best way to develop this necessary, effortless recognition is to encourage children to read, and to provide class time for reading text that is totally the child's choice. Reading and rereading rather easy text seems to be particularly effective.

In addition to working on placing some words into readily available memory, there is sound research suggesting that students can use context clues to help identify unknown words. This body of research further suggests that instruction can help improve students' use of such clues. Frequently, three kinds of context clues are discussed. First, semantic clues require a child to think about the meanings of words, and what is already known about the topic being read. For example, when reading a story about bats, good teachers help children to activate prior knowledge about bats, and to develop an expectation that the selection may contain words associated with bats, such as *swoop*, *wings*, *mammal*, and *nocturnal*. This discussion might help a child gain a sense of what might be reasonable in a sentence. The word order in a sentence might also provide clues. For example, in the sentence, "Bats can _____," the order of the words in the sentence indicates that the missing word must be a verb. Furthermore, the illustrations in the book can often help with the identification of a word. Still, context clues are often not specific enough to predict the exact word. However, when context clues are combined with other clues such as phonics and word-part clues, accurate word identification is usually possible.

Another strategy is to pay attention to letter groups, as there are many groups of letters that frequently occur within words. These clusters of letters can be specifically taught. Common prefixes, suffixes, and inflectional endings should be pointed out to students. Being able to rapidly and accurately associate sounds with a cluster of letters leads to more rapid, efficient word identification.

As young readers build an increasing store of words that they can recognize with little effort, they use the words they know to help them recognize words that are unfamiliar. For example, a child who has seen the word *bat* many times and who knows the sound associated with the consonant *r* will probably have little difficulty recognizing the word *rat*.

The best practice for helping students to gain skill in word-recognition is real reading and writing activities. As children read and reread texts of their own choice, they have many opportunities to successfully decode a word, and realize that each time the letter combination b-a-t is in the selection, it's read as *bat*. With each exposure to that word, the child reads the word more easily. A child who writes a sentence with that word as part of the sentence is developing a greater sensitivity to meaning or context clues. The child attempting to spell that word is reviewing and applying what he knows about letter–sound associations.

Reading Comprehension

Competency 0004

Understand skills and strategies involved in reading comprehension.

The following topics are examples of content that may be covered under this competency.
- Understand factors affecting reading comprehension (e.g., reading rate and fluency, prior knowledge, vocabulary knowledge).
- Demonstrate knowledge of literal, inferential, and evaluative comprehension skills.
- Identify strategies to facilitate comprehension before, during, and after reading (e.g., predicting, selfmonitoring, questioning, rereading).

Helping students read for understanding is the central goal of reading instruction. Comprehension is a complex process involving the text, the reader, the situation, and the purpose for reading. There are a number of factors that come into play as a child attempts to comprehend a passage. First, students cannot understand texts if they cannot read the words. Thus, a teacher who is interested in improving students' comprehension skills needs to teach them to decode well. In addition, children need time during the school day to read texts that are easy for them to read, and have to have time to discuss what has been read. Children need to read and reread easy texts often enough that decoding becomes rapid, easy, and accurate.

It has been noted frequently in the literature that children who comprehend well have bigger vocabularies than children who struggle with reading. In part, this is true because their knowledge of vocabulary develops through contact with new words as they read text that is rich in new words. However, it has also been suggested that simply teaching vocabulary in isolation does not automatically enhance comprehension.

Reading comprehension can be affected by prior knowledge, with many demonstrations that readers who possess rich prior knowledge about the topic of a reading often understand the reading better than classmates with less prior knowledge. Prior knowledge also affects interest. Generally, students like to read about somewhat familiar topics. This is an area in which the skill and interest of the teacher can play a significant role. An able teacher can make a previously unfamiliar topic seem familiar through pre-reading activities during which prior knowledge is activated, new prior knowledge is formed, and interest is stirred up. A good teacher will set a clear purpose for reading, and ask the students to gain an overview of the text before reading, make predictions about the upcoming text, and then read selectively based on their predictions. Best practice suggests that children should be encouraged to generate questions about ideas in text while reading. Successful teachers encourage children to construct mental images representing ideas in text, or to construct actual images from text that lends itself to such an activity. A successful teacher will help readers to process text containing new factual information through reading strategies, helping children to relate that new information to their prior knowledge. A potent mechanism for doing this is elaborative interrogation, wherein the teacher poses "why?" questions, encouraging children to question the author and check the answers through text verification. It is through conversation that children are able to compare their predictions and expectations about text content to what was read. It is through these conversations that children see the need to revise their prior knowledge when compelling new ideas that conflict with prior knowledge are encountered. As part of these ongoing conversations, teachers will become alert to students who are applying errant world knowledge as they read and will be able to encourage use of appropriate knowledge. These conversations lead children to figure out the meanings of unfamiliar vocabulary based on context clues, the opinions of others, and sometimes through the use of appropriate source materials such as glossaries, dictionaries, or an appropriate selection in another text. After reading activities, able teachers encourage children to revisit the text—to reread and make notes and paraphrase—to remember important points, interpret the text, evaluate its quality, and review important points. Children should also be encouraged to think about how ideas encountered in the text might be used in the future. As children gain competence, they enjoy showing what they know.

As a follow-up to the reading of a fictional selection, children should be encouraged to analyze the story using the story-grammar components of setting, characters, problems encountered by characters, attempts at solution to the problem, successful solution, and ending. It has been noted in the literature that even primary-level students, when asked to use comprehension strategies and monitoring, have benefited greatly from it.

As children's comprehension grows more sophisticated, they move from merely attempting to comprehend what is in the text to reading more critically. This means that they grow in understanding that any single text provides but one portrayal of the facts. With skillful instruction, children come to read not only what a text says; they also learn to attend to how that text portrays the subject matter. They recognize the various ways in which every text is the unique creation of a unique author, and they also learn to compare and contrast the treatment of the same subject matter in a number of texts. Teachers help students grow in comprehension through lessons. At first, teachers are happy if children are able to demonstrate their comprehension of what a text says by being able to engage in some after-reading activity that involves restating what was contained in the text in some authentic way. The next level is to have the children ponder what a text does: to describe an author's purpose, to recognize the elements of the text and how the text was assembled. Finally, some children can attain the skill set needed to successfully engage in text interpretation, to be able to detect and articulate tone and persuasive elements, to discuss point of view, and to recognize bias. Over time, and with good instruction, children learn to infer unstated meanings based on social conventions, shared knowledge, shared experience, or shared values. They make sense of text by recognizing implications and drawing conclusions, and they move past the point of believing the content of a selection simply because it was in print.

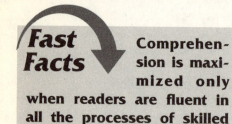

Fast Facts Comprehension is maximized only when readers are fluent in all the processes of skilled reading.

Another piece of the comprehension puzzle is that children need to be taught to monitor their own comprehension, and to decide when they need to exert more effort, or to apply a strategy to make sense of a text. The goal of comprehension instruction is for the children to reach a level at which the application of strategies becomes automatic.

In summary, comprehension is maximized only when readers are fluent in all the processes of skilled reading, from the decoding of words to the articulation and easy, appropriate application of the comprehension strategies used by good readers. Teachers need to teach predicting, questioning, seeking clarification, relating to background knowledge, constructing mental images, and summarizing. The teaching of comprehension strategies has to be conceived as a long-term developmental process, and the teaching of all reading strategies is more successful if they are taught and used by all of the teachers on a staff. In addition, teachers need to allow time for in-school reading, and recognize that good texts are comprehended on a deep level only through rereading and meaty discussions.

Study Skills and Strategies

Competency 0005

Understand reading instruction and study skills in the content areas.

The following topics are examples of content that may be covered under this competency.
- Apply knowledge of reading strategies to promote learning in the content areas (e.g., activating and developing prior knowledge).
- Understand strategies for reading for different purposes.
- Apply knowledge of study skills in the content areas (e.g., note-taking skills, interpretation of graphs, use of reference materials).

Students need to know how to study the information that has been presented to them in texts and other media. Graphic organizers help students to review such material, and help them see the relationships between one bit of information and another. A Venn diagram helps students see how things are alike and different. It can be used to help students see how a single topic is treated in two readings, or how two books, animals, or ecosystems are alike and different. The student labels the two overlapping circles, and lists items that are unique to each one in each respective circle. In the area in the center where there is an overlap, the student records the elements that the two items have in common.

A schematic table strips a story down to the bare bones, and helps students to see the story grammar at work:

Problem	
Who	
What	
Where	
When	
Why	
How	

↓

Attempted solution	result
Attempted solution	result

↓

End result	

Another skill students need to master is note taking. Unless you want to read passages copied directly out of an encyclopedia or other source material, take the time to actively teach note-taking techniques, and think up an authentic task that requires higher-level manipulation of the located information for the students to accomplish. First, help the children to formulate a researchable question. Next, have them highlight the words that might be used as keywords in searching for information. Then have them brainstorm in groups for other words to be used as keywords. Then ask then to list appropriate sources. Then, as they skim articles, they can fill in the chart with little chunks of information. For example:

Bats of North America						
Name	**Location**	**Biome**	**Endangered?**	**Diet**	**Roost**	**Fact**
California leaf-nosed bat	CA, AZ	desert	yes	insects	old mines, caves	
Gray bats	TN, KY, FL	forest	yes	insects	Caves near water	
Big brown bats	All states except Hawaii	varied	no	Beetles insects	Buildings, tunnels, caves, trees	Was seen flying in a snowstorm
Little brown bats	All 50 states	varied	no			Can eat 500 mosquitoes per hour

The next step here is to think up a task in which the student has to think about all the information and use it in some meaningful way.

Students also need to look closely at the structure of text in order to comprehend it. When starting a new unit of study, skillful teachers take the students on a picture, table, and graphic walk-through of the text that will be the object of study, asking questions and pointing out useful text features to the students. Most texts have titles, subtitles, headings, and key words. Where were these placed? What techniques were used to make them stand out? Figuring out the structure of a text helps readers to read more efficiently. Children can anticipate what information will be revealed in a selection when they understand textual structure. Understanding the pattern of the text helps students organize ideas. Authors have a fairly short list of organizational patterns to choose from. The following are the most common patterns:

- Chronological order—relates events in a temporal sequence from beginning to end

- Cause-and-effect relationships between described events, with the causal factors identified or implied

- Problem description, followed by solutions

- Comparisons and/or contrasts to describe ideas to readers

- Sequential materials, presented as a series of directions to be followed in a prescribed order

Genre

Competency 0006

Understand characteristic features of children's literature and strategies to promote students' literary response and analysis.

The following topics are examples of content that may be covered under this competency.
- Demonstrate knowledge of major works, authors, and genres of children's literature.
- Understand strategies to develop students' responses to literature (e.g., guided reading, reading logs, discussions about literature).
- Analyze the use of children's literature to promote respect for and appreciation of diversity.
- Understand elements of literary analysis and criticism (e.g., analyzing story elements, recognizing features of different genres, interpreting figurative language).

A genre is a particular type of literature. Classifications of genre are largely arbitrary—based on conventions that apply a basic category to an author's writing. They give the reader a general expectation of what sort of book is being picked up. Teachers today are expected to share a wide range of texts with children. Charlotte Huck, Susan Hepler, Janet Hickman, and Barbara Kiefer, in their book, *Children's Literature in the Elementary School*, define children's literature as "a book a child is reading." They go on to list picture books, traditional literature, modern fantasy, realistic fiction, historical fiction, nonfiction, biography, and poetry as genres of children's literature. Most genres can be subdivided into a variety of categories, and it is possible that genres could be mixed in a single title.

Picture books are books in which the illustrations and the text work together to communicate the story. There is a huge market for picture books, and they cover many topics. It is a very good idea to share picture books with children in a number of different formats.

Sometimes, able teachers simply read the book to the child without showing any of the pictures. The story is then discussed, and the children are asked if they would like the book to be reread, this time with the pictures being shared. Typically, this technique sparks a lively conversation about why the book with its illustrations is better than hearing the words alone.

Alternatively, teachers may take the children on a picture-walk through the book, allowing them to speculate about the story before reading it to them. Then, once the book is read, the speculations can be confirmed or reassessed.

Using picture books allows teachers to discuss the elements of higher-level comprehension without the burden of reading lengthy prose, for a picture book can be discussed with an eye on many different factors: design, color, space, media choice, cultural conventions, point of view, showing vs. telling, fairness, realism, or concerns. It is a way to raise issues in a classroom community, and it's a subtle way to affirm classroom members. Nearly any lesson worth teaching is better taught with a picture book in hand. Picture books can be very useful tools in a variety of ways: nearly any concept can be both deepened and expanded by reading the appropriate picture books.

Traditional literature comprises the stories that have their roots in the oral tradition of storytelling. This genre also includes the modern versions of these old stories. It is interesting to read and share multiple versions of old stories, and to compare and contrast each version. It is also interesting to read a number of folktales and keep track of the elements that these old stories have in common. It's also interesting to encourage children to notice where these old stories show up in their day-to-day lives. Children enjoy sharing what they notice. These old stories are woven into ads, comic books, jokes, and other selections.

Modern fantasy is a genre that presents make-believe stories that are the product of the author's imagination. The point of origin for all of these stories is the imagination of the author. Often, they are so beyond the realm of everyday life that they can't possibly be true. Extraordinary events take place within the covers of these books. Fantasy allows a child to move beyond the normal, ho-hum life in the classroom, and speculate about a life that never was, and may never be. But, maybe, just maybe, wouldn't it be grand if an owl were to swoop through an open window and drop a fat letter? What if you dumped some cereal into a bowl, and a lump dropped into the bowl with a thud, and it turned out to be a dragon's egg? What if you could step through a wardrobe and be someplace completely different? Fantasy is a genre that typically sparks rather intense discussions, and provides ample opportunities to illuminate the author's craft for the child.

Historical fiction is set in the past. This type of fiction allows children to live vicariously in times and places they do not normally experience any other way. This type of fiction often has real people and real events depicted, with fiction laced around them. Historical fiction informs the study of social studies. The textbook might say, "and then the tea was dumped in the harbor." *Johnny Tremain* vividly brings the event into focus. These books often bring the emotions of the situation into sharp relief. When reading *Pink and Say*, by Patricia Polacco, children are stunned when one of the boys is summarily hanged as he enters Andersonville. *Number the Stars*, by Lois Lowry, begins a conversation about what we would be willing to give up to save a friend.

Nonfiction books have the real world as their point of origin. These books help to expand the knowledge of children when they are studying a topic; however, these books need to be evaluated for accuracy, authenticity, and inclusion of the salient facts. It is a very good idea to include the children in this process, and, when an inaccuracy is detected, it's a good idea to encourage the child or children who spotted the flaw to write to the publisher and relate their findings. Typically, the publisher writes back, thus turning a published flaw into an authentic, empowering writing experience for a child. Again, these books can be the platform for teaching higher-level comprehension skills. Children and their teachers can discuss fact vs. theory. For example, the reintroduction of wolves into Yellowstone is a topic that exists in the real world, and reading materials on the subject are readily available. The *fact* is that wolves are carnivorous predators. The *theory* part of the investigation could be a discussion of the impact that reintroducing wolves into the Yellowstone ecosystem might have. This discussion will need to be supported with documentation. The materials read will need to be evaluated in terms of the intended audience, bias, inclusion of enough information, and text structure. These books can also be powerful in creating a community of learners, as they can be used as a means of gathering information about a topic that children are working on together as part of a cooperative learning group. Since nonfiction books are written at a variety of reading levels, all children can find a book to read, and since different titles have different information, the children end up swapping and talking about the books. It makes for some touching and powerful moments in a classroom.

Biography is a genre that deals with the lives of real people. Autobiography is a genre that deals with the life of the author. These books enliven the study of social studies because, through careful research, they often include information that transforms a name in a textbook into a person that one may like to get to know better. Did you know that George Washington had false teeth carved from the finest hippopotamus ivory? Did you know that Dolley Madison was stripping wallpaper—very expensive hand-painted silk wallpaper, no less—off the walls in the residence in the White House as British warships were moving up the Potomac River? Again, these books can provide a platform for dynamic lessons about higher-level comprehension skills, especially about bias. Consider the treatment of Helen Keller. Was any information included about how feisty and forward-thinking she was?

Poetry is a genre that is difficult to define for children, except as "not-prose." Poetry is the use of words to capture something: a sight, a feeling, or perhaps a sound. Poetry needs to be chosen carefully for a child, as poetry ought to elicit a response from the child—one that connects with the experience of the poem. All children need poetry in their lives. Poetry needs to be celebrated and enjoyed as part of the classroom experience, and a literacy-rich classroom will always include a collection of poetry to read, reread, savor, and enjoy. Some children enjoy the discipline of writing in a poetic format. Reggie Routman has published a series of slim books about teaching children to write poems on their own.

In summary, today there is an overwhelming variety of children's literature to choose from. When selecting books for use in a classroom, a teacher has a number of issues to consider. Is the book accurate? Aesthetically pleasing? Engaging? Bear in mind the idea that all children deserve to see positive images of children like themselves in the books they read, as illustrations can have a powerful influence on their perceptions of the world. Children also have a need to see positive images of children who are not like themselves, as who is or is not depicted in books can have a powerful influence on their perception of the world as well. Teachers ought to provide children with literature that depicts an affirming, multicultural view, and the selection of books available should show many different kinds of protagonists. Both boys and girls, for example, should be depicted as able.

Language Arts

The Writing Process

SUBAREA II—LANGUAGE ARTS

Competency 0007

Understand skills and strategies involved in writing for various purposes.

The following topics are examples of content that may be covered under this competency.

- Analyze factors a writer should consider when writing for a variety of audiences and purposes (e.g., expressive, informative, persuasive), including factors related to selection of topic and mode of written expression.
- Understand steps and procedures associated with given components of the writing process (e.g., prewriting, gathering and synthesizing information, writing a first draft, revising, proofreading).
- Understand developmental stages of a writer, including the use of pictures and developmental spelling.
- Compare characteristic features and requirements associated with written materials in various formats (e.g., letter, essay) and modes (e.g., narrative, descriptive, evaluative).

Since the early 1970s, Dr. Donald Graves, a professor of education at the University of New Hampshire, has been working in classrooms trying to understand why writing seems to be so difficult to master for so many children. Through conversation with many working teachers, children, their parents, university students, and working writers, and via many keen-eyed observations in classrooms, he developed an approach to writing instruction called *process writing*.

His notion was simple: let's teach children to write the way real writers write. What do writers do? Well, to begin with, they tend to write about what they want to write about. Then they may read about the subject, talk about the subject, take notes, or generally fool around with the topic before they compose. Then they may write a draft, knowing up-front that they are not done at this point. They may share the draft with others, and end up writing all over it. They may also go over every sentence, thinking about word choice, and looking for vague spots, or spots where the piece falls off the subject. They may revise the draft again, share it again, revise it again, and so on, until they are satisfied with the product. Then they publish it. Often, they receive feedback before and after the piece is published, which may lead to a new writing effort. Some writers save scraps of writing in a journal. They may save a turn of phrase, a comment overheard on a bus, a new word, good quotes, or an interesting topic.

Doesn't this sound like a process a child might find helpful? Today, it seems a bit obvious. In the 1970s, 1980s, and even into the 1990s it seemed revolutionary. However, it was well received because teachers were pleased with the way students benefited from this kind of instruction. At the same time, in many schools computers were becoming readily available to students, and many teachers were finding that writing instruction and computers were a very happy marriage. Also, there were several excellent books available about helping children to write well. Donald Graves wrote *Writing: Teachers and Children at Work* and *A Fresh Look at Writing*. Lucy Calkins wrote *The Art of Teaching Writing*, and Nancy Atwell contributed *In the Middle: Writing, Reading, and Learning with Adolescents*. All of these and others offered support for this new way to augment children's efforts toward learning to write.

Nancy Atwell was particularly skilled in describing how a literacy-rich environment ought to be established and fostered. Children need to be encouraged to read books for enjoyment, but to also look at the craft of the author. Children need to respond to reading in writing. A great deal of research supported the notion that reading informs the writing process, and that the act of writing informs the reading process.

Donald Graves advised children to think about events in their lives as a good starting point for discovering topics. He liked to talk about Patricia Polacco books. Almost all of her books are reports of real-life events, things that happened to her and her rotten red-haired brother. For example, *Meteor!* was the story of one summer's night when a meteor fell into the yard. It could be told like this: "It was hot. We were outside. A meteor fell, and almost hit us. It didn't." The difference between that account and the published story provides a starting point for a potentially rich discussion about the craft of the writer.

Lucy Calkins, in *The Art of Teaching Writing*, addresses the importance of expecting good writing from children, and then giving them ample time to write, and the needed instruction and encouragement to make it happen. She suggests that children keep a writing notebook where they can keep little scraps of writing that might find their way into a written piece some day. This suggestion also helps with classroom management during a writer's workshop. It gives children something to do instead of wandering around the room or announcing, "I'm done!" and ceasing to write.

Another part of the writing process is to share the writing with a classmate, and allow that peer to edit the piece. Able teachers provide guidance for this process, so that the students do not simply declare the work "good" or leave the classmate in tears because the draft is ruthlessly criticized. Neither end of the spectrum results in the growth of a student's writing ability.

Following an edit for content, the piece is edited for features such as punctuation, capitalization, and spelling. The use of computers has made the entire writing process much easier. Children learn to use a thesaurus, dictionary, and the functions of spelling and grammar. Revisions can be made more easily. One of the best results, however, is that the finished piece *looks* finished. Gone are the days when a child did his or her personal best, only to get the paper back with "messy" scrawled in red across it.

Another aspect of the process is celebration. Children are invited to share their work with the class. After a young author reads their piece, classmates ought to offer affirmations and suggestions. Able teachers ought to have children save each piece of paper generated in the writing process, and store them in a personal portfolio for review.

Analyzing and Revising Texts

Competency 0008

Analyze written work in relation to its stated purpose; evaluate areas in need of improvement; and revise written texts for style, clarity, and organization.

The following topics are examples of content that may be covered under this competency.
- Evaluate revision strategies for improving the effectiveness of written material in relation to a given purpose (e.g., expressive, informative, persuasive).
- Analyze given texts in terms of unity and organization, and make appropriate revisions (e.g., adding topic sentences, reordering sentences or paragraphs, using transitional words and phrases, deleting distracting details).
- Improve the clarity, precision, and effectiveness of given texts through changes in word choice.

Competency 0009

Apply knowledge of English grammar and mechanics in revising texts.

The following topics are examples of content that may be covered under this competency.
- Evaluate given texts in terms of sentence construction, and make appropriate revisions (e.g., revising run-on sentences, misplaced or dangling modifiers, lack of parallel structure).

- Revise texts for subject-verb agreement and pronoun-antecedent agreement.
- Use standard verb forms, pronouns, adverbs, adjectives, and plural and possessive forms of nouns in context.
- Make appropriate revisions involving punctuation and capitalization in a given text.

The test questions for this subarea of the OSAT are very much like the Communications Skills questions on the OGET. To prepare for these questions on the OSAT, you should look at and thoroughly review Chapter 2, pages 33–78, and Chapter 6, pages 125–136, and you should study the information below concerning expository and persuasive essays.

The Expository Essay

An expository essay can encompass a variety of subjects. It may tell how to make or do something, or it may explore an idea. Expository writing conveys information to the reader in such a way as to bring about understanding; its subject may be a process or procedure, or perhaps the writer's ideas about a concept. Here are some samples of topics that you may be asked to write about in an expository essay:

- The ideal vacation

- The qualities of a good friend

- How to plan a lesson or create a syllabus (*Note*: Expository essays could be about "how to" do just about anything, but on the OSAT, you will not be asked how to do something unless you could reasonably be expected to know how to do it—for example, you would not be asked how to bake a cake.)

- Similarities and differences between the younger generation and your own (essays like this are called "comparison-and-contrast essays")

- Characteristics of types of people you have met in school (essays like this are called "classifying essays")

- The reasons that you have decided to become a teacher (essays like this are called "cause-and-effect essays")

The structure of your expository essay will depend somewhat on the topic you are given, but the usual five-paragraph structure is a good starting point.

- Your first paragraph should begin with an attention grabber. For example, the essay about the ideal vacation might start with a sentence or two about something wonderful (or terrible) that you have done on a previous vacation, and the essay about the good friend could start with a very short anecdote about something a friend has done for you. The how-to-plan-a-lesson essay could begin with a humorous story of an unplanned lesson.

- Your first paragraph should end with a thesis statement. Creativity will be rewarded in the opening of the essay, and possibly in the conclusion, but in the thesis statement on a standardized-test essay, it is best to state your thesis as clearly as you can. Because you will be using the five-paragraph structure, try to make your thesis include three major points (for your three body paragraphs). For example, the essay on an ideal friend could include a paragraph on three different friends you've had and the traits of each, or it could focus on three different traits.

  - *This essay will discuss openness and honesty as I have experienced them in my friendships with Amanda, Tom, and Bill.*

  - *The crucial traits of an ideal friend are openness, honesty, and wit, and I shall discuss their value as I have experienced them—or their lack—in my real friendships.*

- Note, from the examples just given, that your thesis will determine the structure of your three body paragraphs. In an expository essay, your body paragraphs are not necessarily carrying an argument, as they are in a persuasive essay. You may arrange the paragraphs in any way that is convenient; just make sure that you include logical transitions between and within the paragraphs. For example, the second thesis statement above would be in an essay that had a paragraph each about openness, honesty, and wit, but you could skip back and forth between friendships in order to illustrate each of the qualities.

- The first part of the conclusion (fifth paragraph) should briefly recap the thesis and body paragraphs. The second part should include a statement that reinforces your position in a meaningful and memorable way. Creativity here will earn you some credit in the grading, but this is probably the least important part of the essay. If you can't think of something clever, don't waste much time trying to do so; the extra time is better spent revising your first four paragraphs.

The Persuasive Essay

The persuasive essay is meant to move its reader to take an action or to form or change an opinion. There are three main reasons it is included on the OSAT:

- It requires thinking skills such as analysis, synthesis, and evaluation.

- It requires writers to take a stand from among two or more alternatives.

- Persuasive writing is a skill that you will have to both teach and use in your professional life.

Because all the persuasive prompts you will receive on a test (and most persuasive writing situations you will encounter in life) ask you to choose a stand from two or more reasonable alternatives, you will have to demonstrate that you understand why the other alternatives are reasonable. More important, though, you will have to make clear that you believe your stand on the issue is better, and you need to present your supporting evidence in such a way that it might convince a reasonable person who believed an alternative stand was preferable.

Persuasive prompts on the OSAT will likely ask you to write for a general audience of educated adults, but it might also ask you to write to an audience of parents or to your principal or school board. Here are some samples of topics that you may be asked to write about in a persuasive essay:

- The effects of television on students' grades—good, bad, negligible?

- Is affirmative action appropriate in hiring and promoting teachers?

- Should national elections take place on a weekend day rather than a Tuesday?

- Should states require students to pass standardized tests in order to begin high school?

- Should high-school athletes be subjected to involuntary drug testing?

- Should students and teachers (i.e., not janitors) be responsible for keeping their school clean?

Note that you may not have a particular opinion about some of these matters. Indeed, you may not know much about the topic; the prompt will, however, typically give you enough information to help you write a good five-paragraph essay.

The structure of your persuasive essay will depend somewhat on the topic you are given, but the usual five-paragraph structure is a good starting point.

- Your first paragraph should begin with an attention grabber. One good strategy is to imagine a world in which the point of view you are against has prevailed. For example, if you take a position for affirmative action in hiring and promoting teachers, you might ask your reader to imagine a school system in which many students would go through high school without ever seeing a principal who looks like them. If you take the other side, you might ask the reader to compare two school systems, one of which had teachers who had scored an average of 20 points higher on their certification tests.

- Your first paragraph should end with a thesis statement. Creativity will be rewarded in the opening of the essay, and possibly in the conclusion, but in the thesis statement on a standardized-test essay, it is best to state your thesis as clearly as you can, especially in the persuasive essay. Because you will be using the five-paragraph structure, try to make your thesis include three major points (for your three body paragraphs). In addition, you want your thesis to state your position very clearly. If you include your summary of the other side's arguments in your thesis statement, you should always do so in a subordinate clause. For example, the thesis of the essay on involuntary drug testing might look like this:

  - *Although involuntary drug testing would be a violation of civil rights if participation in athletics were involuntary, such testing would restore integrity to athletic contests, increase student attendance, and help to protect athletes' health.*

  - *Even though participation in athletics is "voluntary," students should not be given an either-or choice between nonparticipation on the one hand and the loss of privacy and the restriction of their civil rights on the other.*

- Note, from the examples just given, that your thesis will determine the structure of your three body paragraphs. In a persuasive essay, your body paragraphs will carry your argument; you will succeed not on the basis of your eloquence in the introductory and concluding paragraphs, but on how well you organize and state facts that support your argument. It is often best to use your most convincing reason in the final body paragraph. For example, the first thesis statement above would introduce an essay that had a paragraph about doubt that currently exists about whether high-school athletes' skill is based on ability or drugs. The next paragraph would be about the good things that would happen if that doubt were resolved. The final paragraph would then switch to your most important point: that performance-enhancing drugs are bad for athletes' health. As an exercise, can you think of a structure for the three body paragraphs of the essay with the second example above as a thesis statement?

- The first part of the conclusion (fifth paragraph) should briefly recap the thesis and body paragraphs (i.e., your argument). The second part should include a statement that reinforces your position in a meaningful and memorable way. Creativity here will earn you some credit in the grading, but this is probably the least important part of the essay. If you can't think of something clever, don't waste much time trying to do so; the extra time is better spent revising your first four paragraphs.

The Listening Process

Competency 0010

Understand skills and strategies involved in listening for various purposes.

The following topics are examples of content that may be covered under this competency.

- Compare listening strategies in terms of their appropriateness for given contexts and purposes (e.g., acquiring information, appreciating literature read aloud, interpreting and evaluating information).
- Analyze barriers to effective listening and strategies for active listening.
- Apply knowledge of factors affecting the ability to listen effectively and construct meaning from oral messages in various listening situations (e.g., ability to recognize nonverbal cues, to use prior knowledge, to distinguish fact from opinion, to recognize transitions, to identify faulty reasoning).

Language is an intensely complex system for creating meaning through socially shared conventions. Very young children begin to learn language by listening and responding to the people in their lives. This early listening provides a foundation for acquisition of language. Babies are active listeners. Long before they can respond in speech per se, they encourage the person talking to them to continue by waving their arms, smiling, or wriggling, for example. On the other hand, they are also capable of clear communication when they have had enough by dropping eye contact or turning away, among other examples of body language.

Although listening is used extensively in communication, it does not receive much attention at school. Studies suggest that teachers assume that listening develops naturally. One study from 1986 suggests that teachers are not apt to get much training on teaching listening; the survey of 15 textbooks used in teacher education programs revealed that out of a total of 3,704 pages of text, only 82 pages mentioned listening.

While there is no well-defined model of listening to guide instruction, there are some suggestions. Some theorists link listening skills to reading skills. They feel that reading and listening make use of similar language comprehension processes. Listening and reading both require the use of skills in phonology, syntax, semantics, and knowledge of text structure, and seem to be controlled by the same set of cognitive processes.

However, there is an additional factor in play in listening: the recipient of the oral message can elect to listen passively, or listen actively, with active listening being the desired goal. A number of studies suggest that the teaching of listening can be efficiently taught by engaging in the kinds of activities that have been successful in developing reading, writing, and speaking proficiencies and skills such as setting a purpose for listening, giving directions, asking questions about the selection heard, and encouraging children to forge links between the new information that was just heard and the knowledge already in place. In addition, children need to be coached in the use of appropriate volume and speed when they speak, and in learning how to participate in discussions and follow the rules of polite conversation, such as staying on a topic and taking turns.

The Speaking Process

Competency 0011

Understand skills and strategies involved in speaking for various purposes.

The following topics are examples of content that may be covered under this competency.
- Analyze ways in which features of oral language (e.g., choice of language, rate, pitch, tone, volume) and nonverbal cues (e.g., body language, visual aids) affect communication in given situations.
- Evaluate various methods of organizing and presenting thoughts, feelings, ideas, and information for different audiences and purposes (e.g., giving instructions, participating in group discussions, persuading an audience, entertaining).
- Recognize factors affecting oral communication and nonverbal cues in different situations. Apply knowledge of language conventions appropriate to a variety of social situations (e.g., informal conversations, job interviews).

When preparing a speech, children should know the same thing that teachers know about their audience: it is better to have an audience that is actively listening than one that is listening passively. Children should be coached to do the following in order to make them more effective public speakers:

- Speak in a loud voice, but do not shout.

- Speak slowly and pronounce words clearly.

- Pay attention to time—and know your audience's attention span.

- Maintain good eye contact with your audience.

- Use gestures to engage your audience.

- Do not read your speech directly off note cards.

- If you use note cards, keep them down, away from your face.

- Decide which points should be emphasized by changing the tone of your voice (called *intonation*).

- Be prepared to answer any questions that your audience might have.

The use of visual aids is also important. Most schools now have PowerPoint or similar programs for their students to use, and students should probably be giving at least one such presentation a year beginning in the fourth or fifth grade. There is still a place for hand-made visual aids in school, however—certainly for younger children and even for older ones, who should have to manufacture two or three a year (perhaps in groups) so that they do not limit their ingenuity to the prepackaged visuals of a computer program.

In addition, students should learn that the preparation of a speech is very much like writing, with its prewriting, writing, and revising stages preceding the presentation. (The prewriting stage includes audience analysis, which is perhaps even more important in speaking than in writing.) It is a good idea to assess each of these stages through conferences, especially for children who are giving their first speech or are especially nervous about public speaking.

Social Studies

The Social Studies section of the OSAT Subtest 1 includes six test objectives. These objectives represent a broad range of integrated social sciences concepts from the content areas of history, geography, political science, and economics. Embedded within each broad objective are a number of essential social sciences concepts. A thorough understanding of each objective requires deep knowledge of the embedded concepts coupled with the ability to analyze and apply those concepts in a comparative analysis of Oklahoma, U.S., and world contemporary and historic society. For each objective an explanation of the embedded concepts is provided.

When preparing for the social studies portion of the elementary test, you should review the embedded concepts enumerated within each objective. Once you think you have a thorough understanding of each concept you should determine whether or not you can apply your understanding within the context of Oklahoma, U.S., and world contemporary and historic contexts.

SUBAREA III—SOCIAL STUDIES

Competency 0012

Understand major ideas, eras, themes, developments, and turning points in the history of Oklahoma, the United States, and the world; and analyze their significance from multiple perspectives.

The following topics are examples of content that may be covered under this competency.

- Analyze the societal effects of major developments in world history (e.g., the agricultural revolution, the scientific revolution, the industrial revolution, the information revolution).
- Understand the principal political, social, economic, and geographic characteristics of ancient civilizations and the connections and interactions among these civilizations.
- Understand the history of interactions among American Indian peoples and European Americans in Oklahoma and the western United States.
- Analyze the roles and contributions of individuals and groups to U.S. social, political, economic, cultural, and religious life, including historically underrepresented groups.

Competency 0013

Understand geographic concepts and phenomena, and analyze the interrelationships of geography, society, and culture in the development of Oklahoma, the United States, and the world.

The following topics are examples of content that may be covered under this competency.

- Demonstrate an understanding of how the five themes of geography—location, place, relationships within places, movement, and regions—can be used to analyze geographic phenomena and human cultures.
- Recognize the physical characteristics of the earth's surface, and analyze the continual reshaping of the surface by physical processes.
- Analyze the development and interaction of social, political, cultural, and religious systems in different regions of Oklahoma, the United States, and the world.
- Analyze the impact of human activity on the physical environment (e.g., industrial development, population growth, deforestation).

Competency 0014

Understand concepts and phenomena related to human development and interactions (including anthropological, psychological, and sociological concepts).

The following topics are examples of content that may be covered under this competency.

- Evaluate factors that contribute to the development of personal identity (e.g., family, group affiliations, socialization processes).
- Analyze the roles and functions of social groups and institutions in the United States (e.g., ethnic groups, schools, religions) and their influence on individual and group interactions.

- Analyze why individuals and groups hold different or competing points of view on issues, events, and historical developments.
- Understand the processes of social and cultural change.

Competency 0015

Understand economic and political principles, concepts, and systems; and relate this knowledge to historical and contemporary developments in Oklahoma, the United States, and the world.

The following topics are examples of content that may be covered under this competency.

- Analyze the basic structure, fundamental ideas, accomplishments, and problems of the U.S. economic system.
- Analyze values, principles, concepts, and key features of American constitutional democracy (e.g., individual freedom, separation of powers, due process).
- Compare different perspectives regarding economic and political issues and policies in Oklahoma and the United States (e.g., in relation to taxing and spending decisions).
- Analyze relationships between the United States and other nations (e.g., in the development of democratic principles and human rights).

Competency 0016

Understand the roles, rights, and responsibilities of citizenship in the United States and the skills, knowledge, and attitudes necessary for successful participation in civic life.

The following topics are examples of content that may be covered under this competency.

- Analyze the personal and political rights guaranteed in the Declaration of Independence, the U.S. Constitution, the constitution of the state of Oklahoma, and major civil rights legislation.
- Demonstrate an understanding of the U.S. election process and the roles of political parties, pressure groups, and special interests in the U.S. political system.
- Analyze the ways in which citizens participate in and influence the political process in the United States (e.g., the role of public opinion and citizen action in shaping public policy).
- Analyze the factors that affect attitudes toward civic life and that have expanded or limited the role of the individual in U.S. political life during the twentieth century (e.g., female suffrage, discriminatory laws, the growth of presidential primaries, the role of the media in political elections).

Competency 0017

> **Understand and apply skills related to social studies, including gathering, organizing, mapping, evaluating, interpreting, and displaying information.**
>
> The following topics are examples of content that may be covered under this competency.
> - Evaluate the appropriateness of various resources for meeting specified information needs (e.g., atlas, database, surveys, polls, the Internet).
> - Interpret information presented in one or more graphic representations (e.g., graph, table, map), and translate written or graphic information from one form to the other.
> - Summarize the purpose or point of view of a historical text.

History

Developing historical perspective includes knowledge of events, ideas, and people from the past. That knowledge encompasses an understanding of the diversity of race, ethnicity, social and economic status, gender, region, politics, and religion within history. Historic understanding includes the use of historical reasoning, resulting in a thorough exploration of cause-effect relationships to reach defensible historical interpretations through inquiry.

Significant knowledge of events, ideas, and people from the past results from careful analysis of cause and effect relationships in the following chronological eras: beginnings of civilization to 1620; colonization and settlement (1585–1763); revolution and the new nation (1754–1815); expansion and reform (1801–1861); Civil War and Reconstruction (1850–1877); the development of the industrial United States (1870–1900); the emergence of modern America (1890–1930); the Great Depression and World War II (1929–1945); postwar United States (1945–1970); and contemporary United States (1968–present).

Significant knowledge of historical events, ideas, and people from Oklahoma's past would result from careful analysis of cause and effect relationships in the chronological eras listed above for the United States. Included in this knowledge is an understanding of the evolution of political ideas, institutions, and practices in Oklahoma and the influence of technology, agriculture, urbanization, industry, and labor on the development of the Oklahoma economy. For example, pressure brought by European-American settlers on eastern land held by Native nations led to their forced migration to what is now Oklahoma, the most notable example being the Trail of Tears of 1838–1839. It is also necessary to understand the importance of family and local history.

This objective also involves the ability to analyze and interpret the past. Analysis and interpretation result from an understanding that history is logically constructed based upon conclusions resulting from careful analysis of documents, eyewitness accounts, letters, diaries, artifacts, photos, historical sites, and other primary and secondary sources.

Geography

Understanding major geographic concepts involves comprehending both physical features of geography and the cultural aspects of geography. This would include knowledge of the five fundamental themes of geography, comprehension of the relationships within and between places, understanding interdependence within the local, natural, and global communities, and familiarity with global issues and events.

The five themes of geography are: place; human-environmental interaction; location; movement and connections; and regions, patterns, and processes. An understanding of these themes would include the ability to use them to analyze regions within Oklahoma, the United States, and the world to gain a perspective about interrelationships among those regions. The use of the five themes should also result in the ability to compare regions.

An understanding of the theme of location requires knowledge of both absolute and relative location. Absolute location is determined by longitude and latitude. Relative location deals with the interactions that occur between and among places. Relative location involves the interconnectedness among people because of land, water, and technology. For example, knowledge of the history of Oklahoma City includes an understanding of how its location near several important oil fields has contributed to its economic development and vitality.

An understanding of the theme of human-environmental interaction involves consideration of how people rely on the environment, how we alter it, and how the environment may limit what people are able to do. For example, knowledge of how the Oklahoma Territory came to be settled by European-Americans in 1889 includes an understanding of the role of cattle ranching in Oklahoma's history.

An understanding of the theme of location, movement, and connections involves identifying how people are connected through different forms of transportation and communication networks and how those networks have changed over time. This would include identifying channels of the movement of people, goods, and information. For example, the Chisholm Trail used in the Texas cattle drives led to the development of railway and road transportation routes.

An understanding of the theme of regions, patterns, and processes includes identifying climatic, economic, political, and cultural patterns within regions. Understanding why these patterns were created includes understanding how climatic systems, communication networks, international trade, political systems, and population changes contributed to a region's development. An understanding of regions enables a social scientist to study their uniqueness and relationship to other regions.

Understanding global issues and events includes comprehending the interconnectedness of peoples throughout the world. For example, knowledge of the relationship between world oil consumption and oil production would result in an understanding of the impact that increased demand for oil in China would have on the price of a barrel of oil, which in turn could affect the decisions of consumers of new vehicles in the United States.

Economic and Political Principles

An understanding of economics involves exploring the implications of scarcity (the concept that wants are unlimited while resources are limited). Exploration of scarcity involves an understanding of economic principles spanning from personal finance to international trade. Economic understanding is rooted in exploring principles of choice, opportunity costs, incentives, trade, and economic systems. (For a definition of each of the economic principles see the Handy Dandy Guide [HDG] developed by the National Council on Economic Education in 1989. For brief definitions based upon this guide see the Web site *http://ecedweb.unomaha.edu/lessons/handydandy.htm*). This exploration includes analysis of how those principles operate within the economic choices of individuals, households, businesses, and governments.

In addition, economic understanding includes knowledge of the role that price, competition, profit, inflation, economic institutions, money, and interest rates play within a market system. A complete understanding of markets includes knowledge of the role of government within an economic system, including how monetary and fiscal policy impacts the market. (These economic concepts are based upon the *National Content Standards in Economics* published by the National Council on Economic Education. A brief overview and complete list of standards can be found at *http://ncee.net/ea/standards/*).

An understanding of various political systems involves the ability to compare different political systems, their ideologies, structures, institutions, processes, and political cultures. This requires knowledge of alternative ways of organizing constitutional governments from systems of shared power to parliamentarian systems. Systems of shared power include federal systems, where sovereign states delegate powers to a central government; a federal system, where a national government shares power with state and local governments; and Unitarian systems where all power is concentrated in a centralized government.

Understanding local and state governments results from knowledge of the role of federal and state constitutions in defining the power and scope of state and local government. That knowledge should include comprehension of reserved and concurrent powers. Furthermore, an understanding of state and local government results from knowledge of the organization and responsibilities of such governments.

Understanding of the role of law in a democratic society results from a knowledge of the nature of civil, criminal, and constitutional law and how the organization of the judicial system serves to interpret and apply such laws. Essential judicial principles to know include comprehension of rights, such as the right of due process, the right to a fair and speedy trial, and the right to a hearing before a jury of one's peers. Additional judicial principles include an understanding of the protections granted in the Constitution, which include protection from self-incrimination and unlawful searches and seizures.

Understanding global interdependence begins with recognition that world regions include economic, political, historical, ecological, linguistic, and cultural regions. This understanding should include knowledge of military and economic alliances such as NATO, the G8 members, or cartels such as OPEC, and how their existence affects political and economic policies within regions. Knowledge of world regions and alliances leads to identification of issues that affect people in these areas. Common issues that affect people around the world include food production, human rights, resource use, prejudice, poverty, and trade.

Fast Facts

An understanding of economics involves exploring the implications of scarcity.

A true sense of global interdependence results from an understanding of the relationship between local decisions and global issues. For example, how do individual or community actions regarding waste disposal or recycling affect worldwide resource availability? Or how do fuel emissions standards affect air pollution or how fuel standards affect oil supply and gas prices?

Government and the Responsibilities of Citizens

The social sciences portion of the Elementary Education test requires comprehension of the ideals of American democracy, including a core set of values expressed in America's essential founding documents, the Declaration of Independence, the Articles of Confederation, the U.S Constitution, and the Bill of Rights. Those values include life, liberty, pursuit of happiness, common good, justice, equality, truth, diversity, popular sovereignty, and patriotism.

Furthermore, the ideals of American democracy include the following essential Constitutional principles: the rule of law, separation of powers, representative government, checks and balances, individual rights, freedom of religion, federalism, limited government, and civilian control of the military. Essential democratic principles include those principles fundamental to the American judicial system: the right to due process of law, the right to a fair and speedy trial, protection from unlawful search and seizure, and the right to decline to self-incriminate.

Fast Facts → **It is essential for citizens to be active in order to maintain a democratic society.**

Comprehension of the rights and responsibilities of citizens of the United States involves understanding that it is essential for citizens to be active in order to maintain a democratic society. This activity includes participation in voting, providing service to communities, and regulating oneself in accordance with the law.

Diversity

Understanding the role of cultural diversity in shaping Oklahoma, the United States, and the world begins with knowledge of the commonalities and differences among such groups as African-Americans, Asian-Americans, Hispanic-Americans, and Native Americans. Commonalities and differences can be found when analyzing the role of language, education, religion, culture, and struggles for equality within and among groups. Understanding the role of cultural diversity in shaping Oklahoma, the United States, and the world should include an understanding of the struggles various groups undertake to gain equality and recognition within society.

A historical perspective of the role of cultural diversity in shaping the development of Oklahoma and the United States begins by gaining a sense of the types of people who came to Colonial America and their reasons for coming. This understanding can help one gain an appreciation for the diverse peoples that eventually won their independence from Great Britain. Following those people from the east during the various migrations westward can explain how various groups of people settled what today is the American West. Studies of Old Immigration (1830–1850) and New Immigration (1900–1920) further complete the picture of the settling of America that encouraged diverse peoples to come here. Within this historical understanding one should be able to identify examples of how immigrants sought to assimilate themselves into American culture, contributions of immigrant groups to American culture, and ways that immigrants have been exploited.

Diverse cultural groups have shaped world history. Diversity has both positive and negative results—from contributing to disputes over territories, creating alliances that eventually lead to world and regional conflicts, outsourcing of jobs, and relocation of companies from the United States to foreign countries, to more positive examples such as the economic specialization that enhances choice and the modern globalization that results in economic interdependence. The impact of cultural diversity on world history can be explored by careful analysis of the following events, among others: the origin and spread of Christianity and Islam; colonialism and exploration; the beginning of World War I; and contemporary conflict in the Middle East.

Locating, Organizing, and Interpreting Social Sciences Information

The ability to understand and apply skills and procedures related to the study of social sciences involves knowledge of the use of systematic inquiry. Inquiry is essential for use in examining single social sciences topics or integrated social sciences. Being able to engage in inquiry involves the ability to acquire information from a variety of resources, and organize that information, which leads to the interpretation of that information. Inquiry involves the ability to design and conduct investigations, which in turn leads to the identification and analysis of social sciences issues.

In addition, this understanding includes knowledge about and the use of the various resources used in systematic social science inquiry. Those resources include primary and secondary sources, encyclopedias, almanacs, atlases, government documents, artifacts, and oral histories.

Constructed Response

In the final part of OSAT Subtest 1 you will be asked to write a constructed response. Unlike the constructed response in the OGET, knowledge of standard English is *not* a critical part of your score. Instead, the constructed-response item is written to assess your understanding in Subarea I, Reading, which consists of the following competencies:

- Understand the reading process.

- Understand phonological skills and strategies related to reading.

- Understand skills and strategies related to word identification and vocabulary development.

- Understand skills and strategies involved in reading comprehension.

- Understand reading instruction and study skills in the content areas.

- Understand characteristic features of children's literature and strategies to promote students' literary response and analysis.

The Assignment

You will typically be given a problem situation from an educational setting and asked what you would do to solve the problem. The four criteria by which you will be graded are

- Purpose—the extent to which your response fulfills the purpose of the assignment

- Subject matter knowledge—the accuracy and appropriateness with which you apply your knowledge of the subject

- Support—the quality and relevance of your supporting details

- Rationale—the soundness of your arguments and the degree of understanding you demonstrate

Of these four criteria, the most important is "support": you cannot get high scores in either "subject matter knowledge" or "rationale" unless you use the information you are given to marshal examples that will support whatever your argument is.

Here is a sample assignment. Read it through carefully.

Hiru is a fifth grader. His teacher has analyzed his performance on a fifth-grade-level passage that he has read aloud to her. She did this by keeping a running record of his miscues while reading. His accuracy rate was 88%, which is usually considered to be just below a student's instructional level (90%). He read the passage with expression (usually correctly inflected) and enthusiasm. Hiru was able to talk about the passage, but not always accurately, and he was able to make some simple predictions about what might happen next.

He did not self-correct on any of the words he misread. Here is a list of the words he substituted for:

Text	Student
shall	will
tired	tie-red
lie	lay
scratch	scrap
stretched	streaked
radiator	radio
returned	retired

In addition, the teacher had to tell him the word "admonition," and he omitted a "now" and an "and."

Using your knowledge of how to teach word identification and fluency, write a response in which you

- Analyze Hiru's pattern(s) of miscues and his overall reading fluency

- Cite specific examples to back up your analysis

- Describe at least two different types of activities that might improve Hiru's reading fluency

- Explain why these types of activities might work

Preparing to Write

Writing Process for the Constructed Response
• Prewriting
o Jot notes, make diagrams
o Outline
o Reread questions
o Adjust outline to questions if necessary
• Writing
• Revising
o Did you answer the questions?
o Do you have support for all the assertions you make?
o Is your writing clear?
o Is your writing free of grammatical/spelling mistakes?

For this constructed response, it is not necessary to frame your answer with a strong, creative opening and closing; the best strategy here is simply to begin your **prewriting** stage by jotting down notes.

Because the questions in this type of constructed response will typically be rather specific, you should begin by writing down anything that will help you answer each question—in order, if possible. For instance, the first thing you will want to do with this assignment is to organize the facts you need in order to *analyze* the pattern of misreadings. You can use the table that is already provided for you; you might add columns that are headed by "Similar Meaning," "Graphophonically Similar," and "Syntactically Acceptable" and put checkmarks in the table cells that apply. You would have checkmarks under Similar Meaning for the first and third words, and checkmarks under Graphophonically Similar for all but the first word. You would also have checkmarks under Syntactically Acceptable for four of the seven words. (That is, the substitution is the same part of speech as the actual word in the text.) At this point, you're well on the way to answering the first two questions.

Now you want to turn your prewriting attention to what types of activities will help this fifth grader improve his reading and why. His problem seems to be word recognition rather than syntactic comprehension. In addition, he seems to have mastered phonics, at least at the beginnings of words. Thus, he could be given lessons or mini-lessons, either by the teacher or by a peer, on basic word-identification strategies: phonic analysis (beyond the initial sounds), analogies (i.e., making associations with known words), syllabic analysis, and morphemic analysis (i.e., study of roots). Hiru needs to learn to recognize words that an average fifth grader knows so that he can read at grade level or above, so you should choose two strategies/activities that you are most familiar with in order to do that.

Now you are ready to outline. Outlining should not take much time, because the assignment makes a rough outline for you. You do have some choices, though, for example, you could combine the first two questions so that you can present one element of your analysis, along with your reasoning, followed by another element and your reasoning, and so on, rather than simply making an analysis and then going back to your reasons. With this assignment, it is probably better to present your reasons along with each analytic statement. You could use the same kind of organization with questions three and four: for instance, a paragraph on teaching syllabic analysis and a paragraph on giving Hiru extra morphemic analysis work. Thus, your outline might look something like this:

I. Analysis and reasoning

    A. Good overall comprehension—answers questions and reads with enthusiasm, and most errors are nevertheless syntactically correct

    B. Will be at frustration level with fifth-grade texts—too many words he doesn't know

    C. Needs to improve word recognition—although he has a rough understanding of phonics, his ability to recognize words is below grade level

II. Strategies

    A. Lessons on syllabic analysis—miscues show Hiru needs to look beyond initial sounds

    B. Lessons on morphemic analysis—returned–retired pair and scratch–scrap pair have different roots

Conclusion: Hiru needs to learn to recognize words that an average fifth grader knows in order to make use of his ability at comprehension so that he can read at grade level or above, so you should choose two strategies/activities that you are most familiar with in order to do that.

This outline will give you a good start. Now is the time for **writing**: get the ideas down as clearly and as coherently as you can. In your **revising** stage, you should look at what you've written, making sure that you have indeed answered the questions clearly, that you have good examples for everything you wrote, and (even though standard English is not one of the grading criteria), your writing is free of spelling and grammatical errors.

Scoring the Constructed Response

All responses to OSAT constructed-response assignments are scored using scales that describe varying levels of performance. These scales were approved by committees of Oklahoma educators.

Each response is scored by multiple scorers according to standardized procedures during scoring sessions held immediately after each administration of the test. Scorers with relevant professional backgrounds are oriented to these procedures before the scoring session and are carefully monitored during the scoring sessions.

A constructed-response assignment response is designated unscorable if it is blank, not on the assigned topic, illegible or unintelligible, not in the appropriate language, or of insufficient length to score. *If you do not provide a scorable response for each constructed-response assignment on your test, you cannot pass the test regardless of your scores on the other sections of the test.*

Sample Performance Characteristics for Constructed-Response Assignments	
PURPOSE	The extent to which the response achieves the purpose of the assignment
SUBJECT MATTER KNOWLEDGE	Accuracy and appropriateness in the application of subject matter knowledge
SUPPORT	Quality and relevance of supporting details
RATIONALE	Soundness of argument and degree of understanding of the subject matter

Scoring Scale for Constructed-Response Assignments

"4"—The response reflects a thorough knowledge and understanding of the subject matter.

- The purpose of the assignment is fully achieved.
- There is a substantial, accurate, and appropriate application of subject matter knowledge.
- The supporting evidence is sound; there are high-quality, relevant examples.
- The response reflects an ably reasoned, comprehensive understanding of the topic.

"3"—The response reflects a general knowledge and understanding of the subject matter.

- The purpose of the assignment is largely achieved.
- There is a generally accurate and appropriate application of subject matter knowledge.
- The supporting evidence generally supports the discussion; there are some relevant examples.
- The response reflects a general understanding of the topic.

"2"—The response reflects a partial knowledge and understanding of the subject matter.

- The purpose of the assignment is partially achieved.
- There is a limited, possibly inaccurate or inappropriate application of subject matter knowledge.
- The supporting evidence is limited; there are few relevant examples.
- The response reflects a limited, poorly reasoned understanding of the topic.

"1"—The response reflects little or no knowledge and understanding of the subject matter.

- The purpose of the assignment is not achieved.
- There is little or no appropriate or accurate application of subject matter knowledge.
- The supporting evidence, if present, is weak; there are few or no relevant examples.
- The response reflects little or no reasoning about or understanding of the topic.

"U"—The response is unscorable because it is illegible, not written to the assigned topic, written in a language other than English, or of insufficient length to score.

"B"—There is no response to the assignment.

OSAT

Oklahoma Subject Area Test
Elementary Education

Practice Subtest 1

This test for the OSAT is also on CD-ROM in our special interactive OGET/OSAT TEST*ware*®. It is highly recommended that you first take this exam on computer. You will then have the additional study features and benefits of enforced timed conditions and instant, accurate scoring. See page xii for guidance on how to get the most out of our OGET/OSAT book and software.

SUBTEST DIRECTIONS

A sample of the general directions for the OSAT is shown in the box below. You may want to familiarize yourself with the directions, as similar versions will be used for the actual examination.

You should have in front of you:

(1)   a test booklet for the test for which you registered (check the field name on the front cover);

(2)   an answer document (be sure you have signed your answer document and filled in the required information on pages 1 and 3); and

(3)   a No. 2 lead pencil.

IF YOU DO NOT HAVE ALL OF THESE MATERIALS, PLEASE INFORM THE TEST ADMINISTRATOR. REMOVE ALL OTHER MATERIALS FROM YOUR DESK.

GENERAL DIRECTIONS

This test booklet contains two sections: a selected-response section and a writing assignment. You may complete the sections in the order you choose, but it is suggested that you complete the selected-response section of the test first. The directions for each section appear immediately before that section.

Each selected-response question in this booklet has four answer choices. Read each question carefully and choose the ONE best answer. Record your answer on the answer sheet in the space that corresponds to the question number. Completely fill in the space having the same letter as the answer you have chosen. *Use only a No. 2 lead pencil.*

Sample Question:

1.   Which of these cities is farthest north?

    A.   Oklahoma City

    B.   Muskogee

    C.   Tulsa

    D.   Lawton

The correct answer to this question is C. You would indicate that on the answer sheet as follows:

1.   Ⓐ Ⓑ ● Ⓓ

For the writing assignment, you will be asked to prepare a written response to a writing assignment. Record your written response on pages 3 to 6 of the answer document. You may use **ONLY** one answer document. You may either print or write, as long as your handwriting is legible. You must use a pencil. Make sure that you have time to plan, write, review, and revise what you have written.

You should answer all questions. Even if you are unsure of an answer, it is better to guess than not to answer a question at all. You may use the margins of the test booklet for scratch paper, but all of your answers, including your response to the writing assignment, must be recorded in your answer document. Answers that are written in the test booklet will **NOT** be scored.

The words "End of Section" indicate you have completed a section. After you have completed one section, you may go on to the other section. You may go back and review your answers and your written response to the writing assignment, but be sure you have answered all selected-response questions, completed the writing assignment, and rechecked all the information in your answer document, particularly your identification information on pages 1 and 3, before you raise your hand for dismissal. Your test materials must be returned to a test administrator when you finish the test.

FOR TEST SECURITY REASONS, YOU MAY NOT TAKE NOTES OR REMOVE ANY OF THE TEST MATERIALS FROM THE ROOM.

This session will last four hours. You may work at your own pace on the different sections of the test. If you have any questions, please ask them now before you begin the test.

STOP
DO NOT GO ON UNTIL YOU ARE TOLD TO DO SO.

Answer Sheet

1. Ⓐ Ⓑ Ⓒ Ⓓ	11. Ⓐ Ⓑ Ⓒ Ⓓ	21. Ⓐ Ⓑ Ⓒ Ⓓ	31. Ⓐ Ⓑ Ⓒ Ⓓ
2. Ⓐ Ⓑ Ⓒ Ⓓ	12. Ⓐ Ⓑ Ⓒ Ⓓ	22. Ⓐ Ⓑ Ⓒ Ⓓ	32. Ⓐ Ⓑ Ⓒ Ⓓ
3. Ⓐ Ⓑ Ⓒ Ⓓ	13. Ⓐ Ⓑ Ⓒ Ⓓ	23. Ⓐ Ⓑ Ⓒ Ⓓ	33. Ⓐ Ⓑ Ⓒ Ⓓ
4. Ⓐ Ⓑ Ⓒ Ⓓ	14. Ⓐ Ⓑ Ⓒ Ⓓ	24. Ⓐ Ⓑ Ⓒ Ⓓ	34. Ⓐ Ⓑ Ⓒ Ⓓ
5. Ⓐ Ⓑ Ⓒ Ⓓ	15. Ⓐ Ⓑ Ⓒ Ⓓ	25. Ⓐ Ⓑ Ⓒ Ⓓ	35. Ⓐ Ⓑ Ⓒ Ⓓ
6. Ⓐ Ⓑ Ⓒ Ⓓ	16. Ⓐ Ⓑ Ⓒ Ⓓ	26. Ⓐ Ⓑ Ⓒ Ⓓ	36. Ⓐ Ⓑ Ⓒ Ⓓ
7. Ⓐ Ⓑ Ⓒ Ⓓ	17. Ⓐ Ⓑ Ⓒ Ⓓ	27. Ⓐ Ⓑ Ⓒ Ⓓ	37. Ⓐ Ⓑ Ⓒ Ⓓ
8. Ⓐ Ⓑ Ⓒ Ⓓ	18. Ⓐ Ⓑ Ⓒ Ⓓ	28. Ⓐ Ⓑ Ⓒ Ⓓ	38. Ⓐ Ⓑ Ⓒ Ⓓ
9. Ⓐ Ⓑ Ⓒ Ⓓ	19. Ⓐ Ⓑ Ⓒ Ⓓ	29. Ⓐ Ⓑ Ⓒ Ⓓ	39. Ⓐ Ⓑ Ⓒ Ⓓ
10. Ⓐ Ⓑ Ⓒ Ⓓ	20. Ⓐ Ⓑ Ⓒ Ⓓ	30. Ⓐ Ⓑ Ⓒ Ⓓ	40. Ⓐ Ⓑ Ⓒ Ⓓ

Practice Subtest 1

1. When reading, the semantic cueing system refers to _____.

   A. the meaning system of language

   B. the structural system of language

   C. the letter-sound relationships in written language

   D. the social and cultural aspects of language

2. When reading, the syntactical cueing system refers to _____.

   A. the meaning system of language

   B. the structural system of language

   C. the letter-sound relationships in written language

   D. the social and cultural aspects of language

3. When reading, the phonological cueing system refers to_____.

   A. the meaning system of language

   B. the structural system of language

   C. the letter-sound relationships in written language

   D. the social and cultural aspects of language

4. When reading, the pragmatic cueing system refers to _____.

   A. the meaning system of language

   B. the structural system of language

   C. the letter-sound relationships in written language

   D. the social and cultural aspects of language

5. Listening is a process students use to extract meaning out of oral speech. Activities teachers can engage in to assist students in becoming more effective listeners include:

    I. clearly setting a purpose for listening.
    II. allowing children to relax by chewing gum during listening.
    III. asking questions about the selection.
    IV. encouraging students to forge links between the new information and knowledge already in place.

    A. I and II

    B. II, III, and IV

    C. I, III, and IV

    D. All of the above

6. Which of the following describes best practice in writing instruction?

    A. Instruct students in writing, and give them time to write.

    B. Have students complete worksheets about writing.

    C. Have students copy famous speeches.

    D. Have the children create a mural of a story so far, and label all of the characters.

7. Which of the following descriptions best describes the western, Pacific region of Canada comprising British Columbia and the Yukon?

    A. The area contains many uninhabitable areas, including a mix of arid desert-like terrain and rugged mountain ranges that hinder rail and car transportation, resulting in minimal population settlement.

    B. The area contains arid deserts and vast grasslands that are ideal for cattle farming and oil production.

    C. The area contains the vast majority of Canada's natural resources and the majority of Canada's population.

    D. The area contains fifty percent of Canada's population, resulting in seventy percent of Canada's manufacturing.

DIRECTIONS: Read the following passage and answer the question that follows.

The Police believed that Dollree Mapp was hiding a person suspected in a crime. The police went to her home in Cleveland, Ohio, knocked, and requested entry. Mapp refused. After more officers arrived on the scene, police forced their way into Mapp's house. During the police search of the house they found pornographic books, pictures, and photographs. They arrested Mapp and charged her with violating an Ohio law against possession of pornographic materials. Mapp and her attorney appealed the case to the Supreme Court of Ohio. The Ohio Supreme Court ruled in favor of the police. Mapp's case was then appealed to the Supreme Court of the United States. Mapp and her attorney asked the Supreme Court to determine whether or not evidence obtained through a search that violated the Fourth Amendment was admissible in state courts. The U.S. Supreme Court, in the case *Mapp v. Ohio*, ruled that evidence obtained in a search that violates the Fourth Amendment is not admissible. The majority opinion states, "Our decision, founded on reason and truth, gives to the individual no more than that which the Constitution guarantees him, to the police officer no less than that to which honest law enforcement is entitled, and, to the courts, that judicial integrity so necessary in the true administration of justice."

8. The excerpt above best illustrates which of the following features of judicial proceedings in the United States?

    A. due process of law

    B. a fair and speedy trial

    C. judicial review

    D. the exclusionary rule

DIRECTIONS: Read the story, and then respond to the five questions that follow.

BESSIE

I began my days as a cow. Well, a calf, to be more precise. I was born to the world a soft tawny color, with liquid brown eyes and soft, floppy ears that begged to be touched. My days were simple. I spent all my time in the company of other bovine females, most especially my mother. She was a prized breeder, my mother; as a result it was my misfortune to be weaned earlier than most other calves.

Only hours after my weaning, a miraculous event changed the course of my life. Princess Georgette happened to be riding by on her shaggy little pony, alongside her nanny, when she heard my lows of despair and turned.

"Whatever could be making that pitiful noise?" she asked aloud.

One of the farmers called out to her, "'Tis only a wee calf, Highness. She'll not be at it long, I assure you."

"I shall see the creature at once," she ordered, pulling her pony up against the rail and dismounting.

At this point, I had moved hopefully toward the commotion, and, as I inched my tender nose out of the barn to investigate, I came face-to-face with the oddest-looking creature I had seen so far in my somewhat short existence. She had outrageous red curls rioting all over her head, and tumbling down over her shoulders. The thing I noticed most, though, was her hopelessly freckled nose, which, at that moment, was uncomfortably close to my own. So close, in fact, that I decided to remedy my discomfort, and did so by lowing rather loudly in her petulant little face. To my astonishment, she giggled with delight at my rudeness, and reached out to stroke my furry forehead. I found myself nuzzling up to her small chest. "Oh Nan, I must have it. Such a funny furry thing must be kept in my garden where I might entertain myself endlessly with it."

So that is how I became a member of the royal household.

My days fell into an odd sort of routine. I spent my mornings cropping on the lawns and shrubs until Georgette would appear, luring me into the hedge ways with a handful of cresses nipped from the kitchen. As soon as I got close enough and started to nibble, she would shriek, and startle me into a canter, at which she would chase me into the hedges until I was so thoroughly lost, I would have to low helplessly until Georgette found me.

Tragically, calves do not stay calves forever. As the seasons passed, her interest in our games began to wane. The gardeners had, at this time, gotten very tired of working around me as I lumbered through the hedges. They communicated up through the chain of command, straight to the king himself, their wish to be rid of me. He dismissed the problem with an order to have me put down.

Georgette pouted at this and stamped her foot, but her father would not budge an inch. "Now, don't get missish with me, Georgette. I've given the order, and I'll see it done as I've dictated whether you like it or not."

Georgette, during this speech, had become thoughtful. After a long pause, she proposed: "Well, if I must see my Bessie put down as you've said, mightn't I get a handbag and boots out of her at least?"

"Very well," sighed her father.

For my part, it was a stroke of luck that this conversation had taken place just on the other side of the hedge where I had been, only moments before, contently munching on the last bit of clover to be found this season. Naturally, I took exception to being discussed in such a candid manner. In fact, I could not believe my furry, floppy ears. I felt myself slipping into a sort of self-pity, and walked away. When I passed the westernmost gate, it occurred to me that I might not have to face my doom. This door, that was normally latched and guarded, stood open. I was out that gate and on the lane nearby in an instant.

I wandered aimlessly for hours, when I abruptly came upon a little clearing. A stream ran through it, past the coziest of tiny cottages. I trotted straight over to the stream and began drinking in long draughts. After several moments of such behavior, I became aware of another presence nearby. It was a small, old man, leaning toward me in a strange sort of furry robe, and balancing himself on the most incredibly gnarled staff, and holding a silver bucket that steamed and hissed, yet smelled overwhelmingly delicious.

"Hello," he said in a pleasant tone. "I'm happy you have finally arrived. I read it in *The Book*. Would you care to drink from my bucket?" he asked. . . .

9.   This is the beginning of a story. To what genre does it belong?

    A.   poetry

    B.   historical fiction

    C.   nonfiction

    D.   fantasy

10. What is likely to happen next?

    A. Bessie will go to a barn.

    B. Bessie will catch frogs.

    C. Bessie will run away.

    D. Bessie will drink the potion and turn into a brown-eyed girl.

11. How did you know what might happen next?

    A. The nanny never wanted the princess to have a pet cow.

    B. Magical things often happen in stories that begin with a princess.

    C. I read about dysfunctional families often.

    D. The princess will have a new handbag and boots.

12. How should this sort of story be introduced to children?

    A. Complete a K-W-L to activate prior knowledge about fairy tales.

    B. Ask the children to look up vocabulary words in a dictionary.

    C. Read the children a nonfiction book about dairy farming.

    D. Show a video about talking to strangers.

13. If you were going to ask the children to finish this story as a writing activity, what would you do next?

    A. Have them complete a worksheet about the vocabulary words.

    B. Ask them to diagram the first sentence.

    C. Ask them to form small groups, and talk about what might happen next.

    D. Have them complete a Venn diagram about Bessie and a real cow.

> **Read the passage below, written in the style of a newspaper editorial;
> then answer the four questions that follow.**

[1]The zoning regulations of Westown have long been a thorn in the side of local real estate developers. [2]The authors of those regulations apparently believed that their regulations would be appropriate in perpetuity, because they _____ to amend. [3]The result is a growing area of blight bounded on the north by Bradley Avenue and on the east by Randolph Street.

[4]This coming Wednesday the Westown's city council has a chance to bring its zoning practices into the twenty-first century. [5]The decisive votes will come from Council members Putman, Beckett, and Reis. [6]The votes of Putman and Beckett in particular will be of interest to their constituents, because the residents of their wards would stand to gain a great deal from rezoning. [7]The proposed changes would bring the Fourth Ward some much-needed commerce in the currently run-down Randolph-MacKenzie area and would help _____ the Fifth Ward's steady population loss. [8]Although each of these self-styled "progressives" have displayed reluctance to vote for anything that would spur development in the recent past, both have strong opposition in the upcoming election and would do well to consider how their votes on this issue will impact the results of that election.

14. Which of the following changes is needed in the passage above?

    A. Sentence 1: Change "have" to "has"

    B. Sentence 4: Change "Westown's" to "Westown"

    C. Sentence 8: Change the comma after "past" to a semicolon

    D. Sentence 8: Change "how" to "that"

15. Which of the following words would be the best to insert into the blank in sentence 7?

    A. alleviate

    B. accelerate

    C. excoriate

    D. exonerate

16. Which of the numbered sentences should be revised to correct an error in verb form?

    A. sentence 3

    B. sentence 5

    C. sentence 6

    D. sentence 8

17. Which of the following phrases, inserted into the blank in sentence 2, would make sense and would be free of errors?

    A   made the regulations very easy

    B.   ensured that the provisions would be difficult

    C.   made them almost impossible

    D.   said the zoning ordinances will be hard

18. Which of the following statements are true about economic activity in Oklahoma?

    I.   State government, the military, and the manufacturing industry are among Oklahoma's major employers.
    II.   Oklahoma's livestock industry is less profitable than its cotton and wheat crops.
    III.   The petroleum, natural gas, and livestock industries in Oklahoma have contributed directly to the state's manufacturing industry.
    IV.   Tulsa and Oklahoma City are minor regional players in the natural gas and petroleum industry.

    A.   I and II only

    B.   I and III only

    C.   II and III only

    D.   II and IV only

19. Which of the following statements best defines the role of the World Trade Organization (WTO)?

    A.   It resolves trade disputes and attempts to formulate policy to open world markets to free trade through monetary policy and regulation of corruption.

    B.   It is an advocate for human rights and democracy by regulating child labor and providing economic aid to poor countries.

    C.   It establishes alliances to regulate disputes and polices ethnic intimidation.

    D.   It regulates trade within the United States in order to eliminate monopolistic trade practices.

20. The drought of the 1930s that spanned from Texas to North Dakota was caused by

    I.   overgrazing and overuse of farmland.
    II.   natural phenomena, such as below-average rainfall and wind erosion.
    III.   environmental factors, such as changes in the jet stream.
    IV.   the lack of government subsidies for new irrigation technology.

    A.   I and II only

    B.   II and III only

    C.   I and III only

    D.   II and IV only

Read the passage below; then answer the two questions that follow.

[1]Actually, the term "Native American" is incorrect. [2]Indians migrated to this continent from other areas, just earlier than Europeans did. [3]The ancestors of the Anasazi—Indians of the four-state area of Colorado, New Mexico, Utah, and Arizona—probably crossed from Asia into Alaska. [4]About 25,000 years ago, while the continental land bridge still existed. [5]This land bridge arched across the Bering Strait in the last Ice Age. [6]About 500 CE the ancestors of the Anasazi moved onto the Mesa Verde, a high plateau in the desert country of Colorado. [7]The Wetherills, five brothers who ranched in the area, are generally given credit for the first exploration of the ruins in the 1870s and 1880s. [8]There were some 50,000 Anasazi thriving in the four-corners area by the 1200s CE. [9]At their zenith, 700 to 1300 CE, the Anasazi had established widespread communities and built thousands of sophisticated structures—cliff dwellings, pueblos, and kivas. [10]They even engaged in trade with Indians in surrounding regions by exporting pottery and other goods.

21. Which of the following is a nonstandard sentence?

    A.   sentence 1

    B.   sentence 2

    C.   sentence 4

    D.   sentence 5

22. Which of the following draws attention away from the main idea of the paragraph?

    A.   sentence 3

    B.   sentence 4

    C.   sentence 7

    D.   sentence 8

23. Which line on the chart best matches the resources with the historical question that is being asked?

Line	Historical Research Question	Source of Information
1	How many people were living in Boston, MA, during the time of the American Revolution?	Historical atlas
2	What role did Fort Mackinac fulfill during the American Revolution?	Encyclopedia article
3	How did the average temperatures and snowfall during the winter of 1775–1776 compare with previous winters?	Historical almanac
4	When was the first U.S. treaty signed and what were the terms of the treaty?	Diary of a participant

A. line 1

B. line 2

C. line 3

D. line 4

DIRECTIONS: Use the passages below, adapted from Herodotus's *Histories*, to answer the two questions that follow.

Passage A: I think, too, that those Egyptians who dwell below the lake of Moiris and especially in that region which is called the Delta, if that land continues to grow in height according to this proportion and to increase similarly in extent, will suffer for all remaining time, from the Nile not overflowing their land, that same thing which they themselves said that the Hellenes would at some time suffer: for hearing that the whole land of the Hellenes has rain and is not watered by rivers as theirs is, they said that the Hellenes would at some time be disappointed of a great hope and would suffer the ills of famine. This saying means that if the god shall not send them rain, but shall allow drought to prevail for a long time, the Hellenes will be destroyed by hunger; for they have in fact no other supply of water to save them except from Zeus alone. This has been rightly said by the Egyptians with reference to the Hellenes: but now let me tell how matters are with the Egyptians themselves in their turn.

Passage B: If, in accordance with what I before said, their land below Memphis (for this is that which is increasing) shall continue to increase in height according to the same proportion as in the past time, assuredly those Egyptians who dwell here will suffer famine, if their land shall not have rain nor the river be able to go over their fields. It is certain however that now they gather in fruit from the earth with less labour than any other men and also with less than the other Egyptians; for they have no labour in breaking up furrows with a plough nor in hoeing nor in any other of those labours which other men have about a crop; but when the river has come up of itself and watered their fields and after watering has left them again, then each man sows his own field and turns into it swine, and when he has trodden the seed into the ground by means of the swine, after that he waits for the harvest, and when he has threshed the corn by means of the swine, then he gathers it in.

24. Which of the following best states the main issues being discussed in the above passages?

   A. Ancient Egyptians were so dependent upon the Nile River that one's location determined one's prosperity.

   B. The Nile River was so important to the prosperity of ancient Egyptians that it determined where many Egyptians settled.

   C. Egyptians who depend upon the Nile River for irrigation will not suffer from famine as those who depend upon rain.

   D. Egyptians settling in the Delta were dependent upon religion because irrigation from rain was more unpredictable than the Nile.

25. Herodotus, in passage A, could best support assertions made in the passage by presenting which of the following types of evidence?

   A. Data showing the productivity of Egyptian farmers in both the Delta and Memphis regions.

   B. Data showing the average rainfall in the Delta as compared to average rainfall in Memphis.

   C. Data showing the cycle of flooding along the Nile as compared to the cycles of rainfall in the Delta.

   D. Data showing the wealth of Egyptians in the Delta as compared to the wealth of Egyptians in Memphis.

26. Which of the following would be considered a primary source in researching the factors that influenced U.S. involvement in the Korean War?

   I. The personal correspondence of a military man stationed with the 5th Regimental Combat Team (RCT) in Korea.
   II. A biography of Harry S. Truman by David McCullough, published in 1993.
   III. A journal article about the beginning of the Korean War by a noted scholar.
   IV. An interview with Secretary of Defense George Marshall.

   A. I and II only

   B. II and IV only

   C. II and III only

   D. I and IV only

27. Which of the following was *not* a major Native American tribe that resided in Oklahoma before the 1800s?

    A. the Chickasaw

    B. the Osage

    C. the Quapay

    D. the Mound Builders

Read the passage below; then answer the three questions that follow.

[1]We've grown accustomed to seeing this working woman hanging from the subway strap during commuting hours. [2]We may refer disparagingly to her tailored suit and little tie, but we no longer visualize her in a house dress with her hair uncombed. [3]The woman who leaves her children to go to work in the morning is no longer a pariah in her community or her family. [4]Her paycheck is more than pin money; it buys essential family staples and often supports the entire family. [5]But she is not the only beneficiary of the increasing presence of women in the workplace.

[6]The situation for men has also changed as a result of women's massive entry into the work force for the better. [7]Men who would once have felt unrelenting pressure to remain with one firm and climb the career ladder are often freed up by a second income to change careers in midlife. [8]They enjoy greatest intimacy and involvement with their children.

[9]The benefits for business are also readily apparent. [10]No senior manager in the country would deny that the huge generation of women who entered management seven or eight years ago has functioned superbly, often outperforming men.

[11]Yet the prevailing message from the media on the subject of women and business is one filled with pessimism. [12]We hear about women leaving their employers in the lurch when they go on maternity leave. [13]Or we hear the flip side, that women are overly committed to their careers and neglectful of their families. [14]And in fact, it is true that problems arising from women's new work force role do exist, side by side with the benefits.

[15]The problems hurt business as well as individuals and their families, affordable quality childcare, for one example, is still a distant dream. [16]Some women are distracted at work, and men who would have felt secure about their children when their wives were home are also anxious and distracted. [17]Distraction also impedes the productivity of some high-achieving women with the birth of their first child and causes some to depart with the birth of their second.

28. Which of the following sentences displays a nonstandard placement of a modifying phrase?

    A. sentence 1

    B. sentence 3

    C. sentence 6

    D. sentence 7

29. Which of the following sentences displays a nonstandard use of a comparative form?

    A.   sentence 4

    B.   sentence 8

    C.   sentence 10

    D.   sentence 13

30. Which of the following sentences is a nonstandard sentence?

    A.   sentence 14

    B.   sentence 15

    C.   sentence 16

    D.   sentence 17

31. Which of the following best describes a major difference between a state government and the federal government?

    A.   State governments have more responsibility for public education than the federal government.

    B.   State governments are more dependent upon the personal income tax for revenue than the federal government.

    C.   State governments are more dependent upon the system of checks and balances than the federal government.

    D.   State governments are subject to term limits, where as federal government representatives serve unlimited terms.

32. Which of the following were major causes of the Great Depression?
    I.   Hoarding money greatly reduced the money supply, resulting in higher prices on consumer goods.
    II. The gold standard limited the amount of money in supply, reducing money circulation, and causing a drop in prices and wages.
    III. Smoot-Hawley Tariff increased tariffs, which resulted in increased prices for consumer goods.
    IV. The stock market crash reduced the value of companies, causing them to raise prices of consumer goods.

    A.   I and II only

    B.   II and III only

    C.   III and IV only

    D.   I, II, and III

33. Before reading a story about a veterinary hospital to his first-grade class, Mr. Drake constructs a semantic map of related words and terms using the students' input. What is his main intention for doing this?

    A. To demonstrate a meaningful relationship between the concepts of the story and the prior knowledge of the students

    B. To serve as a visual means of learning

    C. To determine the level of understanding the students will have at the conclusion of the topic being covered

    D. To model proper writing using whole words

34. If a teacher is interested in improving the comprehension skills of students, that teacher should
    I. teach students to decode well.
    II. allow time during the day to read and reread selections.
    III. discuss the selections after reading to clarify meaning and make connections.
    IV. tell jokes.

    A. I and II only

    B. I, II, and IV

    C. I, II, and III

    D. All of the above

Read the passage below; then answer the three questions that follow.

---

[1]In the past 30 years, television has become a very popular pastime for almost everyone. [2]From the time the mother places the baby in her jumpseat in front of the television until the time the senior citizen in the retirement home watched Vanna White turn the letters on "Wheel of Fortune," Americans spend endless hours in front of the "boob tube." [3]How did we get to be this way?

[4]When my mother was a little girl, what did children do to entertain themselves? [5]They played. [6]Their games usually involved social interaction with other children as well as imaginatively creating entertainment for themselves. [7]They also developed hobbies like woodworking and sewing. [8]Today, few children really know how to play with each other or entertain themselves. [9]Instead, they sit in front of the television, glued to cartoons that are senseless and often violent. [10]Even if they watch educational programs like "Sesame Street," they don't really have to do anything but watch and listen to what the answer to the question is.

[11]Teenagers, also, use television as a way of avoiding doing things that will be helping them mature. [12]How many kids does much homework anymore? [13]Why not? [14]Because they work part-time jobs and come home from work tired and relax in front of the television.

35. Which of the following sentences uses a nonstandard verb form?

    A. sentence 4

    B. sentence 7

    C. sentence 8

    D. sentence 12

36. Which of the following sentences in the passage is nonstandard?

    A. sentence 2

    B. sentence 7

    C. sentence 10

    D. sentence 14

37. Which of the following changes is needed in the first two paragraphs?

    A. Sentence 1: Change "has become" to "is."

    B. Sentence 2: Change "watched" to "watches."

    C. Sentence 4: Change "When" to "Being that."

    D. Sentence 9: Change "sit" to "sat."

38. The Silk Road did not connect to which of the following countries?

    A. China

    B. Greece

    C. Iran

    D. India

39. When a member of the House of Representatives helps a citizen from his or her district receive federal aid to which that citizen is entitled, the representative's action is referred to as

    A. casework.

    B. pork barrel legislation.

    C. lobbying.

    D. logrolling.

40. Why should children be encouraged to figure out the structure and the features of the text they are attempting to comprehend and remember?

    I. It helps the students to understand the way the author organized the material to be presented.

    II. It helps the students to really look at the features of the text.

    III. Talking about the structure of the text provides an opportunity for the teacher to point out the most salient features to the students.

    IV. The discussions may help the child make connections between the new material in the chapter and what is already known about the topic.

A. I and III

B. II and IV

C. I and IV

D. All of the above

Constructed Response

Use the information below to complete the exercise that follows.

Mrs. Whalen, a fifth-grade teacher, is assessing Demetrius, a new student to the school, for reading fluency and comprehension. She has him read the following passage aloud.

My name is Jake. That's my first name, obviously. I can't tell you my last name. It would be too dangerous. The controllers are everywhere. Everywhere. And if they knew my full name, they could find me and my friends, and then . . . well, let's just say I don't want them to find me. What they do to people who resist them is too horrible to think about.

I won't even tell you where I live. You'll just have to trust me that it is a real place, a real town. It may even be *your* town.

I'm writing this all down so that more people will learn the truth. Maybe then, somehow, the human race can survive until the Algonites return and rescue us, as they promised they would.

Maybe.

My life used to be normal. Normal, that is, until one Friday night at the mall. I was there with Marco, my best friend. We were playing video games and hanging out at this cool store that sells comic books and stuff. The usual.

Demetrius has trouble pronouncing nearly every word longer than two syllables: "obviously," "controllers," and "Algonites," for example. He also needs help in pronouncing the word "resist." He reads with some expression and fairly quickly, except for the words he stumbles over. When questioned about the content of the passage, he answers as follows:

Mrs. Whalen: Can you tell me something about what you were just reading?

Demetrius: There's a guy who likes video games. I think his name is Jake.

Mrs. Whalen: What can you tell me about Jake?

Demetrius: Well, he's scared. He's in trouble.

Mrs. Whalen: How do you know he's in trouble?

Demetrius: He can't give out his last name.

Mrs. Whalen: Do you have any idea what he's afraid of?

Demetrius: Not really—they're An-guh-...

Mrs. Whalen: The Algonites?

Demetrius: Yeah, them. I guess they're after the whole world.

Based on your knowledge of reading comprehension, write a response that:

•   identifies two comprehension needs demonstrated by this student;

•   provides evidence for the needs you identify;

•   suggests two different instructional strategies to address the needs you identify; and

•   explains why these strategies might be effective.

Practice Test Answer Sheets

Begin your essay on this page. If necessary, continue on the next page.

Continue on the next page if necessary.

Continuation of your essay from previous page, if necessary.

OSAT

Oklahoma Subject Area Test
Elementary Education

Answers:
Practice Subtest 1

Answer Key

1. (A)	11. (B)	21. (C)	31. (A)
2. (B)	12. (A)	22. (C)	32. (B)
3. (C)	13. (C)	23. (C)	33. (A)
4. (D)	14. (B)	24. (C)	34. (C)
5. (C)	15. (A)	25. (D)	35. (D)
6. (A)	16. (D)	26. (D)	36. (D)
7. (A)	17. (B)	27. (A)	37. (B)
8. (D)	18. (B)	28. (C)	38. (B)
9. (D)	19. (A)	29. (B)	39. (A)
10. (D)	20. (A)	30. (B)	40. (D)

Practice Subtest

Detailed Explanations of Answers

1. **A**

   Semantic cueing involves using the meaning of the text and the context to figure out an unknown word. The genre of the selection, the illustrations, the reader's knowledge of the topic of the selection, and the context of the written words can provide semantic cues as the reader tries to unlock an unknown word.

2. **B**

   Syntactic cueing involves using the reader's grammatical knowledge of spoken and written language to figure out the significance of an unknown word in a text.

3. **C**

   Phonological cueing involves using the knowledge of matching written symbols with their sounds. This cueing strategy has limitations: it can be used effectively only for words where the letter patterns are known by the reader. The reader must also know how to analyze an unknown word.

4. **D**

   The pragmatic cueing system involves using the understanding that people use language differently in different contexts. This knowledge may help a reader to correctly interpret a text.

5. **C**

Clearly setting a purpose for listening, asking questions about the selection, and encouraging students to forge links between the new information and knowledge already in place are all supported by research as effective strategies.

6. **A**

There is a direct relationship between what is taught in school and what is learned in school. Also, if you want children to improve in writing, they need time to write.

7. **A**

The western or Pacific Coast of Canada is known as the Cordillera region. It receives an exceptional amount of rain and includes some of the tallest and oldest trees in Canada, similar to northern California. The area is full of rugged mountains with high plateaus and desert-like areas. For more information on Canada's regions visit http://www.members.shaw.ca/kcic1/geographic.html.

8. **D**

Due process is the legal concept that every citizen is entitled to equal treatment under the law. The excerpt illustrates one aspect of due process, the exclusionary rule. The exclusionary rule is applied when evidence is seized in violation of due process. So the most correct answer is D, the exclusionary rule.

9. **D**

Many of the classic stories for children exist in the realm of fantasy because of the timeless quality of such tales. Fantasy allows children to explore places and events that have never taken place, and will never take place, yet somehow contain messages that we can discuss, savor, and learn from. Faith Ringgold, an author of books for children, has stated, "One of the things you can do so well with children is to blend fantasy and reality. Kids are ready for it; they don't have to have everything lined up and real. It's not that they don't know it's not real, they just don't care."

10. **D**

Most books that begin with a princess have similar outcomes.

11. **B**

Stories that begin with an issue and a princess in place normally contain many magical events. Please consider some of the following titles: The Paper Bag Princess *by Robert Munsch;* The Frog Prince, Continued *by Jon Scieszka;* Princess Furball *by Charlotte Huck; and* Sleeping Ugly *by Jane Yolen.*

12. **A**

A K-W-L isn't just for content area lessons. Some children come to think of fairy tales as "babyish" or "girlish." This kind of discussion, laced with little chunks of stories being read aloud, helps children to recognize how delightful and charming this genre can be. It also helps them to figure out the rules of the genre, which improves their reading and writing.

13. **C**

This is the next step in the writing process.

14. **B**

The presence of "the" before "Westown's" means that the reference is to the council, not to a council belonging to Westown. The sentences in the other choices are all currently correct, and changing them would make them nonstandard.

15. **A**

The editorial is suggesting that the population loss is a bad thing and that proposed changes would be a good thing. Thus, population loss is something the author wants stopped, or at least lessened, so alleviate, which means to lessen, is the only possible choice.

16. **D**

The subject of the first clause is "each," which is singular, so the verb should be "has."

17. **B**

Choice A is wrong because it makes no sense within the sentence; the zoning regulations cannot be easy to change. Choice C makes sense, but its use of "them" is ambiguous—does it refer to the authors or the regulations? Choice D is wrong because, if the authors said the regulations would be hard to change, the word apparently earlier in the sentence would make no sense. Thus Choice B is the best answer.

18. B

I and III are correct. Among the major employers in Oklahoma are the Oklahoma state government, the U.S. Air Force, and General Motors. Also, Oklahoma's food processing plants, rubber and plastic manufacturing and other heavy industry are directly related to the livestock, petroleum, and natural gas industries in the state. II is incorrect because Oklahoma's livestock industry is more profitable, not less, than agriculture. IV is incorrect because Tulsa and Oklahoma City are among the great natural gas and petroleum centers of the world.

19. A

The main purpose of the WTO is to open world markets to all countries to promote economic development and to regulate the economic affairs between member states.

20. A

Overgrazing, overuse of farmland, and a lack of rainfall caused the drought of the 1930s.

21. C

Choice C is a prepositional phrase, "About 25,000 years ago," which is followed by a subordinate clause. This part should be linked to the previous sentence as it is integral to the migration of the Anasazi. Choices A, B, and D are all complete sentences.

22. C

Choice C has to do with the later history of the Mesa Verde area, after the Anasazi had abandoned it. Because this is so far removed chronologically, sentence 7 should be deleted or further developed in a second paragraph. Choices A and B discuss the very early history of the Indians. Choice D follows the chronological time order from 500 CE and leads into a discussion of the height of the Anasazi civilization.

23. C

Historical almanacs contain yearly data of certain events, including the time at sunrise and sunset along with weather-related data and statistics, so C is correct. Historical atlases contain a collection of historical maps. These maps may or may not include population data, so A is incorrect. Historical population data may best be found in government publications on the census. An encyclopedia article would contain a factual summary of the colonial period and the American Revolution, but may not include an analysis of the role of Fort Mackinac during the American Revolution, as encyclopedias attempt to give overviews rather than interpretations or analysis, so B is incorrect. A secondary source on Michigan during the colonial period may better address this question. Information on when the first treaty was signed and the terms of the treaty would most likely appear in a history book or government publication; a participant's diary may not be as accurate.

24. 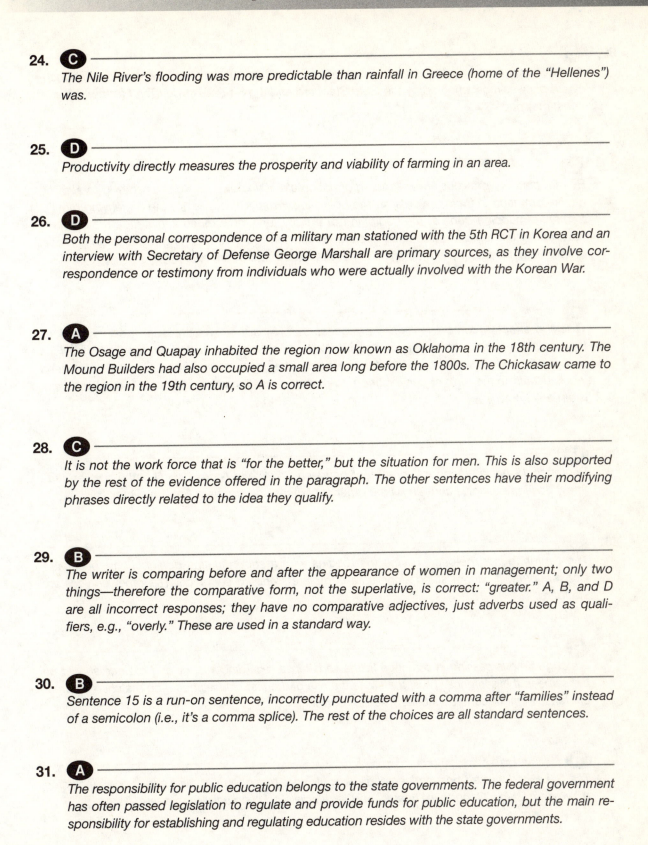 **C**

The Nile River's flooding was more predictable than rainfall in Greece (home of the "Hellenes") was.

25. **D**

Productivity directly measures the prosperity and viability of farming in an area.

26. **D**

Both the personal correspondence of a military man stationed with the 5th RCT in Korea and an interview with Secretary of Defense George Marshall are primary sources, as they involve correspondence or testimony from individuals who were actually involved with the Korean War.

27. **A**

The Osage and Quapay inhabited the region now known as Oklahoma in the 18th century. The Mound Builders had also occupied a small area long before the 1800s. The Chickasaw came to the region in the 19th century, so A is correct.

28. **C**

It is not the work force that is "for the better," but the situation for men. This is also supported by the rest of the evidence offered in the paragraph. The other sentences have their modifying phrases directly related to the idea they qualify.

29. **B**

The writer is comparing before and after the appearance of women in management; only two things—therefore the comparative form, not the superlative, is correct: "greater." A, B, and D are all incorrect responses; they have no comparative adjectives, just adverbs used as qualifiers, e.g., "overly." These are used in a standard way.

30. **B**

Sentence 15 is a run-on sentence, incorrectly punctuated with a comma after "families" instead of a semicolon (i.e., it's a comma splice). The rest of the choices are all standard sentences.

31. **A**

The responsibility for public education belongs to the state governments. The federal government has often passed legislation to regulate and provide funds for public education, but the main responsibility for establishing and regulating education resides with the state governments.

32. **B**

A limited money supply and rising prices were major causes of the Great Depression. The money supply was most affected by the Gold Standard and the Smoot-Hawley Tariff further affected consumer prices.

33. **A**

By mapping out previous knowledge, information already known can be transferred to support new information. Although words on the board are visual (B), this is not the underlying motive. Semantic mapping done at the beginning of a story tests how much knowledge the students have about the topic at the outset, not the conclusion (C). This mapping process does model proper use of words (D), but doing so is not the main intent of the exercise.

34. **C**

Teaching effective comprehension is a process that takes time and practice. It seems obvious that a student cannot comprehend a text if the text cannot be decoded. It also seems obvious that, if you want students to get better at reading, they need time to read. Students also need input, usually in the form of conversation, to make connections between what is read and what is already known.

35. **D**

Sentence 12 has an incorrect agreement between "kids" and "does," so D is the answer. Kids [they] do [something] is correct. All the other sentences use standard English syntax.

36. **D**

The sentence is a rhetorical clause that begins with a subordinating conjunction, "because." Consequently, it cannot stand alone as a complete standard sentence. The other choices are standard.

37. **B**

Although time is passing in sentence 2, the verb tense regarding infancy and old age should be the same in this sentence. Thus, the present tense of the first clause should be matched by present tense in the second ("watches"), so B is correct.

38. **B**

The Silk Road was a transcontinental trade route that branched out over a vast area, including A, western China; C, northern Iran; D, northern India; and eventually the Sahara.

39. **A**

A is the best answer, since the term "casework" is used by political scientists to describe the activities of congressmen on behalf of individual constituents. These activities might include helping an elderly person secure social security benefits, or helping a veteran obtain medical services. Most casework is actually done by congressional staff and may take as much as a third of the staff's time. Congressmen supply this type of assistance for the good public relations it provides. Answer B fails because pork barrel legislation is rarely if ever intended to help individual citizens. Pork barrel legislation authorizes federal spending for special projects, such as airports, roads, or dams, in the home state or district of a congressman. It is meant to help the entire district or state. Also, there is no legal entitlement on the part of a citizen to a pork barrel project, such as there is with social security benefits. C is not the answer because lobbying is an activity directed towards congressmen, not one done by congressmen. A lobbyist attempts to get congressmen to support legislation that will benefit the group that the lobbyist represents. Logrolling, D, is incorrect, because it does not refer to a congressional service for constituents. It refers instead to the congressional practice of trading votes on different bills. Congressman A will vote for Congressman B's pork barrel project and in return B will vote for A's pork barrel project.

40. **D**

Children learn more from a text if the teacher helps them figure out how the book was put together. It makes the text more understandable. It also helps them to read the text critically, as part of the conversation can address the issue of what is missing in the text.

Constructed-Response Answer Earning 4 Points

For Demetrius to read this text at an independent level, he needs better word identification skills and better acquaintance with the passage's genre.

If he does not know the meaning of the word "obviously," he not only misses a clue about Jake's personality, but he also goes into decoding mode, which prevents him from enjoying the text and from making connections between the text and other experiences.

Although Demetrius has two major word identification problems—decoding words phonologically and simply not having a sufficient vocabulary to read this passage—the inability I will concentrate on here is the insufficient vocabulary. Two of the words Demetrius had trouble with—"obviously" and "resist"—should be in a fifth grader's vocabulary, and they both follow somewhat unusual phonological models.

Even with better skills in this area, however, Demetrius will still have trouble with comprehension. This passage appears to be from a science fiction book, and he definitely seems unfamiliar with the genre. Thus, his first response to Mrs. Whalen's question concerning what the passage is about is Jake's affinity for video games, which may be the only thing Demetrius grasps well about the passage. When asked what else he knows about Jake, he concentrates on Jake's trouble rather than the trouble for the human race, probably because Demetrius is more accustomed to reading books in which individuals are in trouble of their own (or maybe he's just used to being "in trouble" himself).

Both strategies that Mrs. Whalen should try could be done on either an individual basis just with Demetrius or on a class-wide (or small-group) basis, depending on how many other readers in the class are at Demetrius's level. The first strategy, to increase his vocabulary, is to work with the student(s) to analyze new and unfamiliar words in all their reading. Assuming Demetrius will be worked with on an individual basis, he should read a book that is at his current instructional level (that is he can read it independently). He should make word lists of the words that he is unfamiliar with. He should define them and try to think of (or find) other words that have similar phonemes. For instance, his words and their phonemic analogies in this passage might be "obviously ↔ previously" and "resist ↔ insist." He may need help finding meanings or analogies, so Mrs. Whalen should have occasional short conferences with him to assess whether the word lists and their analogies are useful or even possible. This strategy will theoretically increase the number of words he knows and his ability to decipher unfamiliar words as well.

A second strategy is one that Mrs. Whalen would probably want to do with the whole class, and that would be to introduce the science fiction genre. Surely many students in the class will be acquainted with science fiction at least through movies and television shows, and they will be able to list a number of standard science fiction plots. Mrs. Whalen should diagram some of these plots on a board or overhead so that students will know what to expect as they read science fiction—for example, that big matters such as human survival are often at stake.

Demetrius already shows that he can make connections between what he reads and his own life, but his connections are flawed because he relies too much on his own life and too little on the text. By learning better word-recognition strategies and by recognizing conventions of the genre he is reading, he can raise his comprehension to a higher level.

Features of the Constructed Response Scoring 4

Purpose. The purpose of the assignment has been achieved. All four bullet points listed in the assignment have been addressed in an orderly way. The essay begins by stating the two comprehension needs, then gives evidence for these needs. It goes on to discuss two strategies, with reasons that the writer expects each to have a chance for success.

Subject Matter Knowledge. By indicating specific methods for implementing both strategies, this essay shows that the writer has an idea of how to improve reading, and how to assess whether the proposed methods are successful.

Support. Specific examples from the reading assessment are cited in describing the needs, and specific examples are given for the supposed strategies.

Rationale. In a sense, the "rationale" part of the scoring is covered by the other three areas: it would be hard to give a convincing argument without answering the question, demonstrating knowledge, or supporting your points. However, this area also includes the organization of the argument, and this essay methodically elucidates its points in a manner that helps the reader keep track of the overall argument.

FOR YOUR REFERENCE ONLY—*The constructed-response item is written to assess understanding in Subarea I, Reading, which consists of the competencies listed below.*

Understand the reading process.

Understand phonological skills and strategies related to reading.

Understand skills and strategies related to word identification and vocabulary development.

Understand skills and strategies involved in reading comprehension.

Understand reading instruction and study skills in the content areas.

Understand characteristic features of children's literature and strategies to promote students' literary response and analysis.

OSAT

Oklahoma Subject Area Test
Elementary Education

Subtest 2 Review

Mathematics

Objectives

SUBAREA I—MATHEMATICS

Competency 0001

> **Understand formal and informal reasoning processes, including logic and simple proofs, and apply problem-solving techniques and strategies in a variety of contexts.**
>
> The following topics are examples of content that may be covered under this competency.
> - Judge the validity or logic of mathematical arguments.
> - Evaluate the sufficiency of information provided to solve a problem.
> - Draw a valid conclusion based on stated conditions.
> - Apply inductive reasoning to make mathematical conjectures.

Competency 0002

> **Use a variety of approaches (e.g., estimation, mental math, modeling, pattern recognition) to explore mathematical ideas and solve problems.**
>
> The following topics are examples of content that may be covered under this competency.
> - Evaluate the appropriateness of using estimation to solve a given problem.
> - Use an appropriate model to illustrate a given problem.
> - Analyze the usefulness of a specific model or mental math procedure for exploring a given mathematical idea or problem.
> - Simplify a problem to facilitate a solution.

Competency 0003

Understand mathematical communication and the historical and cultural contexts of mathematics.

The following topics are examples of content that may be covered under this competency.
- Use mathematical notation to represent a given relationship.
- Use appropriate models, diagrams, and symbols to represent mathematical concepts.
- Use appropriate vocabulary to express given mathematical ideas and relationships.
- Apply knowledge of the role of mathematics in society and the contributions of various cultures toward the development of mathematics.

Competency 0004

Understand skills and concepts related to number and numeration, and apply these skills and concepts to real-world situations.

The following topics are examples of content that may be covered under this competency.
- Use ratios, proportions, and percents to model and solve problems.
- Compare and order fractions, decimals, and percents.
- Solve problems using equivalent forms of numbers (e.g., integer, fraction, decimal, percent, exponential and scientific notation).
- Analyze the number properties used in operational algorithms (e.g., multiplication, long division).

Competency 0005

Understand and apply the principles and properties of linear algebraic relations and functions.

The following topics are examples of content that may be covered under this competency.
- Analyze mathematical relationships and patterns using tables, verbal rules, equations, and graphs.
- Derive an algebraic expression to represent a real-world relationship or pattern, and recognize a real-world relationship that is represented by an algebraic expression.
- Use algebraic functions to describe given graphs, to plot points, and to determine slopes.
- Perform algebraic operations to solve equations and inequalities.

Competency 0006

Understand the principles and properties of geometry, and apply them to model and solve problems.

The following topics are examples of content that may be covered under this competency.
- Apply the concepts of similarity and congruence to model and solve real-world problems.
- Apply knowledge of basic geometric figures to solve real-world problems involving more complex patterns.
- Apply inductive and deductive reasoning to solve real-world problems in geometry.

Competency 0007

Understand concepts, principles, skills, and procedures related to measurement, statistics, and probability; and demonstrate an ability to use this understanding to describe and compare phenomena, to evaluate and interpret data, and to apply mathematical expectations to real-world phenomena.

The following topics are examples of content that may be covered under this competency.
- Estimate and convert measurements using standard and nonstandard units.
- Solve measurement problems involving volume, time, or speed.
- Interpret graphic and nongraphic representations of frequency distributions, percentiles, and measures of central tendency.
- Determine probabilities, and make predictions based on probabilities.

Problem Solving

The ability to render some real-life quandaries into mathematical or logical problems—workable via established procedures—is a key to finding solutions. Because each quandary will be unique, so too will be your problem-solving plan of attack. Still, many real-world problems that lend themselves to mathematical solutions are likely to require one of the following strategies.

1. **Guess and check** (not the same as "wild guessing"). With this problem-solving strategy, make your best guess, and then check the answer to see whether it's right. Even if the guess doesn't immediately provide the solution, it may help to get you closer to it so that you can continue to work on the problem. An example:

    Three persons' ages add up to 72, and each person is one year older than the last person. What are their ages?

    Because the three ages must add up to 72, it is reasonable to take one-third of 72 (24) as your starting point. Of course, even though 24 + 24 + 24 gives a sum of 72, those numbers don't match the information ("Each person is one year older..."). So, you might guess that the ages are 24, 25, and 26. You check that guess by addition, and you see that the sum of 75 is too high. Lowering your guesses by one each, you try 23, 24, and 25, which indeed add up to 72, giving you the solution. There are many variations of the guess and check method.

2.   **Making a sketch or a picture** can help to clarify a problem. Consider this problem:

Mr. Rosenberg plans to put a four-foot-wide concrete sidewalk around his backyard pool. The pool is rectangular, with dimensions 12' by 24'. The cost of the concrete is $1.28 per square foot. How much concrete is required for the job?

If you have exceptional visualization abilities, no sketch is needed. For most of us, however, a drawing like the one shown below may be helpful in solving this and many other real-life problems.

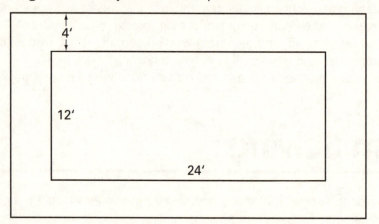

3.   **Make a table or a chart.** Sometimes, *organizing* the information from a problem makes it easier to find the solution; tables and charts can be helpful.

4.   **Making a list**, like making a table or chart, can help to organize information, and perhaps provide or at least hint at a solution. The strategy would work well for solving this problem: "How many different outcomes are there if you roll two regular six-sided dice?"

5.   **Act it out.** Sometimes, literally "doing" a problem, with physical objects, your bodies, and so forth, can help produce a solution. A classic problem that could be solved in this manner is the following: "If five strangers meet, and if everyone shakes everyone else's hand once, how many total handshakes will there be?"

6. **Look for patterns.** This technique encourages you to ask, "What's happening here?" Spotting a pattern would be helpful in solving a problem such as:

Nevin's weekly savings account balance for 15 weeks are as follows: $125, $135, $148, $72, $85, $96, $105, $50, $64, $74, $87, $42, $51, $60, $70. If the pattern holds, (approximately) what might Nevin's balance be the next week?

7. **Working a simpler problem** means finding the solution to a different but simpler problem, hoping that you will spot a way to solve the harder one. *Estimating* can be thought of as working a simpler problem. If you need to know the product of 23 and 184, and no calculator or pencil and paper are handy, you could estimate the product by getting the exact answer to the simpler problem, 20 × 200.

8. **Writing an open math sentence** (an equation with one or more variables, or "unknowns"), then solving it, is often an effective strategy. This is sometimes called "translating" a problem into mathematics. Consider this problem: "Tiana earned grades of 77%, 86%, 90%, and 83% on her first four weekly science quizzes. Assuming all grades are equally weighted, what score will she need on the fifth week's quiz in order to have an average (or mean) score of 88%?" Using the given information, you can set up the following equation, which, when solved, will answer the question:

$$\frac{(77+86+90+83+x)}{5}=88$$

9. **Work backward.** Consider this problem: "If you add 12 to some number, then multiply the sum by 4, you will get 60. What is the number?" You can find a solution by *starting at the end*, with 60. The problem tells you that the 60 came from multiplying a sum by 4. When multiplied by 4, 15 equals 60, so 15 must be the sum referred to. And if 15 is the sum of 12 and something else, the "something else" can only be 3.

There are, of course, hybrid approaches. You can mix and match problem-solving strategies wherever you think they are appropriate. In general, attention to *reasonableness* may be most crucial to problem-solving success, especially in real-life situations.

Mathematical Communication and Mathematical Terminology, Symbols, and Representations

While a review of even basic mathematical terminology and symbolism could fill a book, there are some key points to keep in mind:

Mathematics is, for the most part, a science of precision. When working with math symbols and terminology, meticulousness is in order. For example, "less than" does not mean the same thing as "not greater than." The following two equations are *not* equivalent (every term on both sides of the first equation should be divided by 6.)

$$6m + 2 = 18$$

$$\frac{6m}{6} + 2 = \frac{18}{6}$$

All of this matters, especially in real-life problem situations.

Certain mathematical concepts and terms are frequently misunderstood. Here are a few of the "repeat offenders":

Use care with *hundreds vs. hundredths, thousands vs. thousandths,* and so forth. Remember that the "th" at the end of the word indicates a fraction. "Three hundred" means 300, whereas "three hundredths" means 0.03.

Negative numbers are those less than zero. Fractions less than zero are negative numbers, too.

The *absolute value* of a number can be thought of as its distance from zero on a number line.

Counting numbers can be shown by the set (1, 2, 3, 4, . . .). Notice that 0 is not a counting number.

Whole numbers are the counting numbers, plus 0 (0, 1, 2, . . .).

Integers are all of the whole numbers and their negative counterparts (. . . −2, −1, 0, 1, 2, . . .). Note that negative and positive fractions are not considered integers (unless they are equivalent to whole numbers or their negative counterparts).

Factors are any of the numbers or symbols in mathematics that, when multiplied together, form a product. (The whole number factors of 12 are 1, 2, 3, 4, 6, and 12.) A number with exactly two whole number factors (1 and the number itself) is a *prime number*. The first few primes are 2, 3, 5, 7, 11, 13, and 17. Most other whole numbers are *composite numbers*, because they are *composed* of several whole number factors (1 is neither prime nor composite; it has only one whole number factor).

The *multiples* of any whole number are what are produced when the number is multiplied by counting numbers. The multiples of 7 are 7, 14, 21, 28, and so on. Every whole number has an infinite number of multiples.

Recall that *decimal numbers* are simply certain fractions written in special notation. All decimal numbers are actually fractions whose denominators are powers of 10 (10, 100, 1000, etc.) 0.033, for instance, can be thought of as the fraction $\frac{33}{1000}$.

There is an agreed-upon order of operations for simplifying complex expressions.

First you compute any multiplication or division, left to right. Then you compute any addition or subtraction, also left to right. (If an expression contains any parentheses, all computation within the parentheses should be completed first.) Treat exponential expressions ("powers") as multiplication. Thus, the expression $3 + 7 \times 4 - 2$ equals 29. (Multiply 7 by 4 *before* doing the addition and subtraction.)

Exponential notation is a way to show repeated multiplication more simply. $2 \times 2 \times 2$, for instance, can be shown as 2^3, and is equal to 8. (Note: 2^3 does *not* mean 2×3.)

Scientific notation provides a method for showing numbers using exponents (although it is most useful for very large and very small numbers.) A number is in scientific notation when it is shown as a number between 1 and 10 to a power of 10. Thus, the number 75,000 in scientific notation is shown as 7.5×10^4.

Addends (or *addenda*) can be thought of as "parts of addition problems." When addends are combined, they produce *sums*. Likewise, *factors* can be seen as "parts of multiplication problems." When factors are multiplied, they produce *products*. When two numbers are divided, one into the other, the result is a *quotient*.

Equations are not the same as mathematical *expressions.* $12 + 4 = 16$ and $2x + 7 = 12$ are equations. $(144 - 18)$ and $13y^2$ are expressions. Notice that expressions are "lacking a verb," so to speak (you don't say "is equal to" or "equals" when reading expressions). Inequalities are very much like equations, but "greater than" or "less than" are added, such as in $x \leq 7$.

A *trend* is a pattern over time.

Careful use of mathematical terms and ideas such as those noted above is essential to communicating mathematically.

Fast Facts

Careful use of mathematical terms and ideas is essential to communicating mathematically.

The ability to convert among various mathematical and logical representations (graphic, numeric, symbolic, verbal) is an important skill, and, as with problem solving, precision and care are keys to quality conversions. Consider this number line, which might represent ages of students who are eligible for a particular scholarship:

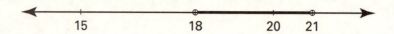

Are 21-year-old students eligible? No, because the conventional notation used on the number line shows a *circle* around the point at 21. That means that 21 is *not* included in the set. Converting the graphic representation to symbolism gives $18 < x < 21$.

Number Skills

Key properties of whole numbers (and some related terms) include the following:

The Commutative Property for Addition and Multiplication states that the order in which addends are added or factors are multiplied does not determine the sum or product. (6×9 gives the same product as 9×6, for instance.) Division and subtraction are not commutative.

The Associative Property for Addition and Multiplication states that "associating" three or more addends or factors in a different fashion will not change the sum or product. For example, $(3 + 7) + 5$ gives the same sum as $3 + (7 + 5)$. Division and subtraction are not associative.

The *Distributive Property of Multiplication over Addition* is shown hereafter in simple notation form:

$$a(b + c) = (a \times b) + (a \times c)$$

An illustration of the Distributive Property is this: multiplying 6 by 47 will give the same result as multiplying 6 by 40, multiplying 6 times 7, then *adding* the products. That is, $6 \times (47) = (6 \times 40) + (6 \times 7)$.

Some pairs of operations are considered to be *inverse*. Addition and subtraction are inverse operations, as are multiplication and division. The operations can be thought of as "undoing" one another: Multiplying 4 by 9 gives 36; dividing 36 by 9 "gives back" 4.

The *Multiplicative Identity Property of One* states that any number multiplied by 1 remains the same. ($34 \times 1 = 34$, for instance.) The number 1 is called the *Multiplicative Identity*.

The *Property of Reciprocals* states that any number (except for zero) multiplied by its reciprocal gives 1. (The *reciprocal* of a number is 1 divided by that number.)

Remember that dividing by zero is considered to have no meaning; avoid doing it when computing or solving equations and inequalities.

The *Additive Identity Property of Zero* states that adding zero to any number will not change the number ($87 + 0 = 87$, for instance). Zero is called the *Additive Identity*.

Division is *partitive* when you know the total and the number of parts or groups but you don't how many are in each part. Consider: "You have 7 containers of bolts and a total of 98 bolts. How many bolts are in each container (assuming the same number in each)?" Arriving at the answer is an example of partitive division.

With *measurement division*, the number of groups is not known. Using the example above, if you knew that there were 14 bolts per container, and that there were 98 bolts altogether, finding the number of containers would require measurement division.

Rational Numbers, Fractions, and Decimals

A property of real numbers is *The Density Property*. It states that, given any two real numbers, there is always another real number between them. (Think of the number line: No matter how close two points are, there is always a point between them.)

Rational numbers are those that can be written as fractions. (This includes integers; 12, for instance, can be written as $\frac{12}{1}$.)

Decimals (or "decimal fractions"), which come to an end when represented exactly, are *terminating decimals* (2.125, for instance). *Repeating decimals* are those in which the digits repeat a pattern endlessly (3.333333 . . . , for example). To use shorthand notation to show repeating decimals, you can write the "repeating block" just once, putting a bar over it. The example above, for instance, can be shown as 3.3̲. (Both terminating and repeating decimals are rational numbers.)

Some numbers are real numbers, but cannot be accurately represented by fractions. The ratio of the length of the diameter of any circle to its circumference, or π, for instance, is irrational. There are useful approximations of π, such as 3.14159, but π cannot be "pinned down" in either fraction or decimal notation.

Fractions, decimal numbers, ratios, and percents can be thought of as different ways of representing values, and any given rational number can be shown any of those ways. It is useful to be able to convert from one to the other. The following are some conversion tips:

The practical method for changing a fraction into a decimal is by dividing the numerator by the denominator. For example, $\frac{1}{4}$ becomes 0.25 when 1 is divided by 4, as follows:

$$
\begin{array}{r}
.25 \\
4\overline{)1.00} \\
\underline{8} \\
20
\end{array}
$$

Naturally, this can be done longhand or with a calculator. (If the decimal number includes a whole number, as with $2\frac{3}{5}$, you can ignore the whole number when doing the division.) The decimal number may terminate or repeat. Converting a simple fraction to a decimal number will never result in an irrational number.

To convert a non-repeating decimal number to a fraction in lowest terms, simply write the decimal as a fraction with the denominator a power of ten, and then reduce to lowest terms. For example, 0.125 can be written as $\frac{125}{1000}$, which reduces to $\frac{1}{8}$.

Any decimal number can be converted to a percent by shifting the decimal point two places to the right and adding the percent symbol. For example, 0.135 becomes 13.5%. (If the number before the percent symbol is a whole number, there is no need to show the decimal point.)

A percent can be converted to a decimal number by shifting the decimal point two places to the left and dropping the percent symbol: 98% becomes 0.98 as a decimal.

A percent can be converted to a fraction simply by putting the percent (without the percent symbol) over 100, then reducing. In this way 20% can be shown as $\frac{20}{100}$, which reduces to $\frac{1}{5}$.

Ratio notation is simply an alternative method for showing fractions. For example, $\frac{2}{5}$ can be rewritten as "2 to 5." Ratio notation is commonly used when you want to emphasize the relationship of one number to another. Ratios are often shown as numbers with a colon between them; 2:5 is the same ratio as 2 to 5 and $\frac{2}{5}$.

To illustrate all of the above equivalencies and conversions at once, consider the fraction $\frac{19}{20}$. Shown as a ratio, it's 19 to 20, or 19:20. As a decimal, you have 0.95; as a percent, 95%.

The rules for performing operations on rational numbers (fractions) parallel in many ways the computational rules for integers. Just as adding –3 and –11 gives –14, adding $-\frac{1}{9}$ and $-\frac{5}{9}$ gives $-\frac{6}{9}$ (or $-\frac{2}{3}$ in reduced form.)

Algebraic Concepts and Methods

An important skill is the ability to represent real problems in algebraic form, and the concept of the *variable* is key. A variable is simply a symbol that represents an unknown value. Most typically x is the letter used, although any letter can be used. By "translating" real problems to algebraic form containing one or more variables (often as equations or inequalities), solutions to many problems can be found mathematically.

Understanding the relationships among values, and being able to accurately represent those relationships symbolically, is another key to algebraic problem solving. Consider the ages of two sisters. If you don't know the age of the younger sister, but know that the older sister is three years older, you can show the information symbolically as follows: The age of the younger sister can be shown as x, and the age of the older sister as $x + 3$. If you are told that the sum of the sisters' ages is, say, 25, you can represent that information via an equation:

$$x + (x + 3) = 25$$

which can be read as "the age of the younger sister plus the age of the older sister totals 25." This sort of translation skill is crucial for using algebra for problem solving.

Some helpful *translation* tips include the following: The word *is* often suggests an equal sign; *of* may suggest multiplication, as does *product*. *Sum* refers to addition; *difference* suggests subtraction; and a *quotient* is obtained after dividing. The key when translating is to make sure that the equation accurately matches the information and relationships given in the word problem.

Operations with algebraic expressions are governed by various rules and conventions. For instance, only *like* algebraic terms can be added or subtracted to produce simpler expressions. For example, $2x^3$ and $3x^3$ can be added together to get $5x^3$ because the terms are like terms; they both have a base of $x3$. You cannot add, say, $7m^3$ and $6m^2$; m^3 and m^2 are unlike bases. (Note: To *evaluate* an algebraic expression means to simplify it using conventional rules.)

When multiplying exponential terms together, the constant terms are multiplied, but the exponents of terms with the same variable bases are *added* together, which is somewhat counterintuitive. For example, $4w^2$ multiplied by $8w^3$ gives $32w^5$ (not $32w^6$, as one might guess).

When like algebraic terms are divided, exponents are subtracted. For example,

$$\frac{2x^7}{5x^3}$$

becomes

$$\frac{2x^4}{5}$$

In algebra, you frequently need to multiply two *binomials* together. Binomials are algebraic expressions of two terms. The FOIL method is one way to multiply binomials. FOIL stands for "first, outer, inner, last": Multiply the first terms in the parentheses, then the outermost terms, then the innermost terms, then the last terms, and then add the products together. For example, to multiply $(x + 3)$ and $(2x - 5)$, you multiply x by $2x$ (the first terms), x by -5 (outer terms), 3 by $2x$ (inner terms), and 3 by 5 (last terms). The four products ($2x^2$, $-5x$, $6x$, and -15) add up to $2x^2 + x - 15$. If the polynomials to be multiplied have more than two terms (*trinomials*, for instance), make sure that *each* term of the first polynomial is multiplied by *each* term of the second.

The opposite of polynomial multiplication is factoring. Factoring a polynomial means rewriting it as the product of factors (often two binomials). The trinomial $x^2 - 11x + 28$, for instance, can be factored into $(x - 4)(x - 7)$. (You can check this by "FOILing" the binomials.)

When attempting to factor polynomials, it is sometimes necessary to find factors common to all terms first. The two terms in $5x^2 - 10$, for example, both contain the factor 5. This means that the expression can be rewritten as $5(x^2 - 2)$.

Factoring is useful when solving some equations, especially if one side of the equation is set equal to zero. Consider $2x^2 - x - 1 = 2$. It can be rewritten as $2x^2 - x - 3 = 0$. This allows the left side to be factored into $(2x - 3)(x + 1)$, giving equation solutions of $\frac{3}{2}$ and -1.

Consider all of the information above as the following problem is first "translated" into an equation, then solved.

Three teachers who are retiring are said to have 78 years of experience among them. You don't know how many years of experience Teacher A has, but you know that Teacher B has twice as many as A, and Teacher C has three more years of experience than B. How many years of experience does each have?

You can start by calling Teacher A's years of experience x. You then consider the relationship to the other two teachers: You can call Teacher B's years of experience $2x$, which allows you to call Teacher C's years of experience $(2x + 3)$. You know that the teachers' years of experience add up to 78, allowing you to write:

$$x + 2x + (2x + 3) = 78$$

Using the rules for solving such an equation, you find that $x = 15$, meaning that the teachers' years of experience are, respectively, 15, 30, and 33 years.

Geometry

A fundamental concept of geometry is the notion of a *point*. A point is a specific location, taking up no space, having no area, and frequently represented by a dot. A point is considered one-dimensional.

Through any two points there is exactly one straight line; straight lines are one-dimensional. Planes (think of flat surfaces without edges) are two-dimensional. From these foundational ideas you can move to some other important geometric terms and ideas.

A segment is any portion of a line between two points on the line. It has a definite start and a definite end. The notation for a segment extending from point *A* to point *B* is $\overline{AB}$. A ray is like a straight segment, except it extends forever in one direction. The notation for a ray originating at point *X* (an *endpoint*) through point *Y* is $\overrightarrow{XY}$.

When two rays share their endpoints, an *angle* is formed. A *degree* is a unit of measure of the angle created. If a circle is divided into 360 even slices, each slice has an angle measure of 1 degree. If an angle has exactly 90 degrees, it is called a *right* angle. Angles of less than 90 degrees are *acute* angles. Angles greater than 90 degrees are *obtuse* angles. If two angles have the same size (regardless of how long their rays might be drawn), they are *congruent*. Congruence is shown this way: $\angle m = \angle n$ (read "angle *m* is congruent to angle *n*").

A polygon is a closed plane figure bounded by straight lines or a closed figure on a sphere bounded by arcs of great circles. In a plane, three-sided polygons are *triangles*, four-sided polygons are *quadrilaterals*, five sides make *pentagons*, six sides make *hexagons*, and eight-sided polygons are *octagons*. (Note that not all quadrilaterals are squares.) If two polygons (or any figures) have exactly the same size and shape, they are *congruent*. If they are the same shape, but different sizes, they are *similar*.

Polygons may have lines of symmetry, which can be thought of as imaginary fold lines which produce two congruent, mirror-image figures. Squares have four lines of symmetry, and non-square rectangles have two, as shown later. Circles have an infinite number of lines of symmetry; a few are shown on the circle.

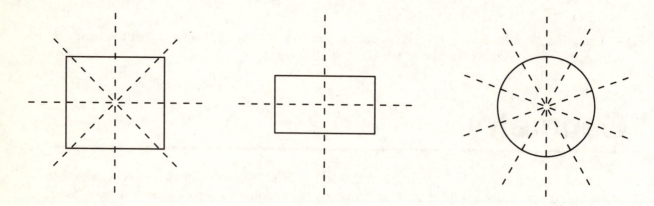

The *diameter* of a circle is a straight line segment that goes from one edge of a circle to the other side, passing through the center. The *radius* of a circle is half of its diameter (from the center to an edge). A *chord* is any segment that goes from one spot on a circle to any other spot (all diameters are chords, but not all chords are diameters).

The *perimeter* of a two-dimensional (flat) shape or object is the distance around the object.

Volume refers to how much space is inside of three-dimensional, closed containers. It is useful to think of volume as how many cubic units could fit into a solid. If the container is a rectangular solid, multiplying width, length, and height together computes the volume. If all six faces (sides) of a rectangular solid are squares, then the object is a cube.

Parallel and perpendicular are key concepts in geometry. Consider the two parallel lines that follow, and the third line (a *transversal*), which crosses them.

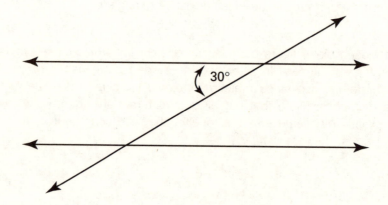

Note that among the many individual angles created, there are only two angle measures: 30° (noted in the figure) and 150° (180° − 30°).

Triangles have various properties. One is that the sum of the measures of the three angles of any triangle is 180°. If, therefore, the measures of two angles are known, the third can be deduced using addition, then subtraction. The Pythagorean theorem states that in any right triangle with legs (shorter sides) *a* and *b*, and hypotenuse (longest side) *c*, the sum of the squares of the sides will be equal to the square of the hypotenuse. In algebraic notation the Pythagorean theorem is given as $a^2 + b^2 = c^2$.

Two important coordinate systems are the number line and the coordinate plane, and both systems can be used to solve certain problems. A particularly useful tool related to the coordinate plane is the Distance Formula, which allows you to compute the distance between any two points on the plane. Consider points C and D in the following figure.

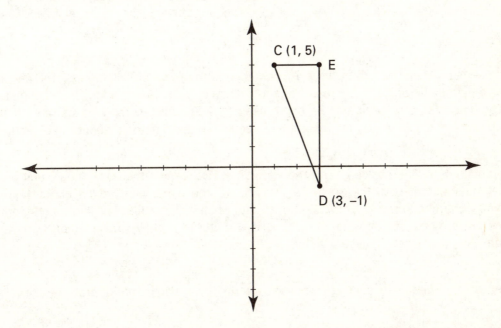

By finding the difference of the points' *x* coordinates (3 − 1, or 2) and the difference of their *y* coordinates (−1 − 5, or −6), you have found the lengths of the sides of triangle CED (2 units and 6 units—you can ignore the negative sign on the 6.) You can now use the Pythagorean theorem to find the length of the hypotenuse of triangle CED, which is the same as the length from point C to D ($2^2 + 6^2 = 40$, and the square root of 40 is approximately 6.3). Here is the distance formula in algebraic form:

$$d = \sqrt{(x_2 - x_1)^2 + (y_2 - y_1)^2}$$

Measurement

Measurement includes estimating and converting measurements within the customary and metric systems; applying procedures for using measurement to describe and compare phenomena; identifying appropriate measurement instruments, units, and procedures for measurement problems involving length, area, angles, volume, mass, time, money, and temperature; and using a variety of materials, models, and methods to explore concepts and solve problems involving measurement.

Here are some key measurement terms and ideas:

Customary units are generally the same as *U.S. units*. Customary units of length include inches, feet, yards, and miles. Customary units of weight include ounces, pounds, and tons. Customary units of capacity (or volume) include teaspoons, tablespoons, cups, pints, quarts, and gallons.

Metric units of length include millimeters, centimeters, meters, and kilometers. The centimeter is the basic metric unit of length, at least for short distances. There are about 2.5 centimeters to 1 inch. The kilometer is a metric unit of length used for longer distances. It takes more than 1.5 kilometers to make a mile. A very fast adult runner could run a kilometer in about three minutes.

Metric units of weight include grams and kilograms. The gram is the basic metric unit of mass (which for many purposes is the same as *weight*). A large paper clip weighs about 1 gram. It takes about 28 grams to make 1 ounce. Metric units of capacity include milliliters and liters. The liter is the basic metric unit of volume (or capacity). A liter is slightly smaller than a quart, so it takes more than four liters to make a gallon.

Here are some frequently used customary-to-metric ratios. Values are approximate.

1 inch = 2.54 centimeters

1 yard = 0.91 meters

1 mile = 1.61 kilometers

1 ounce = 28.35 grams

1 pound = 2.2 kilograms

1 quart = 0.94 liters

Metric-to-customary conversions can be found by taking the reciprocals of each of the factors noted above. For instance, 1 kilometer = 0.62 mile (computed by dividing 1 by 1.61).

An important step in solving problems involving measurement is to decide which area you are in; generally, such problems will fall under one of these categories: length, area, angles, volume, mass, time, money, and temperature. Solving measurement problems will likely have you calling on your knowledge in several other areas of mathematics, especially algebra. The following is one example of a measurement problem that requires knowledge of several math topics:

> Sophie's Carpet Store charges $19.40 per square yard for the type of carpeting you'd like (padding and labor included). How much will you pay to carpet your 9 foot by 12 foot room?

One way to find the solution is to convert the room dimensions to yards (3 yards by 4 yards), then multiply to get 12 square yards. Finally, multiply 12 by the price of $19.40 per square yard, for a total price of $232.80

Statistics and Probability

Measures of central tendency of a set of values include *mean*, *median*, and *mode*. The mean is found by adding all the values, then dividing the sum by the number of values. The median of a set is the middle number when the values are in numerical order. (If there is an even number of values, and therefore no middle value, the mean of the middle two values gives the median.) The mode of a set is the value occurring most often. (Not all sets of values have a single mode; some sets have more than one.) Consider the following set.

6   8   14   5   6   5   5

The mean, median, and mode of the set are 7, 6, and 5, respectively. (Note: The mean is often referred to as the average, but all three measures are averages of sorts.)

Probability theory provides models for chance variations. The *probability* of any event occurring is equal to the number of desired outcomes divided by the number of all possible events. Thus, the probability of blindly pulling a green ball out of a hat (in this case the desired outcome) if the hat contains two green and five yellow balls, is $\frac{2}{7}$ (about 29%). *Odds* are related to probability, but are different. The odds that any given event *will* occur is the ratio of the probability that the event will occur to the probability that the event *will not* occur (typically expressed as a ratio). In the example above, the odds that a green ball will be drawn are 2:5.

Statistics is the branch of mathematics that involves collecting, analyzing, and interpreting data, organizing data to describe them usefully, and drawing conclusions and making decisions. Statistics builds on probability, and typically studies "populations," meaning quantifiable groups of things. Trends and patterns not otherwise noticed may be revealed via statistics.

One key statistical concept is that of *standard deviation*. The standard deviation of a set of values tells how "tightly" all of the values are clustered around the mean of the set. When values are tightly clustered near the mean, the standard deviation is small. If values are widespread, the standard deviation is large. Here is one way to find the standard deviation of a set. Consider the set used earlier:

$$6 \quad 8 \quad 14 \quad 5 \quad 6 \quad 5 \quad 5$$

First find the mean (7). Next, find the difference of each value in the set and the mean (ignoring negative signs). This gives 1, 1, 7, 2, 1, 2, and 2. Now, you square each of those values, giving 1, 1, 49, 4, 1, 4, and 4. You next take the sum of those squares (64) and divide the sum by the number of values ($\frac{64}{7} = 9.14$). Finally, you take the square root of 9.14, giving a standard deviation of 3.02. Think of 3.02 as the amount that the values in the set "typically" vary from the center.

Mathematical Reasoning Processes

Mathematical reasoning includes analyzing problem situations, making conjectures, organizing information, and selecting strategies to solve problems; evaluating solutions to problems; constructing arguments and judging the validity or logic of arguments; and using logical reasoning to draw and justify conclusions from given information.

Problem-solvers must rely on both formal and informal *reasoning processes*. A key informal process relies on *reasonableness*. Consider this problem:

Center Town Middle School has an enrollment of 640 students. One day, 28 students were absent. What percent of the total number of students were absent?

Even if someone forgot how to compute percents, some possible answers could be rejected instantly: 28 is a "small-but-not-tiny" chunk of 640, so answers like 1%, 18%, and 25% are *unreasonable*.

There are also formal reasoning processes, such as *deductive reasoning*. Deductive reasoning is reasoning from the general to the specific, and it is supported by deductive logic. Here is an example of deductive reasoning:

All ducks have wings (a general assertion). Donald is a duck; therefore Donald has wings (a specific proposition).

With *inductive reasoning*, a general rule is inferred from specific observations (which may be limited). Moving from the statement "All boys in this classroom are wearing jeans" (a specific but limited observation) to "All boys wear jeans" (a general assertion) is an example of inductive reasoning. Note that conclusions arrived at via deductive and inductive reasoning are not necessarily true.

Science

Science, Technology, and Society

It is unworthy of excellent men to lose hours like slaves in the labor of calculation which could be relegated to anyone else if machines were used.

Gottfried Wilhelm von Leibniz (1646–1716), German polymath

Science disciplines hold to certain central values that unify them in their philosophy and methodology. Science relies on evidence collected in verifiable experiments, on conclusions validated by replication, and on theories that explain observations and that are capable of making testable predictions. Modern scientific thought traces a significant portion of its development to the work of Western European scientists, much, but far from all. It is important to recognize the contributions made by all peoples and cultures to the development of scientific knowledge. Men and women from all continents and races continue to make meaningful contributions to the advancement of science in all disciplines. Examples are readily available for enrichment and instruction from online resources.

Science can tell us how to do something, not whether we should.

Fast Facts

Technology can be loosely defined as the application of science for the benefit of mankind. For both political and economic reasons not all peoples have the same ready access to clean, safe water supplies nor to adequate food supplies, in spite of the technological capabilities that basic science has provided. Science certainly can benefit, but it too, arguably, can harm mankind and our environment. Science gives us the knowledge and tools to understand nature's principles and that knowledge can often be applied for some useful purpose. Few would debate the benefits of the wheel and axle, the electric light, the polio vaccine, or plastic. The benefits of science and technology become more complicated to evaluate when discussing the applications of gene splicing for genetically modified foods, of cloning, of nuclear energy to replace fossil fuels, or the application of atomic energy to weapons of mass destruction. Science can tell us how to do something, not whether we should.

Scientific literacy helps us participate in the decision-making process of our society as well-informed and contributing members. Real-world decisions have social, political, and economic dimensions, and scientific information is often used to both support and refute these decisions. Understanding that the inherent nature of scientific information is unbiased, and based on experimental evidence that can be reproduced by any laboratory under the same conditions can help us all make better decisions, recognize false arguments, and participate fully as active and responsible citizens.

Scientific knowledge is a body of statements of varying degrees of certainty—some most unsure, some nearly sure, but none absolutely certain . . . Now, we scientists are used to this, and we take it for granted that it is perfectly consistent to be unsure, that it is possible to live and not know.

Richard P. Feynman (1918–1988), Nobel Prize in Physics, 1965

Science education has as its goal the training of a scientifically literate public that fully participates in the economic, political, and cultural functions of our society. Scientifically literate individuals, students and teachers alike, must have knowledge that is connected and useful. The Oklahoma science curriculum, both for the preparation of preservice teachers and for K-12 instruction, is guided by this principle.

The Oklahoma curriculum operationally defines the scientifically literate individual as one who uses scientific knowledge, constructs new scientific knowledge, and reflects on scientific knowledge. Such individuals have specific science content knowledge, they build upon that knowledge through their experiences and activities, and they can evaluate objectively and critically the value and limitations of that knowledge.

SUBAREA II—SCIENCE

Competency 0008

Understand the interrelationships among the physical and life sciences and the connections among science, technology, and society.

The following topics are examples of content that may be covered under this competency.
- Apply principles of mathematics, science, and technology to model a given situation (e.g., the movement of energy and nutrients between a food chain and the physical environment).
- Analyze the effects of changes in environmental conditions (e.g., temperature, availability of water and sunlight) on plant and animal health, growth, and development.
- Analyze the effects of human activities (e.g., burning fossil fuels, clear-cutting forests) on the environment and the benefits and limitations of science and technology.
- Evaluate the use of science and technology in solving problems related to the effects of human activities on the environment (e.g., recycling, energy conservation).

Life Science

I venture to define science as a series of interconnected concepts and conceptual schemes arising from experiment and observation and fruitful of further experiments and observations. The test of a scientific theory is, I suggest, its fruitfulness.

James Bryant Conant (1893–1978), Chemist and Educator

Competency 0009

Understand the principles of life science (including biology and ecology), and use this understanding to interpret, analyze, and explain phenomena.

The following topics are examples of content that may be covered under this competency.
- Infer the life science principle (e.g., adaptation, homeostasis) illustrated in a given situation.
- Analyze relationships among the components of an ecological community.
- Analyze the factors that contribute to change in organisms and species over time.
- Analyze processes that contribute to the continuity of life (e.g., life cycles; the role of growth, repair, and maintenance).

Cells

The concept of a cell is central to our understanding of the life sciences. Cells are the simplest living unit of life, just as atoms are the building blocks of molecules, and molecules of cells. Cell Theory states that all organisms are composed of cells, that all cells arise from preexisting cells, and that the cell is the basic organizational unit of all organisms. Groups of specialized cells, or tissues, may have highly specialized characteristics and functions within an organism. A single organism may comprise only a single cell, or many billions of cells, and cells themselves range in size from the micron to many centimeters in dimension. Growth in most organisms is associated with cell division and replication, in addition to enlargement of the cells.

Classification

A dichotomous key is a tool of science that allows us to organize and classify objects by their observable traits and properties. In the life sciences, classification keys are widely used, and the simplest are based on the gross anatomy of all organisms, including plants, animals, fungi, protists, and two kingdoms of bacteria. Through comparison of the number of wings or legs, habitat, and eating habits we begin, at the earliest levels, to understand patterns in nature, constructing our own understanding of the world around us, and practice the basic elements of scientific thought and discovery.

Scientific knowledge may be classified or organized by grouping similar types of knowledge into thematic concepts. Many concepts are so broad as to find application in multiple disciplines. Cycle, for example, is a powerful concept that has widespread application throughout science, useful for both explanation and prediction. Life cycles are central to the study of biology. The recurring pattern of events in the life cycle links birth, growth, reproduction, and death. The concept of a cycle is also evident in the carbon cycle, nitrogen cycle, Krebs cycle, hydrogeologic cycle, periodic table, and many other processes, including the transformations of energy needed to sustain life. The food chain represents the complex interdependency of all plants and animals on the energy from the Sun, and the recycling of nutrients from simple to complex organisms.

Fast Facts → **Life cycles are central to the study of biology.**

Heredity

The discussion of life cycles brings forward the concept that the offspring of one generation bears likeness to, but also variation from, the previous generation. Some characteristics of the individual parent are passed along, while others appear not to be. We observe the connections between the visible traits of the parents and children, connections evident in all sexually reproducing organisms. It is clear that the offspring of dogs are other dogs, which generally look much like the parent dogs. Details of how such traits are conveyed through genetics are important to understand; yet instruction in these topics is allocated to the curriculum of higher grades.

Evolution

The goal of science education is to develop a scientifically literate public. At the elementary level this involves an understanding of how physical traits promote the survival of a species, how environmental changes affect species that are not adapted to those new conditions, and the role of heredity in passing and modifying the traits of successive generations. There are ample examples available to illustrate these concepts to the elementary student. A rabbit whose coat regularly turns white before the snowfall is at a temporary disadvantage, and is therefore subject to a higher degree of predation. That rabbit may not live to produce other early-white-coated rabbits. Technology, the application of knowledge for man's benefit, includes activities that are designed to select those traits that are intended to lead to healthier, stronger, and more productive crops and animals.

While the tenets of evolution as scientific theory are widely accepted, particularly as they apply to the short-term changes and adaptations within a species, the subject continues to generate some debate. To place the discussion in its proper context, some discussion of the scientific use of terms is appropriate, because the common usage of a term may differ significantly from its scientific usage. A *scientific fact* is an observation that has been repeatedly confirmed. However, scientific facts change if new observations yield new information. Frequently, the development of new, more sophisticated or precise instruments leads to such new information. A *scientific hypothesis* is a testable statement about the natural world, and as such is the starting point for most scientific experimentation. A hypothesis can generally be proven wrong, but is seldom proven right. *Scientific theories*, like atomic theory and cell theory, are well-substantiated explanations of some aspect of the natural world. A scientific theory provides a unified explanation for many related hypotheses. While a theory is generally widely accepted (e.g., through much of human history people accepted a flat Earth circled by a moving Sun), theories remain open to revision or even replacement should a better, more logical, more comprehensive or compelling explanation be found.

> A *scientific fact* is an observation that has been repeatedly confirmed.
>
> **Fast Facts**

Not all issues of our human experience are subject to the analysis and rigors of scientific experimentation and validation. Our understanding of art, poetry, philosophy, and religion rely on ways of thinking and understanding that are not necessarily subject to repeated validation through the controlled scientific experiment, or which may rely more on personal values or deference to authority. The scientifically literate individual will distinguish the role and value of scientific thought from other ways of knowing, while maintaining respect and appreciation for the ways of thinking and understanding practiced in disciplines outside of science.

Ecology

Our surroundings are a complex, interconnected system in which the living organisms exist in relationship with the soil, water, and air, linked together through chemical and physical processes, and in states of continual change or dynamic equilibrium. *Ecosystem* is the term for all the living and nonliving things in a given environment and how they interact. Scientifically literate individuals are aware of their surroundings, the interdependence of each part, and the effects that man's activities can have on those surroundings. Mutualistic and competitive relationships also exist between the organisms in an ecosystem, defining how organisms rely upon each other, and exist in competition and conflict with each other.

Energy transformations are the driving force within an ecosystem. Many organisms obtain energy from light. For example, light drives the process of photosynthesis in green plants. Solar energy also provides necessary heat for cold-blooded animals. Organisms may also derive energy from other organisms, including other plants and/or animals. When one source of energy is depleted in an ecosystem, many organisms must shift their attention to other sources of energy. For example, a bear will eat berries, fish, or nuts depending on the season. The energy pyramid for an ecosystem illustrates these relationships and identifies those organisms that are most dependent on the other organisms in the system. Higher order organisms cannot survive for long without the other organisms beneath them in the energy pyramid. The availability of adequate food within an ecosystem can be used to explain the system's functioning, the size of an animal's territory, or the effects of over-predation of a single species upon those organisms above it in the food chain.

Ecosystems change over time, both from natural processes and from the activities of man. The scientifically literate individual will be able to identify how the environment changes, how those changes impact the organisms that live there, and recognize the differences between long-term and short-term variation. Natural succession is observed when one community replaces another, for example the colonies of fungus that grow, thrive, and then are replaced by different colonies on rodent droppings held under ideal conditions.

Physical Science

All of physics is either impossible or trivial. It is impossible until you understand it, and then it becomes trivial.

Ernest Rutherford (1871–1937), Physicist, Nobel Prize for Chemistry, 1908

Competency 0010

Understand the principles of physical science (including earth science, chemistry, and physics), and use this understanding to interpret, analyze, and explain phenomena.

The following topics are examples of content that may be covered under this competency.
* Analyze factors and processes related to celestial and atmospheric phenomena (e.g., seasonal changes, the phases of the moon).
* Analyze the forces that shape the earth's surface (e.g., volcanism, erosion).

- Distinguish between physical and chemical properties of matter and between physical and chemical changes in matter.
- Infer the physical science principle (e.g., effects of common forces, conservation of energy) illustrated in a given situation.

Geosphere

Scientifically literate individuals have an understanding and appreciation for the world around them. Rocks hold an early fascination, both for their utility: as objects for throwing, skipping; and also for their beauty, texture, and diversity. Physical landforms vary considerably across the face of the Earth, revealed to the observant and thoughtful eye in road cuts, and the scenic viewpoints everywhere. On a small scale, each puddle, rivulet, and mass of sand and gravel in a yard or parking lot reveals the same actions of erosion, deposition, and graded sorting of material by size and mass that are at work on a global scale to form and reform our physical environment. The scientifically literate individual continually constructs new knowledge by study of the geosphere through direct observation, through photographs, models and samples, and through graphical representations (maps). The geosphere is the source for many natural resources essential for modern life, and the recipient of pollution caused by man's activities.

Evidence of physical changes to the geosphere is abundant, and frequently newsworthy. Each landslide, earthquake, or volcanic eruption reveals something about the Earth and its structures. Fossils, preserved remnants of or marks made by plants and animals that were once alive, are one source of evidence about changes in the environment over time. Finding fossils of marine organisms in what is now a desert is an opportunity to discuss scientific ways of knowing, of how science forms and tests hypotheses, and how theories develop to explain the reasons behind observations. The scientifically literate individual understands the concepts of uncertainty in measurement and the basis of scientific theories. Such an understanding may lead the teacher in an elementary classroom to refer to fossils and rocks simply as "very old," to dinosaurs as "living long ago," and to occasionally preface statements of scientific theory with the observation that "many scientists believe . . ."

Hydrosphere

With about seventy-five percent of the Earth's surface covered with water, the hydrosphere defines our planet and its environment. Most people live near the ocean, but few people live on, or have even experienced, the vast reaches of the world's oceans. Closer to our daily lives, and important because of the fresh water necessary to sustain life and commerce, are the rivers that pass through Oklahoma. The hydrosphere includes not just the surface waters described, but the subsurface waters of aquifers, and the water vapor present in the atmosphere. Man has a significant impact on the hydrosphere through activities that contaminate, divert, and attempt to control the flow of water. These activities can benefit one part of the environment or society while harming another.

The scientific concept of cycle is also used to describe the movement of water through its various phases, and through each part of the environment. A climate chamber formed from discarded polyethylene soda bottles can easily demonstrate these changes, and when soil, plants, and small frogs are added, a nearly complete ecosystem is formed if we count the food we add for the frog each day. In this chamber the student can observe the water cycle as liquid water evaporates, then condenses again against an ice-filled chamber to fall back to the surface. Only two phases, solid and liquid, can be observed directly, since the individual molecules of water vapor are too small to be seen by the naked eye. The white cloud visible at the tip of the teakettle, like our breath when we exhale on a cold winter day and fog, are examples of condensed water vapor (liquid water). The supply of fresh water on the Earth is limited, and water is a reusable resource that must be carefully managed. With this in mind, we are grateful for the technology to treat and purify water, which has done much to extend the human lifespan and reduce disease by providing clean and reliable sources of water in some parts of the world.

Atmosphere

The atmosphere is the layer of gases held close to the Earth by gravitational forces. In size, it has been compared with the skin on an apple. The atmosphere is densest close to the surface, where gravity holds the heavier gases and the pressure is greatest. The atmosphere becomes less dense and pressure decreases exponentially as altitude increases. All weather is contained within the lowest layer of the atmosphere (troposphere) and the temperature decreases as one rises through this layer. We can often observe the top of this layer as clouds form anvil-shaped tops when they cannot rise further than the height of the cold boundary between the lowest layer (troposphere) and the overlying layer (stratosphere).

The concept of cycle reappears in the discussion of the recurring patterns of weather, and the progression of the seasons. The basis of the seasons has much more to do with the angle of light striking the Earth, and very little to do with the distance from the Sun. Classroom weather stations and weather charts are useful learning tools, and projects to build thermometers, hygrometers, and barometers are popular in classrooms.

Density variations related to temperature drive the movement of air. Heat energy warms the air and increases water evaporation, warm air expands and rises above cooler surrounding air, rising air cools and water vapor condenses forming clouds and precipitation. Cold, heavy air settles over the polar caps and flows toward the equator, generally leading to weather trends that bring cold northerly winds into Oklahoma for part of the winter. Temperature gradients and the resulting air movement are readily observed at home where the basement is cool, the upstairs warmer, and a draft is often felt when sitting near the stairway.

Space Science

The concept of cycle again finds application in the periodic movement of the Sun and planets. The size of objects, and distances between them, are difficult to represent on the same scale. The National Mall in Washington, D.C., contains a 1/10,000,000,000th-scale solar system model in which the Sun is the size of a grapefruit, and Pluto, located some 650 yards away, is the size of a poppy seed. The openness of space is mirrored at a much smaller scale by vast open spaces between atoms and between nuclei and their electrons.

A ball rolling down the aisle of a school bus appears, to observers sitting on the bus, to swerve to the right and hit the wall as the bus makes a left-hand turn. To an observer outside the bus, the ball continued its straight-line motion until acted upon by a force, often resulting from a collision with the wall. For centuries the best science available held that the Sun rose in the east and set in the west. As scientific instruments developed and improved (telescopes for example), scientists collected new information that challenged old theories. New theories are not always well received, a fact to which Galileo would attest. We now understand that the Sun is the gravitational center of the solar system, and that the planet's motions are defined by their path along an elliptical orbit defined by its speed and its continual gravitational attraction to the Sun.

Matter and Energy

Broadly speaking, our experiences with the world involve interactions with and between matter and energy. The physical sciences give us a clearer understanding and appreciation of our surroundings and the way we interact with and affect those surroundings. Matter can be described and distinguished by its chemical and physical properties. Physical properties, such as color and density, are termed *intrinsic* when they do not change as the amount of the matter changes. Properties like mass or volume do vary when matter is added or removed, and these are termed "extrinsic properties." Mass is the amount of matter in an object, which is sometimes measured using a lever arm balance. Weight, although sometimes incorrectly used interchangeably with mass, is a measure of the force of gravity experienced by an object, often determined using a spring scale. An electronic scale may display an object's mass in grams, but it is dependant on gravity for its operation. Such a device is only accurate after using a calibration mass to adjust the electronics for the unique local gravitational force. While we may say an object is "weightless" as it floats inside the space shuttle, it is still affected by the gravitational forces from both the Earth and Sun, which keep it in orbit around each. The force of gravity is proportional to the product of the masses of the two objects under consideration divided by the square of the distance between them. Earth, being larger and more massive than Mars, has proportionally higher gravitational forces. This is the basis of the observation in H. G. Wells' *The War of the Worlds* that the Martian invaders were "the most sluggish things I ever saw crawl."

Density, the ratio of mass to volume, is an intrinsic property that depends on the matter, but not the amount of matter. Volume is defined as the amount of space an object occupies. The density of a 5-ton cube of pure copper is the same as that of a small copper penny. However, the modern penny is a thin shell of copper over a zinc plug, and the density of this coin is significantly lower than that of the older pure copper coin. Density is related to buoyancy. Objects sink, in liquids or gases alike, if they are denser than the material that surrounds them. Archimedes' principle, also related to density, states that an object is buoyed up by a force equal to the mass of the material the object displaces. Thus, a 160-lb concrete canoe will easily float in water if the volume of the submerged portion is equal to the volume of 20 gallons of water (water is approximately 8 lbs/gal × 20 gal = 160 lbs). Density is not the same as viscosity, a measure of thickness or flowability. The strength of intermolecular forces between molecules determines, for example, that molasses is slow in January, or that hydrogen bromide is a gas in any season.

All matter is composed of atoms, or combinations of atoms selected from among the more than one hundred elements. The atom is the smallest particle of an element that retains the properties of the element; similarly, the molecule is the smallest particle of a compound. Molecules cannot be separated into smaller particles (atoms or smaller) without a chemical change disrupting the chemical bonds that bind the molecule together. Physical separations, through the use of filter paper, centrifuge, or magnet for example, do not affect chemical bonds. The scientific concept of a cycle, in this case without a time dependence, is evident in the fundamental makeup of matter and reflected in the structure of the periodic table. Mendeleev is credited with the development of the modern periodic table, in part for his predicting the existence of then-unknown elements based on the repeating trends in reactivity and physical properties. The concepts associated with atoms and molecules are not found in the elementary benchmarks, but they should be well understood by the elementary teacher nonetheless, as they provide the basis of all our understanding of matter and chemical change.

Energy is loosely scientifically defined as the ability to do work. Kinetic energy is the energy of motion ($KE = 1/2mv^2$), where m is the mass and v the velocity of an object. Chemical energy is stored in the bonds of our food, held for later conversion to kinetic energy and heat in our bodies. Potential energy is held in an icicle hanging off the roof ($PE = mgh$) where m is mass, g is the gravitational force constant, and h is the height. When the icicle falls, its potential energy is converted to kinetic energy, and then to sound energy as it hits the pavement, and additional kinetic energy as the fragments skitter off. At the elementary level, students need to be able to identify the types of energy involved in various phenomena and identify the conversions between types. In the popular Rube Goldberg competitions, students use a number of sequential energy conversions to perform a simple task like breaking a balloon or flipping a pancake. Energy is conserved in each of these normal processes, converted to less useful forms (e.g., heat) but not created nor destroyed. Similarly, matter is never created or destroyed in a normal chemical reaction. Nuclear fusion is an obvious exception to both rules, following Einstein's equation $E = mc^2$; however, these reactions are generally not allowed in the classroom or school laboratory.

Students gain useful experience with energy conversions as they study simple electrical circuits and chemical dry cells. The dry cell produces electrical energy from chemical potential energy. The size of the dry cell is proportional to the amount of starting material, and thus the available current, but not the electromotive force or voltage, which is an intrinsic property. The D cell produces the same 1.5-volt potential as the AAA cell; the difference is in how long they can maintain the flow of current in the circuit. The battery is dead when when one or more of the starting materials has been depleted, or when the essential electrolytic fluid leaks or dries out. The measured cell voltage depends on the oxidation and reduction potentials and of the half-reactions involved and on the concentration of each chemical species. When a cell reaches equilibrium, the measured cell potential and free energy of the cell both reach zero.

Seldom do we find chemical reactants present in the precise quantities to match the stoichiometric ratio indicated by the chemical equation defining a reaction. In a battery, or any reaction for that matter, one of the chemicals will be depleted before the others. The concept of a limiting reactant is important in chemistry, whereby one reactant is consumed before the other, similar to the summer BBQ where hot dogs are in packages of ten, but the buns are in packages of eight. In contrast, how quickly a battery drains is linked to the rates of chemical reactions (kinetics), dependent on temperature, concentration, and the presence of a catalyst. Many chemical reactions involve multiple steps, where one step, the rate-limiting step, controls the rate of the entire process. This is much like the child in the family who is always the last one to get in the car when everyone else is in a hurry.

Simple dry cells do not pose a serious safety hazard—always an issue in hands-on activities—and are thus good for student experiments. A series connection linking dry cells in a chain increases the overall voltage, and thus the brightness of the bulb, a parallel connection with batteries placed in the circuit (like rungs in a ladder) increases the effective size of the cell but the voltage remains the same.

Changes in Matter

Scientific theories have their utility in providing a unified explanation for diverse and varied observations. Atomic theory, which views atoms and molecules as the fundamental building blocks of all matter, would be modified or abandoned if it didn't also explain other observations. Snow tracked into the kitchen quickly melts before either evaporating or being absorbed into someone's socks, which then must be hung by the fire to dry. In either of these changes the fundamental particles of water are the same, an assembly of three atoms held by covalent (shared electron) bonds in a bent molecular geometry associated with polar molecules. New attractions are possible between polar water molecules and the ions formed when some compounds are dissolved in solution. The relative strength of the new attractions to the water overcomes the attractions within the pure solid, allowing the solid to dissolve and in some cases dissociate in solution. Insoluble compounds do not dissolve because the strength of the attractions within the solid exceeds those available between the molecules and/or ions and the solvent.

Phase changes are also explained using atomic theory. Evaporation from a liquid occurs when individual molecules gain sufficient energy to break free from the intermolecular attractions in the liquid phase. The stronger the intermolecular attractions, the lower the vapor pressure and the higher the boiling point. The boiling point is the temperature at which the vapor pressure of molecules leaving solution equals the atmospheric pressure. Lowering the atmospheric pressure above a liquid makes it easier for the highest energy liquid molecules to escape, thus the boiling point is lower. Cooking while camping at high altitudes requires more time and, thus, more fuel because food cooks slower as a result of the lowered boiling temperature.

All matter has a temperature above the theoretical value of absolute zero because all matter is in continual motion. In a balloon filled with nitrogen gas, some molecules are moving relatively fast, others relatively slowly. The temperature of the gas is a measure of this motion, a measure of the average kinetic energy of the particles. Molecules are very small and fast moving, and there are vast empty spaces between them. The average speed of nitrogen molecules at 25°C is over 500 meters per second, whereas the lighter hydrogen molecules have an average speed in excess of 1,900 meters per second. One cubic centimeter of air at room temperature and normal pressure contains roughly 24,500,000,000,000,000,000 molecules (2.45×10^{19} molecules). The same quantity of water would contain roughly 3.34×10^{22} water molecules, while the same one cubic centimeter of copper would contain roughly 8.5×10^{22} copper atoms. The differences between these numbers are not nearly as large as the numbers themselves, yet the differences are readily observable. Gases have significant empty spaces between the molecules and thus can be compressed, whereas liquids and solids have less or no compressibility, respectively. If air enters the lines of hydraulic brake systems, the pedal depresses easily as the trapped gas compresses instead of having the non-compressible liquid transfer the motion into braking power.

While the atoms and molecules of all materials are in constant motion (vibrational energy), those in gases and liquids are also free to move about their own axes (rotational energy), and about the container (translational energy). Increasing the temperature of a solid imparts additional energy, which increases the vibrational energy. Once any particular atom or molecule gains sufficient energy to break free of the intermolecular attractions to the bulk solid or liquid it will slip or fly away (melt or evaporate, respectively). Hotter atoms require more space in which to vibrate. For this reason wagon wheel rims are heated in the forge to expand the metal before slipping the rim onto the wheel, basketballs left outside on a cold night don't bounce well, and in thermometers the expansion of alcohol or mercury is used to indicate temperature.

Motion

The motion of atoms and molecules is essential to our understanding of matter at the molecular level, but we have many examples of motion readily available on the macroscopic level in the world around us. Many an idle moment can be passed with a young child timing small athletic feats: for example, "How long will it take you to run to that tree and back?" or "The time to beat is 8.65 seconds; who can do it faster?" These experiences provide an informal experience with measurements of motion that serve as the basis for more scientific descriptions of speed, direction and changes of speed.

We can use time and motion to evaluate other chemical and physical phenomena. The periodic motion of a pendulum can be timed to determine the period, and experiments devised to explore the effect of pendulum mass, string length or amount of initial deflection. Hook's law can be studied by timing the vibrations of a spring. Chemical kinetics can be studied by timing reactions and observing changes in absorbance, conductivity, or pH. The growth rates of seedlings can be studied as a function of soil, water, and light conditions. Such activities provide a natural framework to teach the concepts of scientific exploration, control of variables, collection, and presentation of data.

Waves and Vibrations

Waves are one mechanism of energy transport from one location to another. We experience waves directly in the forms of light, sound and water, and indirectly through radio and TV, wireless networks, and X-rays. Waves are periodic in their nature, and the concept of periodicity (cycles) is one of the key interdisciplinary concepts that include the motions of planets, the properties of elements, life cycles of plants and animals, and many other events. Energy is transmitted through a material in a translational wave when in water. For example, particles of water move perpendicular to the direction of energy travel. A wave with greater energy has greater amplitude. AM radio refers to amplitude modulation of the radio signal, where the carrier wave amplitude is modified by adding the amplitudes of the voice or music waves to create a cumulative and more complex wave form. The receiver must subtract from this complex waveform the simple sinusoidal waveform of the carrier to leave the voice or music.

Compressional waves, like sound, are characterized by having the media move along the same axis as the direction of energy travel. The speed of sound waves is dependent on the medium through which it travels, faster in denser materials like railroad track, and faster in water than through air, yet faster in warm air than colder air. Cold air is denser, but the gas molecules in warm air move faster and more quickly convey the sound energy. Sound cannot travel in a vacuum (referring to the absence of all matter in a given space) because, as a compressional wave, it needs to have particles to compress as it travels.

Light is energy, and darkness is the absence of that energy. A shadow is not "cast" by an object, but rather the stream of light energy is blocked by the object, leaving an area of darkness. A black light behaves like any other, giving off light energy, yet at frequencies too high and wavelengths too short for our eyes to see (thus the light appears black to us). Some objects held beneath a black light absorb the energy from the ultraviolet light, and reemit this light at slightly lower wavelengths that our eyes can see, giving them the appearance that they glow in the dark. Laundry soaps with whiteners and brighteners contain additives that do something similar, converting portions of the invisible UV radiation from the Sun into lower frequency near-UV and additional visible light to make your "whites whiter." Since deer are more sensitive to near-UV wavelengths than humans, hunters are careful to launder their camouflage hunting clothes with soaps that do not contain such whiteners.

White light comprises all the visible wavelengths. Color is a property that light already has. White light passing through a prism, raindrop, or spectroscope can be separated into its constituent colors. An object appears red because it, or the dye molecules it contains, reflects the red wavelengths constituent in the white light that strike it. If a red shirt is illuminated by a blue light the shirt will appear black because there is no red light for it to reflect. Blue paint reflects blue light from a white source, and yellow paint reflects yellow. Mixing the paints gives a material that reflects blue and yellow light, and our eye sees the mixture as green. A blue filter placed before a white light allows only the blue light to pass, absorbing all other wavelengths. A red shirt, when viewed through a blue filter, will appear black because the shirt can only reflect red light, but the filter can only pass blue light. The phosphors of our TV screen are in sets of red, green, and blue, which when illuminated together release white light.

Principles and Processes of Scientific Investigations

Happy is he who gets to know the reasons for things.

Virgil (70–19 BCE), Roman poet

Competency 0011

Apply inquiry skills and processes to communicate scientific information and interpret natural phenomena.

The following topics are examples of content that may be covered under this competency.

- Draw conclusions and make generalizations based on examination of given experimental results.
- Interpret data presented in one or more graphs, charts, or tables to determine patterns or relationships.
- Apply mathematical rules or formulas (including basic statistics) to analyze given experimental or observational data.
- Evaluate the appropriateness of different types of graphic representations to communicate given scientific data.

Collecting and Presenting Data

The male has more teeth than the female in mankind, and sheep and goats, and swine. This has not been observed in other animals. Those persons which have the greatest number of teeth are the longest lived; those which have them widely separated, smaller, and more scattered, are generally more short lived.

Aristotle (384–322 BCE), Greek philosopher

Scientifically literate individuals have detailed and accurate content knowledge that is the basis of their scientific knowledge. They do not strive to recall every detail of that knowledge, but build conceptual frameworks upon which prior knowledge, as well as new learning, is added. From this framework of facts, concepts, and theories the scientifically literate individual can reconstruct forgotten facts, and use this information to answer new questions not previously considered. The scientifically literate individual is a lifelong learner who asks questions that can be answered using scientific knowledge and techniques.

Science is based upon experimentation, but not all knowledge is derived daily from first principles. The scientifically literate individual is informed by existing knowledge, and is knowledgeable about the sources, accuracy, and value of each source. Not every source is equally reliable, accurate, or valid. Classroom teachers are advised to use trusted educational sites such as those sponsored by the Oklahoma State Department of Education, which lists links at *www.sde.state.ok.us*.

Scientifically literate individuals must be able to evaluate critically the information and evidence they collect, and the conclusions or theories to which that information and evidence leads. Such analysis incorporates an understanding of the limitations to knowledge in general, and the limitations of all measurements and information based on the quality of the experimental design. The literate individual can evaluate claims for scientific merit, identify conflicting evidence and weigh the value and credibility of conflicting information. They can also recognize that not every question can be answered using scientific knowledge, valuing the contributions of other cultures and other ways of knowing, including art, philosophy, and theology.

Scientific information is communicated to nonscientific audiences in order to inform, guide policy and influence the practices that affect all of society. This information is presented through text, tables, charts, figures, pictures, models, and other representations that require interpretation and analysis. Scientifically literate individuals can read and interpret these representations, and select appropriate tools to present the information they gather.

Competency 0012

> **Understand principles and procedures related to the design and implementation of observational and experimental scientific investigations.**
>
> The following topics are examples of content that may be covered under this competency.
> *   Distinguish among the features of a given experimental design (e.g., dependent and independent variables, control and experimental groups).
> *   Formulate hypotheses based on reasoning and preliminary results or information.
> *   Evaluate the validity of a scientific conclusion in a given situation.
> *   Apply procedures for the care and humane treatment of animals and the safe and appropriate use of equipment in the laboratory.

Experimental Design

> *It is a capital mistake to theorise before one has data. Insensibly one begins to twist facts to suit theories instead of theories to suit facts.*
>
> Sherlock Holmes, the fictional creation of Arthur Conan Doyle (1859–1930), British physician and novelist

When a bat bites Gilligan, first mate of TV's ill-fated *S.S. Minnow*, he is convinced that he will turn into a vampire. Seemingly, no amount of reassurance by the Professor will convince him otherwise because, he claims, he saw the movie three times and it always came out the same way. We trust the results of experiments, both formal and informal, to help us understand our surroundings. Unfortunately, without proper control of the variables and a sound experimental design, our observations may lead us to entirely wrong-headed or incorrect conclusions.

Scientific Method

The scientific method is not a specific six-step method that is rigorously followed whenever a question arises that can be answered using the knowledge and techniques of science. Rather, it is a process of observation and analysis that is used to develop a reliable, consistent, and nonarbitrary representation and understanding of our world. We can use the scientific method (observation and description, formulation of hypotheses, prediction based on hypotheses, and tests of predictions) for many, but not all questions. The approach is best applied to situations in which the experimenter can control the variables, eliminating or accounting for all extraneous factors, and perform repeated independent tests wherein only one variable is changed at a time.

The science fair project is a common tool for instruction in the scientific method. Many formal and informal sources, often Web based, provide lists of suggested science fair topics, but not all are experiments. For the youngest students it is appropriate and useful for the focus to be upon models and demonstrations, for example the solar system model, volcano, or clay cross-section of an egg. Later the students should move to true experiments where the focus is on identifying a testable hypothesis, and controlling all experimental variables but the one of interest. Many projects may be elevated from model or demonstration to experiment. A proposal to demonstrate how windmills work can be made an experiment when the student adds quantitative measurements designed to measure one variable while varying only one other and while holding all other variables constant. For example, using an electric fan, the number of rotations per minute can be measured as a function of the fan setting (low, medium, or high). However, while keeping the fan setting constant, several different experiments could vary any one of the following variables: number of fins, size of fins, or shape of fins while in each case measuring the rotational speed.

Health and Safety

Through active, hands-on activities, science instruction is made a richer and more meaningful experience. From simple observations and activities at early grades, through detailed controlled experiments at higher grades, students who do science to learn science understand science better. While students are engaged in the process of discovery and exploration, the teacher must be engaged in protecting the health and safety of these students. The hazards vary with the discipline, and thoughtful planning and management of the activities will significantly reduce the risks to students. In all cases, students must utilize appropriate personal hygiene (hand washing) and wear personal protective equipment (goggles, gloves) while engaged in laboratory or field activities. Substitution of less hazardous materials whenever possible is a high priority. For example, in the physical sciences, replace mercury thermometers with alcohol or electronic, replace glass beakers and graduated cylinders with durable polyethylene, and eliminate or reduce the use of hazardous chemicals. In the earth sciences, rocks and minerals used in class should not contain inherently hazardous materials, students should not be allowed to taste the minerals, and reagents like HCl used for identification of carbonate minerals should be dispensed from spill-proof plastic containers. In the life sciences, special care should be given to topics such as safe practices for sharps, the safe handling of living organisms, and the care and use of microscopes. Experiments or activities involving the collection or culture of human cells or fluids should be discouraged, and proper sterilization procedures followed to prevent the growth or spread of disease agents. When they are possible, outdoor, museum, and other field activities can bring a valuable enrichment to the science curriculum in all disciplines. They also bring additional responsibilities for the safe planning and implementation of activities that increase student learning while maintaining the health and safety of the students.

Chapter 13

Health and Fitness

Competency 0013

Understand basic principles and practices of personal, interpersonal, and community health and safety; and apply related attitudes, knowledge, and skills (e.g., decision making, problem solving) to promote personal well-being.

The following topics are examples of content that may be covered under this competency.

- Apply decision-making and problem-solving skills and procedures in individual and group situations, including situations related to personal well-being, self-esteem, and interpersonal relationships.
- Analyze contemporary health-related problems (e.g., HIV, teenage pregnancy, suicide, substance abuse) in terms of their causes and effects on individuals, families, and society; and evaluate strategies for their prevention.
- Analyze the effects of specific practices (e.g., related to nutrition, exercise) and attitudes on lifelong personal health.
- Analyze relationships between environmental conditions and personal and community health and safety.

Competency 0014

Understand physical education concepts and practices related to the development of personal well-being.

The following topics are examples of content that may be covered under this competency.

- Recognize activities that promote the development of motor skills (e.g., locomotor, manipulative, body mechanics), perceptual awareness skills (e.g., body awareness, spatial and directional awareness), and fitness (e.g., endurance, flexibility).
- Apply safety concepts and practices associated with physical activities (e.g., doing warm-up exercises, wearing protective equipment).
- Understand skills necessary for successful participation in given sports and activities (e.g., dodging, spatial orientation, eye-body coordination).
- Analyze ways in which participation in individual or group sports or physical activities can promote personal well-being (e.g., self-discipline, respect for self and others) and interpersonal skills (e.g., cooperation, leadership).

The health and physical education review section offers a perspective on the importance of maintaining a healthy mind and body as well as demonstrating how the two work in conjunction. This section includes discussions of cardiovascular fitness, nutrition, team sports, and the role of athletics. Preparing your mind through study will leave you in great shape to succeed on test day.

Health and Safety

Benefits of Diet and Exercise

One of the primary reasons for teaching physical education is to instill a willingness to exercise. To that end, it is important to understand the benefits of participating in a lifelong program of exercise and physical fitness.

Fortunately, it is not difficult to find justification for exercising and maintaining a consistently high level of fitness. The benefits of a consistent program of diet and exercise are many. Improved cardiac output, improved maximum oxygen intake, and improvement of the blood's ability to carry oxygen are just a few. Exercise also lowers the risk of heart disease by strengthening the heart muscle, lowering pulse and blood pressure, and lowering the concentration of fat in both the body and the blood. It can also improve appearance, increase range of motion, and lessen the risk of back problems associated with weak bones and osteoporosis.

Good Nutrition

Along with exercise, a knowledge of and participation in a healthy lifestyle are vital to good health and longevity. What constitutes good nutrition, the role of vitamins, elimination of risk factors, and strategies to control weight are all part of a healthy lifestyle.

Complex carbohydrates should constitute at least half the diet. This is important because these nutrients are the primary and most efficient source of energy. Examples of complex carbohydrates are vegetables, fruits, high-fiber breads, and cereals. Fiber in the diet is very important because it promotes digestion, reduces constipation, and has been shown to help reduce the risk of colon cancer. Another benefit of complex carbohydrates is that they are high in water content, which is vital to the functioning of the entire body.

Proteins should constitute about one-fifth of the diet. Protein builds and repairs the body. Sources of protein are beans, peas, lentils, peanuts, and other pod plants. Another source is red meat, which unfortunately contains a great deal of saturated fat.

There are two categories of fat: unsaturated, which is found in vegetables, and saturated, which comes from animals or vegetables. Cocoa butter, palm oil, and coconut oil are saturated fats that come from vegetables. Unsaturated vegetable fats are preferable to saturated fats because they appear to offset the rise in blood pressure that accompanies too much saturated fat. These fats may also lower cholesterol and help with weight loss. Whole milk products contain saturated fat, but the calcium found in them is vital to health. For this reason, most fat-limiting diets suggest the use of skim milk and low-fat cheese.

Research indicates a link between high-fat diets and many types of cancer. Diets high in saturated fats are also dangerous because fats cause the body to produce too much low-density lipoprotein in the system. Cholesterol, a substance found only in animals, is of two different kinds: LDL (low-density lipoproteins) and HDL (high-density lipoproteins). Some cholesterol is essential in order for the body to function properly. It is vital to the brain and is an important component in the creation of certain hormones. LDLs raise the probability of heart disease by encouraging the buildup of plaque in the arteries. HDLs do just the opposite. LDL can be controlled through proper diet, and HDL cholesterol levels can be raised by exercise. The body produces cholesterol in the liver. Excess cholesterol found in the blood of so many people usually comes from cholesterol in their diet rather than from internal production. Triglycerides are another form of fat found in the blood. It is important to monitor them because high triglycerides seem to be inversely proportional to HDLs.

Vitamins and Minerals

Vitamins are essential to good health. One must be careful, however, not to take too much of certain vitamins. Fat soluble vitamins—A, D, E, and K—will be stored in the body, and excessive amounts will cause some dangerous side effects. The remaining vitamins are water soluble and are generally excreted through the urinary system and the skin when taken in excess. A brief synopsis of the vitamins and minerals needed by the body follows:

- Vitamin A: Needed for normal vision, prevention of night blindness, healthy skin, resistance to disease, and tissue growth and repair. Found in spinach, carrots, broccoli and other dark green or yellow orange fruits and vegetables; also found in liver and plums.

- Vitamin D: Promotes absorption of calcium and phosphorus, and needed for normal growth of healthy bones, teeth, and nails. Formed by the action of the sun on the skin.

Also found in halibut liver oil, herring, cod liver oil, mackerel, salmon, and tuna, and is added to many milk products.

- Vitamin E: Protects cell membranes; seems to improve elasticity in blood vessels; also may prevent formation of blood clots and protect red blood cells from damage by oxidation. Found in wheat germ oil, sunflower seeds, raw wheat germ, almonds, pecans, peanut oil, and cod liver oil.

- Thiamin/B_1: Needed for functioning of nerves, muscle growth, and fertility and for production of energy, appetite, and digestion. Found in pork, legumes, nuts, enriched and fortified whole grains, and liver.

- Riboflavin/B_2: Aids in the production of red blood cells, good vision, healthy skin and mouth tissue, and production of energy. Found in lean meat, dairy products, liver, eggs, enriched and fortified whole grains, and green leafy vegetables.

- Niacin/B_3: Promotes energy production, appetite, healthy digestive and nervous system, and healthy skin.

- Pyridoxine/B_6: Promotes red blood cell formation and growth. Found in liver, beans, pork, fish, legumes, enriched and fortified whole grains, and green leafy vegetables.

- Vitamin B_{12}: Promotes healthy nerve tissue, energy production, utilization of folic acid; also aids in the formation of healthy red blood cells. Found in dairy products, liver, meat, poultry, fish, and eggs.

- Vitamin C: Promotes healing and growth, resists infection, increases iron absorption, and aids in bone and tooth formation/repair. Found in citrus fruits, cantaloupe, potatoes, strawberries, tomatoes, and green vegetables.

- Sodium: Maintains normal water balance inside and outside cells; is a factor in blood pressure regulation and electrolyte and chemical balance. Found in salt, processed foods, bread, and bakery products.

- Potassium: Prevents muscle weakness and cramping; important for normal heart rhythm and electrolyte balance in the blood. Found in citrus fruits, leafy green vegetables, potatoes, and tomatoes.

- Zinc: Taste, appetite, healthy skin, and wound healing. Found in lean meat, liver, milk, fish, poultry, whole grain cereals, and shellfish.

- Iron: Red blood cell formation, oxygen transport to the cells; prevents nutritional anemia. Found in liver, lean meats, dried beans, peas, eggs, dark green leafy vegetables, and whole grain cereals.

- Calcium: Strong bones, teeth, nails, muscle tone; prevents osteoporosis and muscle cramping; helps the nerves function and the heart beat. Found in milk, yogurt, and other dairy products, and dark leafy vegetables.

- Phosphorus: Regulates blood chemistry and internal processes; helps build strong bones and teeth. Found in meat, fish, poultry, and dairy products.

- Magnesium: Energy production, normal heart rhythm, nerve/muscle function; prevents muscle cramps. Found in dried beans, nuts, whole grains, bananas, and leafy green vegetables.

Weight Control Strategies

Statistics show that Americans get fatter every year. Even though countless books and magazine articles are written on the subject of weight control, often the classroom is the only place a student gets reliable information about diet. For example, it is an unfortunate reality that fat people do not live as long, on average, as thin ones. Being overweight has been isolated as a risk factor in various cancers, heart disease, gall bladder problems, and kidney disease. Chronic diseases such as diabetes and high blood pressure are also aggravated by, or caused by, being overweight.

Conversely, a great many problems are presented by being underweight. Our society often places too much value on losing weight, especially for women. Ideal weight as well as a good body-fat ratio is the goal when losing weight. Exercise is the key to a good body-fat ratio. Exercise helps to keep the ratio down, thus improving cholesterol levels, and helps in preventing heart disease.

In order to lose weight, calories burned must exceed calories taken in. No matter what kind of diet is tried, this principle applies. There is no easy way to maintain a healthy weight. Here again, the key is exercise. If calorie intake is restricted too much, the body goes into starvation mode and operates by burning fewer calories. Just a 250-calorie drop per day combined with a 250-calorie burn will result in a loss of one pound a week. Crash diets, which bring about rapid weight loss, are not only unhealthy but also ineffective. Slower weight loss is more lasting. Aerobic exercise is the key to successful weight loss. Exercise speeds up metabolism and causes the body to burn calories. Timing of exercise will improve the benefits. Exercise before meals speeds up metabolism and has been shown to suppress appetite. Losing and maintaining weight is not easy. Through education, people will be better able to realize that losing weight is hard work and is a constant battle.

Another aspect of health concerns awareness and avoidance of the health risks that are present in our everyday lives. Some risk factors include being overweight, smoking, using drugs, having unprotected sex, and stress. Students should learn the consequences of using drugs, both legal and illegal, and they should learn at least one of the several ways to reduce stress that are commonly used in most elementary schools. Education is the key to minimizing the presence of these risk factors. Unfortunately, because of the presence of peer pressure and the lack of parental control, the effect of education is sometimes not enough.

Family Health

The role of the family in health education deserves special consideration. The "family" includes people who provide unconditional love, understanding, long-term commitment, and encouragement. Variations in family living patterns in our society include, for example, nuclear and extended families, single-parent families, and blended families. Children from all types of families deserve equal consideration and respect; they should get it at least in the classroom, because they often do not in the larger society.

Community Health

The health of students and their families depends not only on individual and family decisions, but on the factors involving the wider society. One of these factors is advertising, which often encourages children to make unhealthy decisions. Students as young as kindergarten and first grade can learn how to recognize advertisements (e.g., for candy or sugar-laden cereal) that might lead them to unhealthy behavior, and by third or fourth grade, they should be able to demonstrate that they are able to make health-related decisions regarding advertisements in various media.

In addition, any studies of the physical environment—in science, social studies, or other subjects—should be related to health whenever possible. Examples include the effects of pollution on health, occupational-related disease (e.g., "black lung" disease and the effects of chemicals on soldiers), and the differences in health care options available to people in different parts of the world and in different economic circumstances.

Differentiation between communicable and noncommunicable disease can be taught at the youngest grade levels. Very young children should learn to wash their hands frequently, for instance. Older children should be able to explain the transmission and prevention of communicable disease, and all children should learn which diseases cannot be transmitted through casual contact.

Movement and Physical Fitness

Principles of Cardiovascular Fitness

Cardiovascular fitness, or aerobic capacity, is the ability of the entire body to work together efficiently—to be able to do the most amount of work with the least amount of effort. Cardiovascular fitness is composed of four basic components: strength and power; endurance; movement speed and flexibility; and agility. Training is required to develop consistent aerobic capacity, and training is composed of several principles. To begin, a warm-up is essential. An effective warm-up will increase body temperature and blood flow, and it will guard against strains and tears to muscles, tendons, and ligaments. A good warm-up consists of stretching exercises, calisthenics, walking, and slow jogging. Although children have trouble understanding the importance of warm-up, they should get into the habit of doing it, because it will be particularly important as they grow older.

While exercising, a student must be aware of his or her body's adaptations to the demands imposed by training. Some of these adaptations are improved heart function and circulation, improved respiratory function, and improved strength and endurance. All of these lead to improved vigor and vitality. In order to effect these adaptations, the students must exert themselves to a far greater degree than their normal daily activities. This exertion is referred to as *overload*. Despite what this term suggests, it does not imply that children should work beyond healthy limits. However, it does imply that they must push themselves in order to see results. The rate of improvement and adaptation is directly related to the frequency, intensity, and duration of training.

In addition to regular training, you must gear your students' training toward those adaptations that are important to them. This is known as *specificity*. Performance improves when the training is specific to the activity being performed. That is, certain activities will have more effect on cardiovascular health than on overall muscle tone and appearance, and vice versa. Therefore, you should always try to maintain a balance in the exercise you assign.

The body thrives on activity, and therefore the axiom "use it or lose it" certainly holds true. Lack of activity can cause many problems, including flabby muscles, a weak heart, poor circulation, shortness of breath, obesity, and a degenerative weakening of the skeletal system. It is important to note, however, that when many people begin a program of exercise, they expect to see results immediately. More often than not, this is not the case. Individual response to exercise varies greatly from person to person. This can be affected by heredity, age, general cardiovascular fitness, rest and sleep habits, an individual's motivation, environmental influences, and any handicap, disease, or injury that may impede the body's adaptation to training. The sum of all these factors is an individual's potential for maximizing their own cardiovascular fitness. Unfortunately, very few people live up to this full potential.

Finally, a good program of exercise always ends with a cooling-off period. Very much like the warm-up, and just as essential, the same low-impact exercises used during a warm-up may be used to cool off after a period of intense exertion. Without cooling off, blood will pool and slow the removal of waste products. With this basic introduction in mind, let's look at some more specific forms of exercise and the positive effects they have on the body.

Aerobic Exercise

Aerobic exercise involves both muscle contraction and movement of the body. Aerobic exercise requires large amounts of oxygen and, when done regularly, will condition the cardiovascular system. Some aerobic exercises are especially suited to developing aerobic training benefits, with a minimum of skill and time involved. Examples of good aerobic activities are walking, running, swimming, rope skipping, and bicycling. These activities are especially good in the development of fitness because all of them can be done alone and with a minimum of special equipment. In order to be considered true aerobic conditioning, an activity must require a great deal of oxygen, must be continuous and rhythmic, must exercise major muscle groups and burn fat as an energy source, and must last for at least 20 minutes at an individual's target heart rate. You may determine the target heart rate by subtracting 80% of your age from 220 for adolescents; healthy younger children do not need to be restricted to an arbitrary limit on heart rate during exercise.

Interval training is also a good way to develop fitness. This type of exercise involves several different aerobic activities performed at intervals to create one exercise session. If a student learns about interval training, she will be better able to create her own fitness program.

Low-Impact Aerobics

For some people, low-impact aerobics may have some advantages over traditional, or high-impact, aerobics. Because low-impact aerobic exercise is easier to perform, it is an option for all ages and levels of fitness. It is easier to monitor heart rate, and there is less warm-up and cool-down required. Because one foot is on the ground at all times, there is less chance of injury. In all other respects, such as duration and frequency, low-impact aerobic exercise is identical to high-impact.

Anatomy and Physiology

Anatomy describes the structure, position, and size of various organs. Because our bones adapt to fill a specific need, exercise is of great benefit to the skeletal system. Bones that anchor strong muscles thicken to withstand the stress. Weight-bearing bones can develop heavy mineral deposits while supporting the body. Because joints help provide flexibility and ease of movement, it is important to know how each joint moves. Types of joints are ball and socket (shoulder and hip), hinge (knee), pivot (head of the spine), gliding (carpal and tarsal bones), angular (wrist and ankle joints), partially moveable (vertebrae), and immovable (bones of the adult cranium).

Muscles are the active movers in the body. In order to teach any physical education activity properly, the functions and physiology of the muscles must be understood. Since muscles move by shortening, or contracting, proper form should be taught so the student can get the most out of an activity. It is also important to know the location of each muscle. This knowledge will help in teaching proper form while doing all physical education activities. Understanding the concept of antagonistic muscles, along with the related information concerning flexors and extensors, is also vital to the physical educator. Imagine trying to teach the proper form of throwing a ball if you do not understand the mechanics involved. Knowledge of anatomy and physiology is also necessary to teach proper techniques used in calisthenics as well as in all physical activities. Some physical education class standbys are frequently done improperly or done when the exercise itself can cause harm. Examples of these are squat thrusts, straight-leg sit-ups, straight-leg toe touches, straight-leg push-ups for girls, and double leg lifts.

Sports and Games

Individual, dual, and team sports all have a prominent place in a successful physical education curriculum. Since one of the attributes of a quality physical education program is its carryover value, it is easy to justify the inclusion of these activities in a curriculum. Learning the rules and keeping score supplies a framework for goals and for learning how to deal with both victory and defeat. Here are examples of some sports and games that are useful to achieve the aforementioned goals:

Team Sports

- Volleyball—six players, two out of three games. Winner scores 25 points with a margin of 2.

- Basketball—five players. Most points at the end of the game wins.

- Softball—9 or 10 players. Most runs at the end of seven innings wins.

- Field hockey—11 players. Most goals wins.

- Soccer—11 players. Most goals wins.

- Flag football—9 or 11 players (can be modified to fit ability and size of the class). Six points for a touchdown, one or two for a point after, and two for a safety.

Dual Sports

- Tennis—Either doubles or singles. Four "points"—15, 30, 40, and game. Tie at forty—deuce. Winner must win by a margin of two. Remember, *love* means zero points in tennis.

- Badminton—Either doubles or singles. 15 points (doubles) or 21 (singles) by a margin of 2.

- Table tennis—Either doubles or singles. 21 points by a margin of 2.

- Shuffleboard—Either singles or doubles. 50, 75, or 100 points, determined by participants before the game begins.

Individual Sports

- Swimming—Very good for cardiovascular conditioning and can be done almost anywhere there is water.

- Track and field—Scoring varies with event.

- Bowling—Scoring is unique; good math skills are encouraged.

- Weight training—No scoring involved, but the benefits are many. Muscles are toned and strengthened through the use of weight training. Either weight machines or free weights can be used. It is important for students to learn the proper techniques and principles of weight training so they can reap the benefits while avoiding injury. When weight training, participants must consider the concept of muscular balance—this is equal strength in opposing muscle groups. All opposing groups (antagonistic muscles), i.e., triceps and biceps, hamstrings and quadriceps, need to be equal or body parts may become improperly aligned. The responsibility of the physical educator is to teach accurate information about the human body as well as teach ways to prevent injury and achieve efficiency in movement. Understanding that abdominal strength is important to lower back strength can help students create an exercise program to help avoid back injuries.

- Gymnastics—Includes tumbling. Excellent activity for developing coordination and grace. Also requires strength, which is developed by the activities done. This training can begin at a very early age with tumbling activities and progress to gymnastics.

- Golf—A fantastic carryover activity that can be taught on campus, at the golf course, or both. Requires coordination, concentration, and depth perception.

- Rhythmics—Includes ball gymnastics and other activities that may require music. Rhythmics can be taught in early elementary physical education, enabling students to develop music appreciation as well as spatial awareness.

- Dance—Can be done either individually or with a partner. Dance is especially good at developing spatial awareness and the ability to follow instructions. Dance instruction should begin in elementary school. Basic steps are walk and/or skip and are suitable to teach to first and second graders. Skip, slide, and/or run are suitable for second and third graders. The more difficult step-hop can be taught to grades 3 through 6. The ability to dance can also aid in the development of social skills and teamwork. The instructor must be careful not to teach too many steps before the dance is tried with the music. Most students enjoy dance in spite of themselves.

Adaptive Physical Education

Public Law 94-142 provides the legal definition for the term "handicapped children." It includes children who have been evaluated as being mentally impaired, deaf, speech impaired, visually handicapped, emotionally disturbed, orthopedically impaired, multi-handicapped, having learning disabilities, or having other health impairments (anemia, arthritis, etc.). PL 94-142 states that these children need special education and services. The challenge in teaching physical education to handicapped children is tailoring activities to fit each child. For example, blind or partially sighted students can participate in weight lifting, dance, and some gymnastic and tumbling activities. These students can also participate in some other activities with modifications. A beeper ball can be used for softball; a beeper can be used for archery. If a beeper is not available for archery, the teacher can put the student in position and assist in aiming. Many games and activities can be modified for the handicapped. Sometimes all it takes is a little ingenuity to change activities so that handicapped students can enjoy participating.

There are many students who are only temporarily disabled who will benefit from adaptive physical education. Examples of temporary disabilities are pregnancy, broken bones, and recovery from surgery and disease.

Movement Education

Movement education is the process by which a child is helped to develop competency in movement. It has been defined as "learning to move and moving to learn." Movement competency requires the student to manage his or her body. This body management is necessary to develop both basic and specialized activities. Basic skills are needed by the child for broad areas of activity that are related to daily living and child's play. Specialized skills are required to perform sports and have very clear techniques. Basic skills must be mastered before the child can develop specialized ones. The child controls his movement during nonlocomotor (stationary) activities, in movements across the floor or field, through space, and when suspended on an apparatus. To obtain good body management skills is to acquire, expand, and integrate elements of motor control. This is done through wide experiences in movement, based on a creative and exploratory approach. It is important that children not only manage the body with ease of movement but also realize that good posture and body mechanics are important parts of their movement patterns.

Perceptual motor competency is another consideration in body management. Perceptual motor concepts that are relevant to physical education include those that give attention to balance, coordination, lateral movement, directional movement, awareness of space, and knowledge of one's own body. Basic skills can be divided into three categories: locomotor, nonlocomotor, and manipulative skills. A movement pattern might include skills from each category.

Locomotor skills involve moving the body from place to place: walking, running, skipping, leaping, galloping, and sliding. Skills that move the body upward, such as jumping or hopping, are also locomotor skills.

Nonlocomotor skills are done in place or with very little spatial movement. Examples of nonlocomotor skills are bending and stretching, pushing and pulling, raising and lowering, twisting and turning, and shaking and bouncing.

Manipulative skills are skills used when the child handles a play object. Most manipulative skills involve using the hands and the feet, but other parts of the body may be used as well. Hand-eye and foot-eye coordination are improved with manipulative objects. Throwing, batting, kicking, and catching are important skills to be developed using balls and beanbags. Starting a child at a low level of challenge and progressing to a more difficult activity is an effective method for teaching manipulative activities. Most activities begin with individual practice and later move to partner activities. Partners should be of similar ability. When teaching throwing and catching, the teacher should emphasize skill performance, principles of opposition, weight transfer, eye focus, and follow-through. Some attention should be given to targets when throwing because students need to be able to catch and throw to different levels. Reaching is a "point-to-point" arm movement that is very common in our daily activities. In fact, reaching and grasping are typically used together to serve a number of purposes, such as eating, drinking, dressing, or cooking. The reaching/grasping task requires an "eye-hand" coordination and control of movement timing for a successful attempt.

Specialized skills are related to various sports and other physical education activities such as dance, tumbling, gymnastics, and specific games. To teach a specialized skill, the instructor must use explanation, demonstration, and drill. Demonstration can be done by other students, provided the teacher monitors the demonstration and gives cues for proper form. Drills are excellent to teach specific skills but can become tedious unless they are done in a creative manner. Using game simulations to practice skills is an effective method to maintain interest during a practice session.

Teachers must always remember to use feedback when teaching a skill or activity. Positive feedback is much more conducive to skill learning than negative feedback. Feedback means correcting with suggestions to improve. If a student continually hits the ball into the net while playing tennis, he or she is aware that something is not right. The teacher should indicate what the problem is and tell the student how to succeed in getting the ball over the net.

Movement education enables the child to make choices of activity and the method they wish to employ. Teachers can structure learning situations so the child can be challenged to develop his or her own means of movement. The child becomes the center of learning and is encouraged to be creative in carrying out the movement experience. In this method of teaching, the child is encouraged to be creative and progress according to her abilities. The teacher is not the center of learning, but suggests and stimulates the learning environment. Student-centered learning works especially well when there is a wide disparity of motor abilities. If the teacher sets standards that are too high for the less talented students, they may become discouraged and not try to perform.

Basic movement education attempts to develop the children's awareness not only of what they are doing but also how they are doing it. Each child is encouraged to succeed in his or her own way according to his or her own capacity. If children succeed at developing basic skills in elementary school, they will have a much better chance at acquiring the specialized skills required for all sports activities.

Psychological and Social Aspects of Physical Education

Physical education is a very important part of a student's elementary school education. It is not only an opportunity to "blow off steam," but it is also an arena of social interaction. One psychological aspect of physical education is the enhancement of self-esteem. Often students who have limited success in other classes can "shine" in physical education. This does not happen automatically; it is up to the teacher to create situations that enable students to gain self-esteem.

Teachers must also be careful not to damage self-esteem. An example of a potentially damaging situation occurs during the exercise of choosing members of a team. Teachers should not have captains choose the teams in front of the whole class. Nothing is more demeaning than to be the last person chosen. A better method is for the teacher to select the captains (this is also a very good way to separate the superstars: have the six best athletes be the captains). The captains then go to the sidelines and pick the teams from a class list. The teacher can then post or read the team lists after mixing up the order chosen so that no one knows who were the first and last picked.

From a developmental perspective, considerable research evidence suggests that children's participation in exercise or sports results in a number of long-term benefits, including the improvement of self-esteem, or self-confidence for social interactions; the development of sport leadership and sportsmanship; and motivation for participating in lifetime physical activities.

Chapter 14

Fine Arts

SUBAREA IV—FINE ARTS

Competency 0015

Understand concepts, techniques, and materials associated with the visual arts; analyze works of visual art; and understand the cultural dimensions of the visual arts.

The following topics are examples of content that may be covered under this competency.

- Apply knowledge of basic tools, techniques, and technologies in creating different types of artwork.
- Analyze how the illusion of space is created in a given two-dimensional work of art (e.g., linear perspective, overlapping elements).
- Analyze a given two-dimensional or three-dimensional work of art in terms of its unifying elements.
- Analyze how given works of art reflect the cultures that produced them.

Competency 0016

Understand concepts, techniques, and materials for producing, listening to, and responding to music; analyze works of music; and understand the cultural dimensions of music.

The following topics are examples of content that may be covered under this competency.

- Compare various types of instruments (e.g., percussion, woodwind, computerized) in terms of the sounds they produce.
- Apply common musical terms (e.g., pitch, tempo).

- Relate characteristics of music (e.g., rhythm, beat) to musical effects produced.
- Analyze how different cultures have created music reflective of their own histories and societies (e.g., call-and-response songs, ballads, work songs).

Competency 0017

Understand concepts, techniques, and materials related to theater and dance; analyze works of drama and dance; and understand the cultural dimensions of drama and dance.

The following topics are examples of content that may be covered under this competency.
- Compare dramatic and theatrical forms and their characteristics (e.g., pantomime, improvisation).
- Analyze how technical aspects of drama (e.g., the use of masks, costumes, props) affect the message or overall impression created by a dramatic performance.
- Relate types of dance (e.g., ballet, folk dance) to their characteristic forms of movement, expressive qualities, and cultural roles.
- Analyze ways in which different cultures have used drama and dance (e.g., to teach moral lessons, to preserve cultural traditions, to affirm a sense of community, to entertain).

Visual Arts

Why We Create Visual Art

Visual Communication

At its most fundamental level, art—be it opera, ballet, painting, or pantomime—is a form of communication. The realm of visual art encompasses many forms of communication, including sculpture, painting and drawing, ceramics, performance art, printmaking, jewelry, fiber art, photography, and film and video. Each medium or field of specialization communicates differently than the others. Take, for instance, the difference between viewing a sculpture and a tapestry. Sculpture (in the round) requires the viewer to physically move around in space to comprehend the work, whereas a tapestry can generally be viewed from a stationary position. Sculpture is three-dimensional, encompassing height, width, and depth, whereas a tapestry is two-dimensional, encompassing only height and width. While both forms of art can have a strong visual presence, sculpture is unique in that it has the capacity to be fully physically engaging in actual space. Artists choose different disciplines and media because each method and medium has its own communicative potential.

Aesthetics

As viewers, we can be affected by visual art in ways that are difficult to define. The powerful experience of encountering, for example, a huge carved Olmec head sculpture in an outdoor garden in Villahermosa, Mexico, or contemplating a quiet, delicate Vermeer painting in The Hague, Netherlands, is sometimes termed an aesthetic moment or experience. We may try to put into words the experience of these moments—beautiful, colossal, overwhelming, transcendental—but the words often seem inadequate. What the art is communicating is perhaps hard to verbalize, but the feeling is undeniable. As viewers, we are momentarily transported so that we are no longer aware of our surroundings or ourselves. When art communicates to us in such a direct and forceful way, we consider this an aesthetic experience.

Although aesthetics has long been recognized as the branch of philosophy pertaining to beauty, it is impossible to find agreement on what is beautiful. In keeping with the root of the word, aesthetics can be understood more as a study of sensation or feeling than of beauty. This broader understanding of aesthetics has the ability to encompass the range of sensations that one can experience in viewing a work of art. Art is not always beautiful in the traditional sense of the word, and our aesthetic philosophies must be able to encompass this reality.

Current Tendencies in Visual Art

Visual art, like other forms of communication, has the capacity to convey the complexity of issues, ideas, and feelings. What generally (and traditionally) distinguishes visual art from the other disciplines in the arts is the emphasis on the visual. However, there are numerous visual artists who work entirely in sound, for example. What, then, is the factor that distinguishes visual artists from experimental sound artists, video artists from cinematographers, and performance artists from actors or dancers? The categories that distinguish one discipline from another are becoming increasingly blurred. While the traditional areas of fine art study (namely music, theatre, dance, and visual art) still exist, many artists today are what we term *interdisciplinary*. These artists are often conversant with different art disciplines while maintaining an identity in their primary field of study. The interdisciplinary crossover of art forms has opened up many exciting possibilities for music, theatre, dance, and visual art. Indeed, interdisciplinary art has the potential to capture the complexities of our present world differently than was previously possible.

Understanding Art

The Role of Visual Art in Society

From the earliest cave paintings to the most recent art installations, visual art has functioned as a form of commentary on the society from which it springs; consequently, visual art is continually changing. Over the millennia, visual art has played (and continues to play) a key role in the dissemination of aesthetic tendencies, political ideas, religious and spiritual doctrines, cultural beliefs and critiques, and societal norms and trends. Conversely, visual art has changed and adapted to these same influences. In essence, visual art has the capacity to both shape and be shaped by the society in which it exists.

Visual art has also served the vital role of empowering the artist in his or her subject matter. For example, there has been broad speculation about the functions of the animal imagery that adorns the caves of France and Spain: Some suggest that the act of representing the animals gave the creator power over the creature or the creature's soul, while others have postulated that these artistic gestures were an early form of inventory—a means to count, organize, and track the myriad animals that existed in the outside world.

The function of art as an empowering tool is as vital today as it was in past millennia. Much like the cave painters of the past, contemporary artists often use their art as a means to chart and order the complexities, wonders, and inspirations of the present-day world.

Anonymous Artist

Fast Facts The earliest examples of art known to us date back to about 40,000 BCE, and the majority of this art remains anonymous to us.

The earliest examples of art known to us date back to about 40,000 BCE, and the majority of this art remains anonymous to us. For example, all of the extant art from Egypt, of which thousands of examples survive, was created anonymously, in service to the pharaohs, gods, and society of the artists. There are instances of work crews having inscribed their names on the pyramids; however, since the form, subject matter, and imagery were determined by the dictates of that society, this seems to be more about individuals taking pride in their work than a desire for individual recognition. While this began to change during the Greek and Roman eras (wherein we begin to recognize individual artists' styles and artists more commonly signed their names), the role of the artist as an individual creator (and the subject, form, and content of art being determined by the individual artist) is a relatively recent phenomenon.

It is also important to recognize that what remains of a past society like Egypt is always incomplete. We do not have the benefit of knowing what did not survive (e.g., homes, art, and utilitarian objects of everyday life).

How We View Art

A critical aspect of understanding art requires consideration of the context in which the art has been created; indeed, by examining the specifics of an artist's milieu—geographical, political, racial, social, religious, economic, and so forth—it is possible to truly appreciate and comprehend the profound differences that occur among works of art. Moreover, the way we view art is always mitigated by all of these same factors. Throughout history, art has readily been categorized based on some of the above factors, particularly temporal, geographic, and cultural ones. For instance, we tend to distinguish pre-Colombian artifacts by time periods (classical, postclassical), regional stylistic variations (Puuc, Zapotec), and tribal or geographical distinctions (Incan, Mayan, Aztec). These categories exist as a means of organizing and distinguishing the myriad groups of people, objects, styles, and places from which visual art arises. In today's visual art world, these same categories are often incomplete or inappropriate in illuminating the distinctions between art forms: these categories alone omit or underplay the importance of specific cultural context on the work of art. Moreover, there is a long-standing tradition of Western scholars using a Eurocentric, comparative value system when examining the differences between visual arts of various cultures. This system is often biased and generally lacking in that it does not account for the contextual specifics of each culture. Some scholars have relegated or dismissed works of art as "primitive," "naïve," or simply "crude," based upon comparisons with art that is created under the aesthetic traditions of Europe. Comparing visual art from one culture to another is a rich, valuable, and worthwhile form of study, but only if cultural biases are not informing the process.

Consider the world we live in: In less than a day, one can travel to Micronesia, sub-Saharan Africa, or New Zealand. Furthermore, the Internet allows us immediate access to any person, group, country, company, or interest. Our understanding of influences in visual art has to encompass the understanding that the global network that reaches every part of the planet now influences every region of the world. In this global climate, it is not always possible to neatly categorize or even identify the influences that occur in visual art. It is possible, however, to recognize, distinguish and appreciate certain tendencies in visual art.

Concepts And Skills

Principles and Elements

In viewing and creating visual art, there are endless considerations in how to convey ideas, thoughts, and feelings in the visual realm. The elements—point, line, plane, shape, value, texture, color—and principles—balance, harmony, variety, directional thrust, focal area, and so forth—of art play an integral role in creating, viewing, and analyzing visual art. For instance, the choice of a particular color in a painting can change the whole mood of the work. Additionally, the meaning of a certain color in a work of art can change dramatically depending on the period or culture in which the work of art was created.

The color red, for instance, can simultaneously signify love, war, anger, passion, danger, warmth, death, life, and many other things depending on the cultural significance of the color, the context of the color in the work of art, and the intention of the artist. As we view and create visual art, we are constantly fine-tuning our sensibilities so that we are sensitive to the subtleties of the elements and principles of art.

Form and Meaning

As discussed previously, visual art functions as a reflection of the values, beliefs, and tendencies of an individual or society. Naturally, the *form* of art changes in relation to its function or meaning. For instance, the native carvers of Africa's Ivory Coast ascribe specific meaning to forms in the carving of their ceremonial masks. Each formal element on the mask—bulging eyes, elongated nose, perforated cheeks, and so on—serves a spiritual, cultural, and symbolic function during a ceremony, in that the mask creates a connection to the spirit world for both the performer and the tribe.

Figure 1.1   Ivory Coast Ceremonial Mask. Date unknown.

The forms on the mask, therefore, are culturally recognized, determined, and created for a specific purpose. This is very different from the view of visual art that emerged during the nineteenth century in Europe: namely, the role of form in a work of visual art was elevated to a primary level, while subject and content took an increasingly secondary role. The result of this elevation of form in visual art is what was eventually termed *formalist* art in the twentieth century in North America.

Formalism, at its peak with Post-Painterly Abstraction in the 1950s and 1960s, prided itself on its lack of meaning, symbolism, and subject matter: Simply put, it was about form or material and nothing more. It is astounding that one culture can ascribe deep, symbolic meaning to form or material while another culture can revel in its relative meaninglessness. The stark contrast between the beliefs of the Baule and the Post-Painterly Abstractionists indicates the vast differences that occur between art forms from different cultures and the importance of understanding how material associations can affect meaning in a work of art.

Deciphering Clues

Sometimes when viewing a work of art, we are unable to obtain information about the artist or the artist's intentions. In these instances, our role as viewer is akin to being a detective: We must collect as much information about the work of art as possible in order to make an educated guess about its meaning. The following mixed media drawing can be analyzed and understood based solely upon the clues we are given in the artwork.

Figure 1.2   Student work by Regina Chandler

By considering aspects of the art principles and elements in the drawing, we are often able to learn about the artist's intentions. The first thing we may notice in the drawing is the chair, which for many reasons draws the attention of a viewer. It appears to be the closest object to the viewer; it is the largest object (relatively speaking) in the drawing, and it can lead one's eyes into the space behind it. Another noticeable feature is the viewer's relationship to the chair. The chair is drawn in extreme, slightly distorted three-point perspective. The initial point of view that the viewer confronts is one of ambiguity. In one way, the viewer is looking down the stairs and the chair appears to be falling away; in another way, the viewer is looking up the stairs and the chair is falling toward the viewer. Adding to the ambiguity in this drawing are the light source and shadows; indeed, the viewer is given at least two light sources that create shadows on the stairs and on the underside of the chair. Lastly, the viewer of this piece is confronted with the randomly collaged atmosphere of road maps. The predominant theme that seems to emerge from the drawing is one of confusion and ambiguity. One might assume that, based on these observations, the student's intention here was to play with the rules of perspective in order to create an indeterminate space and feeling. The drawing holds one's attention by virtue of its changeability. It is possible that the student had specific intentions about the choice of maps and the illusion of the chair (perhaps a memory or a symbolic reference to somewhere specific), and sometimes we are fortunate enough to learn the inspiration of an artist's work. Yet, in this particular example, one is able to piece together enough clues from the drawing to enjoy and appreciate the work without knowing all of the specifics of the artist's motivation.

Material Factors

Understanding the differences between works of art happens on many levels. As previously discussed, the aesthetic standards by which one assesses a work of art must take into account the many cultural factors that influence visual art. Equally important to aesthetic consideration is knowledge of the many tools, techniques, and materials that artists employ in their art. The number of potential materials for creating works of art has increased exponentially over the past 150 years or so. This situation can be attributed both to industrial innovations and to artists' broadening their scope to include found materials and unusual non-art objects and media. The foregrounding of materiality that occurred with the formalist artists in the twentieth century has further contributed to the recent expanse of materials for art making. The inclusion of uncommon materials in visual art has dramatically changed the criteria by which one assesses visual art; in fact, it is no longer unusual to be confronted with traditionally carved marble sculptures (Louise Bourgeois) and cast and licked chocolate sculptures (Janine Antoni) in the same gallery space. What becomes important in analyzing these diverse works is an understanding of the motivation behind the artwork. It is equally legitimate for one artist to pursue traditional carving in stone while another artist explores conceptual possibilities in cast and licked chocolate. One may be more attracted to one art form over another, but ultimately, it is critical for us to respect the diversity that contributes to the variety, richness and complexity of the art world.

Music

When preparing for this part of the exam, it is important to focus on the objectives to which music is primarily related. They include contexts for the music, concepts and skills involved in experiencing music, and the aesthetic and personal dimensions of music. These constitute a broad overview of the field of music and the musical experience.

One objective is to "understand historical, cultural, and societal contexts for the arts (visual arts, music, drama, dance) and the interrelationships among the arts." This suggests an integration of subject matter that is an opportunity for teachers and students to make connections between social studies, reading or language arts, and the fine arts. For example, when students are reading stories about the American Revolution, they should be aware that it occurred during the period known as the Classical Period in music history. Listening to a work by Haydn or Mozart and talking about how they reflected the "old world" and then comparing the work to a Colonial American tune of the time like "Chester" by William Billings is a great exercise. Similarly, the visual art of Andy Warhol, the music of the Beatles, the assassination of John F. Kennedy, and the war in Vietnam all share the same approximate time frame. In these and the virtually infinite number of other cases or combinations, the students can be asked to find contrasts and similarities or they can attempt to find ways that historical context affected art and ways that art affected and reflected history.

These examples from American History are easy for most to grasp quickly. However, the objective seeks to have teachers and students consider the role of the Arts, to include music, in history and culture beyond the American experience. Listening to music from China, Japan, Germany, Australia, or Africa when studying those cultures can enrich the experience and make it more memorable for students. It is even more valuable to experience live or videotaped performances of the music and dance of these cultures because often the music is performed in traditional costume with traditional instruments (sometimes very different from modern instruments) and seeing the costumes and the movement are an important part of understanding the culture.

According to the objective, merely experiencing the music is not enough. The students must be able to recognize the music or art as part of its historical context and then, through discussion or written exercises that emphasize higher order thinking, they must demonstrate an understanding of the music's place in the historical context and be able to note things that are common and things that are different from context to context—period to period, culture to culture, and so forth—appropriate to their age and level of development. For example, Haydn, Mozart, and Billings used simple melodies in their compositions, but Haydn and Mozart wrote mostly large works like symphonies and operas, whereas Billings wrote mostly psalms and songs. Students must be aware of these facts and then consider why more highly developed forms were preferred in the "old world" while basic psalms and songs were more common in the Colonies. The obvious answer is that colonists did not have the time or the resources to encourage or produce larger musical works. However, the discussion could go beyond that basic step depending on the sophistication of the students.

Another objective is to "understand concepts, techniques, and materials" for producing, listening to, and responding to music. Understanding concepts and techniques suggests more than an appreciation of these concepts and skills. The students ought to experience music making and be taught to listen as musicians listen. They should learn how to put their response to music into accepted music terminology.

Making music is a basic experience. Mothers sing to their babies. Children beat sticks together, make drums, and sing during their play. Adults whistle or sing along with tunes on the radio. People are naturally drawn to sound and music. It is an important part of culture, religious practice, and personal experience for all people. Some people become professional musicians, whereas others whistle, sing, or play for their own enjoyment and nothing more. It is important that students have the opportunity to experience as many forms of music making as possible. It is through the acquisition of basic skills in singing and playing instruments that people can grow in their ability to express themselves through music. As students develop skills, they are also exposed to basic musical concepts such as melody, harmony, rhythm, pitch, and timbre. Then, with experience, they come to make decisions about what is acceptable or not acceptable within a given cultural or historical context and thereby develop their own aesthetic awareness. There is only a very small segment of society that does not make music. These people would likely choose to make music if they could, but are unable as a result of a physical impairment or personal choice (e.g., a vow of silence). Music making is a natural part of human experience.

Listening is a skill that is often taken for granted. There is not a "right" way to listen. However, listening can be much more than allowing the sound to flow past the ears. It can be as basic as listening for melodies and analyzing for form and chord structure or as advanced as critiquing the interpretation on its musical and aesthetic merits. Listening with knowledge and understanding can make the experience of a musical performance much deeper and more meaningful. While music can be experienced and found satisfying, challenging, or beautiful without prior knowledge of a piece or an understanding of its form, cultural significance, and so forth, these things can enrich the experience.

Fast Facts **Music does not provide specific information, instructions, or reactions. People respond to it naturally.**

People respond to music naturally. They do not need prompting or help to respond. They just respond. However, in order to share that response, they must learn how to put their response to music into musical terminology. Some people call music a language, but it does not function as a spoken language. It does not provide specific information, instructions, or reactions. Rather, it sparks thoughts, feelings and emotions. In order to try to put the experience into words, musicians and artists have developed vocabulary and approaches to discussing music and art. This is not to say that there is only one way to respond to or to talk about music or art. However, it is easier to understand music and musicians, art and artists, if the students understand and can use the kind of vocabulary and approaches that musicians or artists use to discuss their work. This includes things as basic as melody and harmony and as profound as the aesthetic experience.

This objective is also about self-expression through and with regard to music. People cannot express themselves or effectively communicate if they do not understand the structures and rules that underlie the "language" that they are trying to use. Although music does not provide the kind of specific communication that spoken language does, it does have structures that can be considered and discussed to help students understand the music and express their responses to the music.

Part of meeting this objective is to understand and promote the aesthetic and personal dimensions related to music. The aesthetic experience is what draws people to music. That experience that everyone has had, but cannot describe because words seem clumsy when it comes to something that can be so profound and wonderful. The type of music or the period or the performer does not necessarily limit the aesthetic experience. It is equally possible to have an aesthetic experience when listening to a child sing a simple melody as it is when listening to a professional orchestra performing a Beethoven symphony. The important thing is to share that aesthetic experience. It is part of what makes music and art special.

There are many ways to encourage exploration of and growth through aesthetic responsiveness. A common experience is a crucial starting point. Have the students listen to several pieces of music and, after listening attentively, ask them to describe how each one made them feel. It is often best to write their response down before starting a discussion. Then, ask them if they can explain why each piece of music made them feel the way they indicated. Younger students will likely provide simple, straightforward emotional responses (e.g., "It made me feel happy!"), while older students should be exploring why it affected the feelings that it did and using both musical concepts (e.g., "It made me feel happy because it was in a major key.) and non-musical associations (e.g., "It made me feel happy because it sounded like a circus and I like to go to the circus."). Through this kind of sharing, along with teacher insights and reading about how other people have responded to music, students can explore and come to a deeper understanding of their personal responses to music, other art forms, and possibly the world. In addition, it should provide them with practical ways to express their responses or reactions to what they experience in life.

According to the objective, having an aesthetic experience, recognizing its value, and being able to grapple with discussing or sharing that experience are not enough. It is also important to promote and develop this part of the musical and artistic experience. Teachers and students must attempt to foster an appreciation for the arts and their ability to create meaning. The arts provide an opportunity to explore and express ideas and emotions through a unique view of life experiences. It is through the experience of music, or any art form, that people begin to transcend the mundane day-to-day experience and reach beyond to a richer life experience.

The objectives that deal with music include contexts for the music, concepts and skills involved in experiencing music, and the aesthetic and personal dimensions of music. Music does not exist in a vacuum. The context (e.g., historical or cultural) of a piece of music is very important. Students should know and be able to discuss the context of music through integration of subject matter. Music ought to be experienced in every way possible. Students must be given opportunities to develop basic performance skills as well as listening skills and vocabulary for responding to music. And, to pull all of these together, teachers and students should develop their aesthetic awareness and help others to do the same. While music and the musical experience can be complex, it is important to remember these basic ideas. In the end, it is not whether someone is a professional musician or an avid listener, but that they know the wonders of music and the arts.

Drama

The arts are a part of the core curriculum, both in terms of Oklahoma standards and the No Child Left Behind federal mandate. Dance, music, drama, and the visual arts are essential parts of a complete education. Study of one or more art forms develops the intellect, provides unique access to meaning, and connects individuals with works of genius, multiple cultures, and contributions to history.

Drama and theatre activities benefit students' educational growth, regardless of their future career.

Fast Facts

Drama and theatre activities offer learners opportunities to experience an art form in many different ways. Whether studying a play, mounting a production, attending a performance, or engaging in creative drama in the classroom, this subject helps students to learn about themselves and their world, develop social skills, strengthen both their verbal and nonverbal communication skills, creatively problem-solve, analyze, and collaborate. Some of the benefits inherent in this instructional methodology include developing concentration skills, analyzing content, demonstrating artistic discipline, improving listening, learning to apply research, communicating information, and making and justifying artistic choices. These are important to a student's educational growth, regardless of that individual's future career. Students who have a chance to learn about and through drama are motivated; their imaginations are engaged and their work is often quite focused.

More specific aesthetic benefits also are acquired. By participating in these activities, students learn about dramatic process and product. They acquire knowledge of theatre artists and their responsibilities. They engage in making artistic choices and learn about the personal discipline that the arts demand. Furthermore, students develop personal aesthetics that are based on informed judgments. They develop insight into cultures and communities, and better understand how this art form is manifest in both their artistic and their everyday lives.

Drama means "to do, act." Drama/theatre is an experiential way to connect to content. Students are engaged physically, mentally, and emotionally. In today's classroom, infusing these techniques into the curriculum allows for hands-on learning that is meaningful and lasting. Young people can learn not only about drama/theatre but also through the art form if it is partnered with another subject. Using these techniques helps children to understand both artistic and paired subject content.

Drama offers multiple approaches to gaining knowledge. Whether a student's preferred learning style is visual (verbal), visual (nonverbal), aural, or tactile/kinesthetic, infusing lessons with drama/theatre expands ways of knowing, especially because of the variety of activities available. Multiple approaches to knowledge acquisition and retention help to insure that all children learn. It should be no surprise, then, that in addition to students who regularly achieve in their studies, even those who generally are less successful may thrive in classrooms where drama/theatre is a regular part of their learning environment. Teaching and learning through and with dramatic art is a unique and effective approach to instruction at all educational levels and with students of varying degrees of academic achievement.

Educators teaching elementary school age children will find that understanding child drama and the continuum of activities that defines it will help them to determine what type of activity is best to use at any given time. While the following comparison helps to distinguish the two major components of this progression, it is important to recognize that one is not better than the other; they are simply different in composition and purpose. Creative drama, children's theatre, and the activities between them offer ample opportunities for integration and demonstrate that the arts are powerful partners for learning.

At one end of the drama/theatre spectrum is creative drama. In this format, process is more important than product; the benefit to the participant is paramount. Creative drama is frequently used in classrooms because it is informal drama that can work in any setting and with any number of children. Scenery, costumes, and/or props are not required. These activities move from teacher-centered to student-centered, from shorter to longer activities and sessions, from unison play to individual play, and from simple beginning activities to more complex story work. Participants need little, if any, previous experience with this approach to curriculum. Once they are introduced to this pedagogy, however, both their interests and their skills will grow.

Here are definitions for the many types of activities that are components of creative drama.

> **Beginning Activities:** These are warm-up activities such as name games, chants, listening games, and other simple exercises designed to relax and motivate participants.

> **Games:** These are more challenging than beginning activities and often focus upon developing players' concentration, imagination, and teamwork skills. Frequently, they are played with students seated or standing in a circle.

> **Sequence Games:** The teacher takes a story or similar material and divides it into particular events or scenes, placing each on an index card. These are randomly distributed to players. When a student recognizes his/her cue being performed, that student goes next. Index cards should have the cue at the top and the new action at the bottom, preferably in a different font or color. The teacher should keep a master list, in order, of cues. This helps students if the correct sequence is interrupted or lost.

> **Pantomime:** Players use their bodies to communicate rather than their voices. Pantomime sentences and stories, creative movement exercises, and miming games are common examples.

Improvisations: These are spontaneously created performances based upon at least two of the following: who (characters), what (conflict), where (setting), when (time), and how (specifics of interpretation). Performed either in pantomime or with dialogue, improvisations should not be planned or rehearsed. Interesting episodes that emerge may be further developed through story creation. Role-playing improvisations deal with problem solving. Students are exposed to differing points of view by replaying and switching roles. Role-playing should not be confused with playing in-role, which is when the teacher enters the dramatization as a character.

Stories: A number of activities can be based upon stories and can range from simple to complex. In the former category, for example, are *noisy stories*. These are simple stories that players help to tell by making sounds or saying words associated with characters. *Story creation* activities require that players develop stories, and these activities can be stimulated by various items, including props, titles, students' own writing, or true events. *Open-ended stories* are those from which students build stories given only a beginning and then share their creations either orally, in writing, or through performance. *Story dramatization* is the most complex informal dramatic activity, as it utilizes players' previously developed skills in service to playing stories. Once proficient here, students move naturally to formal theatrical endeavors.

Several types of activities bridge the gap between creative drama and theatre for youth. These include theatre-in-education (TIE), readers' theatre, and puppetry. Each can be integrated into classroom practice.

Theatre-in-Education (TIE): Originating in Britain, Theatre-in-Education is performed by actor-teachers and students. Using material based upon curriculum or social issues, players assume roles and, through these, explore and problem-solve. TIE's structure is flexible and its focus is educational.

Puppetry: Puppets can range from simple paper bag or sock creations to elaborately constructed marionettes. Puppets can be used for creative drama and theatre activities. Likewise, puppet stages can be as simple as a desktop or table, or they can be intricately constructed with artistically designed settings and theatrical trappings.

Readers Theatre: Called Theatre of the Imagination, Readers Theatre offers performance opportunities without elaborate staging. Traditionally, this type of performance has players sitting on stools, using onstage and/or offstage focus, and employing notebooks or music stands to hold scripts. A narrator may be used and readers may or may not play multiple roles. This type of performance is wedded to literature. A common misconception, however, is that this is simply expressive reading. To truly impact an audience, Readers Theatre must be more than that. Rich characterization, suggested movement, and clear interpretation of the literature are required. In their minds' eyes, audience members complete the stage pictures suggested by the interpreters.

Children's theatre is product-oriented and audience-centered. This theatre for young people can be performed by and for children, by adults for youth, or with a combined cast of adults and young people. In addition, actors can be either amateurs or professionals. Here, dialogue is memorized, the number of characters in the play determines the cast size, and scenery and costumes are generally expected production elements.

Educators may take their students to see plays or they may wish to stage plays in their classrooms or other school facilities. In addition to the familiar format, plays for young people can also be done as participation plays and as story theatre. These last two are especially adaptable to educational venues.

Traditional Theatre: In this most commonly used form of theatre, performers and audience are separate entities. Actors use character and story to communicate and the audience responds with feedback (e.g., laughing, applauding). Typically, actors perform on a stage and are supported by others who contribute the technical elements of theatre.

Participation Theatre: Children are given opportunities to use their voices and bodies within the context of the play. They might be asked for their ideas, invited to join the actors, or given chances to contribute to the play in meaningful ways.

Story Theatre: In this format, actors can function as both characters and narrators, sometimes commenting upon their own actions in role. They can play one role or multiple parts. Scenery, if used, is minimal and costume pieces can suggest a character. Story theatre is classroom friendly and closely linked to literature.

Young people benefit from exposure to theatre, whether as participant or audience member. Opportunities abound for developing vocal skills, vocabulary, imagination, understanding of dramatic structure and types of conflict, physical skills, and empathy. Theatre offers innovative instructional options.

Theatre is not a new art form; it emerged in ancient Greece as a part of religious celebrations. The fact that theatre has evolved over centuries is a testament to its nature; it is both experimental and transitional, allowing innovative elements to be absorbed into the mainstream while continuing to look for new artistic inventions. This is not its only dichotomy.

Theatre is a profession for some and an avocation for others. It is a communal and a collective art form. Regardless of its structure, theatre engages through both visual and auditory stimulation. And because it uses live actors performing for an audience that is "in the moment" with them, it can be repeated but it will never be exactly the same.

How does theatre help students to learn? Plays reflect culture. They hold up a mirror that allows us to travel to different places and time periods, learning about the conditions, people, and viewpoints that have shaped the world of the play. They challenge learners to explore and to deepen their understanding. Theatre introduces children to some characters who are like them and to some who are not. It enriches and broadens a child's way of knowing.

Using drama in the classroom may result in a lively educational environment. Teachers should welcome the energetic chatter and movement indicating students who are learning. They should also recognize that, in this type of experience, there might not be one correct answer or interpretation. Part of the joy and challenge of using drama in the classroom is that it pushes students to think creatively and independently. If teachers view themselves as co-explorers in this process, the journey they take with their students is both productive and fun!

Dance

It has been said, "to dance is human." How true! Dance is one of the most human of endeavors. Throughout history, dance has been rich with meaning and passion. It expresses the depths of humanness across all cultures.

Fast Facts

Dance expresses the depths of humanness across all cultures.

Dance plays important roles among the peoples of the world. There are many ways in which dance is a mirror of culture. Dance may be looked at as a social activity. Dance can also be a performing art. Dance is also a creative pursuit.

Dance as a Mirror of Culture

As far back into ancient times as written records or artwork exist, we have evidence that all cultures dance. From the earliest artwork to that of today, the dancing figure is the artistic subject of many cultures. When we consider why people draw, paint, or sculpt, we learn that they portray what is important to them, what their community or culture values. Dance is important enough to be represented in the art of most cultures from antiquity to today.

Cultural Values

When a culture values strength and power, their dance will show it. When a culture values the community over the individual, it is clear in the dance. When a culture values order and hierarchy in social structure, the dance will give evidence of the same structure. With an observant eye, one can learn a great deal about a culture by studying its dances. This section speaks to many dance-evident cultural values such as gender roles, sexuality, concepts of beauty and aesthetics, community solidarity, and creativity.

Religion

Most cultural dances are historically connected to religion. All over the world we can observe dances of devotion and worship of the deities where movements might include bowing in reverence, lifting arms to the heavens, and gestures of receiving of divine benefits. We can observe dances that tell stories of the power and conquests of deities (e.g., Egyptian, Greek, Indian, Japanese). These movements may include a wide, strong stance with fisted hands and stamping feet. It is also common to see the important stories of the gods told through dance and mime.

We can observe dances that appeal to the gods for survival. For hunting success (e.g., Native American, Inuit) movements may include pantomime of the animal and hunter and the inevitable killing of the animal. For fertile fields and lavish harvest (e.g., Hebrew, Egyptian, European) movements may include pantomime of the planting, tending, and harvesting, as well as lifting or expanding actions that suggest crop growth. For victory in war (e.g., Chinese, Roman, African) movements may include use of swords, spears, or shields and the miming of conflict and victory. In most cultures the power of the dance to cause the gods' positive response is unquestioned.

We can observe dances that ask for divine blessings on life events. For the birth of a child (e.g., African, Polynesian) the movements may include childbearing actions, cradling and "offering" the child up to the deity, and crawling, walking, and running to indicate growth of the child. For initiation into adulthood (e.g., Native American, African) the movements may include shows of strength and manhood for the male and swaying and nurturing gestures for the female. For marriage (in most cultures) movements are jubilant, reflect traditional gender roles for men and women, and may include movements that suggest sexuality and fertility. For funerals (e.g., Egyptian, Cambodian, Zimbabwean) movements may reenact the life story of the deceased and may include grieving as well as celebration of an afterlife. For many cultures, dance is the primary connection between people and their gods.

Gender Roles

How should a man move? How should a woman move? Each culture answers these questions in dance. Most often the rules are unwritten, but they are clear nonetheless. In the dances of the Polynesian culture of the Cook Islands, for example, men keep a pulsing rhythm in their bodies by taking a wide stance and pumping knees open and closed. Their movements are always strong and powerful. The women stand with feet together and sway softly from side to side with undulating hips and rippling arms. In their dances, the man and woman never touch. In fact, they often dance in separate gender groups. In the ballroom dancing of European and American cultures, the man leads the woman by holding her and guiding her. She follows his lead. They move in perfect synchrony and reflect the western cultural ideal of a flawless heterosexual union (led by the man) that is effortless and perfect. Each culture defines gender-specific movements and speaks volumes about the roles of men and women through its dance.

Beauty and Aesthetics

All cultures define beauty in their own way. Dances clearly reflect that ideal (aesthetic) of beauty. Some African dances, for example, feature plump and fleshy women dancers who embody health, fertility, the earth, and beauty to their people. In the European traditional form of ballet, however, the skeletal ballerina is spotlighted to reflect the fragile, ethereal, romantic ideal of female beauty. Another contrast can be made between the traditional court dances of Bali and American Modern dance. In Bali, the court dances have existed for centuries. Dancers train for many years to perform with great serenity, balance, and symmetry. They embody the ideal beauty of Balinese culture. In contemporary America, modern dance can express the very different aesthetic of a driving, off-balance asymmetry. Each image mirrors a cultural definition of what is beautiful. We can all discover many different kinds of beauty through experiencing the dances of various cultures.

Dance as a Social Activity

Social dance has a relatively short history in the human race. Dance has always drawn people together as communicants in a common religion and as celebrants of community events in the context of religion. However, the practice of dance for the primary purpose of gathering people together to enjoy each other's company is only centuries old, rather than millennia-old. When we look at the history of social dance we can clearly see changes in social structure and accepted behavior through changes in the dances.

Folk Dances around the World

Folk dances are cultural dances that have remained quite stable for a long period of time. The music has remained constant and the movements have changed little over the years. Folk dances usually reflect the national traditions of various cultures. They evoke pride in people's traditions and culture by keeping alive the dances of their ancestors. Dancers swell with pride as they perform the dances of their forebears with others that share their heritage. Folk dances are usually about the group, not the specific dancer or couple. Folk dance is a solid connection to the past and a vehicle for "belonging." When one dances a dance, one belongs to the group that has danced that dance through the ages. For some cultures that are being absorbed into western society and swallowed by global culture, such as the Inuits of northern Canada, languages are gradually lost, traditional crafts are lost and ancient religion is lost, but the dances are the last to go. People cling to their dances as the last remnant of a shared past. For the Punjab Indians who immigrated to England in the past century, the dances of their Indian culture are so important to their understanding of their cultural heritage that all children study the dances and the people perform them at social gatherings. People dance their own culture's folk dances to understand who they are and where they came from. It is also valuable to learn the folk dances of other cultures. When we dance the dances of others, we learn about them and gain respect for them by "dancing in their shoes."

Social Dances of Western Cultures

Social dances of Western cultures are usually about the couple and heterosexual courtship. In contrast with folk dance, social dances usually change over time. Through several centuries in Europe and America, changes in social dance have created a fascinating mirror of changing social attitudes toward courtship and gender. When the waltz emerged in full force on the European scene in the nineteenth century, it was soundly condemned as scandalous because the couple was for the first time dancing face to face in an embrace. However, the man continued to lead the dance and the woman followed. Each new social dance has met with similar resistance as the changes in social attitudes toward gender and sexuality have initiated new ways of moving. Embraces become closer, sexual movements become more suggestive, and clothing becomes more revealing as times and social attitudes change.

It is possible to clearly track changes in the social attitude in America by looking at the social dances of various times. The Lindy Hop of the late 1920s and 1930s is a good example. The earliest swing dance, the Lindy Hop emerged from the heart of the African-American culture of Harlem. Its popularity grew and the mainstream white culture was fascinated. White Americans began to flock to Harlem to learn the Lindy Hop. In this time of great separation between the races, the Lindy Hop forged new connections between people of different skin color. Social strictures began to marginally break down.

Another example of the power of social dance to reflect changing social attitudes is the Twist. During the 1960s in America, the Twist emerged and took the social dance scene by storm. Its impact was felt in the fact that the couple did not have to synchronize their movements. In fact, the dancers no longer had to touch each other. Each one danced alone. This dance reflects an important social change in 1960s America when women's liberation and the civil rights movements announced that each person had equal rights regardless of gender or race. The Twist was a revolutionary dance that allowed the individual to pursue her/his own movement. Neither dancer leads nor follows. What a mirror of society!

Dance as a Performing Art

Dance has played another role in history, the role of performing art. In various cultures elite groups of people are designated as dancers/performers. Their occupation is to dance before audiences. There are several examples of performing styles, old and new, among various cultures.

In Japan, Kabuki emerged as a performing art from a long history in the streets. Traditionally, men play all women's roles in elaborate makeup and costume. Highly controlled, stylized movements and lavish costumes represent favorite stories and characters. The theatre art is studied for a lifetime and the popularity of top Kabuki actors/dancers can equal the level of movie stars in Japan.

In India, the Bharata Natyam is a centuries-old dance rooted in the Hindu religion. A solo female dancer who is highly trained in this intricate form of storytelling performs the Bharata Natyam. The dancer utilizes the entire body, but especially the hands and eyes, in a very colorful and expressive dance.

From South Africa comes a style of dance called Gumboots. Out of the dark and silent goldmines and the oppressive lives of the slave laborers emerges a style of dance performed by groups of men wearing miners' gumboots. The dancers leap, turn, and stamp their boots in well-grounded group formations. Their rhythmic and exuberant dance tells of solidarity within adversity and of the workers' amazing endurance.

Finally, out of Irish step-dancing traditions and American innovation comes the Riverdance phenomenon. In this vertically lifted, stylized Irish dancing, the dancers hold their arms tightly at their sides while making quick explosive movements of the legs. They balance mainly on their toes while creating lightning-fast tap rhythms with their hard-soled shoes in kaleidoscopic group patterns.

In Europe and America, the primary performance styles of dance are ballet, modern, jazz, and tap dance.

Ballet, a stylized form in which the body is elongated and extended into space, emerges from the royal courts of Renaissance Europe. Female dancers, or ballerinas, study for years to be able to dance "en pointe," on the tips of their toes. The romantic ballet literally elevates the ballerina to an otherworldly figure unhampered by gravity. Ballet has a long history as an elite form of dance that contains elements of the affectations of royalty. Modern forms of ballet, however, have stretched the limits of the traditional form to include many more movement possibilities.

Modern dance emerged around the turn of the twentieth century, primarily in America, as a reaction against the style restrictions of ballet. It is a "freer" form of dance in which the dancer explores and creates dance with very few stylistic limits. Modern, and now postmodern, dancers and choreographers use many existing movement styles and combine them in innovative ways to create new forms.

Jazz and tap dance emerged in America from a similar source. They both meld the dance styles of Europe, Africa, and various other cultures. Both grow from the fertile cross-cultural ground of nineteenth and twentieth century America to create new dance blends and hybrids. Jazz dance is a performing style that also borrows from American social dance and uses contemporary music, physical power, body-part isolations, and gravity to create strong and rhythmic dances. Tap dance uses metal taps attached to the toes and heels of dance shoes to create intricate and complex rhythms. These four western performing styles have greatly influenced each other throughout the twentieth and into the twenty-first centuries. Choreographers and dancers borrow from each other, style lines become blurred, and new blends between styles are common and exciting. Performing forms are constantly changing through time, but each has a cherished tradition.

Dance as a Creative Pursuit

Creative Problem-Solving

Arguably the earliest creative act of a human being is movement. Long before mastering poetry, visual art, or music, a child creates movement. Fundamentally, in all creative pursuits, we are practicing problem solving. Creative problem solving includes: contemplating a problem, considering various solutions, trying various solutions, choosing one solution, altering and fine-tuning the solution, and finally evaluating the solution. Development of creative problem solving skills is important in human life. All education programs profess the importance of problem solving, and the arts are no exception. The more we use creative movement in the classroom, the greater the learning potential. As students create, they learn about the world, about others, and about themselves.

The Body as the Medium

Dance is an art that requires only the human body, standard equipment for all children. No pen, paintbrush, or musical instrument is needed. As children explore the basics of movement (body, space, time, and relationship), they gain the movement vocabulary to express themselves more and more eloquently. Mastery of the body as a creative medium should be a primary goal in dance education.

Dance Content

Usually, dances are about something. They often have identifiable content. Most dances create meaning in some form, even when quite abstract. When a human being creates a dance, he or she may be expressing such diverse ideas as: community, literary conflict, properties of magnets, regular or irregular rhythms, mathematical patterns, or visual design. A dancer/ choreographer may be exploring feelings such as: alienation, comfort, precision, smooth or bumpy flow, anger, or peace. A choreographer may also be sharing experiences through dance by telling a story or by creating an environment that arises from their life experience. Students are encouraged to create meaning in dance by expressing ideas, exploring feelings, or sharing experiences learn a great deal about themselves while developing their creative problem-solving skills.

Dance in the Classroom and across the Curriculum

Why isn't there more dancing in the schools? General classroom teachers may feel inadequate to teach dance but maybe they define dance too narrowly as merely patterns of intricate steps. Dance in the elementary schools should be about creative movement. Any sensitive teacher can guide students through creative movement that builds upon classroom learning.

For example, in language arts, students can learn spelling and vocabulary words by groups spelling words with their bodies or acting out the meaning of the word. They can *embody* the concept of opposites, for example, by exploring (alone or with a partner) heavy/light, near/far, curved/angular, or symmetrical/asymmetrical. Students can also dance the character or mime the story they are studying.

Movement and math also share much ground. Creative movement studies can use repetition and rhythm to count in multiples or can use partner body sculptures to reflect symmetry and asymmetry, for example.

Science studies can include exploration of gravity, creating a group machine, demonstrating the flow of electrical currents and circuits, or moving within the properties of various types of clouds.

Social studies supply many rich ideas for creative movement, too. Some movement ideas include drawing a map of the classroom and creating a movement "journey" or exploring various occupations, transportation forms, or types of communities through creative movement. Folk dances are always a powerful means to experience other cultures.

Summary

Dance is a powerful force in human life that can express and teach about others, our world, and our selves. Dance is a mirror of culture, cultural values, religion, gender roles, and concepts of beauty. Dance is a social activity that draws people together into belonging and expresses community through folk dance and social dance. Dance is a performing art in many cultures, reflecting cultural ideals through choreography and performance. And finally, dance is a creative pursuit that uses creative problem solving to transform body movement into meaning: expressing ideas, exploring feelings, and sharing experiences. Dance is a powerful teaching tool that can bridge the disciplines of the curriculum.

OSAT

Oklahoma Subject Area Test
Elementary Education

Practice Subtest 2

This test for the OSAT is also on CD-ROM in our special interactive OGET/OSAT TEST*ware*®. It is highly recommended that you first take this exam on computer. You will then have the additional study features and benefits of enforced timed conditions and instant, accurate scoring. See page xii for guidance on how to get the most out of our OGET/OSAT book and software.

SUBTEST DIRECTIONS

A sample of the general directions for the OSAT is shown in the box below. You may want to familiarize yourself with the directions, as similar versions will be used for the actual examination.

You should have in front of you:

(1) a test booklet for the test for which you registered (check the field name on the front cover);

(2) an answer document (be sure you have signed your answer document and filled in the required information on pages 1 and 3); and

(3) a No. 2 lead pencil.

IF YOU DO NOT HAVE ALL OF THESE MATERIALS, PLEASE INFORM THE TEST ADMINISTRATOR. REMOVE ALL OTHER MATERIALS FROM YOUR DESK.

GENERAL DIRECTIONS

This test booklet contains two sections: a selected-response section and a writing assignment. You may complete the sections in the order you choose, but it is suggested that you complete the selected-response section of the test first. The directions for each section appear immediately before that section.

Each selected-response question in this booklet has four answer choices. Read each question carefully and choose the ONE best answer. Record your answer on the answer sheet in the space that corresponds to the question number. Completely fill in the space having the same letter as the answer you have chosen. *Use only a No. 2 lead pencil.*

Sample Question:

1. Which of these cities is farthest north?

    A. Oklahoma City

    B. Muskogee

    C. Tulsa

    D. Lawton

The correct answer to this question is C. You would indicate that on the answer sheet as follows:

1. Ⓐ Ⓑ ● Ⓓ

You should answer all questions. Even if you are unsure of an answer, it is better to guess than not to answer a question at all. You may use the margins of the test booklet for scratch paper, but all of your answers must be recorded in your answer document. Answers that are written in the test booklet will **NOT** be scored.

The words "End of Section" indicate you have completed a section. After you have completed one section, you may go on to the other section. You may go back and review your answers but be sure you have answered all selected-response questions and rechecked all the information in your answer document, particularly your identification information on pages 1 and 3, before you raise your hand for dismissal. Your test materials must be returned to a test administrator when you finish the test.

FOR TEST SECURITY REASONS, YOU MAY NOT TAKE NOTES OR REMOVE ANY OF THE TEST MATERIALS FROM THE ROOM.

This session will last four hours. You may work at your own pace on the different sections of the test. If you have any questions, please ask them now before you begin the test.

STOP

DO NOT GO ON UNTIL YOU ARE TOLD TO DO SO.

Answer Sheet

1. Ⓐ Ⓑ Ⓒ Ⓓ	11. Ⓐ Ⓑ Ⓒ Ⓓ	21. Ⓐ Ⓑ Ⓒ Ⓓ	31. Ⓐ Ⓑ Ⓒ Ⓓ
2. Ⓐ Ⓑ Ⓒ Ⓓ	12. Ⓐ Ⓑ Ⓒ Ⓓ	22. Ⓐ Ⓑ Ⓒ Ⓓ	32. Ⓐ Ⓑ Ⓒ Ⓓ
3. Ⓐ Ⓑ Ⓒ Ⓓ	13. Ⓐ Ⓑ Ⓒ Ⓓ	23. Ⓐ Ⓑ Ⓒ Ⓓ	33. Ⓐ Ⓑ Ⓒ Ⓓ
4. Ⓐ Ⓑ Ⓒ Ⓓ	14. Ⓐ Ⓑ Ⓒ Ⓓ	24. Ⓐ Ⓑ Ⓒ Ⓓ	34. Ⓐ Ⓑ Ⓒ Ⓓ
5. Ⓐ Ⓑ Ⓒ Ⓓ	15. Ⓐ Ⓑ Ⓒ Ⓓ	25. Ⓐ Ⓑ Ⓒ Ⓓ	35. Ⓐ Ⓑ Ⓒ Ⓓ
6. Ⓐ Ⓑ Ⓒ Ⓓ	16. Ⓐ Ⓑ Ⓒ Ⓓ	26. Ⓐ Ⓑ Ⓒ Ⓓ	36. Ⓐ Ⓑ Ⓒ Ⓓ
7. Ⓐ Ⓑ Ⓒ Ⓓ	17. Ⓐ Ⓑ Ⓒ Ⓓ	27. Ⓐ Ⓑ Ⓒ Ⓓ	37. Ⓐ Ⓑ Ⓒ Ⓓ
8. Ⓐ Ⓑ Ⓒ Ⓓ	18. Ⓐ Ⓑ Ⓒ Ⓓ	28. Ⓐ Ⓑ Ⓒ Ⓓ	38. Ⓐ Ⓑ Ⓒ Ⓓ
9. Ⓐ Ⓑ Ⓒ Ⓓ	19. Ⓐ Ⓑ Ⓒ Ⓓ	29. Ⓐ Ⓑ Ⓒ Ⓓ	39. Ⓐ Ⓑ Ⓒ Ⓓ
10. Ⓐ Ⓑ Ⓒ Ⓓ	20. Ⓐ Ⓑ Ⓒ Ⓓ	30. Ⓐ Ⓑ Ⓒ Ⓓ	40. Ⓐ Ⓑ Ⓒ Ⓓ

Practice Test

DIRECTIONS: Use the information below to answer the three questions that follow.

An experiment is planned to test the effect of microwave radiation on the success of seed germination. One hundred corn seeds will be divided into four sets of twenty-five each. Seeds in Group 1 will be microwaved for one minute, seeds in Group 2 for two minutes, and seeds in Group 3 for ten minutes. Seeds in Group 4 will not be placed in the microwave. Each group of seeds will be soaked overnight and placed between the folds of water-saturated newspaper.

1. When purchasing the seeds at the store no single package contained enough seeds for the entire project, most contain about thirty seeds per package. Which of the following is an acceptable approach for testing the hypotheses?
    I. Purchase one packet from each of four different brands of seed, one packet for each test group
    II. Purchase one packet from each of four different brands of seed and divide the seeds from each packet equally among the four test groups
    III. Purchase four packets of the same brand, one packet for each test group
    IV. Purchase four packets of the same brand, and divide the seeds from each packet equally among the four test groups.

    A. I and II only

    B. II and IV only

    C. III and IV only

    D. IV only

2. During the measurement of seed and root length it is noted that many of the roots are not growing straight. Efforts to manually straighten the roots for measurement are only minimally successful as the roots are fragile and susceptible to breakage. Which of the following approaches is consistent with the stated hypothesis?

    A. At the end of the experiment, straighten the roots and measure them

    B. Use a string as a flexible measuring instrument for curved roots

    C. Record the mass instead of length as an indicator of growth

    D. Record only the number of seeds that have sprouted, regardless of length

3. In presenting the results of this experiment, which of the following could be used to present the data to confirm or refute the hypothesis?

    I.   A single bar graph with one bar for each test group indicating the number of days until the first seed sprouts.
    II. A pie chart for each test group showing the percent of seeds in that group that sprouted.
    III. A line graph plotting the total number of sprouted seeds from all test groups vs. time (experiment day).
    IV. A line graph plotting the number of germinated seeds vs. the minutes of time exposed to the microwave.

    A. I only

    B. II only

    C. II and IV only

    D. III and IV only

4. Which equation could be used to answer the following question?

    Together, a pen and a pencil cost $2.59 (ignoring tax). The pen cost $1.79 more than the pencil. What was the cost of the pencil?

    A. $x = (2.59 - 1.79) \times 2$

    B. $2.59 = x - 1.79$

    C. $2.59 = x + (x + 1.79)$

    D. $x = 2.59 - 1.79$

5. Bemus School is conducting a lottery to raise funds for new band uniforms. Exactly 1000 tickets will be printed and sold. Only one ticket stub will be drawn from a drum to determine the single winner of a big-screen television. All tickets have equal chances of winning. The first 700 tickets are sold to 700 different individuals. The remaining 300 tickets are sold to Mr. Greenfield.

    Given the information above, which of the following statements are true?

    I.   It is impossible to tell in advance who will win.
    II. Mr. Greenfield will probably win.
    III. Someone other than Mr. Greenfield will probably win.
    IV. The likelihood that Mr. Greenfield will win is the same as the likelihood that someone else will win.

    A. I and II only

    B. I and III only

    C. II and IV only

    D. III and IV only

DIRECTIONS: The following two questions are based upon this excerpt from Jules Verne's 1870 work *From the Earth to the Moon and Round the Moon* pp. 39–40 (Dodd, Mead & Company 1962), where plans are made to construct a cannon 900 feet long to shoot a projectile to the Moon.

The problem before us is how to communicate an initial force of 12,000 yards per second to a shell of 108 inches in diameter, weighing 20,000 pounds. Now when a projectile is launched into space, what happens to it? It is acted upon by three independent forces: the resistance of the air, the attraction of the earth, and the force of impulsion with which it is endowed. Let us examine these three forces. The resistance of the air is of little importance. The atmosphere of the earth does not exceed forty miles. Now, with the given rapidity, the projectile will have traversed this in five seconds, and the period is too brief for the resistance of the medium to be regarded otherwise than as insignificant. Proceeding, then, to the attraction of the earth, that is, the weight of the shell, we know that this weight will diminish in the inverse ratio of the square of the distance. When a body left to itself falls to the surface of the earth, it falls five feet in the first second; and if the same body were removed 257,542 miles farther off, in other words, to the distance of the moon, its fall would be reduced to about half a line in the first second.

6. Propelling such a large projectile requires a massive force. The "initial force of 12,000 yards per second" is really a reference to the projectile's initial speed. The calculation of force required to move an object with a mass of 20,000 pounds from rest to a speed of 12,000 yards per second in a time span of 0.05 seconds is reflected in which of the following:

    A. $20,000 \times 12,000 / 0.05$

    B. $20,000 \times 12,000 \times 0.05$

    C. $(20,000 \times 9.8) / (20,000 \times 0.05)$

    D. $(20,000 / 9.8) \times (12,000 / 0.05)$

7. The acceleration due to gravity is generally accepted as 9.8 m/sec^2 for objects near the Earth's surface, and the Earth's radius is approximately 4,000 miles. Given that the proposed projectile weighs 20,000 lbs at the surface, what would be the approximate mass at a distance of 8,000 miles from the surface of the Earth?

    A. 20,000 lbs / 2

    B. 20,000 lbs / 4

    C. 20,000 lbs / 8

    D. 20,000 lbs / 16

8. The primary and most efficient energy source of the body comes from

    A.   proteins.

    B.   fats.

    C.   complex carbohydrates.

    D.   simple sugars.

9. Which of the following is a locomotor skill?

    A.   bouncing

    B.   catching

    C.   throwing

    D.   leaping

10. Which is NOT a principle of aerobic conditioning?

    A.   requires oxygen

    B.   continuous and rhythmic

    C.   burns protein for energy

    D.   uses major muscle groups

11. Dance can be a mirror of culture. Which of the following is not an illustration of this statement?

    A.   Women in the Cook Islands dance with their feet together and sway, while the men take a wide stance and flap their knees.

    B.   Movement basics include body, space, time, and relationship.

    C.   In Africa, the birth of a child is an occasion for a dance that asks for divine blessings.

    D.   The court dancers of Bali study for many years to achieve the balance, beauty, and serenity of their dance.

Use the image below to answer the two questions that follow.

Student work by Sara Goodrich

12. As shown in the figure, the technique of gluing imagery to a two-dimensional surface is referred to as

    A. montage.

    B. frottage.

    C. collage.

    D. assemblage.

13. In the above image, the chair is the focal point of the drawing. Why?

    A. It is large, frontal, and drawn in high contrast.

    B. It is highly simplified and minimally detailed.

    C. It is asymmetrically balanced in the drawing.

    D. It is drawn in three-point perspective.

14. In order to achieve lasting weight loss, students should

    A.   enter a commercial diet program.

    B.   combine permanent dietary changes with exercise.

    C.   cut calories to below 1,000 per day.

    D.   exercise for two hours a day.

15. Which of the following vitamins is not fat soluble?

    A.   Vitamin D

    B.   Vitamin C

    C.   Vitamin E

    D.   Vitamin K

16. Of the following, which test does NOT measure muscular strength and endurance in children?

    A.   Pull-ups

    B.   Flexed arm hang

    C.   Grip strength test

    D.   Sit-and-reach test

17. Around the time of World War II the chemical industry developed several new classes of insecticide that were instrumental in protecting our soldiers from pest-borne diseases common to the tropic regions they were fighting in. These same insecticides found widespread use at home to increase production of many agricultural crops by reducing the damage from insects like cotton weevils and grasshoppers. While farmers continued to use the same levels of insecticide, over time it was found that the insect population was increasing. Identify the best explanation for this observation:

    A.   Insecticides, like most chemicals, lose their potency when stored.

    B.   The insect population was increasing to reach the carrying capacity of a given ecosystem.

    C.   The initial doses of pesticide were too low to effectively kill the insects.

    D.   Insects with a tolerance to insecticide survived the initial doses and lived to produce insecticide resistant offspring.

18. Which of the following types of pollution or atmospheric phenomena are correctly matched with their underlying causes?

      I.   global warming – carbon dioxide and methane
      II. acid rain – sulfur dioxide and nitrogen dioxide
      III. ozone depletion – chlorofluorocarbons and sunlight
      IV. aurora borealis – solar flares and magnetism

    A.   I and II only

    B.   II and III only

    C.   I and IV only

    D.   I, II, III, and IV

19. Which of the following characteristics of a sound wave is associated with its pitch?

      I.   Amplitude
      II.   Frequency
      III. Wavelength
      IV. Speed

    A.   I only

    B.   II only

    C.   II and III only

    D.   IV only

20. Which of the following statements correctly describes each group of vertebrates?

      I.   Amphibians are cold-blooded, spending part of their life cycle in water and part on land.
      II.   Reptiles are generally warm-blooded, having scales that cover their skin.
      III. Fish are cold-blooded, breathing with gills, and covered by scales.
      IV. Mammals are warm-blooded with milk glands and hair.

    A.   I and IV only

    B.   I, III, and IV only

    C.   IV only

    D.   I, II, III, and IV

21. Pitch is the relative _____ of a musical sound.

    A.   duration or length

    B.   loudness or softness

    C.   highness or lowness

    D.   rhythm

22. Dance can reflect the religion of a culture by
    I. offering adoration and worship to the deity.
    II. appealing to the deity for survival in war.
    III. asking the deity for success in the hunt.
    IV. miming the actions of planting and harvesting crops.

    A. I and II only

    B. I and III only

    C. II, III, and IV only

    D. I, II, III, and IV

23. Which of the following do the dances of Waltz, Lindy Hop, and Twist have in common?

    A. They became popular in the nineteenth century.

    B. They are forms of "swing" dance.

    C. They reflect changes in social attitudes of their time.

    D. They are danced by couples touching each other.

24. Which of the following is NOT a characteristic of cholesterol?

    A. Cholesterol plays a role in the function of the brain.

    B. Cholesterol is a component in the creation of certain hormones.

    C. Cholesterol is produced in the liver.

    D. Excess cholesterol found in the blood of many people usually comes from internal production.

25. A table tennis game is scored to

    A. 15 points.

    B. 15 points, with a margin of two.

    C. 21 points, with a margin of two.

    D. 21 points.

26. Matt earned the following scores on his first six weekly mathematics tests: 91%, 89%, 82%, 95%, 86%, and 79%.

    He had hoped for an average (mean) of 90% at this point, which would just barely give him an A– in math class on his first report card. How many more total percentage points should Matt have earned over the course of those six weeks to qualify for an A–?

    A.   87

    B.   3

    C.   90

    D.   18

27. The floor of a rectangular room is to be covered in two different types of material. The total cost of covering the entire room is $136.00. The cost of covering the inner rectangle is $80.00. The cost of covering the shaded area is $56.00.

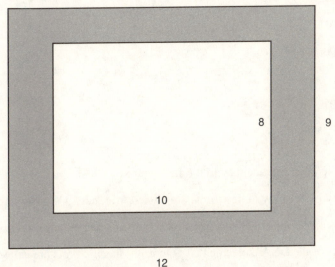

    We wish to determine the cost of material per square foot used to cover the shaded area. What information given below is unnecessary for this computation?

    > I.   The total cost of covering the entire room.
    > II. The cost of covering the inner rectangle.
    > III. The cost of covering the shaded area.

    A.   I only

    B.   II only

    C.   I and II

    D.   I and III

28. Which of the following is an important reason why music should be included in every child's daily classroom activities?

    A.   The imagination, creativity, and aesthetic awareness of a child can be developed through music for more creative living in our mechanized society.

    B.   Students need an opportunity to stay current with today's popular music culture.

    C.   Making and listening to music is part of our cultural experience and provides opportunities for personal aesthetic growth.

    D.   Participating in creatively planned musical activities helps build a child's self-esteem and understanding of others.

29. Harmony results when a melody is accompanied by
        I.   a rhythm instrument.
        II.   a guitar.
        III.   another instrument or singer playing or singing the melody.
        IV.   another instrument playing chords.

    A.   I and II only

    B.   I and III only

    C.   II and III only

    D.   II and IV only

30. Identify the incorrect statement from the following:

    A.   Heredity is the study of how traits are passed from parent to offspring.

    B.   The chemical molecule that carries an organism's genetic makeup is called DNA.

    C.   Sections of the DNA molecule that determine specific traits are called chromosomes.

    D.   The genetic makeup of an organism is altered through bioengineering.

31. Which of the following sources of energy is nonrenewable?

    A.   hydrogen-cell

    B.   geothermal

    C.   nuclear

    D.   hydroelectric

32. To move a heavy book across a tabletop at a constant speed, a person must continually exert a force on the book. This force is primarily used to overcome which of the following forces?

    A.   The force of gravity

    B.   The force of air resistance

    C.   The force of friction

    D.   The weight of the book

33. To complete an effective aerobic workout, exercise should be performed at an individual's target heart rate for a minimum of

    A.   15 minutes.

    B.   20 minutes.

    C.   30 minutes.

    D.   45 minutes.

34. Which of the following statements is not true?

    A.   Infectious diseases are caused by viruses, bacteria, or protists.

    B.   Cancers and hereditary diseases can be infectious.

    C.   Environmental hazards can cause disease.

    D.   The immune system protects the body from disease.

35. Nelson's Menswear Shop was selling sweaters for $40 at the beginning of the year. In March, the price of the sweaters was raised by 10%. In September, the price was raised by an additional 15%. Ignoring tax, what was the price of the sweaters in September?

    A. $50.00

    B. $65.40

    C. $59.00

    D. $50.60

36. Three pounds of cherries cost $4.65. What would five pounds cost (at the same price per pound)?

    A. $7.75

    B. $7.50

    C. $23.00

    D. $23.25

37. You have stepped into an art museum and are drawn to a painting you know nothing about. In order to appreciate the painting, it is helpful to
    I.   know all of the details of the artist's intentions and motivations.
    II. study the clues in the artwork for potential meaning.
    III. determine the cultural significance of every visual clue in the painting.
    IV. consider the art elements and principles in the work of art.

    A. I and II only

    B. I and III only

    C. II and IV only

    D. III and IV only

38. Which one of the following statements is most true regarding the materials of visual art?

    A. Industrial innovations in art-making materials have improved art in the past 150 years.

    B. The use of uncommon materials in art-making has improved art in the past 150 years.

    C. The use of unusual materials in art-making has changed the standards by which we view art.

    D. Industrial innovations in art-making materials have had little influence on visual art.

39. How many ten thousands are there in one million?

    A. 100

    B. 10

    C. 1,000

    D. 10,000

40. An owner of twin Siamese cats knows the following data:

    I.   Cost of a can of cat food

    II. Volume of a can of cat food

    III. Number of cans of cat food eaten each day by one cat

    IV. The weight of the cat food in one can

    Which of the data above can be used to determine the cost of cat food for 7 days for the 2 cats?

    A. I and II only

    B. I and III only

    C. I and IV only

    D. III and IV only

OSAT

Oklahoma Subject Area Test
Elementary Education

Answers:
Practice Subtest 2

Answer Key

1. (B)	11. (B)	21. (C)	31. (C)
2. (D)	12. (C)	22. (D)	32. (C)
3. (C)	13. (A)	23. (C)	33. (B)
4. (C)	14. (B)	24. (D)	34. (B)
5. (B)	15. (B)	25. (C)	35. (D)
6. (A)	16. (D)	26. (D)	36. (A)
7. (B)	17. (D)	27. (C)	37. (C)
8. (C)	18. (D)	28. (C)	38. (C)
9. (D)	19. (C)	29. (D)	39. (A)
10. (C)	20. (B)	30. (C)	40. (B)

Practice Subtest

Detailed Explanations of Answers

1. **B**

   The experiment requires a control of all variables other than the one identified in the hypothesis—exposure to microwave radiation. Seeds from different suppliers may be different; for example, one brand may be treated with a fungicide or a different fungicide. While it is likely that item III might be acceptable, without confirming that all packages are from the same year and production run, the four packages may be significantly different from each other. The best solution is to randomly divide the available seeds equally between the four test groups. Item II allows the experiment to also compare the germination rates between the different brands, but only if the seeds from each packet are isolated within each test group, and the number of seeds large enough to create a statistically significant sample.

2. **D**

   The hypothesis is to evaluate seed germination as a function of microwave irradiation. Recording the overall growth or length of the seed root, while interesting, is not the stated hypothesis. Item C would be a good approach if the hypothesis were to relate seed growth to some variable, as it would more accurately reflect the growth of thicker or multiple roots in a way that root length might not measure.

3. **C**

   Item I will not reflect the success of seed germination overall, one seed in a given sample may germinate early. Reporting the time until the last seed germinates would also not be useful. Item III combines the number of all the sprouted seeds, losing the differentiation of the test groups. Items II and IV maintain the distinction between test groups and indicate the overall success rate of the germination.

4. **C**

The total price of the two items is given as $2.59, hinting that equation B or C may be correct. (In both cases, $2.59 is shown as the sum of two values.)

Examine the right side of equation C: You note that one value is $1.79 higher than the other. That is, in equation C, x could stand for the price of the pencil, and (x + 1.79) could stand for the price of the more expensive pen. Hence, equation C is the right one. None of the others fit the information given.

5. **B**

Statement I is true because the winner could be Mr. Greenfield and it could be someone else. Statement II is not true, even though Mr. Greenfield bought many more tickets than any other individual. He still has a block of only 300; there are 700 ticket stubs in the drum that aren't his. This tells us that statement III is true.

Finally, statement IV is false. Don't confuse the true statement "all tickets have an equal chance of winning" with the false statement that "all persons have an equal chance of winning."

6. **A**

Force is equal to mass multiplied by acceleration (F = ma). The force needed is the product of the object's mass (20,000 lbs) and the acceleration. Acceleration is the change in speed per unit of time. The projectile's acceleration is thus (12,000 yards/second – 0 yards/second) / 0.05 seconds).

7. **B**

The force of gravity is inversely proportional to the square of the distance; thus, doubling the distance reduces the gravitational force by a factor of 4. The mass reduction for this object at the top of the atmosphere, just forty miles above the surface, would be insignificant. However, experience tells us that objects are "weightless" in the space shuttle. This apparent weightlessness is a result of a balance between the forward motion of the shuttle and the gravitational attraction of the Earth. Both the shuttle and the objects in it are moving forward together at a high rate of speed, and falling together under the force of gravity. They are "weightless" only relative to each other. Were the shuttle to cease forward motion it would fall directly and precipitously to Earth under the unrelenting force of gravity.

8. **C**

Complex carbohydrates are the most efficient energy source for the body. While other choices provide some energy, they are not nearly as efficient as complex carbohydrates.

9. **D**

Leaping is the only locomotor skill listed. Bouncing (A), catching (B), and throwing (C) are manipulative movements.

10. C

A, B, and D are principles of aerobic conditioning. C is not.

11. B

The statement "Movement basics include body, space, time, and relationship" is the correct answer because this describes only the dimensions of dance movement; in no way does it speak to how dance reflects the culture of which it is part.

12. C

Choice C is the correct answer. This is a collage.

13. A

It is large, frontal, and drawn in high contrast.

14. B

Permanent dietary changes and exercise are the only way to produce lasting weight loss. Commercial diets (A) do not always include a program of exercise, but rather concentrate on diet. Radically reducing calorie intake (C) will cause the body to go into starvation mode and slow down digestion to conserve energy. Two hours of daily exercise (D) is not very practical and without controlling calorie intake, it would be ineffective.

15. B

Vitamin C is water soluble—the remaining choices are fat soluble.

16. D

The grip strength test (C), pull-ups (for boys) (A), and flexed arm hang (for girls) (B), are all tests to measure muscular strength and endurance. The sit-and-reach test measures flexibility.

17. D

Early doses of pesticide were strong enough to kill most of the insects; only a few survived who, perhaps because of some genetic trait, had a slightly higher tolerance to the poison. When these pesticide-tolerant insects reproduced they passed the tolerance to their offspring, so D is correct. Higher doses of pesticide are initially effective, but again a few individuals survive with tolerance to that new level. Control of pest populations generally requires access to a variety of pesticides that work through different mechanisms, and which are applied in such a way as to minimize buildup of tolerance in the insect population.

18. **D**

All are correctly matched.

19. **C**

The frequency of a wave is associated with pitch. Middle C has a frequency of 440 cycles per second. However, wavelength and frequency are directly related by the relationship $v = c / \lambda$ where v (nu) is the frequency, c is the speed of sound, and λ (lambda) is wavelength.

20. **B**

Reptiles are not generally warm-blooded, so II is incorrect; all other statements are correct.

21. **C**

This question focuses on a specific but very basic musical concept, pitch. Answer C is the best answer and the only correct answer. Answer A refers indirectly to the basic concept of rhythm. This relates to answer D, which is totally wrong because it is another concept and not a descriptor of the concept of pitch. Answer B is wrong because it refers directly to the basic concept of dynamics.

22. **D**

The correct choice is D, statements I, II, III, and IV. Dance can reflect the religion of a culture in many ways on account of its deep historical roots in religious tradition.

23. **C**

The Waltz, Lindy Hop, and the Twist each reflect changes in social attitudes of their time.

24. **D**

Excess cholesterol found in the blood typically comes from cholesterol in a diet rather than internal production. Cholesterol, which is produced in the liver (C), plays a vital role in brain function (A) and is important for creating certain hormones (B).

25. **C**

Table tennis is scored to 21 and must be won by a margin of two points. In doubles play for badminton, the winner must score 15 points (A). Singles badminton is also scored to 21 points with a margin of two points needed for victory.

26. **D**

It is helpful to compute Matt's current average. Adding up his scores, you get 522. Dividing that by 6 (the number of scores), you find that his average is 87%. Similarly, you can multiply 90 by

6 to compute the number of total points it would take to have an average of 90 (90 × 6 = 540). Matt only earned 522 points, so he was 18 shy of the A–.

27. **C**

The total area of the larger rectangle is

   base × height = 12 × 9 = 108 sq. ft.

Therefore, the area of the shaded portion surrounding the inner rectangle is

   108 sq. ft. – 80 sq. ft. = 28 sq. ft.

If the total cost of material used to cover the shaded area is $56 and we have 28 sq. ft., the cost per square foot is $\frac{\$56}{28\text{ sq. ft.}}$ = $2.00 per square foot.

Answers A, B, and D are incorrect. Neither I nor II is necessary to determine the cost per square foot of the shaded area. D is incorrect because III is needed to determine the cost per sq foot.

28. **C**

This question is focused on the music objective as stated in the Oklahoma standards. There-fore, it is important to look for the answer that best reflects the objective. Answer C is the best answer because it covers all parts of the objective in at least a minimal way and is the only one that mentions music's cultural dimensions. Answer A is a good answer and the second best an-swer because it deals with one of the objectives, but the focus on creativity rather than culture keeps it from being the best answer. Answers B and D are not good answers because they do not deal with the objectives.

29. **D**

This question focuses on a basic musical concept, "harmony." Harmony is the performance of two or more different pitches simultaneously. Therefore, when looking at the answers provided, it is good to begin by eliminating answers that have nothing to do with pitch. A rhythm instru-ment is a non-pitched instrument in almost all cases, so choice I is not pitch-related and that means that answers A and B are eliminated because they both include choice I. Since two or more different pitches must be performed simultaneously to have harmony, choice III can also be eliminated because there are two performers, but not two different pitches. That eliminates answer C and leaves answer D as the best and correct answer.

30. **C**

Genes are the sections of the DNA molecule that determine specific traits.

31. **C**

Nuclear energy is nonrenewable. Nuclear energy has potential advantages in providing large quantities of energy from a small amount of source material, but once started the process of radioactive decay is nonreversible.

32. **C**

The force of friction between the book and the table is the primary force that must be overcome to move the book. An experiment to study these frictional forces could keep all other variables (size and weight of the book, speed of travel) constant while measuring the force needed to move the book using a spring scale. Different experiments could change the surface of the book by covering the book with wax paper, construction paper, or sandpaper.

33. **B**

Exercising cardiovascularly for a minimum of 20 minutes per session, as part of an exercise program, will lead to effective physical results with a proper nutritional diet. Forty-five minutes (D) is an effective time period when performing a weight-lifting exercise session.

34. **B**

Diseases caused by viruses, bacteria, or protists that invade the body are called infectious diseases. These disease-causing organisms are collectively referred to as germs. Cancers and hereditary diseases are not infectious.

35. **D**

The first price increase is for 10%. That's the same as one-tenth, and one-tenth of $40 is $4. Adding $4 to $40 gives $44 as the March price.

The next increase is 15% of $44. Multiplying 44 by 0.15 (0.15 being another way to represent 15%) gives 6.6, which is read as $6.60. You then increase the March price of $44 by $6.60, giving you $50.60.

Note that you cannot arrive at the answer by adding the individual percent increases (10 + 15 = 25) and then multiplying by 40.

36. **A**

Finding the answer by setting up a proportion works well here:

$$\frac{3}{4.65} = \frac{5}{x}$$

Proportions often are two fractions set equal to each other, with one "corner" being the unknown value, or x. The equation above can be read as "3 is to 4.65 as 5 is to what?"

One way to solve a proportion (that is; to find the value of x), is to cross-multiply the two corners that have known values (in this case 4.65 and 5). That gives 23.25, which is then divided by the remaining known value (3), giving 7.75.

37. **C**

Choice C, statements II and IV, is correct. You would want to study the clues in the artwork for potential meaning and consider the art elements and principles in the work of art. The more you know about the context in which the artist worked, the more you can appreciate the work itself. Not everything will be immediately evident, so you will want to assume the role of detective.

38. **C**

Choice C is the correct answer. The use of uncommon materials has dramatically changed the criteria by which one assesses visual art.

39. **A**

You know that ten thousand contains 4 zeros, or 10^4 in place value. One million contains 10^6, or six zeros. Thus, 10^6 divided by 10^4 is 10^2 or 100. You may divide out 10,000 into one million, but that is the laborious way to solve this. Choice A is correct.

40. **B**

You are challenged to analyze which data you would need to calculate the cost of feeding 2 cats for 7 days. If you calculate the cost for one cat for 7 days, then double the answer, you will have an approximate cost for 2 cats. The total cost for one cat is the cost of a can of food, times the number of cans of food eaten each day by one cat, times 7 days.

Your Test-Day Checklist

☑ Get a good night's sleep. Tired test-takers consistently perform poorly.

☑ Wake up early.

☑ Dress comfortably. Keep your clothing temperature appropriate. You'll be sitting in yout test clothes for hours. Clothes that are itchy, tight, too warm, or too cold take away from your comfort level.

☑ Eat a good breakfast.

☑ Take these with you to the test center:
- Several sharpened No. 2 pencils. Pencils are not provided at the test center
- Admission ticket
- Proper indentification: current, government-issued identification bearing your photograph and signature, and one additional piece of identification

☑ Arrive at the test center early. Remember, no one is allowed into a test session after the test has begun.

☑ Compose your thoughts and try to relax before the test.

Remember that eating, drinking, and smoking are prohibited. Calculators, dictionaries, textbooks, notebooks, briefcases, and packages are also prohibited.

Index

INSTALLING REA's TEST*ware*®

SYSTEM REQUIREMENTS

Pentium 75 MHz (300 MHz recommended) or a higher or compatible processor; Microsoft Windows 98 or later; 64 MB available RAM; Internet Explorer 5.5 or higher.

INSTALLATION

1. Insert the OGET/OSAT TEST*ware*® CD-ROM into the CD-ROM drive.

2. If the installation doesn't begin automatically, from the Start Menu choose the Run command. When the Run dialog box appears, type d:\setup (where D is the letter of your CD-ROM drive) at the prompt and click OK.

3. The installation process will begin. A dialog box proposing the directory "Program Files\REA\ OGET_OSAT" will appear. If the name and location are suitable, click OK. If you wish to specify a different name or location, type it in and click OK.

4. Start the OGET/OSAT TEST*ware*® application by double-clicking on the icon.

REA's OGET/OSAT TEST*ware*® is **EASY** to **LEARN AND USE**. To achieve maximum benefits, we recommend that you take a few minutes to go through the on-screen tutorial on your computer. The "screen buttons" are also explained here to familiarize you with the program.

TECHNICAL SUPPORT

REA's TEST*ware*® is backed by customer and technical support. For questions about **installation or operation of your software**, contact us at:

> **Research & Education Association**
> **Phone: (732) 819-8880 (9 a.m. to 5 p.m. ET, Monday–Friday)**
> **Fax: (732) 819-8808**
> **Website:** *http://www.rea.com*
> **E-mail: info@rea.com**

Note to Windows XP Users: In order for the TEST*ware*® to function properly, please install and run the application under the same computer administrator-level user account. Installing the TEST*ware*® as one user and running it as another could cause file-access path conflicts.

NOTES

NOTES

NOTES

NOTES

NOTES

NOTES

REA's Test Prep Books Are The Best!
(a sample of the <u>hundreds of letters</u> REA receives each year)

(more on next page)

REA's Test Prep Books Are The Best!
(a sample of the <u>hundreds of letters</u> REA receives each year)

" I used [*the REA study guide*] to study for the LSAT and ATS-W tests—and passed them both with *perfect scores*. This book provided excellent preparation ... "
Student, New York, NY

" The reviews in [the REA book] were outstanding ... If it wasn't for your excellent prep, I would not have stood a chance [of passing the NYSTCE]. "
Student, Elmira, New York

" I did well because of your wonderful prep books... I just wanted to thank you for helping me prepare for these tests. "
Student, San Diego, CA

" My students report your chapters of review as the most valuable single resource they used for review and preparation. "
Teacher, American Fork, UT

" Your book was such a better value and was so much more complete than anything your competition has produced—and I have them all! "
Teacher, Virginia Beach, VA

" Compared to the other books that my fellow students had, your book was the most helpful in helping me get a great score. "
Student, North Hollywood, CA

" Your book was responsible for my success on the exam, which helped me get into the college of my choice... I will look for REA the next time I need help. "
Student, Chesterfield, MO

" Just a short note to say thanks for the great support your book gave me in helping me pass the test... I'm on my way to a B.S. degree because of you! "
Student, Orlando, FL

(more on previous page)

Brief Contents

Detailed Contents

Lab

3 Managing and Analyzing a Workbook EX3.1

Working Together 1: Linking and Embedding between Word 2007 and Excel 2007 EXWT1.1

Acknowledgments

We would like to extend our thanks to the professors who took time out of their busy schedules to provide us with the feedback necessary to develop the 2007 Edition of this text. The following professors offered valuable suggestions on revising the text:

Adida Awan, Savannah State University

Jacqueline Bakal, Felician College

Chet Barney, Southern Utah University

Bruce W. Bryant, University of Arkansas Community College Morrilton

Kelly D. Carter, Mercer University

Cesar Augusto Casas, St. Thomas Aquinas College

Sally Clements, St. Thomas Aquinas College

Donna N. Dunn, Beaufort County Community College

Donna Ehrhart, Genesee Community College

Saiid Ganjalizadeh, The Catholic University of America

Dr. Jayanta Ghosh, Florida Community College

Carol Grazette, Medgar Evers College/CUNY

Susan Gundy, University of Illinois at Springfield

Greg R. Hodge, Northwestern Michigan College

Christopher M. J. Hopper, Bellevue Community College

Ginny Kansas, Southwestern College

Robert Kemmerer, Los Angeles Mission College

Diana I. Kline, University of Louisville

Linda Klisto, Broward Community College North Campus

Nanette Lareau, University of Arkansas Community College Morrilton

Deborah Layton, Eastern Oklahoma State College

Keming Liu, Medgar Evers College/CUNY

J. Gay Mills, Amarillo College

Kim Moorning, Medgar Evers College/CUNY

Dr. Belinda J. Moses, University of Phoenix/Baker College/Wayne County Community College

Lois Ann O'Neal, Rogers State University

Andrew Perry, Springfield College

Michael Philipp, Greenville Technical College

Julie Piper, Bucks County Community College

Brenda Price, Bucks County Community College

Thali N. Rajashekhara, Camden County College

Dr. Marcel Marie Robles, Eastern Kentucky University

Jose (Joe) Sainz, Naugatuck Valley Community College

Pamela J. Silvers, Asheville-Buncombe Technical Community College

Glenna Stites, Johnson County Community College

Joyce Thompson, Lehigh Carbon Community College

Michelle G. Vlaich-Lee, Greenville Technical College

Mary A. Walthall, St. Petersburg College

We would like to thank those who took the time to help us develop the manuscript and ensure accuracy through pain-staking edits: Brenda Nielsen of Mesa Community College–Red Mountain, Rajiv Narayana of SunTech Info-Labs, and Craig Leonard.

Our thanks also go to Linda Mehlinger of Morgan State University for all her work on creating the PowerPoint presentations to accompany the text. We are grateful to Harry Knight of Franklin University, the author of the Instructor's Manual and Testbank, for his careful revision of these valuable resources and creation of online quizzing materials.

Finally, we would like to thank team members from McGraw-Hill, whose renewed commitment, direction, and support have infused the team with the excitement of a new project. Leading the team from McGraw-Hill are Sarah Wood, Marketing Manager, and Developmental Editors Kelly Delso and Alaina Grayson.

The production staff is headed by Marlena Pechan, Project Manager, whose planning and attention to detail have made it possible for us to successfully meet a very challenging schedule; Srdjan Savanovic, Designer; Jason Huls, Production Supervisor; Ben Curless, Media Producer; Jeremy Cheshareck, Photo Researcher; and Betsy Blumenthal, copyeditor—team members whom we can depend on to do a great job.

Preface

The 20th century brought us the dawn of the digital information age and unprecedented changes in information technology. There is no indication that this rapid rate of change will be slowing—it may even be increasing. As we begin the 21st century, computer literacy is undoubtedly becoming a prerequisite in whatever career you choose.

The goal of the O'Leary Series is to provide you with the necessary skills to efficiently use these applications. Equally important is the goal to provide a foundation for students to readily and easily learn to use future versions of this software. This series does this by providing detailed step-by-step instructions combined with careful selection and presentation of essential concepts.

Times are changing, technology is changing, and this text is changing too. As students of today, you are different from those of yesterday. You put much effort toward the things that interest you and the things that are relevant to you. Your efforts directed at learning application programs and exploring the Web seem, at times, limitless.

On the other hand, students often can be shortsighted, thinking that learning the skills to use the application is the only objective. The mission of the series is to build upon and extend this interest by not only teaching the specific application skills but by introducing the concepts that are common to all applications, providing students with the confidence, knowledge, and ability to easily learn the next generation of applications.

Instructor's Resource CD-ROM

The **Instructor's Resource CD-ROM** contains a computerized Test Bank, an Instructor's Manual, and PowerPoint Presentation Slides. Features of the Instructor's Resource are described below.

- **Instructor's Manual CD-ROM**   The Instructor's Manual, authored by Harry Knight of Franklin University, contains lab objectives, concepts, outlines, lecture notes, and command summaries. Also included are answers to all end-of-chapter material, tips for covering difficult materials, additional exercises, and a schedule showing how much time is required to cover text material.

- **Computerized Test Bank**   The test bank, authored by Harry Knight, contains over 1,300 multiple choice, true/false, and discussion questions. Each question will be accompanied by the correct answer, the level of learning difficulty, and corresponding page references. Our flexible EZ Test software allows you to easily generate custom exams.

- **PowerPoint Presentation Slides** The presentation slides, authored by Linda Mehlinger of Morgan State University, include lab objectives, concepts, outlines, text figures, and speaker's notes. Also included are bullets to illustrate key terms and FAQs.

Online Learning Center/Web Site

Found at **www.mhhe.com/oleary,** this site provides additional learning and instructional tools to enhance the comprehension of the text. The OLC/Web site is divided into these three areas:

- **Information Center** Contains core information about the text, supplements, and the authors.

- **Instructor Center** Offers instructional materials, downloads, and other relevant links for professors.

- **Student Center** Contains data files, chapter competencies, chapter concepts, self-quizzes, flashcards, additional Web links, and more.

Simnet Assessment for Office Applications

Simnet Assessment for Office Applications provides a way for you to test students' software skills in a simulated environment. Simnet is available for Microsoft Office 2007 and provides flexibility for you in your applications course by offering:

Pre-testing options

Post-testing options

Course placement testing

Diagnostic capabilities to reinforce skills

Web delivery of test

MCAS preparation exams

Learning verification reports

For more information on skills assessment software, please contact your local sales representative, or visit us at **www.mhhe.com.**

O'Leary Series

The O'Leary Application Series for Microsoft Office is available separately or packaged with *Computing Essentials*. The O'Leary Application Series offers a step-by-step approach to learning computer applications and is available in both brief and introductory versions. The introductory books are MCAS Certified and prepare students for the Microsoft Certified Applications Specialist exam.

Computing Concepts

Computing Essentials 2008 offers a unique, visual orientation that gives students a basic understanding of computing concepts. *Computing Essentials* encourages "active" learning with exercises, explorations, visual illustrations, and inclusion of screen shots and numbered steps. While combining the "active" learning style with current topics and technology, this text provides an accurate snapshot of computing trends. When bundled with software application lab manuals, students are given a complete representation of the fundamental issues surrounding the personal computing environment.

GUIDE TO THE O'LEARY SERIES

The O'Leary Series is full of features designed to make learning productive and hassle free. On the following pages you will see the kind of engaging, helpful pedagogical features that have helped countless students master Microsoft Office Applications.

EASY-TO-FOLLOW INTRODUCTORY MATERIALS

INTRODUCTION TO MICROSOFT OFFICE 2007

Each text in the O'Leary Series opens with an Introduction to Office 2007, providing a complete overview of this version of the Microsoft Office Suite.

What Is the 2007 Microsoft Office System?

Microsoft's 2007 Microsoft Office System is a comprehensive, integrated system of programs, servers, and services designed to solve a wide array of business needs. Although the programs can be used individually, they are designed to work together seamlessly, making it easy to connect people and organizations to information, business processes, and each other. The applications include tools used to create, discuss, communicate, and manage projects. If you share a lot of documents with other people, these features facilitate access to common documents. This version has an entirely new user interface that is designed to make it easier to perform tasks and help users more quickly take advantage of all the features in the applications. In addition, the communication and collaboration features and integration with the World Wide Web have been expanded and refined.

The 2007 Microsoft Office System is packaged in several different combinations of programs or suites. The major programs and a brief description are provided in the following table.

Program	Description
Word 2007	Word Processor program used to create text-based documents
Excel 2007	Spreadsheet program used to analyze numerical data
Access 2007	Database manager used to organize, manage, and display a database
PowerPoint 2007	Graphics presentation program used to create presentation materials
Outlook 2007	Desktop information manager and messaging client
InfoPath 2007	Used to create XML forms and documents
OneNote 2007	Note-taking and information organization tools
Publisher 2007	Tools to create and distribute publications for print, Web, and e-mail
Visio 2007	Diagramming and data visualization tools
SharePoint Designer 2007	Web site development and management for SharePoint servers
Project 2007	Project management tools
Groove 2007	Collaboration program that enables teams to work together

The four main components of Microsoft Office 2007—Word, Excel, Access, and PowerPoint—are the applications you will learn about in this series of labs. They are described in more detail in the following sections.

Overview of Microsoft Office Word 20[07]

What Is Word Processing?

Office Word 2007 is a word processing software application whose p[urpose] is to help you create any type of written communication. A word pro[cessor] can be used to manipulate text data to produce a letter, a report, a [memo,] an e-mail message, or any other type of correspondence. Text data [is any] letter, number, or symbol that you can type on a keyboard. The grou[ping of] the text data to form words, sentences, paragraphs, and pages [of text] results in the creation of a document. Through a word processor, y[ou can] create, modify, store, retrieve, and print part or all of a document.

Word processors are one of the most widely used application software programs. Putting your thoughts in writing, from the simplest note to the most complex book, is a time-consuming process. Even more time-consuming is the task of editing and retyping the document to make it better. Word processors make errors nearly nonexistent—not because they are not made, but because they are easy to correct. Word processors let you throw away the correction fluid, scissors, paste, and erasers. Now, with a few keystrokes, you can easily correct errors, move paragraphs, and reprint your document.

Word 2007 Features

Word 2007 excels in its ability to change or edit a document. Editing involves correcting spelling, grammar, and sentence-structure errors. In addition, you can easily revise or update existing text by inserting or deleting text. For example, a document that lists prices can easily be updated to reflect new prices. A document that details procedures can be revised by deleting old procedures and inserting new ones. This is especially helpful when a document is used repeatedly. Rather than recreating the whole document, you change only the parts that need to be revised.

Revision also includes the rearrangement of selected areas of text. For example, while writing a report, you may decide to change the location of a single word or several paragraphs or pages of text. You can do it easily by cutting or removing selected text from one location, then pasting or placing the selected text in another location. The selection also can be copied from one document to another.

To help you produce a perfect document, Word 2007 includes many additional support features. The AutoCorrect feature checks the spelling and grammar in a document as text is entered. Many common errors are corrected automatically for you. Others are identified and a correction suggested. A thesaurus can be used to display alternative words that have a meaning similar or opposite to a word you entered. A Find and Replace feature can be used to quickly locate specified text and replace it with other text throughout a document. In addition, Word 2007 includes a

WDO.1

INTRODUCTION TO WORD 2007

Each text in the O'Leary Series also provides an overview of the specific application features.

ENGAGING LAB INTRODUCTIONS

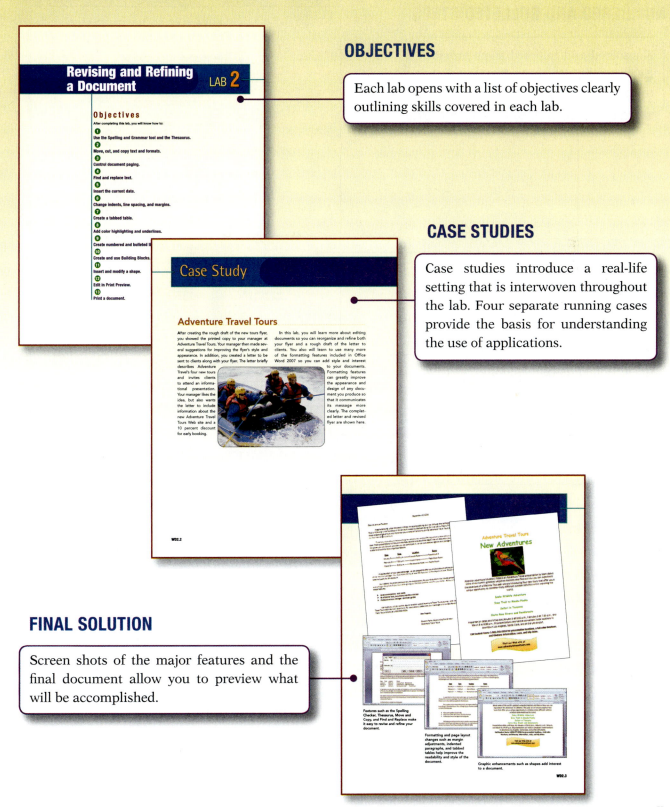

OBJECTIVES

Each lab opens with a list of objectives clearly outlining skills covered in each lab.

CASE STUDIES

Case studies introduce a real-life setting that is interwoven throughout the lab. Four separate running cases provide the basis for understanding the use of applications.

FINAL SOLUTION

Screen shots of the major features and the final document allow you to preview what will be accomplished.

STEP-BY-STEP INSTRUCTION

NUMBERED AND BULLETED STEPS

Numbered and bulleted steps provide clear step-by-step instructions on how to complete a task, or series of tasks.

All steps and bullets appear in the left-hand margin, making it easy not to miss a step.

AND EASY-TO-FOLLOW DESIGN

TABLES

Tables provide quick summaries of concepts and procedures for specific tasks.

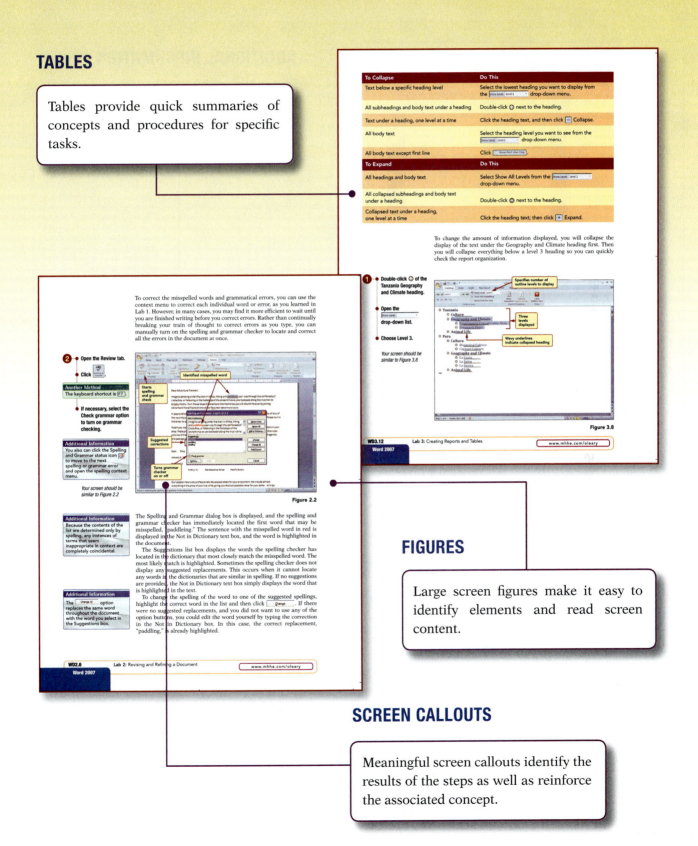

Figure 2.2

Figure 3.8

FIGURES

Large screen figures make it easy to identify elements and read screen content.

SCREEN CALLOUTS

Meaningful screen callouts identify the results of the steps as well as reinforce the associated concept.

SUPPORTIVE MARGIN NOTES

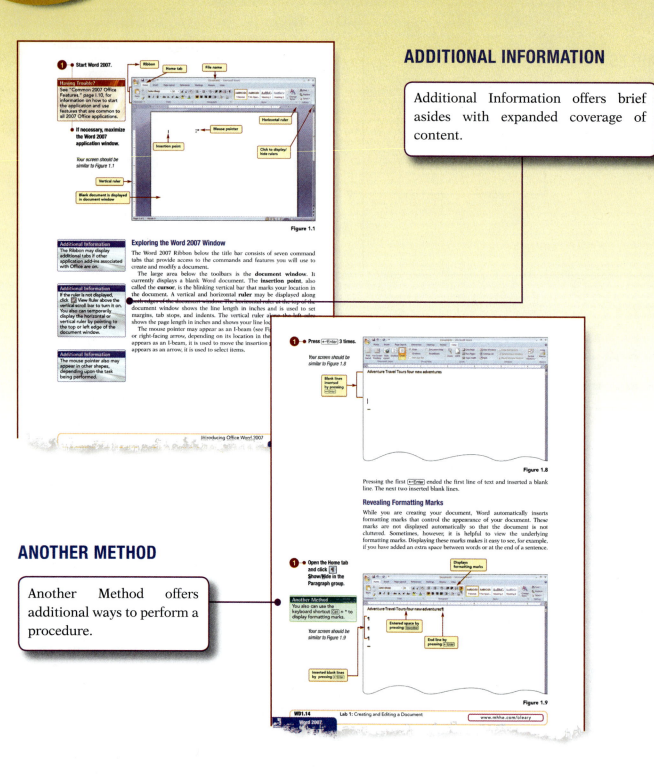

ADDITIONAL INFORMATION

Additional Information offers brief asides with expanded coverage of content.

ANOTHER METHOD

Another Method offers additional ways to perform a procedure.

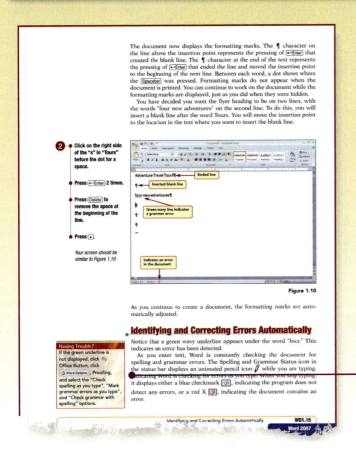

Figure 1.10

HAVING TROUBLE

Having Trouble helps resolve potential problems as students work through each lab.

MORE ABOUT

New to this edition, the More About icon directs students to the More About appendix found at the end of the book. Without interrupting the flow of the text, this appendix provides additional coverage required to meet MCAS certification.

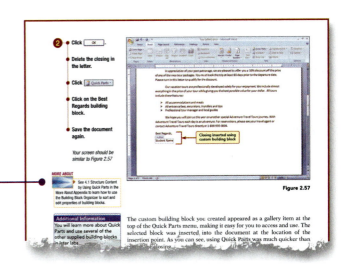

Figure 2.57

REAL-WORLD APPLICATION

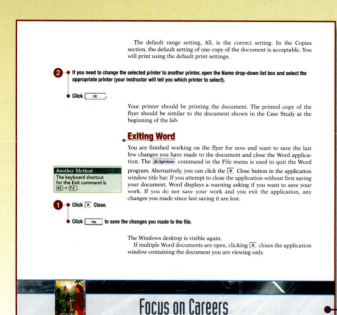

The default range setting, All, is the correct setting. In the Copies section, the default setting of one copy of the document is acceptable. You will print using the default print settings.

2 • If you need to change the selected printer to another printer, open the Name drop-down list box and select the appropriate printer (your instructor will tell you which printer to select).

• Click [OK].

Your printer should be printing the document. The printed copy of the flyer should be similar to the document shown in the Case Study at the beginning of the lab.

Exiting Word

You are finished working on the flyer for now and want to save the last few changes you have made to the document and close the Word application. The [X Exit Word] command in the File menu is used to quit the Word program. Alternatively, you can click the [X] Close button in the application window title bar. If you attempt to close the application without first saving your document, Word displays a warning asking if you want to save your work. If you do not save your work and you exit the application, any changes you made since last saving it are lost.

Another Method
The keyboard shortcut for the Exit command is [Alt] + [F4].

1 • Click [X] Close.

• Click [Yes] to save the changes you made to the file.

The Windows desktop is visible again.
If multiple Word documents are open, clicking [X] closes the application window containing the document you are viewing only.

Focus on Careers

EXPLORE YOUR CAREER OPTIONS

Food Service Manager
Have you noticed flyers around your campus advertising job positions? Many of these jobs are in the food service industry. Food service managers are traditionally responsible for overseeing the kitchen and dining room. However, these positions increasingly involve administrative tasks, including recruiting new employees. As a food service manager, your position would likely include creating newspaper notices and flyers to attract new staff. These flyers should be eye-catching and error-free. The typical salary range of a food service manager is $34,000 to $41,700. Demand for skilled food service managers is expected to increase through 2010.

Exiting Word | WD1.71
Word 2007

FOCUS ON CAREERS

Focus on Careers provides an example of how the material covered may be applied in the "real world."

Each lab highlights a specific career, ranging from forensic science technician to food services manager, and presents job responsibilities and salary ranges for each.

Case Study

Adventure Travel Tours

Adventure Travel Tours provides information on their tours in a variety of forms. Travel brochures, for instance, contain basic tour information in a promotional format and are designed to entice potential clients to sign up for a tour. More detailed regional information packets are given to people who have already signed up for a tour, so they can prepare for their vacation. These packets include facts about each region's climate, geography, and culture. Additional informational formats include pages on Adventure Travel's Web site and scheduled group presentations.

Part of your responsibility as advertising coordinator is to gather the information that Adventure Travel will publicize about each regional tour. Specifically, you have been asked to provide background information for two of the new tours: the Tanzania Safari and the Machu Picchu trail. Because this information is used in a variety of formats, your research needs to be easily adapted. You will therefore present your facts in the form of a general report on Tanzania and Peru.

In this lab, you will learn to use many of the features of Office Word 2007 that make it easy to create an attractive and well-organized report. A portion of the completed report is shown here.

WD3.2

CONTINUING CASE STUDIES

Within each series application, the same Case Study is used to illustrate concepts and procedures.

AND INTEGRATION

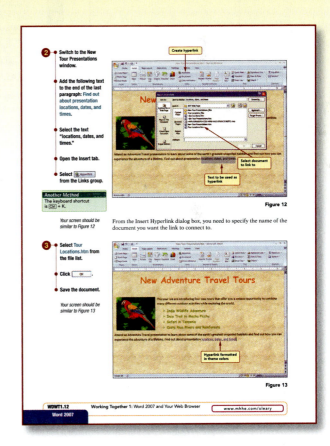

WORKING TOGETHER LABS

At the completion of the brief and introductory texts, a final lab demonstrates the integration of Microsoft Office applications. Each Working Together lab also includes end-of-chapter materials.

REINFORCED CONCEPTS

CONCEPT PREVIEW

Concept Previews provide an overview to the concepts that will be presented throughout the lab.

Concept Preview

The following concepts will be introduced in this lab:

1. **Grammar Checker** The grammar checker advises you of incorrect grammar as you create and edit a document, and proposes possible corrections.
2. **Spelling Checker** The spelling checker advises you of misspelled words as you create and edit a document, and proposes possible corrections.
3. **AutoCorrect** The AutoCorrect feature makes some basic assumptions about the text you are typing and, based on these assumptions, automatically corrects the entry.
4. **Word Wrap** The word wrap feature automatically decides where to end a line and wrap text to the next line based on the margin settings.
5. **Font and Font Size** Font, also commonly referred to as a typeface, is a set of characters with a specific design that has one or more font sizes.
6. **Alignment** Alignment is the positioning of text on a line between the margins or indents. There are four types of paragraph alignment: left, centered, right, and justified.
7. **Graphics** A graphic is a nontext element or object such as a drawing or picture that can be added to a document.

Introducing Office Word 2007

Adventure Travel Tours has recently upgraded their computer systems at all locations across the country. As part of the upgrade, they have installed the latest version of the Microsoft Office 2007 suite of applications. You are very excited to see how this new and powerful application can help you create professional letters and reports as well as eye-catching flyers and newsletters.

Starting Office Word 2007

... on Microsoft Office Word 2007
... and presentations.

CONCEPT BOXES

Concept boxes appear throughout the lab providing clear, concise explanations and serving as a valuable study aid.

3. Click outside the menu to close it.

   Open the spelling context menu for "lern" and choose "learn".

The spelling is corrected, and the spelling indicator in the status bar indicates that the document is free of errors.

Using Word Wrap

Now you will continue entering more of the paragraph. As you type, when the text gets close to the right margin, do not press ←Enter to move to the next line. Word will automatically wrap words to the next line as needed.

Concept 4

Word Wrap

4. The word wrap feature automatically decides where to end a line and wrap text to the next line based on the margin settings. This feature saves time when entering text because you do not need to press ←Enter at the end of a full line to begin a new line. The only time you need to press ←Enter is to end a paragraph, to insert blank lines, or to create a short line such as a salutation. In addition, if you change the margins or insert or delete text on a line, the program automatically readjusts the text on the line to fit within the new margin settings. Word wrap is common to all word processors.

Enter the following text to complete the sentence.

1. Press End to move to the end of the line.

www.mhhe.com/oleary

REINFORCED CONCEPTS (CONTINUED)

CONCEPT SUMMARIES

The Concept Summary offers a visual summary of the concepts presented throughout the lab.

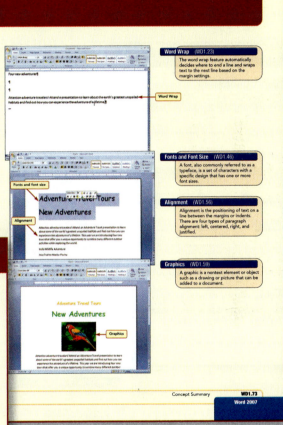

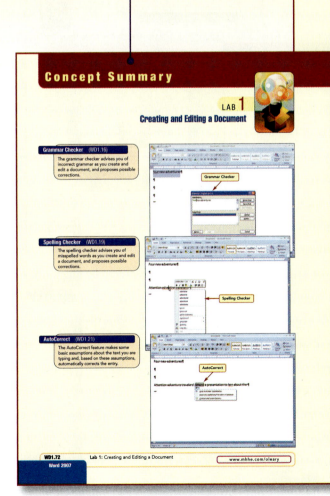

LAB REVIEW

KEY TERMS

Includes a list of all bolded terms with page references.

COMMAND SUMMARY

Command Summaries provide a table of commands, shortcuts, and their associated action for all commands used in the lab.

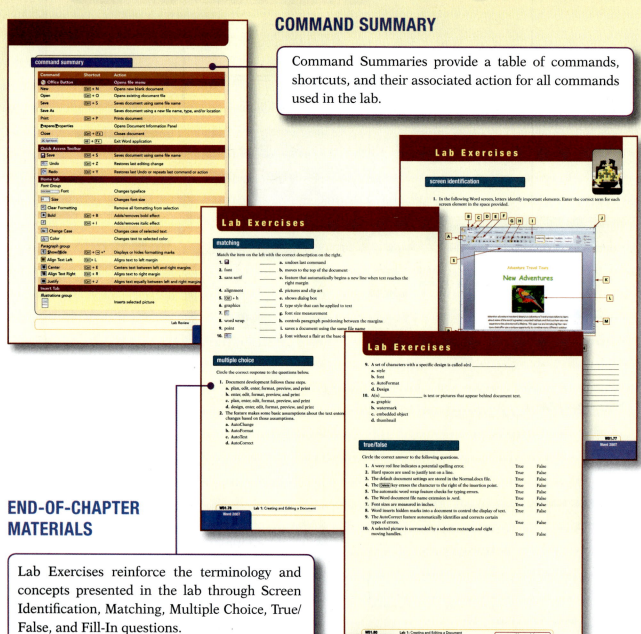

END-OF-CHAPTER MATERIALS

Lab Exercises reinforce the terminology and concepts presented in the lab through Screen Identification, Matching, Multiple Choice, True/False, and Fill-In questions.

AND SKILL DEVELOPMENT

LAB EXERCISES

Lab Exercises provide hands-on practice and develop critical-thinking skills through step-by-step and on-your-own practice exercises. Many cases in the practice exercises tie to a running case used in another application lab. This helps demonstrate the use of the four applications across a common case setting. For example, the Adventure Tours case used in Word is continued in practice exercises in Excel, Access, and PowerPoint.

ON YOUR OWN

STEP-BY-STEP

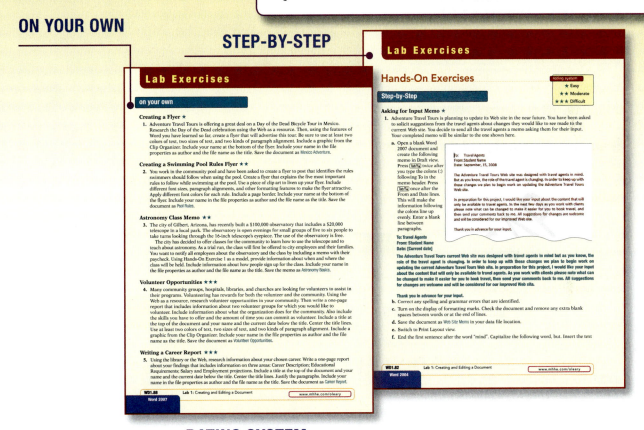

RATING SYSTEM

These exercises have a rating system from easy to difficult and test your ability to apply the knowledge you have gained in each lab. Exercises that build off of previous exercises are noted with a Continuing Exercises icon.

END-OF-BOOK RESOURCES

2007 Word Brief Command Summary

Command	Shortcut	Action
Office Button		Opens File menu
New	Ctrl + N	Opens new document
Open	Ctrl + O	Opens existing document file
Save	Ctrl + S, 🔲	Saves document using same file name
Save As	F12	Saves document using a new file name, type, and/or location
Save as/Save As type/ Web Page		Saves file as a Web page document
Print	Ctrl + P	Specify print settings before printing document
Print/Print Preview		Displays document as it will appear when printed
Print/Quick Print		Prints document using default printer settings
Prepare/Properties		Opens Document Information Panel
Close	Ctrl + F4	Closes document
Word Options/Proofing		Changes settings associated with Spelling and Grammar checking
Word Options/Advanced/ Mark formatting inconsistencies		Checks for formatting inconsistencies
Exit Word	Alt + F4, ✕	Closes the Word application
Quick Access Toolbar		
🔲 Save		Saves document using same file name
↶ Undo	Ctrl + Z	Restores last editing change
↷ Redo	Ctrl + Y	Restores last Undo or repeats last command or action
Home tab		
Clipboard Group		
✂ Cut	Ctrl + X	Cuts selection to Clipboard
📋 Copy	Ctrl + C	Copies selection to Clipboard
📋	Ctrl + V	Pastes item from Clipboard
🖌 Format Painter		Copies format to selection

COMPREHENSIVE COMMAND SUMMARY

Provides a table of commands, shortcuts, and their associated action for all commands used throughout each text in the O'Leary Series.

Glossary of Key Terms

active window The window containing the insertion point and that will be affected by any changes you make.

alignment How text is positioned on a line between the margins or indents. There are four types of paragraph alignment: left, centered, right, and justified.

antonym A word with the opposite meaning.

author The process of creating a Web page.

AutoCorrect A feature that makes basic assumptions about the text you are typing and automatically corrects the entry.

bibliography A listing of source references that appears at the end of the document.

browser A program that connects you to remote computers and displays the Web pages you request.

building blocks Document fragments that include text and formatting and that can be easily inserted into a document.

bulleted list Displays items that logically fall out from a paragraph into a list, with items preceded by bullets.

caption A title or explanation for a table, picture, or graph.

case sensitive The capability to distinguish between uppercase and lowercase characters.

cell The intersection of a column and row where data are entered in a table.

character formatting Formatting features such as bold and color that affect the selected characters only.

citations Parenthetical source references that give credit for specific information included in a document.

Click and Type A feature available in Print Layout and Web Layout views that is used to quickly insert text, graphics, and other items in a blank area of a document, avoiding the need to enter blank lines.

clip art Professionally drawn graphics.

control A graphic element that is a container for information or objects.

cross-reference A reference in one part of a document related to information in another part.

cursor The blinking vertical bar that shows you where the next character you type will appear. Also called the insertion point.

custom dictionary A dictionary of terms you have entered that are not in the main dictionary of the spelling checker.

default The initial Word document settings that can be changed to customize documents.

destination The location to which text is moved or copied.

Document Map A feature that displays the headings in the document in the navigation window.

document properties Details about a document that describe or identify it and are saved with the document content.

document theme A predefined set of formatting choices that can be applied to an entire document in one simple step.

document window The area of the application window that displays the contents of the open document.

drag and drop A mouse procedure that moves or copies a selection to a new location.

drawing layer The layer above or below the text layer where floating objects are inserted.

drawing object A simple object consisting of shapes such as lines and boxes.

edit The process of changing and correcting existing text in a document.

GLOSSARY

Bolded terms found throughout each text in the O'Leary Series are defined in the glossary.

MORE ABOUT APPENDICES

A More About appendix appears at the end of the brief and introductory texts. This appendix offers students additional coverage needed to meet MCAS requirements. Skills pertaining to additional MCAS coverage are denoted by a More About icon in the margins of the text.

REFERENCE 1 - DATA FILE LIST

The Data File List is a reference guide that helps organize data and solution files. It identifies the names of the original and saved files.

REFERENCE 2 - MCAS CERTIFICATION GUIDE

Links all MCAS objectives to text content and end-of-lab exercises. You will always know which MCAS objectives are being covered. Introductory texts are MCAS certified.

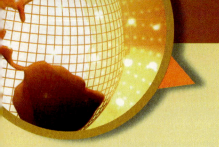

ONLINE LEARNING CENTER (OLC)

www.mhhe.com/oleary

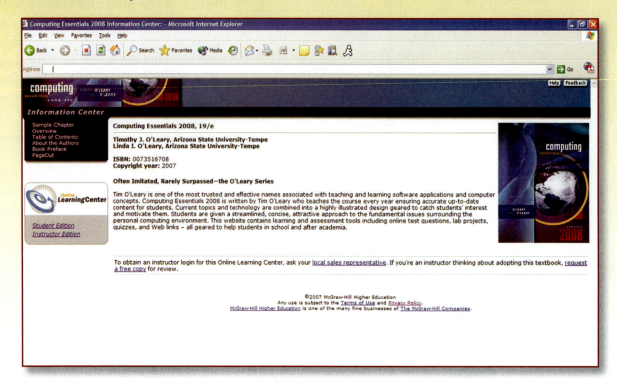

The Online Learning Center follows The O'Leary Series lab by lab, offering all kinds of supplementary help for you. OLC features include:

- Learning Objectives
- Student Data Files
- Chapter Competencies
- Chapter Concepts
- Self-Grading Quizzes
- Additional Web Links

ABOUT THE AUTHORS

Tim and Linda O'Leary live in the American Southwest and spend much of their time engaging instructors and students in conversation about learning. In fact, they have been talking about learning for over 25 years. Something in those early conversations convinced them to write a book, to bring their interest in the learning process to the printed page. Today, they are as concerned as ever about learning, about technology, and about the challenges of presenting material in new ways, in terms of both content and method of delivery.

A powerful and creative team, Tim combines his 25 years of classroom teaching experience with Linda's background as a consultant and corporate trainer. Tim has taught courses at Stark Technical College in Canton, Ohio, and at Rochester Institute of Technology in upstate New York, and is currently a professor at Arizona State University in Tempe, Arizona. Linda offered her expertise at ASU for several years as an academic advisor. She also presented and developed materials for major corporations such as Motorola, Intel, Honeywell, and AT&T, as well as various community colleges in the Phoenix area.

Tim and Linda have talked to and taught numerous students, all of them with a desire to learn something about computers and applications that make their lives easier, more interesting, and more productive.

Each new edition of an O'Leary text, supplement, or learning aid has benefited from these students and their instructors who daily stand in front of them (or over their shoulders). The O'Leary Series is no exception.

DEDICATION

We dedicate this edition to Nicole and Katie who have brought love and joy to our lives.

Introduction to Microsoft Office 2007

Objectives

After completing the Introduction to Microsoft Office 2007, you should be able to:

1 Describe the 2007 Microsoft Office System.

2 Describe the Office 2007 applications.

3 Start an Office 2007 application.

4 Recognize the basic application features.

5 Use menus, context menus, and shortcut keys.

6 Use the Ribbon, dialog boxes, and task panes.

7 Use Office Help.

8 Exit an Office 2007 application.

What Is the 2007 Microsoft Office System?

Microsoft's 2007 Microsoft Office System is a comprehensive, integrated system of programs, servers, and services designed to solve a wide array of business needs. Although the programs can be used individually, they are designed to work together seamlessly, making it easy to connect people and organizations to information, business processes, and each other. The applications include tools used to create, discuss, communicate, and manage projects. If you share a lot of documents with other people, these features facilitate access to common documents. This version has an entirely new user interface that is designed to make it easier to perform tasks and help users more quickly take advantage of all the features in the applications. In addition, the communication and collaboration features and integration with the World Wide Web have been expanded and refined.

The 2007 Microsoft Office System is packaged in several different combinations of programs or suites. The major programs and a brief description are provided in the following table.

Program	Description
Word 2007	Word Processor program used to create text-based documents
Excel 2007	Spreadsheet program used to analyze numerical data
Access 2007	Database manager used to organize, manage, and display a database
PowerPoint 2007	Graphics presentation program used to create presentation materials
Outlook 2007	Desktop information manager and messaging client
InfoPath 2007	Used to create XML forms and documents
OneNote 2007	Note-taking and information organization tools
Publisher 2007	Tools to create and distribute publications for print, Web, and e-mail
Visio 2007	Diagramming and data visualization tools
SharePoint Designer 2007	Web site development and management for SharePoint servers
Project 2007	Project management tools
Groove 2007	Collaboration program that enables teams to work together

The four main components of Microsoft Office 2007—Word, Excel, Access, and PowerPoint—are the applications you will learn about in this series of labs. They are described in more detail in the following sections.

Word 2007

Word 2007 is a word processing software application whose purpose is to help you create text-based documents. Word processors are one of the most flexible and widely used application software programs. A word processor can be used to manipulate text data to produce a letter, a report, a memo, an e-mail message, or any other type of correspondence.

Two documents you will produce in the first two Word 2007 labs, a letter and flyer, are shown here.

A letter containing a tabbed table, indented paragraphs, and text enhancements is quickly created using basic Word features.

September 15, 2008

Dear Adventure Traveler:

Imagine camping under the stars in Africa, hiking and paddling your way through the rainforests of Costa Rica, or following in the footsteps of the ancient Inca as you backpack along the Inca trail to Machu Picchu. Turn these dreams of adventure into memories you will cherish forever by joining Adventure Travel Tours on one of our four new adventure tours.

To tell you more about these exciting new adventures, we are offering several presentations in your area. These presentations will focus on the features and cultures of the region. We will also show you pictures of the places you will visit and activities you can partici... to attend one of the following presentations:

Date	Time
January 5	8:00 p.m.
February 5	7:30 p.m.
March 8	8:00 p.m.

In appreciation of your past patronage, we a... of the new tour packages. You must book the trip at... letter to qualify for the discount.

Our vacation tours are professionally develo... everything in the price of your tour while giving you... these features:

➢ All accommodations and meals
➢ All entrance fees, excursions, transfers and...
➢ Professional tour manager and local guides

We hope you will join us this year on anothe... Travel Tours each day is an adventure. For reservatio... Travel Tours directly at 1-800-555-0004.

A flyer incorporating many visual enhancements such as colored text, varied text styles, and graphic elements is both eye-catching and informative.

Adventure Travel Tours

New Adventures

Attention adventure travelers! Attend an Adventure Travel presentation to learn about some of the earth's greatest unspoiled habitats and find out how you can experience the adventure of a lifetime. This year we are introducing four new tours that offer you a unique opportunity to combine many different outdoor activities while exploring the world.

India Wildlife Adventure

Inca Trail to Machu Picchu

Safari in Tanzania

Costa Rica Rivers and Rainforests

Presentation dates and times are January 5 at 8:00 p.m., February 3 at 7:30 p.m., and March 8 at 8:00 p.m. All presentations are held at convenient hotel locations in downtown Los Angeles, Santa Clara, and at the LAX airport.

Call Student Name 1-800-555-0004 for presentation locations, a full color brochure, and itinerary information, costs, and trip dates.

Visit our Web site at
www.adventuretraveltours.com

The beauty of a word processor is that you can make changes or corrections as you are typing. Want to change a report from single spacing to double spacing? Alter the width of the margins? Delete some paragraphs and add others from yet another document? A word processor allows you to do all these things with ease.

Word 2007 includes many group collaboration features to help streamline how documents are developed and changed by group members. You also can create and send e-mail messages directly from within Word using all its features to create and edit the message. In addition, you can send an entire document as your e-mail message, allowing the recipient to edit the document directly without having to open or save an attachment.

Word 2007 is closely integrated with the World Wide Web, detecting when you type a Web address and automatically converting it to a hyperlink. You also can create your own hyperlinks to locations within documents, or to other documents, including those at external locations such as a Web site or file server. It also includes features that help you quickly create Web pages and blog entries.

Excel 2007

Excel 2007 is an electronic worksheet that is used to organize, manipulate, and graph numeric data. Once used almost exclusively by accountants, worksheets are now widely used by nearly every profession. Marketing professionals record and evaluate sales trends. Teachers record grades and calculate final grades. Personal trainers record the progress of their clients.

Excel 2007 includes many features that not only help you create a well-designed worksheet, but one that produces accurate results. Formatting features include visual enhancements such as varied text styles, colors, and graphics. Other features help you enter complex formulas and identify and correct formula errors. You also can produce a visual display of data in the form of graphs or charts. As the values in the worksheet change, charts referencing those values automatically adjust to reflect the changes.

Excel 2007 also includes many advanced features and tools that help you perform what-if analysis and create different scenarios. And like all Office 2007 applications, it is easy to incorporate data created in one application into another. Two worksheets you will produce in Labs 2 and 3 of Excel 2007 are shown on the next page.

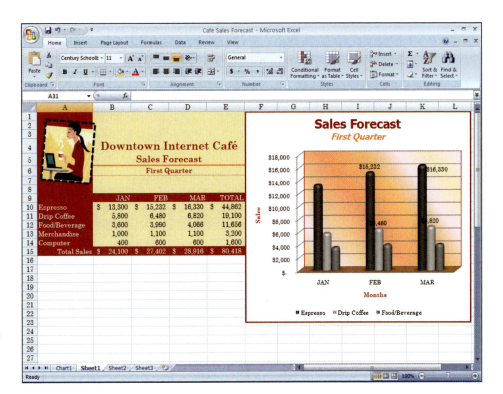

A worksheet showing the quarterly sales forecast containing a graphic, text enhancements, and a chart of the data is quickly created using basic Excel 2007 features.

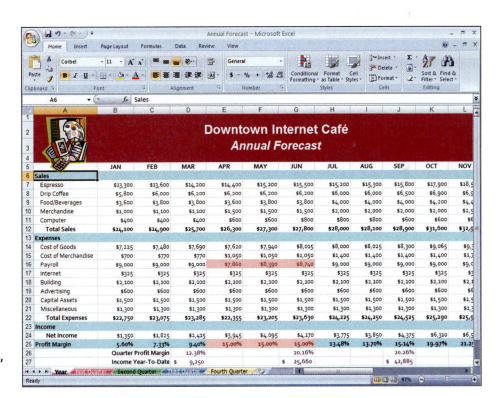

A large worksheet incorporating more complex formulas, visual enhancements such as colored text, varied text styles, and graphic elements is both informative and attractive.

What Is the 2007 Microsoft Office System?   I.5

Excel 2007

You will see how easy it is to analyze data and make projections using what-if analysis and what-if graphing in Lab 3 and to incorporate Excel data in a Word document as shown in the following figures.

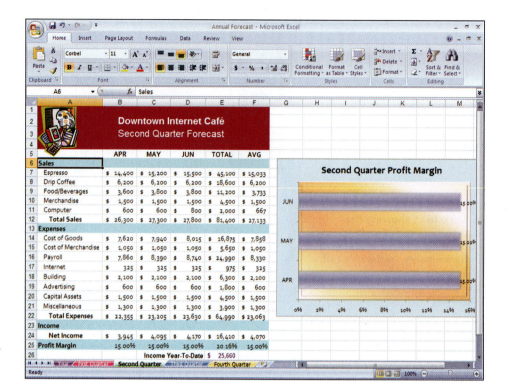

Changes you make in worksheet data while performing what-if analysis are automatically reflected in charts that reference that data.

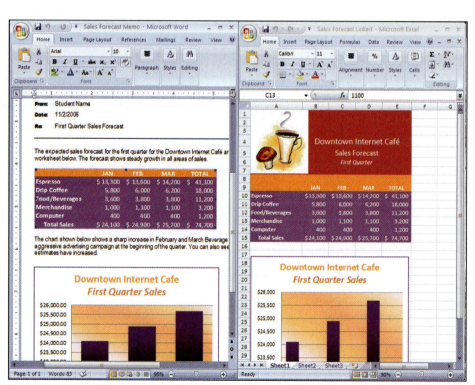

Worksheet data and charts can be copied and linked to other Office documents such as a Word document.

Access 2007

Access 2007 is a relational database management application that is used to create and analyze a database. A database is a collection of related data. In a relational database, the most widely used database structure, data is organized in linked tables. Tables consist of columns (called *fields*) and rows (called *records*). The tables are related or linked to one another by a common field. Relational databases allow you to create smaller and more manageable database tables, since you can combine and extract data between tables.

The program provides tools to enter, edit, and retrieve data from the database as well as to analyze the database and produce reports of the output. One of the main advantages of a computerized database is the ability to quickly add, delete, and locate specific records. Records also can be easily rearranged or sorted according to different fields of data, resulting in multiple table arrangements that provide more meaningful information for different purposes. Creation of forms makes it easier to enter and edit data as well. In the Access labs, you will create and organize the database table shown below.

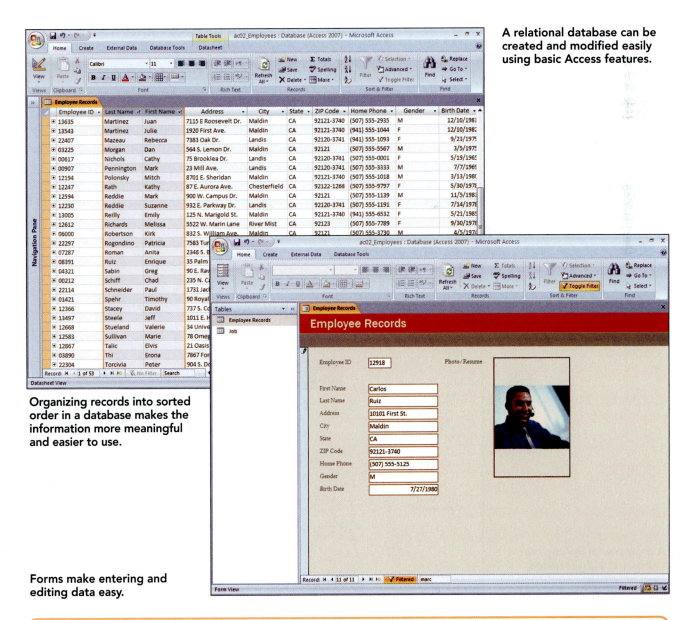

A relational database can be created and modified easily using basic Access features.

Organizing records into sorted order in a database makes the information more meaningful and easier to use.

Forms make entering and editing data easy.

Another feature is the ability to analyze the data in a table and perform calculations on different fields of data. Additionally, you can ask questions or query the table to find only certain records that meet specific conditions to be used in the analysis. Information that was once costly and time-consuming to get is now quickly and readily available. This information can then be quickly printed out in the form of reports ranging from simple listings to complex, professional-looking reports in different layout styles, or with titles, headings, subtotals, or totals.

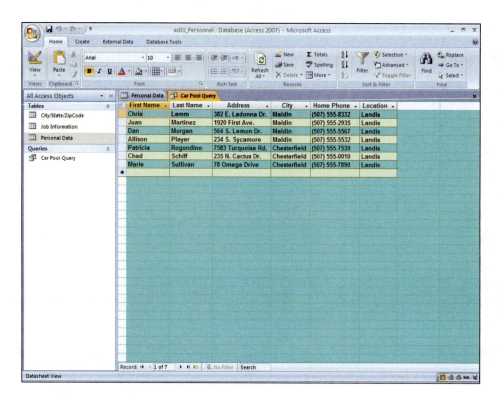

A database can be queried to locate and display only specified information.

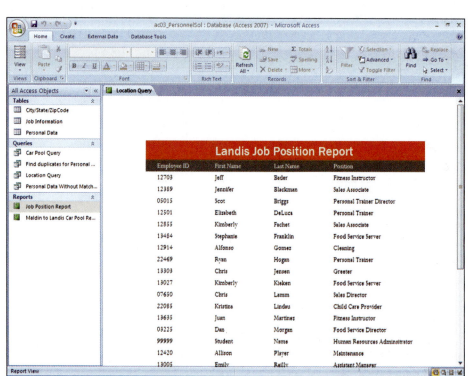

A professional-looking report can be quickly generated from information contained in a database.

PowerPoint 2007

PowerPoint 2007 is a graphics presentation program designed to help you produce a high-quality presentation that is both interesting to the audience and effective in its ability to convey your message. A presentation can be as simple as overhead transparencies or as sophisticated as an on-screen electronic display. In the first two PowerPoint labs, you will create and organize the presentation shown below.

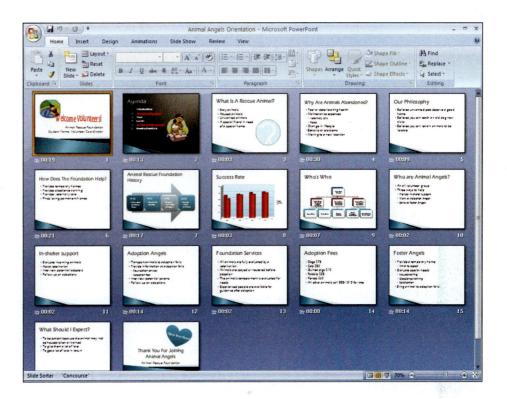

A presentation consists of a series of pages or "slides" presenting the information you want to convey in an organized and attractive manner.

When running an on-screen presentation, each slide of the presentation is displayed full-screen on your computer monitor or projected onto a screen.

What Is the 2007 Microsoft Office System?   I.9

Excel 2007

Common Office 2007 Interface Features

Additional Information

Please read the Before You Begin and Instructional Conventions sections in the Overview of Microsoft Office Excel 2007 (EXO.3) before starting this section.

Now that you know a little about each of the applications in Microsoft Office 2007, we will take a look at some of the interface features that are common to all Office 2007 applications. This is a hands-on section that will introduce you to the features and allow you to get a feel for how Office 2007 works. Although Word 2007 will be used to demonstrate how the features work, only common **user interface** features, a set of graphical images that represent various features, will be addressed. These features include using the File menu, Ribbon, Quick Access Toolbar, task panes, and Office Help, and starting and exiting an application. The features that are specific to each application will be introduced individually in each application text.

Starting an Office 2007 Application

There are several ways to start an Office 2007 application. The two most common methods are by using the Start menu or by clicking a desktop shortcut for the program if it is available. If you use the Start menu, the steps will vary slightly depending on the version of Windows you are using.

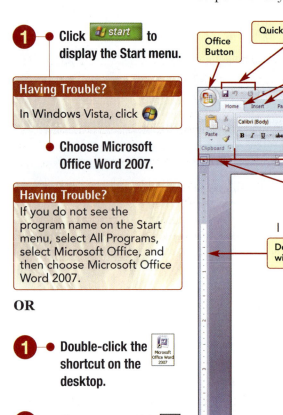

1 ● Click 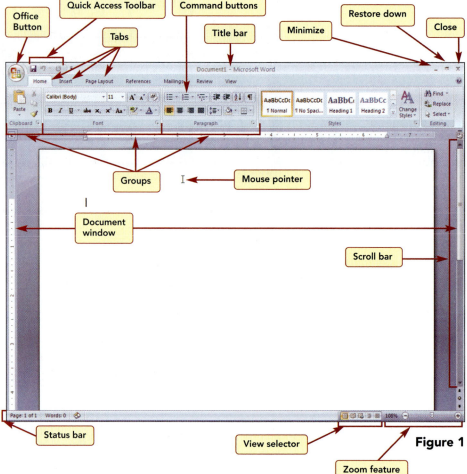 to display the Start menu.

Having Trouble?

In Windows Vista, click 🔵

● Choose Microsoft Office Word 2007.

Having Trouble?

If you do not see the program name on the Start menu, select All Programs, select Microsoft Office, and then choose Microsoft Office Word 2007.

OR

1 ● Double-click the shortcut on the desktop.

2 ● If necessary, click ☐ Maximize in the title bar to maximize the window.

Your screen should be similar to Figure 1

Having Trouble?

Your screen may look slightly different based on your Windows operating system settings.

Figure 1

The Word 2007 program is started and displayed in a window on the desktop. The application window title bar displays the file name followed by the program name, Microsoft Word. The right end of the title bar displays the [-] Minimize, [▫] Restore Down, and [x] Close buttons. They perform the same functions and operate in the same way as all Windows versions.

Below the title bar is the **Ribbon**, which provides a centralized area that makes it easy to find ways to work in your document. The Ribbon has three basic parts: tabs, groups, and commands. **Tabs** are used to divide the Ribbon into major activity areas. Each tab is then organized into **groups** that contain related items. The related items are commands that consist of command buttons, a box to enter information, or a menu. As you use the Office applications, you will see that the Ribbon contains many of the same groups and commands across the applications. You also will see that many of the groups and commands are specific to an application.

The upper left area of the window's title bar displays the ⊕ Office Button and the Quick Access Toolbar. Clicking ⊕ Office Button opens the File menu of commands that allows you to work *with* your document, unlike the Ribbon that allows you to work *in* your document. For example, it includes commands to open, save, and print files. The **Quick Access Toolbar** (QAT) provides quick access to frequently used commands. By default, it includes the ▫ Save, ▫ Undo, and ▫ Redo buttons, commands that Microsoft considers to be crucial. It is always available and is a customizable toolbar to which you can add your own favorite buttons.

The large center area of the program window is the **document window** where open application files are displayed. Currently, there is a blank Word document open. In Word, the mouse pointer appears as I when positioned in the document window and as a ↖ when it can be used to select items.

On the right of the document window is a vertical scroll bar. A **scroll bar** is used with a mouse to bring additional lines of information into view in a window. The vertical scroll bar is used to move up or down. A horizontal scroll bar is also displayed when needed and moves side to side in the window. At the bottom of the window is the **status bar**, a view selector, and a document zoom feature. Similar information and features are displayed in this area for different Office applications. You will learn how these features work in each individual application.

Using the File Menu

Clicking the ⊕ Office Button opens the File menu of commands that are used to work with files.

Your screen should be similar to Figure 2

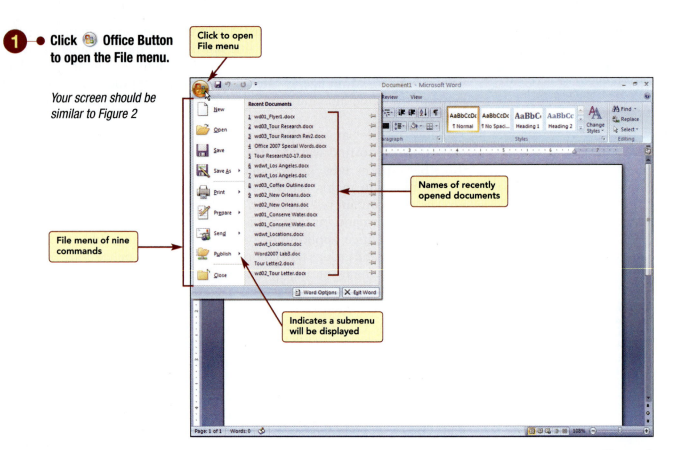

Click to open File menu

Names of recently opened documents

File menu of nine commands

Indicates a submenu will be displayed

Figure 2

The menu lists nine commands that are used to perform tasks associated with files. Notice that each command displays an underlined letter. This identifies the letter you can type to choose the command. Five commands display a ▶, which indicates the command includes a submenu of options. The right side of the command list currently displays the names of recently opened files (your list will display different file names). The default program setting displays a maximum of 17 file names. Once the maximum number of files is listed, when a new file is opened, the oldest is dropped from the list.

Once the File menu is open, you can select a command from the menu by pointing to it. A colored highlight bar, called the **selection cursor**, appears over the selected command.

2 **Point to the Open command.**

Your screen should be similar to Figure 3

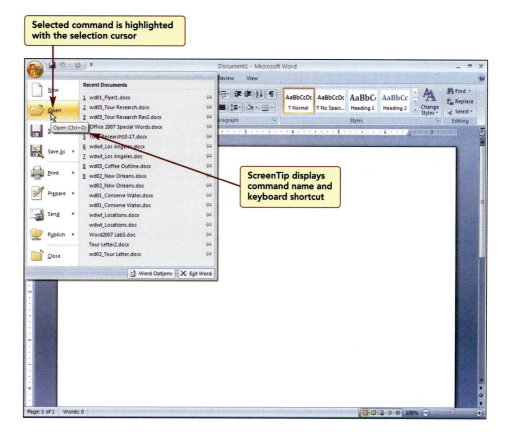

Selected command is highlighted with the selection cursor

ScreenTip displays command name and keyboard shortcut

Figure 3

A **ScreenTip**, also called a **tooltip**, briefly appears displaying the command name and the keyboard shortcut, [Ctrl] + O. The keyboard shortcut can be used to execute this command without opening the menu. In this case, if you hold down the [Ctrl] key while typing the letter O, you will access the Open command without having to open the File menu first. ScreenTips also often include a brief description of the action a command performs.

Next you will select a command that will display a submenu of options.

3 • **Point to the Prepare command.**

• **Point to the Mark as Final submenu option.**

Your screen should be similar to Figure 4

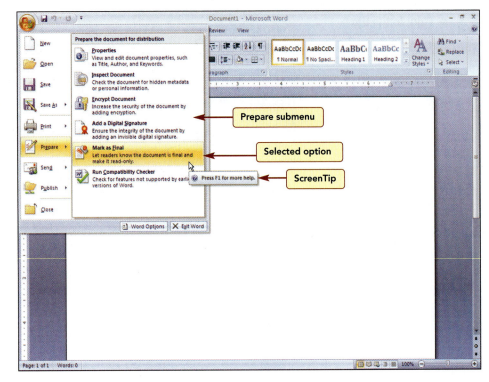

Figure 4

The submenu lists the six Prepare command submenu options and the Mark as Final option is selected. A ScreenTip provides information about how to get help on this feature. You will learn about using Help shortly.

4 • **Point to the Print command.**

• **Point to the of the Print command.**

Your screen should be similar to Figure 5

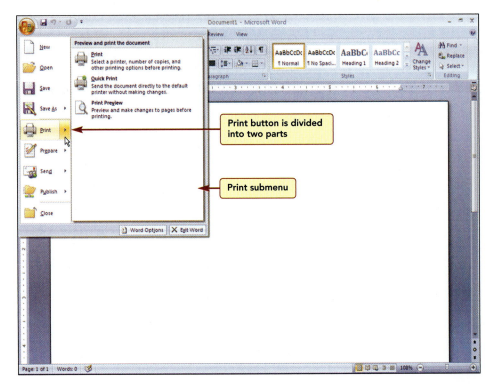

Figure 5

Introduction to Microsoft Office 2007

www.mhhe.com/oleary

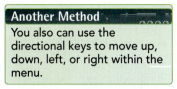
5 ● **Click the Print command.**

Your screen should be similar to Figure 6

So far you have only selected commands; you have not chosen them. To choose a command, you click on it. When the command is chosen, the associated action is performed. Notice the Print command is divided into two parts. Clicking the Print section on the left will choose the command and open the Print dialog box. Clicking ⊡ in the right section has no effect.

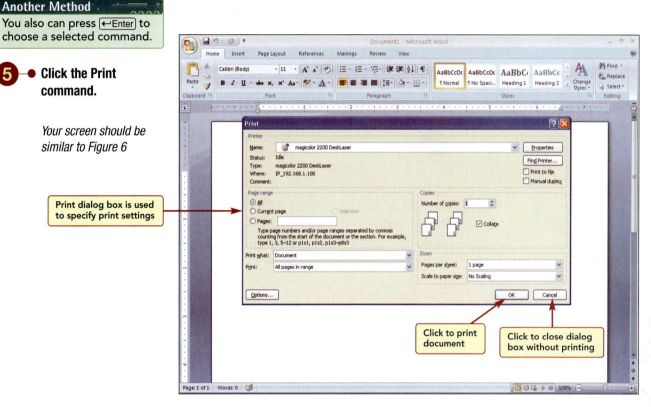

Print dialog box is used to specify print settings

Click to print document

Click to close dialog box without printing

Figure 6

In the Print dialog box, you would specify the print settings and click ⎓ OK ⎓ to actually print a document. In this case, you will cancel the action and continue to explore other features of the Office 2007 application.

6 ● **Click** ⎓ Cancel ⎓ .

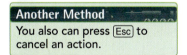
Using Context Menus

Another way to access some commands is to use a context menu. A **context menu** is opened by right-clicking on an item on the screen. This menu is context sensitive, meaning it displays only those commands relevant to the item. For example, right-clicking on the Quick Access Toolbar will display the commands associated with using the Quick Access Toolbar only. You will use this method to move the Quick Access Toolbar.

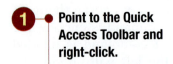

1 ● Point to the Quick Access Toolbar and right-click.

Another Method

You also can click ▾ at the end of the Quick Access toolbar to open the menu.

● Click the Show Quick Access Toolbar below the Ribbon option.

Your screen should be similar to Figure 7

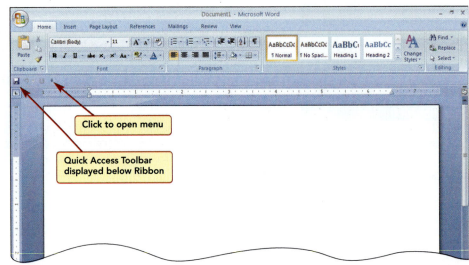

Click to open menu

Quick Access Toolbar displayed below Ribbon

Figure 7

The Quick Access Toolbar is now displayed full size below the Ribbon. This is useful if you have many buttons on the toolbar; however, it takes up document viewing space. You will return it to its compact size using the toolbar's drop-down menu.

2 ● Click ▾ on the right end of the Quick Access Toolbar.

● Choose Show Above the Ribbon.

Your screen should be similar to Figure 8

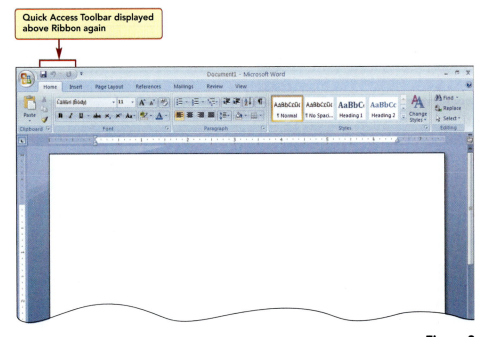

Quick Access Toolbar displayed above Ribbon again

Figure 8

MORE ABOUT

▶ See the More About appendix to learn how to customize the Quick Access Toolbar.

The Quick Access Toolbar is displayed above the Ribbon again. The toolbar's drop-down menu contains a list of commands that are often added to the toolbar. Clicking on the command selects it and adds it to the toolbar.

Using the Ribbon

The Ribbon displays tabs that organize similar features into groups. In Word, there are seven tabs displayed. To save space, some tabs, called **contextual** or **on-demand tabs**, are displayed only as needed. For example, when you are working with a picture, the Picture Tools tab appears. The contextual nature of this feature keeps the work area uncluttered when the feature is not needed and provides ready access to it when it is needed.

Opening Tabs

The Home tab is open when you first start the application or open a file. It consists of five groups: Clipboard, Font, Paragraph, Styles, and Editing. Each group contains command buttons that when clicked on perform their associated action or display a list of additional commands. The commands in the Home tab help you perform actions related to creating the content of your document.

1 ● **Click on the Insert tab.**

Your screen should be similar to Figure 9

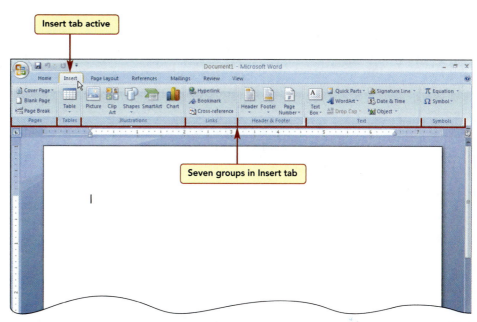

Figure 9

This Insert tab is now the active tab. It contains seven groups whose commands have to do with inserting items into a document.

2 ● **Click on each of the other tabs, ending with the View tab, to see their groups and commands.**

Your screen should be similar to Figure 10

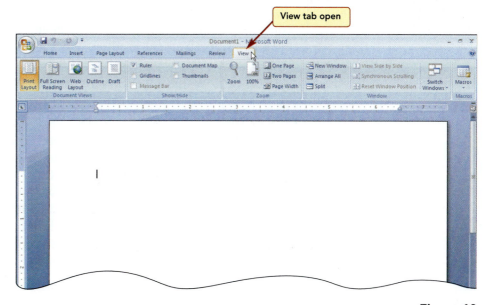

Figure 10

Each tab relates to a type of activity; for example, the View tab commands perform activities related to viewing the document. Within each tab, similar commands are grouped together to make finding the commands you want to use much easier.

Displaying Super Tooltips

Many command buttons immediately perform the associated action when you click on them. The buttons are graphic representations of the action they perform. To help you find out what a button does, you can display the button's ScreenTip.

1 Open the Home tab.

• Point to the upper part of the ⬚ Paste button in the Clipboard group.

• Point to the lower part of the Paste button in the Clipboard group.

• Point to ⬚ Format Painter in the Clipboard group.

Your screen should be similar to Figure 11

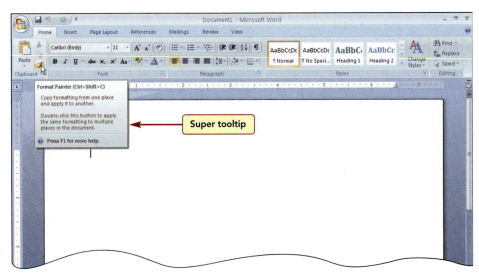

Super tooltip

Figure 11

Additional Information

Not all commands have shortcut keys.

Additional Information

You will learn about using Help shortly.

The ⬚ Paste button is a split button; clicking the upper section of the button immediately performs the action and clicking the lower section displays a menu of options. Both parts of the Paste button display tooltips containing the button name, the shortcut key combination, Ctrl + V, and a brief description of what the button does. Pointing to ⬚ Format Painter displays a **super tooltip** that provides more detailed information about the command. Super tooltips may even display information such as procedures or illustrations. You can find out what the feature does without having to look it up in Help. If a feature has a Help article, you can automatically access it by pressing F1 while the super tooltip is displayed.

Using Galleries and Lists

Many commands in the groups appear as a **gallery** that displays small graphics that represent the result of applying a command. For example, in the Styles group, the command buttons to apply different formatting styles to text display examples of how the text would look if formatted using that command. These are called **in-Ribbon galleries** because they appear directly in the Ribbon. Other commands include multiple options that appear in **drop-down galleries** or drop-down lists that are accessed by clicking the ⬚ button on the right side of the command button. To see an example of a drop-down gallery, you will open the ⬚ Bullets drop-down gallery.

1 ● Click ⬚ in the ⬚ Bullets button.

Your screen should be similar to Figure 12

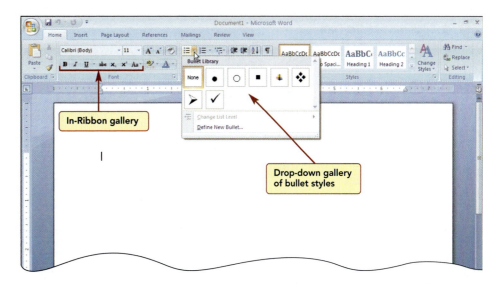

In-Ribbon gallery

Drop-down gallery of bullet styles

Figure 12

A drop-down gallery of different bullets is displayed. The drop-down gallery will disappear when you make a selection or click on any other area of the window. To see an example of a drop-down list, you will open the `11 ▾` Font Size drop-down list.

2 ● Click outside the Bullet gallery to clear it.

● Click ⬚ in the `11 ▾` Font Size button.

Your screen should be similar to Figure 13

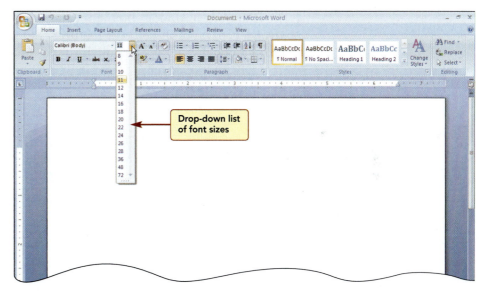

Drop-down list of font sizes

Figure 13

If you click on the button itself, not the ⬚ section of the button, the associated command is performed.

Using the Dialog Box Launcher

Because there is not enough space, only the most used commands are displayed in the Ribbon. If there are more commands available, a ⬚ button, called the **dialog box launcher**, is displayed in the lower-right corner of the group. Clicking ⬚ opens a dialog box or **task pane** of additional options.

1 ● **Click outside the Font size list to clear it.**

● **Point to the 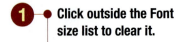 of the Paragraph group to see the tooltip.**

● **Click 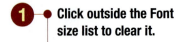 of the Paragraph group.**

Your screen should be similar to Figure 14

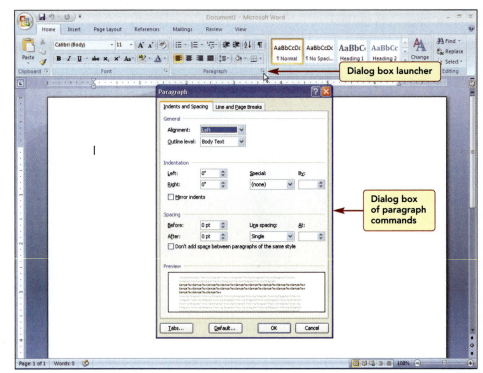

Figure 14

The Paragraph dialog box appears. It provides access to the more advanced paragraph settings features. Selecting options from the dialog box and clicking [OK] will close the dialog box and apply the settings as specified. To cancel the dialog box, you can click [Cancel] or [X] in the dialog box title bar.

2 ● **Click [Cancel] to close the dialog box.**

● **Click 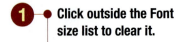 in the Clipboard group.**

Your screen should be similar to Figure 15

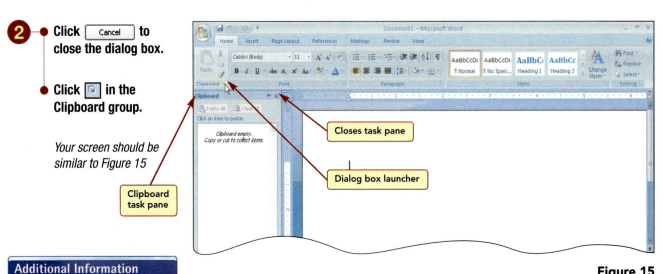

Figure 15

Additional Information
You will learn about using dialog boxes, task panes, and the Clipboard as they are used in the labs.

A task pane is open that contains features associated with the Clipboard. Unlike dialog boxes, task panes remain open until you close them. This allows you to make multiple selections from the task pane while continuing to work on other areas of your document.

3 ● **Click [X] in the upper-right corner of the task pane to close it.**

Using Access Key Shortcuts

Another way to use commands on the Ribbon is to display the access key shortcuts by pressing the [Alt] key and then typing the letter for the feature you want to use. Every Ribbon tab, group, and command has an access key.

● Press [Alt].

Another Method
You also can press [F10] to display the access keys.

Your screen should be similar to Figure 16

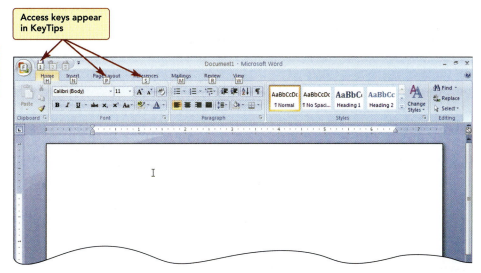

Access keys appear in KeyTips

Figure 16

The letters are displayed in **KeyTips** over each available feature. Now typing a letter will access that feature. Then, depending on which letter you pressed, additional KeyTips may appear. To use a Ribbon command, press the key of the tab first, then the group, and then continue pressing letters until you press the letter of the specific command you want to use. You will use KeyTips to display the Paragraph dialog box again.

● Type the letter **H** to access the Home tab.

● Type the letters **PG** to access the Paragraph group and open the dialog box.

Your screen should be similar to Figure 17

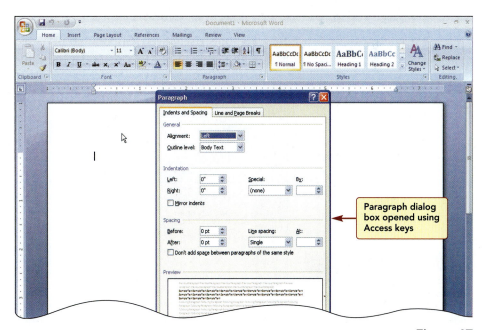

Paragraph dialog box opened using Access keys

Figure 17

Three keystrokes opened the Paragraph dialog box.

Once the Access key feature is on, you can also use the [←] or [→] directional key to move from one tab to another, and the [↓] key to move from a tab to a group and the [↑] key to move from a group to a tab. You can use all four directional keys to move among the commands in a Ribbon. [Tab ⇄] and [⇧ Shift] + [Tab ⇄] also can be used to move right or left. Once a command is selected, you can press [Spacebar] or [←Enter] to activate it.

Minimizing the Ribbon

Sometimes you may not want to see the entire Ribbon so that more space is available in the document area. You can minimize the Ribbon by double-clicking the active tab.

1 ● Click ❌ to close the Paragraph dialog box.

● Double-click the Home tab.

Your screen should be similar to Figure 18

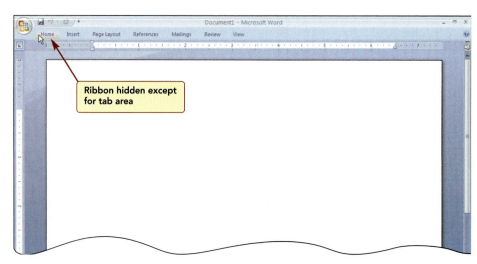

Ribbon hidden except for tab area

Figure 18

Now, the only part of the Ribbon that is visible is the tab area. This allows you to quickly reopen the Ribbon and, at the same time, open the selected tab.

2 ● Double-click the Insert tab.

Your screen should be similar to Figure 19

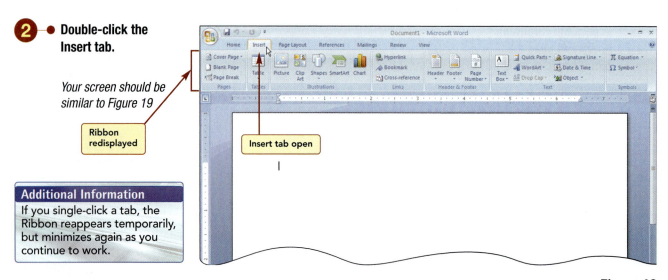

Ribbon redisplayed

Insert tab open

Figure 19

The full Ribbon reappears and the Insert tab is open and ready for use.

Using the Mini Toolbar

Another method of accessing commands is through the Mini toolbar. The **Mini toolbar** appears automatically when you select text in a document and provides commands that are used to format (enhance) text. It also appears along with the context menu when you right-click an item in a document. Both the Mini toolbar and context menus are designed to make it more efficient to execute commands.

You can see what these features look like by right-clicking in a blank area of the document window.

1 ● **Right-click the blank document window space.**

Your screen should be similar to Figure 20

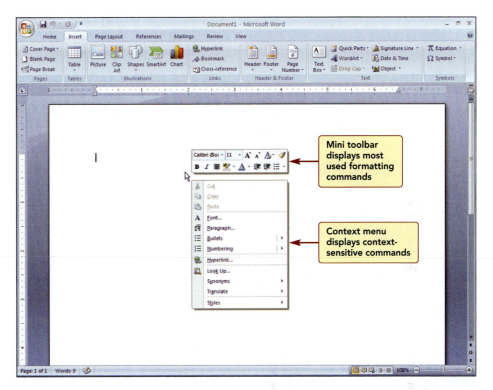

Mini toolbar displays most used formatting commands

Context menu displays context-sensitive commands

Figure 20

The Mini toolbar displays the most frequently used formatting commands. For example, when the Home tab is closed, you can use the commands in the Mini toolbar to quickly change selected text without having to reopen the Home tab to access the command. When the Mini toolbar appears automatically, it is faded so that it does not interfere with what you are doing, but changes to solid (as it is here) when you point at it.

The context menu below the Mini toolbar displays a variety of commands that are quicker to access than locating the command on the Ribbon. The commands that appear on this menu change depending on what you are doing at the time.

Using Office Help

Another Method
You also can press F1 to access Help.

Notice the [?] in the upper-right corner of the Ribbon. This button is used to access the Microsoft Help system. The Help button is always visible even when the Ribbon is hidden. Because you are using the Office Word 2007 application, Office Word Help will be accessed.

1 ●— **Click** ⊙ **Microsoft Office Word Help.**

● **If a Table of Contents list is displayed along the left side of the Help window, click** ⊡ **in the Help window toolbar to close it.**

Additional Information

You will learn about using the Table of Contents shortly.

Your screen should be similar to Figure 21

Additional Information

Clicking the scroll arrows scrolls the text in the window line by line, and dragging the scroll bar up or down moves to a general location within the window area.

Additional Information

Because Help is an online feature, the information is frequently updated. Your screens may display slightly different information than those shown in the figures in this lab.

Having Trouble?

In addition to being connected to the Internet, the feature to show content from the Internet must be selected. If necessary, click the 🔵 Offline button at the bottom of the Help window and choose Show content from Office Online.

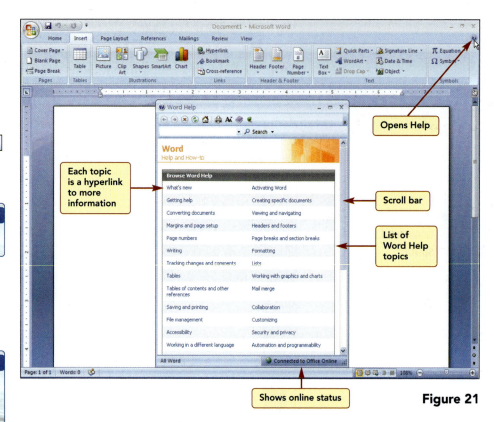

Figure 21

The Microsoft Word Help feature is opened and displayed in a separate window. The Help window on your screen will probably be a different size and arrangement than in Figure 21. Depending on the size of your Help window, you may need to scroll the window to see all the Help information provided.

It displays a listing of Help topics. If you are connected to the Internet, the Microsoft Office Online Web site is accessed and help information from this site is displayed in the window. If you are not connected, the offline help information that is provided with the application and stored on your computer is located and displayed. Generally, the listing of topics is similar but fewer in number.

Selecting Help Topics

There are several ways you can get help. The first is to select a topic from the listing displayed in the Help window. Each topic is a **hyperlink** or connection to the information located on the Online site or in Help on your computer. When you point to the hyperlink, it appears underlined and the mouse pointer appears as ⟨🖑⟩. Clicking the hyperlink accesses and displays the information associated with the hyperlink.

The information on the selected subtopic is displayed. Clicking the table of contents link jumped directly to this section of the window, saving you time by not having to scroll. The ▶ preceding the subtopic has changed to ▼, indicating the subtopic content is displayed.

Additional Information

In Windows Vista, these buttons are ⊞ Show All and ⊟ Hide All .

You can continue to click on the subtopic headings to display the information about each topic individually. Likewise, clicking on an expanded topic hides the information. Additionally you can click ▶ Show All located at the top of the window to display all the available topic information and ▼ Hide All to hide all expanded information.

Searching Help Topics

Another method to find Help information is to conduct a search by entering a sentence or question you want help on in the Search text box of the Help window. Although you also can simply enter a word in the Search box, the best results occur when you type a phrase, complete sentence, or question. A very specific search with 2–7 words will return the most accurate results.

When searching, you can specify the scope of the search by selecting from the Search scope drop-down menu. The broadest scope for a search, All Word, is preselected. You will narrow the scope to search Word Help only.

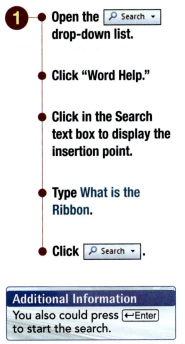

1 ● Open the 🔍 Search ▾ drop-down list.

● Click "Word Help."

● Click in the Search text box to display the insertion point.

● Type **What is the Ribbon.**

● Click 🔍 Search ▾ .

Additional Information

You also could press ←Enter to start the search.

Your screen should be similar to Figure 26

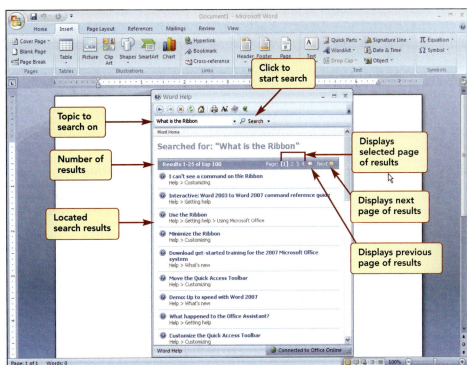

Figure 26

The first 25 located results of the top 100 are displayed in a window. There are four pages of results. The results are shown in order of relevance, with the most likely matches at the top of the list. Now you can continue to locate the information you need by selecting from the topic links provided. To see the next page of results, you can click **Next** or ➡ or click the specific page number you want to see from the Page count area. To see the previous page of results, click ⬅ .

Topics preceded with  indicate the window will display the related Help topic. Those preceded with a ⊞ indicate a tutorial about the topic is available from the Microsoft Training Web site.

2 ● **Click "Use the Ribbon."**

Your screen should be similar to Figure 27

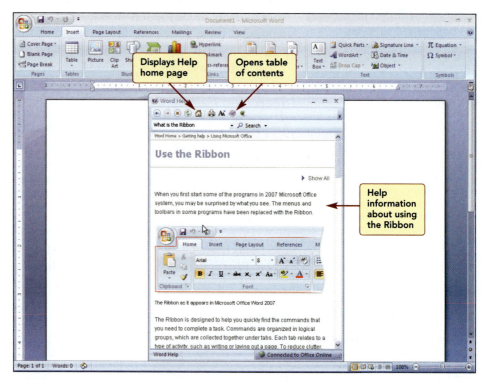

Figure 27

The same Help information you saw previously is displayed.

Using the Help Table of Contents

A third source of help is to use the Help table of contents. Using this method allows you to browse the entire list of Help topics to locate topics of interest to you.

1 ● Click 🏠 **Home in the Help window toolbar to return to the opening Help window.**

● Click 🔽 **Show Table of Contents from the Help window toolbar.**

Additional Information

You also could click ⬅ Back in the Help window toolbar to return to the previous page, page by page.

Your screen should be similar to Figure 28

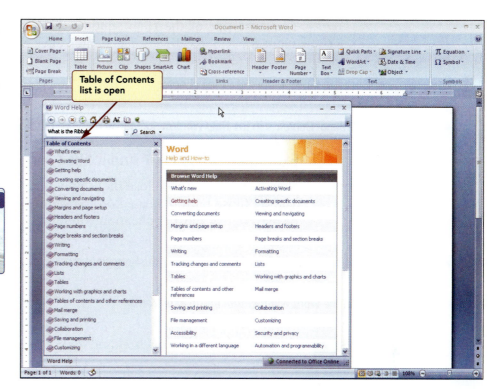

Figure 28

Additional Information

Pointing to an item in the Table of Contents displays a ScreenTip of the entire topic heading.

The entire Word Help Table of Contents is displayed in a pane on the left side of the Help window. Clicking on an item preceded with a 🔽 Closed Book icon opens a chapter, which expands to display additional chapters or topics. The 📖 Open Book icon identifies those chapters that are open.

Clicking on an item preceded with 🔘 displays the specific Help information.

2 ● Click "Getting help" to open this chapter.

● Click "Using Microsoft Office."

● Scroll the table of contents list and click "Use the Ribbon."

Your screen should be similar to Figure 29

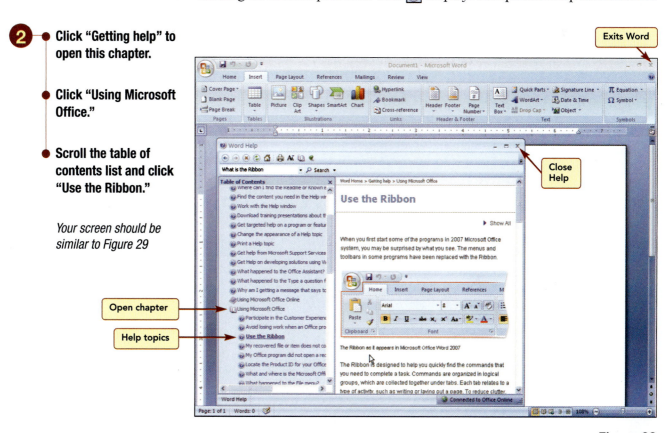

Figure 29

The right side of the Help window displays the same Help information about the Ribbon. To close a chapter, click the ⊡ icon.

3 ● Click ⊡ to close the Using Microsoft Office chapter.

● Click ⊡ Hide Table of Contents in the Help window toolbar to hide the table of contents list again.

Exiting an Office 2007 Application

Now you are ready to close the Help window and exit the Word program. The ⊠ Close button located on the right end of the window title bar can be used to exit most application windows.

1 ● Click ⊠ Close in the Help window title bar to close the Help window.

● Click ⊠ Close in the Word window title bar to exit Word.

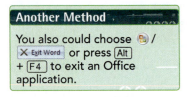

Another Method

You also could choose ▣ / ✕ Exit Word or press [Alt] + [F4] to exit an Office application.

The program window is closed and the desktop is visible again.

Lab Review

Introduction to Microsoft Office 2007

command summary

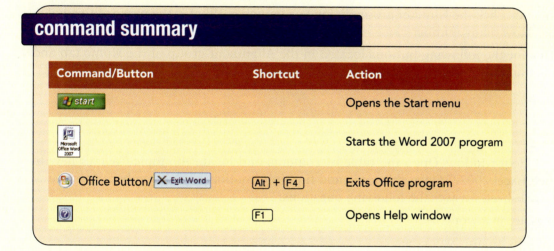

Command/Button	Shortcut	Action
start		Opens the Start menu
Microsoft Office Word 2007		Starts the Word 2007 program
Office Button/ ✕ Exit Word	Alt + F4	Exits Office program
❓	F1	Opens Help window

Lab Exercises

step-by-step

Using an Office Application ★

1. All Office 2007 applications have a common user interface. You will explore the Excel 2007 application and use many of the same features you learned about while using Word 2007 in this lab.

   a. Use the Start menu or a shortcut icon on your desktop to start Office Excel 2007.

   b. What shape is the mouse pointer when positioned in the document window area? _____

   c. Excel has _____ tabs. Which tabs are not the same as in Word? _____

   d. Open the Formulas tab. How many groups are in the Formulas tab? _____

   e. Which tab contains the group to work with charts? _____

   f. From the Home tab, click the Number group dialog box launcher. What is the name of the dialog box that opens? How many number categories are there? _____ Close the dialog box.

   g. Display ToolTips for the following buttons located in the Alignment group of the Home tab and identify what action they perform.

   ▤ _____

   ▤ _____

   ▤ _____

   h. Open the Excel Help window. Open the table of contents and locate the topic "What's new in Microsoft Office Excel 2007?" Open this topic and find information on the number of rows and columns in a worksheet. Answer the following questions:

   How many rows are in a worksheet? _____

   How many columns are in a worksheet? _____

   What are the letters of the last column? _____

   i. Close the table of contents. Close the Help window. Exit Excel.

on your own

Exploring Microsoft Help ★

1. In addition to the Help information you used in this lab, Office 2007 Online Help also includes many interactive tutorials. Selecting a Help topic that starts a tutorial will open the browser program on your computer. Both audio and written instructions are provided. You will use one of these tutorials to learn more about using Word 2007.

   Start Word 2007. Open Help and open the topic "What's New?" Click on the topic "Up to speed with Word 2007." Follow the directions in your browser to run the tutorial. When you are done, close the browser window, close Help, and exit Word 2007.

Overview of Microsoft Office Excel 2007

What Is an Electronic Spreadsheet?

The electronic spreadsheet, or worksheet, is an automated version of the accountant's ledger. Like the accountant's ledger, it consists of rows and columns of numerical data. Unlike the accountant's ledger, which is created on paper using a pencil and a calculator, the electronic spreadsheet is created by a computer system running spreadsheet application software.

In contrast to word processing software that manipulates text, spreadsheet programs manipulate numerical data. The first spreadsheet program, VisiCalc, was introduced in 1979. Since then, spreadsheets have evolved into a powerful business tool that has revolutionized the business world.

The electronic spreadsheet eliminates the paper, pencil, and eraser. With a few keystrokes, the user can quickly change, correct, and update the data. Even more impressive is the spreadsheet's ability to perform calculations from very simple sums to the most complex financial and mathematical formulas. The calculator is replaced by the electronic spreadsheet. Analysis of data in the spreadsheet has become a routine business procedure. Once requiring hours of labor and/or costly accountants' fees, data analysis is now available almost instantly using electronic spreadsheets.

Nearly any job that uses rows and columns of numbers can be performed using an electronic spreadsheet. Typical uses include the creation of budgets and financial planning for both business and personal situations.

Excel 2007 Features

Spreadsheet applications help you create well-designed spreadsheets that produce accurate results. These programs not only make it faster to create spreadsheets, they also produce professional-appearing results. Their advantages include the ability to quickly edit and format data, perform calculations, create charts, and print the spreadsheet. Using Excel 2007, you can quickly analyze and manage data and communicate your findings to others.

The Microsoft Office Excel 2007 spreadsheet program uses a workbook file that contains one or more worksheets. Each worksheet can be used to organize different types of related information. Numeric or text data is entered into the worksheet in a location called a cell. These entries can then be erased, moved, copied, or edited. Formulas can be entered that perform calculations using data contained in specified cells. The results of the calculations are displayed in the cell containing the formula. Columns and rows can be inserted and deleted. The cell width can be changed to accommodate entries of varying lengths.

The design and appearance of the worksheet can be enhanced in many ways. There are many commands that control the format or display of a cell. For instance, numeric entries can be displayed with dollar signs or with a set number of decimal places. Text or label entries can be displayed centered, left-, or right-aligned to improve the spreadsheet's appearance. You can further enhance the appearance of the worksheet by changing the font style and size and by adding special effects such as bold, italic, borders, boxes, drop shadows, and shading to selected cells. You also can use cell styles to quickly apply predefined combinations of these formats to selections. Additionally, you can select from different document themes, predefined combinations of colors, fonts, and effects, to give your workbooks a consistent, professional appearance.

You can change the values in selected cells and observe their effect on related cells in the worksheet. This is called what-if or sensitivity analysis. Questions that once were too expensive to ask or took too long to answer can now be answered almost instantly and with little cost. Planning that was once partially based on instinct has been replaced to a great extent with facts. However, any financial planning resulting from the data in a worksheet is only as accurate as that data and the logic behind the calculations. Once your data is set, you can add conditional formatting to ranges of cells to emphasize data based on a set of criteria you establish and to highlight trends.

You also can produce a visual display of data in the form of graphs or charts. As the values in the worksheet change, charts referencing those values automatically adjust to reflect the changes. You also can enhance the appearance of a graph by using different type styles and sizes, adding three-dimensional effects, and including text and objects such as lines and arrows.

Finally, Excel 2007 offers many ways to share data and communicate information to others. The most common ways to share are by sending workbooks through e-mail, by faxing workbooks, and by printing and distributing copies of workbooks. You can set up workbooks to allow multiple users to edit and modify the workbook simultaneously. Alternatively, you can distribute multiple copies of workbooks and then merge the changes from several of the copies. You can review the changes and accept or reject them as needed.

Case Study for Office Excel 2007 Labs

The Downtown Internet Café is a new concept in coffeehouses, combining the delicious aromas of a genuine coffeehouse with the fun of using the Internet. You are the new manager for the coffeehouse and are working with the owner, Evan, to develop a financial plan for the next year.

Lab 1: Your first project is to develop a forecast for the Café showing the estimated sales and expenses for the first quarter. You will learn to enter numbers, perform calculations, copy data, label rows and columns, and format entries in a spreadsheet using Office Excel 2007.

Lab 2: After creating the first-quarter forecast, you decide to chart the sales data to make it easier to see the trends and growth patterns. You also want to see what effect a strong advertising promotion of the new Café features will have on the forecasted sales data.

Lab 3: You have been asked to revise the workbook to include forecasts for the second, third, and fourth quarters. Additionally, the owner wants you to create a composite worksheet that shows the entire year's forecast and to change the data to achieve a 15 percent profit margin in the second quarter.

Working Together 1: Your analysis of sales data for the first quarter has shown a steady increase in total sales. Evan, the Café owner, has asked you for a copy of the forecast that shows the growth in sales if a strong sales promotion is mounted. You will include the worksheet and chart data in a Word memo to the owner.

Before You Begin

To the Student

The following assumptions have been made:

- Microsoft Office Excel 2007 has been properly installed on your computer system.

- You have the data files needed to complete the series of Excel 2007 labs and practice exercises. These may be supplied by your instructor and are also available at the online learning center Web site found at www.mhhe.com/oleary.

- You are already familiar with how to use Microsoft Windows XP or Vista and a mouse.

To the Instructor

A complete installation of Microsoft Office Excel 2007 is required in which all components are available to students while completing the labs. In several labs, an online connection to the Web is needed to fully access a feature.

Please be aware that the following settings are assumed to be in effect for the Office Excel 2007 program. These assumptions are necessary so that the screens and directions in the labs are accurate. These settings are made using Office Button/ Excel Options in the categories shown below.

Popular

- The Mini Toolbar feature is active.

- The Live Preview feature is enabled.

- ClearType is on.

- The color scheme setting is blue.

- Show feature descriptions in ScreenTips is selected.

- Body Font is the selected font for a new workbook in a font size of 11 points.

- New sheets are displayed in Normal view.

- Three sheets are included in a new workbook file.
- Language is set to English (US).

Formulas

- Workbook calculation is set to Automatic.
- Formula AutoComplete is on.
- Use table names in formulas is on.
- Use GetPivotData functions for PivotTable references is on.
- Background error checking is on and errors are indicated using green.
- All error checking rules are on except Formulas referring to empty cells.

Proofing

- All AutoCorrect options are on.
- All AutoFormat options are on.
- SmartTags is off.
- Ignore words in Uppercase is on.
- Ignore words that contain numbers is on.
- Ignore Internet and file addresses is on.
- Flag repeated words is on.

Advanced/Editing Options

- All editing options are on except Automatically insert a decimal point and Zoom on roll with IntelliMouse.
- The selection moves Down after pressing Enter.

Advanced/Cut, Copy, and Paste

- All options are on.

Advanced/Display

- All options are on with the following settings:
  - Show 17 Recent Documents.
  - Ruler units is set to Default Units.
  - Cell comments show comments and indicators.

Advanced/Display options for this workbook: Book 1

- All options are on.

Advanced/Display options for this worksheet: Sheet 1

- All options are on except:
  - Show formulas in cells instead of their calculated results.
  - Show page breaks.
- Gridline color is set to black.

Advanced/Formulas

- All options are on.

Advanced/When calculating this workbook: Book 1

- Update links to other documents is on.
- Save external link values is on.

Advanced/General

- Ask to update automatic links is on.
- Scale content for A4 or 8.5 × 11" paper sizes is on.

Customize

- The Quick Access toolbar displays the Save, Undo, and Redo buttons.

Finally, the feature to access Online Help is on. (From the Help window, open the Connection Status menu and choose Show Content from Office Online.)

All figures in the text reflect the use of a display monitor set at 1024 by 768 and the Windows XP operating system. If other monitor display settings are used, there may be more or fewer lines of information displayed in the windows than in the figures. If the Windows Vista operating system is used, some features may look slightly different.

Instructional Conventions

Hands-on instructions you are to perform appear as a sequence of numbered steps. Within each step, a series of bullets identifies the specific actions that must be performed. Step numbering begins over within each topic heading throughout the lab. Four types of margin notes appear throughout the labs. Another Method notes provide alternate ways of performing the same command. Having Trouble? notes provide advice or cautions for steps that may cause problems. Additional Information notes provide more information about a topic. More About notes refer you to the More About Excel 2007 appendix for additional information about related features.

Commands

Commands that are initiated using a command button and the mouse appear following the word "Click." The icon (and the icon name if the icon does not include text) is displayed following "Click." If there is another way to perform the same action, it appears in an Another Method margin note when the action is first introduced, as shown in Example A.

As you become more familiar with the application, commands will appear as shown in Example B.

Example A

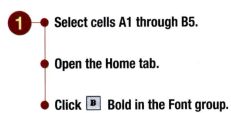

1. Select cells A1 through B5.

   Open the Home tab.

   Click **B** Bold in the Font group.

Another Method
The keyboard shortcut is
Ctrl + B.

Example B

1 ● Select cells A1:B5.

● Click 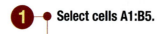 **B** Bold in the Font group of the Home tab.

OR

1 ● Bold cells A1:B5.

File Names and Information to Type

Plain blue text identifies file names you need to select or enter. Information you are asked to type appears in blue and bold. (See Example C.)

Example C

1 ● **Open the workbook** ex01_Cafe Sales.xlsx.

● **Type** Downtown Internet Café **in cell B2.**

 Office Button

Clicking on the Microsoft Office button  will open the File menu of commands. Commands that are to be selected follow the word "Select" and appear in black text. You can select an item by pointing to it using the mouse or by moving to it using the directional keys. When an option is selected, it appears highlighted. Commands that you are to choose to perform the associated action appear following the word "Choose." You can choose a command by clicking on it using the mouse or by pressing the ←Enter key once it is selected. Initially these commands will appear as in Example A. As you become more familiar with the application, commands will appear as shown in Example B.

Example A

1 — ● Click  Office Button.

   ● Select Print.

   ● Choose Print Preview.

Example B

1 —● Click  Office Button, select Print, and choose Print Preview.

   OR

1 —● Preview the worksheet.

Creating and Editing a Worksheet

LAB 1

Objectives

After completing this lab, you will know how to:

1 Enter, edit, and clear cell entries.

2 Adjust column widths.

3 Save, close, and open workbooks.

4 Spell-check a worksheet.

5 Use the thesaurus.

6 Copy and move cell entries.

7 Specify ranges.

8 Enter formulas and functions.

9 Insert and delete rows and columns.

10 Change cell alignment.

11 Format cells.

12 Enter and format a date.

13 Preview and print a worksheet.

Case Study

Downtown Internet Café

You are excited about your new position as manager and financial planner for a local coffeehouse. Evan, the owner, has hired you as part of a larger effort to increase business at the former Downtown Café. Evan began this effort by completely renovating his coffeehouse and installing a wireless network. He plans to offer free Wi-Fi service for customers to use with their own laptop computers. In addition, he has set up several computer kiosks for customers to use who do not have laptops and has provided a printer and copier for all customers to use. He also has decided to rent an MP3 download kiosk for customers who may want to update the music on their iPods or PDAs. Finally, to reflect the new emphasis of the café, he has changed its name to the Downtown Internet Café.

You and Evan expect to increase sales by attracting techno-savvy café-goers, who you hope will use the Downtown Internet

Café as a place to meet, study, work, or download music for their iPods and PDAs. You also believe the rental computers will be a draw for vacationers who want to check e-mail during their travels.

Evan wants to create a forecast estimating sales and expenses for the first quarter. As part of a good business plan, you and Evan need a realistic set of financial estimates and goals.

In this lab, you will help with the first quarter forecast by using Microsoft Office Excel 2007, a spreadsheet application that can store, manipulate, and display numeric data. You will learn to enter numbers, perform calculations, copy data, and label rows and columns as you create the basic structure of a worksheet for the Downtown Internet Café. You will then learn how to enhance the worksheet using formatting features and by adding color as shown here.

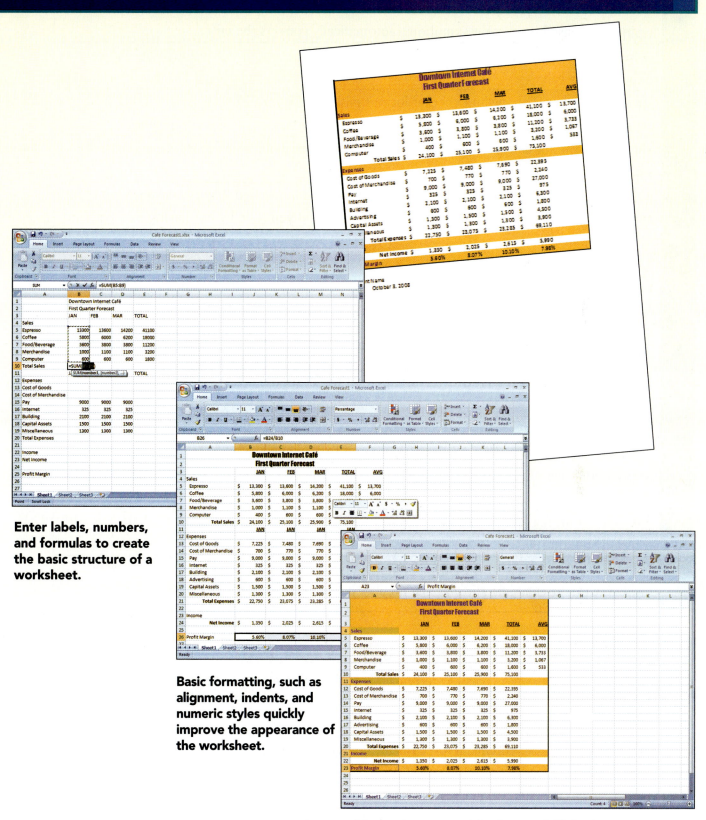

Enter labels, numbers, and formulas to create the basic structure of a worksheet.

Basic formatting, such as alignment, indents, and numeric styles quickly improve the appearance of the worksheet.

Adding color text and background fill further enhances the appearance of the worksheet.

Concept Preview

The following concepts will be introduced in this lab:

1. **Data Entries** The basic information or data you enter in a cell can be text or numbers.

2. **AutoCorrect** The AutoCorrect feature makes some basic assumptions about the text you are typing and, based on these assumptions, automatically corrects the entry.

3. **Column Width** The size or width of a column controls the amount of information that can be displayed in a cell.

4. **Spelling Checker** The spelling checker locates misspelled words, duplicate words, and capitalization irregularities in the active worksheet and proposes the correct spelling.

5. **Thesaurus** The thesaurus is a reference tool that provides synonyms, antonyms, and related words for a selected word or phrase.

6. **Copy and Move** The contents of worksheet cells can be duplicated (copied) or moved to other locations in the worksheet or between worksheets, saving you time by not having to retype the same information.

7. **Range** A selection consisting of two or more cells on a worksheet is a range.

8. **Formula** A formula is an equation that performs a calculation on data contained in a worksheet.

9. **Relative Reference** A relative reference is a cell or range reference in a formula whose location is interpreted in relation to the position of the cell that contains the formula.

10. **Function** A function is a prewritten formula that performs certain types of calculations automatically.

11. **Recalculation** When a number in a referenced cell in a formula changes, Excel automatically recalculates all formulas that are dependent upon the changed value.

12. **Alignment** Alignment settings allow you to change the horizontal and vertical placement and the orientation of an entry in a cell.

13. **Font and Font Size** A font, also commonly referred to as a typeface, is a set of characters with a specific design.

14. **Number Formats** Number formats change the appearance of numbers onscreen and when printed, without changing the way the number is stored or used in calculations.

Introducing Office Excel 2007

As part of the renovation of the Downtown Internet Café, Evan upgraded the office computer with the latest version of the Microsoft Office System suite of applications, Office 2007. You are very excited to see how this new and powerful application can help you create professional budgets and financial forecasts for the Café.

Starting Excel 2007

You will use the spreadsheet application Excel 2007 included in the Microsoft Office 2007 System suite to create the first-quarter forecast for the Café.

1
- Start Office Excel 2007.
- If necessary, maximize the Excel application window.

Having Trouble?
See "Common 2007 Office Features" page I.10, for information on how to start the application and for a discussion of features common to all 2007 Microsoft Office applications.

Your screen should be similar to Figure 1.1

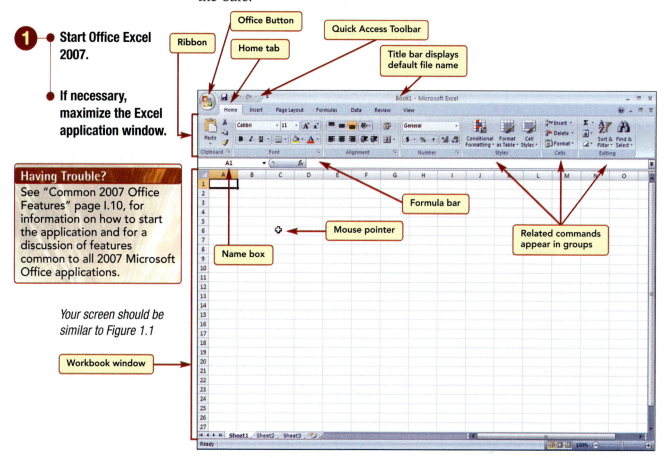

- Office Button
- Ribbon
- Home tab
- Quick Access Toolbar
- Title bar displays default file name
- Formula bar
- Mouse pointer
- Name box
- Related commands appear in groups
- Workbook window

Figure 1.1

After a few moments, the Excel application window is displayed. Because Excel remembers many settings that were in use when the program was last closed, your screen might look slightly different.

Exploring the Excel Window

The Excel application window title bar displays the default file name, Book1, and program name. It also displays the Office Button and the Quick Access Toolbar, two features that are common to all Office 2007 applications. The Ribbon below the title bar consists of seven tabs that provide access to the commands and features you will use to create and modify a worksheet. Each tab is divided into groups that contain related items. The related items include commands that consist of command buttons, a box to enter information, or a drop-down gallery of options from which you select.

Below the Ribbon is the formula bar. The **formula bar** displays entries as they are made and edited in the workbook window. The **Name box**, located at the left end of the formula bar, provides information about the selected item.

Additional Information
Because the Ribbon can adapt to the screen resolution and orientation, your Ribbon may look slightly different. It also may display additional tabs if other application add-ins associated with Office 2007 are on.

Additional Information
You will learn all about using these features throughout these labs.

The large center area of the program window is the **workbook window**. A **workbook** is an Excel file that stores the information you enter using the program. You will learn more about the different parts of the workbook window shortly.

The mouse pointer can appear as many different shapes. The mouse pointer changes shape depending upon the task you are performing or where the pointer is located on the window. Most commonly it appears as a ⬚ or ✛. When it appears as a ✛, it is used to move to different locations in the workbook window and when it appears as a ⬚, it is used to choose items, such as commands from the Ribbon.

1 ● Move the mouse pointer into the center of the workbook window to see it appear as ✛.

● Move the mouse pointer to the Ribbon to see it appear as ⬚.

Your screen should be similar to Figure 1.2

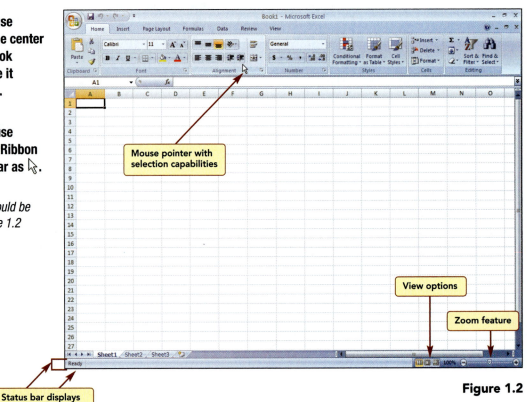

Mouse pointer with selection capabilities

View options

Zoom feature

Status bar displays current mode

Figure 1.2

The status bar at the bottom of the Excel window displays information about various Excel settings. The left side of the status bar displays the current mode or state of operation of the program, in this case, Ready. When Ready is displayed, you can move around the workbook, enter data, use the function keys, or choose a command. As you use the program, the status bar displays the current mode. The right side of the status bar contains buttons to change the view and a zoom feature.

Exploring the Workbook Window

When you first start Excel 2007, the workbook window displays a new blank workbook that has many predefined settings. These settings, called **default** settings, are stored in the default workbook template file named Book.xlt. A **template** is a file that contains settings that are used as the basis for a new file you are creating.

The default workbook file includes three blank sheets. A **sheet** is used to display different types of information, such as financial data or charts. Whenever you open a new workbook, it displays a worksheet. A **worksheet**, also commonly referred to as a **spreadsheet**, is a rectangular grid of **rows** and **columns** used to enter data. It is always part of a workbook and is the primary type of sheet you will use in Excel. The worksheet is much larger than the part you are viewing in the window. The worksheet actually extends 16,384 columns to the right and 1,048,576 rows down.

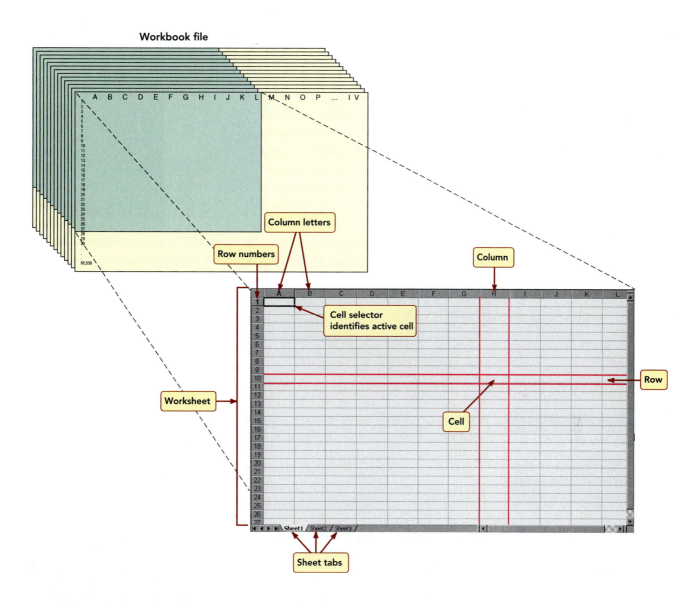

The **row numbers** along the left side and the **column letters** across the top of the workbook window identify each worksheet row and column. The intersection of a row and column creates a **cell**. Notice the black border, called the **cell selector**. surrounding the cell located at the intersection of column A and row 1. This identifies the **active cell**, which is the cell your next entry or procedure affects. Additionally, the Name box in the formula bar displays the **cell reference**, consisting of the column letter and row number of the active cell. The reference of the active cell is A1.

Each sheet in a workbook is named. Initially, the sheets are named Sheet1, Sheet2, and so on, displayed on **sheet tabs** at the bottom of the workbook window. The name of the **active sheet**, which is the sheet you can work in, appears bold. The currently displayed worksheet in the workbook window, Sheet1, is the active sheet.

1 ● **Click the Sheet2 tab.**

Another Method
You also can press Ctrl + Page Down to move to the next sheet and Ctrl + Page Up to move to the previous sheet.

Your screen should be similar to Figure 1.3

Blank worksheet in Sheet2

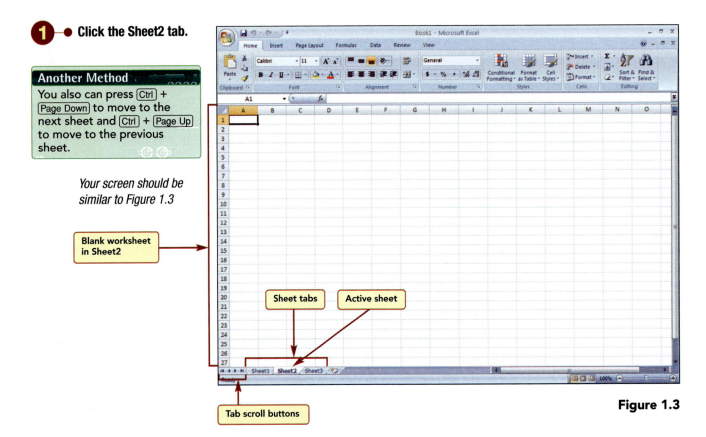

Sheet tabs

Active sheet

Tab scroll buttons

Figure 1.3

Additional Information
Do not be concerned if your workbook window displays more or fewer column letters and row numbers than shown here. This is a function of your computer monitor settings.

An identical blank worksheet is displayed in the window. The Sheet2 tab letters are bold, the background is highlighted, and it appears in front of the other sheet tabs to show it is the active sheet.

The sheet tab area also contains **tab scroll buttons**, which are used to scroll tabs right or left when there are more sheet tabs than can be seen. You will learn about these features throughout the labs.

Moving around the Worksheet

Additional Information
You can use the directional keys in the numeric keypad (with NumLock off) or, if you have an extended keyboard, you can use the separate directional keypad area.

The mouse or keyboard commands can be used to move from one cell to another in the worksheet. To move using a mouse, simply point to the cell you want to move to and click the mouse button. Depending upon what you are doing, using the mouse to move may not be as convenient as using the keyboard, in which case the directional keys can be used. You will make Sheet1 active again and use the mouse, then the keyboard to move in the worksheet.

1 ● **Click the Sheet1 tab to make it the active sheet again.**

● **Click cell B3.**

● **Press → (3 times).**

● **Press ↓ (4 times).**

Your screen should be similar to Figure 1.4

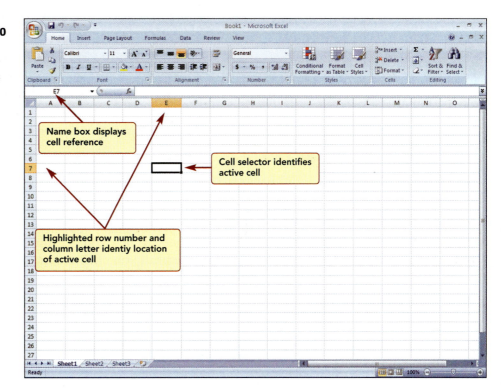

Name box displays cell reference

Cell selector identifies active cell

Highlighted row number and column letter identiy location of active cell

Figure 1.4

Cell E7 is outlined in black, indicating this cell is the active cell. The Name box displays the cell reference. In addition, the row number and column letter are gold to further identify the location of the active cell.

As you have learned, the worksheet is much larger than the part you are viewing in the window. To see an area of the worksheet that is not currently in view, you need to scroll the window. Either the keyboard or the mouse can be used to quickly scroll a worksheet. Again, both methods are useful depending upon what you are doing. The keyboard and mouse procedures shown in the tables that follow can be used to move around the worksheet.

Additional Information

Keys joined with a + indicate that you need to hold down the first key while pressing the second.

Keyboard	Action
Page Down	Moves down one full window
Page Up	Moves up one full window
Alt + Page Down	Moves right one full window
Alt + Page Up	Moves left one full window
Home	Moves to beginning of row
Ctrl + Home	Moves to upper-left corner cell of worksheet
Ctrl + End	Moves to last used cell of worksheet
End →	Moves to last-used cell in row
End ↓	Moves to last-used cell in column

Mouse	Action
Click scroll arrow	Scrolls worksheet one row/column in direction of arrow
Click above/below scroll box	Scrolls worksheet one full window up/down
Click right/left of scroll box	Scrolls worksheet one full window right/left
Drag scroll box	Scrolls worksheet multiple windows up/down or right/left
Hold down ⇧Shift and drag scroll box	Scrolls quickly through multiple rows/columns

In addition, if you hold down the arrow keys, the [Alt] + [Page Up] or [Alt] + [Page Down] keys, or the [Page Up] or [Page Down] keys, you can quickly scroll through the worksheet. When you use the scroll bar, however, the active cell does not change until you click on a cell that is visible in the window.

You will scroll the worksheet to see the rows below row 25 and the columns to the right of column L.

2 ● Press [Page Down] (3 times).

● Press [Alt] + [Page Down] (3 times).

Having Trouble?
Do not use the numeric keypad [Page Up] and [Page Down] keys, as this may enter a character in the cell.

Your screen should be similar to Figure 1.5

Rows 82 through 108

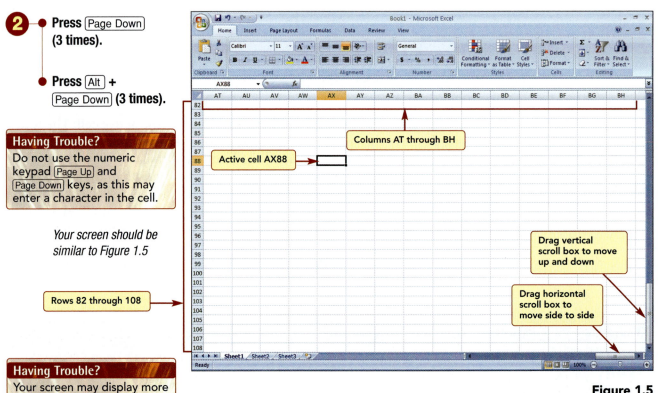

Columns AT through BH

Active cell AX88

Drag vertical scroll box to move up and down

Drag horizontal scroll box to move side to side

Figure 1.5

Having Trouble?
Your screen may display more or fewer rows and columns and the active cell may be a different cell. This is a function of your screen and system settings.

Additional Information
If you have a mouse with a scroll wheel, rotating the wheel forward or back scrolls up or down a few rows at a time.

The worksheet scrolled downward and left three full windows, and the window displays rows 82 through 108 and columns AT through BH of the worksheet. The active cell is cell AX88. As you scroll the worksheet using the keyboard, the active cell also changes.

It is even more efficient to use the scroll bar to move long distances.

3 ● Slowly drag the vertical scroll box up the scroll bar until row 1 is displayed.

● Slowly drag the horizontal scroll box left along the scroll bar until column A is displayed.

Your screen should be similar to Figure 1.6

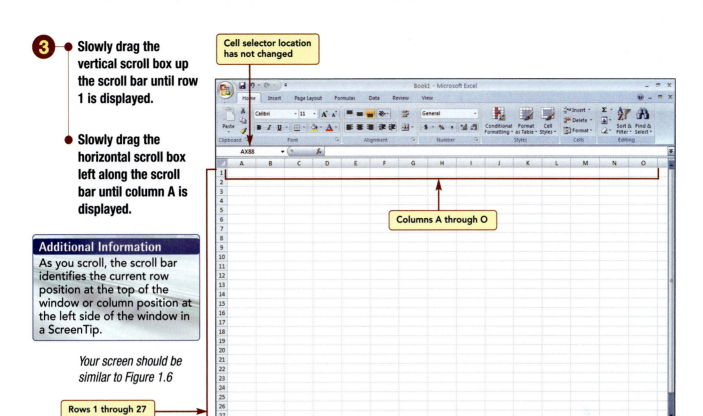

Cell selector location has not changed

Columns A through O

Rows 1 through 27

Figure 1.6

Notice that the Name box displays the active cell location as AX88. When you use the scroll bar to scroll the worksheet, the active cell does not change.

4 ● Practice moving around the worksheet using the keys presented in the table on page EX1.9.

● Press Ctrl + Home to move to cell A1.

You can use the mouse or the keyboard with most of the exercises in these labs. As you use both the mouse and the keyboard, you will find that it is more efficient to use one or the other in specific situations.

Creating New Worksheets

Now that you are familiar with the parts of the workbook and with moving around the worksheet, you are ready to create a worksheet showing the forecast for the first three months of operation for the Downtown Internet Café.

Developing a Worksheet

Worksheet development consists of four steps: planning, entering and editing, testing, and formatting. The objective is to create well-designed worksheets that produce accurate results and are clearly understood, adaptable, and efficient.

Step	Description
1. Plan	Specify the purpose of the worksheet and how it should be organized. This means clearly identifying the data that will be input, the calculations that are needed to achieve the results, and the output that is desired. As part of the planning step, it is helpful to sketch out a design of the worksheet to organize the worksheet's structure. The design should include the worksheet title and row and column headings that identify the input and output. Additionally, sample data can be used to help determine the formulas needed to produce the output.
2. Enter and edit	Create the structure of the worksheet using Excel by entering the worksheet labels, data, and formulas. As you enter information, you are likely to make errors that need to be corrected or edited, or you will need to revise the content of what you have entered to clarify it or to add or delete information.
3. Test	Test the worksheet for errors. Use several sets of real or sample data as the input, and verify the resulting output. The input data should include a full range of possible values for each data item to ensure the worksheet can function successfully under all possible conditions.
4. Format	Enhance the appearance of the worksheet to make it more readable or attractive. This step is usually performed when the worksheet is near completion. It includes many features such as boldface text, italic, and color.

As the complexity of the worksheet increases, the importance of following the design process increases. Even for simple worksheets like the one you will create in this lab, the design process is important. You will find that you will generally follow these steps in the order listed above for your first draft of a worksheet. However, you will probably retrace steps such as editing and formatting as the final worksheet is developed.

During the planning phase, you have spoken with the Café manager, Evan, regarding the purpose of the worksheet and the content in general. The primary purpose is to develop a forecast for sales and expenses for the next year. First, Evan wants you to develop a worksheet for the first-quarter forecast and then extend it by quarters for the year. After reviewing past budgets and consulting with Evan, you have designed the basic layout for the first-quarter forecast for the Café, as shown on the next page.

Downtown Internet Café
First Quarter Forecast

Sales:

Beverage   January   February   March   Total
     $ 13,600 $14,600 $15,600 $43,800
                                     (sum of beverage sales)

Food   xx,xxx

Total Sales $ xx,xxx $xx,xxx $xx,xxx $xxx,xxx
     (sum of monthly sales)   (sum of total sales)

Expenses:

Cost of Goods $(.25 * beverage sales + 50 * food sales) $(sum of cost of goods)

Salary

Total Expenses $xx,xxx $xx,xxx $xx,xxx $xxx,xxx
     (sum of monthly expenses)   (sum of total expenses)

Income

Net Income $(Total Sales - Total Expenses)

Profit Margin $(Total Expenses ÷ Total Sales)

Entering and Editing Data

Now that you understand the purpose of the worksheet and have a general idea of the content, you are ready to begin entering the data. When you first start Office Excel 2007, a new blank Excel workbook file is opened containing three blank worksheets. Each worksheet is like a blank piece of paper that already has many predefined settings. These settings, called **default** settings, are generally the most commonly used settings.

You will use the blank worksheet with the default settings to create the worksheet for the Café.

As you can see, the budget you designed above contains both descriptive text entries and numeric data. These are two types of data you can enter in a worksheet.

Concept 1

Data Entries

1   The basic information or data you enter in a cell can be text or numbers. Text entries can contain any combination of letters, numbers, spaces, and any other special characters. **Number** entries can include only the digits 0 to 9 and any of the special characters, + – ( ) , . / $ % ? =. Number entries can be used in calculations.

Text and number entries generally appear in the cell exactly as they are entered. However, some entries such as **formulas** direct Excel to perform a calculation on values in the worksheet. In these cases, the result of the formula appears in the cell, not the formula itself. You will learn about formulas later in the lab.

Entering Text

You enter data into a worksheet by moving to the cell where you want the data displayed and typing the entry using the keyboard. First, you will enter the worksheet headings. Row and column **headings** are entries that are used to create the structure of the worksheet and describe other worksheet entries. Generally, headings are text entries. The column headings in this worksheet consist of the three months (January through March) and a total (sum of entries over three months) located in columns B through E. To enter data in a worksheet, you must first select the cell where you want the entry displayed. The column heading for January will be entered in cell B2.

1 • **Click on cell B2 to move to it.**

• **Type January.**

Your screen should be similar to Figure 1.7

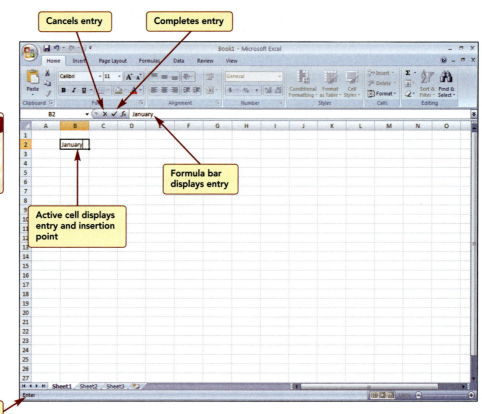

Cancels entry

Completes entry

Formula bar displays entry

Active cell displays entry and insertion point

Mode indicator

Figure 1.7

Several changes have occurred in the window. As you type, the entry is displayed both in the active cell and in the formula bar. An insertion point appears in the active cell and marks your location in the entry. Two new buttons, ☒ and ☑, appear in the formula bar. They can be used with a mouse to cancel your entry or complete it.

Notice also that the mode displayed in the status bar has changed from Ready to Enter. This notifies you that the current mode of operation in the worksheet is entering data.

Although the entry is displayed in both the active cell and the formula bar, you need to press the ⏎Enter key or click ☑ to complete your entry. If you press Esc or click ☒, the entry is cleared and nothing appears in the cell. Since your hands are already on the keyboard, it is quicker to press ⏎Enter than it is to use the mouse to click ☑.

2 • **Press ⏎Enter.**

Your screen should be similar to Figure 1.8

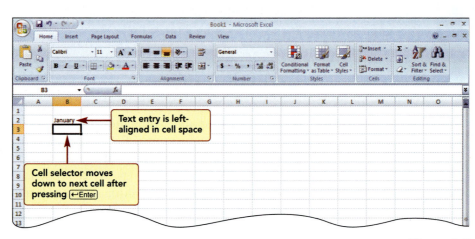

Text entry is left-aligned in cell space

Cell selector moves down to next cell after pressing ⏎Enter

Figure 1.8

The entry January is displayed in cell B2, and the mode has returned to Ready. In addition, the active cell is cell B3. Whenever you use the ←Enter key to complete an entry, the selection moves down one cell.

Notice that the entry is positioned to the left side of the cell space. This is one of the worksheet default settings.

Clearing an Entry

After looking at the entry, you decide you want the column headings to be in row 3 rather than in row 2. This will leave more space above the column headings for a worksheet title. The Delete key can be used to clear the contents from a cell. You will remove the entry from cell B2 and enter it in cell B3.

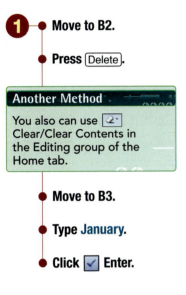

Additional Information

Pressing ⇧Shift + ←Enter to complete an entry moves up a cell, and Ctrl + ←Enter completes the entry without moving to another cell.

1 ● Move to B2.

● Press Delete.

Another Method

You also can use ⟨⟩ Clear/Clear Contents in the Editing group of the Home tab.

● Move to B3.

● Type January.

● Click ✓ Enter.

Your screen should be similar to Figure 1.9

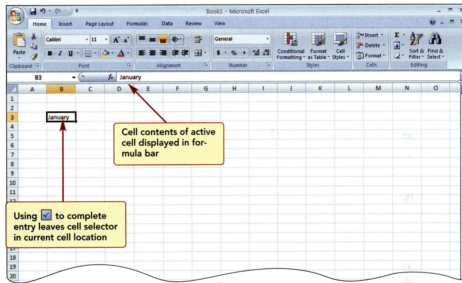

Cell contents of active cell displayed in formula bar

Using ✓ to complete entry leaves cell selector in current cell location

Figure 1.9

The active cell does not change when you use ✓ to complete an entry. Because the active cell contains an entry, the cell content is displayed in the formula bar.

Editing an Entry

Next, you decide to change the heading from January to JAN. An entry in a cell can be entirely changed in the Ready mode or partially changed or edited in the Edit mode. To use the Ready mode, you move to the cell you want to change and retype the entry the way you want it to appear. As soon as a new character is entered, the existing entry is cleared.

Generally, however, if you need to change only part of an entry, using the Edit mode is quicker. To change to Edit mode, double-click on the cell whose contents you want to edit.

1 ● **Double-click B3.**

Having Trouble?
The mouse pointer must be ✚ when you double-click on the cell.

Another Method
Pressing the F2 key also will change to Edit mode. The insertion point is positioned at the end of the entry.

Your screen should be similar to Figure 1.10

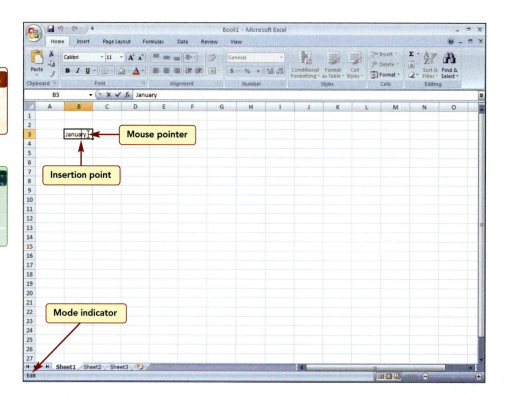

Figure 1.10

The status bar shows that the new mode of operation is Edit. The insertion point appears at the location you clicked in the entry, and the mouse pointer changes to an I-beam when positioned on the cell.

The mouse pointer can now be used to move the insertion point in the entry by positioning the I-beam and clicking. You also can use the arrow keys located on the numeric keypad or the directional keypad to move the insertion point. The keyboard directional keys used to move within text are described in the following table.

Key	Movement
→	One character to right
←	One character to left
↑	One line up
↓	One line down
Ctrl + →	One word to right
Ctrl + ←	One word to left
Home	Left end of line
End	Right end of line

Holding down a directional key or key combination moves quickly in the direction indicated, saving multiple presses of the key. Many of the insertion point movement keys can be held down to execute multiple moves.

After the insertion point is appropriately positioned, you can edit the entry by removing the incorrect characters and typing the correct characters. The [Delete] key erases characters to the right of the insertion point, and the [Backspace] key erases characters to the left of the insertion point. You will change this entry to JAN.

2 • **If necessary, move the insertion point to after the "y" in January.**

• **Press** [Backspace] **(4 times).**

• **Press** [Home].

• **Press** [→].

• **Press** [Caps Lock].

• **Press** [Insert].

• **Type AN.**

• **Press** [←Enter].

Your screen should be similar to Figure 1.11

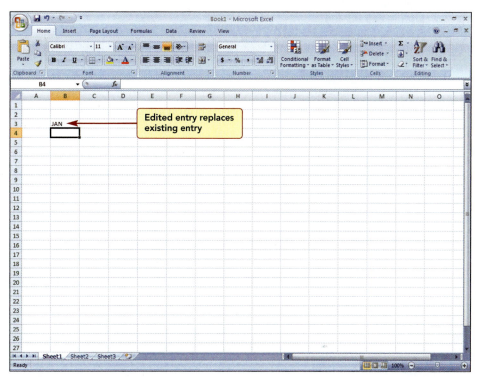

Figure 1.11

The four characters at the end of the entry were deleted using [Backspace]. Turning on the Caps Lock feature produced the uppercase letters AN without having to hold down [⇧Shift]. Finally, by pressing [Insert], the program switched from inserting text to overwriting text as you typed. The insertion point changed to a highlight to show that the character will be replaced.

The new heading JAN is entered into cell B3, replacing January. As you can see, editing will be particularly useful with long or complicated entries.

Next, you will enter the remaining three headings in row 3. You also can complete an entry by moving to any other worksheet cell.

3 • Click on cell C3.

• Type feb.

• Press → or Tab ⇥ or click D3.

• Complete the column headings by entering MAR in cell D3 and TOTAL in cell E3.

• Press Caps Lock to turn off this feature.

Your screen should be similar to Figure 1.12

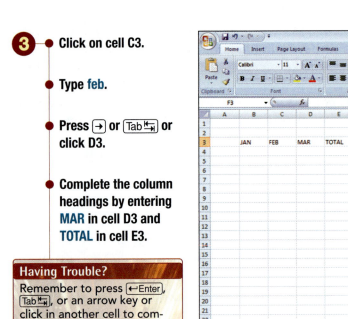

Figure 1.12

The column headings are now complete for the first quarter. Above the column headings, you want to enter a title for the worksheet. The first title line will be the café name, Downtown Internet Café.

4 • Move to B1.

• Type Downtown Cafe.

• Click ✓ Enter.

• Double-click on cell B1 to change to Edit mode.

• Move the insertion point to the beginning of the word Café.

• Type Internet followed by a space.

• Press Ctrl + ←Enter.

Your screen should be similar to Figure 1.13

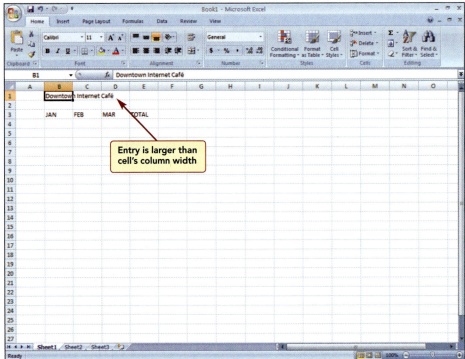

Entry is larger than cell's column width

Figure 1.13

Because you did not change to Overtype mode, the new text was inserted between the existing text in the entry. Also notice that the entry is longer than the cell's column width and overlaps into the cell to the right. As long as the cell to the right is empty, the whole entry will be displayed. If the cell to the right contains an entry, the overlapping part of the entry is not displayed.

Using AutoCorrect

Next, you will enter the second title line, First Quarter Report. When you complete an entry in a cell, Excel checks the entry for accuracy. This is part of the automatic correcting feature of Excel.

Concept 2

AutoCorrect

2 The **AutoCorrect** feature makes some basic assumptions about the text you are typing and, based on these assumptions, automatically corrects the entry. The AutoCorrect feature automatically inserts proper capitalization at the beginning of sentences and in the names of days of the week. It also will change to lowercase letters any words that were incorrectly capitalized because of the accidental use of the Caps Lock key. In addition, it also corrects many common typing and spelling errors automatically.

One way the program automatically makes corrections is by looking for certain types of errors. For example, if two capital letters appear at the beginning of a word, the second capital letter is changed to a lowercase letter. If a lowercase letter appears at the beginning of a sentence, the first letter of the first word is capitalized. If the name of a day begins with a lowercase letter, the first letter is capitalized.

Another way the program makes corrections is by checking all entries against a built-in list of words that are commonly spelled incorrectly or typed incorrectly. If it finds the entry on the list, the program automatically replaces the error with the correction. For example, the typing error "aboutthe" is automatically changed to "about the" because the error is on the AutoCorrect list. You also can add words that you want to be automatically corrected to the AutoCorrect list. Words you add are added to the list on the computer you are using and will be available to anyone who uses the machine later.

As you enter the second title line, you will intentionally misspell two words to demonstrate how the AutoCorrect feature works.

1 ● Move to B2.

● Type **Firts Quater Forecast.**

● Press ←Enter.

Your screen should be similar to Figure 1.14

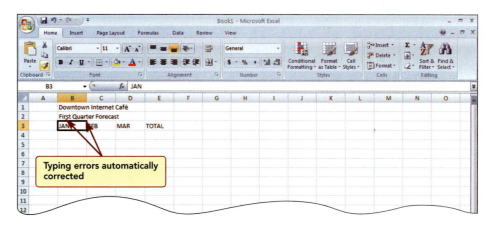

Figure 1.14

The two typing errors were automatically corrected as soon as you completed a word by pressing space.

Next, the row headings need to be entered into column A of the worksheet. The row headings and what they represent are shown in the following table.

Heading	Description
Sales	
Espresso	Income from sales of espresso-based drinks
Coffee	Income from drip coffee sales
Food/Beverage	Income from sales of baked goods, sandwiches, and salads and other beverages
Merchandise	Income from sales of mugs, books, magazines, candy, etc.
Computer	Income from computer rental usage, printing, copier use, and MP3 downloads
Total Sales	Sum of all sales
Expenses	
Cost of Goods	Cost of espresso, coffee, and food items sold
Cost of Merchandise	Cost of merchandise other than food and beverage
Wages	Manager and labor costs
Internet	Wi-Fi access, MP3 kiosk rental, etc.
Building	Lease, insurance, electricity, water, etc.
Capital Assets	Equipment leases, interest, depreciation
Miscellaneous	Maintenance, phone, office supplies, outside services, taxes, etc.
Income	
Net Income	Total sales minus total expenses
Profit Margin	Net income divided by total sales

2 • Complete the row headings for the Sales portion of the worksheet by entering the following headings in the indicated cells.

Cell	Heading
A4	**Sales**
A5	**Espresso**
A6	**Coffee**
A7	**Food/Beverage**
A8	**Merchandise**
A9	**Computer**
A10	**Total Sales**

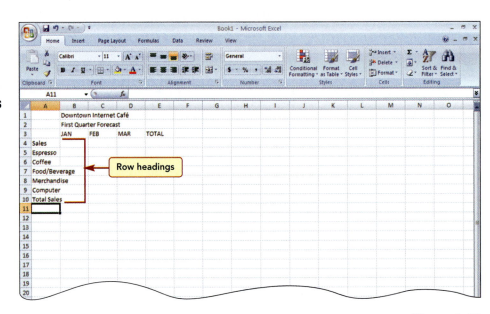

Your screen should be similar to Figure 1.15

Figure 1.15

Lab 1: Creating and Editing a Worksheet

www.mhhe.com/oleary

Entering Numbers

Next, you will enter the expected Espresso sales numbers for January through March into cells B5 through D5. As you learned earlier, number entries can include the digits 0 to 9 and any of these special characters: + − ( ), . / $ % ? =. When entering numbers, it is not necessary to type the comma to separate thousands or the currency ($) symbol. You will learn about adding these symbols shortly.

You will enter the expected espresso sales for January first. Unlike text entries, Excel displays number entries right-aligned in the cell space by default.

1 ● **Move to B5.**

● **Type 13300 and press**
   ⏎Enter.

● **In the same manner,**
enter the January
sales numbers for the
remaining items using
the values shown
below.

Cell	Number
B6	5800
B7	3600
B8	1000
B9	600

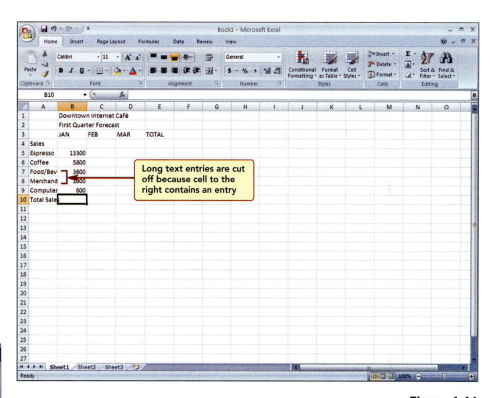

Figure 1.16

Your screen should be similar to Figure 1.16

After entering the numbers for January in column B, any long headings in column A are cut off or interrupted. Notice that the entries in cells A7 and A8 are no longer completely displayed. They contain long text entries and because the cells to the right now contain an entry, the overlapping part of the entry is shortened. However, the entire entry is fully displayed in the formula bar. Only the display of the entry in the cell has been shortened.

Changing Column Widths

To allow the long text entries in column A to be fully displayed, you can increase the column's width.

Concept 3

Column Width

3 The size or width of a column controls the amount of information that can be displayed in a cell. A text entry that is larger than the column width will be fully displayed only if the cells to the right are blank. If the cells to the right contain data, the text is interrupted. On the other hand, when numbers are entered in a cell, the column width is automatically increased to fully display the entry.

The default column width setting is 8.43. The number represents the average number of digits that can be displayed in a cell using the standard type style. The column width can be any number from 0 to 255. If it is set to 0, the column is hidden.

When the worksheet is printed, it appears as it does currently on the screen. Therefore, you want to increase the column width to display the largest entry. Likewise, you can decrease the column width when the entries in a column are short.

There are several ways to change the column width. Using the mouse, you can change the width by dragging the boundary of the column heading. You also can set the column width to an exact value or to automatically fit the contents of the column.

Dragging the Column Boundary

The column width can be quickly adjusted by dragging the boundary line located to the right of the column letter. Dragging it to the left decreases the column width, while dragging it to the right increases the width. As you drag, a temporary column reference line shows where the new column will appear and a ScreenTip displays the width of the column.

1 • Point to the boundary line to the right of the column letter A and when the mouse pointer changes to ↔, click and drag the mouse pointer to the right.

• When the ScreenTip displays 18.00, release the mouse button.

Your screen should be similar to Figure 1.17

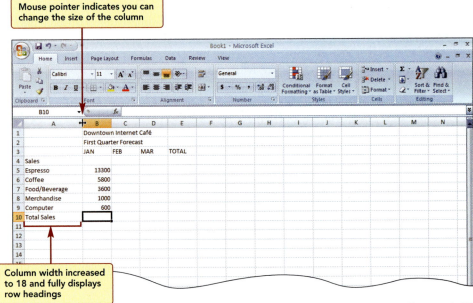

Figure 1.17

Now column A is more than wide enough to fully display all the row headings.

Lab 1: Creating and Editing a Worksheet

www.mhhe.com/oleary

Setting Column Width to a Specified Value

Next, you will reduce the width of column A to 15.

1 • Move to any cell in column A.

• Click  in the Cells group and choose Column Width.

• Type **15** in the Column width text box and click ⬚ OK ⬚.

Your screen should be similar to Figure 1.18

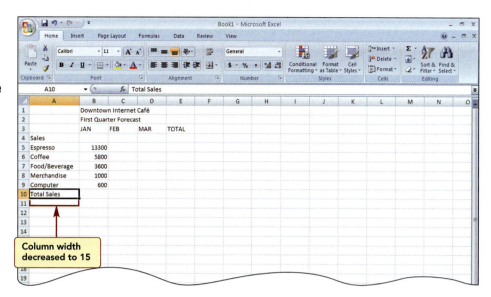

> Column width decreased to 15

Figure 1.18

Additional Information
You can quickly return the column width to the default width setting using 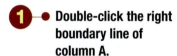 /Default Width.

Although this is close, you would like to refine it a little more.

Using AutoFit

Another way to change the column width is to use the **AutoFit** feature to automatically adjust the width to fit the column contents. When using AutoFit, double-click the boundary to the right of the column heading of the column you want to fit to contents.

1 • Double-click the right boundary line of column A.

Having Trouble?
Make sure the mouse pointer changes to ↔ before you double-click on the column boundary line.

Your screen should be similar to Figure 1.19

Another Method
You also can use 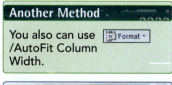 /AutoFit Column Width.

Additional Information
You can adjust the size of any row by dragging the row divider line, by using ⬚Format⬚ /Height, or by using ⬚Format⬚ /AutoFit Row Height.

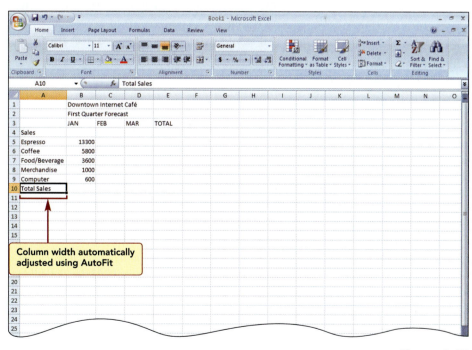

> Column width automatically adjusted using AutoFit

Figure 1.19

The column width is sized to just slightly larger than the longest cell contents. You also can adjust the height of a row using the same procedures you used to adjust the column width.

Saving, Closing, and Opening Workbooks

You have a meeting you need to attend shortly, so you want to save your work to a file and then close the file. As you enter and edit data to create a new workbook, the changes you make are immediately displayed onscreen and are stored in your computer's memory. However, they are not permanently stored until you save your work to a file on a disk. After a workbook is saved as a file, it can be closed and opened again at a later time to be further edited.

As a backup against the accidental loss of work because of power failure or other mishap, Office 2007 applications include an **AutoRecover** feature. When this feature is on, as you work you may see a pulsing disk icon briefly appear in the status bar. This icon indicates that the program is saving your work to a temporary recovery file. The time interval between automatic saving can be set to any period you specify; the default is every 10 minutes. When you start up again, the recovery file is automatically opened containing all changes you made up to the last time it was saved by AutoRecover. You then need to save the recovery file. If you do not save it, it is deleted when closed. While AutoRecover is a great feature for recovering lost work, it should not be used in place of regularly saving your work.

Saving a New Workbook

You will save the work you have completed so far on the workbook. The Save and Save As commands on the File menu are used to save files. The Save command or the 🖫 Save button will save the active file using the same file name by replacing the contents of the existing file with the document as it appears on your screen. The Save As command is used to save a file with a new file name or to a new location. This action leaves the original file unchanged.

When a workbook is saved for the first time, either command can be used. It is especially important to save a new file very soon after you create it as the AutoRecover feature is not functional until a file name has been specified.

1 • Click  **Office Button.**

• **Choose Save As.**

Your screen should be similar to Figure 1.20

Having Trouble?
In Windows Vista, the dialog box layout will be different; however, the same information will be displayed.

Additional Information
Do not be concerned if your dialog box displays a different Save In location and additional file information, such as the size, type, and date modified. These features are determined by the Folder and dialog box 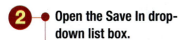 Views settings on your computer.

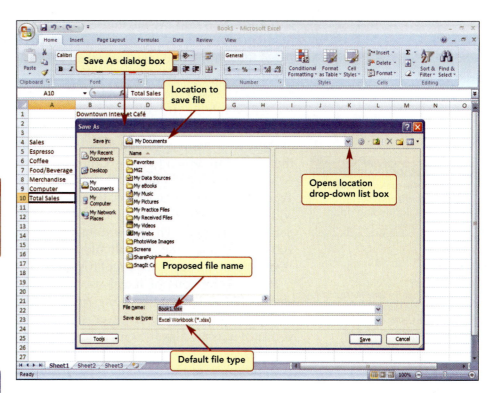

Figure 1.20

This Save As dialog box is used to specify the location to save the file and the file name. The Save In drop-down list box displays the default folder as the location where the file will be saved, and the File Name text box displays the proposed file name. The file list box displays the names of any Excel workbook files in the default location. Only Excel workbook files are listed, because the selected file type in the Save As Type list box is Excel Workbook. First you need to change the location where the file will be saved.

2 • **Open the Save In drop-down list box.**

• **Select the appropriate location to save the file.**

Your screen should be similar to Figure 1.21

Having Trouble?
If you are saving to a storage device/disk and an error message is displayed, check that it is properly inserted in the drive and click [OK].

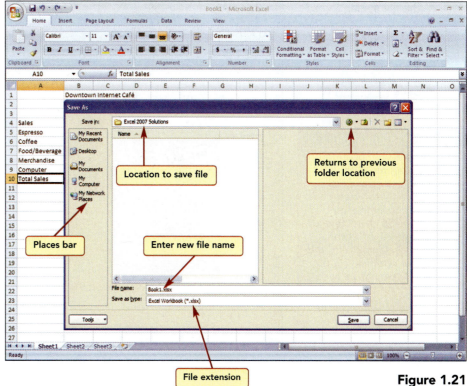

Figure 1.21

If the location you are saving to does not contain other Excel files, your file list will be empty, as shown here. Otherwise, your file list may display Excel file names. You also can select the location to save your file from the Places bar along the left side of the dialog box. The icons bring up a list of recently accessed files and folders, the contents of the My Documents and Favorites folder, the Windows desktop, and folders that reside on a network or Web through My Network Places. Selecting a folder from one of these lists changes to that location. You also can click the  button in the toolbar to return to folders that were previously opened.

Next, you need to enter a file name and specify the file type. The Save as Type box displays Excel Workbook as the default format in which the file will be saved. The File Name box displays Book1.xlsx, the file name of the default workbook. The file extension .xlsx identifies the file as an Excel 2007 workbook. The default file type saves the workbook file in XML (Extensible Markup Language) format.

Previous versions of Excel used the .xls file extension. If you plan to share a file with someone using Excel 2003 or earlier, you can save the file using the .xls file type; however, some features may be lost. Otherwise, if you save it as an .xlsx file type, the recipient may not be able to view all the features.

In addition to the .xlsx file type, Excel workbooks also can be saved in several different file formats that have different file extensions. The file type you select determines the file extension that will be automatically added to the file name when the file is saved.

You will change the file name to Forecast and use the default file type setting.

MORE ABOUT

See 5.4 Save Workbooks in the More About appendix to learn how to identify document features that are not supported by previous versions using the Compatibility Checker.

MORE ABOUT

To learn about XML and other Excel file types, see 5.4 Save Workbooks in the More About appendix.

3 • Triple-click on the file name in the File Name text box to highlight the file name.

• Type **Cafe Forecast**.

• Click [Save] or press [← Enter].

Additional Information
The file name can be entered in either uppercase or lowercase letters and will appear exactly as you type it. Windows documents can have up to 256 characters in the file name. Names can contain letters, numbers, and spaces; the symbols /, ?, :, *, ", <, and > cannot be used.

Your screen should be similar to Figure 1.22

New file name

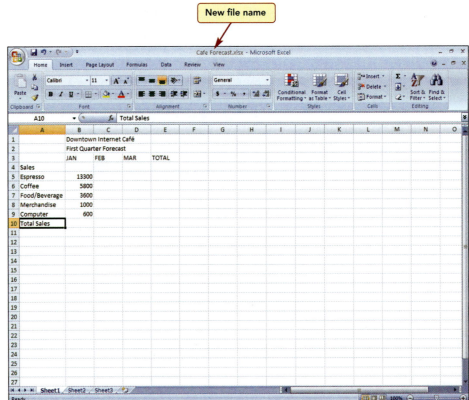

Figure 1.22

The new file name is displayed in the application window title bar. The worksheet data that was on your screen and in the computer's memory is now saved at the location you specified in a new file called Forecast.

Closing a Workbook

You are now ready to close the workbook file.

1  Click ⬛ Office Button and choose Close.

Because you did not make any changes to the document since saving it, the document window is closed immediately and the Excel window displays an empty workbook window. If you had made additional changes, Excel would ask if you wanted to save the file before closing it. This question prevents the accidental closing of a file that has not been saved first.

Opening an Existing Workbook

After attending your meeting, you continued working on the Café forecast. To see what has been done so far, you will open the workbook file named ex01_CafeForecast1. When you open a file, the Open dialog box is displayed. It has many of the same features as in the Save As dialog box. You will select the location and name of the file you want to open from the Look In drop-down menu.

1 Click ⬛ Office Button and choose Open.

● Select the location containing your data files from the Look In drop-down list box.

● Select ex01_Cafe Forecast1.

Your screen should be similar to Figure 1.23

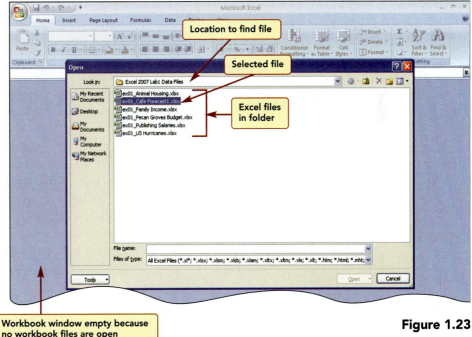

Workbook window empty because no workbook files are open

Figure 1.23

A list of the Excel 2007 files located in your selected folder location is displayed. Your list may display more information, such as file details, depending on the dialog box view settings.

2 • Click [Open ▾].

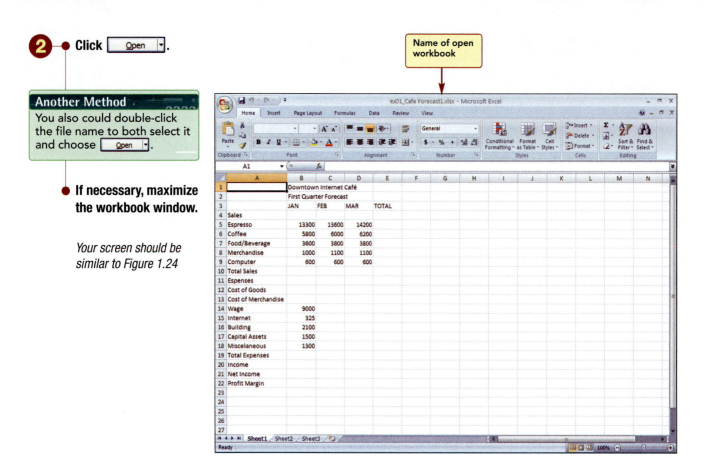

Another Method
You also could double-click the file name to both select it and choose [Open ▾].

• If necessary, maximize the workbook window.

Your screen should be similar to Figure 1.24

Name of open workbook

Figure 1.24

The workbook is opened and displayed in the workbook window. The workbook contains the additional sales values for February and March, the expense row headings, and several of the expense values for the month of January.

Using Proofing Tools

When entering information into a worksheet, you are likely to make spelling and typing errors. To help locate and correct these errors, the spelling checker feature can be used. Additionally, you may find that the descriptive headings you have entered may not be exactly the word you want. The thesaurus can suggest better words to clarify the meaning of the worksheet.

Checking Spelling

In your rush to get the row headings entered you realize you misspelled a few words. For example, the Expenses label is spelled "Espenses." Just to make sure there are no other spelling errors, you will check the spelling of all text entries in this worksheet.

Concept 4

Spelling Checker

4   The **spelling checker** locates misspelled words, duplicate words, and capitalization irregularities in the active worksheet and proposes the correct spelling. This feature works by comparing each word to a dictionary of words, called the **main dictionary**, that is supplied with the program. You also can create a **custom dictionary** to hold words you commonly use but that are not included in the main dictionary. If the word does not appear in the main dictionary or in a custom dictionary, it is identified as misspelled.

When you check spelling, the contents of all cell entries in the entire active sheet are checked. If you are in Edit mode when you check spelling, only the contents of the text in the cell are checked. The Spell Checker does not check spelling in formulas or in text that result from formulas.

Excel begins checking all worksheet entries from the active cell forward.

1 • If necessary, move to A1.

• Open the **Review** tab.

• Click  in the Proofing group.

Another Method
The keyboard shortcut is F7.

Your screen should be similar to Figure 1.25

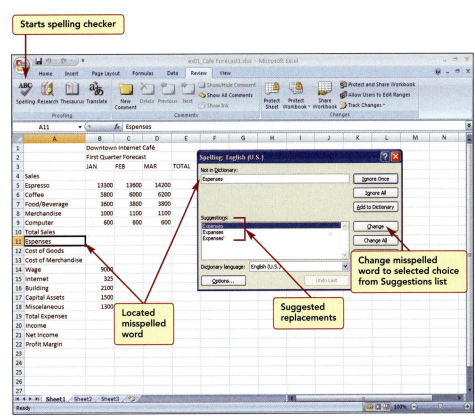

Starts spelling checker

Located misspelled word

Suggested replacements

Change misspelled word to selected choice from Suggestions list

Figure 1.25

Additional Information
Spell checking operates the same way in all Office 2007 programs. The dictionaries are shared between Office applications.

The spelling checker immediately begins checking the worksheet for words that it cannot locate in its main dictionary. The first cell containing a misspelled word, in this case Espences, is now the active cell and the Spelling dialog box is displayed. The word it cannot locate in the dictionary is displayed in the Not in Dictionary text box. The Suggestions text box displays a list of possible replacements. If the selected replacement is not correct, you can select another choice from the suggestions list or type the correct word in the Not in Dictionary text box.

The option buttons shown in the table below have the following effects:

Option	Effect
Ignore Once	Leaves selected word unchanged
Ignore All	Leaves this word and all identical words in worksheet unchanged
Add to Dictionary	Adds selected word to a custom dictionary so Excel will not question this word during subsequent spell checks
Change	Changes selected word to word highlighted in Suggestions box
Change All	Changes this word and all identical words in worksheet to word highlighted in Suggestions box
AutoCorrect	Adds a word to the AutoCorrect list so the word will be corrected as you type

You want to accept the suggested replacement, Expenses.

2 ● **Click**  .

Your screen should be similar to Figure 1.26

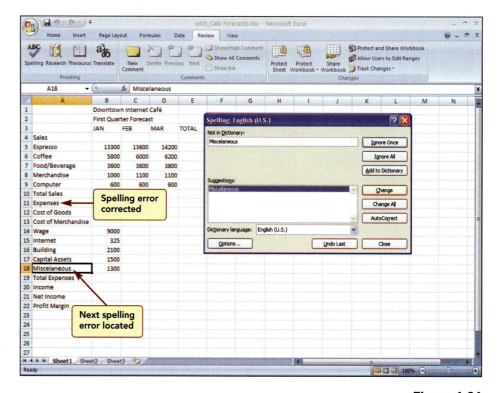

Figure 1.26

The correction is made in the worksheet, and the program continues checking the worksheet and locates another error, Miscelaneous. You will make this correction. When no other errors are located, a dialog box is displayed, informing you that the entire worksheet has been checked.

3 ● **Change this word to Miscellaneous.**

● **Click** [OK] **to end spell checking.**

The worksheet is now free of spelling errors.

Using the Thesaurus

The next text change you want to make is to find a better word for "Wage" in cell A14. To help find a similar word, you will use the thesaurus tool.

Concept 5

Thesaurus

5 The **thesaurus** is a reference tool that provides synonyms, antonyms, and related words for a selected word or phrase. **Synonyms** are words with a similar meaning, such as "cheerful" and "happy." **Antonyms** are words with an opposite meaning, such as "cheerful" and "sad." Related words are words that are variations of the same word, such as "cheerful" and "cheer." The thesaurus can help to liven up your documents by adding interest and variety to your text.

To use the thesaurus, first move to the cell containing the word you want to change. If a cell contains multiple words, you need to select the individual word in the cell.

1 ● **Move to A14.**

● **Click** 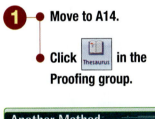 **in the Proofing group.**

> **Another Method**
> You also can hold down Alt while clicking on the cell containing the word you want looked up to access the Thesaurus in the Research task pane.

Your screen should be similar to Figure 1.27

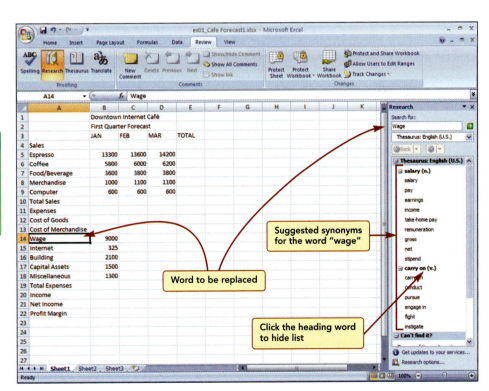

Suggested synonyms for the word "wage"

Word to be replaced

Click the heading word to hide list

Figure 1.27

The Research task pane opens and the word in the active cell, Wage, is entered in the Search for text box and the list box displays words in the Thesaurus that have similar meanings for this word. The list contains synonyms for "wage" used as a noun or as a verb. The first word at the top of each group is the group heading and is closest in meaning. It is preceded with a ⊟ symbol and the word is bold. The ⊟ indicates the list of synonyms is displayed. Clicking the heading word will hide the list of synonyms. Because you want to find a synonym for "wage" used as a noun, you will hide those for "wage" used as a verb.

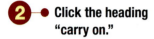

Click the heading "carry on."

Your screen should be similar to Figure 1.28

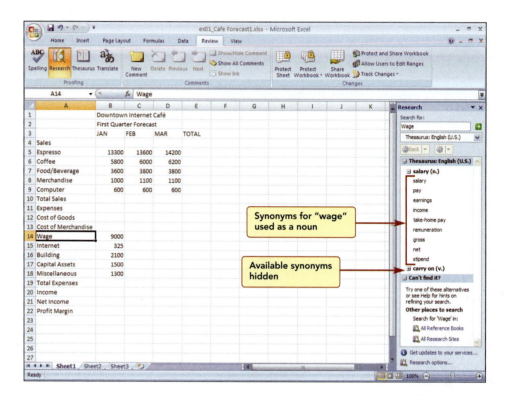

Figure 1.28

Now a ⊞ symbol appears before the group heading, indicating all available words are hidden. Only the synonyms for the word used as a noun are displayed.

When you point to a word in the list, a drop-down list of three menu options, Insert, Copy, and Lookup, become available. The Insert option inserts the word into the active cell. The Copy option is used to copy and then paste the word into any worksheet cell. The Lookup option displays additional related words for the current word. You decide to use the word "pay" and will insert the word into cell A14 in place of "Wage."

Additional Information

Clicking on the word is the same as using the Lookup menu option.

3 ● Point to "pay" and click ☑ to display the menu.

● Choose Insert.

● Click ☒ in the title bar of the Research task pane to close it.

Your screen should be similar to Figure 1.29

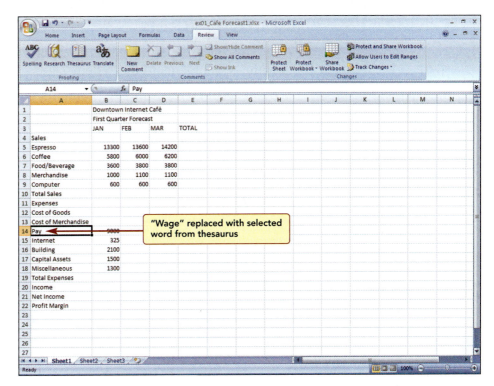

Figure 1.29

The word "Wage" is replaced with the selected word from the thesaurus. Notice the replacement word is capitalized correctly. This is because the replacement text follows the same capitalization as the word it replaces.

Duplicating Cell Contents

Next, you want to enter the estimated expenses for salary, computers, lease, and miscellaneous for February and March. They are the same as the January expense numbers. Because these values are the same, instead of entering the same number repeatedly into each cell you can quickly copy the contents of one cell to another. You also want to move information from one location in the worksheet to another.

Concept 6

Copy and Move

6 The contents of worksheet cells can be duplicated (copied) or moved to other locations in the worksheet or between worksheets, saving you time by not having to retype the same information. An entry that is copied leaves the original, called the **source** or **copy area**, and inserts a duplicate at a new location, called the **destination** or **paste area**. A selection that is moved is removed or cut from the original location in the source and inserted at the destination.

When a selection is cut or copied, the selection is stored in the system Clipboard, a temporary Windows storage area in memory. The system Clipboard contents are then inserted at the new location specified by the location of the insertion point. The system Clipboard can hold only one copied item at a time. The Office 2007 applications also include an Office Clipboard that can store up to 24 items. This allows you to insert multiple items from various Office files and paste all or part of the collection of items into another file.

Using Copy and Paste

When copying and pasting entries, you first use the  Copy command to copy the cell contents to the system Clipboard. Then you move to the new location where you want the contents copied and use the Paste command to insert the system Clipboard contents into the selected cells. Be careful when pasting to the new location because any existing entries are replaced.

To use the Copy command, you first must select the cell or cells in the source containing the data to be copied. You will copy the Pay value in cell B14 into cells C14 and D14.

Additional Information

The Paste button is a split button. Clicking the upper part of the button pastes using the default settings. Clicking the lower part displays a menu of options.

1 ● Move to B14.

● Open the Home tab.

● Click 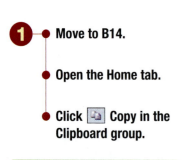 Copy in the Clipboard group.

Another Method

The shortcut key is Ctrl + C. Copy is also available on the context menu.

Your screen should be similar to Figure 1.30

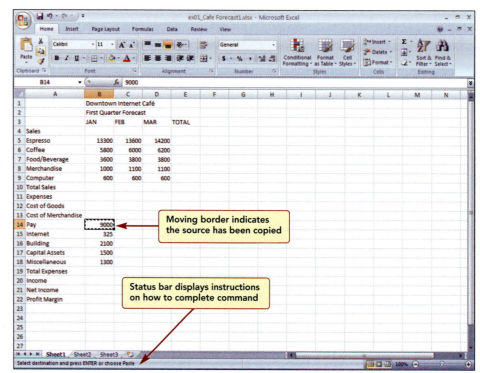

Moving border indicates the source has been copied

Status bar displays instructions on how to complete command

Figure 1.30

A moving border identifies the source and indicates that the contents have been copied to the system Clipboard. The instructions displayed in the status bar tell you to select the destination where you want the contents copied. You will copy it to cell C14.

2 • Move to C14.

• Click the upper part of
the 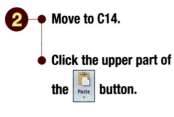 button.

Another Method

The shortcut key is Ctrl + V.
Paste is also available on the
context menu and on the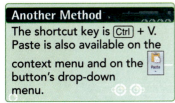
button's drop-down
menu.

*Your screen should be
similar to Figure 1.31*

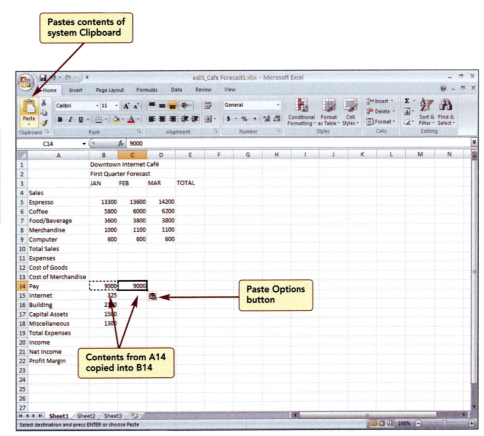

Pastes contents of
system Clipboard

Paste Options
button

Contents from A14
copied into B14

Figure 1.31

Additional Information

You will learn about the
different paste options in
later labs.

The contents of the system Clipboard are inserted at the specified
destination location. Each time the paste command is used, the Paste
Options button is available. Clicking on the button opens the Paste
Options menu that allows you to control how the information you are
pasting is inserted.

The moving border is still displayed, indicating the system Clipboard
still contains the copied entry. Now you can complete the data for the Pay
row by pasting the value again from the system Clipboard into cell D14.
While the moving border is still displayed, you also can simply press
←Enter to paste. However, as this method clears the contents of the system
Clipboard immediately, it can only be used once.

3 ● Move to D14.

● Press ⏎Enter.

Your screen should be similar to Figure 1.32

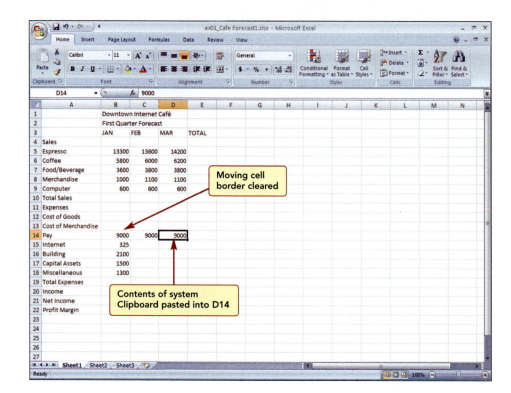

Figure 1.32

The contents of the system Clipboard are inserted at the specified destination location and the moving border is cleared, indicating the system Clipboard is empty.

Selecting a Range

Now you need to copy the Internet value in cell B15 to February and March. You could copy and paste the contents individually into each cell as you did with the Pay values. A quicker method, however, is to select a range and paste the contents to all cells in the range at once.

Concept 7

Range

7 A selection consisting of two or more cells on a worksheet is a **range**. The cells in a range can be adjacent or nonadjacent. An **adjacent range** is a rectangular block of adjoining cells. A **nonadjacent range** consists of two or more selected cells or ranges that are not adjoining. In the example shown below, the shaded areas show valid adjacent and nonadjacent ranges. A **range reference** identifies the cells in a range. A colon is used to separate the first and last cells of an adjacent range reference. For example, A2:C4 indicates the range consists of cells A2 through C4. Commas separate the cell references of a nonadjacent range. For example, A10,B12,C14 indicates the range consists of cells A10, B12, and C14 of a nonadjacent range.

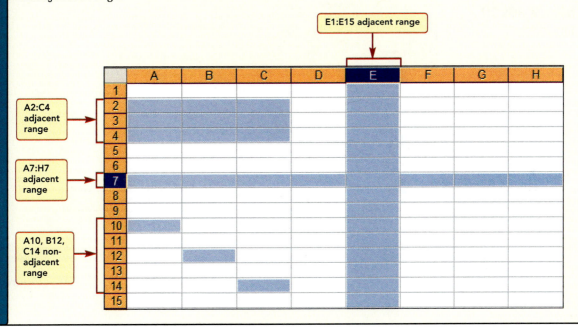

You can select a range using the mouse procedures shown in the following table. You also can select using the keyboard by moving to the first cell of the range, holding down ⬆Shift or pressing F8 and using the navigational keys to expand the highlight. Using the F8 key turns on and off Extend mode. When this mode is on, Extend Selection appears in the status bar.

To Select	Mouse
A range	Click first cell of range and drag to the last cell.
A large range	Click first cell of range, hold down ⬆Shift, and click last cell of range.
All cells on worksheet	Click the ▱ All button located at the intersection of the row and column headings.
Nonadjacent cells or ranges	Select first cell or range, hold down Ctrl while selecting the other cell or range.
Entire row or column	Click the row number or column letter heading.
Adjacent rows or columns	Drag across the row number or column letter headings.
Nonadjacent rows or columns	Select first row or column, hold down Ctrl, and select the other rows or columns

To complete the data for the Internet row, you want to copy the value in cell B15 to the system Clipboard and then copy the system Clipboard contents to the adjacent range of cells C15 through D15.

1 • Move to **B15**.

• Click 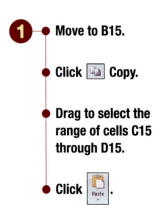 Copy.

• Drag to select the range of cells C15 through D15.

• Click **Paste**.

Your screen should be similar to Figure 1.33

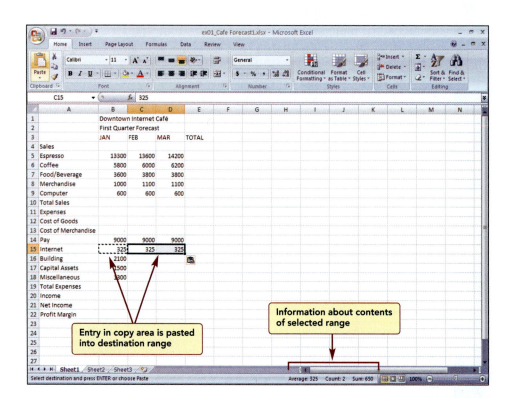

Entry in copy area is pasted into destination range

Information about contents of selected range

Figure 1.33

The destination range is highlighted and identified by a dark border surrounding the selected cells. The entry copied from cell B15 was pasted into the selected destination range. Also notice the status bar now displays the average, count, and sum of values in the selected range.

Using the Fill Handle

Next, you will copy the January Building expenses to cells C16 through D16, the Capital Assets expenses to cells C17 through D17, and the Miscellaneous expenses to cells C18 through D18. You can copy all values at the same time across the row by first specifying a range as the source. Another way to copy is to drag the **fill handle**, the black box in the lower-right corner of a selection.

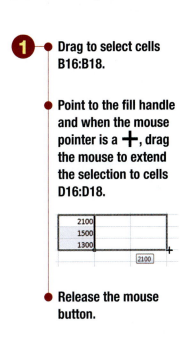

1 • **Drag to select cells B16:B18.**

• **Point to the fill handle and when the mouse pointer is a ✚, drag the mouse to extend the selection to cells D16:D18.**

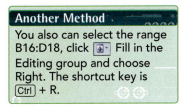

• **Release the mouse button.**

Another Method

You also can select the range B16:D18, click [⬛▾] Fill in the Editing group and choose Right. The shortcut key is Ctrl + R.

Your screen should be similar to Figure 1.34

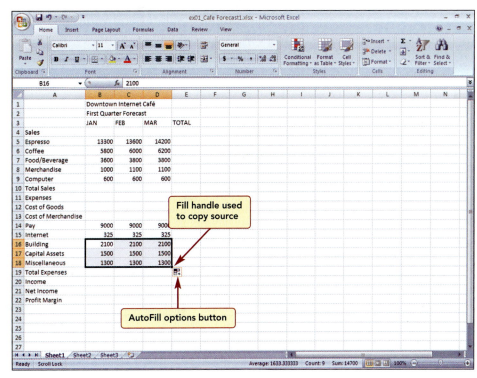

Figure 1.34

Additional Information

You will learn more about the AutoFill feature in later labs.

The range of cells to the right of the source is filled with the same values as in the source range. The Fill Series command does not copy the source to the system Clipboard and therefore you cannot paste the source multiple times. When you copy by dragging the fill handle, the AutoFill Options button 🔳 appears. Its menu commands are used to modify how the fill operation was performed. It will disappear as soon as you make an entry in the worksheet.

Inserting Copied Cells

You also decide to include another row of month headings above the expenses to make the worksheet data easier to read. To do this quickly, you can insert copied data between existing data. To indicate where to place the copied content, you move the cell selector to the upper-left cell of the area where you want the selection inserted.

The column headings you want to copy are in cells B3 through E3. You will also copy the blank cell, A3, so that a blank cell is inserted in column A when you paste the contents.

1 • **Copy the contents of cells A3 through E3.**

• **Move to A11.**

• **Click** Insert ▾ **in the Cells group.**

Your screen should be similar to Figure 1.35

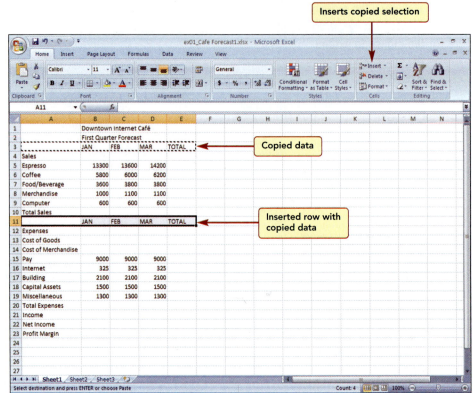

Figure 1.35

The copied data is inserted into the existing row (11) and all entries below are moved down one row.

Cutting and Moving Entries

Next, you decide the Income, Net Income, and Profit Margin rows of data would stand out more if a blank row separated them from the expenses. Also, the Profit Margin row of data would be better separated from the Net Income row by a blank row. You will first remove the cell contents of the three cells using Cut and then paste the contents from the system Clipboard into the new location. You will use the keyboard shortcuts for these commands to complete this process.

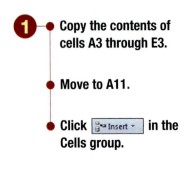

Additional Information

You also can insert cut selections between existing cells by choosing Insert Cut Cells from the Insert ▾ drop-down menu.

1 • Press `Esc` to clear the moving border.

• Select cells A21 through A23.

• Press `Ctrl` + X.

• Move to cell A22.

• Press `Ctrl` + V.

 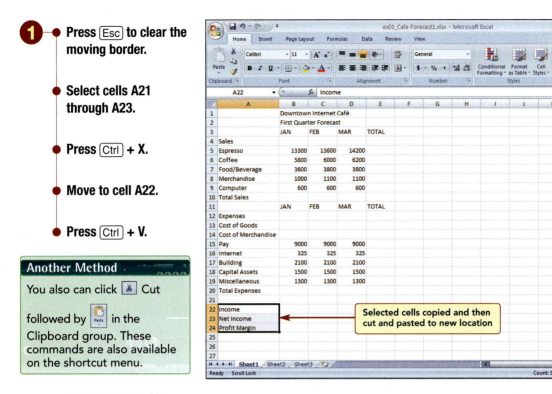
Your screen should be similar to Figure 1.36

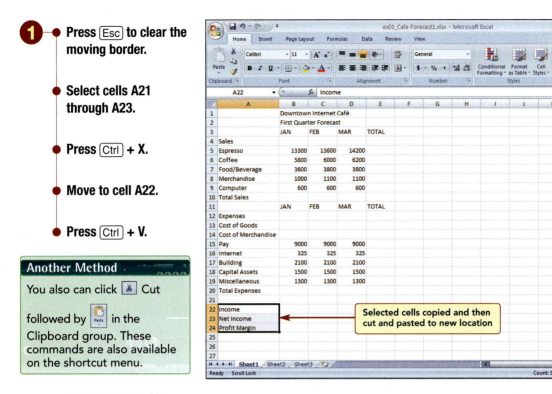

Selected cells copied and then cut and pasted to new location

Figure 1.36

The contents of the three selected cells are copied to the system Clipboard. Then, when you paste, the cell contents are removed and inserted at the new location, copying over any existing content.

Another way you can cut and paste is to use drag and drop editing to move the cell contents. This method is quickest and most useful when the distance between cells is short and they are visible within the window, whereas cut and paste is best for long-distance moves. You will use this method to move the Profit Margin entry down one cell.

2 ● **Move to cell A24.**

● **Point to the border of the selection and when the mouse pointer shape is ⬍, drag the selection down one row to cell A25 and release the mouse button.**

Additional Information

As you drag, an outline of the cell selection appears and the mouse pointer displays the cell reference to show its new location in the worksheet.

● **Click ⬛ Office Button and choose Save As.**

● **Save the changes you have made to the workbook as Café Forecast1 to your solution file location.**

Your screen should be similar to Figure 1.37

Additional Information

You also can hold down Ctrl and drag a selection to copy it to a new location. The mouse pointer appears as ⬈⁺ as you drag when copying.

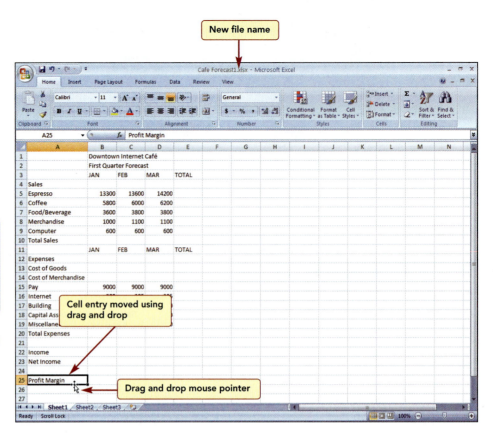

New file name

Cell entry moved using drag and drop

Drag and drop mouse pointer

Figure 1.37

The cell contents were moved into cell A25 and cleared from the original cell.

Note: If you are running short on lab time, this is an appropriate place to end your session.

Review of Copying and Moving Methods

To review, you have learned three methods to copy or move an entry:

1. Use the Copy, Cut, and Paste commands: ⬛ Copy (Ctrl + C), ✂ Cut (Ctrl + X), and ⬛ Paste (Ctrl + V), or choose Copy, Cut, and Paste from the selection's context menu.

2. Use the ⬛ Fill command: Right, Left, Up, or Down or drag the fill handle.

3. Drag the cell border of the selection to move. Hold down Ctrl while dragging the cell border of a selection to copy.

When you use the Copy and Cut commands, the contents are copied to the system Clipboard and can be copied to any location in the worksheet, another workbook, or a document in another application multiple times. When you use 🔳 Fill or drag the fill handle, the destination must be in the same row or column as the source, and the source is not copied to the system Clipboard. Dragging the cell border to move or copy also does not copy the source to the system Clipboard.

Working with Formulas

The remaining entries that need to be made in the worksheet are formula entries.

Concept 8

Formula

8 A **formula** is an equation that performs a calculation on data contained in a worksheet. A formula always begins with an equal sign (=) and uses arithmetic operators. An **operator** is a symbol that specifies the type of numeric operation to perform. Excel includes the following operators: + (addition), – (subtraction), / (division), * (multiplication), % (percent), and ^ (exponentiation). The calculated result from formulas is a **variable** value because it can change if the data it depends on changes. In contrast, a number entry is a **constant** value. It does not begin with an equal sign and does not change unless you change it directly by typing in another entry.

In a formula that contains more than one operator, Excel calculates the formula from left to right and performs the calculation in the following order: percent, exponentiation, multiplication and division, and addition and subtraction (see Example A). This is called the **order of precedence**. If a formula contains operators with the same precedence (for example, addition and subtraction), they are again evaluated from left to right. The order of precedence can be overridden by enclosing the operation you want performed first in parentheses (see Example B). When there are multiple sets of parentheses, Excel evaluates them working from the innermost set of parentheses out.

Example A: =5*4–3   Result is 17 (5 times 4 to get 20, and then subtract 3 for a total of 17)
Example B: =5*(4–3)   Result is 5 (4 minus 3 to get 1, and then 1 times 5 for a total of 5)

The values on which a numeric formula performs a calculation are called **operands**. Numbers or cell references can be operands in a formula. Usually cell references are used, and when the numeric entries in the referenced cell(s) change, the result of the formula is automatically recalculated.

Entering Formulas

The first formula you will enter will calculate the total Espresso sales for January through March (cell E5) by summing the numbers in cells B5 through D5. You will use cell references in the formula as the operands and the + arithmetic operator to specify addition. A formula is entered in the cell where you want the calculated value to be displayed. As you enter the formula, Excel helps you keep track of the cell references by identifying the referenced cell with a colored border and using the same color for the cell reference in the formula.

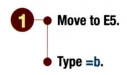

1 — **Move to E5.**

— **Type =b.**

Your screen should be similar to Figure 1.38

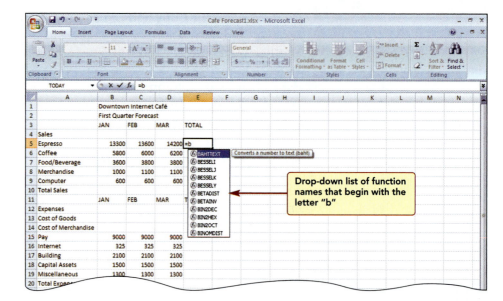

Drop-down list of function names that begin with the letter "b"

Figure 1.38

A drop-down list of function names that begin with the letter "b" are displayed. Functions are a type of formula entry that you will learn about shortly.

2 — **Type 5+c5+d5.**

Additional Information

Cell references can be typed in either uppercase or lowercase letters. Spaces between parts of the formula are optional.

Your screen should be similar to Figure 1.39

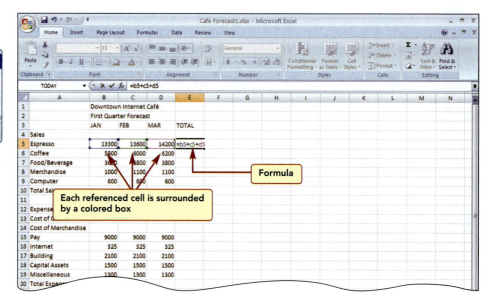

Formula

Each referenced cell is surrounded by a colored box

Figure 1.39

As you enter the formula, each cell that is referenced in the formula is surrounded by a colored box that matches the color of the cell reference in the formula.

3 ● Press `Ctrl` + `←Enter` or click ☑ Enter in the Formula bar.

Your screen should be similar to Figure 1.40

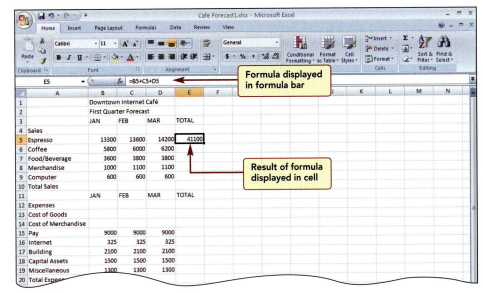

Figure 1.40

The number 41100 is displayed in cell E5, and the formula that calculates this value is displayed in the formula bar.

Copying Formulas

The formulas to calculate the total sales for rows 6 through 9 can be entered next. Just as you can with text and numeric entries, you can copy formulas from one cell to another.

1 ● Copy the formula in cell E5 to cells E6 through E9 using any of the copying methods.

● Move to E6.

● If necessary, press `Esc` to clear the moving border.

Your screen should be similar to Figure 1.41

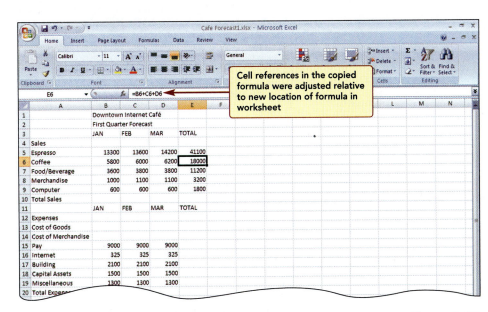

Figure 1.41

The calculated result, 18000, is displayed in the cell. The formula displayed in the formula bar is =B6+C6+D6. The formula to calculate the Coffee total sales is not an exact duplicate of the formula used to calculate the Espresso total sales (=B5+C5+D5). Instead, the cells referenced in the formula have been changed to reflect the new location of the formula in row 6. This is because the references in the formula are relative references.

Concept 9

Relative Reference

9 A **relative reference** is a cell or range reference in a formula whose location is interpreted by Excel in relation to the position of the cell that contains the formula. When a formula is copied, the referenced cells in the formula automatically adjust to reflect the new worksheet location. The relative relationship between the referenced cell and the new location is maintained. Because relative references automatically adjust for the new location, the relative references in a copied formula refer to different cells than the references in the original formula. The relationship between cells in both the copied and the pasted formulas is the same although the cell references are different.

For example, in the figure here, cell A1 references the value in cell A4 (in this case, 10). If the formula in A1 is copied to B2, the reference for B2 is adjusted to the value in cell B5 (in this case, 20).

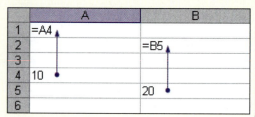

2 • Move to cell E7, E8, and then to cell E9.

Your screen should be similar to Figure 1.42

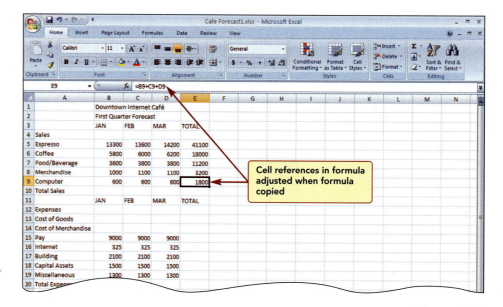

Figure 1.42

The formulas in these cells also have changed to reflect the new row location and to appropriately calculate the total based on the sales.

Entering Functions

Next, you will calculate the monthly total sales. The formula to calculate the total sales for January needs to be entered in cell B10 and copied across the row. You could use a formula similar to the formula used to calculate the category sales in column E. The formula would be =B5+B6+B7+B8+B9. However, it is faster and more accurate to use a function.

Concept 10

Function

10 A **function** is a prewritten formula that performs certain types of calculations automatically. The **syntax** or rules of structure for entering all functions is

=Function name (argument1, argument2, . . .)

The function name identifies the type of calculation to be performed. Most functions require that you enter one or more arguments following the function name. An **argument** is the data the function uses to perform the calculation. The type of data the function requires depends upon the type of calculation being performed. Most commonly, the argument consists of numbers or references to cells that contain numbers. The argument is enclosed in parentheses, and commas separate multiple arguments. The beginning and ending cells of a range are separated with a colon.

Some functions, such as several of the date and time functions, do not require an argument. However, you still need to enter the opening and closing parentheses; for example, =NOW(). If a function starts the formula, enter an equal sign before the function name; for example, =SUM(D5:F5)/25.

Additional Information
Use Help for detailed explanations of every function.

Excel includes several hundred functions divided into 11 categories. Some common functions from each category and the results they calculate are shown in the following table.

Category	Function	Calculates
Financial	PMT	Calculates the payment for a loan based on constant payments and a constant interest rate
	PV	Returns the present value of an investment—the total amount that a series of future payments is worth now
	FV	Returns the future value of an investment—the total amount that a series of payments will be worth
Date & Time	TODAY	Returns the serial number that represents today's date
	DATE	Returns the serial number of a particular date
	NOW	Returns the serial number of the current date and time
Math & Trig	SUM	Adds all the numbers in a range of cells
	ABS	Returns the absolute value of a number (a number without its sign)
Statistical	AVERAGE	Returns the average (arithmetic mean) of its arguments
	MAX	Returns the largest value in a set of values; ignores logical values and text
	MIN	Returns the smallest value in a set of values; ignores logical values and text
	COUNT	Counts the number of cells in a range that contain numbers
	COUNTA	Counts the number of cells in a range that are not empty
	COLUMNS	Returns the number of columns in an array or reference

Category	Function	Calculates
Lookup & Reference	HLOOKUP	Looks for a value in the top row of a table and returns the value in the same column from a row you specify
	VLOOKUP	Looks for a value in the leftmost column of a table and returns the value in the same row from a column you specify
Database	DSUM	Adds the numbers in the field (column) or records in the database that match the conditions you specify
	DAVERAGE	Averages the values in a column in a list or database that match conditions you specify
Text	PROPER	Converts text to proper case in which the first letter of each word is capitalized
	UPPER	Converts text to uppercase
	LOWER	Converts text to lowercase
	SUBSTITUTE	Replaces existing text with new text in a text string
Logical	IF	Returns one value if a condition you specify evaluates to TRUE and another value if it evaluates to FALSE
	AND	Returns TRUE if all its arguments are TRUE; returns FALSE if any arguments are FALSE
	OR	Returns TRUE if any arguments are TRUE; returns FALSE if all arguments are FALSE
	NOT	Changes FALSE to TRUE or TRUE to FALSE
	IFERROR	Returns value-if-error if expression is an error and the value of the expression itself otherwise
Information	ISLOGICAL	Returns TRUE if value is a logical value, either TRUE or FALSE
	ISREF	Returns TRUE if value is a reference
Engineering	BIN2DEC	Converts a binary number to decimal
	CONVERT	Converts a number from one measurement system to another
Cube	CUBESETCOUNT	Returns the number of items in a set

You will use the SUM function to calculate the total sales for January. Because the SUM function is the most commonly used function, it has its own command button.

1 Move to B10.

Click **Σ ▾** Sum in the Editing group.

Another Method

Pressing [Alt] + = is the keyboard shortcut for Sum. This function is also available on the Formulas tab.

Your screen should be similar to Figure 1.43

Function name   **Range argument**   **Calculates a sum automatically**

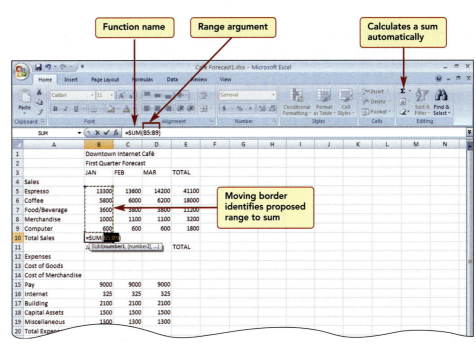

Moving border identifies proposed range to sum

Additional Information

The **Σ ▾** Sum button also can calculate a grand total if the worksheet contains subtotals. Select a cell below or to the right of a cell that contains a subtotal and then click **Σ ▾** Sum.

Figure 1.43

Excel automatically proposes a range based upon the data above or to the left of the active cell. The formula bar displays the name of the function followed by the range argument enclosed in parentheses. You will accept the proposed range and enter the function.

2 Click ✓ Enter.

Your screen should be similar to Figure 1.44

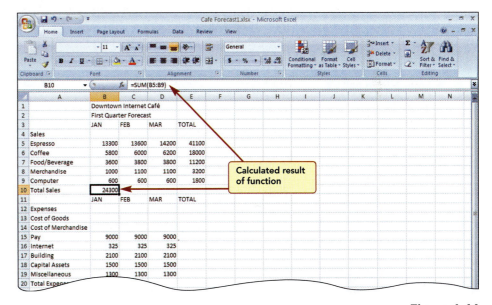

Calculated result of function

Figure 1.44

The result, 24300, calculated by the SUM function is displayed in cell B10. Next you need to calculate the total sales for February and March and the Total column.

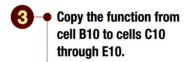

3 ● Copy the function from cell B10 to cells C10 through E10.

● Move to C10.

Your screen should be similar to Figure 1.45

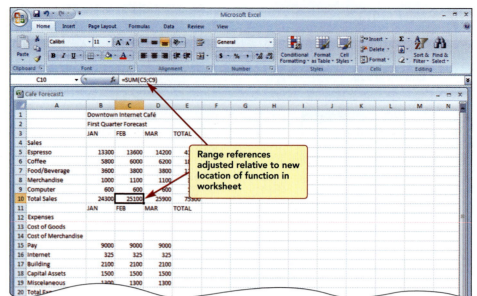

> Range references adjusted relative to new location of function in worksheet

Figure 1.45

The result calculated by the function, 25100, is displayed in cell C10 and the copied function is displayed in the formula bar. The range reference in the function is adjusted relative to its new cell location because it is a relative reference.

You also decide to calculate the minimum, maximum, and average sales for each sales category. You will add appropriate column headings and enter the functions in columns F, G, and H. The Σ Sum button also includes a drop-down menu from which you can select several other common functions. As you enter these functions, the proposed range will include the Total cell. Simply select another range to replace the proposed range.

4 ● Enter MIN in cell F3, MAX in cell G3, and AVG in cell H3.

● Move to F5.

● Open the Σ Sum drop-down menu and choose Min.

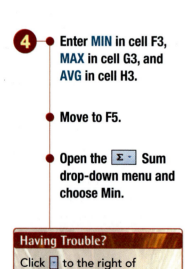

Having Trouble?

Click ▾ to the right of the button to open the drop-down menu.

● Select the range B5:D5 and click ✓ Enter.

Your screen should be similar to Figure 1.46

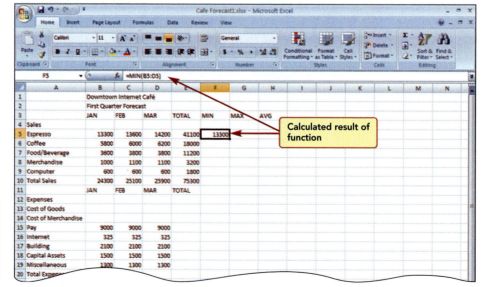

> Calculated result of function

Figure 1.46

The MIN function correctly displays 13300, the smallest value in the range.

Next you will enter the MAX and AVG values for the Espresso sales. Then you will copy the functions down the column through row 9.

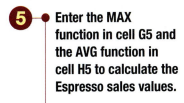

5 ● Enter the MAX function in cell G5 and the AVG function in cell H5 to calculate the Espresso sales values.

● Copy the functions in cells F5:H5 to F6 through H9.

● Move to H9.

Your screen should be similar to Figure 1.47

H9 ▾ (*fx* =AVERAGE(B9:D9)

	A	B	C	D	E	F	G	H	I	J	K	L	M	N
1		Downtown Internet Café												
2		First Quarter Forecast												
3		JAN	FEB	MAR	TOTAL	MIN	MAX	AVG						
4	Sales													
5	Espresso	13300	13600	14200	41100	13300	14200	13700						
6	Coffee	5800	6000	6200	18000	5800	6200	6000						
7	Food/Beverage	3600	3800	3800	11200	3600	3800	3733.333						
8	Merchandise	1000	1100	1100	3200	1000	1100	1066.667						
9	Computer	600	600	600	1800	600	600	600						
10	Total Sales	24300	25100	25900	75300									
11		JAN	FEB	MAR	TOTAL									
12	Expenses													
13	Cost of Goods													
14	Cost of Merchandise													
15	Pay	9000	9000	9000										
16	Internet	325	325	325										
17	Building	2100	2100	2100										
18	Capital Assets	1500	1500	1500										
19	Miscellaneous	1300	1300	1300										
20	Total Expense													

Cell references adjusted when functions copied

Figure 1.47

MORE ABOUT

▶ To learn how to use the COUNT and COUNTA functions, see 3.2 Summarize Data Using a Formula in the More About appendix.

The minimum, maximum, and average values for the five sales categories have been calculated.

Using Pointing to Enter a Formula

Next, you will enter the formula to calculate the cost of goods for espresso, coffee, and food and beverages sold. These numbers are estimated by using a formula to calculate the number as a percent of sales. Evan suggested using estimated percents for this worksheet so he could get an idea of what to expect from the first three months after the remodel. He wants you to calculate espresso expenses at 25 percent of espresso sales, coffee expenses at 30 percent of coffee sales, and food and beverage expenses at 60 percent of food sales.

Rather than typing in the cell references for the formula, you will enter them by selecting the worksheet cells. In addition, to simplify the process of entering and copying entries, you can enter data into the first cell of a range and have it copied to all other cells in the range at the same time by using Ctrl + ←Enter to complete the entry. You will use this feature to enter the formulas to calculate the beverage expenses for January through March. This formula needs to calculate the beverage cost of goods at 25 percent first and add it to the food cost of goods calculated at 50 percent.

1
- Select B13 through D13.
- Type =.
- Click cell B5.

Your screen should be similar to Figure 1.48

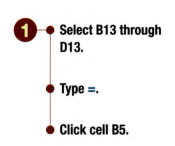

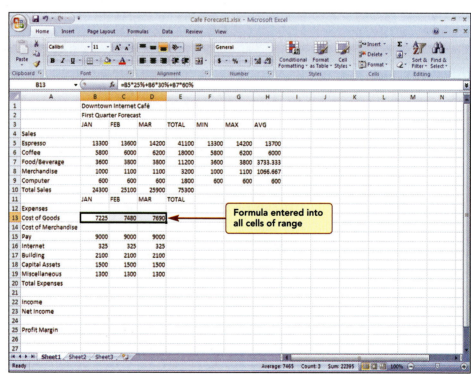

Callouts in figure: "Cell reference of selected cell is entered in formula", "Moving border surrounds selected cell", "Mode indicator"

Figure 1.48

Notice that the status bar displays the current mode as Point. This tells you that the program is allowing you to select cells by highlighting them. The cell reference, B5, is entered following the = sign. You will complete the formula by entering the percentage value to multiply by and adding the Food percentage to the formula.

2
- Type *25%+.
- Click on B6.
- Type *30%+.
- Click on B7.
- Type *60%.
- Press Ctrl + ↵Enter.

Your screen should be similar to Figure 1.49

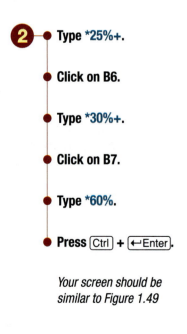

Callout in figure: "Formula entered into all cells of range"

Figure 1.49

The formula to calculate the January cost of goods expense was entered in cell B13 and copied to all cells of the selected range.

Now you will enter the cost of merchandise by multiplying the value in B8 by 70%. Then you will calculate the total expenses in row 20 and column E. To do this quickly, you will preselect the range and use the [Σ ▾] Sum button.

3 ● Select cells B14 through D14.

● Type =.

● Click on B8.

● Type *70%.

● Press [Ctrl] + [←Enter].

● Select B13 through E20.

● Click [Σ ▾] Sum.

● Select B23 through E23.

● Enter the formula =B10-B20.

● Press [Ctrl] + [←Enter].

Your screen should be similar to Figure 1.50

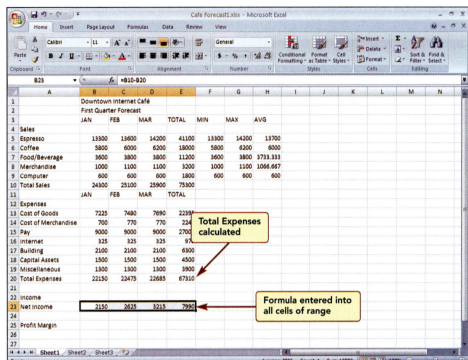

Figure 1.50

The formula is quickly entered into all cells of the range.

Finally, you will enter the formulas to calculate the net income and profit margin. Net income is calculated by subtracting total expenses from total sales and profit margin is calculated by dividing net income by total sales.

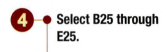

4 • Select B25 through E25.

• Enter the formula **=B23/B10**.

• Press Ctrl + ←Enter.

Your screen should be similar to Figure 1.51

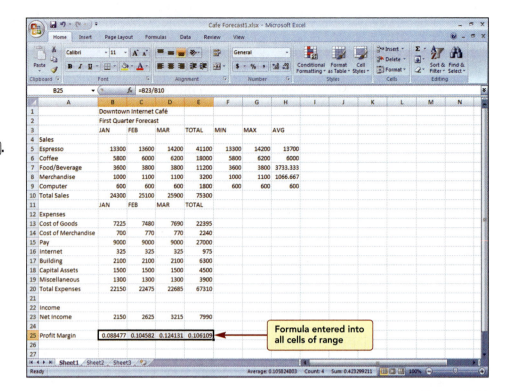

Figure 1.51

The net income and profit margins are calculated and displayed in the worksheet.

Recalculating the Worksheet

Now that you have created the worksheet structure and entered some sample data for the forecasted sales for the first quarter, you want to test the formulas to verify that they are operating correctly. A simple way to do this is to use a calculator to verify that the correct result is displayed. You can then further test the worksheet by changing values and verifying that all cells containing formulas that reference the value are appropriately recalculated.

Concept 11

Recalculation

11 When a number in a referenced cell in a formula changes, Excel automatically **recalculates** all formulas that are dependent upon the changed value. Because only those formulas directly affected by a change in the data are recalculated, the time it takes to recalculate the workbook is reduced. Without this feature, in large worksheets it could take several minutes to recalculate all formulas each time a number is changed in the worksheet. Recalculation is one of the most powerful features of electronic worksheets.

After considering the sales estimates for the three months, you decide that the estimated sales generated from Computer usage for January are too high and you want to decrease this number from 600 to 400.

1 ● Change the entry in cell B9 to **400** and press Ctrl + ←Enter to complete the edit.

Your screen should be similar to Figure 1.52

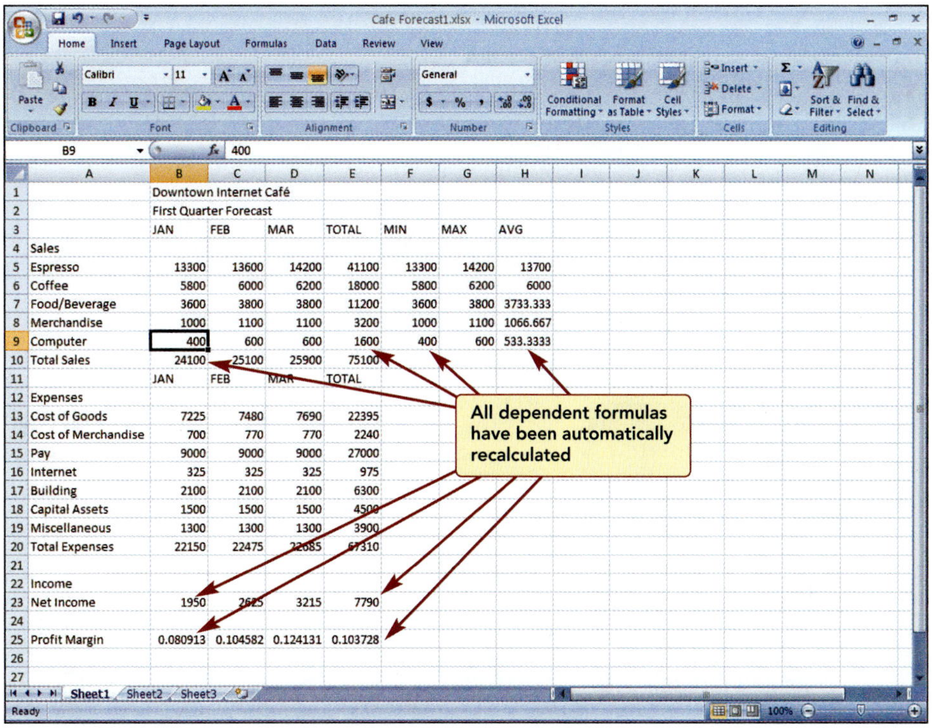

Figure 1.52

The Computer total in cell E9 has been automatically recalculated. The number displayed is now 1600. The MIN and AVG values in cells F9 and H9 have been recalculated to 400 and 533.3333 respectively. Likewise, the January total in cell B10 of 24100 and the grand total in cell E10 of 75100 each decreased by 200 to reflect the change in cell B9. Finally, the Net Income and Profit Margin values also have adjusted appropriately.

The formulas in the worksheet are correctly calculating the desired result. The Sales portion of the worksheet is now complete.

Inserting and Deleting Rows and Columns

As you are developing a worksheet, you may realize you forgot to include information or decide that other information is not needed. To quickly add and remove entire rows and columns of information, you can insert and delete rows and columns. A new blank row is inserted above the active cell location and all rows below it shift down a row. Similarly, you can insert blank cells and columns in a worksheet. Blank cells are inserted above or to the left of the active cell and blank columns are inserted to the left of the active cell. Likewise, you can quickly delete selected cells, rows, and columns and all information in surrounding cells, rows, or columns automatically shifts appropriately to fill in the space.

Additionally, whenever you insert or delete cells, rows, or columns, all formula references to any affected cells adjust accordingly.

Inserting Rows

Finally, you realize that you forgot to include a row for the Advertising expenses. To add this data, you will insert a blank row above the Capital Assets row.

1 • Move to A18.

• Open the [Insert] drop-down menu in the Cells group and choose Insert Sheet Rows.

Another Method

You also can choose Insert from the active cell's context menu.

• Enter the heading **Advertising** in cell A18 and the value **600** in cells B18 through D18.

• Copy the function from cell E17 to E18 to calculate the total advertising expense.

• Move to cell B21.

• Click 💾 Save to save the worksheet using the same file name.

Your screen should be similar to Figure 1.53

Additional Information

Click [Insert ▾] to insert blank cells, shifting existing cells down, and [Insert ▾]/Sheet Columns to insert blank columns, shifting existing columns right.

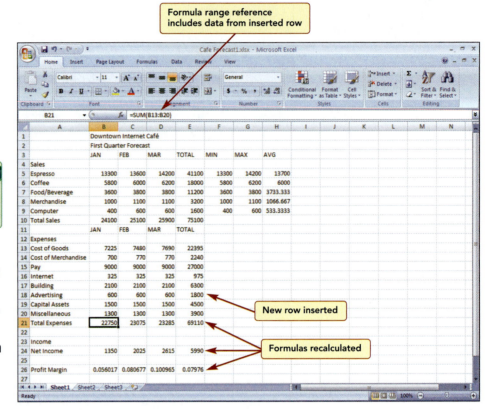

Formula range reference includes data from inserted row

New row inserted

Formulas recalculated

Figure 1.53

A blank row was inserted in the worksheet and the cell references in all formulas and functions below the inserted row adjusted appropriately. The range in the formula to calculate monthly total expenses in row 21 has been adjusted to include the data in the inserted row and the total expense for the first quarter is 69110. Additionally, the net income in row 24 and the profit margin in row 26 have been recalculated to reflect the change in data.

Deleting Columns

As you look at the worksheet data, you decide the minimum and maximum values are not very useful since this data is so easy to see in this small worksheet. You will delete these two columns from the worksheet to remove this information. To specify which column to delete, select any cell in the column.

1 ● **Select cells F21 and G21.**

● **Open the** [Delete ▾] **drop-down menu in the Cells group and choose Delete Sheet Columns.**

Your screen should be similar to Figure 1.54

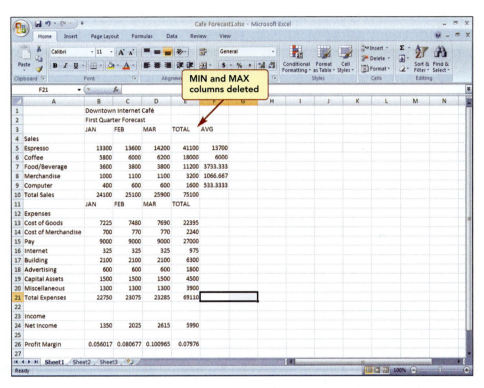

MIN and MAX columns deleted

Figure 1.54

The two columns have been removed and the columns to the right of the deleted columns automatically shifted to the left.

Formatting the Worksheet

Now that the worksheet data is complete, you want to improve the appearance of the worksheet. Applying different formatting to text and numbers can greatly enhance the appearance of the document. **Format** controls how entries are displayed in a cell and includes such features as the position of data in a cell, character font and color, and number formats such as commas and dollar signs.

You want to change the appearance of the row and column headings and apply formatting to the numbers. Applying different formats greatly improves both the appearance and the readability of the data in a worksheet.

Changing Cell Alignment

You decide the column headings would look better if they were right-aligned in their cell spaces, so that they would appear over the numbers in the column. Alignment is a basic format setting that is used in most worksheets.

Concept 12

Alignment

12 **Alignment** settings allow you to change the horizontal and vertical placement and the orientation of an entry in a cell.

Horizontal placement allows you to left-, right-, or center-align text and number entries in the cell

Text	Text	Text

space. Entries also can be indented within the cell space, centered across a selection, or justified. You also can fill a cell horizontally with a repeated entry.

Text		Text
	Text	

Vertical placement allows you to specify whether the cell contents are displayed at the top, the bottom, or the center of the vertical cell space or justified vertically.

Text	Text	Text	Text

You also can change the angle of text in a cell by varying the degrees of rotation.

The default workbook horizontal alignment settings left-align text entries and right-align number entries. The vertical alignment is set to Bottom for both types of entries, and the orientation is set to zero degrees rotation from the horizontal position. You want to change the horizontal alignment of the month headings in rows 3 and 11 to right-aligned.

The Alignment group contains commands to control the horizontal and vertical placement of entries in a cell. You can quickly apply formatting to a range of cells by selecting the range first. A quick way to select a range of filled cells is to hold down ⇧Shift and double-click on the edge of the active cell in the direction in which you want the range expanded. For example, to select the range to the right of the active cell, you would double-click the right border. You will use this method to select and right-align these entries.

Additional Information

If you do not hold down ⇧Shift while double-clicking on a cell border, the active cell moves to the last-used cell in the direction indicated.

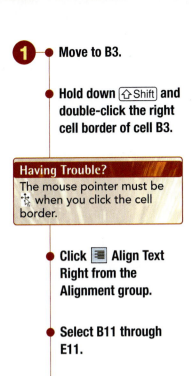

1 **Move to B3.**

Hold down ⇧Shift **and double-click the right cell border of cell B3.**

Having Trouble?

The mouse pointer must be ⟷ when you click the cell border.

Click ▤ **Align Text Right from the Alignment group.**

Select B11 through E11.

Click ▤ **Align Text Right.**

Your screen should be similar to Figure 1.55

Additional Information

You also can select entire nonadjacent rows or columns by holding down Ctrl while selecting the rows or columns.

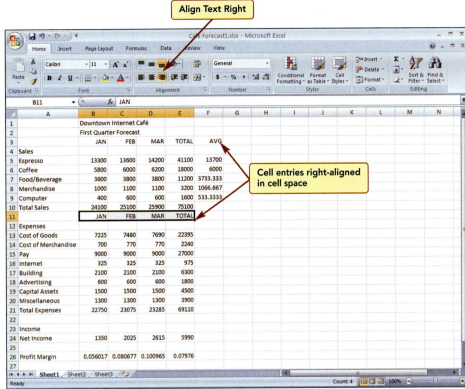

Figure 1.55

The entries in the selected ranges are right-aligned in their cell spaces.

Indenting Entries

Next, you would like to indent the row headings in cells A5 through A9 and A13 through A20 to increase the space between the cell border and the entry. You want to indent the headings in both ranges at the same time. To select nonadjacent cells or cell ranges, after selecting the first cell or range, hold down Ctrl while selecting each additional cell or range. You will select the cells and indent their contents.

1

- Select A5 through A9.

- Hold down Ctrl.

- Select A13 through A20.

- Release Ctrl.

- Click ▤ Increase Indent in the Alignment group.

- AutoFit the width of column A.

Your screen should be similar to Figure 1.56

Increase Indent

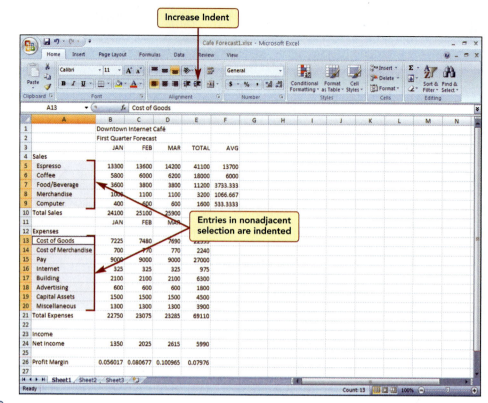

Entries in nonadjacent selection are indented

Figure 1.56

Additional Information

Clicking ▤ Increase Indent multiple times indents the selection in two-space increments. Clicking ▤ Decrease Indent reduces the margin between the border and the text in the cell.

Each entry in the selected range is indented two spaces from the left edge of the cell. Finally, you want to right-align the Total Sales, Total Expenses, and Net Income headings.

2

- Select A10, A21, and A24.

- Click ▤ Align Text Right.

Your screen should be similar to Figure 1.57

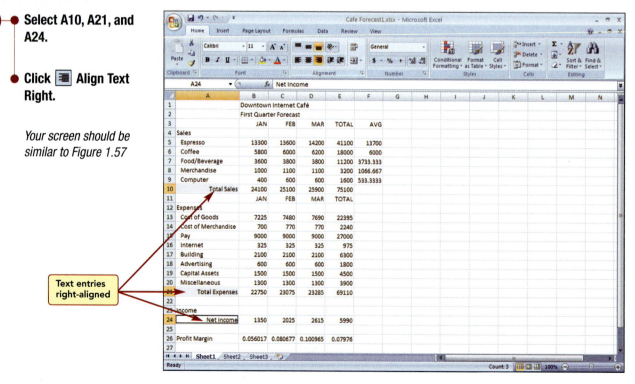

Text entries right-aligned

Figure 1.57

Centering across a Selection

Next, you want to center the worksheet titles across columns A through E so they are centered over the worksheet data. To do this, you will merge or combine the cells in the range over the worksheet data (A1 through E1) into a single large **merged cell** and then center the contents of the range in the merged cell. This process is easily completed in one simple step using the Merge and Center command.

1 • Select A1 through F1.

• Click  Merge and Center in the Alignment group.

Another Method

The Format Cells dialog box also can be used to center across a selection: Format/Cells/Alignment/Horizontal/Center Across Selection/Merge cells.

Your screen should be similar to Figure 1.58

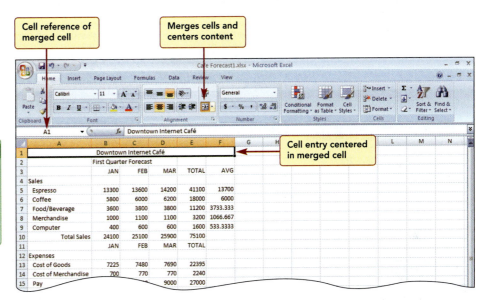

Figure 1.58

The six cells in the selection have been combined into a single large cell and the entry that was in cell B1 is centered within the merged cell space. Only the contents of the first cell containing an entry in the upper-leftmost section of the selected range are centered in the merged cell. If other cells to the right of that cell contain data, it would be deleted. The cell reference for a merged cell is the upper-left cell in the original selected range, in this case A1.

2 • Merge and center the second title line across columns A through F.

Your screen should be similar to Figure 1.59

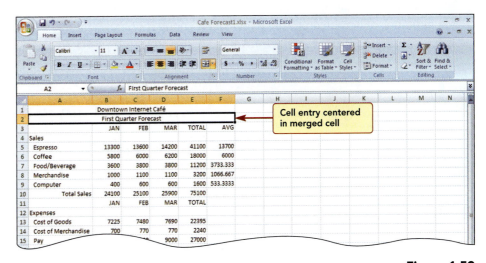

Figure 1.59

You also can use the commands in the 🔲▾ Merge and Center drop-down menu shown in the following table to control a merge. You can merge cells horizontally and vertically.

Merge Menu	Action
🔲 Merge and Center	Merges cells and centers entry
🔳 Merge Across	Merges cells horizontally
🔲 Merge Cells	Merges cells horizontally and vertically
🔲 UnMerge Cells	Splits cells that have been merged back into individual cells

Changing Fonts and Font Sizes

Finally, you want to improve the worksheet appearance by enhancing the appearance of the title. One way to do this is to change the font and font size used in the title.

Concept 13

Font and Font Size

13 A **font**, also commonly referred to as a **typeface**, is a set of characters with a specific design. The designs have names such as Times New Roman and Courier. Using fonts as a design element can add interest to your document and give readers visual cues to help them find information quickly.

There are two basic types of fonts: serif and sans serif. **Serif** fonts have a flair at the base of each letter that visually leads the reader to the next letter. Two common serif fonts are Roman and Times New Roman. Serif fonts generally are used in paragraphs. **Sans serif** fonts do not have a flair at the base of each letter. Arial and Helvetica are two common sans serif fonts. Because sans serif fonts have a clean look, they are often used for headings in documents. It is good practice to use only two types of fonts in a worksheet, one for text and one for headings. Too many styles can make your document look cluttered and unprofessional.

Each font has one or more sizes. **Size** is the height and width of the character and is commonly measured in **points**, abbreviated pt. One point equals about 1/72 inch, and text in most worksheets is 10 pt or 12 pt.

Here are several examples of the same text in various fonts and sizes.

Typeface	Font Size (12 pt/18 pt)
Calibri (Sans Serif)	This is 12 pt. **This is 18 pt**
Times New Roman (Serif)	This is 12 pt. This is 18 pt.
Book Antigua (Serif)	This is 12 pt. This is 18 pt.

First you will try a different font for the title and a larger font size.

1 • **Select A1 and A2.**

• **Open the** [Calibri ▼] **Font drop-down list box in the Font group.**

Your screen should be similar to Figure 1.60

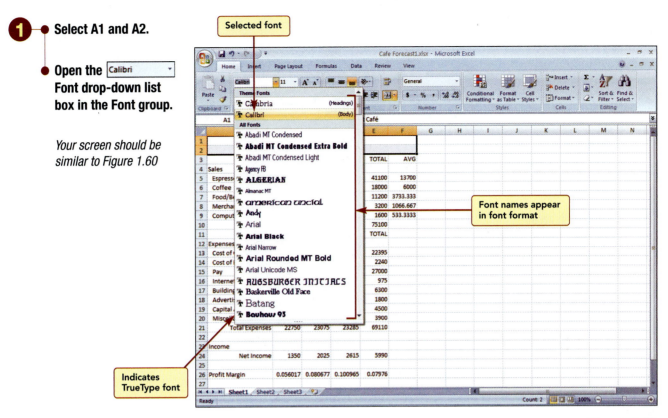

Selected font

Font names appear in font format

Indicates TrueType font

Figure 1.60

The Font drop-down list displays examples of the available fonts on your system in alphabetical order. The default worksheet font, Calibri, is highlighted. Notice the **T** preceding the font name. This indicates the font is a TrueType font. TrueType fonts appear onscreen as they will appear when printed. They are installed when Windows is installed. Fonts that are preceded with a blank space are printer fonts. These fonts are supported by your printer and are displayed as closely as possible to how they will appear onscreen but may not match exactly when printed. You will change the font and increase the font size to 14. As you point to the font options, the selected text in the worksheet displays how it will appear if chosen. This is the **Live Preview** feature of Excel.

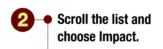

2 • Scroll the list and choose Impact.

Having Trouble?
You will not be able to see the Fonts Live Preview because the drop-down menu covers the selection to be formatted.

• Open the `11 ▼` Font Size drop-down list box.

• Point to several different font sizes in the list to see the Live Preview.

• Choose 14.

Your screen should be similar to Figure 1.61

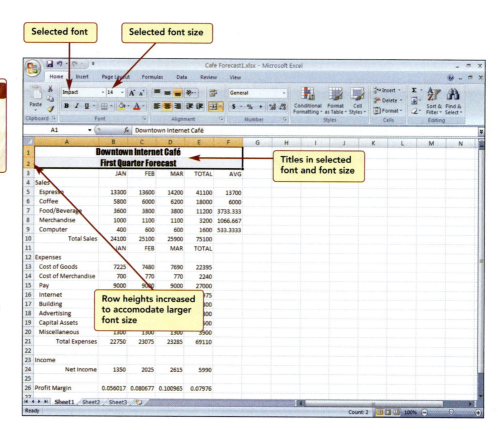

Figure 1.61

Another Method
The Font and Font Size commands are also available on the Mini toolbar; however, they do not display a Live Preview.

The title appears in the selected typeface and size and the Font and Size buttons display the name of the font and the size used in the active cell. Notice that the height of the row has increased to accommodate the larger font size of the heading.

Applying Character Effects

In addition to changing font and font size, you can apply different **character effects** to enhance the appearance of text. The table below describes some of the effects and their uses.

Format	Example	Use
Bold	**Bold**	Adds emphasis
Italic	*Italic*	Adds emphasis
Underline	<u>Underline</u>	Adds emphasis
Strikethrough	~~Strikethrough~~	Indicates words to be deleted
Superscript	"To be or not to be."[1]	Used in footnotes and formulas
Subscript	H_2O	Used in formulas
Color	Color Color Color	Adds interest

You want to add bold, italic, and underlines to several worksheet entries.

1 ● **Select B3 through F3.**

● **Click** B **Bold.**

● **Click** U ▾ **Underline.**

*Your screen should be
similar to Figure 1.62*

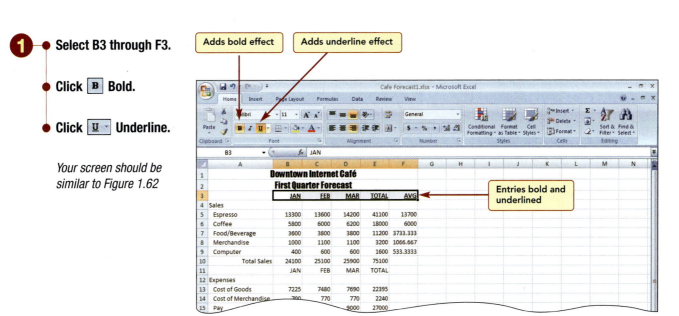

Figure 1.62

Many of the formatting commands are also available on the Mini toolbar that appears when you display the shortcut menu. To use the Mini toolbar, choose command buttons just as you would from the Ribbon.

2 ● **Select A5 through A9.**

● **Right-click on the
selection to display
the Mini toolbar.**

● **Click** B **Bold.**

● **Click** I **Italic.**

Another Method
The keyboard shortcut for bold is Ctrl + B; for italic, it is Ctrl + I; and for underline, it is Ctrl + U.

*Your screen should be
similar to Figure 1.63*

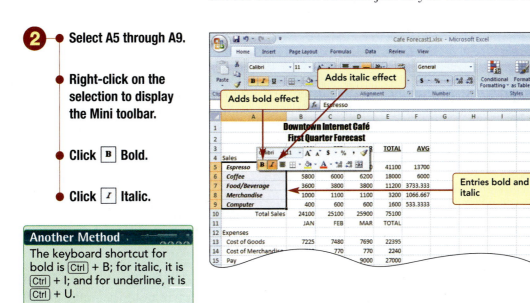

Figure 1.63

Using Undo

Sometimes formatting changes you make do not have the expected result. In this case, you feel that the sales category names would look better without the formatting. One way to remove the format from the cells is to use [2▾] Clear in the Editing group and choose Clear Formats. Because you just performed these actions, you can quickly clear the formats by undoing the last two actions you performed.

1 • Open the ⟲ Undo drop-down list in the Quick Access Toolbar.

• Move the mouse pointer down the list to highlight the Italic and Bold actions.

• Click on the highlighted selection.

Another Method

The keyboard shortcut for Undo is Ctrl + Z. You also can click ⟲ Undo repeatedly to undo the actions in the list one by one.

Your screen should be similar to Figure 1.64

Additional Information

The keyboard shortcut for Redo is Ctrl + Y. You also can click ⟳ Redo repeatedly to undo the actions in the list one by one.

Additional Information

You can remove both formatting and content using ⟲ Clear/Clear All.

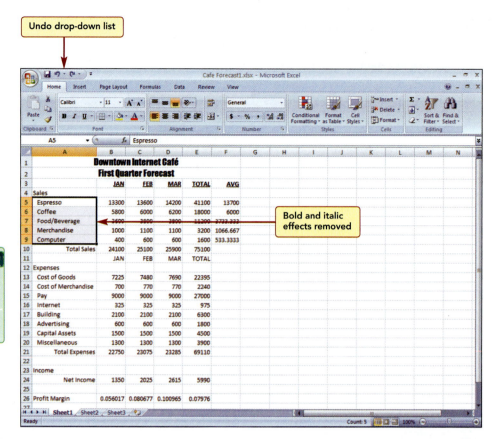

Figure 1.64

The two actions you selected are undone. Undo reverses the selected actions regardless of the current cell pointer location. If you change your mind after you Undo an action, the ⟳ Redo button is available so that you can restore the action you just undid. Undo is convenient if the actions you want to reverse were recently performed; however, if you have performed several other actions since performing the ones you want to undo, those actions also will be reversed. In that case, it would be better to remove the formats using ⟲ Clear/Clear Formats.

Using Format Painter

You do think, however, that the Total Sales, Total Expenses, and Net Income headings would look good in bold. You will bold the entry in cell A10 and then copy the format from A10 to the other cells using **Format Painter**. This feature applies the formats associated with the current selection to new selections. To turn on the feature, move the insertion point to the cell whose formats you want to copy and click the 🖌 Format Painter button. Then you select the cell to which you want the formats applied. The formats are automatically applied to the entire cell contents simply by clicking on the cell. If you double-click the 🖌 Format Painter button, you can apply the formats multiple times. You also will format the headings in row 11.

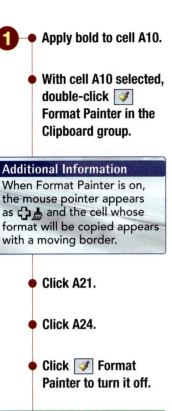

1 • Apply bold to cell A10.

• With cell A10 selected, double-click [icon] Format Painter in the Clipboard group.

Additional Information
When Format Painter is on, the mouse pointer appears as [icon] and the cell whose format will be copied appears with a moving border.

• Click A21.

• Click A24.

• Click [icon] Format Painter to turn it off.

Another Method
You also can press [Esc] to turn off Format Painter.

• Move to B3.

• Single-click on [icon] Format Painter and copy the format to cells B11 through E11.

Your screen should be similar to Figure 1.65

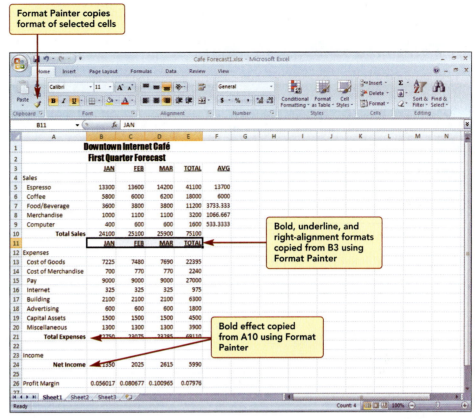

Figure 1.65

The formatting was quickly added to each cell or range as it was selected.

Formatting Numbers

You also want to improve the appearance of the numbers in the worksheet by changing their format.

Concept 14

14 **Number formats** change the appearance of numbers onscreen and when printed, without changing the way the number is stored or used in calculations. When a number is formatted, the formatting appears in the cell while the value without the formatting is displayed in the formula bar.

The default number format setting in a worksheet is General. General format, in most cases, displays numbers just as you enter them, unformatted. Unformatted numbers are displayed without a thousands separator such as a comma, with negative values preceded by a − (minus sign), and with as many decimal place settings as cell space allows. If a number is too long to be fully displayed in the cell, the General format will round numbers with decimals and use scientific notation for large numbers.

First, you will change the number format of cells B5 through F10 to display as currency with dollar signs, commas, and decimal places.

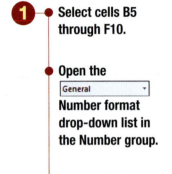

1 • Select cells B5 through F10.

• Open the **General** **Number format** drop-down list in the Number group.

• Choose **Currency**.

Your screen should be similar to Figure 1.66

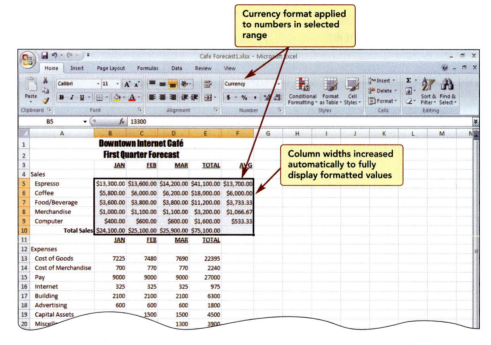

Figure 1.66

Another Method
Excel will also automatically apply a format to a cell based on the symbols you use when entering the number. For example, entering 10,000 in a cell formats the cell to Comma format, and entering $102.20 formats the cell to Currency with two decimal places.

The number entries in the selected range appear with a currency symbol, comma, and two decimal places. The column widths increased automatically to fully display the formatted values.

A second format category that displays numbers as currency is Accounting. You will try this format next on the same range. Additionally, you will specify zero as the number of decimal places because most of the values are whole values. To specify settings that are different than the default setting for a format, you need to use the Format Cells dialog box.

2 • **Click** [icon] **in the Number group to open the Format Cells Number dialog box.**

• **From the Category list box, choose Accounting.**

• **Reduce the decimal places to 0.**

• **Click** [OK] **.**

Your screen should be similar to Figure 1.67

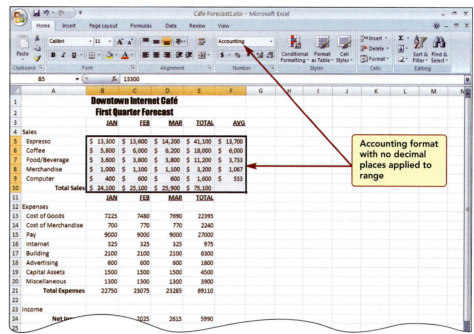

Figure 1.67

The numbers now appear in Accounting format. The primary difference between the Accounting and the Currency formats is that the Accounting format aligns numbers at the decimal place and places the dollar sign in a column at the left edge of the cell space. In addition, it does not allow you to select different ways of displaying negative numbers but displays them in black in parentheses.

You decide the Accounting format will make it easier to read the numbers in a column and you will use this format for the rest of the worksheet. An easier way to apply the Accounting format with 0 decimals is to use the commands in the Number group.

3 • **Select the range B13 through E21.**

• **Click** [$ ▾] **Accounting Number Format in the Number group.**

• **Click** [icon] **Decrease Decimal twice.**

Your screen should be similar to Figure 1.68

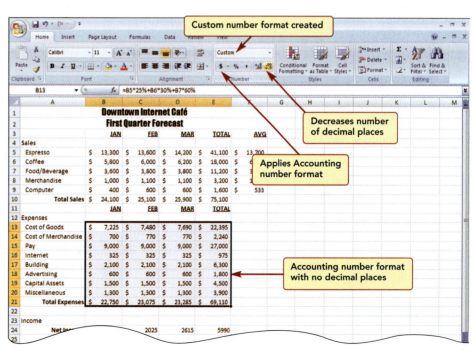

Figure 1.68

Formatting the Worksheet   **EX1.69**

Excel 2007

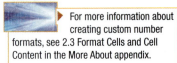
Notice the Number Format box displays Custom because you modified a copy of the existing Accounting number format code. The custom number format is added to the list of number format codes. Between 200 and 250 custom formats can be added depending on the language version of Excel you are using. You can then reapply the custom format by selecting it from the Custom category of the Format Cells Number dialog box. This is useful for complicated formats, but not for formats that are easy to recreate.

Finally, you will format the Net Income as Accounting with zero decimal places and the Profit Margin values to percentages with two decimal places. You will do this using the Mini toolbar. This feature is particularly helpful when working at the bottom of the worksheet window.

4 ● Select B24 through E24.

● Click $ Accounting Number Format on the Mini toolbar.

Having Trouble

Right-click on the selection to display the Mini toolbar.

● Click Decrease Decimal twice on the Mini toolbar.

● Select B26 through E26.

● Click % Percent Style on the Mini toolbar.

● Click Increase Decimal twice on the Mini toolbar.

Your screen should be similar to Figure 1.69

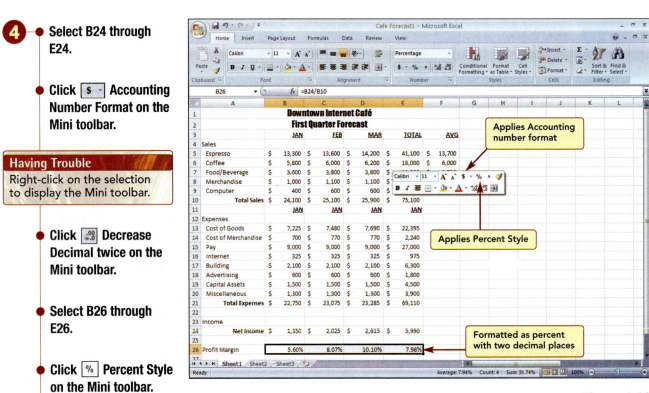

Figure 1.69

Adding Font Color

The last formatting change you would like to make to the worksheet is to add color to the text of selected cells. Font color can be applied to all the text in a selected cell or range or to selected words or characters in a cell.

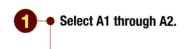

1 • Select A1 through A2.

• Open the  Font Color drop-down menu in the Font group.

Another Method

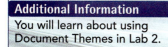 Font Color is also available on the Mini toolbar.

Your screen should be similar to Figure 1.70

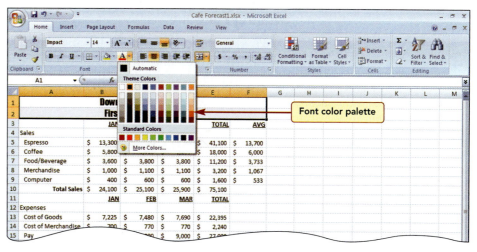

Figure 1.70

A palette of colors is displayed. Automatic is the default text color setting. This setting automatically determines when to use black or white text. Black text is used on a light background and white text on a dark background. The center area of the palette displays the Theme colors. Theme colors are a set of colors that are associated with a document theme, a predefined set of fonts, colors, and effects that can be applied to an entire worksheet. If you change the theme, the theme colors change. The Standard Colors bar displays 10 colors that are always the same.

As you point to a color, the entry in the selected cell changes color so you can preview how the selection would look. A ScreenTip displays the name of the standard color or the description of the theme color as you point to it.

Additional Information

You will learn about using Document Themes in Lab 2.

---

2 • Choose purple from the Standard Colors bar.

Your screen should be similar to Figure 1.71

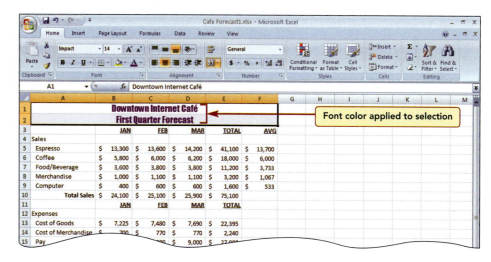

Figure 1.71

The font color of all the text in cells A1 and A2 has changed to the selected color. The selected color appears in the button and can be applied again simply by clicking the button.

Adding Fill Color

Next, you will change the cell background color, also called the fill color, behind the titles and in several other areas of the worksheet. Generally, when adding color to a worksheet, use a dark font color with a light fill color or a light font color with a dark fill color.

1 ● Select cells A1 through F4.

● Open the Fill Color drop-down color palette.

● Point to several colors to see a Live Preview.

● Select the orange color from the Standard Colors bar.

● Select cells A11 through F12 and click Fill Color to apply the last selected fill color.

● Apply the same fill color to A23:F23 and A26:F26.

Your screen should be similar to Figure 1.72

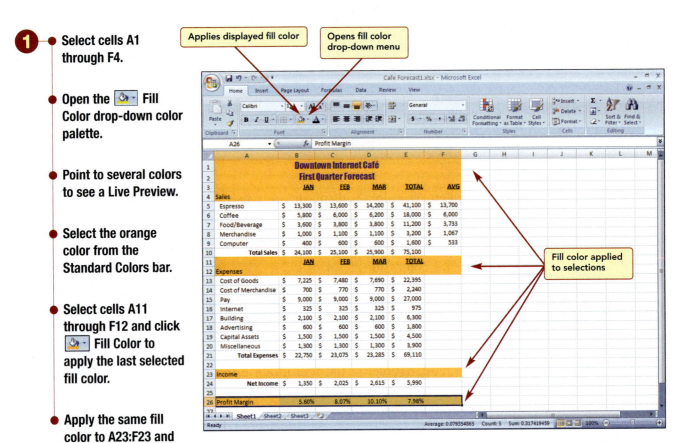

Applies displayed fill color

Opens fill color drop-down menu

Fill color applied to selections

Figure 1.72

The color highlight helps distinguish the different areas of the worksheet.

Adding and Removing Cell Borders

Finally, you decide to add a border around the entire worksheet area. Excel includes many predefined border styles that can be added to a single cell or to a range of cells. Then you will make several additional formatting changes to improve the appearance and readability of the worksheet.

1 • **Select the range A1 through F26.**

• **Open the** ⊞ **Borders drop-down menu in the Font group and choose the Thick Box Border style.**

• **Click outside the range to see the border.**

Your screen should be similar to Figure 1.73

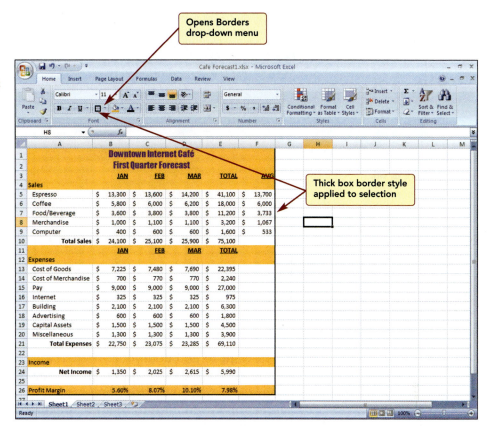

Figure 1.73

The range is considered a single block of cells and the box border surrounds the entire worksheet selection.

When adding borders, the border also is applied to adjacent cells that share a bordered cell boundary. In this case, cells G1 through G26 acquired a left border and cells A27 through F27 acquired a top border. When pasting a cell that includes a cell border, the border is included unless you specify that the paste does not include the border. To see how this works, you will first copy a cell and its border, and then you will copy it again without the border.

2 • Copy cell A1 and paste it in cell G2.

• Move to G4, open the 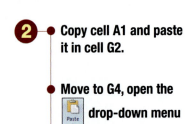 drop-down menu and choose No Borders.

• Move to G6.

Your screen should be similar to Figure 1.74

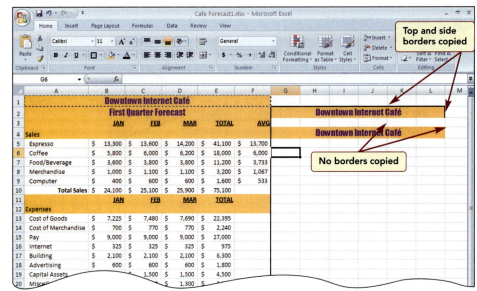

Figure 1.74

If you want to add additional borders or replace an existing border with another, select the range and then add the border. However, if you want to remove a border style from one area of a selection and add a border to another area, you need to remove all borders first and then apply the new border styles. You will try these features next on the entry in cell G2.

3 • Move to G2 and choose No Border from the 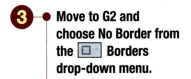 Borders drop-down menu.

• Apply a Bottom Double Border to the selection.

• Move to G6 to see the changes.

Your screen should be similar to Figure 1.75

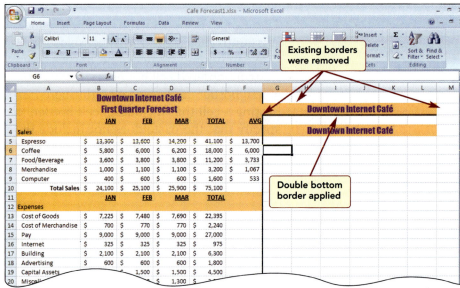

Figure 1.75

All existing borders were removed, including those that share a cell boundary, and the new double bottom border is applied to the selection. You will restore the worksheet to how it was prior to copying the title using Undo and then make some final adjustments to the worksheet.

4

- Undo your last four actions.

- Drag the row 3 bottom boundary line down to increase the row height to 22.50.

- Move to any cell in row 11 and choose Delete Sheet Rows from the ⟦Delete ▾⟧ drop-down menu in the Cells group.

- In the same manner, delete rows 21 and 23.

- Add bold and purple font color to cells A4, A11, A21, and A23.

- Click 💾 Save to save the worksheet changes.

Your screen should be similar to Figure 1.76

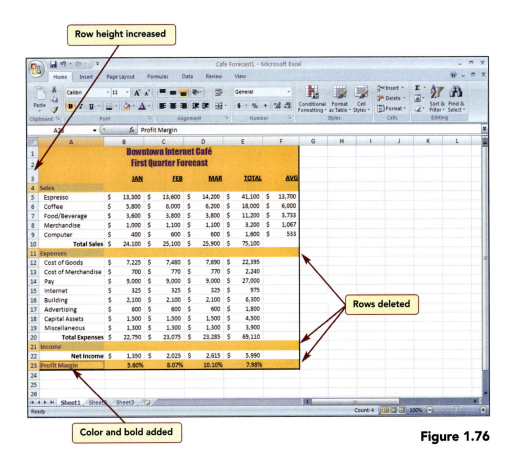

Figure 1.76

Entering the Date

Now that the worksheet is complete, you want to include your name and the date in the worksheet as documentation. There are many ways to enter the date. For example, you could type the date using the format mm/dd/yy or as month dd, yyyy. When a date is entered as text, Excel converts the entry to a numeric entry that allows dates to be used in calculations. Excel stores all dates as **serial values** with each day numbered from the beginning of the 20th century. The date serial values are consecutively assigned beginning with 1, which corresponds to the date January 1, 1900, and ending with 2958465, which is December 31, 9999.

1 • **Enter your first and last name in cell A25.**

• **Enter the current date as mm/dd/yy in cell A26.**

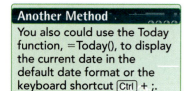
Another Method
You also could use the Today function, =Today(), to display the current date in the default date format or the keyboard shortcut [Ctrl] + ;.

Your screen should be similar to Figure 1.77

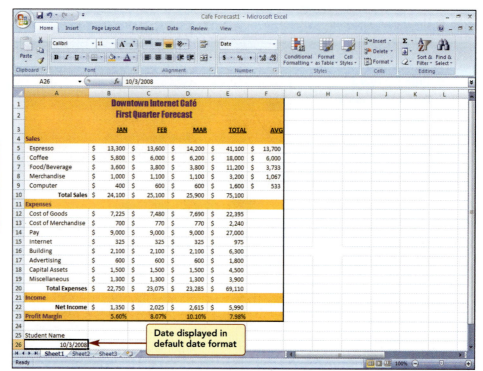

Figure 1.77

The date is displayed using the default date format, which is based on the settings in Windows. It is right-aligned in the cell because it is a numeric entry. You can change the date format in the worksheet without changing the Windows settings using the Format Cells Number dialog box.

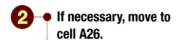

2 • **If necessary, move to cell A26.**

• **Click** 🔲 **in the Number group to open the Format Cells dialog box.**

• **Choose the month xx, xxxx (March 14, 2001) date format from the Type list.**

Your screen should be similar to Figure 1.78

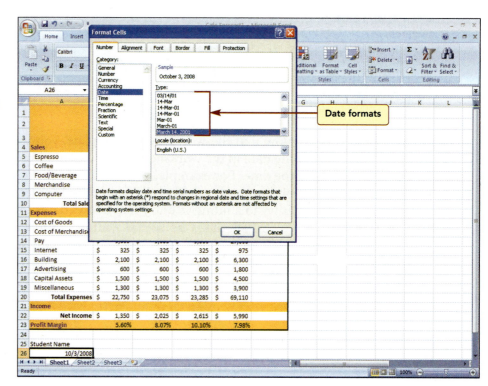

Figure 1.78

3 • **Click** [OK] **.**

The date appears in the specified format.

Previewing and Printing a Worksheet

Although you still plan to make more changes to the worksheet, you want to print a copy of the estimated first-quarter forecast for the owner to get feedback regarding the content and layout. While creating this worksheet, you have been using Normal view, which is designed for onscreen viewing and working. Another view, Print Preview, shows you how the worksheet will appear on the printed page. To save time and unnecessary printing and paper waste, it is always a good idea to first preview onscreen how your worksheet will appear when printed.

Previewing the Worksheet

Previewing a worksheet allows you to look over each page and make necessary adjustments before printing it.

1 ● Click [Office Button icon] **Office Button.**

● **Select Print and choose Print Preview from the Print submenu.**

Your screen should be similar to Figure 1.79

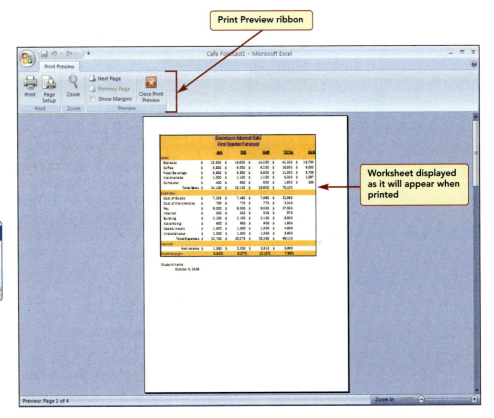

Print Preview ribbon

Worksheet displayed as it will appear when printed

Figure 1.79

The print preview window displays the worksheet as it will appear on the printed page. Notice that the row and column gridlines are not displayed and will not print. This is one of the default print settings. Your worksheet may appear slightly different from that shown in Figure 1.79. This is because the way pages appear in the preview window depends on the available fonts, the resolution of the printer, and the available colors.

The preview window also includes its own Ribbon. While previewing, you can change from full-page view to a magnified view using 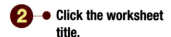 or by clicking on the preview page.

2 ● **Click the worksheet title.**

Your screen should be similar to Figure 1.80

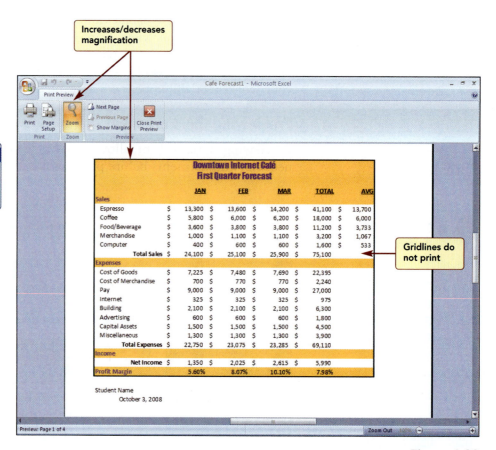

Figure 1.80

The worksheet is displayed in the actual size it will appear when printed.

Printing the Worksheet

The worksheet looks good and does not appear to need any further modifications immediately. Now you are ready to print the worksheet.

1 • Click on the worksheet again to return to full-page view.

• Click 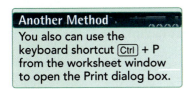.

Your screen should be similar to Figure 1.81

Another Method

You also can use the keyboard shortcut Ctrl + P from the worksheet window to open the Print dialog box.

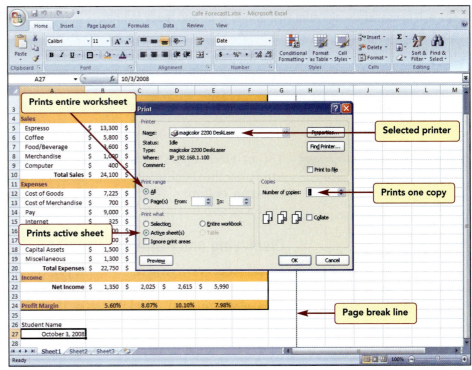

Figure 1.81

Note: Please consult your instructor for printing procedures that may differ from the following directions.

From the Print dialog box, you need to specify the printer you will be using and the document settings. The printer that is currently selected is displayed in the Name drop-down list box in the Printer section of the dialog box.

The Print Range area lets you specify how much of the worksheet you want printed. The range options are described in the following table:

Option	Action
All	Prints the entire worksheet
Pages	Prints pages you specify by typing page numbers in the text box
Selection	Prints selected range only
Active Sheet	Prints the active worksheet
Entire Workbook	Prints all worksheets in the workbook

The default settings of All and Active sheet(s) are correct. In the Copies section, the default setting of one copy of the worksheet is acceptable.

2 ● **If necessary, make sure your printer is on and ready to print.**

● **If you need to change the selected printer to another printer, open the Name drop-down list box and select the appropriate printer.**

● **Click** [OK] **.**

The printed copy should be similar to the document shown in the Case Study at the beginning of the lab. Notice the dotted line that appears between columns G and H. This is the automatic page break line that shows where one printed page ends and the next begins.

Displaying and Printing Formulas

Often, when verifying the accuracy of the data in a worksheet, it is helpful to display all the formulas in a worksheet rather than the resulting values. This way you can quickly verify that the formulas are referencing the correct cells and ranges.

1 ● **Open the Formulas tab.**

● **Click** [Show Formulas] **in the Formula Auditing group.**

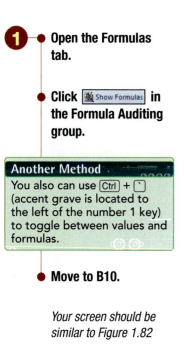

Another Method
You also can use [Ctrl] + [`] (accent grave is located to the left of the number 1 key) to toggle between values and formulas.

● **Move to B10.**

Your screen should be similar to Figure 1.82

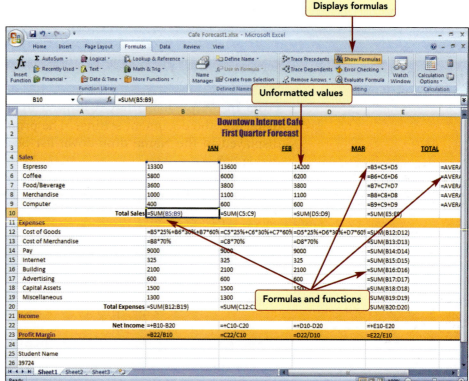

Figure 1.82

The display of the worksheet has changed to display unformatted values and the formulas and functions. It has automatically increased the column widths so the formulas and text do not overflow into the adjacent cells.

Changing Page Orientation and Scaling

Next, you will print the worksheet with formulas. Because the worksheet is so much wider, you will need to change the **orientation** or the direction the output is printed on a page. The default orientation is **portrait**. This setting prints across the width of the paper. You will change the orientation to **landscape,** which prints across the length of the paper. Then you will reduce the scale of the worksheet so it fits on one page. The scaling feature will reduce or enlarge the worksheet contents by a percentage or to fit it to a specific number of pages by height and width. You want to scale the worksheet to fit on one page.

1 • Click 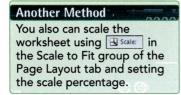 Office Button.

• Point to Print and choose Print Preview.

• Click 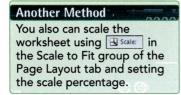 and choose Landscape.

• Choose Fit to.

• Click [OK].

Your screen should be similar to Figure 1.83

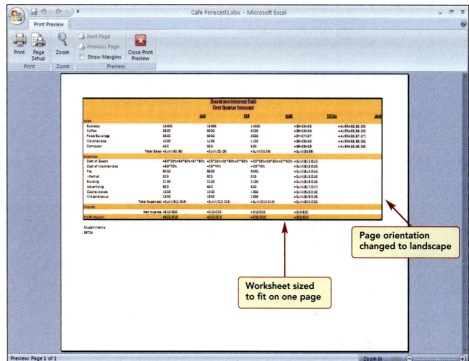

Page orientation changed to landscape

Worksheet sized to fit on one page

Figure 1.83

Another Method
You also can scale the worksheet using [Scale:] in the Scale to Fit group of the Page Layout tab and setting the scale percentage.

The size of the worksheet has been reduced so that it now fits on a single page.

The entire worksheet will easily print across the length of the page when printed using landscape orientation and scaled to fit a single page.

2 • Print the worksheet.

• Press [Ctrl] + [`] to return the display to values.

Exiting Excel 2007

The Exit command in the File menu is used to quit the Excel program. Alternatively, you can click the ☒ Close button in the application window title bar. If you attempt to close the application without first saving the workbook, Excel displays a warning asking whether you want to save your work. If you do not save your work and you exit the application, all changes you made from the last time you saved are lost.

1

• Move to cell A1.

• Click ☒ Close (in the application window title bar).

• Click [Yes] to resave the worksheet.

> **Additional Information**
> Excel saves the file with the cell selector in the same cell location it is in at the time it is saved.

Because you added the date since last saving the worksheet, you were prompted to save it again before closing it.

Focus on Careers

EXPLORE YOUR CAREER OPTIONS

Fan Coordinator

Did you know that 40 percent of the advertised positions in sports are for marketing and promotion? A marketing graduate hired as a basketball fan coordinator would use Excel to keep track of the income and expenses for coordinated half-time activities at professional sporting events. These worksheets would provide valuable information for promoting sponsors' products and services at games. A fan coordinator might start out as an unpaid intern, but after graduation could expect to earn from $25,000 to $32,000.

Concept Summary

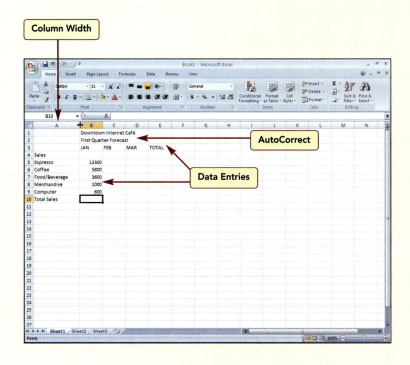

Column Width

AutoCorrect

Data Entries

Data Entries   (EX1.13)

The basic information or data you enter in a cell can be text or numbers.

AutoCorrect   (EX1.19)

The AutoCorrect feature makes some basic assumptions about the text you are typing and, based on these assumptions, automatically corrects the entry.

Column Width   (EX1.22)

The size or width of a column controls the amount of information that can be displayed in a cell.

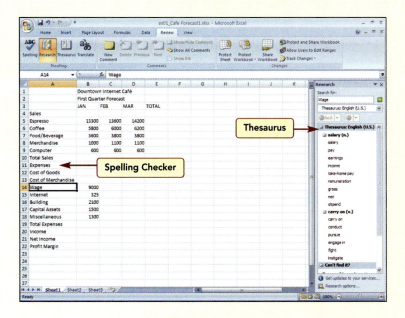

Thesaurus

Spelling Checker

Spelling Checker   (EX1.29)

The spelling checker locates misspelled words, duplicate words, and capitalization irregularities in the active worksheet and proposes the correct spelling.

Thesaurus   (EX1.31)

The thesaurus is a reference tool that provides synonyms, antonyms, and related words for a selected word or phrase.

Copy and Move (EX1.33)

The contents of worksheet cells can be duplicated (copied) or moved to other locations in the worksheet or between worksheets, saving you time by not having to retype the same information.

Range (EX1.37)

A selection consisting of two or more cells on a worksheet is a range.

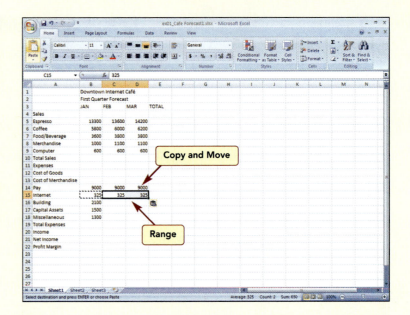

Formula (EX1.43)

A formula is an equation that performs a calculation on data contained in a worksheet.

Relative Reference (EX1.46)

A relative reference is a cell or range reference in a formula whose location is interpreted in relation to the position of the cell that contains the formula.

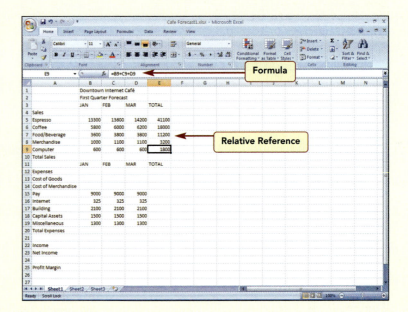

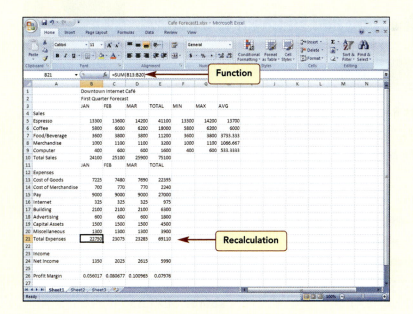

Function (EX1.47)

A function is a prewritten formula that performs certain types of calculations automatically.

Recalculation (EX1.54)

When a number in a referenced cell in a formula changes, Excel automatically recalculates all formulas that are dependent upon the changed value.

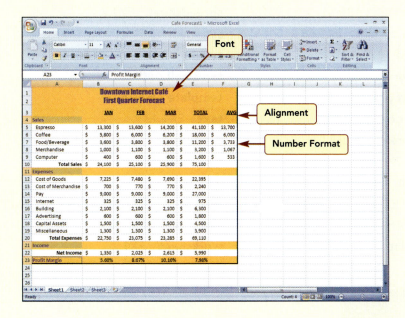

Alignment (EX1.58)

Alignment settings allow you to change the horizontal and vertical placement and the orientation of an entry in a cell.

Font and Font Size (EX1.62)

A font, also commonly referred to as a typeface, is a set of characters with a specific design.

Number Format (EX1.68)

Number formats change the appearance of numbers onscreen and when printed, without changing the way the number is stored or used in calculations.

Lab Review

LAB 1

Creating and Editing a Worksheet

key terms

active cell EX1.7	Format Painter EX1.66	relative reference EX1.46
active sheet EX1.8	formula EX1.43	row EX1.7
adjacent range EX1.37	formula bar EX1.5	row number EX1.7
alignment EX1.58	function EX1.47	sans serif EX1.62
antonym EX1.31	heading EX1.13	serial value EX1.75
argument EX1.47	landscape EX1.81	serif EX1.62
AutoCorrect EX1.19	Live Preview EX1.63	sheet EX1.7
AutoFit EX1.23	main dictionary EX1.29	sheet tab EX1.8
AutoRecover EX1.24	merged cell EX1.61	size EX1.62
cell EX1.7	Name box EX1.5	source EX1.33
cell reference EX1.7	nonadjacent range EX1.37	spelling checker EX1.29
cell selector EX1.7	number EX1.13	spreadsheet EX1.7
character effect EX1.64	number format EX1.68	synonym EX1.31
column EX1.7	operand EX1.43	syntax EX1.47
column letter EX1.7	operator EX1.43	tab scroll buttons EX1.8
constant EX1.43	order of precedence EX1.43	template EX1.6
copy area EX1.33	orientation EX1.81	text EX1.13
custom dictionary EX1.29	paste area EX1.33	thesaurus EX1.31
default EX1.6	point EX1.62	typeface EX1.62
destination EX1.33	portrait EX1.81	variable EX1.43
fill handle EX1.38	range EX1.37	workbook EX1.6
font EX1.62	range reference EX1.37	workbook window EX1.6
format EX1.57	recalculation EX1.54	worksheet EX1.7

MCAS Skills

The Microsoft Certified Applications Specialist (MCAS) certification program is designed to measure your proficiency in performing basic tasks using the Office 2007 applications. Getting certified demonstrates that you have the skills and provides a valuable industry credential for employment. See Reference 2 MCAS Certification Guide for a complete list of the skills that were covered in Lab 1.

command summary

Command	Shortcut	Action
🏢 Office Button		
New	Ctrl + N	Opens a new blank workbook
Open	Ctrl + O	Opens an existing workbook file
Save	Ctrl + S	Saves file using same file name
Save As	F12	Saves file using a new file name
Print	Ctrl + P	Prints a worksheet
Print/Print Preview		Displays worksheet as it will appear when printed
Close	Ctrl + F4	Closes open workbook file
Excel Options		Displays and changes program settings
Exit Excel	× or Alt + F4	Exits Excel program
Quick Access Toolbar		
💾 Save	Ctrl + S	Saves document using same file name
↩ Undo	Ctrl + Z	Reverses last editing or formatting change
↪ Redo	Ctrl + Y	Restores changes after using Undo
Home tab		
Clipboard group		
Paste	Ctrl + V	Pastes selections stored in system Clipboard
✂ Cut	Ctrl + X	Cuts selected data from the worksheet
📋 Copy	Ctrl + C	Copies selected data to system Clipboard
🖌 Format Painter		Copies formatting from one place and applies it to another
Font group		
Calibri Font		Changes text font
11 Font Size		Changes text size
B Bold	Ctrl + B	Bolds selected text
I Italic	Ctrl + I	Italicizes selected text
U Underline	Ctrl + U	Underlines selected text
Border		Adds border to specified area of cell or range

Lab Review

command summary

Command	Shortcut	Action
Fill Color		Adds color to cell background
Font Color		Adds color to text
Alignment group		
Align Text Left		Left-aligns entry in cell space
Center		Center-aligns entry in cell space
Align Text Right		Right-aligns entry in cell space
Increase Indent		Indents cell entry
Decrease Indent		Reduces the margin between the left cell border and cell entry.
Merge & Center		Combines selected cells into one cell and centers cell contents in new cell
Number group		
General / Number Format		Applies selected number formatting to selection
$ / Accounting		Applies Accounting number format to selection
% / Percent Style		Applies Percent Style format to selection
Increase Decimal		Increases number of decimal places
Decrease Decimal		Decreases number of decimal places
Cells group		
Insert /Insert Cells		Inserts blank cells, shifting existing cells down
Insert /Insert Cut Cells		Inserts cut row of data into new worksheet row, shifting existing rows down
Insert /Insert Copied Cells		Inserts copied row into new worksheet row, shifting existing rows down
Insert /Insert Sheet Rows		Inserts blank rows, shifting existing rows down
Insert /Insert Sheet Columns		Inserts blank columns, shifting existing columns right
Delete /Delete Sheet Rows		Deletes selected rows, shifting existing rows up
Delete /Delete Sheet Columns		Deletes selected columns, shifting existing columns left
Format /Row Height		Changes height of selected row
Format /AutoFit Row Height		Changes row height to match the tallest cell entry
Format /Column Width		Changes width of selected column

command summary

Command	Shortcut	Action
Format /AutoFit Column Width		Changes column width to match widest cell entry
Format /Default Width		Returns column width to default width
Editing group		
Σ Sum		Calculates the sum of the values in the selected cells
Σ Sum/Average		Calculates the average of the values in the selected range
Σ Sum/Min		Returns the smallest of the values in the selected range
Σ Sum/Max		Returns the largest of the values in the selected range
Fill/Right	Ctrl + R	Continues a pattern to adjacent cells to the right
Clear		Removes both formats and contents from selected cells
Clear/Clear Formats		Clears formats only from selected cells
Clear/Clear Contents	Delete	Clears contents only from selected cells

Formulas tab

Command	Shortcut	Action
Formula Auditing group		
Show Formulas	Ctrl + `	Displays and hides worksheet formulas

Review tab

Command	Shortcut	Action
Proofing group		
ABC Spelling	F7	Spell-checks worksheet
Thesaurus		Opens the Thesaurus for the selected word in the Research task pane

Print Preview tab

Command	Shortcut	Action
Print	Ctrl + P	Opens Print dialog box
Page Setup		Shows the Page tab of the Page Setup dialog box
Page Setup /Landscape		Changes page orientation to landscape
Page Setup /Fit To		Scales the worksheet to fit a specified number of pages
Zoom		Changes the zoom level of the document preview
Close Print Preview		Closes Print Preview and returns to editing document

screen identification

1. In the following Excel 2007 screen, letters identify important elements. Enter the correct term for each screen element in the space provided.

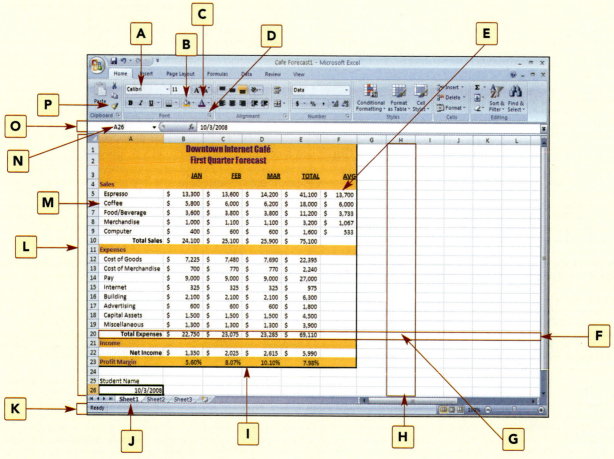

Possible answers for the screen identification are

Column   Formula bar   A. _____   I. _____
Status bar   Active sheet   B. _____   J. _____
Font color   Text label   C. _____   K. _____
Numeric entry   Cell reference   D. _____   L. _____
Fill color   Format painter   E. _____   M. _____
Font   Ribbon   F. _____   N. _____
Range   View buttons   G. _____   O. _____
Formula   Zoom feature   H. _____   P. _____
Row   Border
Column labels   Sheet tabs
Workbook window   Office button
Cell

matching

Match the lettered item on the right with the numbered item on the left.

1. source   _____   **a.** an arithmetic operator

2. /   _____   **b.** a set of characters with a specific design

3. [icon]   _____   **c.** the cell you copy from

4. font   _____   **d.** Excel workbook file name extension

5. .xlsx   _____   **e.** two or more worksheet cells

6. [icon]   _____   **f.** enters a SUM function

7. =C19*A21   _____   **g.** adds a cell border

8. [icon]   _____   **h.** merges cells and centers entry

9. D11   _____   **i.** a formula multiplying the values in two cells

10. [Σ icon]   _____   **j.** a cell reference

11. range

true/false

Circle the correct answer to the following questions.

1. The spell checker can only find misspelled words if they are entered in the main dictionary.   True   False

2. The default column width setting is 10.12.   True   False

3. An adjacent range is two or more selected cells or ranges that are adjoining.   True   False

4. A function is a prewritten formula that performs a calculation.   True   False

5. When a selection is cut, it is stored in the system Clipboard.   True   False

6. When a formula containing relative references is copied, the cell references in the copied formula refer to the same cells that are referenced in the original formula.   True   False

7. A colon is used to separate cell references in nonadjacent ranges.   True   False

8. Recalculation is one of the most powerful features of electronic worksheets.   True   False

9. Cell alignment allows you to change the horizontal and vertical placement and the orientation of an entry in a cell.   True   False

10. Number formats affect the way that numbers are used in calculations.   True   False

Lab Exercises

fill-in

Complete the following statements by filling in the blanks with the correct key terms.

1. The _____ displays the cell selector and will be affected by the next entry or procedure.

2. _____ are integers assigned to the days from January 1, 1900, through December 31, 2099, that allow dates to be used in calculations.

3. Cells or ranges that are included in the same selection but are not located next to each other are part of a _____.

4. The _____ is the location that receives the data from the copy area.

5. A(n) _____ window is used to display an open workbook file.

6. The _____ dictionary holds words the user enters that are not included in the main dictionary.

7. A(n) _____ cell is a cell made up of several selected cells combined into one.

8. A(n) _____ is a rectangular grid of rows and columns.

9. A(n) _____ entry is used to perform a calculation.

10. _____ fonts have a flare at the base of each letter to lead the reader to the next character.

multiple choice

Circle the correct response to the questions below.

1. The _____ is the place to which a selection is moved or copied.
   a. destination area
   b. source area
   c. copy area
   d. source

2. _____ consist of typefaces and sizes that can be applied to characters to improve their appearance.
   a. Cells
   b. Headings
   c. Objects
   d. Fonts

3. _____ entries can contain any combination of letters, numbers, spaces, and any other special characters.
   a. Number
   b. Variable
   c. Constant
   d. Text

4. Which of the following is a valid Excel formula?
   a. =(5 + 8)(2 + 1)
   b. 5 + 8*2 + 1
   c. =5 + 8(2 + 1)
   d. =(5 + 8)*(2 + 1)

5. The amount of information that is displayed in a cell is determined by the _____.
   a. column size
   b. row size
   c. column width
   d. row height

6. Whenever a formula containing _____ references is copied, the referenced cells are automatically adjusted.
   a. relative
   b. automatic
   c. fixed
   d. variable

7. The _____ feature in Excel automatically inserts proper capitalization at the beginning of sentences and in the names of days of the week.
   a. AutoName
   b. AutoCorrect
   c. CorrectWords
   d. Word Wrap

8. When a number in a referenced cell is changed, all the formulas that use the cell reference are _____.
   a. recalculated
   b. reformatted
   c. redefined
   d. left unchanged

9. The _____ is a reference tool that provides synonyms and related words for a selected word.
   a. synonym locator
   b. thesaurus
   c. spelling checker
   d. research book

10. The Currency number format can display _____.
    a. dollar signs
    b. commas
    c. decimal places
    d. all of the above

Hands-on Exercises

step-by-step

Animal Rescue Foundation Adoption Analysis ★

1. Edward Corwin works for the Animal Rescue Foundation. One of his responsibilities is to collect and analyze data on the animals that enter the shelters. He has compiled a list of the cost of housing animals by the local shelters for four different years. After following the directions below to complete the worksheet, your solution will be similar to that shown here.

   a. Open the workbook ex01_Animal Housing. Spell check the worksheet and correct any misspelled words.

   b. Modify the title in cell B2 so the first letter of each word is capitalized. Increase the font size to 14 point. Merge and center both title lines across columns A through E.

   c. Bold and center the headings in row 5. Format cells B5 and C5 to text. Insert a blank row above row 6.

   d. In row 17, enter a function to total the data under the 2007 column and a function to total the data under the 2008 column.

   e. Format the numbers in rows 7 and 17 using the Accounting style with zero decimal places. Format the numbers in rows 8 through 16 using the Comma style with zero decimal places.

   f. Adjust the column widths so all the data is fully displayed. Insert a blank row above row 17.

   g. Edward has just received the information for the last two years. Enter the following data in the cells indicated.

Row	Col D	Col E
5	2009	2010
7	142600	152800
8	213500	220300
9	12500	14700
10	2200	4200
11	1400	1600
12	148500	142400
13	11700	10500
14	18900	25300
15	14200	13500
16	26700	29900

h. Format the column heads to match the style of the corresponding information in columns B and C.

i. Copy the Total function in cell B18 to calculate the total for each of the new years. Increase the indent in cell A18 and add font and fill colors to the worksheet, as you like. Add a thick box border around A1:E18.

j. Enter your name in cell A20 and the current date in cell A21. Format cell A21 to display the month, day, and year (March 14, 2001) date format.

k. Move to cell A1. Save the workbook as Animal Housing Analysis to your solution file location. Preview and print the worksheet.

l. Print the worksheet with formulas using landscape orientation so that it fits on one page.

Hurricane Analysis Worksheet ★

2. Mary Ellen is a manager for an insurance agency. One of her responsibilities is to collect and analyze data on weather conditions in geographical areas. She has compiled a list of hurricanes from the National Weather Service. After following the directions below to complete the worksheet, your solution will be similar to that shown here.

a. Open the workbook ex01_US Hurricanes. Spell check the worksheet and correct any misspelled words.

b. Modify the title in cell A1 so the first letter of each word is capitalized, except "by." Merge and center the two worksheet titles across columns A through I. Increase the font size to 12 point. Bold the titles.

c. Enter the heading **% Major to All** in cell I3 and increase the widths of columns H and I to fully display their headings.

d. Merge and center cells A3 and A4. Merge and center cells I3 and I4.

e. Adjust the width of column A so all the data is fully displayed.

f. Insert new rows above row 1 and below row 3.

g. Bold the titles in rows 5 and 6. Center the titles in B5:H5. Underline and center the titles in cells B6 through H6.

Hurricane Direct Hits by Saffir/Simpson Category 1851-2004

Area	1	2	3	4	5	All (1-5)	Major (3-5)	% Major to All
U.S. (Texas to Maine)	109	72	71	18	3	273	92	33.7%
Texas	23	17	12	7	0	59	19	32.2%
(North)	12	6	3	4	0	25	7	28.0%
(Central)	7	5	2	2	0	16	4	25.0%
(South)	9	5	7	1	0	22	8	36.4%
Louisiana	17	14	13	4	1	49	18	36.7%
Mississippi	2	5	7	0	1	15	8	53.3%
Alabama	11	5	6	0	0	22	6	27.3%
Florida	43	32	27	6	2	110	35	31.8%
(Northwest)	27	16	12	0	0	55	12	21.8%
(Northeast)	13	8	1	0	0	22	1	4.5%
(Southwest)	16	8	7	4	1	36	12	33.3%
(Southeast)	13	13	11	3	1	41	15	36.6%
Georgia	12	5	2	1	0	20	3	15.0%
South Carolina	19	6	4	2	0	31	6	19.4%
North Carolina	21	13	11	1	0	46	12	26.1%
Virginia	9	2	1	0	0	12	1	8.3%
Maryland	1	1	0	0	0	2	0	0.0%
Delaware	2	0	0	0	0	2	0	0.0%
New Jersey	2	0	0	0	0	2	0	0.0%
Pennsylvania	1	0	0	0	0	1	0	0.0%
New York	6	1	5	0	0	12	5	41.7%
Connecticut	4	3	3	0	0	10	3	30.0%
Rhode Island	3	2	4	0	0	9	4	44.4%
Massachusetts	5	2	3	0	0	10	3	30.0%
New Hampshire	1	1	0	0	0	2	0	0.0%
Maine	5	1	0	0	0	6	0	0.0%

Student Name
10/03/08

h. Enter the formula **=H7/G7** in cell I7. Copy the formula down column I for the rest of the states. Format the numbers in column I as a percent with one decimal place.

i. Center the data in cells B7 through I33.

j. Add font and fill colors to the worksheet as you like. Locate the five states with the highest percent of major hurricanes and fill the cells containing the percentages with a different fill color and surround the cells with a thick box border.

k. Enter your name and the current date on separate rows just below the worksheet. Format the date to day/month/year (03/14/01) date format.

l. Move to cell A1. Save the workbook as US Hurricanes Analysis to your solution file location. Preview and print the worksheet.

m. Print the worksheet again with formulas using landscape orientation.

Comparative Median Income for Four-Person Families ★★

3. Terrence Lewis works for an employment agency and needs to provide information about salaries in different states for his clients. He has started a worksheet with data from the years 2003–2005. After following the directions below to complete the worksheet, the first page of your solution will be similar to that shown here.

a. Open the workbook ex01_Family Income. Spell check the worksheet and correct any misspelled words.

b. Edit the title in cell A1 by capitalizing the first letter of each word except the words "for" and "by" and by deleting the comma following "Families." Merge and center the title across columns A through F. Increase the font size to 12, and bold and apply a font color of your choice to the title.

c. Center-align and underline the column headings in row 2. Adjust the width of column A to fully display the labels. Insert blank rows above and below the title.

Median Income for 4-person Families by State

Calendar year	2003	2004	2005	Average	% Change
United States	$62,732	$63,278	$62,228	$62,746	0.81%
Alabama	$53,754	$54,594	$51,451	$53,266	4.48%
Alaska	$69,868	$71,395	$66,874	$69,379	4.48%
Arizona	$56,857	$56,067	$55,663	$56,196	2.15%
Arkansas	$49,551	$47,838	$44,537	$47,309	11.26%
California	$65,766	$63,761	$63,206	$64,244	4.05%
Colorado	$68,089	$67,634	$66,624	$67,449	2.20%
Connecticut	$81,891	$82,517	$82,702	$82,370	-0.98%
Delaware	$69,469	$73,301	$69,360	$70,710	0.16%
District of Columbia	$55,692	$61,799	$63,406	$60,299	-12.17%
Florida	$57,473	$56,824	$55,351	$56,549	3.83%
Georgia	$60,676	$59,497	$59,489	$59,887	2.00%
Hawaii	$67,564	$66,014	$65,872	$66,483	2.57%
Idaho	$54,279	$51,098	$53,722	$53,033	1.04%
Illinois	$69,168	$66,507	$68,117	$67,931	1.54%
Indiana	$63,022	$63,573	$62,079	$62,891	1.52%
Iowa	$61,238	$61,656	$57,921	$60,272	5.73%
Kansas	$61,926	$61,686	$56,784	$60,132	9.06%
Kentucky	$54,030	$54,319	$51,249	$53,199	5.43%
Louisiana	$52,299	$51,234	$47,363	$50,299	10.42%
Maine	$58,802	$58,425	$56,186	$57,804	4.66%
Maryland	$77,938	$82,879	$77,562	$79,460	0.48%
Massachusetts	$78,312	$80,247	$78,025	$78,861	0.37%
Michigan	$67,995	$68,337	$68,740	$68,357	-1.08%
Minnesota	$72,379	$72,635	$70,553	$71,856	2.59%
Mississippi	$47,847	$46,810	$46,331	$46,996	3.27%
Missouri	$59,764	$61,036	$61,173	$60,658	-2.30%
Montana	$51,791	$48,078	$46,142	$48,670	12.24%
Nebraska	$60,129	$60,626	$57,040	$59,265	5.42%
Nevada	$59,588	$59,283	$59,614	$59,495	-0.04%
New Hampshire	$72,369	$72,606	$71,661	$72,212	0.99%
New Jersey	$82,406	$80,577	$78,560	$80,514	4.90%
New Mexico	$48,422	$46,596	$47,314	$47,444	2.34%
New York	$65,461	$66,498	$64,520	$65,493	1.46%
North Carolina	$58,227	$56,500	$57,203	$57,310	1.79%
North Dakota	$57,070	$55,138	$53,140	$55,116	7.40%
Ohio	$63,934	$64,282	$62,251	$63,489	2.70%
Oklahoma	$51,377	$53,949	$48,459	$51,262	6.02%
Oregon	$60,262	$58,737	$58,315	$59,105	3.34%
Pennsylvania	$64,310	$66,130	$65,411	$65,284	-1.68%
Rhode Island	$67,646	$70,446	$68,418	$68,837	-1.13%
South Carolina	$56,110	$59,212	$56,294	$57,205	-0.33%

d. Right-align cells B5 through D56 and format the cells as Accounting with zero decimal places. Autofit column D.

e. Enter the heading **Average** in cell E4. Center and underline the heading. Calculate the average income in cell E5 using the function = Average(B5:D5). Copy the formula to cells E6 through E56.

f. Next, you would like to calculate the percent of change from 2003 to 2005. Enter the heading **% Change** in cell F4. Center and underline the title. Enter the formula **=(B5-D5)/D5** in cell F5. Format the cell as a percentage with two decimal places. Copy the formula to cells F6 through F56.

g. AutoFit columns B through F.

h. Add font and fill colors to the worksheet as you like. Locate the state with the highest positive % change and the state with the highest negative % change. Surround their entire rows with a thick box border.

i. Enter your name and the current date on separate rows just below the last lines. Format the date to day, month, year (14-Mar-01) date format.

j. Move to cell A1. Save the workbook as Family Income to your solution file location. Preview and print the worksheet.

k. Print the worksheet again with formulas on one page using landscape orientation.

Publishing Industry Salary Analysis ★★

4. Enrico Torres is researching an article for the school newspaper on jobs in the publishing industry. He has found some data on salaries for jobs in publishing. He has entered this data into a worksheet but still needs to format the data and perform some analysis of the information. After following the directions below to complete the worksheet, your solution will be similar to that shown here.

a. Open the workbook ex01_Publishing Salaries. Spell check the worksheet and correct any misspelled words.

b. Insert a row below the title in row 1. Merge and center the title in row 1 over columns A through E. Format the title to Tahoma 14 point and AutoFit the row height. Apply a font color of your choice.

c. Adjust the width of column A to 40.00. Adjust the widths of the other columns so that text in each of the cells in row 3 is fully displayed. Center and bold the column heads.

Publishing Industry Salary Analysis table showing occupations with Employment, Hourly Median, Hourly Mean, Deviation, and Annual Mean columns. Student Name, 10/03/08.

d. Edit the column titles by removing Hourly from cells C3 and D3 and entering **Hourly** into cell C2. Merge and center C2 over columns C and D. Bold the entry. Move Annual from cell E3 to E2. Bold and center the text in E2. Apply a font color of your choice to the column headings.

e. Format the data in column B using the Comma style and no decimal places. Format the data in columns C through D to Currency with two decimal places. Format the data in column E to Currency with no decimal places. Right-align the data in cells C4 through E35.

f. Insert a new column between D and E. Label the new column **Deviation** in cell E3. Enter a formula in cell E4 to calculate the difference between the Median Hourly rate and the Mean Hourly rate and copy the formula down the column.

g. Enter **Average** in A36. Right-align and format to match the column heads.

h. In cell B36, use a function to calculate the average of the data in column B. Copy this formula to columns C, D, E, and F. Format the cells containing the average values to match the format used for the other numbers in their columns. AutoFit the columns for the data including the column headings.

i. Apply different fill colors to the title, occupation row headings, data, and the average row. Surround cells A4 through F36 with an All Borders border.

j. Enter your name and the current date on separate rows below the worksheet.

k. Move to cell A1. Save the workbook file as Publishing Salaries to your solution file location. Preview and print the worksheet.

l. Print the worksheet again with formulas on one page using landscape orientation.

Pecan Groves Homeowners Association ★★★

5. The Pecan Groves Homeowners Association is planning a large building project and wants to project how much there is likely to be in the cash budget after expenses. Using last year's final budget numbers, you will create a projected budget for 2008. After following the directions below to complete the worksheet, your solution will be similar to that shown here.

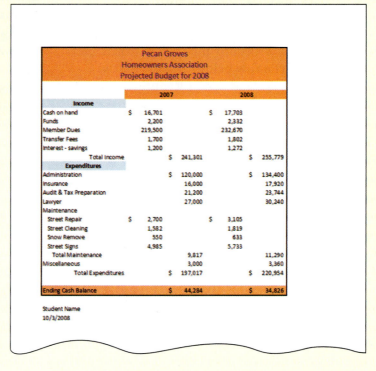

a. Open the workbook file ex01_Pecan Groves Budget. Spell check the worksheet and correct any misspelled words.

b. Change the font type, size, and color and fill color of the three worksheet title lines to a format of your choice. Merge and center the titles across columns A through E.

c. Set the width of column A to 25. Insert a column between columns B and C. Merge and center cell B5 across columns B and C. Merge and center cell D5 across columns D and E. Set the fill color of cells B5 and D5 to match the fill color in the titles.

d. Center the text in cell A6 and change the font color and fill color to a color of your choice. Apply the same formats to cell A13.

e. Right-justify the text in cells A12 and A25. Indent the text in cells A19:A23. Indent the text in cell A23 again. Move the data in cells B14:B17 to C14:C17. Move the data in cell B24 to C24.

f. In cell C12, sum the income data. In cell C23, sum the maintenance expenditure data. In cell C25, sum all the expenditures items. In cell C27, enter a formula to calculate the ending cash balance. (Hint: =C12-C25)

g. Each of the 2008 Income items is projected to increase by 6 percent over the previous year. Enter a formula in cell D7 to calculate the increase in cash on hand. (Hint: =B7*1.06) Copy this formula down column D to the other Income items. Enter the appropriate function into cell E12 to calculate the 2008 total income value.

h. Each of the 2008 expenditure items except for the maintenance expenditures is projected to increase by 12 percent over the previous year. Enter the appropriate formulas in column E to reflect this change. Each maintenance expense is projected to increase 15 percent. Enter the appropriate formulas in column D. Enter the appropriate function in cell E23 to calculate the total maintenance expenses. Use formulas to calculate the value for 2008's total expenditures and ending cash balance.

i. Format cells B7, B19, C12, C14, C25, C27, D7, D19, E12, E14, E25, and E27 as Accounting with zero decimal places. Format all other cells containing numbers except for B5 and D5 to comma with zero decimal places. Set the column widths of columns B through E to 12. Fill the cells A27:E27 with the same fill color used for the titles. Delete column F. Surround the entire worksheet with a thick box border.

j. Enter your name and the current date on separate rows just below the worksheet.

k. Save the workbook file as Pecan Groves Budget to your solution file location. Preview and print the worksheet.

l. Print the worksheet again with formulas using landscape orientation.

on your own

Tracking Your Calories ★

1. A worksheet can be used to track your calories for the day. Design and create a worksheet to record the food you consume and the exercise you do on a daily basis. The worksheet should include your food consumption for all meals and snacks and the activities you performed for a week. Use the Web as a resource to find out the calorie values for the items you consumed, or refer to the calorie information on the product packaging, and to find out the caloric expenditure for the exercises you do. Include an appropriate title, row and column headings, and formulas to

calculate your total calorie intake and expenditure on a daily basis. Include a formula to calculate the percent deviation from your recommended daily calorie intake. Format the worksheet appropriately using features presented in this lab. Enter real or sample data. Include your name and date above the worksheet. Spell check the worksheet. Save the workbook as Calorie Tracking and print the worksheet.

Creating a Personal Budget ★

2. In a blank Excel 2007 workbook, create a personal three-month budget. Enter an appropriate title and use descriptive labels for your monthly expenses (food, rent, car payments, insurance, credit card payments, etc.). Spell check your worksheet. Enter your monthly expenses (or, if you prefer, any reasonable sample data). Use formulas to calculate total expenses for each month and the average monthly expenditures for each expense item. Add a column for projection for the next year showing a 4 percent increase in the cost of living. Enhance the worksheet using features you learned in this lab. Enter your name and the current date on separate rows just below the worksheet. Save the workbook as Personal Budget. Preview and print the worksheet.

Tracking Project Hours ★★

3. Samantha Johnson is the project manager for a small publishing company. She has four part-time employees (Melanie, Bob, Vanessa, and Rudy). Using the steps in the planning process, plan and create a worksheet for Samantha that can be used to record and analyze the hours each employee works per day during the month on two projects: magazine and brochure. Hours-worked data for each employee will be entered into the worksheet. Using that data, the worksheet will calculate the total number of hours for each person per project. Additionally, it will calculate the total weekly hours for each project. Write a short paragraph describing how you used each of the planning steps. Enter sample data in a worksheet. Include your name and the current date on separate rows just below the worksheet. Spell check the worksheet. Save the workbook as Project Hours. Preview and print the worksheet.

Music Analysis ★★★

4. Use the library and/or the Web to locate information on trends in CD sales versus music downloads on the Internet. Create a worksheet to display information relating to the increasing usage by country, age group, or any other trend you locate. Calculate totals or averages based on your data. Enhance the worksheet using features you learned in this lab. Enter your name and the current date on separate rows just below the worksheet. Spell check the worksheet. Save the workbook as Music Analysis. Preview and print the worksheet.

Home Electronics Analysis ★★★

5. A national electronics retailer wants to analyze the trend in home electronics sales and usage for the past three years. Design and create a worksheet to record the number of households (one-person, two-person, and four-person) who have computers, Internet access, televisions, and cable TV access. Include an appropriate title, row and column headings, and formulas to calculate average by category and by year. Include a formula to calculate the percent growth over the three years. Format the worksheet appropriately using features presented in this tutorial. Enter sample data for the three years. Include your name and date above the worksheet. Spell check the worksheet. Save the workbook as Home Electronics Analysis and print the worksheet.

Charting Worksheet Data

Objectives

After completing this lab, you will know how to:

 1 Apply and customize themes.

 2 Use cell styles.

 3 Insert and size a graphic.

 4 Create a chart.

 5 Move, size, and format a chart.

 6 Change the type of chart.

 7 Create, explode, and rotate a pie chart.

 8 Apply patterns and color to a chart.

9 Document a workbook.

10 Size and align a sheet on a page.

11 Add predefined headers and footers

Case Study

Downtown Internet Café

Evan is impressed with how quickly you were able to create the first-quarter sales forecast for the Downtown Internet Café. He made several suggestions to improve the appearance of the worksheet, including applying different formats and adding a graphic. Evan also expressed concern that the sales values seem a little low and has asked you to contact several other Internet cafés to inquire about their startup experiences.

While speaking with other Internet café managers, you heard many exciting success stories. Internet connections attract more customers, and the typical customer stays longer at an Internet café than at a regular café. As a result, they spend more money.

You would like to launch an aggressive advertising campaign to promote the new Internet aspect of the Café. The new Café features include free Wi-Fi connection, computer rentals, and printing and copying services. You believe that the campaign will lead to an increase in customers and subsequently to an increase in sales. To convince Evan, you need an effective way to illustrate the sales growth you are forecasting. You will use Excel 2007's chart-creating and formatting features to produce several different charts of your sales estimates, as shown on the following page.

Graphics and document themes add visual interest to a worksheet.

Many different types of charts can be created and modified to visually represent worksheet data.

Features such as data labels, fill colors, textures, and shadows add a professional appearance to your charts.

Concept Preview

The following concepts will be introduced in this lab:

① Graphics A graphic is a nontext element or object such as a drawing or picture that can be added to a document.

② Theme A theme is a predefined set of formatting choices that can be applied to an entire worksheet in one simple step.

③ Cell Style A cell style is a predefined theme-based combination of formats that have been named and that can be quickly applied to a selection.

④ Chart A chart is a visual representation of data that is used to convey information in an easy-to-understand and attractive manner. Different types of charts are used to represent data in different ways.

⑤ Chart Elements A chart consists of a number of elements that are used to graphically display the worksheet data.

⑥ Chart Object A chart object is a graphic object that is created using charting features. A chart object can be inserted into a worksheet or into a special chart sheet.

⑦ Chart Layout A chart layout is a predefined set of chart elements that can be quickly applied to a chart.

⑧ Chart Style A chart style is a predefined set of chart formats that can be quickly applied to a chart.

⑨ Group A group is two or more objects that behave as a single object when moved or sized. A chart consists of many separate objects.

⑩ Data Labels Data labels provide additional information about a data marker. They can consist of the value of the marker, the name of the data series or category, a percent value, or a bubble size.

⑪ Headers and Footers Headers and footers provide information that typically appears at the top and bottom of each page and commonly include information such as the date and page number.

Improving the Appearance of the Worksheet

To focus Evan's attention solely on the sales values for the Downtown Internet Café, you created a new worksheet containing only those values. Although you have added some formatting to the worksheet already, you still want to improve its appearance by adding a graphic, changing the theme, and applying different cell styles. Then you will create the charts to help Evan visualize the sales trends better.

Inserting a Graphic

You saved the sales portion of the worksheet in a new workbook file.

1 ● Start Office Excel 2007.

● If necessary, maximize the Excel application window.

● Open the file ex02_Cafe Sales.

Your screen should be similar to Figure 2.1

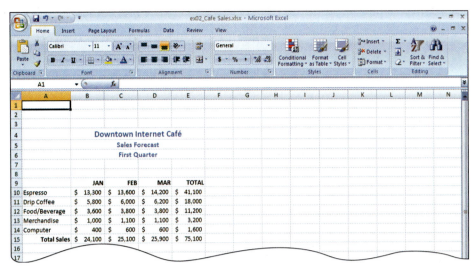

Figure 2.1

First you want to add a graphic next to the worksheet title to add interest.

Concept 1

Graphics

1 A **graphic** is a nontext element or object such as a drawing or **picture** that can be added to a document. An **object** is an item that can be sized, moved, and manipulated. A picture is a file (such as a metafile) that you can ungroup and manipulate as two or more objects or a file that stays as a single object (such as bitmaps) A clip is a single media file, including art, sound, animation, or movies.

A graphic can be a simple drawing object consisting of shapes, such as lines and boxes, that can be created using features on the Drawing toolbar. A **drawing object** is part of the Excel workbook. A picture is an illustration such as a scanned photograph. Pictures are graphics that were created from another program and inserted in the worksheet as embedded objects. An **embedded object** becomes part of the Excel workbook and can be opened and edited using the **source program**, the program in which it was created.

drawing object

graphic illustration

photograph

Add graphics to your worksheets to help the reader understand concepts, to add interest, and to make your worksheet stand out from others.

Graphic files can be obtained from a variety of sources. Many simple drawings called **clip art** are available in the Clip Organizer, a Microsoft Office tool that arranges and catalogs clip art and other media files stored on the computer's hard disk. Additionally, you can access Microsoft's Clip Art and Media Web site for even more graphics. You also can create graphic files using a scanner to convert any printed document, including photographs, to an electronic format. Most images that are scanned are stored as Windows bitmap files (.bmp). All types of graphics, including clip art, photographs, and other types of images, can be found on the Internet. These files are commonly stored as .jpg or .pcx files. Keep in mind that any images you locate on the Internet may be protected by copyright and should be used only with permission. You also can purchase CDs containing graphics for your use.

You want to insert a picture to the left of the title in the worksheet. You located a picture at Microsoft's Clip Art and Media Web site and saved a copy of the picture on your computer.

Additional Information

You also can locate and insert graphics of all types from the ClipArt gallery using 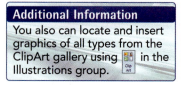 in the Illustrations group.

2 • Open the Insert tab.

• Click 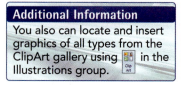 in the Illustrations group.

• Change the Look In location to the location of your data files.

• Select ex02_Internet Cafe.wmf.

• If necessary, click 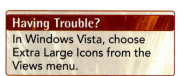 Views and choose Preview from the drop-down menu.

Having Trouble?

In Windows Vista, choose Extra Large Icons from the Views menu.

Your screen should be similar to Figure 2.2

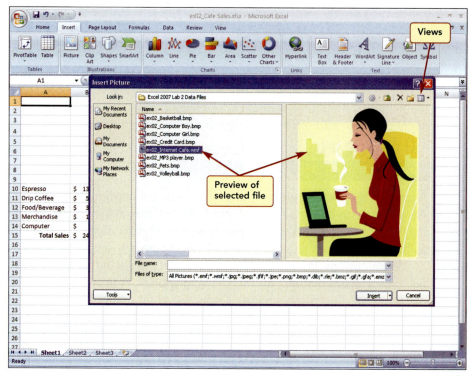

Figure 2.2

A preview of the selected picture is displayed. You think this picture illustrates the concept of a café and that it will look good in the worksheet.

3 Click  .

Your screen should be similar to Figure 2.3

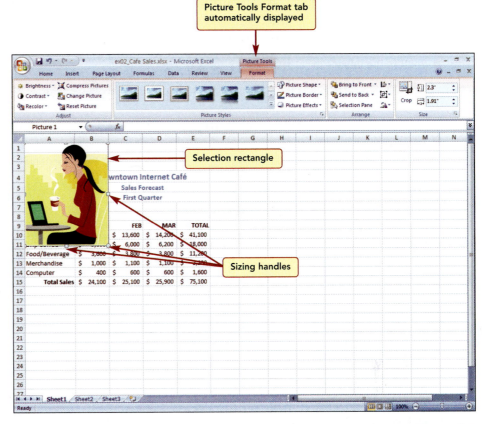

Figure 2.3

The picture is inserted in the worksheet at the location of the cell selector. Notice the picture is surrounded by a **selection rectangle** and eight squares and circles, called **sizing handles**, indicating it is a selected object and can now be deleted, sized, moved, or modified. The Picture Tools Format tab is automatically displayed and can be used to modify the selected picture object.

Sizing a Graphic

Usually, when a graphic is inserted, its size will need to be adjusted. To size a graphic, you select it and drag the sizing handles to increase or decrease the size of the object. The mouse pointer changes to ↖ when pointing to a corner handle and ↔ or ↕ when pointing to a side handle. The direction of the arrow indicates the direction in which you can drag to size the graphic. Dragging a corner handle maintains the scale of the picture by increasing both the width and length of the graphic equally. You also can move a graphic object by pointing to the graphic and dragging it to the new location. The mouse pointer changes to ⛶ when you can move the graphic.

Another Method

You also can size a picture to an exact measurement using commands in the Size group of the Picture Tools tab.

You want to reduce the size of the graphic and position it next to the title.

- ● **Point to the lower-right corner sizing handle.**

- ● **With the pointer as a ↘, drag the mouse inward to reduce the size of the graphic until the bottom of the graphic is even with row 6.**

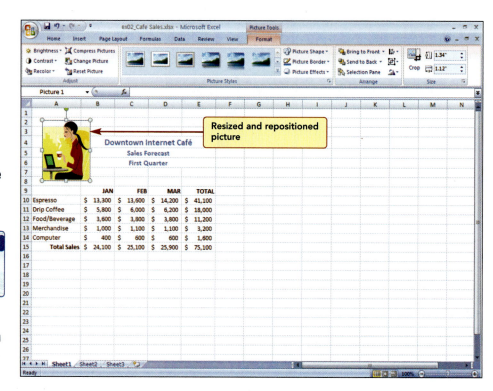

Figure 2.4

Additional Information
When you drag to size the graphic, the mouse pointer shape changes to a ╬.

- ● **Point to the center of the graphic and, when the mouse pointer is ⛶, drag the graphic to position it as in Figure 2.4.**

Additional Information
When you drag to move the graphic, the mouse pointer shape changes to a ⬌.

Your screen should be similar to Figure 2.4

Additional Information
A selected graphic object can be deleted by pressing Delete.

The picture is smaller and moved to the left of the title as you want it.

Modifying the Picture

Next, you want to enhance the picture using features on the Picture Tools Format tab. You decide to enhance it by applying a picture style to it. Picture styles are combinations of border, shadow, and shape effects that can be applied in one simple step. You also can create your own picture style effects by selecting specific style elements such as borders and shadow individually using the Picture Shape, Picture Border, and Picture Effects commands.

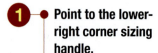

1 • If necessary, open the Format tab.

• Click ▾ More to open the Picture Styles gallery.

• Point to several styles to see the Live Preview.

Your screen should be similar to Figure 2.5

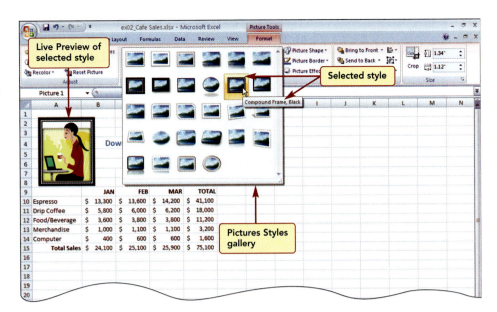

Figure 2.5

When you point to a style, the style name appears in a ScreenTip and the Live Preview shows how the selected picture style will look with your graphic. As you can see, many are not appropriate. However, you decide that the rotated style with a white border will enhance the graphic and the worksheet.

2 • Choose  Rotated, White.

• Click outside the graphic to deselect the object.

Your screen should be similar to Figure 2.6

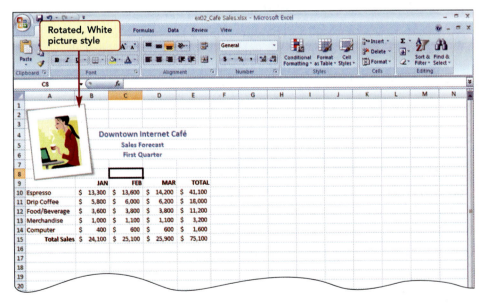

Figure 2.6

After seeing the changes, you decide to further modify the border to add more color and interest.

❸ ● Click on the graphic to select it again.

● Open the Format tab and click 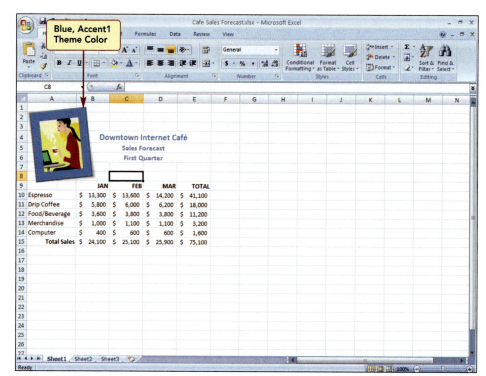 Picture Border ▾ .

● Choose the Blue, Accent1 color from the Theme Colors category.

● Click outside the graphic to deselect the object.

● Save the revised worksheet as Café Sales Forecast to your solution file location.

Your screen should be similar to Figure 2.7

Figure 2.7

Using Themes

The addition of a graphic adds a nice touch to the worksheet title. Now, you want to continue to improve the worksheet appearance by selecting a different theme.

Concept 2

Theme

2 A **theme** is a predefined set of formatting choices that can be applied to an entire workbook in one simple step. Excel includes 20 named built-in themes. Each theme includes three subsets of themes: colors, fonts, and effects. Each color theme consists of 12 colors that are applied to specific elements in a document. Each fonts theme includes different body and heading fonts. Each effects theme includes different lines and fill effects. You also can create your own custom themes by modifying an existing document theme and saving it as a custom theme. The default worksheet uses the Office theme.

Using themes gives your documents a professional and modern look. Because themes are shared across Office 2007 applications, all your office documents can have the same uniform look.

---

1 • Open the Page Layout tab.

• Click 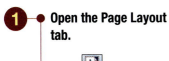 from the Themes group.

Your screen should be similar to Figure 2.8

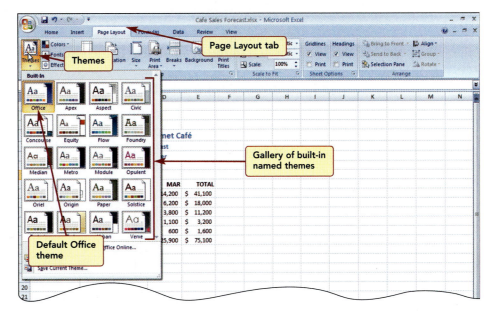

Figure 2.8

A gallery of 20 built-in named themes is displayed. A sample shows the color and font effects included in each theme. The Office theme is highlighted because it is the default theme. Pointing to each theme will display a Live Preview of how it will appear in the document.

2 • Point to several themes to preview them.

• Choose the Solstice theme.

Your screen should be similar to Figure 2.9

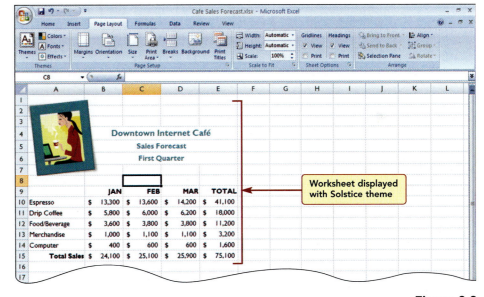

Figure 2.9

Additional Information

If the border and font colors were colors on the Standard colors bar, the color would not have updated to the new theme design.

The formatting settings associated with the selected theme have been applied to the worksheet. Most noticeable is the color change of the picture border and titles to a different shade of blue. This is because the colors in the theme category have been updated to the Solstice theme colors. Additionally, the font has changed from Calibri to Gill Sans MT.

As you add other features to the worksheet, they will be formatted using the Solstice theme colors and effects. The same theme also has been applied to the other sheets in the workbook file.

Customizing a Theme

Sometimes, you cannot find just the right combination of design elements in a built-in theme. To solve this problem, you can customize a theme by changing the color scheme, fonts, and effects. Although you like much of the Solstice theme design, you decide to try customizing the theme by changing the color scheme. Each theme has an associated set of colors that you can change by applying the colors from another theme to the selected theme.

1. Click **Colors** in the Themes group.

Your screen should be similar to Figure 2.10

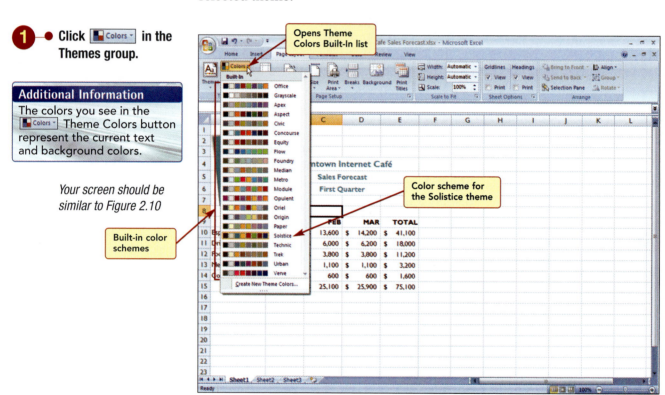

Figure 2.10

The colors used in each of the themes are displayed in the Built-In drop-down list. The set of eight colors that appears next to each theme color name represent the text, background, accent, and hyperlink colors. The Solstice color scheme is selected because it is the color scheme currently in use. Notice that the fourth color from the left in the Solstice color bar is the Accent1 color that is used in the picture border. Although you like that color, you think some of the other colors are drab. Instead, you want to see how the Oriel color scheme would look.

Modifying Cell Styles

Although you like the font size change and the colored bottom border line, you feel the titles could be improved by changing the font color to the same color as the fill color used in column A. Again, you like how the modified cell styles look and want to save the changes to these styles so that they will be easily available again.

1 ● Click [Cell Styles] and right-click on the Title cell style.

● Choose Modify from the shortcut menu.

● Click [Format...] and open the Font tab.

● Open the Color gallery and choose Red, Accent3 from the Theme Colors category.

● Click [OK] twice.

● Modify the Heading 1 and Heading 2 cell styles in the same manner.

Your screen should be similar to Figure 2.17

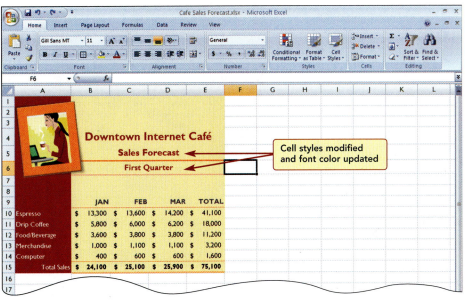

Figure 2.17

The three title lines have been updated to the new color associated with the three cell styles you modified. The changes to cell styles are saved with the current workbook file only.

Applying a Number Cell Style

The final change you want to make is to change the format of some of the worksheet values. Currently all the values are formatted using the Accounting style with zero decimal places. The Cell Styles gallery also includes five predefined number format styles. Examples of the five predefined number styles are shown below.

Style	Example
Comma	89,522.00
Comma [0]	89,522
Currency	$ 89,522.00
Currency [0]	$ 89,522
Percent	89.52200%

You will use the Comma [0] style for the four middle rows of values.

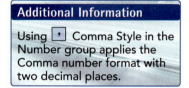

- Select B11:E14.

- Open the Cell Styles gallery.

- Choose Comma [0].

- Clear the selection.

- Save the file.

 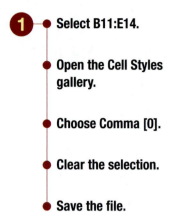
Your screen should be similar to Figure 2.18

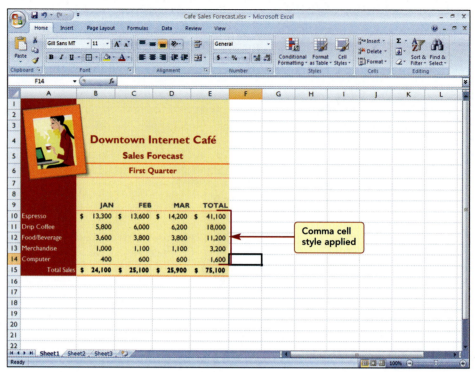

Figure 2.18

The Comma [0] style applies the comma number format with zero decimal places. Using a style applies many formats in one easy step making it quicker to apply formats to cells.

Working with Charts

Although the worksheet shows the sales data for each category, it is difficult to see how the different categories change over time. To make it easier to see the sales trends, you decide to create a chart of this data.

Concept 4

Charts

4 A **chart** is a visual representation of data that is used to convey information in an easy-to-understand and attractive manner. Different types of charts are used to represent data in different ways. The type of chart you create depends on the type of data you are charting and the emphasis you want the chart to impart.

Excel 2007 can produce 14 standard types of graphs or charts, with many different subtypes for each standard type. In addition, Excel includes professionally designed, built-in custom charts that include additional formatting and chart refinements. The basic chart types and how they represent data are described in the following table.

Type	Description	Type	Description
	Area charts show the magnitude of change over time by emphasizing the area under the curve created by each data series.		**Doughnut charts** are similar to pie charts except that they can show more than one data series.
	Bar charts display data as evenly spaced bars. The categories are displayed along the Y axis and the values are displayed horizontally, placing more emphasis on comparisons and less on time.		**Radar charts** display a line or area chart wrapped around a central point. Each axis represents a set of data points.
	Column charts display data as evenly spaced bars. They are similar to bar charts, except that categories are organized horizontally and values vertically to emphasize variation over time.		**XY (scatter) charts** are used to show the relationship between two ranges of numeric data.
			Surface charts display values in a form similar to a rubber sheet stretched over a 3-D column chart. These are useful for finding the best combination between sets of data.
	Line charts display data along a line. They are used to show changes in data over time, emphasizing time and rate of change rather than the amount of change.		**Bubble charts** compare sets of three values. They are similar to a scatter chart with the third value displayed as the size of bubble markers.
	Pie charts display data as slices of a circle or pie. They show the relationship of each value in a data series to the series as a whole. Each slice of the pie represents a single value in the series.		**Stock charts** illustrate fluctuations in stock prices or scientific data. They require three to five data series that must be arranged in a specific order.

Creating a Single Data Series Chart

All charts are drawn from data contained in a worksheet. To create a new chart, you select the worksheet range containing the data you want displayed as a chart plus any row or column headings you want used in the chart. Excel then translates the selected data into a chart based upon the shape and contents of the worksheet selection.

A chart consists of a number of parts or elements that are important to understand so that you can identify the appropriate data to select in the worksheet.

Concept 5

Chart Elements

5   A **chart** consists of a number of elements that are used to graphically display the worksheet data. In a two-dimensional chart, the selected worksheet data is visually displayed within the X- and Y-axis boundaries. The X axis, also called the **category axis**, is the bottom boundary line of the chart and is used to label the data being charted. The left boundary line of the chart is the Y axis, also called the **value axis**. This axis is a numbered scale whose numbers are determined by the data used in the chart. Typically, the X-axis line is the horizontal line and the Y-axis line is the vertical line. In 3-D charts, there also can be an additional axis, called the **Z axis**, that allows you to compare data within a series more easily. This axis is the vertical axis, while the X and Y axes depict the horizontal surface of the chart.

Other basic elements of a two-dimensional chart are

Element	Description
Data labels	Labels that correspond to the headings for the worksheet data that is plotted along the X axis
Plot area	The area within the X- and Y-axis boundaries where the chart appears
Data series	Related data points that are distinguished by different colors or patterns
Chart gridlines	Lines extending from the axis line across the plot area that make it easier to read the chart data
Legend	A box that identifies the chart data series and data markers
Chart title	A descriptive label displayed above the charted data that explains the contents of the chart
Category-axis title	A descriptive label displayed along the X axis
Value-axis title	A descriptive label displayed along the Y axis

(continued)

---

5 The basic parts of a two-dimensional chart are shown in the figure below.

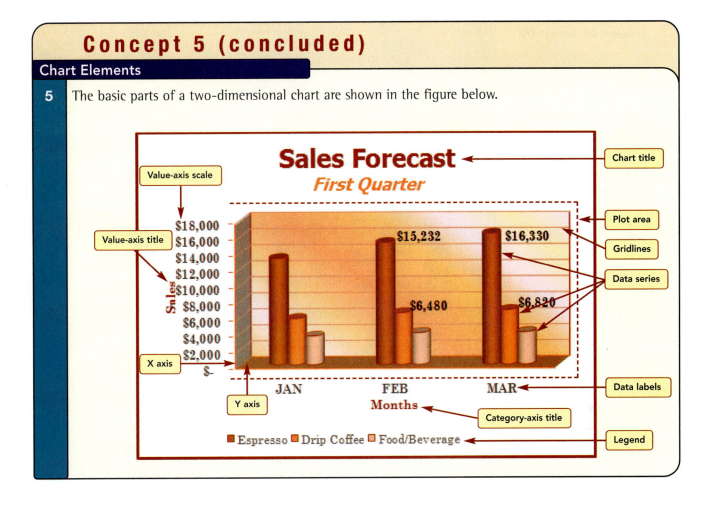

Selecting the Data to Chart

The first chart you want to create will show the total sales pattern over the three months. This chart will use the month headings in cells B9 through D9 to label the X axis. The numbers to be charted are in cells B15 through D15. In addition, the heading Total Sales in cell A15 will be used as the chart legend, making the entire range A15 through D15.

Notice that the two ranges, B9 through D9 and A14 through D14, are not adjacent and are not the same size. When plotting nonadjacent ranges in a chart, the selections must form a rectangular shape. To do this, you will include the blank cell A9 in the selection. You will specify the range and create the chart.

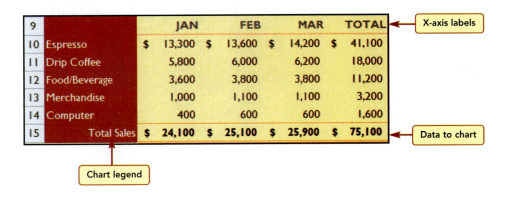

9		JAN	FEB	MAR	TOTAL
10	Espresso	$ 13,300	$ 13,600	$ 14,200	$ 41,100
11	Drip Coffee	5,800	6,000	6,200	18,000
12	Food/Beverage	3,600	3,800	3,800	11,200
13	Merchandise	1,000	1,100	1,100	3,200
14	Computer	400	600	600	1,600
15	Total Sales	$ 24,100	$ 25,100	$ 25,900	$ 75,100

1 • **Select A9 through D9.**

• **Hold down** Ctrl**.**

• **Select A15 through D15.**

Your screen should be similar to Figure 2.19

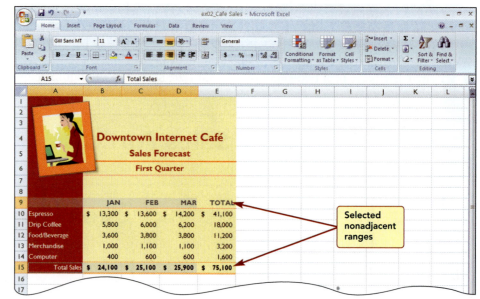

Figure 2.19

Selecting the Chart Type

The next step is to select the chart type from the Charts group, which displays the most commonly used charts as buttons. Each type of chart includes many variations. The  button accesses the less commonly used charts, and the Charts dialog box displays all the available charts in one place.

1 • **Open the Insert tab.**

• **Click**  **in the Charts group.**

Your screen should be similar to Figure 2.20

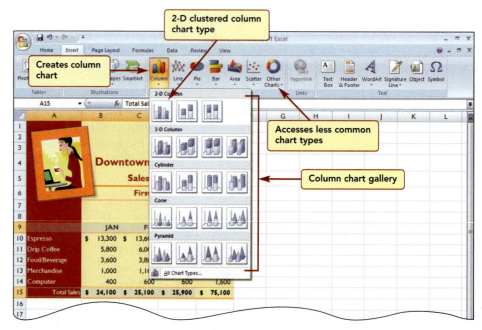

Figure 2.20

The column gallery contains five categories of column charts. You decide to use the two-dimensional clustered column. A Super ScreenTip containing a description of the selected column chart types displays as you point to each chart type.

2 ● Choose **Clustered Column from the 2-D Column category.**

Your screen should be similar to Figure 2.21

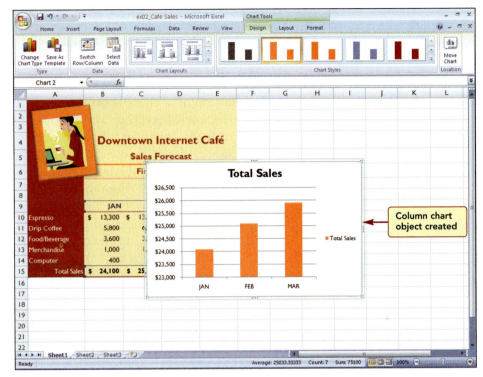

Figure 2.21

The column chart is created using the data from the worksheet and displayed as a chart object in the worksheet.

Concept 6

Chart Object

6 A **chart object** is a graphic object that is created using charting features. A chart object can be inserted into a worksheet or into a special chart sheet. By default, Excel inserts the chart object into the worksheet. Charts that are inserted into a worksheet are embedded objects. An **embedded chart** becomes part of the sheet in which it is inserted and is saved as part of the worksheet when you save the workbook file. Like all graphic objects, an embedded chart object can be sized and moved in a worksheet. A worksheet can contain multiple charts.

A chart that is inserted into a separate chart sheet also is saved with the workbook file. Only one chart can be added to a chart sheet and it cannot be sized and moved.

Excel decides which data series to plot along the X and Y axes based on the type of chart selected and the number of rows and columns defined in the series. The worksheet data range that has the greater number of rows or columns appears along the X axis and the smaller number is charted as the Y data series. When the data series is an equal number of rows and columns, as it is in this case, the default is to plot the rows. The first row defines the X-axis category labels and the second row the plotted data. The content of the first cell in the second row is used as the chart title and legend text.

Moving and Sizing a Chart

Notice that the new chart is on top of the worksheet data. As objects are added to the worksheet, they automatically **stack** in individual layers. The stacking order is apparent when objects overlap. Stacking allows you to create different effects by overlapping objects. Because you can rearrange the stacking order, you do not have to add or create the objects in the order in which you want them to appear.

First you want to move the chart so that it is displayed to the right of the worksheet data. In addition, you want to increase the size of the chart. A chart is moved by dragging the chart border and sized just like a graphic object. The sizing handles of a chart object are the dots that appear in the center and corners of the selected chart's border. If you hold down [Alt] while dragging to move and size a chart object, the chart automatically snaps into position or aligns with the closest worksheet cell when you release the mouse button. Release the mouse button before you release [Alt].

1 ● Point to the chart border and drag the chart object so the upper-left corner is in cell F1.

● Point to the bottom-center sizing handle, hold down [Alt], and drag the chart border line down until it is even with the bottom of row 15.

Your screen should be similar to Figure 2.22

Three Chart Tools tabs

Chart object moved and sized

Figure 2.22

It is now easy to see how the worksheet data you selected is represented in the chart. Each column represents the total sales for that month in row 15. The month labels in row 9 have been used to label the X-axis category labels. The range or scale of values along the Y axis is determined from the data in the worksheet. The upper limit is the maximum value in the worksheet rounded upward to the next highest interval.

Three new Chart Tools tabs appear on the Ribbon to help you modify the chart. The Design tab contains options to change the chart orientation, redefine the source data, and change the chart location or type. The Layout tab commands are used to change the display of chart elements by modifying or adding features such as chart titles, text boxes, callout lines, and pictures. The Format tab is used to add embellishments such as fill colors and special effects to the chart.

Applying Chart Layouts

Next, you want to improve the appearance of the chart. To help you do this quickly, Excel includes many predefined chart layouts and styles (also called quick layouts and quick styles) from which you can select. First, you want to change the chart layout.

Concept 7

Chart Layout

7 A **chart layout** is a predefined set of chart elements that can be quickly applied to a chart. The elements include chart titles, a legend, a data table, or data labels. These elements are displayed in a specific arrangement in the chart. Each chart type includes a variety of layouts. You can then modify or customize these layouts further to meet your needs. However, the custom layouts cannot be saved.

To see the different chart layouts for a column chart, you will open the chart layout gallery.

1 Click ▾ More in the Chart Layouts group of the Chart Tools Design tab.

Your screen should be similar to Figure 2.23

Additional Information
The three chart layouts shown in the Ribbon are the most recently selected chart layouts.

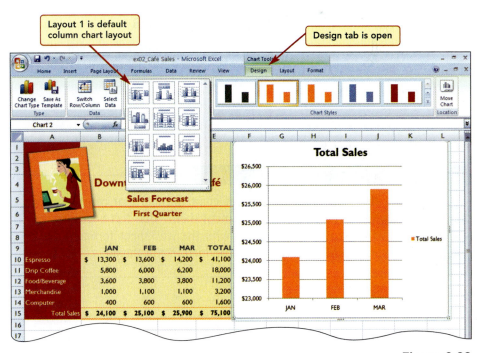

Figure 2.23

The chart layout gallery displays the 11 chart layouts for a column chart. The default chart layout is Layout 1. Since this chart contains only three columns, you decide to try Layout 10 because it shows a chart with wider columns and data labels.

2 ● **Choose Layout 10.**

Your screen should be similar to Figure 2.24

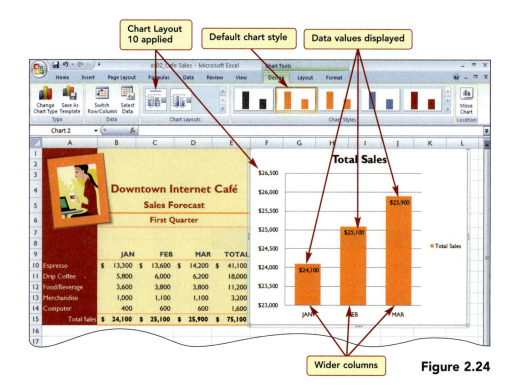

Figure 2.24

The columns are now wider and include the data values.

Applying Chart Styles

Next, you want to change the color of the columns to further enhance the chart. Color is one of the main formats that are included in the predefined chart styles.

Concept 8

Chart Styles

8 A **chart style** is a predefined set of chart formats that can be quickly applied to a chart. The available chart styles are based on the document theme that has been applied. This ensures that the formats you apply to the chart will coordinate with the worksheet formatting. The chart styles use the same colors, fonts, line, and fill effects that are defined in the theme.

The default chart style is selected in the Chart Style group in the Ribbon. You want to see all available choices.

1 ● Click  **More in the Chart Styles group.**

Your screen should be similar to Figure 2.25

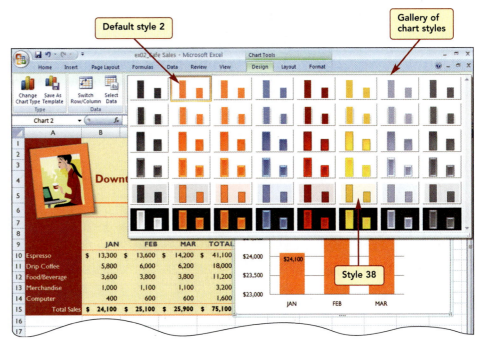

Figure 2.25

The gallery of chart styles consists of 48 sample chart styles with different color columns, background shadings, column shapes, and three-dimensional effects. You want to change the column color and add a background shading to the plot area.

2 ● Choose  **Style 38.**

Your screen should be similar to Figure 2.26

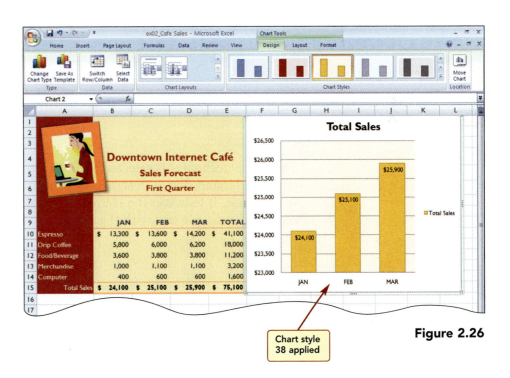

Figure 2.26

The columns are gold and with a shaded background in the plot area.

Adding Chart Labels

Finally, you want to change the appearance of the legend and titles. The Labels group on the Layout tab contains options to modify chart elements. To clarify the data in the chart, you will add titles along the X and Y axes, as well as a more descriptive chart title.

By default, the X- and Y-axis titles do not display. You want to add titles to further explain the data.

1 ● **Open the Chart Tools Layout tab.**

● **In the Labels group, click** [icon] **.**

● **Select Primary Horizontal Axis Title.**

● **Choose Title Below Axis.**

Your screen should be similar to Figure 2.27

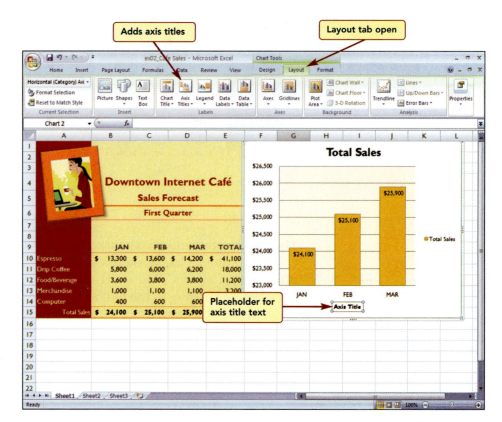

Adds axis titles

Layout tab open

Placeholder for axis title text

Figure 2.27

The title placeholder is selected and displays Axis Title. A **placeholder** is a graphic element that is designed to contain specific types of information. In this case, it tells you the element should display the axis title. You will replace the sample text with the axis title.

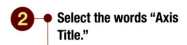

Select the words "Axis Title."

● **Type Months.**

● **Click anywhere on the chart to deselect the placeholder.**

Your screen should be similar to Figure 2.28

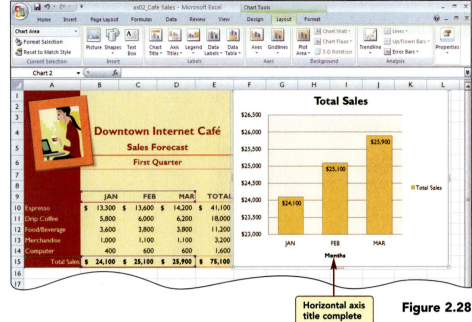

Figure 2.28

Next, you would like to add a title to the Y axis.

Click 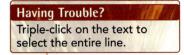 **and select Primary Vertical Axis Title.**

● **Choose Vertical Title.**

● **Select the text and type Total Sales.**

● **Click anywhere on the chart to deselect the text.**

Your screen should be similar to Figure 2.29

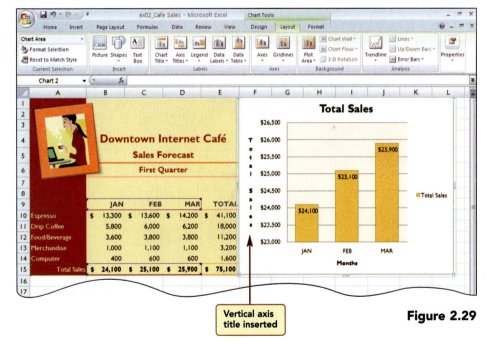

Figure 2.29

You decide the Y-axis title text would look better if it were rotated.

4 ● Click .

● **Select Primary Vertical Axis Title.**

● **Choose Rotated Title.**

Your screen should be similar to Figure 2.30

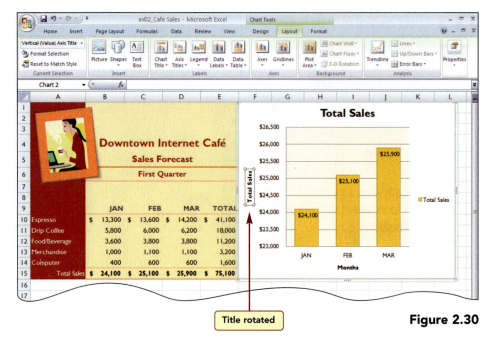

Title rotated

Figure 2.30

The titles clearly describe the information displayed in the chart. Now, because there is only one data range, and the category title fully explains this data, you decide to remove the display of the legend.

Changes placement of legend

5 ● Click  and choose **None.**

Your screen should be similar to Figure 2.31

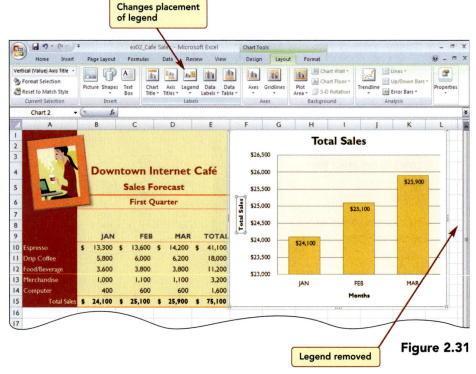

Legend removed

Figure 2.31

The legend is removed and the chart area resized to occupy the extra space.

Finally, you want to add a more descriptive title to the chart. The ![Chart Title] button changes the location of the title on the chart, but the default selection of Above Chart works well. You just need to change the text, which you can do directly on the chart. When you point to different areas in the chart, a chart ScreenTip appears that identifies the chart element that will be affected by your action.

6

• Point to the chart title to see the ScreenTip.

• Click on the chart title to select it.

• Replace the existing text with **Downtown Internet Cafe Sales**.

• Select the text and point to the Mini toolbar.

Additional Information

The Mini toolbar appears automatically when you select text and is dim until you point to it.

• Change the font size to 16 and the font color to Red, Accent3.

• Click anywhere in the chart to clear the selection.

Your screen should be similar to Figure 2.32

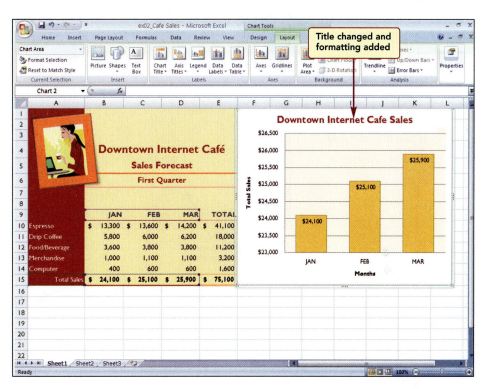

Figure 2.32

Changing the Chart Location

Although this chart compares the total sales for the three months, you decide you are more interested in seeing a comparison for the sales categories. You could delete this chart simply by pressing Delete while the chart is selected. Instead, however, you will move it to a separate worksheet in case you want to refer to it again.

1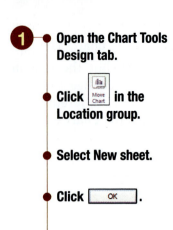

● Open the Chart Tools Design tab.

● Click [Move Chart] in the Location group.

● Select New sheet.

● Click [OK].

● Save the workbook.

Your screen should be similar to Figure 2.33

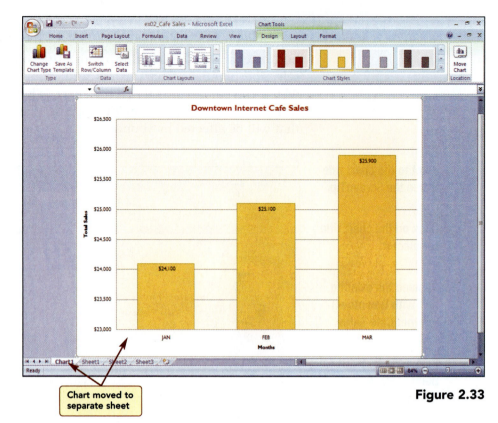

Chart moved to separate sheet

Figure 2.33

The column chart is now an object displayed in a separate chart sheet. Generally, you display a chart in a chart sheet when you want the chart displayed separately from the associated worksheet data. The chart is still automatically linked to the worksheet data from which it was created. The new chart sheet, named Chart1, was inserted to the left of the worksheet, Sheet1. The chart sheet is the active sheet, or the sheet in which you are currently working.

Creating a Multiple Data Series Chart

Now you are ready to continue your analysis of sales trends. You want to create a second chart to display the sales data for each category for the three months. You could create a separate chart for each category and then compare the charts; however, to make the comparisons between the categories easier, you will display all the categories on a single chart.

The data for the three months for the four categories is in cells B10 through D14. The month headings (X-axis data series) are in cells B9 through D9 and the legend text is in the range A10 through A14.

1. Click the Sheet1 tab.

• Select A9 through D14.

• Open the Insert tab.

• Click 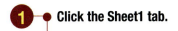 **Column** from the Charts group and choose 3-D Clustered Column.

Your screen should be similar to Figure 2.34

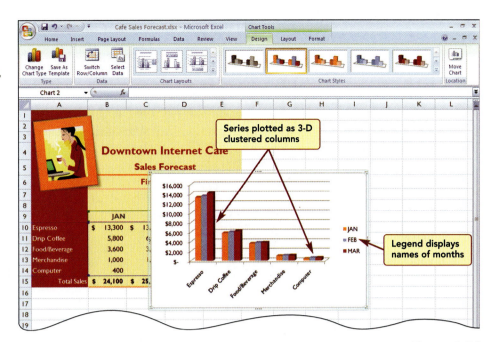

Figure 2.34

A three-dimensional column chart is drawn showing the monthly sales for each category. A different column color identifies each data series, and the legend identifies the categories. When plotting the data for this chart, Excel plotted the three months as the data series because the data range has fewer columns than rows. This time, however, you want to change the data series so that the months are along the X axis.

2. Click  in the Data group of the Chart Tools Design tab.

Your screen should be similar to Figure 2.35

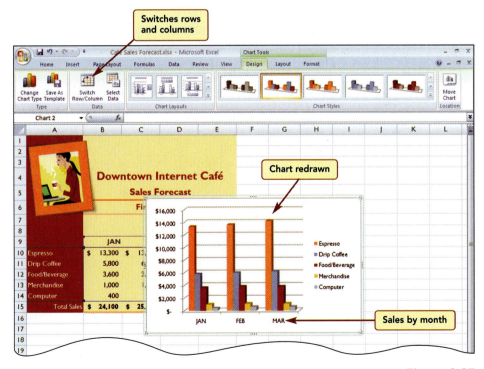

Figure 2.35

The chart is redrawn with the new orientation. The column chart now compares the sales by month rather than by category. The legend displays the names of the sales categories.

Next, you will specify the chart titles and finish the chart.

3 • Change the chart style to Style 18.

• Change the chart layout to Layout 9.

• Replace the placeholder labels with the titles shown below:

Title	Entry
Chart title	Sales Forecast
Horizontal Axis	Months
Vertical Axis	Sales

• Move and size the chart until it covers cells F2 through L15.

Your screen should be similar to Figure 2.36

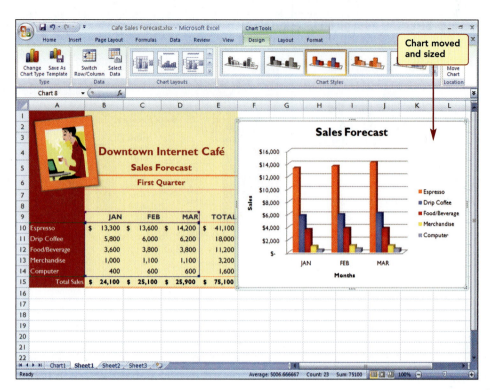

Figure 2.36

The column chart shows that sales in all categories are increasing, with the greatest increase occurring in espresso sales.

Changing the Data Source

As you look at the chart, you see that the Computer and Merchandise sales values are inconsequential to the forecast because they are so small and do not change much. You will remove these data series from the chart.

Your screen should be similar to Figure 2.37

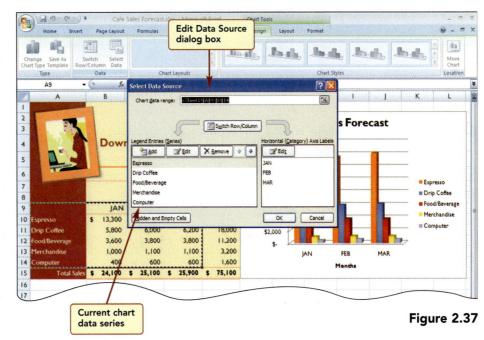

Figure 2.37

In the Select Data Source dialog box, you can change the chart data range, switch the Row and Column orientation, and add, edit, and remove specific data series. You will remove the Computer and Merchandise data series.

2 • Select the Merchandise series name and click ✗ Remove.

• Select the Computer series name and click ✗ Remove.

• Click OK.

Your screen should be similar to Figure 2.38

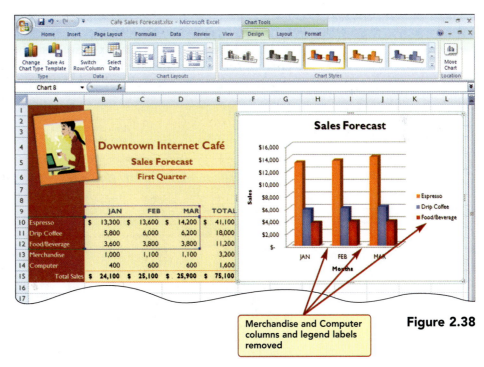

Merchandise and Computer columns and legend labels removed

Figure 2.38

The columns representing the Merchandise and Computer series were removed from the chart along with the legend labels.

Changing the Chart Type

Next, you would like to see how the same data displayed in the column chart would look as a line chart. A line chart displays data as a line and is commonly used to show trends over time. You can change the chart type easily using the  button on the Design tab.

1 ● Click  in the Type group.

Your screen should be similar to Figure 2.39

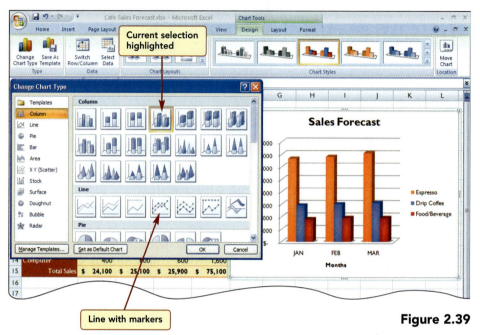

Figure 2.39

The Change Chart Type box displays all the available chart types. The current selection, Clustered Column, is highlighted. You want to change it to a line chart.

2 ● Choose Line with Markers.

● Click [OK].

Your screen should be similar to Figure 2.40

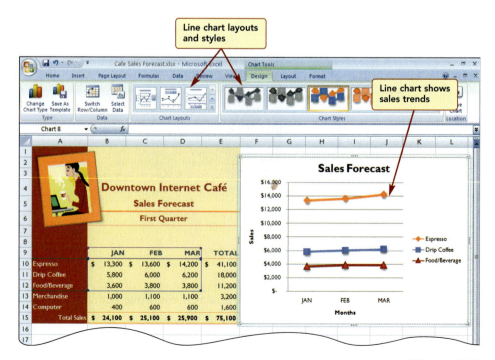

Figure 2.40

The line chart shows the sales trends from month to month. Notice the chart layouts and chart styles in the Ribbon reflect layouts and styles that are available for line charts. You do not find this chart very interesting, so you will change it to a 3-D bar chart next.

3 • **Click** .

• **Choose Bar from the chart type category list.**

• **Choose Clustered Bar in 3-D.**

• **Click** OK

Your screen should be similar to Figure 2.41

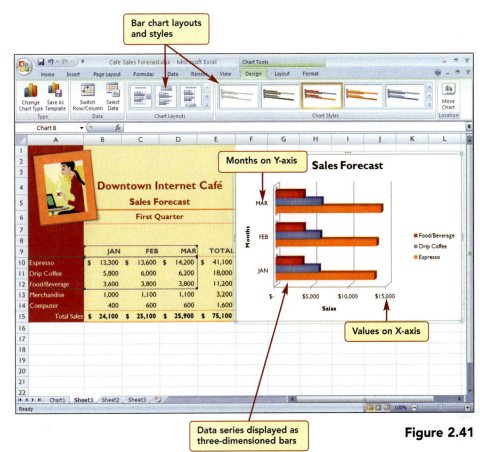

Figure 2.41

The 3-D bar chart reverses the X and Y axes and displays the data series as three-dimensional bars. As you can see, it is very easy to change the chart type and format after the data series are specified. The same data can be displayed in many different ways. Depending upon the emphasis you want the chart to make, a different chart style can be selected.

Although the 3-D bar chart shows the sales trends for the three months for the sales categories, again it does not look very interesting. You decide to look at several other chart types to see whether you can improve the appearance. First you would like to see the data represented as an area chart. An area chart represents data the same as a line chart, but, in addition, it shades the area below each line to emphasize the degree of change.

4 • Click .

• Choose Stacked Area.

• Click [OK].

Your screen should be similar to Figure 2.42

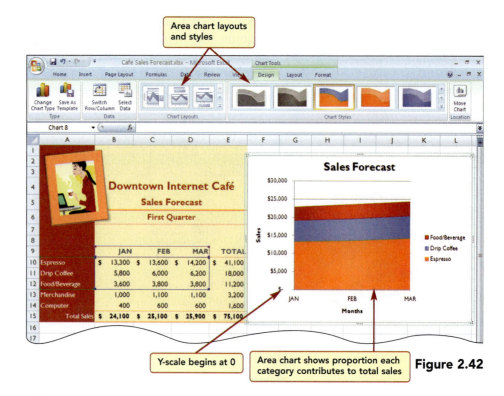

Area chart layouts and styles

Y-scale begins at 0

Area chart shows proportion each category contributes to total sales

Figure 2.42

The Y-axis scale has changed to reflect the new range of data. The new Y-axis range is the sum of the four categories or the same as the total number in the worksheet. Using this chart type, you can see the magnitude of change that each category contributes to the total sales in each month.

Again, you decide that this is not the emphasis you want to show and will continue looking at other types of charts. You want to see how this data will look as a stacked-column chart. You also can double-click a chart type to select it.

5 • Click 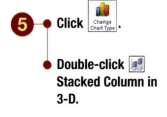.

• Double-click Stacked Column in 3-D.

Your screen should be similar to Figure 2.43

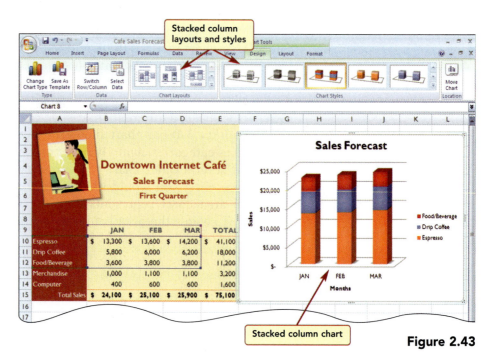

Stacked column layouts and styles

Stacked column chart

Figure 2.43

The chart is redrawn showing the data as a **stacked-column chart.** This type of chart also shows the proportion of each sales category to the total sales.

Although this chart is interesting, you feel that the data is difficult to read and want to see how the data will be represented in several other chart types.

6 • Choose several other chart types to see how the data appears in the chart.

• Change the chart to ▦ Clustered Cylinder in the Column category.

Your screen should be similar to Figure 2.44

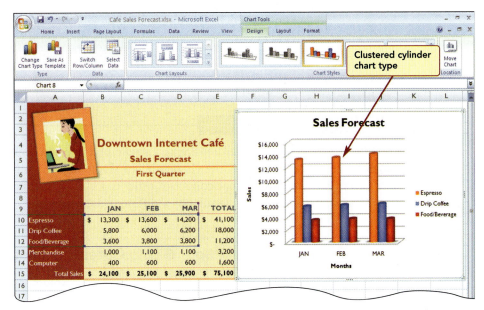

Figure 2.44

You like both the appearance of the clustered cylinders and how the data is represented.

Moving the Legend

While looking at the chart, you decide to move the legend below the X axis.

1 • Open the Chart Tools Layout tab.

• Click 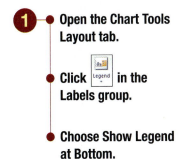 in the Labels group.

• Choose Show Legend at Bottom.

Your screen should be similar to Figure 2.45

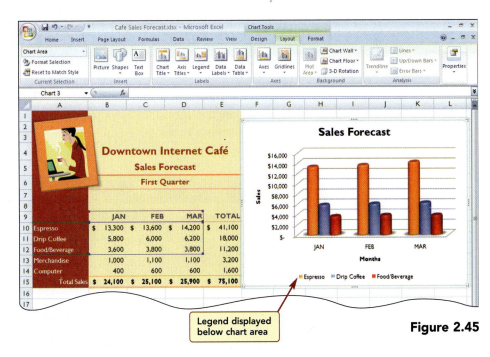

Figure 2.45

The legend appears below the plot area of the chart.

Formatting Chart Elements

Next, you want to further improve the appearance of the chart by applying additional formatting to the chart titles. The chart is an object made up of many different objects or chart elements. Each element of a chart can be enhanced individually to create your own custom style chart. Because a chart consists of many separate objects, it is a group.

Concept 9

Group

9   A **group** is two or more objects that behave as a single object when moved or sized. A chart consists of many separate objects. For example, the chart title is a single object within the chart object. Some of the objects in a chart are also groups that consist of other objects. For example, the legend is a group object consisting of separate items, each identifying a different data series.

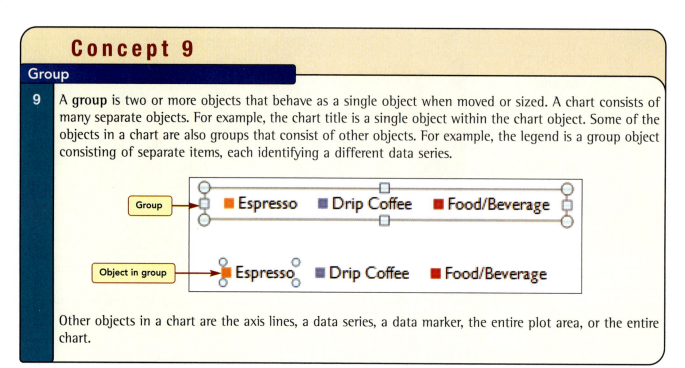

Other objects in a chart are the axis lines, a data series, a data marker, the entire plot area, or the entire chart.

There are several methods you can use to select chart elements. One is to click on the element. To help you select the correct chart element, the element name displays when you point to a chart element. Another is to select the element from the `Chart Area ▾` drop-down list in the Format tab. Finally, you also can use the arrow keys located on the numeric keypad or the directional keypad to cycle from one element to another. The keyboard directional keys used to select chart elements are described in the following table.

Press	To
↓	Select the previous group of elements in a chart.
↑	Select the next group of elements in a chart.
→	Select the next element within a group.
←	Select the previous element within a group.
Esc	Cancel a selection.
Tab	Select the next object or shape in the chart.
Shift + Tab ⇤	Select the previous object or shape in the chart.

There are also several different methods you can use to format chart elements. These methods will be demonstrated as you add formatting to the chart.

The first formatting change you want to make is to increase the font size and add color to the chart title.

1 ● Right-click on the chart title to select it and open the shortcut menu.

● From the Mini toolbar, select Tahoma as the font type.

● Change the font size to 20.

● Select the Orange, Accent 1, Darker 25% theme font color.

Your screen should be similar to Figure 2.46

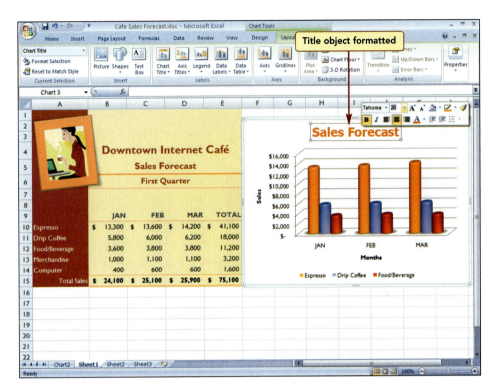

Figure 2.46

Your formatting selections were applied to all the text in the selected object.

Next, you want to add a subtitle below the main title. It will be in a smaller font size and italicized. You also can select individual sections of text in an object and apply formatting to them just as you would format any other text entry.

2 ● **Click at the end of the title to place the insertion point.**

● **Press** ⏎Enter**.**

● **Type** First Quarter**.**

● **Triple-click on the second title line to select it.**

● **Use the Mini toolbar to italicize the selection.**

● **Change the font size to 14.**

● **Apply the Red, Accent 3 theme color to the subtitle.**

● **In a similar manner, apply the Red, Accent 3 theme color to the axis titles.**

Your screen should be similar to Figure 2.47

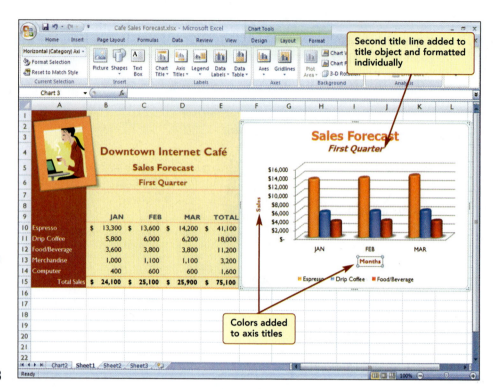

Figure 2.47

Next you decide to add some formatting enhancements to the chart walls and floor.

3 • Open the [Chart Area ▾] **Chart Elements drop-down list in the Current Selection group.**

• **Choose Back Wall.**

• **Click** [Format Selection] **in the Current Selection group.**

Your screen should be similar to Figure 2.48

Figure 2.48

From the Format Wall dialog box, you can change the wall fill colors, outside border, and style, and add shadow, 3-D format, and rotation effects. Fill is the currently selected category and shows that the fill colors use the default fill settings that were automatically set by Excel. You decide to add a gradient fill to the background and a solid line around the chart wall. A **gradient** is a gradual progression of colors and shades that can be from one color to another or from one shade to another of the same color. Excel includes several preset colors that include combinations of gradient fills.

4 ● Choose Gradient Fill.

● Open the Preset colors gallery and choose Wheat.

● Open the Direction gallery and choose the ▦ Linear Diagonal option (top row, option 3).

● Select Border Color from the category list and choose Solid line.

● Click [Close].

Your screen should be similar to Figure 2.49

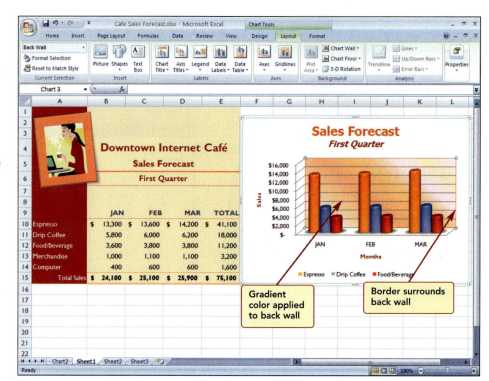

Figure 2.49

Next you will format the side wall and floor using a solid fill color with a slight transparency.

⑤ ● Press ← to select the chart side wall.

● **Click**  .

● **Choose Solid Fill.**

● **Increase the Transparency to 40%.**

● **Click on the chart floor to select it.**

● **Change the chart floor to the same color and transparency as the side wall.**

● **Click** Close .

Your screen should be similar to Figure 2.50

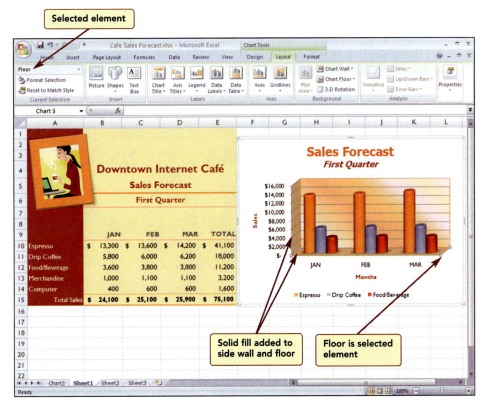

Figure 2.50

The last formatting change you will make is to modify the border line around the entire chart object.

6 ● Click on the chart area (the white background) to select the entire chart.

● Open the Format tab.

● Click [Shape Outline ▾] in the Shape Styles group.

● Select Weight and choose 2¼ points.

● Click [Shape Outline ▾].

● Choose the Red, Accent 3 theme color.

● Click outside the chart to deselect it.

Your screen should be similar to Figure 2.51

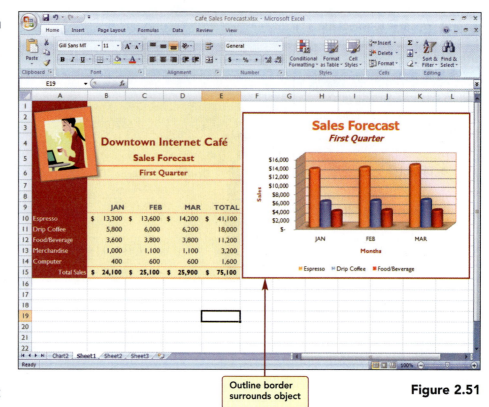

Outline border surrounds object

Figure 2.51

Additional Information

You also can use [Shape Fill ▾] or [Shape Effects ▾] to add fill color or special effects to a shape.

You have modified and enhanced many of the chart elements individually, creating a unique, professional-looking chart.

Adding and Formatting Data Labels

Finally, to make sure that Evan sees your projected increase in espresso and coffee sales, you will include data labels containing the actual numbers plotted on the column chart.

Concept 10

Data Labels

10 Data labels provide additional information about a **data marker**. They can consist of the value of the marker, the name of the data series or category, a percent value, or a bubble size. The different types of data labels that are available depend on the type of chart and the data that is plotted.

Value data labels are helpful when the values are large and you want to know the exact value for one data series. Data labels that display a name are helpful when the size of the chart is large and when the data point does not clearly identify the value. The percent data label is used when you want to display the percent of each series on charts that show parts of the whole. Bubble size is used on bubble charts to help the reader quickly see how the different bubbles vary in size.

You want to display the Espresso and Drip Coffee values as data labels for the months of February and March.

1
- Click on any Espresso data column to select the series.

- Right-click the selection and choose Add Data Labels.

- Add data labels for the Drip Coffee sales.

Another Method

You also could use 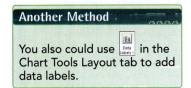 in the Chart Tools Layout tab to add data labels.

Your screen should be similar to Figure 2.52

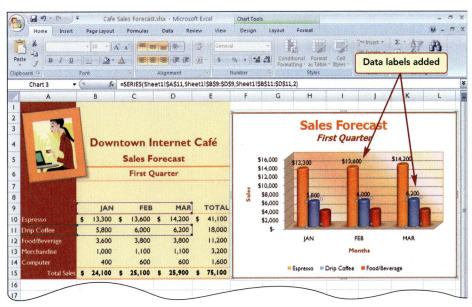

Figure 2.52

Data labels containing the actual values for Espresso and Drip Coffee sales are displayed above the appropriate sales columns on the chart. They use the same formatting as the values in the worksheet.

Data labels, like other chart elements, can be further enhanced by adding fill colors, shadows, 3-D effects, lines, and text orientation to the data label. You will use this feature to add the currency symbol to the Drip Coffee data label so the format matches the Espresso labels.

2
- Right-click on the Drip Coffee data labels and choose Format Data Labels from the shortcut menu.

- Select the Number category and choose Currency.

- Reduce the decimal places to 0.

- Click [Close].

Your screen should be similar to Figure 2.53

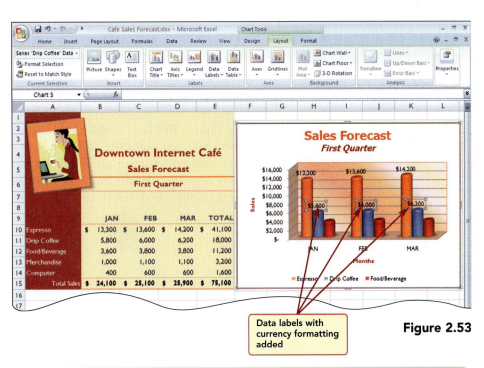

Data labels with currency formatting added

Figure 2.53

Next, you will reposition all the data labels so that they appear to the right of each column. Each data label needs to be selected and moved individually.

3 • Click on the January Drip Coffee data label to select it and drag to position it as in Figure 2.54.

• In the same manner, select the February and March Drip Coffee data labels and drag to position them as in Figure 2.54.

Having Trouble?
To select an individual data label, first click on a data label to select the entire series, and then click on the individual label.

• Select each Espresso data label and drag to position it as in Figure 2.54.

Your screen should be similar to Figure 2.54

Additional Information
You can delete individual data labels or the entire series by selecting the data label or series and pressing Delete or choosing Delete from the shortcut menu.

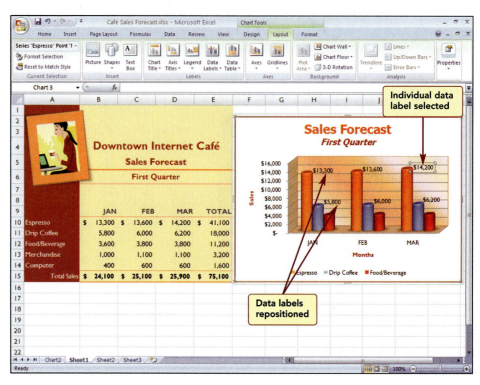

Individual data label selected

Data labels repositioned

Figure 2.54

The data labels are positioned to the top-right of each column.

Changing Worksheet Data

So far, the charts you have created reflect your original sales estimates for the quarter. You are planning to heavily promote the new Internet aspect of the Café and anticipate that Espresso, Coffee, and Food/Beverage sales in February and March will increase dramatically and then level off in the following months. You want to change the worksheet to reflect these increases.

1 ● Increase the February and March Espresso sales by 12% and 15% respectively.

Having Trouble?
Change the entry to a formula by inserting an = sign at the beginning of the entry and then multiply by 1+ increase; for example, a 12 percent increase in the February Espresso sales is = 13600*1.12.

● Increase the February and March Drip Coffee sales by 8% and 10%.

● Increase the February and March Food/Beverage sales by 5% and 7%.

Your screen should be similar to Figure 2.55

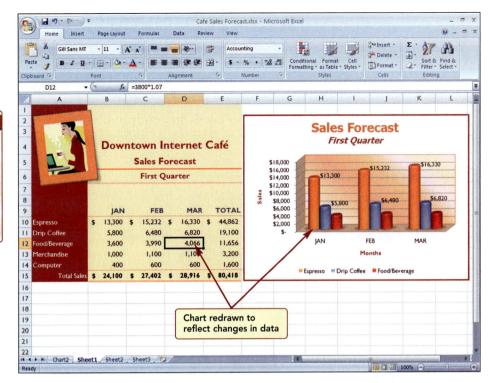

Figure 2.55

The worksheet has been recalculated, and the chart columns that reference those worksheet cells have been redrawn to reflect the change in the sales data. Because the chart is linked to the source data, changes to the source data are automatically reflected in the chart. Likewise, the values in the data labels reflect the revised data.

2 ● Move the chart to its own chart sheet.

● Make Sheet1 active again.

● Save the workbook.

Creating and Formatting a Pie Chart

The last chart you will create will use the Total worksheet data in column E. You want to see what proportion each type of sales is of total sales for the quarter. The best chart for this purpose is a pie chart.

A pie chart compares parts to the whole in a similar manner to a stacked-column chart. However, pie charts have no axes. Instead, the worksheet data that is charted is displayed as slices in a circle or pie. Each slice is displayed as a percentage of the total.

Selecting the Pie Chart Data

The use of X (category) and data series settings in a pie chart is different from their use in a column or line chart. The X series labels the slices of the pie rather than the X axis. The data series is used to create the slices in the pie. Only one data series can be specified in a pie chart.

The row labels in column A will label the slices, and the total values in column E will be used as the data series.

Additional Information

You also can create a chart using the default chart type (column) in a new chart sheet by selecting the data range and pressing F11.

● **1** ● Select A10:A14 and E10:E14.

Having Trouble?

Hold down Ctrl while selecting nonadjacent ranges.

● Open the Insert tab.

● Click  and choose

 Pie in 3-D.

● Move and size the pie chart to be displayed over cells F1 through L15.

Additional Information

Hold down Alt while moving to snap the chart to the cells.

Your screen should be similar to Figure 2.56

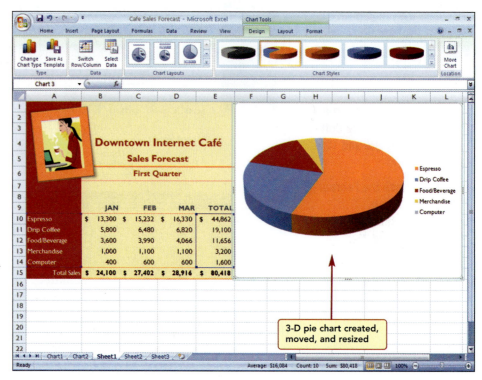

Figure 2.56

A three-dimensional pie chart is drawn in the worksheet. Each value in the data series is displayed as a slice of the pie chart. The size of the slice represents the proportion of total sales that each sales category represents.

Adding Titles and Data Labels

To clarify the meaning of the chart, you need to add a chart title. In addition, you want to remove the legend and display data labels to label the slices of the pie instead. You will take a look at the predefined chart layouts to see if there is a layout that will accomplish all these things in one step.

1 ● **Click** ☑ **More in the Charts Layout group of the Design tab.**

● **Choose Layout 1.**

Your screen should be similar to Figure 2.57

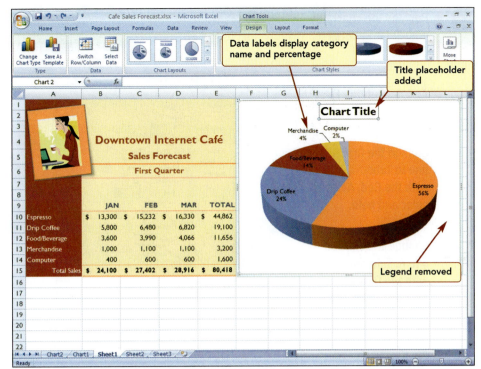

Figure 2.57

The legend has been removed and replaced with data labels that display the category name and the percentage each category is of total sales. The data labels display the category name on a separate line from the value and, if needed, include a leader line to identify the associated wedge. Also, a chart title placeholder has been added to the pie chart.

Next, you will add a title and then you will improve the appearance of the data labels by adding a gradient fill to the labels.

2 ● Replace the chart title with **Total Sales by Category**.

● Add the subtitle **First Quarter**.

● Change the first title line to Tahoma, 18 pt with the Red, Accent 3 color and bold.

● Change the subtitle line to Tahoma, 14 pt, with the Orange, Accent 1 color, and italic.

● Click on one of the data labels to select the data label series.

● Choose Format Data Label Series from the context menu.

● Choose the Fill category and choose Gradient Fill.

● Move the dialog box to see the chart.

Your screen should be similar to Figure 2.58

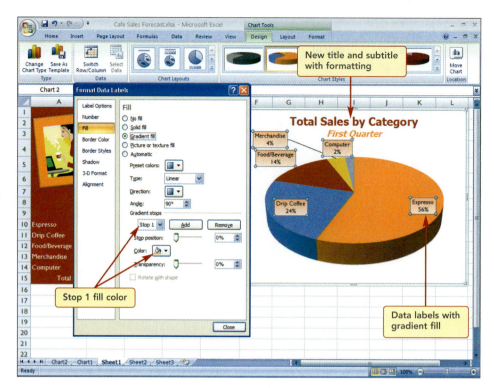

Figure 2.58

The default gradient fill has been added to each data label. You want to change the fill to a gradient fill composed of two colors. Each color is specified as a separate gradient stop. The Stop 1 fill color of orange is already correctly specified. You will change the Stop 2 color to gold.

3 • Open the Gradient Stops drop-down menu and choose Stop 2.

• Open the Color gallery and choose Gold, Accent 4, Lighter 40%.

• Click [Close].

Your screen should be similar to Figure 2.59

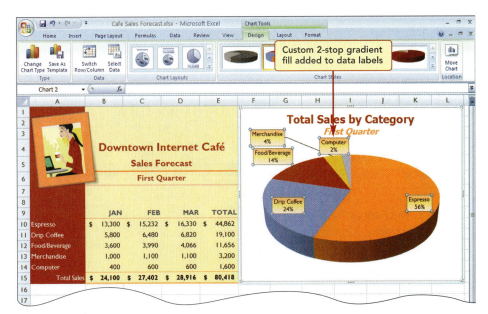

Figure 2.59

The data labels now include a gradient fill background that coordinates well with the chart colors.

The pie chart clearly shows the percent each category is of the total sales. The industry standard for a successful espresso café generates 60 percent of sales from espresso-based drinks. With your suggested advertising campaign, your sales forecast is very close to this standard.

Exploding and Rotating the Pie

Next, you want to separate slightly or **explode** the slices of the pie to emphasize the data in the categories.

1 • Right-click the pie chart and choose Change Series Chart Type.

• Choose 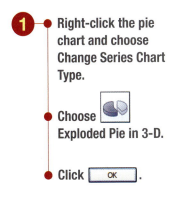 Exploded Pie in 3-D.

• Click [OK].

Your screen should be similar to Figure 2.60

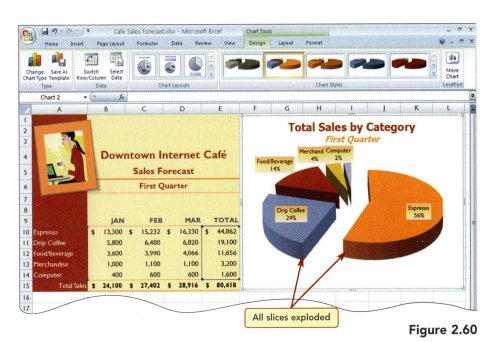

Figure 2.60

All slices are exploded from the center of the pie chart.

You decide you only want to explode the espresso slice to give emphasis to the increase in sales in that category.

2 ● Click ↺▾ **Undo** to cancel your last action.

● **Select the Espresso slice.**

● **Choose Format Data Point from the context menu.**

Having Trouble?
If Format Data Point is not displayed, the slice is not selected. Double-click on the slice to select it.

Your screen should be similar to Figure 2.61

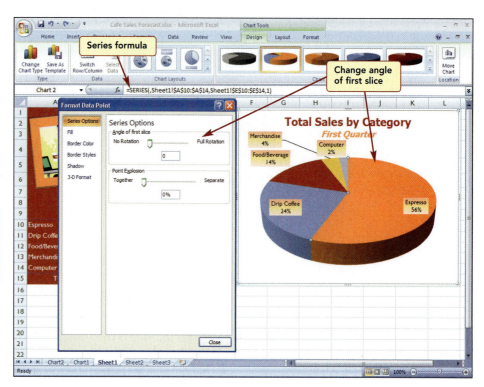

Figure 2.61

Notice that the formula bar displays a **series formula.** A series formula links the chart object to the source worksheet, in this case, Sheet1. The formula contains four arguments: a reference to the cell that includes the data series name (used in the legend), references to the cells that contain the categories (X-axis numbers), references to the numbers plotted, and an integer that specifies the number of data series plotted.

The Format Data Point dialog box has options to rotate the pie and control the amount of explosion of the slices. You want to rotate the pie approximately 330 degrees so that the Espresso slice is more to the right side of the pie. When a pie chart is created, the first data point is placed to the right of the middle at the top of the chart. The rest of the data points are placed in order to the right until the circle is complete. To change the order in which the slices are displayed, you rotate the pie chart. Then you will explode the Espresso slice.

3 • Increase the Angle of first slice to 330 degrees.

• Increase the Point Explosion to 10%.

• Click [Close].

Another Method
You also can drag a slice away from the pie to explode it.

Your screen should be similar to Figure 2.62

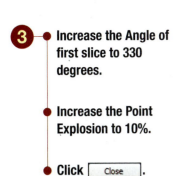
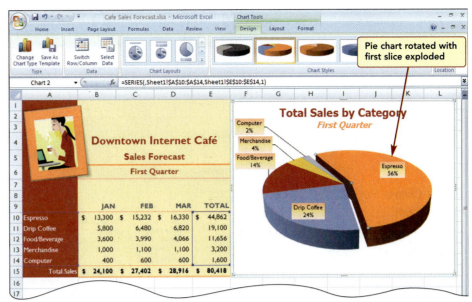

Figure 2.62

Even though the program tries to determine the best position for the data labels, many of the labels are close together and look crowded. In pie charts, you can fix this by changing the position of the data labels.

4 • Select the data label series and choose **Format Data Labels** from the context menu.

• Choose Outside End from the Label Position area.

• Click [Close].

• Drag the Computer, Espresso, and Drip Coffee labels to the positions shown in Figure 2.63.

Your screen should be similar to Figure 2.63

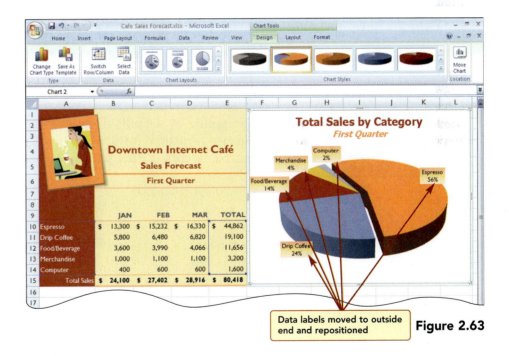

Figure 2.63

Now the labels are more evenly positioned on the pie chart.

Applying Color and Texture

The last change you would like to make is to change the color of the Drip Coffee slice and add a fill to the Espresso slice to make it stand out even further. First, you will enhance the Espresso slice by adding a texture.

1
- Select and then right-click on the Espresso slice.

- Choose Format Data Point.

- Choose Picture or texture fill from the Fill category.

- Open the Texture gallery.

Your screen should be similar to Figure 2.64

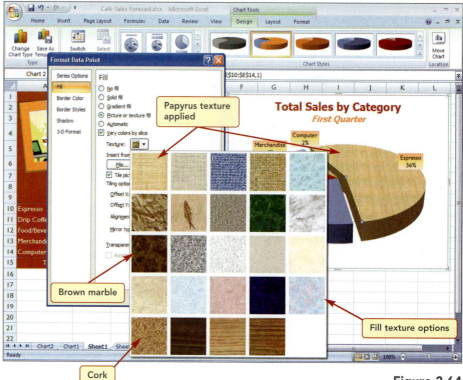

Figure 2.64

A variety of pictures and textures is displayed in the gallery. The Papyrus texture is applied by default. If none of the provided choices is suitable, you could use a picture from a file or ClipArt as the fill. You think the brown marble or cork texture may look good.

2 ● Choose several texture designs to see how they will look.

Having Trouble?
You will need to reopen the Texture gallery again after each selection.

● Choose the Brown Marble texture.

● Choose the Cork texture.

● Select the Drip Coffee slice.

● Choose Gradient fill from the Fill category.

● Click [Close].

Your screen should be similar to Figure 2.65

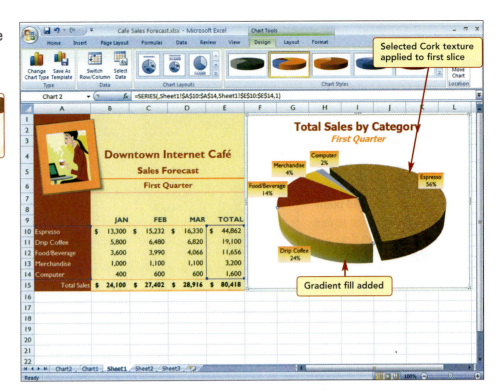

Figure 2.65

The last-used gradient fill colors are automatically applied. You decide, however, that the gradient fill does not look good and instead will try using a Shape Style. Shape Styles consist of predefined combinations of fills, outlines, and effects much like chart styles. Shape styles affect only the selected element.

3 • **If necessary, select the Drip Coffee slice.**

• **Open the Format tab.**

• **Open the Shape Styles gallery in the Shape Styles group and point to several styles to see their effect on the slice.**

• **Choose the Subtle Effect – Accent 1 Shape Style (4th row, 2nd column).**

Your screen should be similar to Figure 2.66

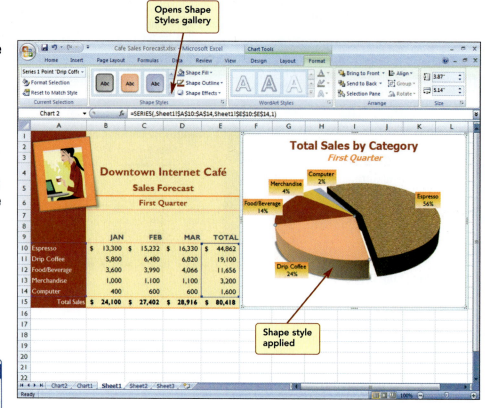

Figure 2.66

Finally, you will add a colored outline border around the entire chart, like the one you used in the column chart. Then you will move the column chart from the chart sheet back into the worksheet.

4 Select the chart area.

• Click ✎ Shape Outline ▾ and increase the Weight to 2¼ points.

• Click ✎ Shape Outline ▾ and change the line color to the Red, Accent 3 color.

• Make the Chart2 sheet active.

• Click 📊 Move Chart in the Location group of the Design tab.

• Choose Object in and select Sheet1 from the drop-down menu.

• Click ⬛ OK .

• Move and size the column chart to fit A17 through F33.

• Move and size the pie chart to fit A35 through F50.

• Deselect the chart.

Your screen should be similar to Figure 2.67

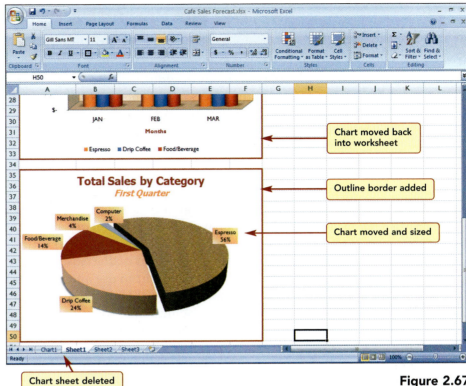

Chart moved back into worksheet

Outline border added

Chart moved and sized

Chart sheet deleted

Figure 2.67

The column chart was moved back into the sheet as an embedded object and the chart sheet it occupied was deleted.

Setting File Properties

You are finished working on the worksheet for now and want to save the changes you have made to the file. Along with the content of the file, each file can include additional **file properties** or settings that are associated with the file. Some of these properties are automatically generated. These include statistics such as the date the file was created and last modified. Others, such as the author of the file, are properties that you can add to the file.

Documenting a Workbook

The information you can associate with the file includes a title, subject, author, keywords, and comments about the workbook file. Additionally, you can specify that a picture of the first page of the file be saved for previewing in the Open dialog box. This information helps you locate the workbook file you want to use and helps indicate the objectives and use of the workbook. You will look at the standard and advanced file properties and add documentation to identify you as the author and to specify a title and keywords for the document. **Keywords** are descriptive words that you associate with the file that can be used to search for all files that have that keyword. This information is entered in the Document Information Panel that will appear above the column letters.

1 ● Click 🔘 Office Button, select Prepare, and choose Properties.

● Enter the following information in the appropriate boxes of the Document Information Panel:

Author	Your name
Title	Downtown Internet Cafe
Subject	First quarter sales forecast
Keywords	sales projections

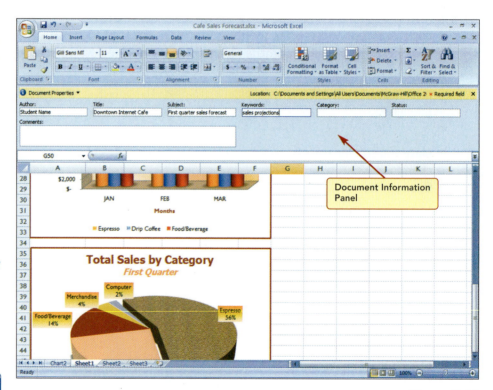

Figure 2.68

Your screen should be similar to Figure 2.68

The Document Information Panel is used to enter and display the standard properties associated with the file.

Next, you will look at the other information that is stored with the file properties.

2 • Click `Document Properties ▼` and choose Advanced Properties from the menu.

• Select each tab in the Properties dialog box and look at the recorded information.

• Open the Summary tab.

• Select the Save preview picture option, if necessary.

Additional Information
Saving a preview picture with your file increases the file size.

Your screen should be similar to Figure 2.69

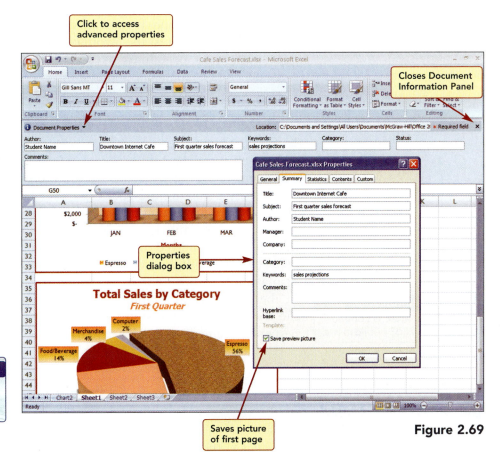

Figure 2.69

The General tab displays information about the type, location, and size of the document as well as about when the document was created and modified. The Statistics tab identifies who last saved the document, the revision number, and the total editing time in minutes. The Summary tab displays much of the same information that appears in the Document Information Panel, plus a few additional properties such as manager and company name that you can define.

You have completed adding the properties to the document. Not until the file is saved are the new properties you added saved with the file.

3 • Click `OK` to close the Properties dialog box.

• Click `×` to close the Document Information Panel.

• Move to the top of the worksheet and save the workbook.

Preparing the Worksheet and Charts for Printing

Before printing a large worksheet or a worksheet that contains charts, you can quickly fine-tune it in Page Layout view. Using this view, you can change the layout and format of data just as in Normal view, but, in addition, you can adjust the layout of the data on the page by changing the page orientation, page margins, scaling, and alignment. Additionally, you can easily add headers and footers.

Using Page Layout View

To get the worksheet ready for printing, you will first make several adjustments to the layout in Page Layout view. While in this view, you also will zoom in on the worksheet to see more information in the workbook window by adjusting the zoom percentage. The default zoom setting is 100 percent. This setting displays data onscreen the same size that it will appear on the printed page. You can reduce or enlarge the amount of information displayed onscreen by changing the magnification from between 10 and 400 percent. You want to decrease the zoom percent to display more information in the window.

There are several methods to zoom the window. Clicking ⊕ or ⊖ on the zoom slider in the status bar increases or decreases the zoom by 10 percent increments. You also can drag the slider to change the percentage.

Additional Information

The Zoom feature is common in all Office 2007 applications.

1 ● Click 🔲 **Page Layout view (in the status bar).**

Another Method

You also can use 📄 Page Layout in the View tab.

● Click ⊖ **Zoom Out in the status bar six times to reduce the zoom to 40%.**

Your screen should be similar to Figure 2.70

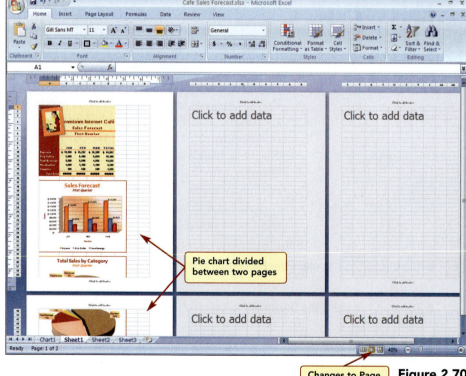

Pie chart divided between two pages

Changes to Page Layout view

Figure 2.70

This view shows how the data and charts lay out on each page of the worksheet and because you reduced the zoom, you can quickly see that the pie chart is divided between two pages. You also notice that the worksheet and charts are not centered on the page. In Page Layout view, horizontal and vertical rulers are displayed so you can make exact measurements of cells, ranges, and objects in the worksheet. You will make several changes to the layout of the page to correct these problems.

First you will reduce the scale of the worksheet until all the data fits on one page. Because the width is fine, you will only scale the height.

2 ● **Open the Page Layout tab.**

● **Open the** Height: Automatic ▾ **drop-down menu and choose 1 page.**

Your screen should be similar to Figure 2.71

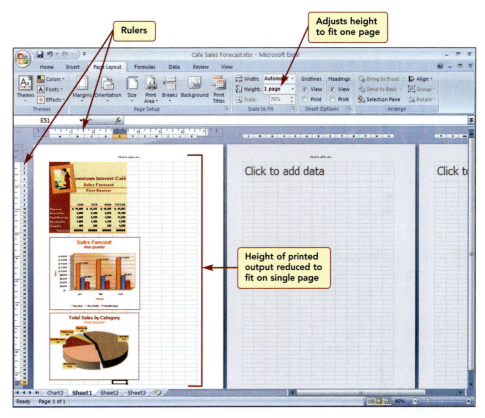

Figure 2.71

The height of the printed worksheet has been reduced to fit on a single page.

Adding Predefined Headers and Footers

Next, you want to include your name and the date in a header.

Concept 11

Headers and Footers

11 Headers and footers provide information that typically appears at the top and bottom of each page and commonly include information such as the date and page number. A **header** is a line or several lines of text that appear at the top of a page just above the top margin line. The header usually contains the file name or worksheet title. A **footer** is a line or several lines of text that appear at the bottom of a page just below the bottom margin line. The footer usually contains the page number and perhaps the date. Headers and footers also can contain graphics such as a company logo. Each worksheet in a workbook can have a different header and footer.

You can select from predefined header and footer text or enter your own custom text. The information contained in the predefined header and footer text is obtained from the file properties associated with the workbook and from the program and system settings.

Header and footer text can be formatted like any other text. In addition, you can control the placement of the header and footer text by specifying where it should appear: left-aligned, centered, or right-aligned in the header or footer space.

You will add a predefined header to the worksheet that displays your name, the date, and page number.

1
- Increase the zoom to 90% and scroll to the top of the worksheet.

- Click in the Header area to activate the header.

- Click [Header] in the Header and Footer group of the Header & Footer Tools Design tab.

Your screen should be similar to Figure 2.72

> Displays predefined headers

> Header & Footer Tools Design tab

> Prepared by header

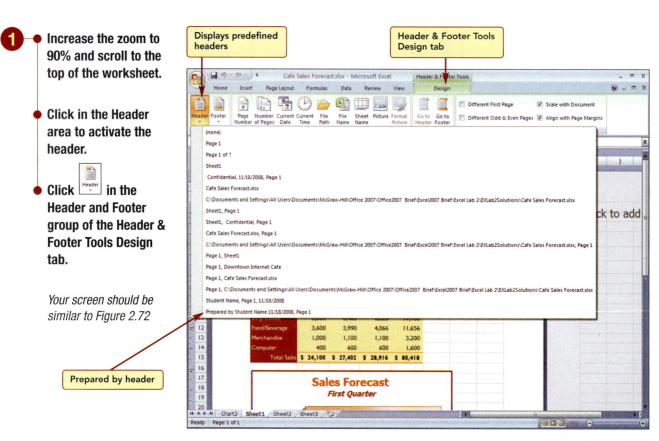

Figure 2.72

Activating the worksheet header displays the Header & Footer Tools Design tab. It contains commands to add elements to, format, or navigate between a header or footer. The 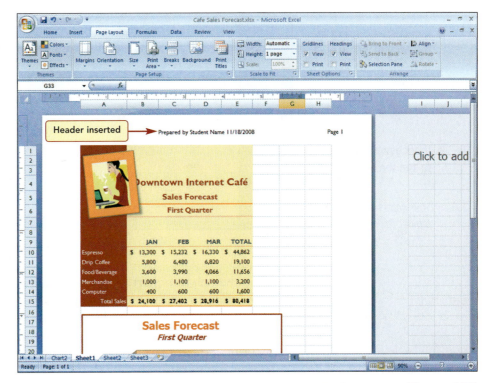 drop-down list includes many predefined headers that can be quickly inserted into the header. Notice that several of the predefined headers include information that was entered in the document properties.

2 ● **Choose the Prepared by [your name] [date], Page 1 option.**

Your screen should be similar to Figure 2.73

Figure 2.73

The selected header is displayed in the header area of the dialog box. It could then be edited or formatted to meet your needs.

Previewing the Entire Workbook

Finally, you are ready to print the workbook. Because it includes a chart sheet and a worksheet, you will preview the entire workbook. To preview all sheets in a workbook at once, you first need to change the print setting to print the entire workbook.

1 • Click 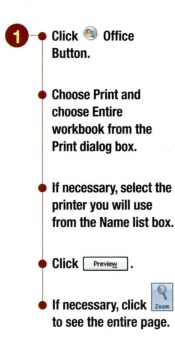 Office Button.

• Choose Print and choose Entire workbook from the Print dialog box.

• If necessary, select the printer you will use from the Name list box.

• Click [Preview].

• If necessary, click [Zoom] to see the entire page.

Your screen should be similar to Figure 2.74

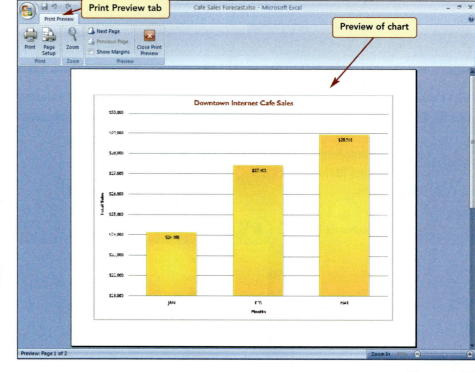

Figure 2.74

Because the column chart is on a separate chart sheet, it is displayed on a page by itself. In addition, if you are not using a color printer, the preview displays the chart colors in shades of gray as they will appear when printed on a black-and-white printer. The Print Preview tab commands are used to access many print and page layout changes while you are previewing a document.

You decide to add a footer to the chart sheet. Each sheet can have its own header and footer definitions.

2 • Click [Page Setup].

• Open the Header/Footer tab.

Your screen should be similar to Figure 2.75

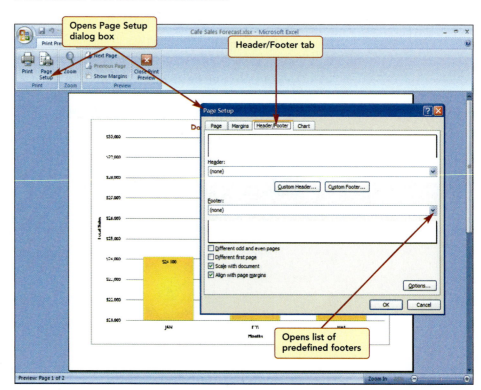

Figure 2.75

Many of the same elements that were available when adding a header in Page Layout view are available in the Page Setup dialog box. You will add a predefined footer to the chart sheet.

3 • Click ☑ in the Footer section to open the list of predefined footers.

• Scroll the list and choose the footer that displays your name, Page 1, and date.

• Click [OK] to close the Page Setup dialog box.

Your screen should be similar to Figure 2.76

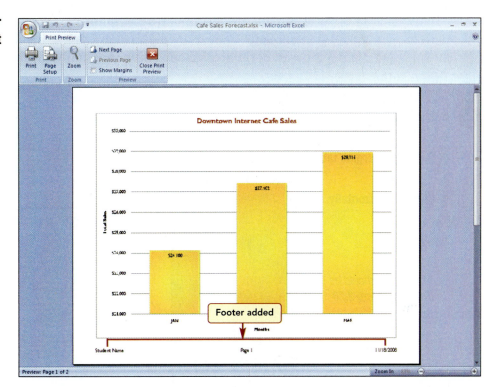

Figure 2.76

4 • Click [Next Page] in the Preview group to see the worksheet and charts in Sheet1.

Your screen should be similar to Figure 2.77

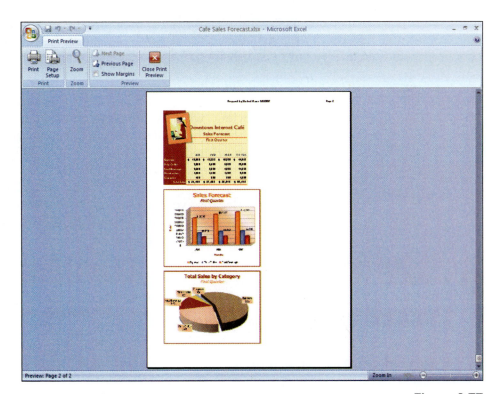

Figure 2.77

The preview shows the header you added to the worksheet and because the worksheet was scaled vertically, all the data fits on a single page.

Aligning a Sheet on a Page

You also would like to center the worksheet horizontally on the page. The default worksheet margin settings include 1-inch top and bottom margins and 0.75-inch right and left margins. The **margins** are the blank space outside the printing area around the edges of the paper. The worksheet contents appear in the printable area inside the margins. You want to center the worksheet data horizontally within the existing margins.

1 ● Click  .

● Open the Margins tab.

● Choose Horizontally.

● Click [OK] .

Your screen should be similar to Figure 2.78

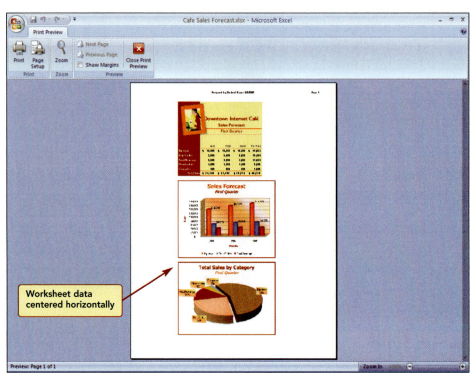

Worksheet data centered horizontally

Figure 2.78

The preview window displays the worksheet centered horizontally between the right and left margins. It now appears the way you want it to look when printed.

Now that the workbook is set up the way you want it for printing, you will print a copy of the worksheet and chart from the print preview window. Because you previewed the workbook from the Print dialog box, the worksheets will print immediately using the specified print settings. Then you will exit the application and save the file at the same time.

2 ● Click  .

● Change to Normal view and move to cell A9 of Sheet1.

● Exit Excel, saving the workbook again.

The page layout settings you specified have been saved with the workbook file.

Focus on Careers

EXPLORE YOUR CAREER OPTIONS

Financial Advisor

With the stock market fluctuations in the last few years, investors are demanding more from their financial advisors than ever before. An advisor needs to promote the company's potential and growth in order to get investors to buy stock. One way to do this is to create a worksheet of vital information and to chart that information so the investor can see why the stock is a good investment. The position of Financial Advisor usually requires a college degree and commands salaries from $24,000 to $50,000, depending on experience.

Concept Summary

LAB 2
Charting Worksheet Data

Graphics (EX2.5)

A graphic is a nontext element or object, such as a drawing or picture, that can be added to a document.

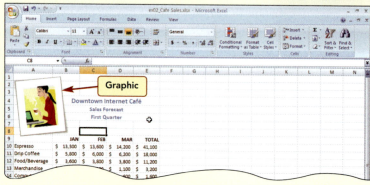

Theme (EX2.10)

A theme is a predefined set of formatting choices that can be applied to an entire document in one simple step.

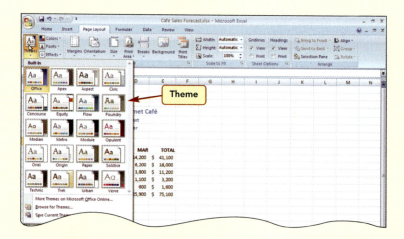

Cell Style (EX2.14)

A cell style is a predefined theme-based combination of formats that have been named and that can be quickly applied to a selection.

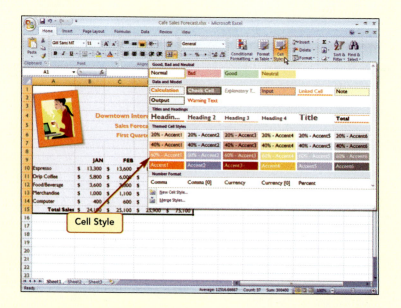

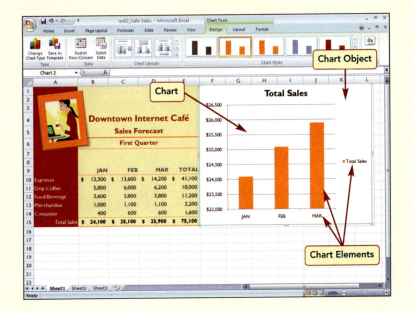

Chart (EX2.19)

A chart is a visual representation of data that is used to convey information in an easy-to-understand and attractive manner. Different types of charts are used to represent data in different ways.

Chart Elements (EX2.20)

A chart consists of a number of elements that are used to graphically display the worksheet data.

Chart Object (EX2.23)

A chart object is a graphic object that is created using charting features. A chart object can be inserted into a worksheet or into a special chart sheet.

Chart Layout (EX2.25)

A chart layout is a predefined set of chart elements that can be quickly applied to a chart.

Chart Style (EX2.26)

A chart style is a predefined set of chart formats that can be quickly applied to a chart.

Concept Summary

Group (EX2.40)

A group is two or more objects that behave as a single object when moved or sized. A chart consists of many separate objects.

Data Labels (EX2.46)

Data labels provide additional information about a data marker. They can consist of the value of the marker, the name of the data series or category, a percent value, or a bubble size.

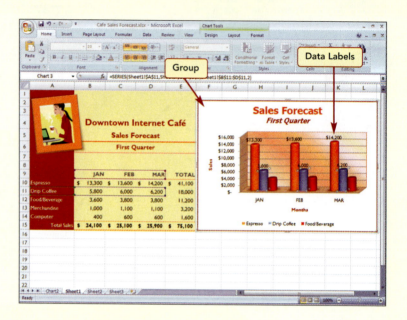

Headers and Footer (EX2.64)

Headers and footers provide information that typically appears at the top and bottom of each page and commonly includes the date and page number.

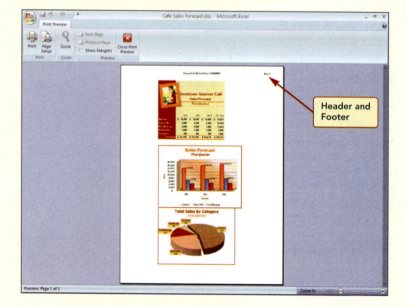

Lab Review

key terms

area chart   EX2.19

bar chart   EX2.19

bubble chart   EX2.19

category axis   EX2.20

category-axis title   EX2.20

cell style   EX2.13

chart   EX2.19, EX2.20

chart gridlines   EX2.20

chart layout   EX2.25

chart object   EX2.23

chart style   EX2.26

chart title   EX2.20

clip art   EX2.6

column chart   EX2.19

data label   EX2.20, EX2.46

data marker   EX2.46

data series   EX2.20

doughnut chart   EX2.19

drawing object   EX2.5

embedded chart   EX2.23

embedded object   EX2.5

explode   EX2.53

file property   EX2.60

footer   EX2.64

gradient   EX2.43

graphic   EX2.5

group   EX2.40

header   EX2.64

keyword   EX2.60

legend   EX2.20

line chart   EX2.19

margin   EX2.68

object   EX2.5

picture   EX2.5

pie chart   EX2.19

placeholder   EX2.28

plot area   EX2.20

radar chart   EX2.19

selection rectangle   EX2.7

series formula   EX2.54

sizing handle   EX2.7

source program   EX2.5

stack   EX2.24

stacked-column chart   EX2.38

stock chart   EX2.19

surface chart   EX2.19

theme   EX2.10

value axis   EX2.20

value-axis title   EX2.20

X axis   EX2.20

XY (scatter) chart   EX2.19

Y axis   EX2.20

Z axis   EX2.20

MCAS skills

The Microsoft Certified Applications Specialist (MCAS) certification program is designed to measure your proficiency in performing basic tasks using the Office 2007 applications. Getting certified demonstrates that you have the skills and provides a valuable industry credential for employment. See Reference 2 MCAS Certification Guide for a complete list of the skills that were covered in Lab 2.

Lab Review

Command	Shortcut	Action
Office Button		
Prepare/Properties		View and edit document properties
Home tab		
Styles group		
Cell Styles		Applies predefined combinations of colors, effects, and formats to selected cells
Cell Styles /Modify		Modifies existing cell style
Insert tab		
Illustrations group		
Picture		Inserts a picture from a file
Clip Art		Inserts selected graphic from Clip Organizer and Microsoft's Clip Art and Media Web site
Charts group		
Column		Inserts a column chart
Pie		Inserts a pie chart
Page Layout tab		
Themes group		
Themes		Applies selected theme to worksheet
Themes /Save Current Theme		Saves modified theme settings as a custom theme
Scale to Fit group		
Width:		Scales worksheet width to specified number of pages
Height:		Scales worksheet height to specified number of pages
Scale:		Scales worksheet by entering a percentage

command summary

Command	Shortcut	Action
View tab		
Workbook Views group		
Page Layout	[icon]	Displays document as it will appear when printed
Picture Tools Format tab		
Picture Styles group		
Picture Shape ▾		Changes shape of drawing, preserving all formatting
Picture Border ▾		Specifies color, width, and line style for outline of shape
Picture Effects ▾		Adds glow, shadow, and other effects to pictures
Chart Tools Design tab		
Type group		
Change Chart Type		Changes to a different type of chart
Data group		
Switch Row/Column		Swap the data over the axes
Select Data		Change the data range included in chart
Location group		
Move Chart		Moves chart to another sheet in the workbook
Chart Tools Layout tab		
Labels group		
Chart Title ▾		Adds, removes, or positions the chart title
Axis Titles ▾		Adds, removes, or positions the axis titles
Legend ▾		Adds, removes, or positions the chart legend

Lab Review

Command	Shortcut	Action
Data Labels		Adds, removes, or positions the data labels
Background group		
Chart Wall		Formats chart walls
Chart Tools Format tab		
Current Selection group		
Chart Area		Selects an element on the chart
Format Selection		Opens Format dialog box for selected element
Shape Styles group		
/More		Opens Shape Styles gallery
Shape Fill		Adds selected fill to shape
Shape Outline		Specifies color, weight, and type of outline
Shape Effects		Adds selected effect to shape
Print Preview tab		
Print group		
Print	Ctrl + P	Prints selection, worksheets, or workbook
Page Setup /Header/Footer tab		Adds header or footer to worksheet
Page Setup /Margins tab/Horizontally		Horizontally aligns worksheet between margins
Zoom group		
Zoom		Magnifies worksheet
Preview group		
Next Page		Displays next page
Previous Page		Displays previous page

Lab Exercises

matching

Match the lettered item on the right with the numbered item on the left.

1. theme   _____   **a.** bottom boundary line of the chart

2. value axis   _____   **b.** numbered scale along the left boundary line of the chart

3. explode   _____   **c.** identifies each number represented in a data series

4. X axis   _____   **d.** area of chart bounded by X and Y axes

5. legend   _____   **e.** applies a set of colors, fonts, and effects

6. plot area   _____   **f.** identifies the chart data series and data markers

7. column chart   _____   **g.** a chart that displays data as vertical columns

8. data marker   _____   **h.** a gradual progression of colors and shades

9. category ranges   _____   **i.** to separate a slice slightly from other slices of the pie

10. gradient   _____   **j.** identifies the data along the X axis

true/false

Circle the correct answer to the following questions.

1. A group is two or more objects that behave as a single object when moved or sized.	True	False
2. Sizing a chart also adjusts the size of the chart elements.	True	False
3. The chart title is visually displayed within the X- and Y-axis boundaries.	True	False
4. A line chart displays data commonly used to show trends over time.	True	False
5. The X-axis title line is called the category-axis title.	True	False
6. You cannot edit or format data in Page Layout view.	True	False
7. A data series links the chart object to the source worksheet.	True	False
8. A pie chart is best suited for data that compares parts to the whole.	True	False
9. Exploding a slice of a pie chart emphasizes the data.	True	False
10. A header is a line or several lines of text that appear at the bottom of each page just above the bottom margin.	True	False

Lab Exercises

fill-in

Complete the following statements by filling in the blanks with the correct key terms.

1. The small circles and squares that surround a selected object are called _____.
2. A(n) _____ is a named combination of formats.
3. _____ is a collection of graphics that is usually bundled with a software application.
4. A(n) _____ is an object that contains other objects.
5. The X axis of a chart is also called the _____ axis.
6. A(n) _____ formula is a formula that links a chart object to the source worksheet.
7. The axis of the chart that usually contains numerical values is called the _____ or _____.
8. _____ provide more information about a data marker.
9. A(n) _____ is text displayed at the top of each page.
10. The _____ is the part of the chart that gives a description of the symbols used in a chart.

multiple choice

Circle the correct response to the questions below.

1. A visual representation of data in an easy-to-understand and attractive manner is called a(n) _____.
    a. object
    b. picture
    c. chart
    d. drawing

2. 3-D charts have an additional axis called the _____.
    a. W axis
    b. X axis
    c. Y axis
    d. Z axis

3. A chart consists of a number of _____ that are used to graphically display the worksheet data.
    a. elements
    b. groups
    c. gridlines
    d. titles

4. A group is one or more _____ that behave as one when moved or sized.
   a. objects
   b. lines
   c. data markers
   d. symbols

5. A chart that is inserted in a worksheet is an _____ object and becomes part of the worksheet.
   a. attached
   b. enabled
   c. embedded
   d. inserted

6. _____ provide additional information about information displayed in the chart.
   a. Data masks
   b. Data labels
   c. Headers
   d. Chart titles

7. A(n) _____ describes the symbols used within the chart to identify different data series.
   a. X axis
   b. legend
   c. Y axis
   d. chart title

8. The _____ of a chart usually displays a number scale determined by the data in the worksheet.
   a. Z axis
   b. value axis
   c. X axis
   d. category axis

9. A _____ chart shows the relationship of each value in a data series to the series as a whole.
   a. line
   b. bar
   c. pie
   d. bubble

10. A _____ is a line of text that appears at the top of a page just below the top margin line.
    a. footer
    b. header
    c. footing
    d. heading

Lab Exercises

Hands-On Exercises

step-by-step

Teens and Credit ★

1. Max's economics paper is on teens and credit. He has some data saved in a worksheet on how much teens charge to a credit card per month. He has asked you to help him chart the data and make the worksheet look more attractive. The completed worksheet with charts is shown here. (Your solution may look different depending upon the formatting selections you have made.)

   a. Open the workbook ex02_Credit Data. Apply a theme of your choice. Use cell styles and adjust column widths as needed.

   b. Format the data in column C to Percent style with one decimal place.

   c. Insert a graphic of your choice to the left of the worksheet data (or use ex02_Credit Card.bmp) and size it appropriately. Apply a picture style of your choice. Save the workbook as Teens and Credit to your solution file location.

   d. Create a clustered-column chart and move it below the worksheet data.

   e. Enter the chart title **How Much Teens Charge** on the first line and **Per Month** on the second. Turn off the display of the legend.

   f. Change the chart type to Clustered Bar in 3-D. Select a chart style of your choice.

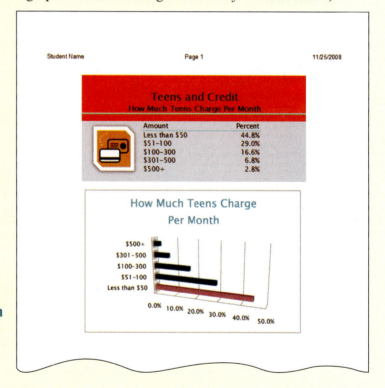

   g. Add color to the chart title and reduce the font size. Change the color for the Less than $50 data series.

   h. Size the chart to the same width as the worksheet. Document the workbook; include your name as the author.

   i. Preview the worksheet. Add a predefined header to the worksheet that displays your name, page number, and date. Center the worksheet horizontally on the page.

   j. Print the worksheet on one page.

   k. Save the workbook again.

Music Download Analysis ★★

2. The Downtown Internet Café is considering providing MP3 download kiosks in the café. To help with the decision, you have collected some data on the number of people who download music. You want to graph the data to get a better idea of the popularity of this activity. The completed worksheet with charts is shown here. (Your completed solution may be slightly different

depending upon the formatting choices you make.)

a. Open the workbook file ex02_Music Download Analysis.

b. Insert a clip art image of your choice to the left of the data. Size the image as necessary. If you do not have an image, you can use ex02_MP3 Player.bmp.

c. Change the theme to Verve with the Aspect font. Apply cell styles and adjust column widths as needed.

d. Create a line chart using the data in cells A5 through C9. Title the chart appropriately.

e. Change the chart type to a bar chart of your choice. Apply a chart style of your choice. Adjust and format the chart title as needed and add a text color of your choice. Display the legend at the bottom of the chart.

f. Position the chart below the worksheet data and size it appropriately. Add borders around the worksheet and chart.

g. Save the workbook as Music Download Analysis to your solution file location.

h. Create a 3-D column chart showing the total percentage. Select the Style 27 chart style. Title the chart appropriately using font sizes and colors of your choice.

i. While reviewing the charts, you realize that the Male and Female columns of data were transposed. Correct the data using the table below.

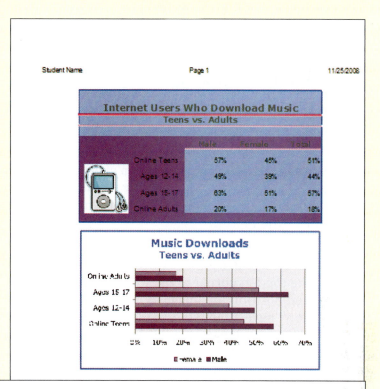

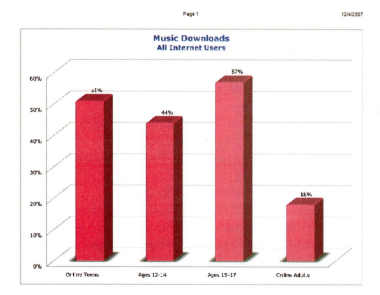

	Male	Female
Online teens	57	45
Ages 12–14	49	39
Ages 15–17	63	51
Online Adults	20	17

j. Move the chart to a separate chart sheet. Add data labels centered above each column. Remove the legend.

k. Document the workbook file by adding your name as author and include a preview picture.

Lab Exercises

l. Preview the workbook. Add a predefined header to the worksheet and chart sheet that displays your name, page number, and date. Center the worksheet horizontally on the page. Print the worksheet. Print the chart sheet.

m. Save the workbook again.

Tracking Animal Adoptions ★★

3. Richard Phillipe volunteers for Animal Angels, a volunteer group that supports the Animal Rescue Agency. He has compiled a worksheet of the number of adoptions in the downtown shelter for the last year. He would like to create a chart that shows how the adoptions differ by month and a chart that shows the total number of adoptions this year. The completed worksheet with charts is shown here. (Your completed solution may be slightly different depending upon the formatting choices you make.)

a. Open the file ex02_Adoptions.

b. Insert a clip art image of your choice in the top-left corner of the worksheet. Size and position the image as necessary. If you don't have an image, use ex02_Pets.bmp. Hint: Use Recolor in the Adjust group and choose Set transparent color to change the picture background to transparent.

c. Save the workbook as Adoption Tracking to your solution file location.

d. Chart the monthly data for the three animal categories as a column chart.

e. Enter the chart title **Adoptions by Month** and the value (Y) axis title **Number of Animals**. Display the legend below the chart.

f. Position the chart over cells A16 through N35.

g. Change the chart type to a line chart with markers.

h. Create a 3-D pie chart of the data in columns A11:A13 and N11:N13. Title the chart **Total Adoptions**. Turn off the legend and use the category names and percentages to label the data series.

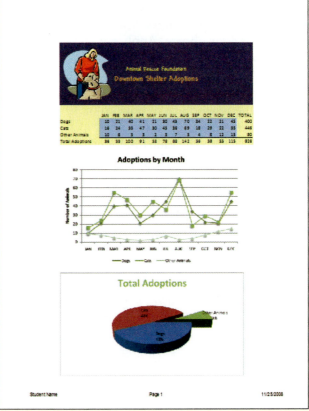

i. Position the chart over cells A38 through N55. Add color and font refinements to the chart title as you like. Rotate the chart so the Dogs slice is at the front of the chart. Explode the Other Animals slice. Apply a chart style of your choice to the pie chart.

j. Richard found an error in the data. Change the value of Other Animals in June to **3** and Dogs to **22** in October.

k. Document the workbook file by adding your name as author and include a preview picture.

l. Save the workbook.

m. Preview the worksheet. Scale the worksheet and charts to fit on one page. Add a predefined footer to the worksheet that displays your name, page number, and date. Center the worksheet horizontally on the page. Print the worksheet.

n. Save the workbook file again.

Children's Sports Participation ★★★

4. Mary Ellen is the program coordinator for Lifestyle Fitness, a physical conditioning and health center. She is proposing to management that they increase their emphasis on child fitness. To reinforce the need for this type of investment, she has compiled some recent data about growth in the number of children (in millions) participating in sports. She wants to create several charts of this data to emphasize the demand. (Your completed solution may be slightly different depending upon the formatting choices you make.)

a. Create a worksheet in columns A through D of the following data.

	2002	2004	2006
Baseball	3494	3976	4772
Basketball	7420	7543	8674
In-line Skating	8276	8311	8975
Running/Jogging	3257	3432	4290
Slow-pitch Softball	4261	4644	5572
Soccer	3510	3864	5950
Touch Football	4263	4647	5111
Volleyball	4395	4654	5584

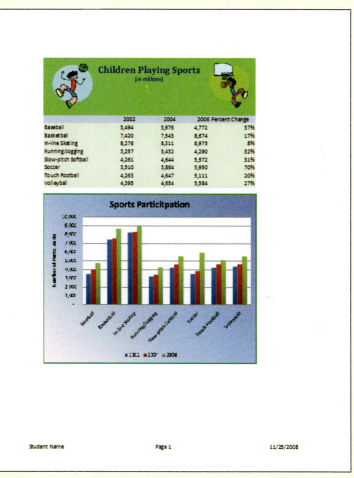

b. Add an appropriate title over the data and format the numbers to show commas with no decimal places. Calculate the percent change from 2002 to 2006 in column E ((2006 value – 2002 value)/2002 value). Add a column heading for the percent change column. Change the cell formatting of column E to percentage with no decimal places. Enhance the worksheet as you like to improve its appearance with font and fill colors and clip art (you can use ex02_Basketball.bmp and ex02_Volleyball.bmp) Hint: Use Recolor in the Adjust group and choose Set transparent color to change the picture background to transparent. Save the workbook as Youth Sports Data to your solution file location.

c. Create a column chart of the worksheet data in columns A through D. Enter a chart title and Y-axis title. Enhance the chart using features presented in the lab.

d. Move the chart below the worksheet and resize it appropriately.

e. Create a 3-D column chart in the worksheet showing the percent change data for the sports. Include the title **Percent Change in Participation 2002–2006**. Use Chart Layout 2 and a chart style of your choice. Remove the legend.

f. Enhance the chart using features presented in the lab. Move the chart to a new chart sheet.

g. Document the workbook by adding your name as author. Save the workbook with a picture preview.

Lab Exercises

h. Preview the workbook. Add a predefined footer to the worksheet that displays your name, page number, and date on both sheets. Center the worksheet horizontally on the page. Print the workbook.

i. Save the workbook again.

Internet Experience ★ ★ ★

5. Wendy Murray's class is studying Internet technology. She has discovered some intriguing research that shows how teens using the Internet has changed over the years. She would like to share this information with her students.

a. Create a worksheet of the data in the table below. Average the rows. Add an appropriate heading for the averaged row.

Teen Online Activities

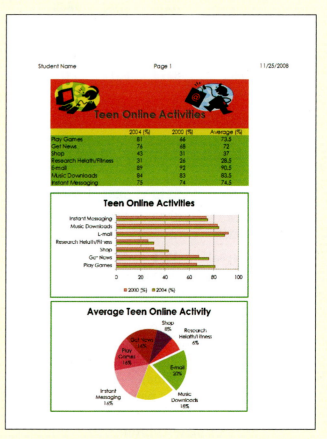

	2004 (%)	2000 (%)
Play Games	81	66
Get News	76	68
Shop	43	31
Research Health/Fitness	31	26
E-mail	89	92
Music Downloads	84	83
Instant Messaging	75	74

b. Format the worksheet using the features you have learned. Add fill color behind the data. Insert clip art graphics of your choice, or use ex02_Computer Girl.bmp and ex02_Computer Boy.bmp.

Hint: Use [Recolor ▾] in the Adjust group and choose Set transparent color to change the picture background to transparent.

c. Save the workbook as Teen Online Activities.

d. Create a bar chart for the activities for both years. Move the legend to the bottom of the chart. Include an appropriate chart title.

e. Display the chart below the worksheet. Change the color of the chart to colors that match the worksheet. Size the chart appropriately.

f. Create a pie chart of the average data. Include an appropriate title. Remove the legend and display data labels for the category names and values. Move the chart below the bar chart. Size it appropriately. Format the pie chart to be similar to your bar chart. Explode a slice of the pie. Rotate the pie to display the exploded slice at the right.

g. Add colored borders around both charts.

h. Document the workbook file by adding your name as author. Include a preview picture.

i. Preview the worksheet. Add a predefined header to the worksheet that displays your name, page number, and date. Center the worksheet horizontally on the page. Scale the worksheet to fit on one page. Print the worksheet.

j. Save the workbook file again.

Job Market Seminar ★

1. Nancy Fernandez is preparing for an upcoming job market seminar she is presenting. She has collected data comparing the mean hourly pay rate for several computer and mathematical jobs in the Midwest and Northeast to the U.S. average rates. Open the workbook ex02_ Job Market. Calculate the percent difference between the Midwest states and U.S. average in column E. Calculate the percent difference between the Northeast states and U.S. average in column F. Add appropriate fill and font colors to the worksheet. Add a graphic to the top-left corner of the worksheet. Nancy thinks the information would be much more meaningful and have greater impact if it were presented in a chart. Create an appropriate chart of the average hourly wage for Computer Programmers, Computer Support Specialists, Computer Systems Analysts, and Database Administrators on a separate chart sheet. Include appropriate chart titles. Add a pattern to the data series and change the plot area fill color. Enhance the chart in other ways using different font sizes and font colors. Position the legend at the bottom of the chart. Add a predefined header to the chart sheet that displays your name, page number, and date. Save the workbook as Seminar and print the chart.

Grade Tracking ★

2. Create a worksheet that tracks your GPA for at least four semesters or quarters. (If necessary, use fictitious data to attain four grading periods.) Create a chart that best represents your GPA trends. Use the formatting techniques you have learned to change the appearance of the worksheet and the chart. Save the workbook as Grades. Include a header or footer that displays your name and the current date in the worksheet. Print the worksheet with the chart.

Stock Market Workbook ★ ★

3. You are interested in the stock market. Use Help to learn more about the Stock chart type. Pick five related mutual funds and enter data about their performance over a period of time. Create a stock chart of the data. Save the worksheet with the chart as Mutual Funds. Include a header or footer that displays your name and the current date in the worksheet. Print the worksheet and the chart.

Graduate School Data ★ ★ ★

4. Andrew Romine is considering graduate school at Ohio State and has gathered some data to present to his parents to make a case for paying part of his tuition and fees. Open the file ex02_Graduate School, which has two worksheets, one that shows Earnings and the other Payback data if Andrew chooses Ohio State. Using what you learned in the lab, create two charts from the data on the Earnings worksheet. One chart should represent the lifetime earnings potential of people based on their level of education and the other should represent median earning by level. Create a pie chart on the Payback worksheet to represent the number of years after graduation that it will take to earn back what he paid for the higher education. Use the difference in Salary as the data labels. Use the features you have learned to enhance the appearance of the worksheets and charts. Include a header on both worksheets that displays your name and the current date. Save the worksheet as Graduate School2. Print the worksheet with the charts.

Insurance Comparisons ★★★

5. Roberto Sanchez is thinking about purchasing a new car. However, he is concerned about the insurance rates. Before purchasing, he wants to find out the insurance rates on the cars he is evaluating. Select three different car manufacturers and models. Use the Web and select three different comparable insurance companies to get the insurance premium cost information for different amounts of coverage (minimum required). Use your own personal information as the basis for the insurance quotes. Create a worksheet that contains the cost of minimum coverage, cost of optional coverage, deductibles available, and insurance premium quotes for each vehicle. Create a chart of the data that shows the coverage and premiums. Enhance the chart appropriately. Add a picture of the cars. Include a header or footer that displays your name and the current date in the worksheet. Save the workbook as Insurance. Print the worksheet and chart.

Managing and Analyzing a Workbook

Objectives

After completing this lab, you will know how to:

1 Correct worksheet errors.

2 Use absolute references.

3 Copy, move, name, and delete sheets.

4 Use AutoFill.

5 Reference multiple sheets.

6 Use Find and Replace.

7 Zoom the worksheet.

8 Split windows and freeze panes.

9 Use what-if analysis and Goal Seek.

10 Control page breaks.

11 Change page orientation.

12 Add custom headers and footers.

13 Print selected sheets and areas.

Downtown Internet Café

You presented your new, more-optimistic, first-quarter sales forecast for the Downtown Internet Café to Evan. He was impressed with the charts and projected increase in sales if an aggressive advertising promotion is launched. However, because the Café's funds are low due to the cost of the recent renovations, he has decided to wait on launching the advertising campaign.

Evan wants you to continue working on the Café forecast using the original, more-conservative projected sales values for the first quarter. In addition, he asks you to include an average calculation and to extend the forecast for the next three quarters.

After discussing the future sales, you

agree that the Café will likely make a small profit during the first quarter of operations. Then the Café should show increasing profitability. Evan stresses that the monthly profit margin should reach 20 percent in the second quarter.

As you develop the Café's financial forecast, the worksheet grows in size and complexity. You will learn about features of Office Excel 2007 that help you manage a large workbook efficiently. You also will learn how you can manipulate the data in a worksheet to reach a goal using the what-if analysis capabilities of Excel. The completed annual forecast is shown here.

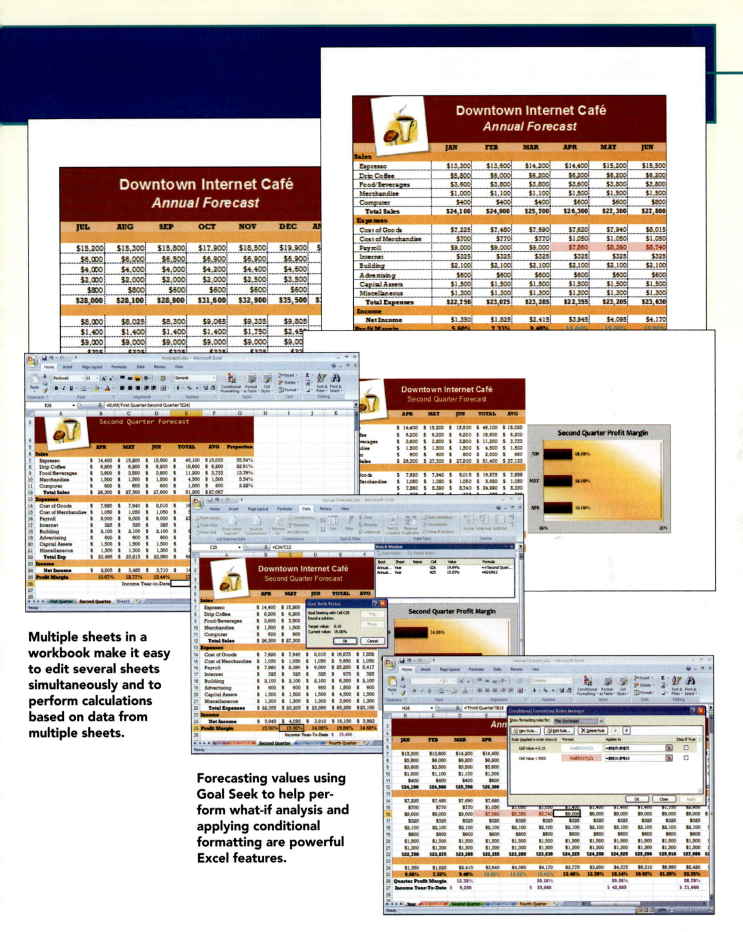

Multiple sheets in a workbook make it easy to edit several sheets simultaneously and to perform calculations based on data from multiple sheets.

Forecasting values using Goal Seek to help perform what-if analysis and applying conditional formatting are powerful Excel features.

Conditional formatting allows you to quickly emphasize worksheet data based on specified conditions.

Concept Preview

The following concepts will be introduced in this lab:

1 **Absolute Reference** An absolute reference is a cell or range reference in a formula whose location does not change when the formula is copied.

2 **Sheet Name** Each sheet in a workbook can be assigned a descriptive sheet name to help identify the contents of the sheet.

3 **AutoFill** The AutoFill feature makes entering a series of headings easier by logically repeating and extending the series. AutoFill recognizes trends and automatically extends data and alphanumeric headings as far as you specify.

4 **Sheet and 3-D References** A formula that contains references to cells in other sheets of a workbook allows you to use data from multiple sheets and to calculate new values based on this data. The formula contains a sheet reference consisting of the name of the sheet, followed by an exclamation point and the cell or range reference.

5 **Find and Replace** The Find and Replace feature helps you quickly find specific information and automatically replace it with new information.

6 **Split Window** The split window feature allows you to divide a worksheet window into sections, making it easier to view different parts of the worksheet at the same time.

7 **Freeze Panes** Freezing panes prevents the data in the pane from scrolling as you move to different areas in a worksheet.

8 **What-If Analysis** What-if analysis is a technique used to evaluate the effects of changing selected factors in a worksheet.

9 **Goal Seek** The Goal Seek tool is used to find the value needed in one cell to attain a result you want in another cell.

10 **Conditional Formatting** Conditional formatting changes the appearance of a range of cells based on a condition that you specify.

Correcting Worksheet Errors

After talking with Evan, the owner of the Café, about the first-quarter forecast, you are ready to begin making the changes he suggested. Evan returned the workbook file to you containing several changes he made to the format of the worksheet.

1

Start Office Excel 2007.

Open the workbook ex03_First Quarter Forecast.

If necessary, maximize the application and workbook windows.

Your screen should be similar to Figure 3.1

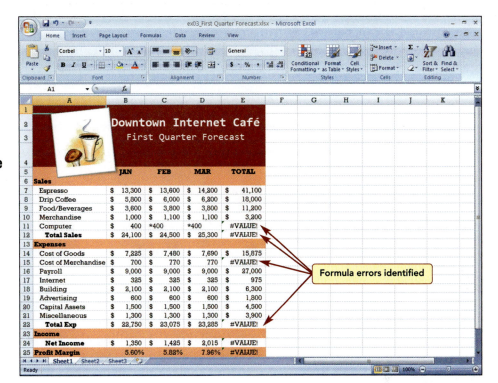

Figure 3.1

As you can see, Evan made several formatting changes to the worksheet. He changed the theme, fill, and text colors and made several changes to the row headings. For example, the Pay heading has been replaced with Payroll. Evan also decided to decrease the Computer sales values to $400 for February and March. He included an asterisk (*) in the cells to make sure you saw the change. However, this has resulted in a formula error.

Excel 2007 includes several tools to help you find and correct errors in formula entries. These tools provide the capability to display the relationships between formulas and cells and to identify and suggest corrections to potential problems in formulas.

Using the Formula Error Checker

As you check the worksheet, you notice a problem in cell E11. When a formula cannot properly calculate a result, an error value is displayed and a green triangle appears in the top-left corner of the cell. Each type of error value has a different cause, as described in the following table.

Error Value	Cause
#####	Column not wide enough to display result, or negative date or time is used
#VALUE!	Wrong type of argument or operand is used
#DIV/0!	Number is divided by zero
#NAME?	Text in formula not recognized
#N/A	Value not available
#REF!	Cell reference is not valid
#NUM!	Invalid number values
#NULL!	Intersection operator is not valid

You can correct each identified error individually or use Excel's formula error checker tool to check them all, one at a time. The formula error checker is similar to the spelling checker in that it goes to each location in the worksheet containing a formula error, identifies the problem, and suggests corrections. You will use the formula error checker to correct this error and check the entire worksheet for others.

1 ● **Open the Formulas tab.**

● **Click** ❖ Error Checking ▾ **in the Formula Auditing group.**

● **If necessary, move the dialog box to see the located formula error.**

Your screen should be similar to Figure 3.2

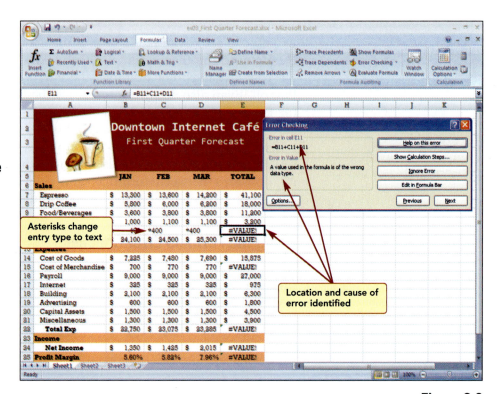

Figure 3.2

The Error Checking dialog box identifies the location and cause of the error. In this case, when Evan changed the February and March computer sales values, he included an asterisk in the cell entries to make sure you noticed the change. This caused Excel to interpret the entry as a text entry, which cannot be used in this formula. To correct the problem, you need to enter the values correctly.

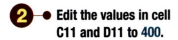 **Edit the values in cell C11 and D11 to 400.**

Your screen should be similar to Figure 3.3

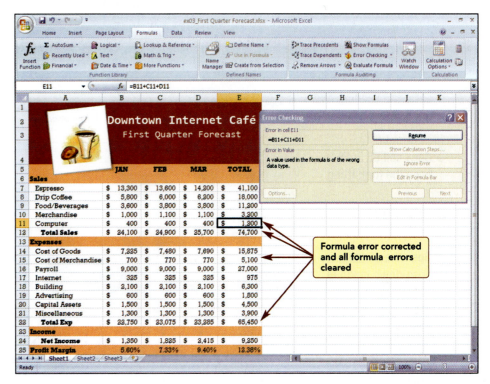

Figure 3.3

Cell E11 now displays the correctly calculated result. Additionally, all other cells that displayed errors also are fixed because their formulas no longer reference cells containing text entries. You will continue checking the worksheet for formula errors.

 **Click** Resume .

Click OK .

No other errors were located. You are now ready to make several of the changes requested by Evan.

Calculating an Average

First you will add a column showing the average values for the first quarter. You will start by entering a new column heading. Then you will enter the Average function to calculate the average for Espresso sales.

In addition to using $\Sigma \cdot$ Sum in the Home tab to enter commonly used functions, you can use Σ AutoSum $\cdot$ in the Function Library group of the Formulas tab.

1 ● Enter the heading **AVG** in cell F5.

● Copy cell E6 to F6 to copy the formatting.

● Move to F7.

● Open the Σ AutoSum $\cdot$ drop-down menu in the Function Library group and choose Average.

Your screen should be similar to Figure 3.4

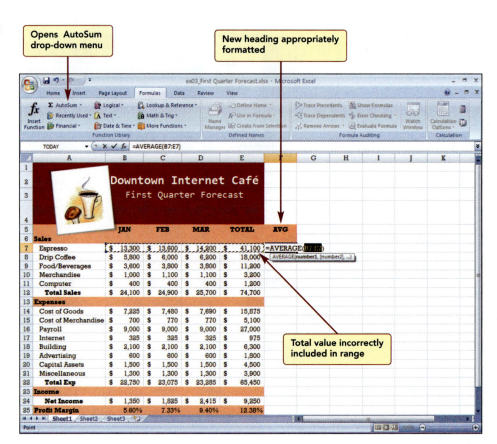

Figure 3.4

Notice that the AVG heading is already appropriately formatted to bold and centered. This is because Excel automatically extends formats to new cells if the format of at least three of the last five preceding cells in the row appears that way.

Excel identifies the range of cells B7 through E7 for the function argument. Because it incorrectly includes the total value in cell E7, you need to specify the correct range.

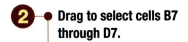

2 • Drag to select cells B7 through D7.

• Click ✓ Enter.

Your screen should be similar to Figure 3.5

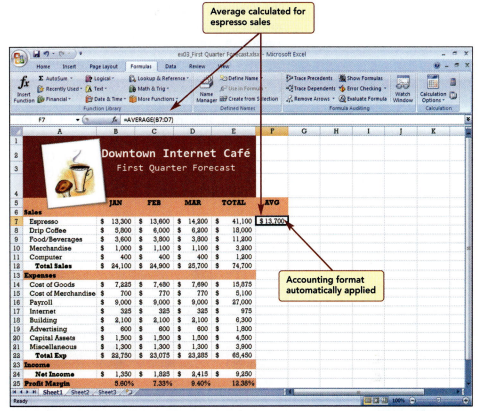

Average calculated for espresso sales

Accounting format automatically applied

Figure 3.5

The average of the Espresso sales for the quarter, $13,700, is calculated and displayed in cell F7. Notice that Excel again extended the format to the new cell, saving you the step of applying the Accounting format.

Next you need to copy the function down column F.

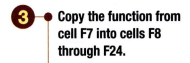

3 • Copy the function from cell F7 into cells F8 through F24.

• Move to cell F13.

Your screen should be similar to Figure 3.6

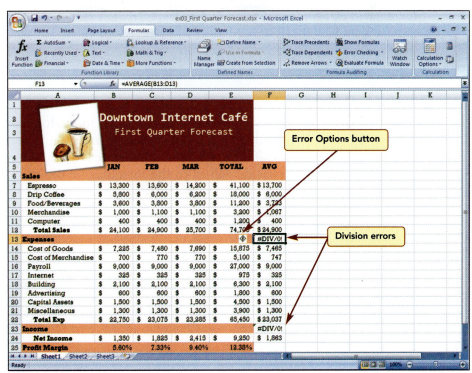

Error Options button

Division errors

Figure 3.6

The average value has been correctly calculated for each row. Notice, however, that two cells display the error value #DIV/0!, indicating the cells contain a formula error. In addition, the ◇▾ Error Options button appears when you select a cell containing an error.

Correcting Formula Errors Individually

To correct this problem, you need to find out the cause of the error. Pointing to the Error Options button displays a ScreenTip identifying the cause of the error; in this case, the formula is attempting to divide by zero or empty cells. This time you will individually correct the error.

1 • **Point to ◇▾ Error Options to see the ScreenTip.**

• **Click ◇▾ Error Options.**

• **Choose Edit in Formula Bar.**

Your screen should be similar to Figure 3.7

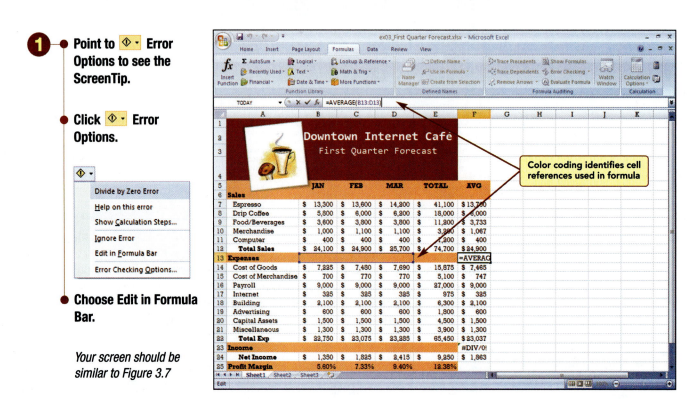

Figure 3.7

Notice that the cell references in the formula are color coded to match the borders Excel displays around the referenced worksheet cells. It is designed to provide visual cues to the relationships between the cells that provide values to the formulas or the cells that depend on the formulas.

Lab 3: Managing and Analyzing a Workbook

www.mhhe.com/oleary

You can now easily see the error is caused by references to blank cells when the function was copied. Since you do not need this formula, you will delete it. Likewise, you need to delete the function that was copied into cell F23. You will clear the entry in this cell using the fill handle.

2 ● **Press** Esc.

● **Press** Delete.

● **Move to cell F23.**

● **Point to the fill handle and when the mouse pointer changes to +, drag upward until the cell is gray.**

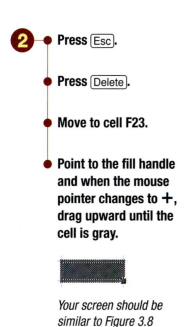

Your screen should be similar to Figure 3.8

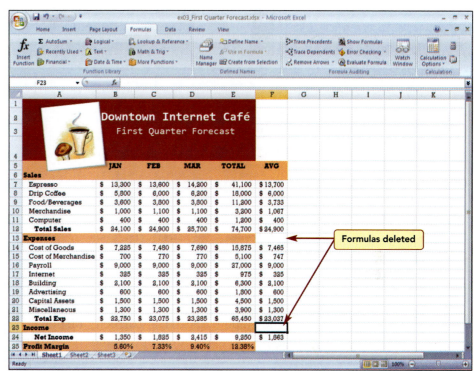

Figure 3.8

Using Absolute References

While looking at the sales data in the worksheet, you decide it may be interesting to know what contribution each sales item makes to total sales. To find out, you will enter a formula to calculate the proportion of sales by each in column G. You will start by entering a new column heading in cell G5 and adding formatting to G6 using the AutoFill feature. Then you will enter the formula = Total Espresso Sales/Total Sales to calculate the proportion for Espresso sales in G7 and copy it to G8 to calculate the proportion for Drip Coffee sales.

1

- Enter the heading **Proportion** in cell G5.

- Drag the fill handle of cell G5 to copy the entry into cell G6.

- Open the 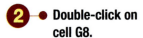 drop-down menu and choose Fill Formatting Only.

- Best fit column G.

- Enter the formula **=E7/E12** in cell G7.

- Drag the fill handle to copy the formula in cell G7 to G8.

Your screen should be similar to Figure 3.9

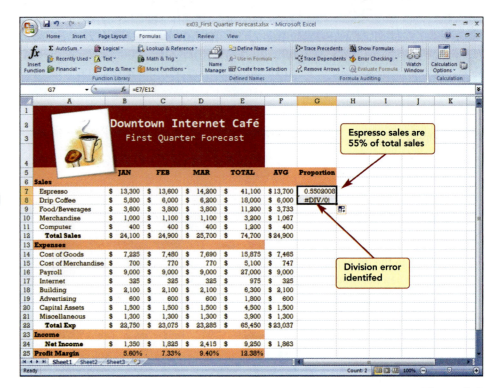

Figure 3.9

The value 0.550201 is correctly displayed in cell G7. This shows that the Espresso sales are approximately 55 percent of Total Sales. However, a division error has occurred in cell G8. You will quickly check the formula in that cell by changing to Edit mode.

2

- Double-click on cell G8.

Your screen should be similar to Figure 3.10

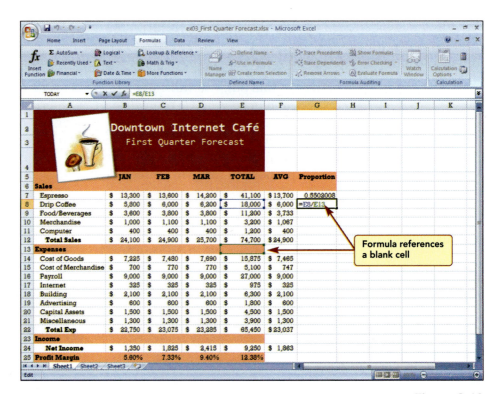

Figure 3.10

In Edit mode, the formula references are again color coded to the worksheet cells. You can now see the error occurred because the relative reference to cell E12 adjusted correctly to the new location when the formula was copied and now references cell E13, a blank cell. The formula in G7 needs to be entered so that the reference to the Total Sales value in cell E12 does not change when the formula is copied. To do this, you need to make the cell reference absolute.

Concept 1

Absolute Reference

1 An **absolute reference** is a cell or range reference in a formula whose location does not change when the formula is copied.

To stop the relative adjustment of cell references, enter a $ (dollar sign) character before the column letter and row number. This changes the cell reference to absolute. When a formula containing an absolute cell reference is copied to another row and column location in the worksheet, the cell reference does not change. It is an exact duplicate of the cell reference in the original formula.

A cell reference also can be a **mixed reference**. In this type of reference, either the column letter or the row number is preceded with the $. This makes only the row or column absolute. When a formula containing a mixed cell reference is copied to another location in the worksheet, only the part of the cell reference that is not absolute changes relative to its new location in the worksheet.

The table below shows examples of relative and absolute references and the results when a reference in cell G8 to cell E8 is copied to cell H9.

Cell Contents of G8	Copied to Cell H9	Type of Reference
$E$8	$E$8	Absolute reference
E$8	F$8	Mixed reference
$E8	$E9	Mixed reference
E8	F9	Relative reference

You will change the formula in cell G7 to include an absolute reference for cell E11. Then you will copy the formula to cells G8 through G10.

You can change a cell reference to absolute or mixed by typing in the dollar sign directly or by using the ABS (Absolute) key, F4. To use the ABS key, the program must be in Edit mode and the cell reference that you want to change must be selected. If you continue to press F4, the cell reference will cycle through all possible combinations of cell reference types.

3 ● Press [Esc] to exit Edit mode.

● Move to G7.

● Click on the reference to E12 in the formula bar to enter Edit mode and select the reference.

● Press [F4] four times to cycle through all reference types.

● Press [F4] again to display an absolute reference.

Your screen should be similar to Figure 3.11

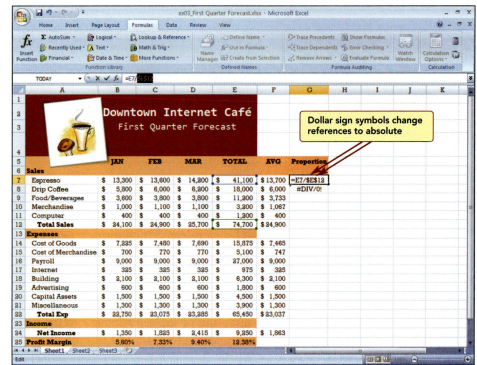

Figure 3.11

MORE ABOUT

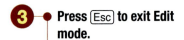

► To learn how to create a formula with a mixed cell reference, see 3.1 Reference Data in Formulas in the More About appendix.

The cell reference now displays $ characters before the column letter and row number, making this cell reference absolute. Leaving the cell reference absolute, as it is now, will stop the relative adjustment of the cell reference when you copy it again.

4 ● Click ☑ Enter.

● Copy the revised formula to cells G8 through G11.

● Double-click on cell G8.

Your screen should be similar to Figure 3.12

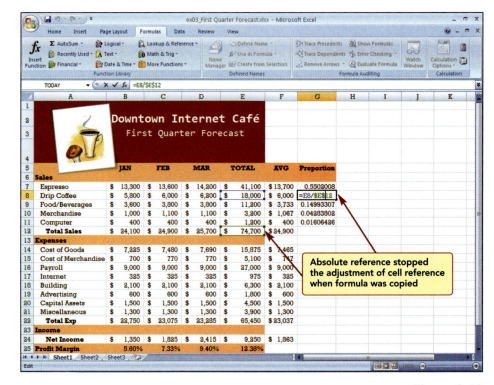

Figure 3.12

The formula when copied correctly adjusted the relative cell reference to Drip Coffee sales in cell E8 and did not adjust the reference to E12 because it is an absolute reference.

The last change you need to make to the proportion data is to format it to the Percent style.

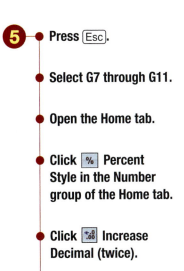

5 ● Press Esc.

● Select G7 through G11.

● Open the Home tab.

● Click % Percent Style in the Number group of the Home tab.

● Click Increase Decimal (twice).

● Extend the fill in the title area to columns F and G.

Having Trouble?
Use fill series with formatting only or Format Painter to copy the fill colors.

● Extend the fill in rows 13, 23, and 25 to columns F and G.

● Move to cell A6 and save the workbook as Forecast3 to your solution file location.

Your screen should be similar to Figure 3.13

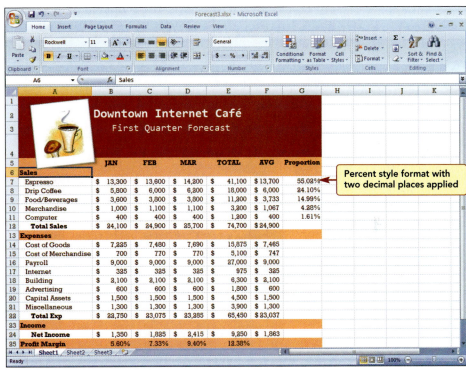

Figure 3.13

The calculated proportion shows the same values that a pie chart of this data would show.

Working with Sheets

Next, you want to add the second-quarter forecast to the workbook. You want this data in a separate sheet in the same workbook file. To make it easier to enter the forecast for the next quarter, you will copy the contents of the first-quarter forecast in Sheet1 into another sheet in the workbook.

Then you will change the month headings, the title, and the number data for the second quarter. Finally, you want to include a formula to calculate a year-to-date total for the six months.

Copying between Sheets

You want to copy the worksheet data from Sheet1 to Sheet2. Copying between sheets is the same as copying within a sheet, except that you switch to the new sheet to specify the destination.

1 ● Select the worksheet range A1 through G25.

Having Trouble?

A quick way to select this range is to move to cell A1, hold down ⇧Shift, and click on cell G25.

● Click 📋 Copy.

● Click on the Sheet2 tab.

● Click 📋 Paste .

Your screen should be similar to Figure 3.14

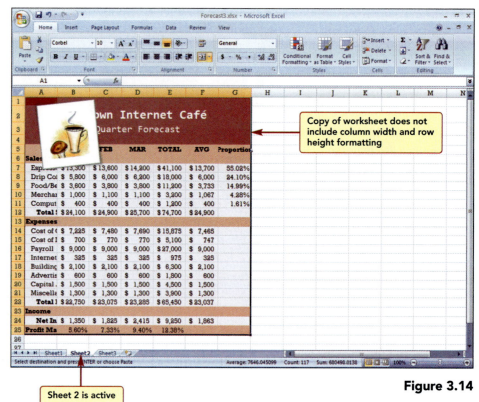

Copy of worksheet does not include column width and row height formatting

Sheet 2 is active

Figure 3.14

All the worksheet data, graphic objects, and formatting, except for the column width settings, are copied into the existing Sheet2. You want to include the column width settings from the source. Notice also that the extra row height of row four was not copied. You will need to manually adjust the height.

2 ● Open the  menu and choose Paste Special.

● Choose Column Widths.

● Click [OK].

● Increase the row height of row 4 to 39 points (52 pixels).

● Click in the worksheet to clear the selection.

Your screen should be similar to Figure 3.15

MORE ABOUT

▶ To learn about other Paste Special options, see 1.3 Modify Cell Contents and Formats in the More About appendix.

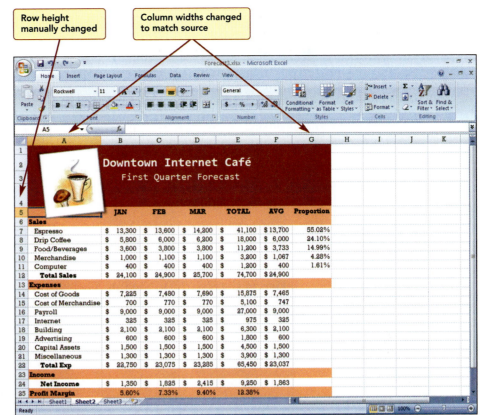

Row height manually changed

Column widths changed to match source

Figure 3.15

Another Method

You also can use  /Move or Copy Sheet in the Cells group or hold down [Ctrl] while dragging the active sheet tab to copy an entire sheet. All formatting, including column widths, is copied into the destination sheet.

The column widths from the copied selection are pasted into the new sheet. Sheet2 now contains a duplicate of the first-quarter forecast in Sheet1.

Renaming Sheets and Coloring Sheet Tabs

As more sheets are added to a workbook, remembering what information is in each sheet becomes more difficult. To help clarify the contents of the sheets, you can rename the sheets.

Concept 2

Sheet Name

2 Each sheet in a workbook can be assigned a descriptive **sheet name** to help identify the contents of the sheet. The following guidelines should be followed when naming a sheet. A sheet name

- Can be up to 31 characters.
- Can be entered in uppercase or lowercase letters or a combination (it will appear as entered).
- Can contain any combination of letters, numbers, and spaces.
- Cannot contain the characters : ? * / \.
- Cannot be enclosed in square brackets [ ].

Double-clicking the sheet tab makes the sheet active and highlights the existing sheet name in the tab. The existing name is cleared as soon as you begin to type the new name. You will change the name of Sheet1 to First Quarter and Sheet2 to Second Quarter.

- Double-click the Sheet1 tab.

- Type **First Quarter**.

- Press ⏎Enter.

- Change the name of the Sheet2 tab to **Second Quarter**.

Another Method

You also can use 🖫 Format ▾ /Rename Sheet in the Cells group of the Home tab

Your screen should be similar to Figure 3.16

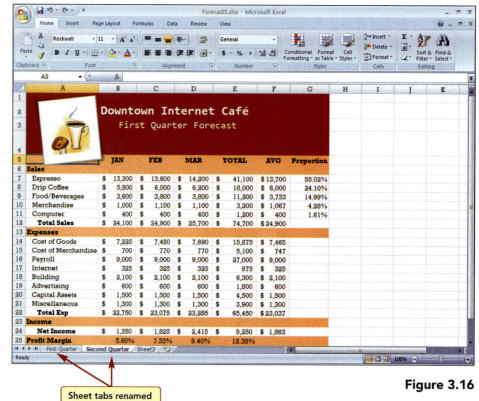

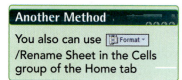
Sheet tabs renamed

Figure 3.16

To further differentiate the sheets, you can add color to the sheet tabs.

2 • **Right-click on the First Quarter tab.**

• **Select Tab Color from the shortcut menu.**

• **Choose the Turquoise, Accent 1 theme color from the color palette.**

• **In the same manner, change the color of the Second Quarter sheet tab to the Red, Accent 2 theme color.**

Another Method

You also can use [Format ▾] / Tab Color in the Cells group.

Your screen should be similar to Figure 3.17

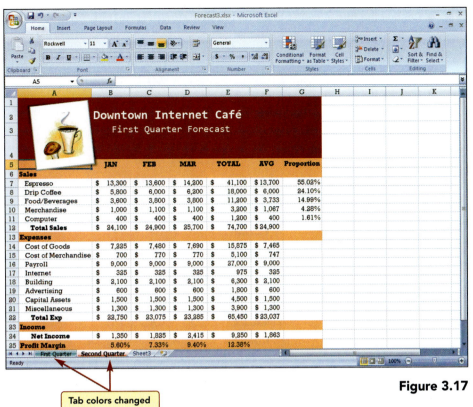

Tab colors changed

Figure 3.17

The sheet tab name of the selected sheet is underlined in the tab color of red and the First Quarter sheet tab is blue. When a sheet is not selected, the sheet tab is displayed with the background color.

Filling a Series

Now you can change the worksheet title and data in the Second Quarter sheet. First you will change the worksheet title to identify the worksheet contents as the second-quarter forecast. Then you will change the month headings to the three months that make up the second quarter: April, May, and June.

1 • Change the title in cell B3 to **Second Quarter Forecast.**

• Change the month heading in cell B5 to **APR.**

Your screen should be similar to Figure 3.18

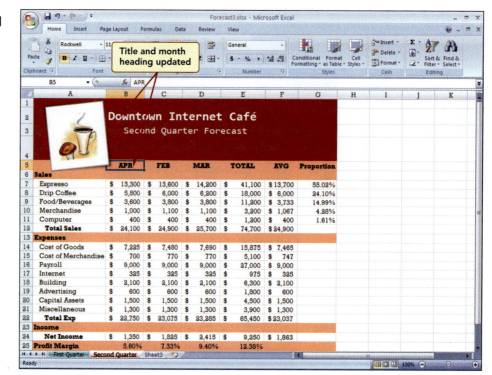

Figure 3.18

Now you need to change the remaining month headings to MAY and JUN. You will use the AutoFill feature to enter the month headings.

Concept 3

AutoFill

3 The **AutoFill** feature makes entering a series of numbers, numbers and text combinations, dates, or time periods easier by logically repeating and extending the series. AutoFill recognizes trends and automatically extends data and alphanumeric headings as far as you specify.

Dragging the fill handle activates the AutoFill feature if Excel recognizes the entry in the cell as an entry that can be incremented. When AutoFill extends the entries, it uses the same style as the original entry. For example, if you enter the heading for July as JUL (abbreviated with all letters uppercase), all the extended entries in the series will be abbreviated and uppercase. Dragging down or right increments in increasing order, and up or left increments in decreasing order. A linear series increases or decreases values by a constant value, and a growth series multiplies values by a constant factor. Examples of how AutoFill extends a series are shown in the table below.

Initial Selection	Extended Series
Qtr1	Qtr2, Qtr3, Qtr4
Mon	Tue, Wed, Thu
Jan, Apr	Jul, Oct, Jan

A starting value of a series may contain more than one item that can be incremented, such as JAN-02, in which both the month and year can increment. You can specify which value to increment by selecting the appropriate option from the AutoFill Options menu.

The entry in cell B5, APR, is the starting value of a series of months. You will drag the fill handle to the right to increment the months. The mouse pointer displays the entry that will appear in each cell as you drag.

2 ● Drag the fill handle of cell B5 to extend the range from cell B5 through cell D5.

● Save the workbook.

Your screen should be similar to Figure 3.19

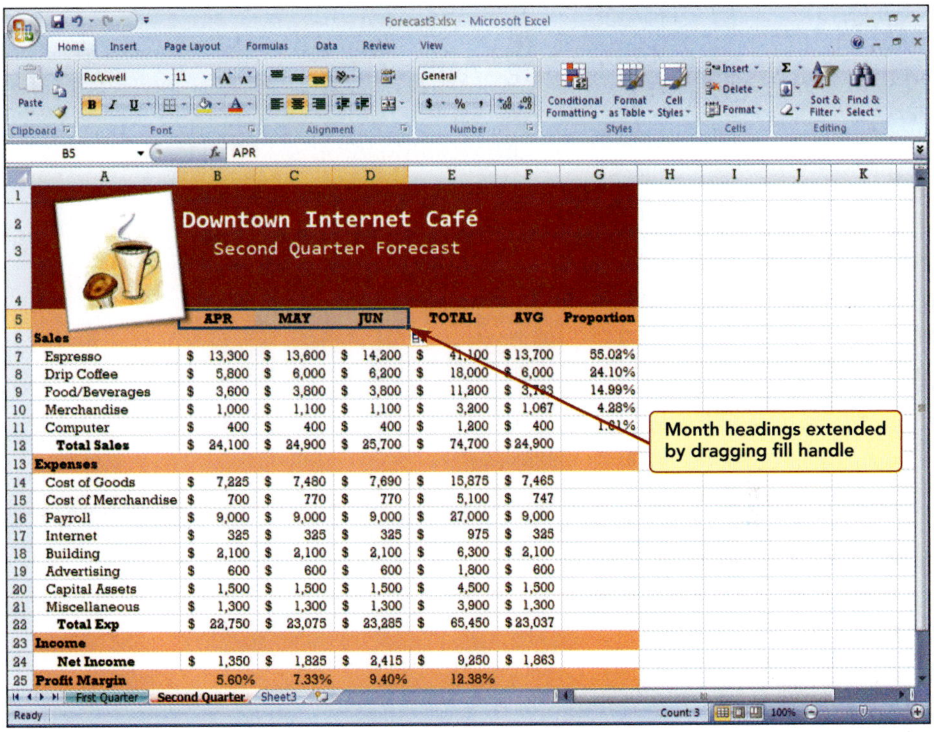

Figure 3.19

Additional Information

If you do not want a series created when you drag the fill handle, hold down Ctrl as you drag and the entries will be copied, not incremented. Alternatively, you can choose Copy Cells from the AutoFill Options menu.

The month headings now correctly reflect the three months for the second quarter. This is because the entry in cell B5 was a month that was recognized as an entry that can be incremented. Additionally, the months appear in uppercase characters, the same as the starting month. This is because AutoFill copies formatting when extending the series.

Referencing Multiple Sheets

Finally, you need to update the forecast to reflect the April through June sales. Then you will enter a formula to calculate the year-to-date income total using data from both sheets.

1 **Enter the following values in the specified cells.**

Sales	Cell	Number
Espresso	B7	14400
	C7	15200
	D7	15500
Drip Coffee	B8	6200
	C8	6200
	D8	6200
Food/Beverages	B9	3600
	C9	3800
	D9	3800
Merchandise	B10	1500
	C10	1500
	D10	1500
Computer	B11	600
	C11	600
	D11	600

Your screen should be similar to Figure 3.20

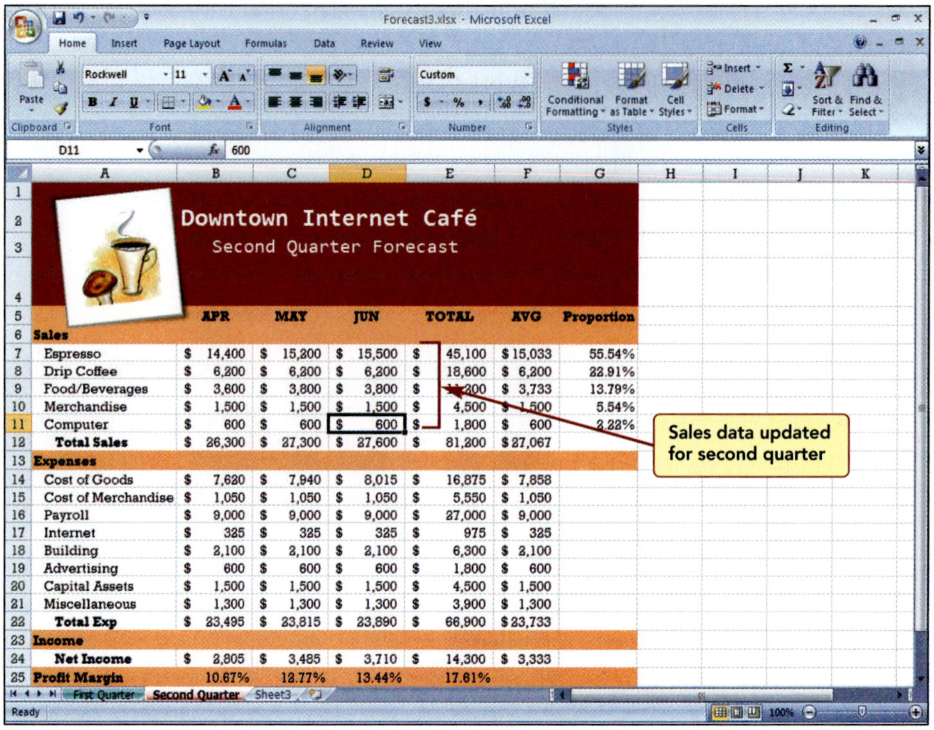

Figure 3.20

The worksheet now contains the data for the second quarter and all dependent formulas have been recalculated.

Now you can enter the formula to calculate a year-to-date income total. The formula to make this calculation will sum the total income numbers from cell E24 in the First Quarter sheet and cell E24 in the Second Quarter sheet. To reference data in another sheet in the same workbook, you enter a formula that references cells in other worksheets.

Concept 4

Sheet and 3-D References

4 A formula that contains references to cells in other sheets of a workbook allows you to use data from multiple sheets and to calculate new values based on this data. The formula contains a **sheet reference** consisting of the name of the sheet, followed by an exclamation point and the cell or range reference. If the sheet name contains nonalphabetic characters, such as a space, the sheet name (or path) must be enclosed in single quotation marks.

If you want to use the same cell or range of cells on multiple sheets, you can use a 3-D reference. A **3-D reference** consists of the names of the beginning and ending sheets enclosed in quotes and separated by a colon. This is followed by an exclamation point and the cell or range reference. The cell or range reference is the same on each sheet in the specified sheet range. If a sheet is inserted or deleted, the range is automatically updated. 3-D references make it easy to analyze data in the same cell or range of cells on multiple worksheets.

Reference	Description
=Sheet2!B17	Displays the entry in cell B17 of Sheet2 in the active cell of the current sheet
=Sheet1!A1 + Sheet2!B2.	Sums the values in cell A1 of Sheet1 and B2 of Sheet2
=SUM(Sheet1:Sheet4!H6:K6)	Sums the values in cells H6 through K6 in Sheets 1, 2, 3, and 4
=SUM(Sheet1!H6:K6)	Sums the values in cells H6 through K6 in Sheet1
=SUM(Sheet1:Sheet4!H6)	Sums the values in cell H6 of Sheets 1, 2, 3, and 4

Just like a formula that references cells within a sheet, a formula that references cells in multiple sheets is automatically recalculated when data in a referenced cell changes.

You will enter a descriptive text entry in cell D25 and then use a 3-D reference in a SUM function to calculate the year-to-date total in cell E25.

The SUM function argument will consist of a 3-D reference to cell E24 in the First and Second Quarter sheets. Although a 3-D reference can be entered by typing it using the proper syntax, it is much easier to enter it by pointing to the cells on the sheets. To enter a 3-D reference, select the cell or range in the beginning sheet and then hold down ⇧Shift and click on the sheet tab of the last sheet in the range. This will include the indicated cell range on all sheets between and including the first and last sheets specified.

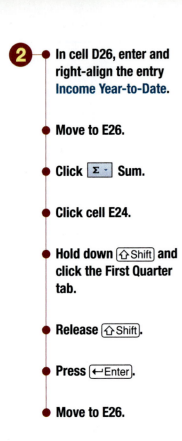

2 • In cell D26, enter and right-align the entry **Income Year-to-Date**.

• Move to E26.

• Click **Σ ·** Sum.

• Click cell E24.

• Hold down ⇧Shift and click the First Quarter tab.

• Release ⇧Shift.

• Press ←Enter.

• Move to E26.

Your screen should be similar to Figure 3.21

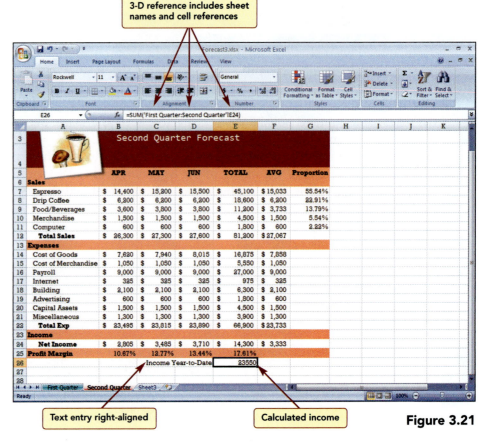

3-D reference includes sheet names and cell references

Text entry right-aligned

Calculated income

Figure 3.21

The calculated number 23550 appears in cell E26, and the function containing a 3-D reference appears in the formula bar.

Hiding Gridlines and Headings

Just as you completed the forecast for the first half of the year, Evan, the Café owner, stopped in and you decide to show him the forecast. To simplify the screen display while showing Evan the worksheet, you will hide the gridlines and column and row headings.

1 ● **Move to cell A1 and open the View tab.**

● **Choose** ☑ Gridlines **from the Show/Hide group to clear the selection.**

● **Choose** ☑ Headings **from the Show/Hide group to clear the selection.**

Your screen should be similar to Figure 3.22

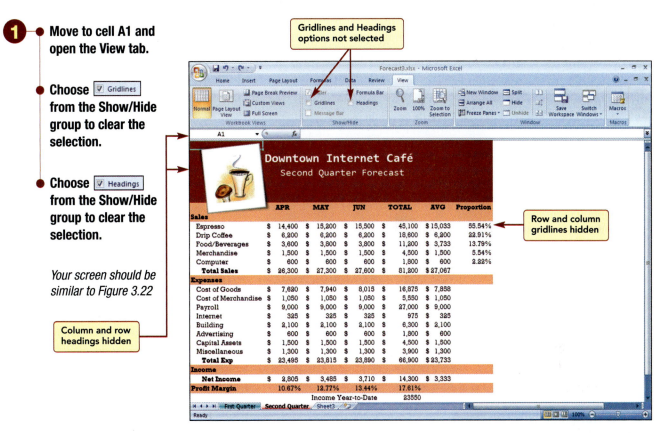

Gridlines and Headings options not selected

Row and column gridlines hidden

Column and row headings hidden

Figure 3.22

While these features are off, you will format the year-to-date income value to Accounting with zero decimal places. Rather than opening the Home tab to access these features, you will copy the format from another cell. The Paste Special menu option, Formatting only, will do this quickly for you.

2 ● **Select any cell that is formatted in the Accounting format and choose Copy from the context menu.**

● **Right-click on cell E26 and choose Paste Special from the context menu.**

● **Choose Formats and click** OK .

Your screen should be similar to Figure 3.23

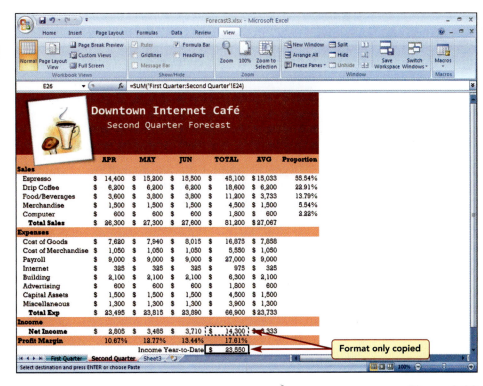

Format only copied

Figure 3.23

Hiding gridlines and headers is convenient for presenting the worksheet to others; however, it is not as easy to work in the sheet with these features off. You will turn them back on and then print a copy of the workbook for Evan.

3 ● Choose [Gridlines] from the Show/Hide group to select it.

● Choose [Headings] from the Show/Hide group to select it.

● Enter the following information in the workbook properties.

Author	your name
Title	Downtown Internet Cafe
Subject	First and second quarter forecasts

> **Having Trouble?**
> Click 🔵 Office Button, point to Prepare, and choose Properties to open the Document Information Panel.

● Preview the entire workbook.

● Add a predefined header containing your name, page number, and the date to both sheets.

● Print the workbook.

● Move to cell A6 in both sheets and save the workbook.

● Close the workbook.

Note: If you are running short on lab time, this is an appropriate place to end this session and begin again at a later time.

Deleting and Moving Sheets

You presented the completed first- and second-quarter forecasts to Evan. He is very pleased with the results and now wants you to create worksheets for the third and fourth quarters and a combined annual forecast. Additionally, Evan has asked you to include a column chart of the data for each quarter. Finally, after looking at the forecast, Evan wants the forecast to show a profit margin of 15 percent for each month in the second quarter.

You have already made several of the changes requested and saved them as a workbook file. You will open this file to see the revised and expanded forecast.

1 ● **Open the workbook file** ex03_Annual Forecast**.**

Your screen should be similar to Figure 3.24

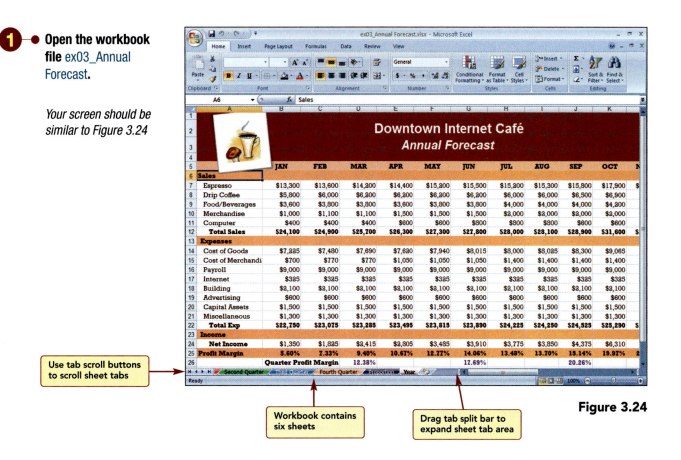

Use tab scroll buttons to scroll sheet tabs

Workbook contains six sheets

Drag tab split bar to expand sheet tab area

Figure 3.24

The workbook file now contains six sheets: First Quarter, Second Quarter, Third Quarter, Fourth Quarter, Proportion, and Year. The Proportion sheet contains the proportion of sales values from the first and second quarters. The Year sheet contains the forecast data for the entire 12 months. Each quarter sheet also includes a chart of the profit margin for that quarter.

Notice also that the First Quarter sheet tab is not entirely visible. This is because there is not enough space in the sheet tab area to display all the tabs. To see the tabs, you can drag the tab split bar located at the right edge of the sheet tab area to expand the area or use the sheet tab scroll buttons to scroll the tabs into view.

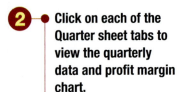

2 • Click on each of the Quarter sheet tabs to view the quarterly data and profit margin chart.

• Display the Proportion sheet.

Your screen should be similar to Figure 3.25

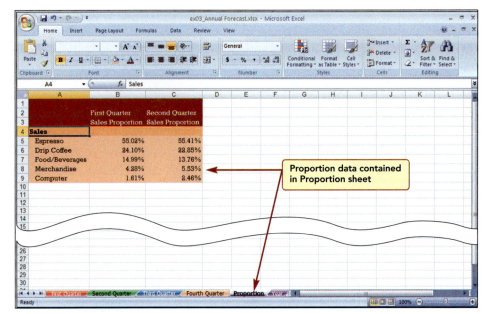

Proportion data contained in Proportion sheet

Figure 3.25

You decide this data, although interesting, is not needed in the forecast workbook and want to delete the entire sheet.

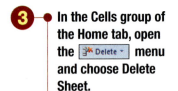

3 • In the Cells group of the Home tab, open the [Delete ▼] menu and choose Delete Sheet.

• Click [Delete] to confirm that you want to permanently remove the sheet.

Another Method
You also can choose Delete from the sheet tab's shortcut menu to delete a sheet.

Your screen should be similar to Figure 3.26

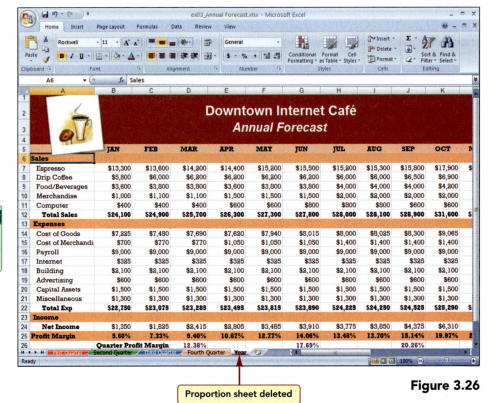

Proportion sheet deleted

Figure 3.26

Additional Information
You can insert a blank new sheet using [Insert ▼] and choosing Insert Sheet. It is inserted to the left of the active sheet.

The entire sheet is deleted, and the Year sheet is now the active sheet. Next you want to move the Year sheet from the last position in the workbook to the first. You can quickly rearrange the order of sheets in a workbook by dragging the selected sheet tab along the row of sheet tabs to the new location.

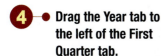

4 Drag the Year tab to the left of the First Quarter tab.

Your screen should be similar to Figure 3.27

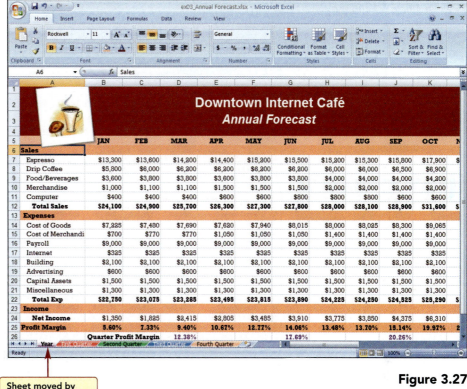

Sheet moved by dragging sheet tab

Figure 3.27

The Year sheet is now the first sheet in the workbook.

Finding and Replacing Information

As you look over the worksheets, you notice that the only abbreviation used in the entire workbook is for expenses in the Total Exp row heading. You want to change it to "Expenses" in all worksheets in the workbook.

You could change the word in each sheet by changing the text directly on the worksheet cells. However, the larger your workbook becomes, the more difficult it will be to find the data you want to modify. Therefore, you will use the Find and Replace feature to quickly locate the word and make the change.

Concept 5

Find and Replace

5 The **Find and Replace** feature helps you quickly find specific information and automatically replace it with new information. The Find command locates all occurrences of the text or numbers you specify. The Replace command is used with the Find command to locate the specified entries and replace the located occurrences with the replacement text you specify. You also can find cells that match a format you specify and replace the format with another. Finding and replacing data and formats is both fast and accurate, but you need to be careful when replacing that you do not replace unintended matches.

Finding Information

First, you will locate and correct the abbreviation using the Find command. This command can be used to locate data in any type of worksheet.

1 • Click  in the Editing group and choose Find.

• If necessary, click Options >> to display the additional search options.

Another Method

The keyboard shortcut is Ctrl + F.

Your screen should be similar to Figure 3.28

Figure 3.28

In the Find and Replace dialog box, you enter the information you want to locate in the Find What text box. It must be entered exactly as it appears in the worksheet. The additional options in the dialog box can be combined in many ways to help locate information. They are described in the table below.

Option	Effect
Within	Searches the active worksheet or workbook.
Search	Specifies the direction to search in the worksheet: By Columns searches down through columns and By Rows searches to the right across rows.
Look in	Looks for a match in the specified worksheet element: formulas, values, comments.
Match case	Finds words that have the same pattern of uppercase letters as entered in the Find What text box. Using this option makes the search case sensitive.
Match entire cell contents	Looks for an exact and complete match of the characters specified in the Find What text box.
Format	Used to specify a cell format to locate and replace. A sample of the selected format is displayed in the preview box.

You will enter the text to find, exp, and will search using the default options.

2 ● Type **exp** in the Find What box.

● Click [Options >>] to hide the additional search options.

● Click [Find Next].

Your screen should be similar to Figure 3.29

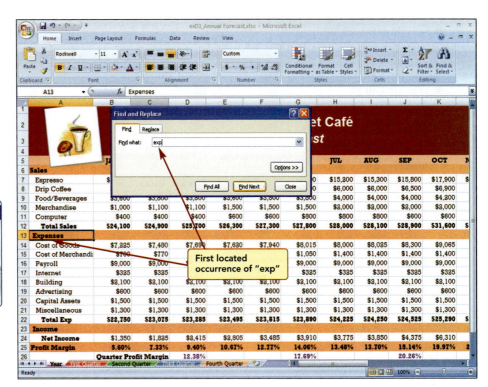

Figure 3.29

The cell selector jumps to the first occurrence of "exp," in cell A13, which contains the word "Expenses." It located this word because the first three letters match. However, this is not the entry you are trying to locate. You will continue the search to locate the next occurrence. Then you will edit the cell to display the word "Expenses."

3 ● Click [Find Next].

● **Double-click on the selected cell.**

● **Change Exp to Expenses.**

● **Click** ☑ **Enter or press** [←Enter].

Your screen should be similar to Figure 3.30

Located text changed

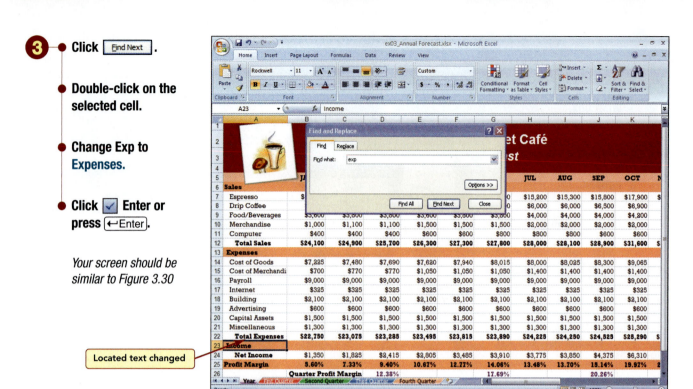

Figure 3.30

You manually made the correction to the label in cell A22. Next, you want to locate the word in all the other sheets and correct the entries.

Replacing Information

You realize that "exp" will be located twice in every worksheet. Since you want to change only the Total Exp headings, you will refine your search term to locate only this heading and use the Replace command to make the correction automatically on the other sheets. The replacement text must be entered exactly as you want it to appear.

First, you will select all four quarter sheets as a group so that any changes you make are made to all selected sheets. To select two or more adjacent sheets click on the tab for the first sheet and click on the last sheet tab while holding down [⇧ Shift]. You can select nonadjacent sheets by holding down [Ctrl] while clicking on each sheet. The title bar displays "[Group]" whenever multiple sheets are selected.

1 ● **Click on the First Quarter sheet tab, hold down** ⬆Shift**, and click on the Fourth Quarter tab.**

● **Change the entry in the Find What box to total exp.**

● **Open the Replace tab.**

● **Type Total Expenses in the Replace With box.**

● **Click** [Find Next]**.**

● **Click** [Replace All]**.**

 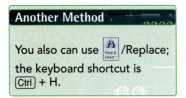
Your screen should be similar to Figure 3.31

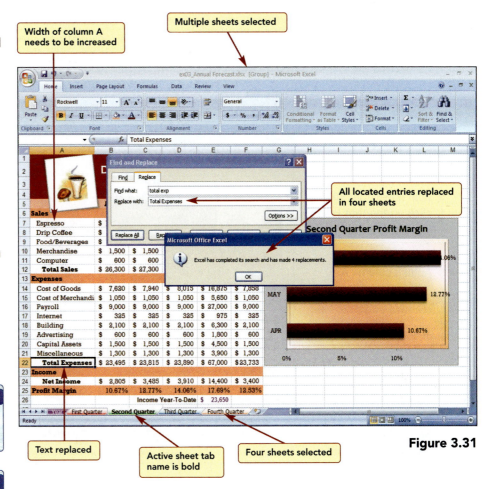

Multiple sheets selected

Width of column A needs to be increased

All located entries replaced in four sheets

Text replaced

Active sheet tab name is bold

Four sheets selected

Figure 3.31

Four replacements were made, indicating that the heading was corrected on all four sheets. It is much faster to use Replace All than to confirm each match separately. However, exercise care when using Replace All because the search text you specify might be part of another word and you may accidentally replace text you want to keep.

Now, you also notice that the labels in column A are not fully displayed, so you need to increase the column width. You will expand the group selection to include the Year sheet and adjust the width of column A on all worksheets at the same time.

2 ● Click **OK** .

● Click **Close** .

● Hold down [Ctrl] and click on the Year tab to add it to the group.

● AutoFit column A.

Having Trouble?
Double-click on the column border of column A when the mouse pointer is a ↔.

● Right-click on the Second Quarter tab and choose Ungroup Sheets to cancel the group selection and make it active.

Another Method
You also can click on any unselected sheet tab to cancel a group selection.

Your screen should be similar to Figure 3.32

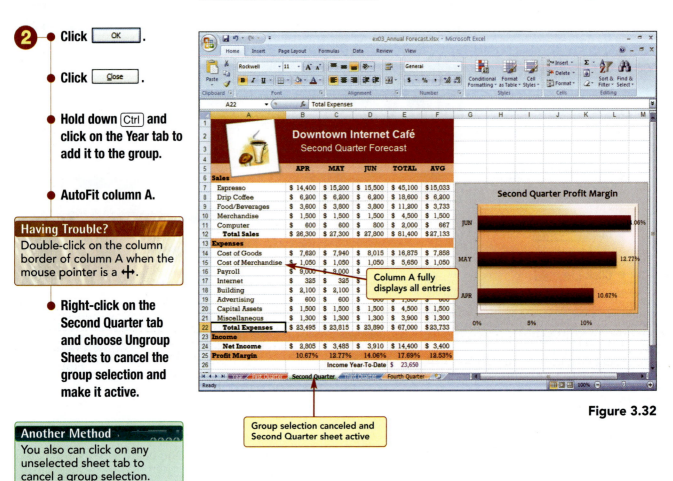

Column A fully displays all entries

Group selection canceled and Second Quarter sheet active

Figure 3.32

You can now see that the width of column A has been adjusted and that the Total Exp label has been replaced with Total Expenses, as it has in all other sheets. When multiple sheets are selected, be careful when making changes, as all selected sheets are affected.

Saving to a New Folder

You have made several changes to the workbook, and before continuing, you want to save it. Since the workbook is for projected forecasts, you decide to save it in a separate folder from the rest of the Café's financial workbooks. You will save the file to a new folder named Forecasts.

1 ● Display the Year sheet.

● Click 🔘 Office Button and choose Save As.

● If necessary, change the location to where you save your files.

● Enter Annual Forecast as the file name.

● Click 📁 Create New Folder in the Save As dialog box.

Additional Information

In Windows Vista, click New Folder.

Your screen should be similar to Figure 3.33

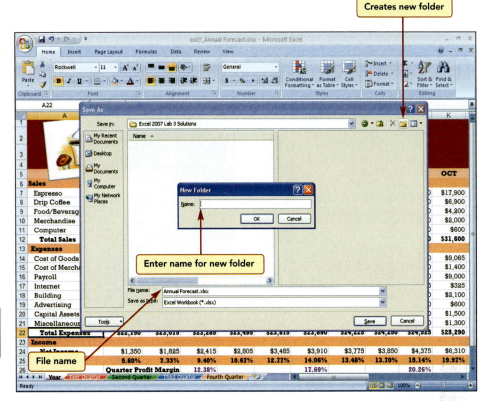

Figure 3.33

Additional Information

You also can rename an existing folder from the Save As dialog box by choosing Rename from the folder's shortcut menu and entering the new name.

The New Folder dialog box enables you to create and name a new folder.

2 ● Type Café Forecasts in the Name text box.

● Click [OK].

● Click [Save].

The Annual Forecast workbook is saved in the new Café Forecasts folder.

Managing Large Worksheets

Now that the Year worksheet is much larger, you are finding that it takes a lot of time to scroll to different areas within the worksheet. To make managing large worksheets easier, you can zoom a worksheet, split the workbook window, and freeze panes.

The Year worksheet displays all of the quarterly data. The entire worksheet, however, is not visible in the window.

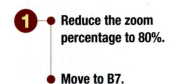

1 • **Reduce the zoom percentage to 80%.**

• **Move to B7.**

Another Method

You also can use 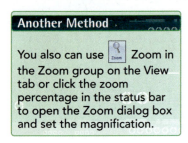 Zoom in the Zoom group on the View tab or click the zoom percentage in the status bar to open the Zoom dialog box and set the magnification.

Your screen should be similar to Figure 3.34

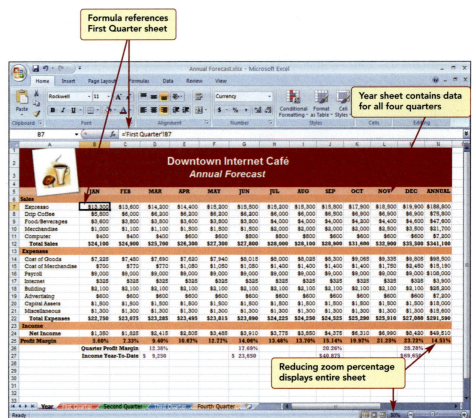

Figure 3.34

You can now see the entire worksheet. Most of the monthly values in the Year sheet, such as cell B7, contain linking formulas that reference the appropriate cells in the appropriate quarter sheets.

Going to a Specific Cell

The only formulas that do not reference cells outside the Year worksheet are those in the Annual column, N. Because you reduced the zoom, it is easy to see the values in column N and to move to a cell by clicking on the cell. However, when the worksheet is at 100 percent zoom, you would need to scroll the worksheet first. You will return the zoom to 100 percent and then use the Go To feature to quickly move to a cell that is not currently visible in the window.

1 ● **Return the zoom to 100%.**

● **Click in the Name box and type N16.**

● **Press** [←Enter].

Your screen should be similar to Figure 3.35

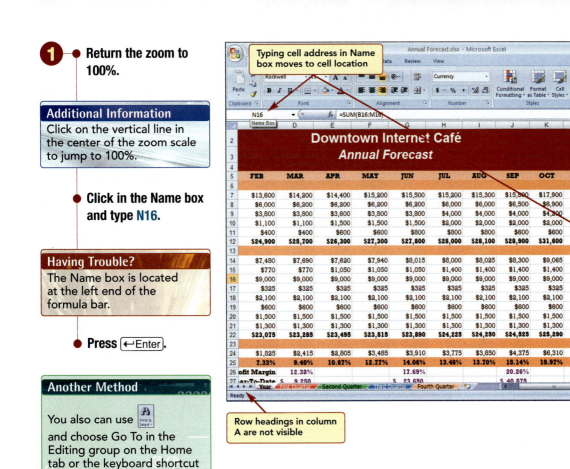

Figure 3.35

The cell selector jumps directly to cell N16 in the Annual column. The formula in this cell calculates the total of the values in row 16 and does not reference another sheet. However, it is difficult to know what the numbers represent in this row because the row headings are not visible. For example, is this number the total for the lease expenses, advertising expenses, or miscellaneous expenses? Without scrolling back to see the row headings, it is difficult to know.

Splitting Windows

Whenever you scroll a large worksheet, you will find that information you may need to view in one area scrolls out of view as you move to another area. Although you could reduce the zoom percent to view more of a worksheet in the window, you still may not be able to see the entire worksheet if it is very large. And as you saw, continuing to reduce the zoom makes the worksheet difficult to read. To view different areas of the same worksheet at the same time, you can split the window.

Concept 6

Split Window

6 The **split window** feature allows you to divide a worksheet window into sections, making it easier to view different parts of the worksheet at the same time. The sections of the window, called **panes**, can consist of any number of columns or rows along the top or left edge of the window. You can divide the worksheet into two panes either horizontally or vertically, or into four panes if you split the window both vertically and horizontally.

Each pane can be scrolled independently to display different areas of the worksheet. When split vertically, the panes scroll together when you scroll vertically, but scroll independently when you scroll horizontally. Horizontal panes scroll together when you scroll horizontally, but independently when you scroll vertically.

Panes are most useful for viewing a worksheet that consists of different areas or sections. Creating panes allows you to display the different sections of the worksheet in separate panes and then to quickly switch between panes to access the data in the different sections without having to repeatedly scroll to the areas.

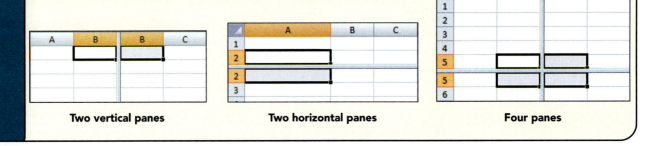

Two vertical panes   Two horizontal panes   Four panes

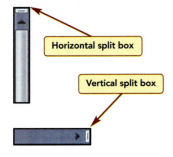

Horizontal split box

Vertical split box

Dragging the split box at the top of the vertical scroll bar downward creates a horizontal split, and dragging the split box at the right end of the horizontal scroll bar leftward creates a vertical split.

You will split the window into two vertical panes. This will allow you to view the headings in column A at the same time as you are viewing data in column N.

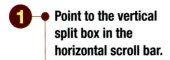

1 • Point to the vertical split box in the horizontal scroll bar.

• Drag the split box to the left and position the bar between columns D and E.

Your screen should be similar to Figure 3.36

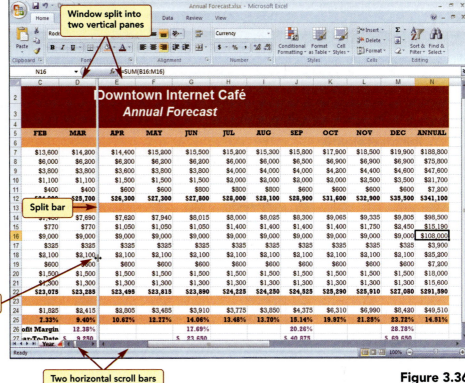

Figure 3.36

There are now two vertical panes with two separate horizontal scroll bars. The highlighted cell selector is visible in the right pane. The left pane also has a cell selector in cell N16, but it is not visible because that area of the worksheet is not displayed in the pane. When the same area of a worksheet is visible in multiple panes, the cell selector in the panes that are not active is highlighted whereas the cell selector in the active pane is clear. The active pane will be affected by your movement horizontally. The cell selector moves in both panes, but only the active pane scrolls.

You will scroll the left pane horizontally to display the month headings in column A.

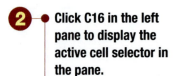

2 • Click C16 in the left pane to display the active cell selector in the pane.

• Press ← twice.

Your screen should be similar to Figure 3.37

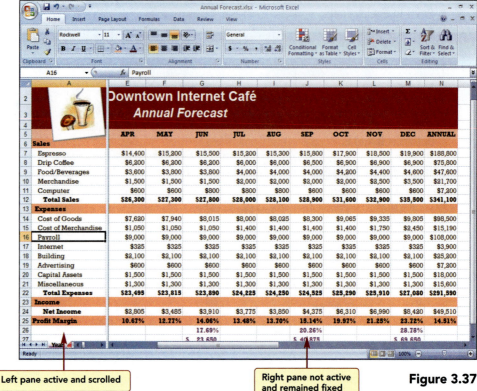

Left pane active and scrolled

Right pane not active and remained fixed

Figure 3.37

The right pane did not scroll when you moved horizontally through the left pane to display the row headings. The cell selector in the right pane is in the same cell location as in the left pane (A16), although it is not visible. You want to change the location of the split so that you can view an entire quarter in the left pane in order to more easily compare quarters.

3 • Drag the split bar to the right three columns.

• Click cell E16 in the right pane.

• Press [End] →.

• Press → (four times).

Your screen should be similar to Figure 3.38

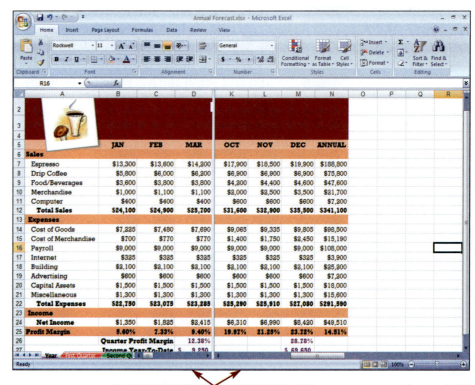

Split windows make comparing distant areas of a large worksheet easier

Figure 3.38

Now you can easily compare the first-quarter data to the last-quarter data. As you can see, creating panes is helpful when you want to display and access distant areas of a worksheet quickly. After scrolling the data in the panes to display the appropriate worksheet area, you can then quickly switch between panes to make changes to the data that is visible in the pane. This saves you the time of scrolling to the area each time you want to view it or make changes to it. You will clear the vertical split from the window.

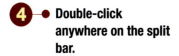

4 ● **Double-click anywhere on the split bar.**

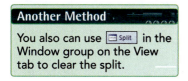

Another Method

You also can use [Split] in the Window group on the View tab to clear the split.

Your screen should be similar to Figure 3.39

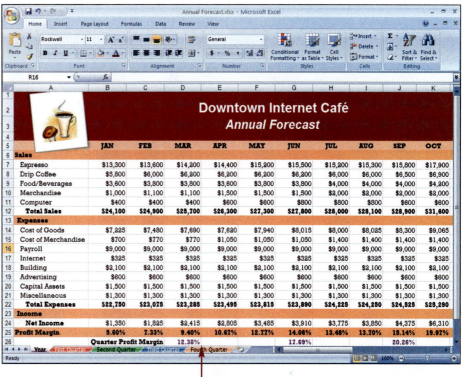

Double-clicking on split bar removes vertical split

Figure 3.39

Freezing Panes

Another way to manage a large worksheet is to freeze panes.

Concept 7

Freeze Panes

7 **Freezing panes** prevents the data in the pane from scrolling as you move to different areas in a worksheet. You can freeze the information in the top and left panes of a window only. This feature is most useful when your worksheet is organized using row and column headings. It allows you to keep the titles on the top and left edge of your worksheet in view as you scroll horizontally and vertically through the worksheet data.

You want to keep the month headings in row 5 and the row headings in column A visible in the window at all times while looking at the Income and Profit Margin data beginning in row 22. To do this, you will create four panes with the upper and left panes frozen.

When creating frozen panes, first position the worksheet in the window to display the information you want to appear in the top and left panes. This is because data in the frozen panes cannot be scrolled like data in regular panes. Then move to the location specified in the following table before using the ⊞ Freeze Panes ▾ command in the Window group on the View tab to create and freeze panes.

To Create	Cell Selector Location	Example
Two horizontal panes with the top pane frozen	Move to the leftmost column in the window and to the row below where you want the split to appear.	 **Top Pane Frozen**
Two vertical panes with the left pane frozen	Move to the top row of the window and to the column to the right of where you want the split to appear.	 **Left Pane Frozen**
Four panes with the top and left panes frozen	Move to the cell below and to the right of where you want the split to appear.	 **Top and Left Panes Frozen**

You want to split the window into four panes with the month column headings at the top of the window and the row headings in column A at the left side of the window.

1 ● Move to B6.

● Open the View tab.

● Click [Freeze Panes ▾] in the Window group and choose Freeze Panes.

Your screen should be similar to Figure 3.40

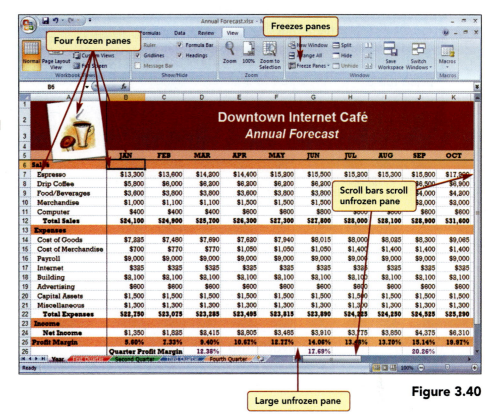

Four frozen panes

Freezes panes

Scroll bars scroll unfrozen pane

Large unfrozen pane

Figure 3.40

The window is divided into four panes at the cell selector location. Only one set of scroll bars is displayed because the only pane that can be scrolled is the larger lower-right pane. You can move the cell selector into a frozen pane, but the data in the frozen panes will not scroll. Also, there is only one cell selector that moves from one pane to another over the pane divider, making it unnecessary to click on the pane to make it active before moving the cell selector in it.

Because Evan has asked you to adjust the Profit Margin values, you want to view this area of the worksheet only.

2 • Use the vertical scroll bar to scroll the window until row 25 is below row 5.

• Move to cell G25.

Your screen should be similar to Figure 3.41

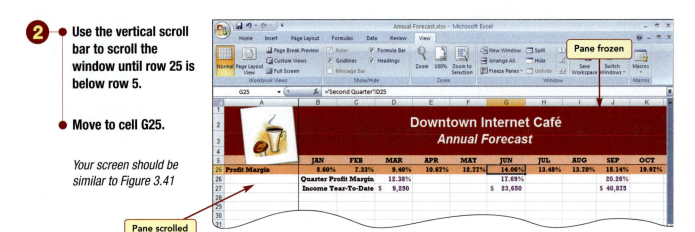

Figure 3.41

Now the Income and Profit Margin data are displayed immediately below the month headings in row 5. The data in rows 6 through 24 is no longer visible, allowing you to concentrate on this area of the worksheet.

Watching Cells

While using a workbook with large worksheets and/or multiple sheets, you may want to keep an eye on how changes you make to values in one area affect cells in another. For example, if you change a value in one sheet that is referenced in a formula in another, you can view the effect on the calculated value using the Watch Window toolbar.

You will be changing values in the Second Quarter sheet next and want to be able to see the effect on the second-quarter profit margin (G26) and Annual Profit Margin (N25) in the Year sheet at the same time.

1 • Select cells G26 and N25.

• Open the Formulas tab.

• Click [Watch Window] in the Formula Auditing group.

• If the Watch Window toolbar is docked along an edge of the window, drag it into the workbook window area.

• Click [Add Watch...] from the Watch Window toolbar.

Your screen should be similar to Figure 3.42

Figure 3.42

The Add Watch dialog box is used to specify the cells you want to see in the Watch Window toolbar. The currently selected cells are identified with a moving border. You will add these cells to the Watch Window.

2 • Click [Add].

• If necessary, move the Watch Window toolbar to the upper-right corner of the worksheet window below the column headings.

Your screen should be similar to Figure 3.43

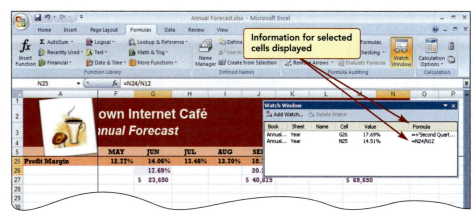

Figure 3.43

The values in the selected cells as well as the formula and location information are displayed in the Watch Window. The Watch Window toolbar will remain open on top of the worksheet as you move from one sheet to another.

Forecasting Values

Evan has asked you to adjust the forecast for the second quarter to show a profit margin of at least 15 percent for each month. After some consideration, you decide you can most easily reduce monthly payroll expenses by carefully scheduling the hours employees work during these three months. Reducing the monthly expense will increase the profit margin for the quarter. You want to find out what the maximum payroll value you can spend during that period is for each month to accomplish this goal. The process of evaluating what effect changing the payroll expenses will have on the profit margin is called what-if analysis.

Concept 8

What-If Analysis

8 | **What-if analysis** is a technique used to evaluate the effects of changing selected factors in a worksheet. This technique is a common accounting function that has been made much easier with the introduction of spreadsheet programs. By substituting different values in cells that are referenced by formulas, you can quickly see the effect of the changes when the formulas are recalculated.

You can perform what-if analysis by manually substituting values or by using one of the what-if analysis tools included with Excel.

Performing What-If Analysis Manually

To do this, you will enter different payroll expense values for each month and see what the effect is on that month's profit margin. You will adjust the April payroll value first.

Select the Second Quarter sheet.

Type 7000 in cell B16.

Press ←Enter.

Your screen should be similar to Figure 3.44

Reducing Payroll expenses increases Profit Margin

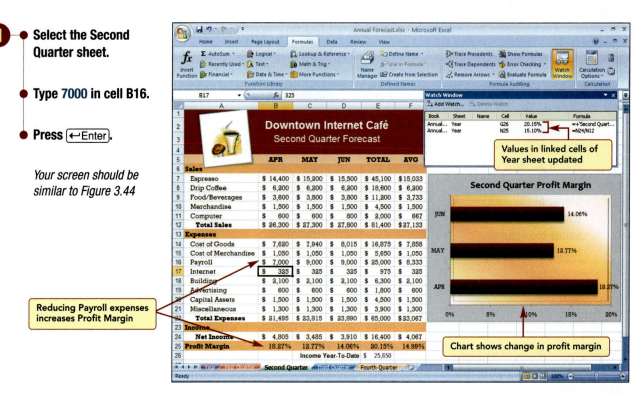

Values in linked cells of Year sheet updated

Chart shows change in profit margin

Figure 3.44

Now by looking in cell B25, you can see that decreasing the payroll expenses has increased the profit margin for the month to 18.27 percent. This is more than you need. Also notice the chart has changed to reflect the change in April's profit margin. The Watch Window shows that the values in the two linked cells in the Year sheet were updated accordingly.

You will continue to enter payroll values until the profit margin reaches the goal.

Type 7900 in cell B16.

Click ☑ Enter.

Type 7850 in cell B16.

Click ☑ Enter.

Type 7860 in cell B16.

Click ☑ Enter.

Save the workbook.

Your screen should be similar to Figure 3.45

Reducing April Payroll to 7860 achieved the 15% Profit Margin

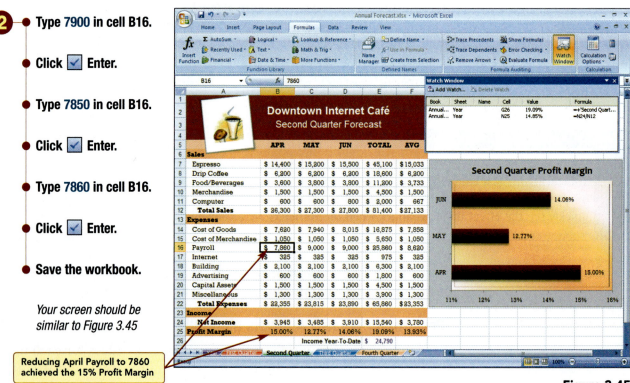

Figure 3.45

That's it! Reducing the payroll value from 9000 to 7860 will achieve the 15 percent profit margin goal for the month. Also notice that the column chart reflects the change in the April profit margin.

Using Goal Seek

It usually takes several tries to find the appropriate value when manually performing what-if analysis. A quicker way is to use the what-if analysis Goal Seek tool provided with Excel.

Concept 9

Goal Seek

9   The **Goal Seek** tool is used to find the value needed in one cell to attain a result you want in another cell. Goal Seek varies the value in the cell you specify until a formula that is dependent on that cell returns the desired result. The value of only one cell can be changed.

You will use this method to find the payroll value for May that will produce a 15 percent profit margin for that month. The current profit margin value is 12.77 percent in cell C25.

1 ● Move to C25.

● Open the Data tab.

● Click What-If Analysis in the Data Tools group.

● Choose Goal Seek.

Your screen should be similar to Figure 3.46

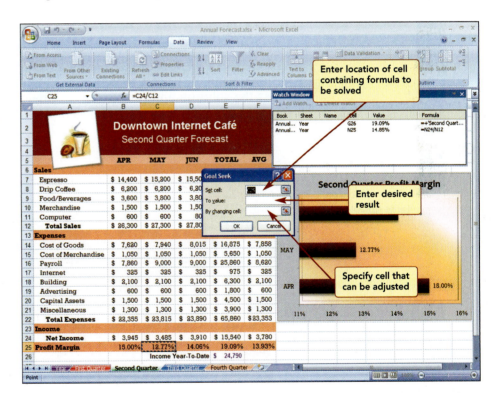

Figure 3.46

In the Goal Seek dialog box, you need to specify the location of the cell containing the formula to be solved, the desired calculated value, and the cell containing the number that can be adjusted to achieve the result. You want the formula in cell C25 to calculate a result of 15 percent by changing the payroll number in cell C16. The Set Cell text box correctly displays the current cell as the location of the formula to be solved. You will enter the information needed in the Goal Seek dialog box.

2 • Click in the To Value text box and enter **15.00%**.

• Click in the By Changing Cell text box and then click on cell C16 in the worksheet to enter the cell reference.

• Click [OK].

Your screen should be similar to Figure 3.47

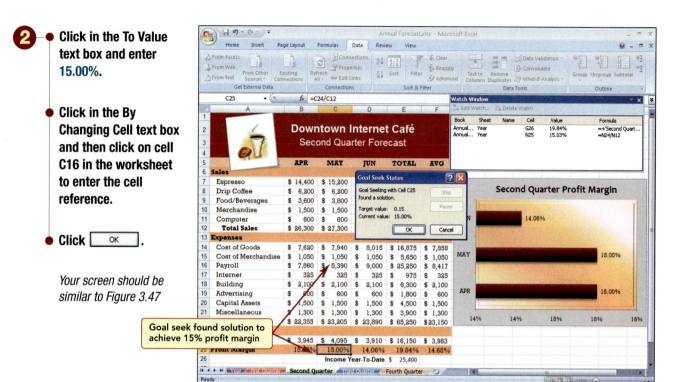

Goal seek found solution to achieve 15% profit margin

Figure 3.47

The Goal Seek dialog box tells you it found a solution that will achieve the 15 percent profit margin. The payroll value of 8390 that will achieve the desired result has been temporarily entered in the worksheet. You can reject the solution and restore the original value by choosing [Cancel]. In this case, however, you want to accept the solution.

3 • Click [OK].

Your screen should be similar to Figure 3.48

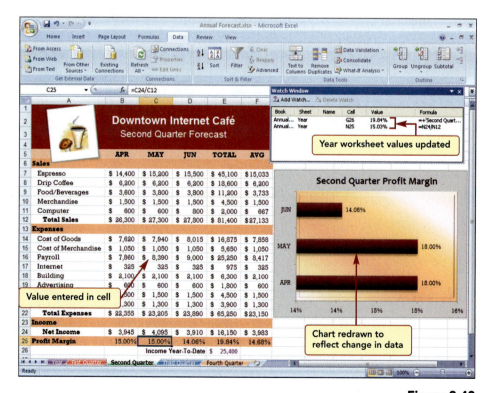

Year worksheet values updated

Value entered in cell

Chart redrawn to reflect change in data

Figure 3.48

The payroll value is permanently updated and the chart redrawn to reflect the change in the May profit margin. Finally, you will adjust the June payroll value. When you are finished, you will close the Watch Window and unfreeze the Year sheet window.

4

- **In a similar manner, use Goal Seek to adjust the June payroll value to achieve a 15% profit margin.**

- **Select both watch cell entries in the Watch Window and click** Delete Watch **.**

- **Click** × **Close to close the Watch Window.**

- **Make the Year sheet active to further verify that the profit margin values for the second quarter were updated.**

- **Open the View tab.**

- **Click** Freeze Panes **in the Window group and choose Unfreeze panes.**

- **Save the workbook file again.**

Your screen should be similar to Figure 3.49

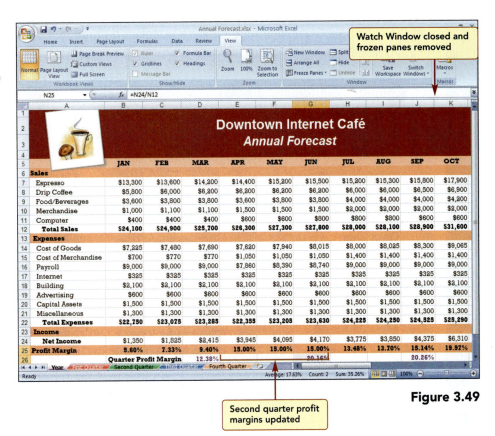

Figure 3.49

Second quarter profit margins updated

The second-quarter values are now at the 15 percent profit margin objective.

Using Conditional Formatting

Next, you want to highlight or emphasize certain values in the worksheet to help visualize the data and quickly analyze information in a worksheet. To do this, you can use conditional formatting.

10 **Conditional formatting** changes the appearance of a range of cells based on a condition that you specify. If the cells in the range meet the conditions (the condition is true), they are formatted. If they do not meet the conditions (the condition is false), they remain unformatted. There are several different ways you can apply conditional formatting as described in the following table.

Conditional Formatting	Description
Cell Rules	Highlights cells based on rules you specify, such as greater than or less than, between, or equal to. It also can highlight cells that contain certain text, dates, and duplicate values.
Top/Bottom Rules	Highlights the highest and lowest values in a range by number, percent, or average based on a cutoff value that you specify.
Data Bars	Displays a color bar in a cell to help you see the value of a cell relative to other cells. The length of the bar represents the value in the cell. A longer bar is a higher value and a shorter bar, a lower value.
Color Scales	Applies a two- or three-color graduated scale to compare values in a range. A two-color scale uses two different colors to represent high or low values and a three-color scale uses three colors to represent high, mid, and low values.
Icon Sets	Displays different color icons in the cell to classify data into three to five categories. Each icon represents a range of values.

Creating Cell Rules

You will use the cell rules conditional formatting to highlight the payroll values that are less than 9,000 a month and profit margin values equal to 15.00%.

1 • Select cells B16 through M16.

• Open the Home tab.

• Click 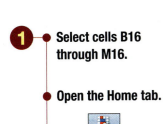 in the Styles group.

• Select Highlight Cells Rules.

• Choose Less Than.

Your screen should be similar to Figure 3.50

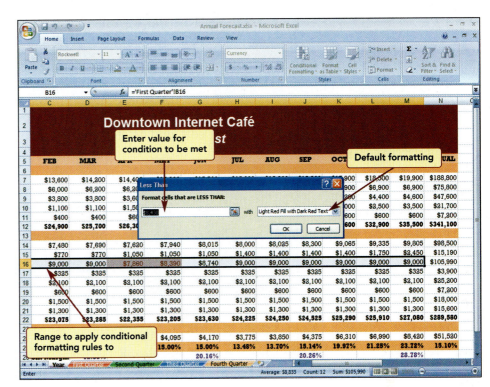

Figure 3.50

In the Less Than dialog box, you enter the value that will be used to determine which cells to highlight. In this case, you will enter the value 9000 so that all values below this amount in the selected range will be highlighted. It also lets you select the formatting to apply to those cells meeting the condition. The default formatting, a light red fill with dark red text, is acceptable.

2 • Type **9000** in the Less Than box.

• Click OK.

• Click cell H16 to clear the selection.

Your screen should be similar to Figure 3.51

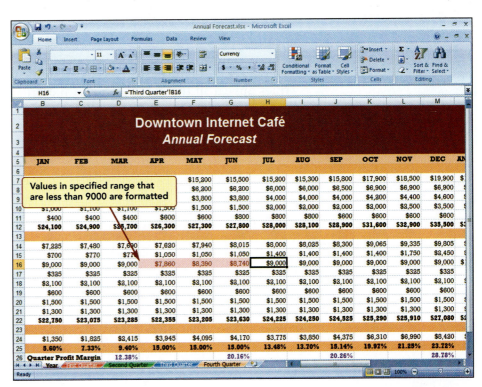

Figure 3.51

Only those cells in the Payroll row whose value is less than 9,000 are formatted using the light-red highlight and dark-red font color.

Using Rules Manager

Next you will use the Rules Manager to add a cell rule to highlight the profit margin values that are equal to 15 percent. The Rules Manager is used to create, edit, and delete conditional formatting rules in a worksheet.

1 ● **Click**  **and choose Manage Rules.**

Your screen should be similar to Figure 3.52

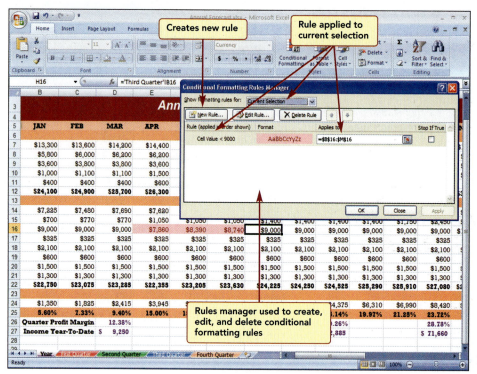

Figure 3.52

MORE ABOUT

▶ To learn how to allow more than one rule to be true, see 4.3 Apply Conditional Formatting in the More About appendix.

The cell rule you just created is listed in the dialog box. The order in which rules appear in the list determines the order in which they are applied in the worksheet. New rules are always added to the top of the list and take precedence over any rules that are below it. You will create a new rule to highlight the 15 percent profit margin values.

② **Click**  .

● **Choose Format only cells that contain from the Select a Rule Type list.**

Your screen should be similar to Figure 3.53

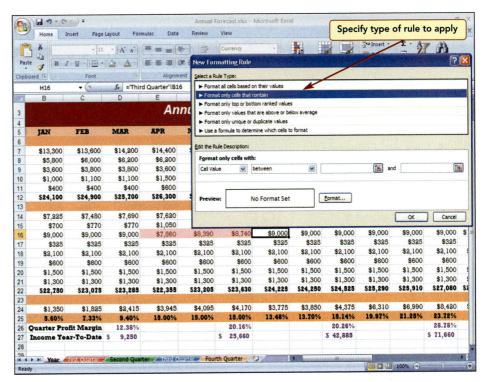

Figure 3.53

In the Edit the Rule Description area of the dialog box, you specify the type of rule to use and the condition value. You can enter a value or select it from the worksheet.

③ ● **Choose Equal To from the condition type list box.**

● **Type 15.00% in the value area.**

● **Click** Format... **and select the Turquoise, Accent 1 font color.**

● **Click** OK .

Your screen should be similar to Figure 3.54

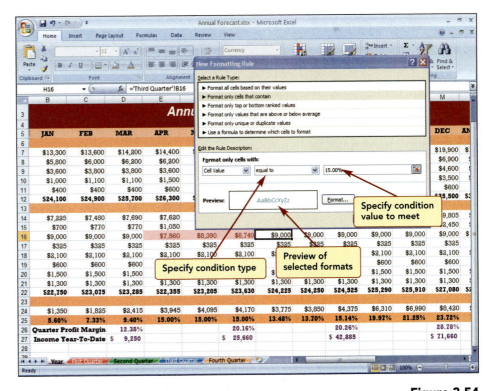

Figure 3.54

When the rule conditions are met, these cells will be formatted in blue font color. The last item you need to specify is the range.

4 ● Click [OK].

● Click  Collapse Dialog in the Applies to box to temporarily hide the dialog box and allow you to select the range.

● Select B25:N25.

● Click 📄 Expand Dialog to display the dialog box again.

● Click [Apply].

● Choose This Worksheet from the Show formatting rules drop-down list to display all the formatting rules in the worksheet.

Your screen should be similar to Figure 3.55

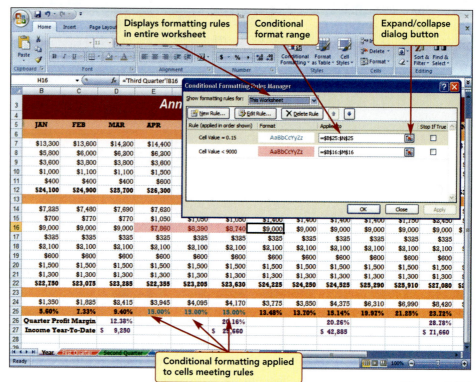

Figure 3.55

Additional Information
You can remove a rule by selecting it and clicking
✕ Delete Rule .

Only those cells whose profit margin value is exactly 15 percent are formatted in blue. You decide it would be more informational to highlight all months that have a profit margin of 15 percent or greater. To do this, you can edit the rule.

5 ● Select the first cell rule in the list (Cell Value = 0.15) and click [Edit Rule...] .

● Change the rule type to Greater than or equal to.

● Click [OK] and click [Apply] .

Your screen should be similar to Figure 3.56

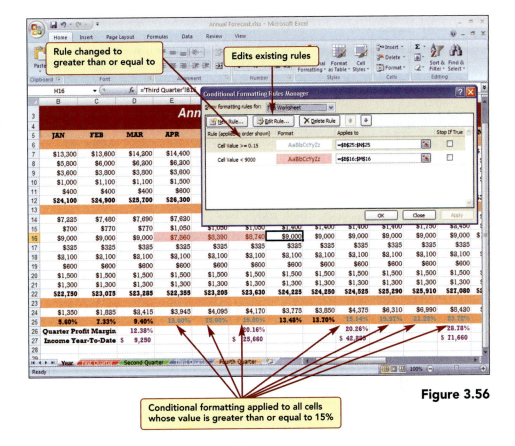

Conditional formatting applied to all cells whose value is greater than or equal to 15%

Figure 3.56

Now all profit margin values that are 15 percent or greater are formatted.

MORE ABOUT

► To learn how to add top and bottom rules, color scales, and icon set conditional formatting, see 4.3 Apply Conditional Formatting in the More About appendix.

Creating Data Bars

The next area you want to emphasize is the income year-to-date values. For this, you will apply the data bars conditional formatting. This option displays colored bars similar to a bar chart within each cell to show the relative values of the cell.

1 Click [Close] to close the dialog box.

● Select D27 through M27.

● Click .

● Select Data Bars and point to the different data bar colors to see the live preview.

● Choose the Light Blue Data Bar color.

Your screen should be similar to Figure 3.57

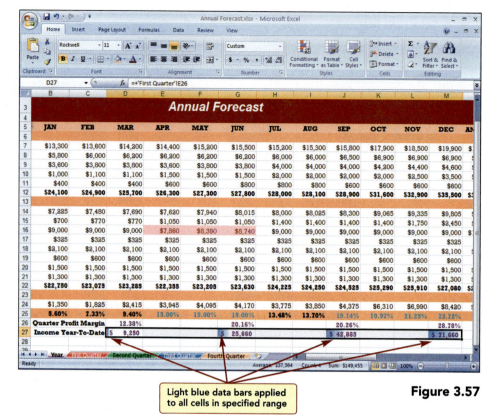

Light blue data bars applied to all cells in specified range

Figure 3.57

Color bars appear in each cell containing a number. The size of the number determines the length of the bar; the larger the value, the longer the bar. Because you do not feel this adds much to the worksheet, you will delete the rule.

2 ● Click [Conditional Formatting] and select Clear Rules.

● Choose Clear Rules from Selected Cells.

● Clear the selection and save the workbook.

Your screen should be similar to Figure 3.58

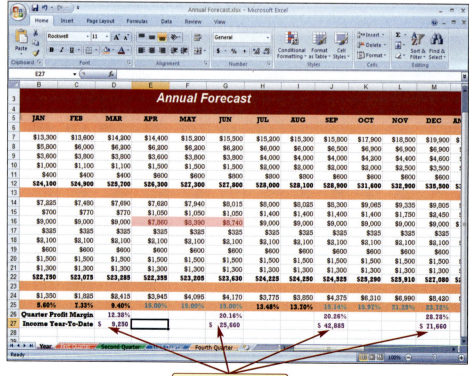

Data bars rule deleted and data bars removed

Figure 3.58

The data bar formatting is removed and the rule is deleted.

Customizing Print Settings

Now you are ready to print the workbook. Just because your worksheet looks great on the screen, this does not mean it will look good when printed. Many times you will want to change the default print and layout settings to improve the appearance of the output. Customizing the print settings by controlling page breaks, changing the orientation of the page, centering the worksheet on the page, hiding gridlines, and adding custom header and footer information are just a few of the ways you can make your printed output look more professional.

Controlling Page Breaks

First you want to preview the Year sheet.

1 • **Display the Year sheet in Print Preview.**

• **Click** Next Page .

Your screen should be similar to Figure 3.59

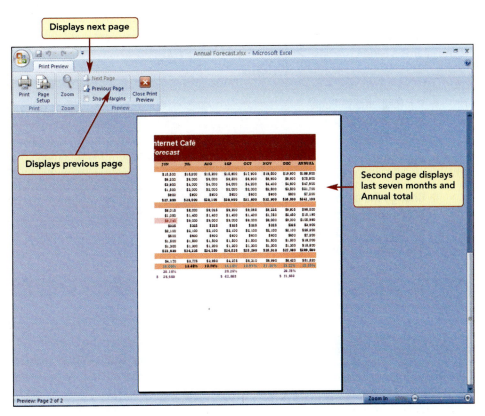

Figure 3.59

The first page of the Year worksheet displays the first five months, and the second page, the remaining months and the annual total. Although you could change the orientation to landscape and use the Fit To feature to compress the worksheet to a single page, this would make the data small and difficult to read. Instead, you decide to leave the printout as two pages, but you want the second six months to appear on the second page.

To do this, you will change the location of the **page break,** the place where one printed page ends and another starts. Excel inserts automatic page breaks based on the paper size, margin settings, and orientation when the worksheet exceeds the width of a page. You can change the location of the automatic page break by inserting a manual page break location. To help you do this, Page Break Preview is used to adjust the location of page breaks.

2 ● **Close Print Preview.**

● **Open the View tab.**

● **Click** [Page Break Preview] **in the Workbook Views group.**

Another Method

You also could click in the status bar to change to Page Break Preview.

● **If a Welcome to Page Break Preview box appears, click** OK **.**

● **Change the zoom to 80% and scroll the window horizontally to see the entire sheet.**

Your screen should be similar to Figure 3.60

Additional Information

You can work in Page Break Preview just like in Normal view.

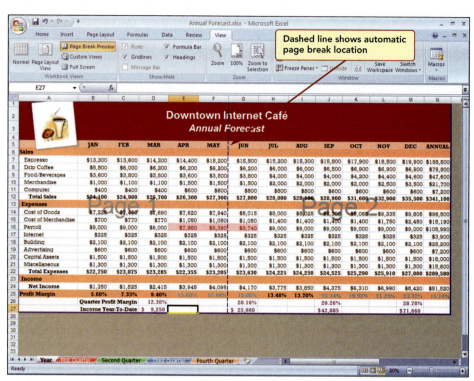

Figure 3.60

Now you can easily see the page break location. The dashed line indicates the location of the automatic page break. You can change the location by dragging the page break line. When you move an automatic page break location to another location, the page break line changes to a solid line, indicating it is a manual page break. Additionally, you realize that even when you move the page break location to column H, the worksheet title will be split between the two pages. You will fix this by unmerging the cells and moving the title to the left on page 1 and copying the title to page 2.

3 ● Point to the page break line and when the mouse pointer is ←→, drag the line to the right between columns G and H.

Another Method

You also can insert page breaks by moving to the column location in the worksheet where you want the break inserted and using 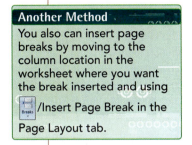/Insert Page Break in the Page Layout tab.

● Select the two merged cells.

● Open the Home tab.

● Open the Merge and Center drop-down menu and choose Unmerge Cells.

● Copy the contents of D2:D3 to K2:K3.

● Press [Esc] to clear the selection and move to cell K4.

Your screen should be similar to Figure 3.61

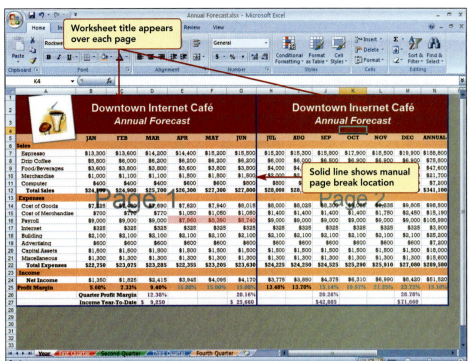

Figure 3.61

Unmerging the cells split the merged cell into its original cells and moved the contents into the upper-left cell of the range of split cells. The center formatting was not removed.

Adding a Custom Header and Footer

You also would like to add a custom header to this sheet. You will do this in Page Layout view because you can add the header simply by clicking on the header area of the page and typing the header text.

Additional Information

You also can add a custom footer by clicking in the footer area of the page.

1 • **Switch to Page Layout view at 70% zoom.**

• **Click on the left end of the header area of page 1.**

Your screen should be similar to Figure 3.62

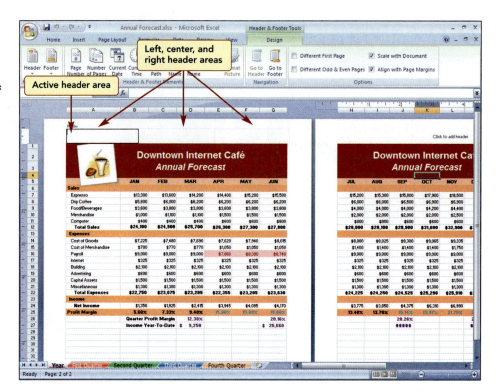

Figure 3.62

The header area is divided into three sections. The left section text box will display the text you enter aligned with the left margin; the center section will center the text; and the right section will right-align the text. You want to enter your name in the left section, class in the center, and the date in the right section. You will enter your name and class information by typing it directly in the box. You will enter the current date using the Current Date feature on the Header & Footer Tools Design tab.

2 — Type **Created by your name.**

● Press Tab.

Another Method

You also could click on the section to move to it.

● Enter the name of your class and the section or time.

● Press Tab.

● Click [Current Date] in the **Header & Footer Elements** group.

Your screen should be similar to Figure 3.63

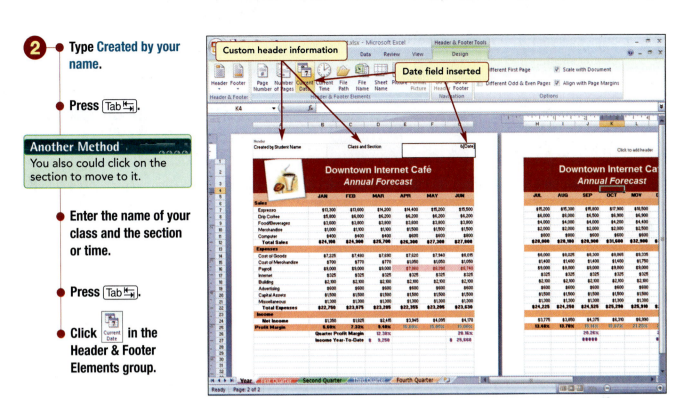

Figure 3.63

Additional Information

Custom headers and footers also can be added using the Header/Footer tab of the Page Setup dialog box.

Additional Information

Be careful when making changes to multiple sheets as these changes may replace data on other sheets.

The Date field is entered in the header. It will enter the current date whenever the worksheet is opened. The actual date will display when you leave the header area.

Next, you want to add footers to the quarter sheets. It is faster to add the footer to all sheets at the same time. If you make changes to the active sheet when multiple sheets are selected, the changes are made to all other selected sheets.

3 Display the First Quarter sheet.

● Select the four quarter sheets.

● Open the Page Layout tab.

● Open the Page Setup dialog box.

● Open the Header/Footer tab.

● Click ⌈ C̲ustom Footer... ⌉ .

Additional Information

The quarter sheets are displayed in Normal view. The view you are using applies only to the individual sheet.

Your screen should be similar to Figure 3.64

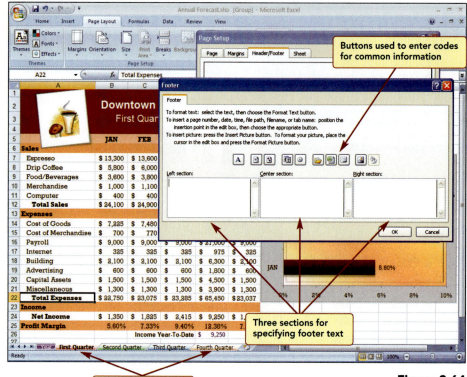

Buttons used to enter codes for common information

Three sections for specifying footer text

Four sheets selected

Figure 3.64

Just like in Page Layout view, the footer area consists of three sections. The buttons above the section boxes are used to enter the codes for common header and footer information. The insertion point is currently positioned in the Left Section text box.

You will enter your name in the left section, the file name in the middle section, and the date in the right section.

4 ● **Type your name.**

● **Press** Tab ⇆.

● **Click** 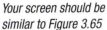 **Insert File Name.**

● **Press** Tab ⇆.

● **Click** 🔲 **Insert Date.**

Your screen should be similar to Figure 3.65

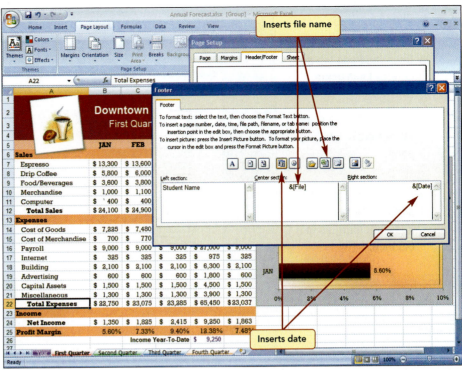

Figure 3.65

Next you will change the orientation of the four sheets to landscape, change the margins to 0.5 inch, and scale the sheets to fit the page. Then you want to make one final check to see how the worksheets will look before printing the workbook.

5 • Click [OK] .

• Open the Page tab and choose Landscape.

• Choose Fit to, to scale the sheets to one page.

• Open the Margins tab and reduce the left and right margins to 0.5 inch.

Having Trouble?
Use the scroll buttons to increase or decrease the margin size.

• Click [Print Preview] .

• Look at the four sheets to confirm that the footer and orientation changes were added to them as well.

Your screen should be similar to Figure 3.66

Additional Information
You also could drag the right or left border of the margin area in the ruler while in Page Layout view to adjust the size of the margins.

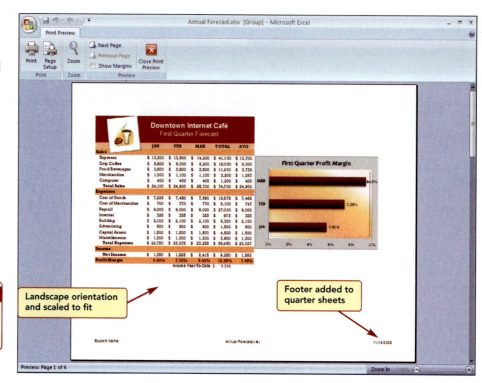

Figure 3.66

The footer as you entered it appears on all selected worksheets and the page layout changes were made as well.

Printing Selected Sheets

You want to print the Year and Second Quarter worksheets only. Because the Annual worksheet is large, you also feel the worksheet may be easier to read if the row and column gridlines were printed. Although gridlines are displayed in Page Layout View and Normal view, they do not print unless you turn on this feature.

1 ● Close the Print Preview window.

● Right-click on a sheet tab and choose Ungroup Sheets.

● Make the Year sheet active.

● Select Print in the Gridlines section of the Sheet Options group in the Page Layout tab.

Another Method
You also can print gridlines by choosing Gridlines from the Page Setup dialog box.

Additional Information
The gridlines appear slightly darker when they are set to print.

● Save the workbook again.

● Hold down [Ctrl] and click the Second Quarter sheet tab to add it to the selection of sheets to print.

● Preview and then print the worksheets.

Having Trouble?
If you do not need to specify print settings that are different from the default settings on your system, use Office Button and choose Quick Print to print the worksheet.

Your printed output should look like that shown in the Case Study at the beginning of the lab.

Printing Selected Areas

You are finished printing the Year and Second Quarter sheets and you have the information Evan requested. However, you think Evan also would like a printout of the First Quarter worksheet without the chart displayed. To print a selected area, you first select the cell range that you want to print.

1 ● Select the First Quarter sheet.

● Select cells A1 through F25.

● Click  in the Page Setup group and choose Set Print Area.

Your screen should be similar to Figure 3.67

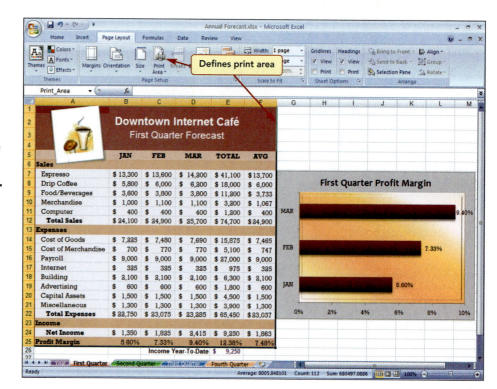

Figure 3.67

The area you selected, called the **print area**, is surrounded with a heavy line that identifies the area.

2 ● Display the Print Preview window.

Your screen should be similar to Figure 3.68

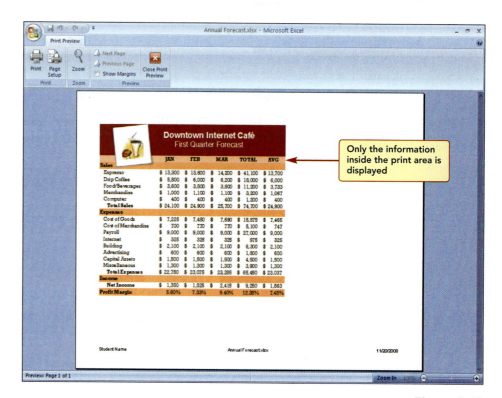

Figure 3.68

Lab 3: Managing and Analyzing a Workbook

The Print Preview window displays only the information contained in the defined print area. The print area is saved with the worksheet and will be used automatically whenever you print the worksheet. It can be cleared using Clear Print Area in the ▣ menu.

3 ● Click ▣ **Print** .

● Specify any print settings and click [OK] .

● Close and save the workbook and exit Excel.

Focus on Careers

EXPLORE YOUR CAREER OPTIONS

Medical Sales Accountant

Medical sales accountants visit doctors and clinics to promote the pharmaceuticals and supplies made by the company they represent. The accountants usually specialize in a few pharmaceuticals or products so that they can help the doctor understand the benefits and risks associated with their products. Medical sales accountants must keep careful and complete records of the samples they have in inventory and what they have delivered to doctors. An Excel workbook is a useful tool to keep track of the many doctors and deliveries made. A career as a medical sales accountant can start with a salary of $35,000 and go up to over $90,000 plus car and travel benefits.

Absolute Reference (EX3.13)

An absolute reference is a cell or range reference in a formula whose location does not change when the formula is copied.

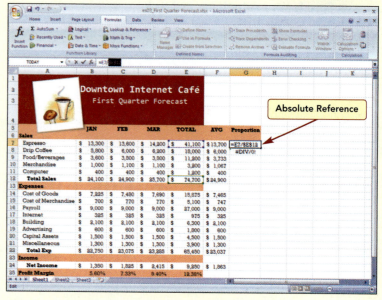

Sheet Name (EX3.18)

Each sheet in a workbook can be assigned a descriptive sheet name to help identify the contents of the sheet.

AutoFill (EX3.20)

The AutoFill feature makes entering a series of headings easier by logically repeating and extending the series. AutoFill recognizes trends and automatically extends data and alphanumeric headings as far as you specify.

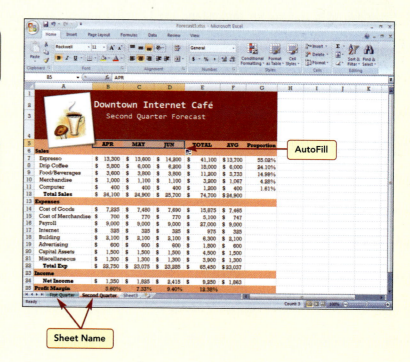

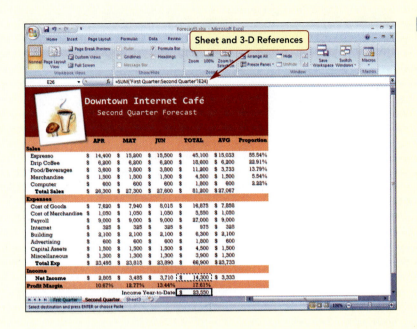

Sheet and 3-D References (EX3.23)

A formula that contains references to cells in other sheets of a workbook allows you to use data from multiple sheets and to calculate new values based on this data. The formula contains a sheet reference consisting of the name of the sheet, followed by an exclamation point and the cell or range reference.

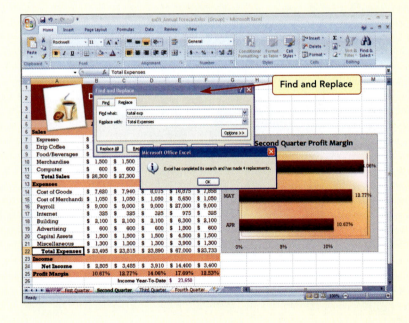

Find and Replace (EX3.29)

The Find and Replace feature helps you quickly find specific information and automatically replace it with new information.

Concept Summary

Split Window   (EX3.38)

The split window feature allows you to divide a worksheet window into sections, making it easier to view different parts of the worksheet at the same time.

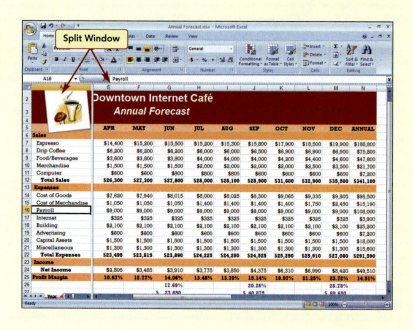

Freeze Panes   (EX3.41)

Freezing panes prevents the data in the pane from scrolling as you move to different areas in a worksheet.

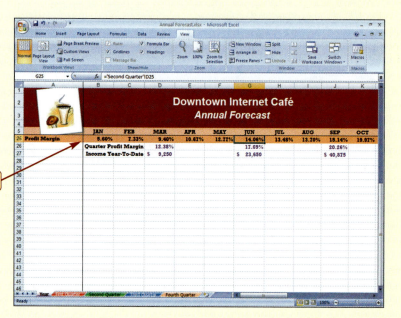

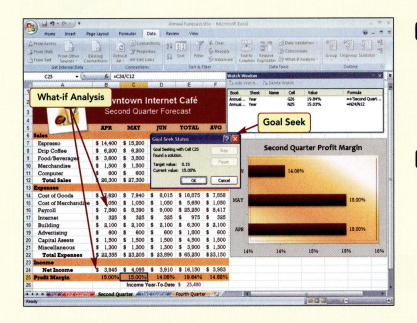

What-If Analysis (EX3.45)

What-if analysis is a technique used to evaluate the effects of changing selected factors in a worksheet.

Goal Seek   (EX3.47)

The Goal Seek tool is used to find the value needed in one cell to attain a result you want in another cell.

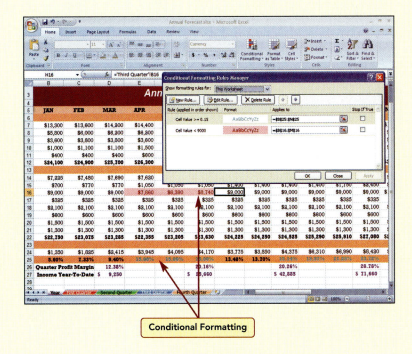

Conditional Formatting   (EX3.50)

Conditional formatting changes the appearance of a range of cells based on a condition that you specify.

Lab Review

LAB 3
Managing and Analyzing a Workbook

key terms

3-D reference EX3.23	**freeze panes** EX3.41	**print area** EX3.66
absolute reference EX3.13	**Goal Seek** EX3.47	**sheet name** EX3.18
AutoFill EX3.20	**mixed reference** EX3.13	**sheet reference** EX3.23
conditional formatting EX3.50	**page break** EX3.57	**split window** EX3.38
Find and Replace EX3.29	**pane** EX3.38	**what-if analysis** EX3.45

MCAS skills

The Microsoft Certified Applications Specialist (MCAS) certification program is designed to measure your proficiency in performing basic tasks using the Office 2007 applications. Getting certified demonstrates that you have the skills and provides a valuable industry credential for employment. See Reference 2 MCAS Certification Guide for a complete list of the skills that were covered in Lab 3.

command summary

Command	Shortcut	Action
File menu		
Print/Quick Print		Prints document using the default printer settings
Home tab		
Styles group		
Conditional Formatting /Highlight Cells Rules		Applies Data Bars, Color Scales, and Icons Sets to selected cells based on criteria
Conditional Formatting /Manage Rules		Opens Rules Manager to create, edit, and delete cell rules
Cells group		
Delete /Delete Sheet		Deletes entire sheet
Format /Rename Sheet		Renames sheet
Format /Move or Copy Sheet		Moves or copies selected sheet
Format /Tab Color		Changes color of sheet tabs
Editing group		
Find & Select /Find	Ctrl + F	Locates specified text, numbers, and/or formats
Find & Select /Replace	Ctrl + H	Locates specified characters or formats and replaces them with specified replacement characters or format
Find & Select /Go To	Ctrl + G	Goes to a specified cell location in worksheet

Lab Review

command summary

Command	Shortcut	Action
Page Layout tab		
Page Setup group		
Margins /Narrow		Changes margin settings
Margins /Custom Margins/Horizontally		Centers worksheet horizontally on page
Margins /Custom Margins/Vertically		Centers worksheet vertically on page
Print Area /Set Print Area		Sets print area to selected cells
Breaks /Insert Page Break		Inserts page break at cell pointer location
Breaks /Remove Page Break		Removes page break at cell pointer location
Breaks /Reset all Page Breaks		Restores automatic page breaks
Scale to Fit group		
Height: /1 page		Scales worksheet vertically to fit one page
Sheet Options group		
Print Gridlines		Displays/hides gridlines for printing
Formulas tab		
Function Library group		
Σ AutoSum		Enters Sum, Average, Minimum, Maximum, or Count function
Formula Auditing group		
Error Checking		Checks worksheet for formula errors
Watch Window		Opens Watch Window toolbar
Data tab		
Data Tools group		
What-If Analysis /Goal Seek		Adjusts value in specified cell until a formula dependent on that cell reaches specified result

command summary

Command	Shortcut	Action
View tab		
Workbook Views group		
Normal		Changes worksheet view to Normal
Page Layout		Displays worksheet as it will appear when printed
Page Break Preview		Displays where pages will break when a worksheet is printed
Show/Hide group		
☑ Gridlines		Turns on/off display of gridlines
☑ Headings		Turns on/off display of row and column headings
Zoom group		
Zoom		Changes magnification of window
Window group		
Freeze Panes ▾ /Freeze Panes		Freezes top and/or leftmost panes
Freeze Panes ▾ /Unfreeze Panes		Unfreezes window panes
Split		Divides window into four panes at active cell or removes split

Lab Exercises

matching

Match the lettered item on the right with the numbered item on the left.

1. 'Second Quarter'!A13   _____   **a.** applies formatting based on cell rules
2. Goal Seek   _____   **b.** 3-D reference
3. Sheet1:Sheet3!H3:K5   _____   **c.** sheet reference
4. freezing panes   _____   **d.** the sections of a divided window
5. conditional formatting   _____   **e.** mixed cell reference
6. panes   _____   **f.** pane that contains the cell selector
7. active pane   _____   **g.** prevents data in pane from scrolling
8. $M$34   _____   **h.** a what-if analysis tool
9. $B12   _____   **i.** absolute cell reference
10. #DIV/0!   _____   **j.** indicates division by zero error

true/false

Circle the correct answer to the following questions.

1. Dragging the sizing handle activates the AutoFill feature and recognizes the cell entry as one that can be incremented. True False

2. If you hold down Ctrl while you drag the fill handle, the entries will not be incremented. True False

3. You can freeze the information in the top and right panes of a window only. True False

4. The sheet reference consists of the name of the sheet separated from the cell reference by a question mark. True False

5. =SUM(Sheet15:Sheet50!H6) averages the values in cell H6 of sheets 15 and 50. True False

6. To create two horizontal panes with the left pane frozen, move the cell selector in the top row of the window and select the column to the right of where you want the split to appear. True False

7. Color bars apply a two- or three-color graduated scale to compare values in a range. True False

8. $G8 is an absolute reference. True False

9. What-if analysis varies the value in the cell you specify until a formula
   that is dependent on that cell returns the desired result.   True   False

10. A relative reference is a cell or range reference in a formula whose
    location does not change when the formula is copied.   True   False

fill-in

Complete the following statements by filling in the blanks with the correct key terms.

1. A $ character in front of either the column or the row reference in a formula creates a(n)
   _____ reference.

2. A(n) _____ reference is created when the reference is to the same cell or range on multiple
   sheets in the same workbook.

3. _____ formatting changes the appearance of a range of cells based on a set of conditions
   you specify.

4. When specified rows and columns are _____, they are fixed when you scroll.

5. A worksheet window can be divided into _____, either horizontal or vertical, through
   which different areas of the worksheet can be viewed at the same time.

6. The _____ feature logically repeats and extends a series.

7. The _____ is used to create, edit, and delete cell rules.

8. _____ consist of the name of the sheet enclosed in quotes, and are separated from the cell
   reference by an exclamation point.

9. The _____ tool is used to find the value needed in one cell to attain a result you want in
   another cell.

10. A technique used to evaluate what effect changing one or more values in formulas has on other
    values in the worksheet is called _____.

multiple choice

Circle the correct response to the questions below.

1. The number 32534 displayed with the Currency style would appear as _____ in a cell.
   a. $32534
   b. 32,534
   c. $32,534
   d. $32,534.00

2. The _____ function key will change a selected cell reference to absolute.
   a. F4
   b. F7
   c. F3
   d. F10

3. The _____ error value indicates that the wrong type of argument or operand was used.
   a. #####
   b. #DIV/0
   c. #N/A
   d. #VALUE!

4. The cell reference to adjust row 8 without adjusting column E is
   a. E8
   b. $E$8
   c. $E8
   d. E$8

5. Which of the following is NOT a valid sheet name?
   a. Second Quarter
   b. Qtr 1
   c. 3/12/04
   d. Week 8 - 10

6. The _____ feature enters a series of headings by logically repeating and extending the series.
   a. ExtendSelect
   b. AutoFill
   c. AutoRepeat
   d. ExtendFill

7. The information in the worksheet can be _____ in the top and left panes of a window only.
   a. fixed
   b. frozen
   c. aligned
   d. adjusted

8. A division of the worksheet window that allows different areas of the worksheet to be viewed at the same time is called a
   a. part
   b. pane
   c. window
   d. section

9. A cell address that is part absolute and part relative is a(n) _____
   a. absolute reference
   b. frozen cell
   c. mixed reference
   d. relative reference

10. _____ is used to evaluate the effects of changing selected factors in a worksheet.
    a. Value analysis
    b. AutoCalculate
    c. What-if analysis
    d. AutoFill

Hands-On Exercises

step-by-step

Juice Bar Sales Forecast ★

1. Marjon Brady owns seven Juice Bar franchises. She has created a worksheet to record each store's first-quarter sales. Now she would like to create a second worksheet in the workbook to record the projected second-quarter sales for each store. The completed worksheets should be similar to those shown here.

a. Open the workbook ex03_Juice Bar.

b. Calculate the total sales for each location and for each month. Adjust column widths as needed.

c. Copy the worksheet data from Sheet1 to Sheet2 and maintain the column width settings. Rename the Sheet1 tab to **1st Quarter Sales** and rename the Sheet2 tab to **2nd Quarter Sales**. Add color to the tabs. Delete Sheet3.

d. In the 2nd Quarter Sales sheet, change the monthly labels to Apr, May, and June using AutoFill. Change the subtitle line to **Second Qtr Sales**. Enter and bold the heading **(Projected)** in cell A4. Merge and center the heading between columns A through E.

e. Enter the following projected April sales figures:

Location	Number
The Arboretum	9600
South Congress	14350
The Triangle	13100
Barton Springs Mall	14100
Lakeland Mall	5350
Brodie Oaks	3600
Lamar Place	7900

Student Name - 11/24/2008

Juice Bar
First Quarter Sales

Location	Jan	Feb	Mar	Total
The Arboretum	$ 7,600	$ 7,850	$ 8,100	$ 23,550
South Congress	$ 14,400	$ 14,350	$ 13,950	$ 42,700
The Triangle	$ 10,100	$ 10,300	$ 10,100	$ 30,500
Barton Springs Mall	$ 12,300	$ 12,600	$ 12,940	$ 37,840
Lakeland Mall	$ 4,600	$ 3,850	$ 4,250	$ 12,700
Brodie Oaks	$ 5,400	$ 5,450	$ 5,100	$ 15,950
Lamar Place	$ 10,100	$ 10,600	$ 9,850	$ 30,550
Total	$ 64,500	$ 65,000	$ 64,290	$ 193,790

Student Name - 11/24/2008

Juice Bar
Second Quarter Sales
(Projected)

Location	Apr	May	Jun	Total
The Arboretum	$ 9,600	$ 10,560	$ 12,144	$ 32,304
South Congress	$ 14,350	$ 15,785	$ 18,153	$ 48,288
The Triangle	$ 13,100	$ 14,410	$ 16,572	$ 44,082
Barton Springs Mall	$ 14,100	$ 15,510	$ 17,837	$ 47,447
Lakeland Mall	$ 5,350	$ 5,885	$ 6,768	$ 18,003
Brodie Oaks	$ 3,600	$ 3,960	$ 4,554	$ 12,114
Lamar Place	$ 7,900	$ 8,690	$ 9,994	$ 26,584
Total	$ 68,000	$ 74,800	$ 86,020	$ 228,820

Sales Year-To-Date: $ 422,610

Lab Exercises

f. A new advertising campaign for May and June is expected to increase monthly sales. May sales for each location are expected to be 10 percent more than April sales, and June sales are expected to be 15 percent more than May. Enter formulas to calculate May and June sales for the "The Arboretum" location and then copy these formulas into the other appropriate cells.

g. Select both sheets and make the following changes:
- Add a thick bottom border below the headings in row 5.
- Apply the Total cell style to the Total row heading and Total row values.
- Use the Find and Replace command to change "Qtr" to "Quarter."
- Reduce the font size of the subtitle line to 14 points.

h. In the Second Quarter sheet, enter, bold, italicize, and right-align the heading **Sales Year-To-Date:** in cell D14. In cell E14, enter a formula to calculate the total sales for the first six months by summing cells E13 on both sheets. Remove the fill color from cell E14.

i. Document the workbook to include your name as the author.

j. In Page Layout view, add a custom header with your name and the date right-aligned to both worksheets.

k. Preview the workbook. Print the 2nd Quarter Sales worksheet.

l. Save the workbook as Juice Bar.

Forecasting Sales ★ ★

2. The Cookie Time bakery has decided to add brownies to their offerings and wants to know the impact on sales. You are in the process of creating a worksheet of the cookie sales for the last six months. In addition, you want to add brownies to the items for sale and project how much of this item you would need to sell to increase the net income to $2,000 a month. Then, you want to set up a second sheet that you will use to enter the sales information for the second six months when it is available. When you are done, your completed worksheets should be similar to those shown here.

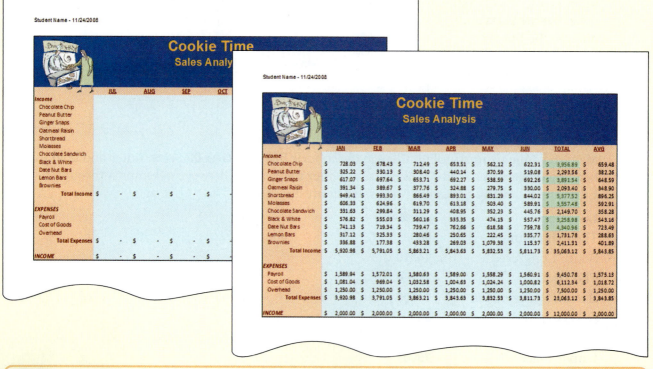

a. Open the workbook ex03_ Cookie Time. Use AutoFill to complete the month headings. Save the workbook as Cookie Time.
b. Add a blank row below row 15 for brownies. Add the row heading **Brownies** in A16.
c. Edit the formula in B17 to include B16 and copy it across the row through column G.
d. Increase the cost of goods by 12 percent for each month to account for the added goods needed to make the brownies.
e. Enter the formulas to calculate the Total Expenses in row 23.
f. Correct all the formula errors in row 25.
g. Enter the functions to calculate the Total and Average values in row 6. Copy the functions down the columns through row 25. Clear the formulas from all cells that reference blank cells, except for row 16.
h. Freeze the window with the titles in column A and above row 5 frozen so you can scroll to see the Income values in row 25 while working on the brownie sales next.
i. Assuming other cookie sales remain the same, you want to know how much brownie sales would be necessary to generate a monthly net income of $2,000. Use Goal Seek to answer these questions and calculate the brownie sales figures. (Hint: Net income is displayed in row 25.)
j. Unfreeze the window.
k. Using conditional formatting, create a cell rule that will highlight those cookies that have total sales greater than $3,000. Use a highlight color of your choice.
l. You will soon be working on the sales figures for the second six months and want to set up a second sheet to hold this information when it is available. Copy the entire worksheet from Sheet1 to Sheet2, retaining the original column widths. Increase the row height of row 3 to 35.25 points. Change the month headings using AutoFill for the second six months (JUL to DEC).
m. Rename Sheet1 to **January-June Sales**. Rename Sheet2 to **July-December Sales**. Add tab colors of your choice. Delete the extra sheet in the workbook.
n. In the July-December Sales sheet, delete the contents only in cells B6:G16 and B20:G22. In cell H6, enter a formula that adds the total from January through June with the monthly figures from July through December. Copy the formula down the column. Change the average formula to average the 12 months. Clear the formula from all cells that reference blank cells. Clear the conditional formatting from all cells in the July-December Sales sheet. Check the formulas by entering (and then removing) some sample data. Change the label in H4 to **Annual TOTAL** and I4 to **Annual AVG**. Best fit both columns.
o. Add a custom header with your name and the date left-aligned to both sheets. Use the Find and Replace command to change "bars" to "Bars" in both sheets.
p. Preview the workbook. Change the print orientation to landscape. Print both worksheets.
q. Add workbook documentation and save the workbook.

Paris Tour Cost Analysis ★★

3. Colleen, a travel analyst for Adventure Travel Tours, is evaluating the profitability of a planned Paris Tour package. She has researched competing tours and has determined that a price of $5,900 is appropriate. Colleen has determined the following costs for the package.

Item	Cost
Air transport	$1,800 per person
Ground transportation	$460 per person
Lodging	$1,475 per person
Food	$900 per person
Tour guides	$3,000
Administrative	$1,200
Miscellaneous	$2,000

She has started a worksheet to evaluate the revenues and costs for the Paris Tour. She wants to know how many travelers are needed to break even (revenues equal costs), how many are needed to make $5,000, and how many are needed to make $10,000. When completed your Break Even and $10,000 Profit worksheets should be similar to those shown here.

a. Open the workbook ex03_Paris Tour. Notice that Alice has already entered the tour price and an estimated number of travelers.

b. Revenue from reservations is calculated by multiplying the tour price times the number of travelers. Enter this formula into C9. Save the workbook as Paris Tour in a folder named Tour Analysis.

c. Based on Alice's cost information, air transportation is $1,800 times the number of travelers. Enter this formula into C12. Enter formulas into C13, C14, and C15 for the other expenses (see table above) related to the number of travelers.

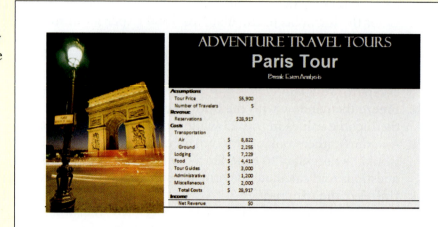

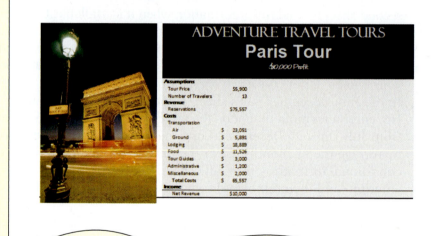

d. Enter the remaining expenses into cells C16, C17, and C18.

e. Calculate total costs in cell C19. Net revenue is the difference between revenue from reservations and total costs. Enter this formula into cell C21.

f. Format the currency values in the worksheet to Accounting with no decimal places.

g. Use Goal Seek to determine the number of travelers needed to just break even (net revenue equals zero).

h. Rename the Sheet1 tab to **Break Even**. Copy the data in the Break Even sheet to Sheet2, preserving column width settings. Rename the Sheet2 tab **$5,000**. Add color to both sheet tabs.

i. In the $5000 sheet, change the title in B3 to **$5,000 Profit**. Use Goal Seek to determine the number of travelers needed to attain net revenues of $5,000.

j. Copy the $5000 sheet data to Sheet3 and rename the tab of the copy to **$10,000**. Change the tab color. Change the title in B3 to **$10,000 Profit**. Use Goal Seek to determine the number of travelers needed to attain net revenues of $10,000.

k. Use the Find and Replace command to change Trip Guides to Tour Guides in all sheets.

l. Select all three sheets and change the page layout to landscape. Change the left and right margins to 0.5 inch and scale the worksheet to fit on one printed page. Add a custom footer to the three sheets with your name and the date center-aligned.

m. Preview the worksheets. Adjust the picture size if needed.

n. Save the workbook. Print the Break Even sheet and the $10,000 sheet.

Calculating Total Points and GPA ★★★

4. Ray Schultz is a college student who has just completed the first two years of his undergraduate program as an architecture major. He has decided to create a worksheet that will calculate semester and cumulative totals and GPA for each semester. The completed Spring 2008 worksheet should be similar to the one shown here.

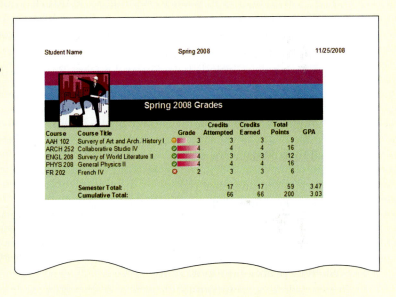

a. Open the workbook ex03_Grade Report. Look at the four sheets. Rename the sheet tabs **Fall 2006**, **Spring 2007**, **Fall 2007**, and **Spring 2008**. Add color to the tabs. Save the workbook as Grade Report in a folder named Grade Analysis.

b. You need to enter the formulas to calculate the Total Points and GPA for the four semesters. You will do this for all four sheets at the same time. Select the four sheets. In the Fall 2006 sheet, multiply the Grade by the Credits Earned to calculate Total Points for Collaborative Studio I. Copy that formula down the column. Sum the Credits Attempted, Credits Earned, and Total Points columns and display the results in the Semester Total row.

c. In cell G13, divide the Semester Total's Total Points by the Semester Total's Credits Earned to calculate the GPA for the semester. Format the GPA to two decimal places. Ungroup the sheets.

d. Use what-if analysis to see the grade Ray would have had to earn in Western Civilization to get an overall 3.0 GPA for the Fall 2006 semester. Change the grade back to a 2.

e. Look at each sheet to see that the formulas were entered and the calculations performed.

f. Go to cell D14 in the Fall 2006 sheet. Enter the reference formula =D13 to copy the Semester Total Credits Attempted number to the Cumulative Total row. Copy the formula to cells E14 and F14 to calculate Credits Earned and Total Points.

g. Go to the Spring 2007 sheet and calculate a Cumulative Total for Credits Attempted by summing the Spring 2007 and Fall 2006 Semester Totals. (Hint: You can use pointing to enter the Cumulative Totals formula.)

h. Copy that formula to the adjacent cells to calculate Cumulative Totals for Credits Earned and Total Points. Repeat this procedure on the Fall 2007 and Spring 2008 sheets.

i. Go to the Fall 2006 sheet. Select all four sheets. In cell G14, calculate the GPA for the Cumulative Total. Format the Cumulative Total GPA to display two decimals. Look at each sheet to see the cumulative GPA for each semester. (Hint: Roy's cumulative GPA at the end of the Spring 2008 semester is 3.03.)

j. In each sheet, you want to highlight the information in the grade earned column. In the Fall 2006 sheet, apply a Color Scale conditional formatting to the grade column. In the Spring 2007 sheet, apply a Data Bars conditional formatting to the grade column. In the Fall 2007 sheet, apply the 5 Arrows (Colored) Icon Set to the grade column. In the Spring 2008 sheet, apply the 3 Symbols (Circled) Icon Set and a Data Bars conditional formatting to the grade column.

k. Add a custom header with your name left-aligned, the sheet name centered, and the date right-aligned to all sheets.

l. Save the workbook. Print the Spring 2008 sheet.

Year-to-Date Sales Analysis ★★★

5. Jin Lee is the owner of the Doggie Day Care Center, which offers full- and half-day care for dogs as well as grooming and training services. She has been asked to prepare a report on the year-to-date accounting totals. She has already entered the figures for January through June. Next, she will create a worksheet for the July through December data and compile the year's totals. Your completed worksheet should be similar to that shown here.

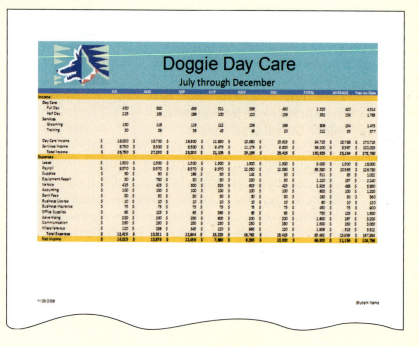

a. Open the file ex03_Doggie Day Care. Adjust the zoom to display all the data. Correct the formula errors. Save the workbook as Doggie Day Care.

b. Enter formulas in cells H9 and H10 to calculate the services totals.

c. Enter the following formula in cell B12 to calculate the income from day care for January: =(B6*$B$32)+(B7*$B$33). Copy the formula across the row to calculate the Day Care income. Enter the appropriate formulas in the Total column to calculate the total income figures.

d. Enter formulas in cells H16 through H28 to calculate the total expenses. In cell H29, total the expenses.

e. In cell B30 enter a formula that subtracts the Total Expenses from the Total Income. Copy the formula across the row.

f. Enter the heading **AVERAGE** in cell I3. Adjust the formatting of the new column to match the other columns in the sheet. Enter a formula to calculate the average number of full-day dogs in cell I6. Copy the formula down the column. Delete the division by zero errors. Adjust the formatting of the sheet as needed.

g. Select the range A1:I30 and copy it to Sheet2, maintaining the original column widths. Adjust the graphic size and the row height to accommodate the graphic. Rename the new sheet **Jul-Dec**. Add tab colors to both sheets.

h. Change the title in the Jul-Dec sheet to **July through December**. Change the month heading in cell B3 to **JUL**. Use AutoFill to change the remaining month headings.

i. Adjust the references in the formulas of rows 12 and 13 by adding the sheet reference.

j. Select cells I14 and I30 and use Watch Window to view the changes made when you enter the following values in the specified cells:

	Jul	Aug	Sep	Oct	Nov	Dec
Full Day	450	500	436	321	386	402
Half Day	225	247	185	100	120	136
Grooming	130	142	116	122	156	166
Training	30	36	36	45	45	20

k. Delete the watch cells and close the Watch Window. Move to cell J3 and enter the heading **Year-to-Date**. In cell J6, enter a formula to compute the total full-day care in the first and second six-month periods. Copy the formula down the column to find the year-to-date totals for all of the rows. Adjust the formatting in column J to match the others in the sheet.

l. Delete Sheet3. Use Find and Replace to change the Marketing labels to **Advertising** in both sheets.

m. Use Goal Seek to calculate the number of full-day dogs needed to increase the Net Income for December to $10,000.

n. Add a custom footer with your name and the date to both sheets. Save the workbook.

o. Print the Jul-Dec sheet on one page.

on your own

Expanding Budget Projections ★

1. In On Your Own exercise 2 of Lab 1, you created a Personal Budget workbook for a three-month budget. Extend the worksheet to add three more months for a total of six months. Add two additional sheets. One sheet will contain a budget for the next six months. The final sheet will present a full year's summary using 3-D references to the values in the appropriate sheets. You need to budget for a vacation. On a separate line below the total balance in the summary sheet, enter the amount you would need. Subtract this value from the total balance. If this value is negative, reevaluate your expenses and adjust them appropriately. Format the sheets using the features you have learned in the first three labs. Add your name in a custom header on all sheets. Preview, print, and save the workbook as Personal Budget2.

Company Expense Comparisons ★

2. Using the Internet or the library, obtain yearly income and expense data for three companies in a related business. In a workbook, record each company's data in a separate sheet. In a fourth sheet, calculate the total income, total expenses, and net income for each company. Also in this sheet, calculate the overall totals for income, expense, and net income. Format the sheets using the features you have learned in the first three labs. Add your name in a custom header on all sheets. Preview, print, and save the workbook as Company Expenses in a folder named Business.

House Analysis ★★

3. Select three cities in which you would consider living after you graduate. Using the Internet or the library, select one price point of housing and determine each house's asking price, square footage, acreage, number of bedrooms, and number of bathrooms. In a workbook containing four sheets, record each city's housing prices and statistics in separate worksheets. In a fourth sheet, calculate the average, standard deviation, and maximum and minimum for each city. Also, in the final sheet, chart the average data for the three cities. Format the sheets using the features you have learned in the first three labs. Add your name in a custom header on all sheets. Preview, print, and save the workbook as House Analysis in a folder named Housing.

Inventory Tracking ★★★

4. It's a good idea to have an inventory of your personal items for safe keeping. Design a worksheet that will keep track of your personal items divided by category; for example: living room, dining room, bedroom, and so forth. Each category may have as many detail lines as needed to represent

the items. For example: sofa, vases, art, and so on. The worksheet should keep track of the number of items; the price paid for each item; the extended price (items * price), if applicable; and the replacement value. Determine the percentage increase in replacement value. Sum the price paid and replacement value in each category and the total value. Format the sheet using the features you have learned in the first three labs. Add your name in a custom header on all sheets. Change the worksheet orientation if necessary; preview, print, and save the workbook as Inventory Tracking.

Start Your Own Business ★ ★ ★

5. Owning and managing a small business is a dream of many college students. Do some research on the Web or in the library and choose a business that interests you. Create a projected worksheet for four quarters in separate worksheets. In a fifth sheet, show the total for the year. Include a year-to-date value in each quarterly sheet. In the last-quarter sheet, depending on the business you select, determine how many customers or sales you need in the last quarter to break even and to end the year with a 10 percent profit. Format the sheets using the features you have learned in the first three labs. Add your name in a custom header on all sheets. Preview, print, and save the workbook as My Business.

Working Together 1: Linking and Embedding between Word 2007 and Excel 2007

Case Study

Downtown Internet Café

Your analysis of the sales data for the first quarter of operations for the Downtown Internet Café projects a small, steady increase in sales each month. If an advertising campaign promoting the new Internet aspect of the Café is mounted, you forecast that coffee and food sales in that quarter will increase sharply.

Evan, the Cafe owner, is still trying to decide if he should advertise and has asked you to send him a memo containing the worksheet data showing the expected sales without an advertising campaign and the chart showing the projected sales with an advertising campaign. Additionally, Evan wants a copy of

the second-quarter forecast showing the 15 percent profit margins for each month. He also wants a copy of the workbook file so that he can play with the sales values to see their effects on the profit margin.

You will learn how to share information between applications while you create these memos. Your completed documents will look like those shown below.

Note: This lab assumes that you know how to use Word 2007 and that you have completed Labs 2 and 3 of Excel 2007.

Memo

To: Professor's Name
From: Student Name
Date: 11/21/2008
Re: First Quarter Sales Forecast

The expected sales forecast for the first quarter for the Downtown Internet Café are shown in the worksheet below. The forecast shows steady growth in all areas of sales.

	JAN	FEB	MAR	TOTAL
Espresso	$ 13,300	$ 13,600	$ 14,200	$ 41,100
Drip Coffee	5,800	6,000	6,200	18,000
Food/Beverages	3,600	3,800	3,800	11,200
Merchandise	1,000	1,100	1,100	3,200
Computer	400	400	400	1,200
Total Sales	$ 24,100	$ 24,900	$ 25,700	$ 74,700

The following chart of the worksheet data shows how expected total sales would increase in February and March if an aggressive advertising campaign is launched at the beginning of the quarter.

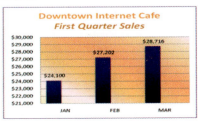

INTEROFFICE MEMORANDUM

TO: EVAN
FROM: STUDENT NAME
SUBJECT: SECOND QUARTER FORECAST
DATE: NOVEMBER 21, 2008

The sales forecast for the second quarter for the Downtown Internet Café is shown in the worksheet below. The forecast shows a 15% profit margin for each month in this quarter. The profit margin value was arrived at by reducing payroll expenses (shown in red).

Downtown Internet Café
Second Quarter Forecast

	APR	MAY	JUN	TOTAL	AVG
Sales					
Espresso	$ 14,400	$ 15,200	$ 15,500	$ 45,100	$ 15,033
Drip Coffee	$ 6,200	$ 6,200	$ 6,200	$ 18,600	$ 6,200
Food/Beverages	$ 3,600	$ 3,800	$ 3,800	$ 11,200	$ 3,733
Merchandise	$ 1,500	$ 1,500	$ 1,500	$ 4,500	$ 1,500
Computer	$ 600	$ 600	$ 800	$ 2,000	$ 667
Total Sales	$ 26,300	$ 27,300	$ 27,800	$ 81,400	$ 27,133
Expenses					
Cost of Goods	$ 7,620	$ 7,940	$ 8,015	$ 16,875	$ 7,858
Cost of Merchandise	$ 1,050	$ 1,050	$ 1,050	$ 5,650	$ 1,050
Payroll	$ 7,860	$ 8,390	$ 8,740	$ 24,990	$ 8,330
Internet	$ 325	$ 325	$ 325	$ 975	$ 325
Building	$ 2,100	$ 2,100	$ 2,100	$ 6,300	$ 2,100
Advertising	$ 600	$ 600	$ 600	$ 1,800	$ 600
Capital Assets	$ 1,500	$ 1,500	$ 1,500	$ 4,500	$ 1,500
Miscellaneous	$ 1,300	$ 1,300	$ 1,300	$ 3,900	$ 1,300
Total Expenses	$ 22,355	$ 23,205	$ 23,630	$ 64,990	$ 23,063
Income					
Net Income	$ 3,945	$ 4,095	$ 4,170	$ 16,410	$ 4,070
Profit Margin	15.00%	15.00%	15.00%	20.16%	15.00%

This workbook is embedded in this document and can be edited by double-clicking on the worksheet.

Sharing Information between Applications

All Microsoft Office 2007 applications have a common user interface such as similar Ribbon commands and galleries. In addition to these obvious features, they have been designed to work together, making it easy to share and exchange information between applications. For example, the same commands and procedures to copy information within an Office Excel 2007 worksheet are used to copy information to other Office 2007 applications such as Word. The information can be pasted in many different formats such as a worksheet object, a bitmap, a picture, a linked object, or an embedded object. How you decide to paste the object depends on what you want to be able to do with the data once it is inserted in the Word document.

Copying between Excel and Word

The memo to Evan about the analysis of the sales data has already been created using Word 2007 and saved as a document file.

1 • **Start Office Word 2007 and open the document** exwt1_Sales Forecast Memo.docx**.**

• **In the memo header, replace [Professor's Name] with your instructor's name and Student Name with your name.**

• **Save the file as** Sales Forecast Memo**.**

Your screen should be similar to Figure 1

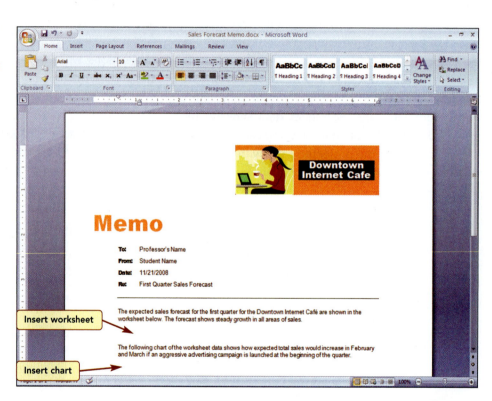

Figure 1

As you can see, you still need to add the Excel worksheet data and chart to the memo. To insert the information from the Excel workbook file into the Word memo, you need to open the workbook. You will then tile the two open application windows to make it easier to see and work with both files.

2 • **Start Excel and open the workbook** exwt1_Sales Charts.

Your screen should be similar to Figure 2

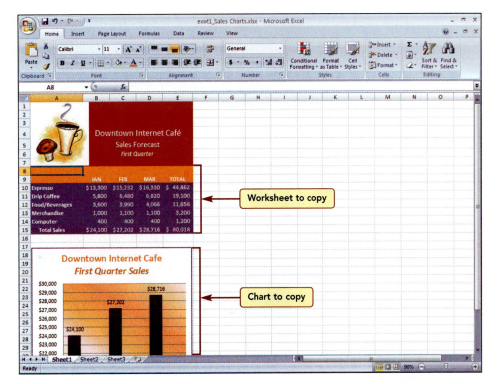

Figure 2

There are now two open applications, Word and Excel. You will insert the worksheet data of the first-quarter sales forecast below the first paragraph. Below the second paragraph, you will display the chart.

You will begin by copying the chart from Excel into the Word document. While using Excel, you have learned how to use cut, copy, and paste to move or copy information within and between worksheets. You also can perform these operations between files in the same application and between files in different Office applications. You want to insert the chart as a picture object that can be edited using the Picture Tools commands in Word.

3 ● Select the column chart.

● Click 🗐 **Copy** to copy the selected chart object to the Clipboard.

● Switch to the Word document.

Having Trouble?
Click the Word document button in the taskbar.

● Move the insertion point to the second blank line below the last paragraph of the memo.

● Click 📋 to copy the contents from the Clipboard into the memo.

● Open the 📋 **Paste Options** menu and choose Paste as Picture.

● Open the Picture Tools Format tab.

● Click 🔲 **Text Wrapping ▾** and choose Top and Bottom.

● Adjust the size of the chart and position it as in Figure 3.

Your screen should be similar to Figure 3

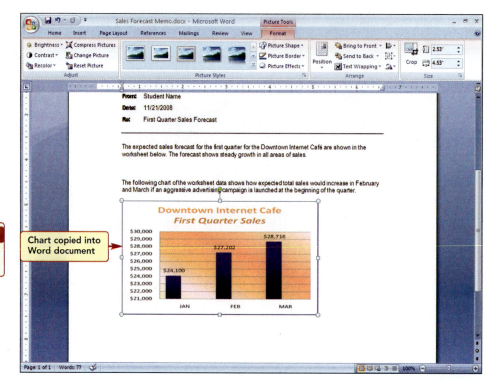

Figure 3

A copy of the chart has been inserted as a picture object into the Word document. It can be formatted, sized, and moved like any other picture object.

Linking between Applications

Next, you want to copy the worksheet showing the sales trends to below the first paragraph in the memo. You will insert the worksheet into the memo as a **linked object**. Information created in one application also can be inserted as a linked object into a document created by another application. When an object is linked, the data is stored in the **source file** (the document in which it was created). A graphic representation or picture of the data is displayed in the **destination file** (the document in which the object is inserted). A connection between the information in the destination file to the source file is established by the creation of an **external reference**, also called a **link**. The link contains references to the location of the source file and the selection within the document that is linked to the destination file.

When changes are made in the source file that affect the linked object, the changes are reflected automatically in the destination file when it is opened. This is called a **live link**. When you create linked objects, the date and time on your machine should be accurate. This is because the program refers to the date of the source file to determine whether updates are needed when you open the destination file.

You will copy the worksheet as a linked object so that it will be updated automatically if the source file is edited. To make it easier to work with the two applications, you will tile the two open application windows.

1 • Right-click on a blank area of the taskbar and choose Tile Windows Vertically from the shortcut menu.

• Click in the Excel window and select cells A9 through E15.

• Click 🗐 Copy.

• Click in the Word document and move to the center blank line between the paragraphs of the memo.

• Open the 📋 Paste menu and choose Paste Special.

• Choose Paste link from the Paste Special dialog box.

Your screen should be similar to Figure 4

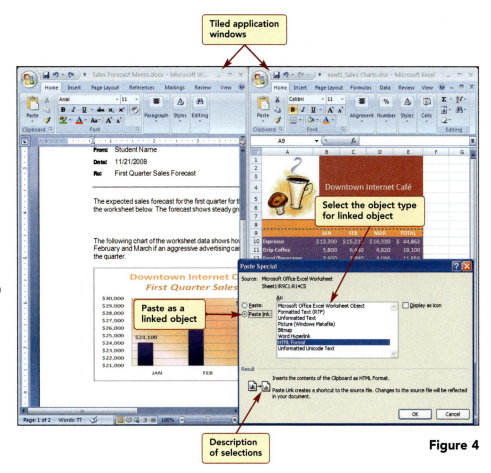

Tiled application windows

Select the object type for linked object

Paste as a linked object

Description of selections

Figure 4

The Paste Special dialog box displays the type of object contained in the Clipboard and its location in the Source area. From the As list box, you select the type of format for the object you want inserted into the destination file. There are many different object types from which you can select. It is important to select the appropriate object format so that the link works correctly when inserted in the destination. In this case, you want to use the Microsoft Office Excel Worksheet Object format.

The Result area describes the effect of your selections. In this case, the object will be inserted as a picture, and a link will be created to the chart in the source file. Selecting the Display as Icon option changes the display of the object in the destination file from a picture to an icon. When inserted in this manner, double-clicking the icon displays the object picture.

2 ● Choose **Microsoft Office Excel Worksheet Object.**

● Click [OK].

Your screen should be similar to Figure 5

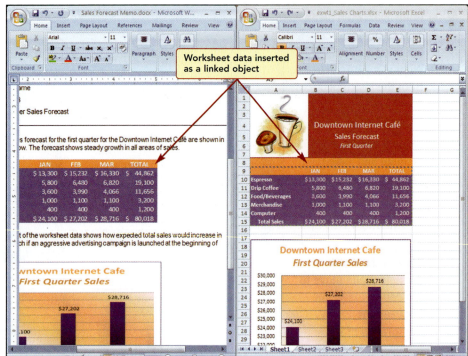

Figure 5

The worksheet data has been copied into the Word document as an object that can be sized and moved like any other object.

Updating a Linked Object

Next, you want to return the sales data in the Excel worksheet to the original forecasted values assuming an aggressive marketing campaign is not mounted.

1 ● Switch to the Excel window.

● Press [Esc] to clear the moving border.

● Change the entry in C10 to 13600 (you are removing the formula).

● In the same manner, change the formulas in the following cells to the values shown.

Cell	Value
D10	14,200
C11	6,000
D11	6,200
C12	3,800
D12	3,800

Your screen should be similar to Figure 6

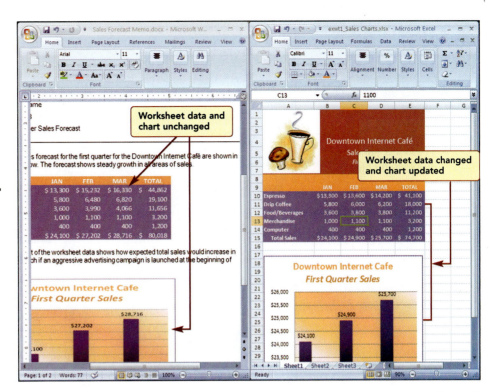

Figure 6

The Excel worksheet and chart have been updated; however, the worksheet data and chart in the Word document still reflect the original values. You will update the worksheet in the Word document next.

2 • **Switch to the Word window.**

• **Select the worksheet object.**

• **Press F9 to update the linked object.**

Another Method
You also can choose Update Link from the linked object's shortcut menu.

Your screen should be similar to Figure 7

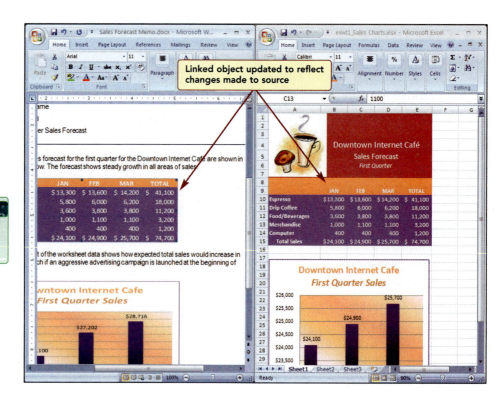

Linked object updated to reflect changes made to source

Figure 7

The linked worksheet object in the memo now reflects the changes you made in Excel for the sales data. This is because any changes you make in Excel will be reflected in the linked object in the Word document. Next, you will see if the chart has been updated also.

3 ● If necessary, scroll the memo to see the entire chart.

● Click on the chart and press F9.

● Deselect the chart.

Additional Information

The chart may have moved to the next page when the worksheet data was inserted. If this happened, reduce the size of the chart object.

Your screen should be similar to Figure 8

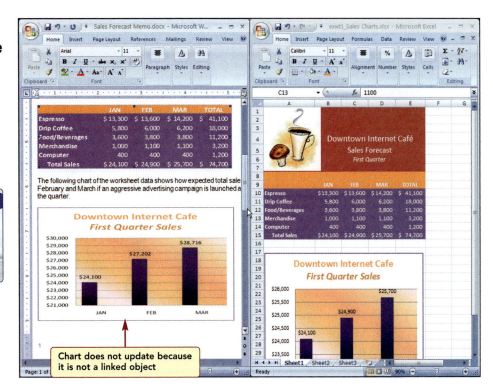

Chart does not update because it is not a linked object

Figure 8

Because the chart in the Word document is not a linked object, it does not update to reflect the changes in data that you made in Excel.

Editing Links

When a document is opened that contains links, the application looks for the source file and automatically updates the linked objects. If the document contains many links, updating can take a lot of time. Additionally, if you move the source file to another location or perform other operations that may interfere with the link, your link will not work. To help with situations like these, you can edit the settings associated with links. You will look at the links to the worksheet data created in the Word document.

1 • Maximize the Word window.

• If necessary, adjust the size of the chart to the same width as the worksheet object.

• Right-click the worksheet object and select Linked Worksheet Object.

• Choose Links from the submenu.

Your screen should be similar to Figure 9

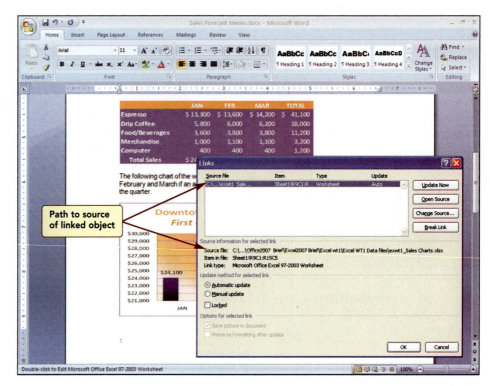

Figure 9

The Links dialog box displays the object path for all links in the document in the list box. The field code specifies the path and name of the source file, the range of linked cells or object name, the type of file, and the update status. Below the list box, the details for the selected link are displayed.

The other options in this dialog box are described in the table below.

Option	Effect
Automatic update	Updates the linked object whenever the destination document is opened or the source file changes. This is the default.
Manual update	The destination document is not automatically updated and you must use the Update Now command button to update the link.
Locked	Prevents a linked object from being updated.
Open Source	Opens the source document for the selected link.
Change Source	Used to modify the path to the source document.
Break Link	Breaks the connection between the source document and the active document.

The links in the Word document are to the exwt1_Sales Charts workbook file. Now that the memo is complete, you will save the documents. Then you will recheck the link settings.

2 ● Click [Cancel] .

● **Switch to the Excel window.**

● **Maximize the window.**

● **Save the Excel workbook as** Sales Forecast Linked**.**

● **Close the workbook file.**

● **Switch to the Word window.**

Having Trouble?
Click the application taskbar button to switch between windows.

● **From the worksheet object's shortcut menu, choose Linked Worksheet Object/Links.**

Your screen should be similar to Figure 10

3 ● Click [Cancel] .

● **Preview the document and make any needed adjustments to the layout.**

● **Print and then close the document, saving any changes if needed.**

Figure 10

You can now see that the link has been edited to reflect the new workbook file name.

Embedding an Object

Additional Information
The source data is stored in an Excel worksheet that is incorporated in the Word file.

Having Trouble?
Refer to Concept 6: Chart Objects in Lab 2 to review embedded objects.

The last thing you need to send Evan is a memo that describes and shows the second-quarter forecast. To do this, you will open the memo already created for you in Word and embed the sections from the Annual Forecast Revised workbook that Evan wants in the appropriate locations. An **embedded object** is stored in the destination file and becomes part of that document. The entire file, not just the selection that is displayed in the destination file, becomes part of the document. This means that you can modify it without affecting the source document where the original object resides.

1
- Open the Word document exwt1_Second Quarter Memo.docx.

- In the memo header, replace Student Name with your name.

- Save the document as Second Quarter Memo.

- Switch to Excel and open the workbook file exwt1_Second Quarter.

Your screen should be similar to Figure 11

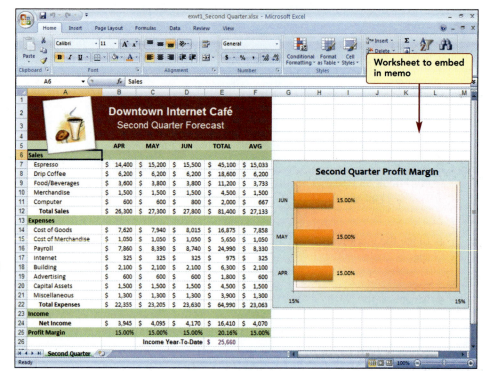

Figure 11

You will embed the second-quarter forecast worksheet in the Word document.

2
- Copy the range A1 through F25.

- Switch to the Word window.

- Move to the middle blank line below the first paragraph of the memo.

- Open the Paste menu and choose Paste Special.

Your screen should be similar to Figure 12

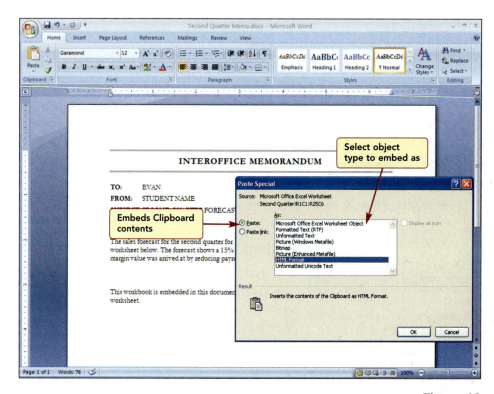

Figure 12

The Paste option inserts or embeds the Clipboard contents in the format you specify from the As list box. To embed the contents of the Clipboard into a document so it can be edited using the source program, select the option that displays the source name, in this case Excel.

3 • **Select Microsoft Office Excel Worksheet Object.**

• **Click** [OK].

Your screen should be similar to Figure 13

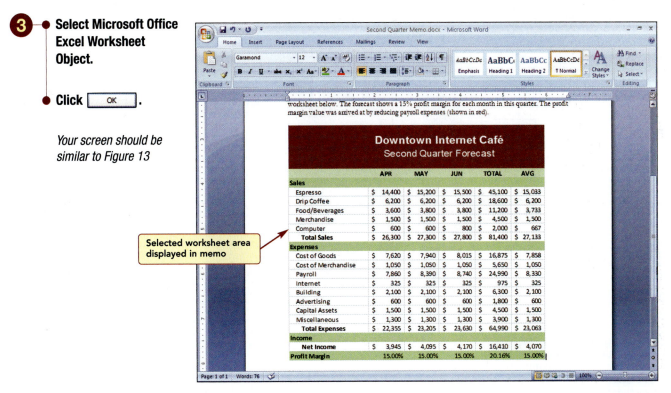

Selected worksheet area displayed in memo

Figure 13

The selected portion of the worksheet is displayed in the memo at the location of the insertion point.

Updating an Embedded Object

You want to add color to the payroll range of cells you adjusted to arrive at the 15 percent profit margin. Because the worksheet is embedded, you can do this from within the Word document. The source program is used to edit data in an embedded object. To open the source program and edit the worksheet, you double-click the embedded object.

1 • Double-click the worksheet object in Word.

Having Trouble?

If the worksheet does not fully display the numbers, click outside the worksheet to return to the document, make the worksheet object larger, and then open the source program again.

Your screen should be similar to Figure 14

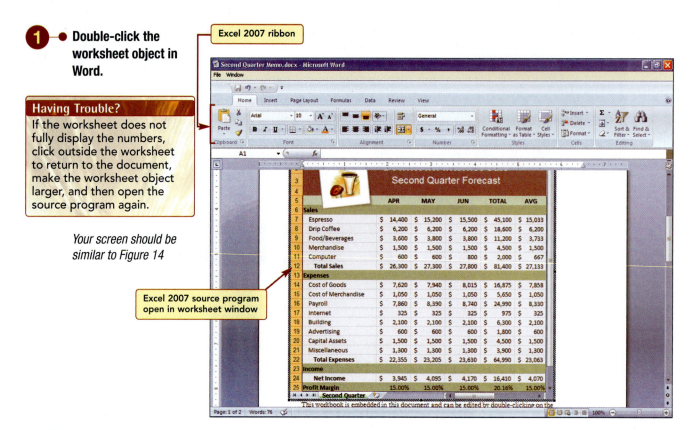

Excel 2007 ribbon

Excel 2007 source program open in worksheet window

Figure 14

Additional Information

The source program must be installed on the computer system to be able to open and edit the embedded object.

The source program, in this case Excel 2007, is opened. The Excel Ribbon replaces the Word Ribbon and the embedded object is displayed in an editing worksheet window. Now you can use the source program commands to edit the object.

2 • Change the font color of cells B15 through D15 to Red, Accent 2 theme color.

• Close the source program by clicking anywhere outside the object.

• Save the document.

Your screen should be similar to Figure 15

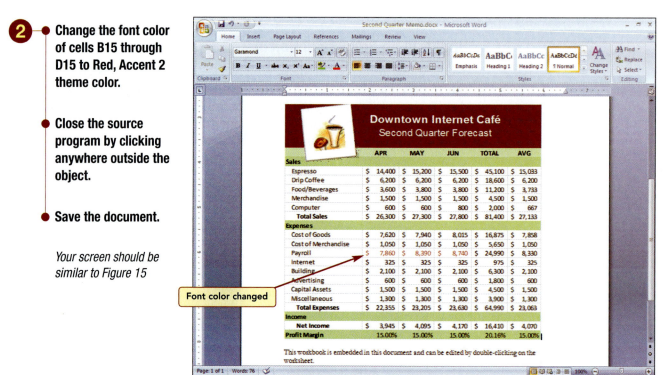

Font color changed

Figure 15

The embedded object in the memo is updated to reflect the changes you made. However, the Excel worksheet is unchanged.

3 ● **Preview and print the memo.**

● **Exit Word and Excel.**

Deciding When to Link or Embed Objects

Linking documents is a very handy feature, particularly in documents whose information is updated frequently. If you include a linked object in a document that you are giving to another person, make sure the user has access to the source file and application. Otherwise the links will not operate correctly.

Keep the following in mind when deciding whether to link or embed objects.

Use linking when:	Use embedding when:
File size is important.	File size is not important.
Users have access to the source file and application.	Users have access to the application but not to the source file.
The information is updated frequently.	The data changes infrequently. You do not want the source data to change.

key terms

destination file EXWT1.4	**link** EXWT1.4	**live link** EXWT1.4
embedded object EXWT1.11	**linked object** EXWT1.4	**source file** EXWT1.4
external reference EXWT1.4		

MCAS Skills

The Microsoft Certified Applications Specialist (MCAS) certification program is designed to measure your proficiency in performing basic tasks using the Office 2007 applications. Getting certified demonstrates that you have the skills and provides a valuable industry credential for employment. See Reference 2 MCAS Certification Guide for a complete list of the skills that were covered in Working Together 1.

command summary

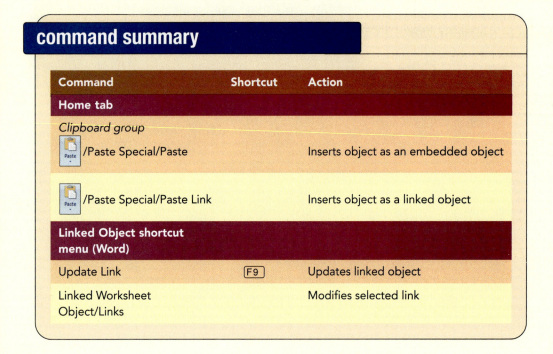

Command	Shortcut	Action
Home tab		
Clipboard group		
/Paste Special/Paste		Inserts object as an embedded object
/Paste Special/Paste Link		Inserts object as a linked object
Linked Object shortcut menu (Word)		
Update Link	F9	Updates linked object
Linked Worksheet Object/Links		Modifies selected link

Lab Exercises

Hands-On Exercises

rating system

★ Easy

★★ Moderate

★★★ Difficult

step-by-step

Rescue Foundation Income Memo ★★

1. The Animal Rescue Foundation's agency director has asked you to provide her with information about income for 2007. She is particularly interested in the two pet show fund-raising and membership drive events that are held in April and October. You will create a memo to her that will include a copy of the worksheet analysis of this data. Your completed memo will be similar to that shown here.

   a. Start Word and open the document exwt1_Rescue Memo.docx.

   b. In the memo header, replace the From placeholder with your name.

   c. Start Excel and open the workbook exwt1_Contributions.

   d. Insert both worksheets as Microsoft Excel Worksheet Object links below the first paragraph in the Word memo. Reduce the size of the worksheets until the memo fits on one page.

   e. You notice the April raffle ticket sales value looks low and after checking your records, you see it was entered incorrectly. In Excel, change the April raffle ticket sales income to **$3,120**.

   f. In the memo, update the linked worksheet.

   g. Save the Excel workbook as Contributions. Exit Excel.

   h. Save the Word document as Rescue Memo Linked. Preview and print the document.

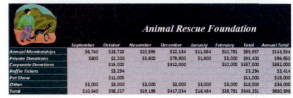

Memo

To:	Barbara Wood, Director
From:	Student Name
CC:	Mark Wilson
Date:	11/21/2008
Re:	Income

Below is the completed income analysis for 2007. As you can see, the income for Fall/Winter is much higher due to corporate donations.

Animal Rescue Foundation

	March	April	May	June	July	August	Total
Annual Memberships	$9,200	$18,783	$8,595	$9,934	$5,684	$5,781	$57,977
Private Donations	$625	$1,400		$1,225			$3,250
Corporate Donations		$17,000	$15,000		$4,000	$9,000	$45,000
Raffle Tickets		$3,120					$3,120
Pet Show		$8,000					$8,000
Other	$3,000	$3,000	$3,000	$3,000	$3,000	$3,000	$18,000
Total	$12,825	$51,303	$26,595	$14,159	$12,684	$17,781	$135,347

Animal Rescue Foundation

	September	October	November	December	January	February	Total	Annual Total
Annual Memberships	$6,740	$23,723	$10,595	$22,134	$11,584	$10,781	$85,557	$143,534
Private Donations	$800	$2,200	$5,600	$79,900	$1,900	$3,000	$93,400	$96,650
Corporate Donations		$16,000		$312,000		$10,000	$337,000	$382,000
Raffle Tickets		$3,294					$3,294	$3,414
Pet Show		$11,000					$11,000	$19,000
Other	$3,000	$3,000	$3,000	$3,000	$3,000	$3,000	$18,000	$36,000
Total	$10,540	$58,217	$19,195	$417,034	$16,484	$26,781	$548,251	$680,998

Also, the pet show fundraising events have been very successful in boosting income during the slow periods of each year.

1

Tour Status Memo ★★

2. Adventure Travel Tours travel agency sends a monthly status report to all subsidiary offices showing the bookings for the hiking tours. Previously, the worksheet data was printed separately from the memo. Now you want to include the worksheet in the same document as the memo. Your completed memo will be similar to that shown here.

a. Start Word and open the exwt1_Tour Status Report.docx document. Replace Student Name with your name on the From line in the heading.

b. Start Excel and open the exwt1_Adventure Travel Status workbook.

c. Copy the worksheet as a linked object to below the paragraph of the memo.

d. In Excel, enter the data shown below for the March bookings worksheet.

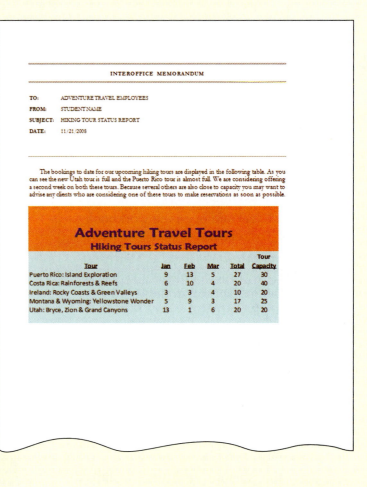

Tour	March Data
Puerto Rico: Island Exploration	5
Costa Rica: Rainforests & Reefs	4
Ireland: Rocky Coasts & Green Valleys	4
Montana & Wyoming: Yellowstone Wonders	3
Utah: Bryce, Zion & Grand Canyons	6

e. Save the workbook as Adventure Travel Status. Exit Excel.

f. Update the linked worksheet object.

g. Save the Word document as March Status Report. Print the memo.

Home Sale Price Memo ★★

3. Jennifer works in the marketing department for a local real estate company. She has recently researched the average home prices and number of days on the market over the last three years for existing homes in the local market area. She has created a worksheet and column charts of the data. Now Jennifer wants to send a memo containing the information to her supervisor. The completed memo will be similar to that shown here.

   a. Start Word and open the document exwt1_Home Price Memo.docx.

   b. In the header, replace the CC: placeholder information in brackets with your name.

   c. Start Excel and open the workbook exwt1_Real Estate Prices. Embed the worksheet data including the charts below the paragraph in the Word memo. Exit Excel.

   d. Open the embedded object in Word and scroll to see the column chart of the Average Price. Increase the size of the object to fully display the chart. Change the chart type to a clustered cylinder. Close the embedded object, leaving the chart displayed in the memo.

   e. Save the Word document as Home Price Memo. Preview and print the document.

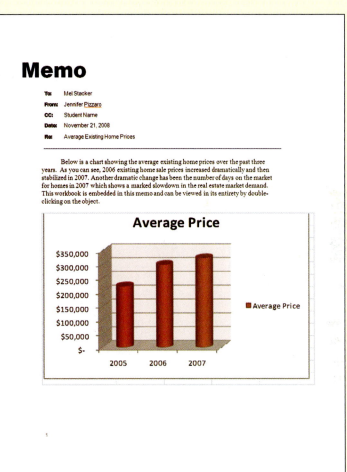

Using Solver, Creating Templates, and Evaluating Scenarios

LAB 4

Objectives

After completing this lab, you will know how to:

1

Use Solver.

2

Create an Answer report.

3

Create customized templates.

4

Protect a worksheet.

5

Open and use multiple workbooks.

6

Link workbooks.

7

Hide worksheets.

8

Create SmartArt.

9

Create, edit, and use scenarios.

10

Create a Scenario Summary report.

11

Use the Insert Function feature.

Case Study

Downtown Internet Café

After further discussion with Evan, the owner of the Downtown Internet Café, you continued to refine the forecast analysis. Based on Evan's input, you revised the third-quarter sales to show a 16 percent monthly profit margin. You also increased the fourth-quarter sales to show a 10 percent increase over third-quarter sales and increased the fourth-quarter payroll expenses.

Evan thinks these changes are more realistic but wants you to further refine the fourth-quarter analysis to show a fourth-quarter profit margin of 25 percent and an annual profit margin of 15 percent. You will use the Solver tool to help determine these values.

Once the annual forecast for the current year (2008) is complete, Evan wants you to use the same procedure to create

the forecast for the following year (2009). You will use the current year annual forecast worksheet to create a template for the next year's forecast. Then you will use the template to create the first-quarter forecast for that year.

Additionally, Evan wants you to create a graphic that will illustrate how the five sales categories are related. You will use the SmartArt feature to create a drawing of a pyramid to show how the four sales are related.

Finally, you have been asked to create three different scenarios that will show the best, worst, and most likely scenarios for the first-quarter forecast for the following year. The completed scenario summary report is shown here.

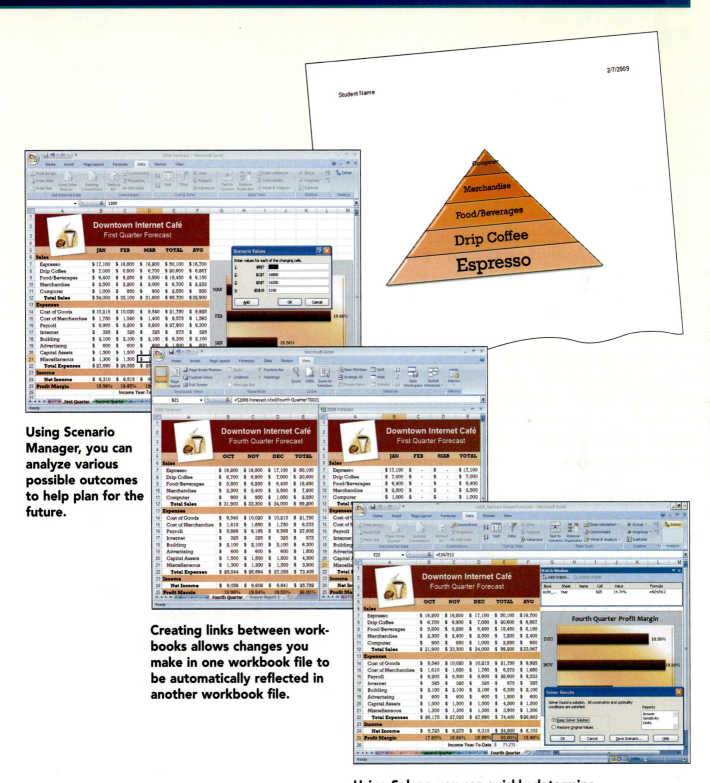

Using Scenario Manager, you can analyze various possible outcomes to help plan for the future.

Creating links between workbooks allows changes you make in one workbook file to be automatically reflected in another workbook file.

Using Solver, you can quickly determine the effect of changing values in two or more cells on another cell.

Concept Preview

The following concepts will be introduced in this lab:

1 **Solver** Solver is a tool used to perform what-if analysis to determine the effect of changing values in two or more cells on another cell.

2 **Custom Template** Custom templates are specialized templates or files containing settings that are used as a pattern for creating similar worksheets in new workbooks.

3 **Protection** The protection feature controls what information can be changed in a workbook.

4 **Window Arrangement** The window arrangement feature displays all open workbook files in separate windows on the screen, making it easy to view and work with information in different workbooks.

5 **Link** A link creates a connection between files that automatically updates the data in one file whenever the data in the other file changes.

6 **SmartArt** A SmartArt graphic is a graphic object that can be used to illustrate concepts and to enhance the workbook.

7 **Scenario** A scenario is a named set of input values that you can substitute in a worksheet to see the effects of a possible alternative course of action.

Analyzing the Worksheet

After seeing how the payroll values changed each month to achieve higher second- and third-quarter profit margins, Evan would like you to do a similar analysis on the fourth quarter. First you want to look at the current profit margin value for the fourth quarter.

1 ● Start Excel 2007.

● Open the workbook file ex04_Revised Annual Forecast.

● Make the Fourth Quarter sheet active.

● Select cell E25.

Your screen should be similar to Figure 4.1

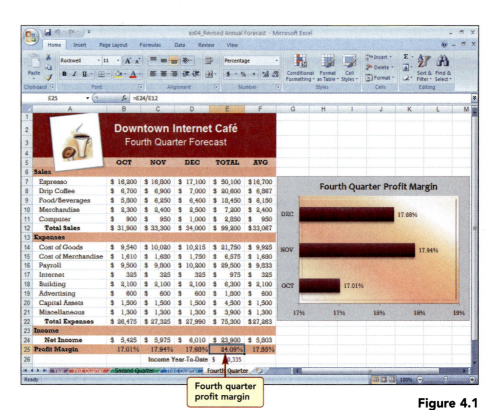

Fourth quarter profit margin

Figure 4.1

The current total profit margin for the fourth quarter is 24.09 percent. Evan would like to achieve a 25 percent quarterly profit margin. Again, to do this, you will need to reduce the monthly payroll expenses. While you are making changes to the quarterly worksheet, you will display the Watch Window to see how the changes affect the annual profit margin.

2 • Display the Year sheet.

• Select cell N25.

• Open the Watch Window.

• If necessary, select any existing watch cells in the Watch Window and click [Delete Watch] to delete them.

• Add cell N25 to the Watch Window.

• If necessary, size and position the Watch Window as in Figure 4.2.

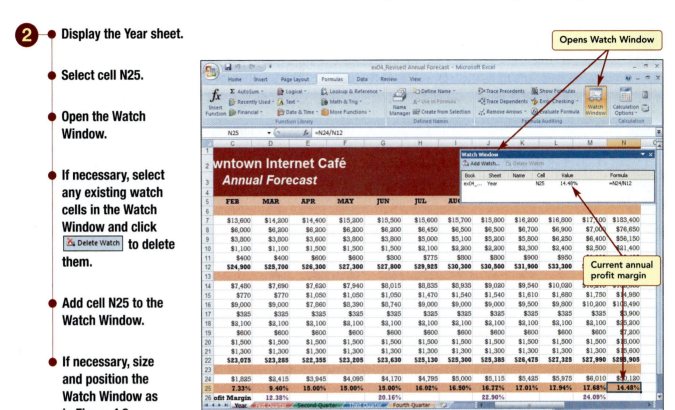

Figure 4.2

Having Trouble?

Click [icon] in the Formula Auditing group of the Formulas tab. Click [Add Watch...] and then [Add] to set the watch cell.

Your screen should be similar to Figure 4.2

The annual profit margin is currently 14.48 percent. Evan also would like to see this value closer to 15 percent for the year.

Using Solver

Although you could manually perform what-if analysis or use the Goal Seek feature to determine the desired profit margin value for the fourth quarter, it would be much quicker to use the Solver tool.

1 **Solver** is a tool used to perform what-if analysis to determine the effect of changing values in two or more cells, called the **adjustable cells**, on another cell, called the **target cell**. Solver calculates a formula to achieve a given value by changing one of the variables that affect the formula. To do this, Solver works backward from the result of a formula to find the numbers. The cells you select must be related through formulas on the worksheet. If they are not related, changing one will not change the other. You also can include constraints to restrict the values Solver can use. The constraints can refer to other cells that affect the target cell formula.

Solver also can produce three types of reports about the solution: Answer, Sensitivity, and Limits. In an Answer report, the original and final values of the target cell and adjustable cells are listed along with any constraints and information about the constraints. Information about how sensitive the solution is to small changes in the target cell formula or in the constraints is provided in a Sensitivity report. A Limits report includes the original and target values of the target cell and adjustable cells. It also lists the lower limit, or the smallest value that the adjustable cell can take while holding all other adjustable cells fixed and still satisfying the constraints and upper or greatest value.

Solver is an Excel Add-in tool that does not appear on the Ribbon until you install it. If 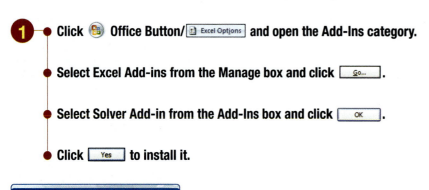 is not displayed in the Analysis group of the Data tab, you will need to install it according to the instructions in Step 1. Otherwise, skip to Step 2.

1 ● **Click** 🔵 **Office Button/** [📄 Excel Options] **and open the Add-Ins category.**

● **Select Excel Add-ins from the Manage box and click** [Go...].

● **Select Solver Add-in from the Add-Ins box and click** [OK].

● **Click** [Yes] **to install it.**

Additional Information
You may need the original install CD if you are using your own computer to load this add-in.

2 Display the Fourth Quarter sheet.

● Open the Data tab and click **Solver** in the Analysis group.

● Move the Solver Parameters dialog box to the bottom right side of the screen.

Your screen should be similar to Figure 4.3

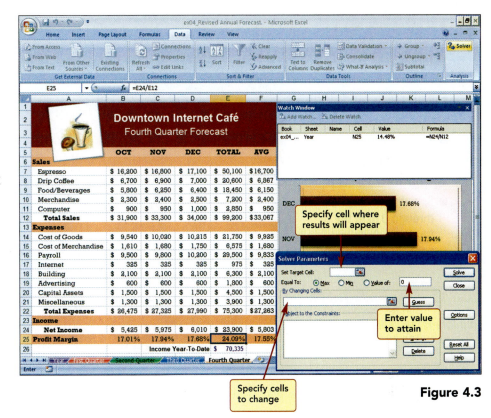

Specify cell where results will appear

Specify cells to change

Enter value to attain

Figure 4.3

In the Solver Parameters dialog box, you need to supply three items of information: the target cell where the result will appear, the desired result value, and the cell or cells that will be changed to achieve the result.

The cell reference of the cell containing the formula you want to solve is entered in the Set Target Cell text box. The number you want as the result of the formula is entered in the Equal To text box. You can set the number to be a maximum, a minimum, or an exact number. The maximum option sets the target cell to the highest possible number, while the minimum option sets the target cell to the lowest possible number.

The final information needed is the cell or cell range whose contents can be changed when the formula is computed. This range is entered in the By Changing Cells text box.

In the fourth-quarter sheet, you are looking for a profit margin value of 25 percent in cell E25 by changing the payroll values in the range of cells B16 through D16.

3 • If necessary, specify cell E25 as the Set Target Cell.

• Select Value of.

• Type **.25** in the Value of text box.

• Specify the range B16 through D16 in the By Changing Cells text box.

Having Trouble?
You can minimize the dialog box using the ⬛ Collapse Dialog button and select the range by highlighting it in the worksheet.

Your screen should be similar to Figure 4.4

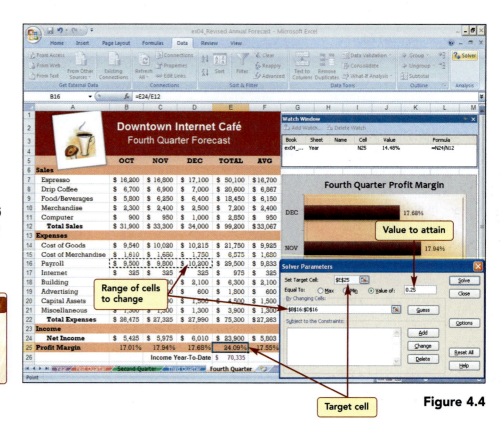

Figure 4.4

Now you are ready to have Solver find the values to meet the parameters you specified.

4 • Click  .

Your screen should be similar to Figure 4.5

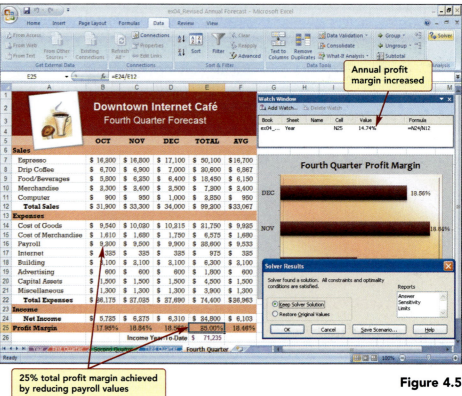

Figure 4.5

The Solver Results dialog box tells you that Solver found a solution. The new payroll numbers are entered in the worksheet range and the worksheet is automatically recalculated. By reducing the payroll expenses slightly each month, the total profit margin for the quarter is 25.0 percent. As you can see in the Watch Window, the profit margin for the year increased from 14.48 to 14.74 percent as a result of reducing payroll expenses in the fourth quarter.

You think the revised payroll values are reasonable. However, using these values does not attain the 15 percent annual profit margin that Evan wants. You decide to run Solver again and set the quarterly profit margin to 26 percent to see if this attains the desired annual profit margin.

From the Solver Results dialog box, you can choose whether to keep the solution or restore the original values. You will keep the proposed solution before running Solver again.

Additional Information
You cannot undo the Solver solution values once you accept them. If you are not sure that you want to keep the proposed values, use the Restore Original Values option or cancel the Solver results.

● Click [OK] to keep the Solver solution.

● **Run Solver again using a profit margin value of 26 percent.**

Your screen should be similar to Figure 4.6

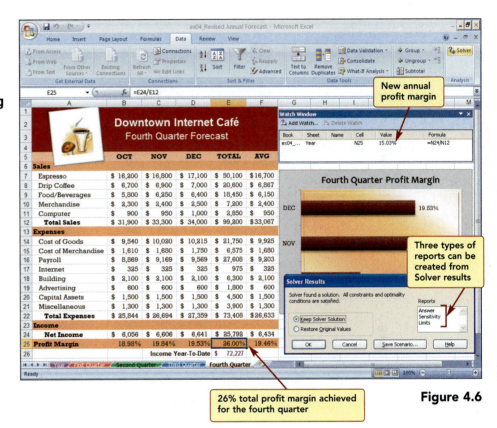

Figure 4.6

This time the Solver solution increases the annual profit margin to 15.03 percent by reducing the payroll expenses for the fourth quarter.

Creating an Answer Report

In addition to generating Solver solutions, you can have Solver create Answer, Sensitivity, or Limits reports. Reports are created in a new sheet in the workbook.

Report Type	Report Content
Answer	Lists target cell and adjustable cells with their original and final values
Sensitivity	Provides information about how sensitive the solution is to small changes in the formula in the Set Target Cell.
Limits	Lists target cell and adjustable cells with their respective values, lower and upper limits, and target values.

To show Evan the results of the analysis, you will keep the new solution and create an Answer report.

1 ● **Select Answer from the Reports list box.**

● **Click** [OK] **.**

● **Make the Answer Report 1 sheet active.**

Your screen should be similar to Figure 4.7

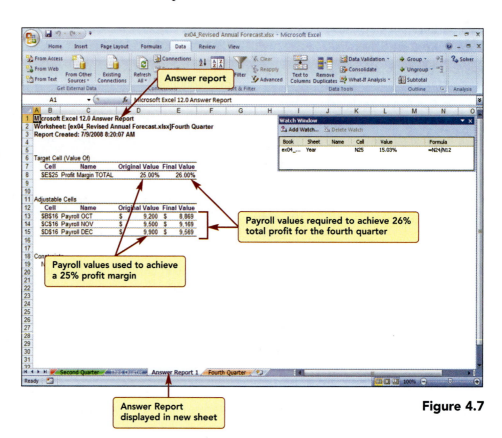

Figure 4.7

The Answer Report 1 sheet displays the Answer report that was generated. The target cell section of the report shows the original profit margin value of 25 percent and the final value of 26.00 percent. The Adjustable Cells area shows the original and final values for each cell that was changed to achieve the profit margin of 26.00 percent.

Wrapping Text

You decide to include a note to Evan to clarify the information in the report. As you enter the text, it will wrap on the screen as it reaches the right edge of the workspace.

1 • **In cell F10 type**
Note: Setting the fourth quarter profit margin to 26% achieves a 15% annual profit margin. Setting the profit margin to 25% achieves a 14.74% annual profit margin. However, I believe that the payroll values that are needed to achieve the 26% profit margin are unrealistically low.

• **Press** Ctrl + ← Enter.

Your screen should be similar to Figure 4.8

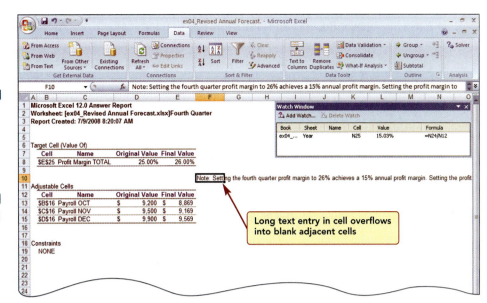

Figure 4.8

Long text entry in cell overflows into blank adjacent cells

Although the text wrapped as you typed it, when the entry is completed it is displayed as a long text entry in the blank cells to the right. You want to change the format of the text to wrap on several lines within the cell space. To do this, you will first increase the width of column F and then set text wrapping for the cell.

2 • **Increase the column width of column F to 40.**

Having Trouble?
A screen tip appears showing the column width setting as you drag the column border line.

• **Click**  **Wrap Text in the Alignment group of the Home tab.**

• **Increase the column width to 60.**

• **Select cell F17.**

Your screen should be similar to Figure 4.9

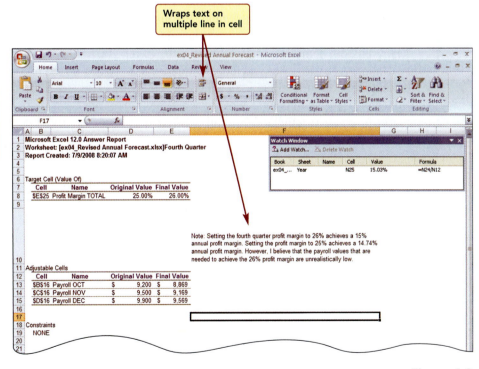

Wraps text on multiple line in cell

Note: Setting the fourth quarter profit margin to 26% achieves a 15% annual profit margin. Setting the profit margin to 25% achieves a 14.74% annual profit margin. However, I believe that the payroll values that are needed to achieve the 26% profit margin are unrealistically low.

Figure 4.9

The data in the cell wraps to fit the column width and adjusts automatically when you resize the column. The forecast for 2008 is now complete.

3 ● Move the Answer Report 1 sheet after the Fourth Quarter sheet.

● Close the Watch Window.

● Make the Year sheet active.

● Move to cell A6 and save the workbook file as 2008 Forecast.

Creating a Custom Template

After seeing the effects of your analyses on the Year sheet, Evan has found Solver to be a valuable tool for planning and managing operations. He has asked you to create a new workbook containing a forecast for the following year. You could create this new forecast workbook by starting all over again, specifying the formats and formulas. However, as the current workbook already contains this information, you decide to use it as a model or template for future forecasts.

Concept 2

Custom Template

2   **Custom templates** are specialized template files containing settings that are used as a pattern for creating similar worksheets in new workbooks. Custom templates are useful in applications where input and output are required using the same format. By not having to redesign the worksheet form each time the same information is needed, you save time and increase accuracy.

     Many custom templates are included with Excel 2007 and more are available from the Microsoft Office Online Web site. They include templates that create different styles of balance sheets, expense statements, loan amortizations, sales invoices, and timecards, to name a few, and are designed to help you quickly create professional-looking workbooks. You also can design and save your own workbook templates or create a template from an existing workbook.

A well-designed template allows you to enter information into the appropriate locations while protecting formulas and basic formats. Since the basic workbook design you want to use for your template is already in place, you will modify the worksheets in the workbook to create the template. The first steps are to eliminate the Answer Report 1 sheet and to change the values in the quarter sheets to zeros.

1 • Delete the Answer Report 1 sheet.

• Select the First Quarter through Fourth Quarter sheets.

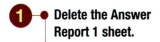

Having Trouble?

Hold down ⇧Shift to extend the sheet selection.

• Enter 0 in cells B7 through D11 and cells B16 through D21 in the First Quarter sheet.

• Move to cell B22.

Your screen should be similar to Figure 4.10

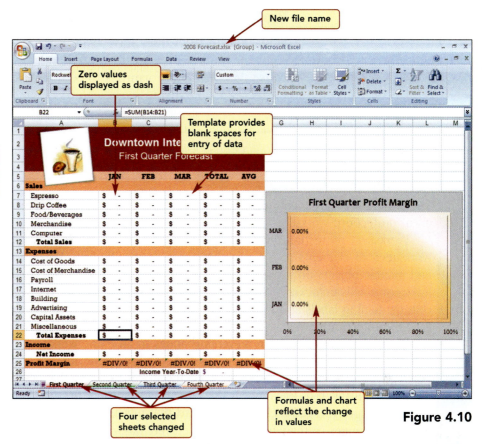

Figure 4.10

The cell format used in the quarter sheets displays cells containing zero values with a dash symbol. All other worksheet cells containing formulas as well as the chart reflect the change in the values.

2 • Look at each of the three other quarter sheets to verify that the values have been replaced.

• Make the Year sheet active and move to cell B7.

Your screen should be similar to Figure 4.11

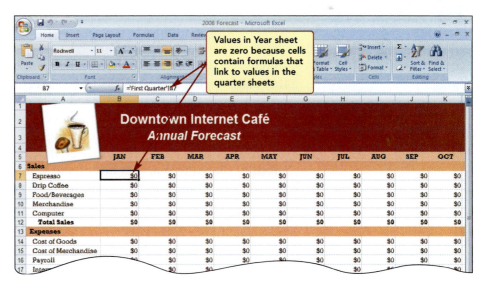

Figure 4.11

Because the Year sheet contains formulas that link to the values in the quarter sheets, this sheet also displays zero values. However, the cell format used in the Year sheet sets the display to show 0 rather than a dash.

Now, whenever you are creating another annual forecast, you will simply enter the new values in place of the blanks in the quarter sheets and the annual sheet will automatically be completed.

Protecting the Worksheet

Now that all the values have been removed and the template is ready to use, you want to prevent unwanted changes to the worksheets that would cause headings and formulas to be altered or cleared. To do this, you can protect the worksheet.

Concept 3

Protection

3 The **protection** feature controls what information can be changed in a workbook. Excel includes two levels of protection: worksheet protection and workbook protection.

Worksheet protection prevents users from changing a worksheet's contents by protecting the entire worksheet, or elements of the worksheet such as specific cells. When a worksheet is protected, all cells and graphic objects on it are locked. The contents of a locked cell cannot be changed. If you want to leave some cells unlocked for editing, such as in a worksheet that you use as an entry form, you can lock cells containing labels and formulas but unlock the entry fields so that other users can fill them in. This type of protection prevents you from entering or changing an entry in any locked cells.

Workbook-level protection prevents changes to an entire workbook in two ways. First, you can protect the structure of a workbook so that sheets cannot be moved or deleted or new sheets inserted. Second, you can protect a workbook's windows. This prevents changes to the size and position of windows and ensures that they appear the same way each time the workbook is opened.

In addition, you can include a **password** that prevents any unauthorized person from either viewing or saving changes to the workbook. Two separate passwords can be used: one to open and view the file and another to edit and save the file. Strong passwords combine uppercase and lowercase letters, numbers, and symbols and are at least eight characters in length. If you use a password, you must remember the password in order to use the workbook or worksheet or to turn protection off in the future. Because passwords cannot be retrieved, it is recommended that you write down and store your passwords in a secure place away from the information they protect or use a strong password that you can remember.

Initially all cells in a worksheet are locked. However, you can enter data in the cells because the worksheet protection feature is not on. When protection is turned on, all locked cells are protected. Therefore, before protecting this sheet, you need to unlock the areas in the worksheet where you want to allow users to make changes to information.

The only area of the Year sheet that needs to be unprotected is the subtitle where the year will be entered when the template is used. You will unlock the cell containing the subtitle and add protection to the rest of the worksheet.

Lab 4: Using Solver, Creating Templates, and Evaluating Scenarios

www.mhhe.com/oleary

1 ● Move to cell D3.

● Click  in the Alignment group to open the Format Cells dialog box.

● Open the Protection tab.

● Clear the Locked option.

Your screen should be similar to Figure 4.12

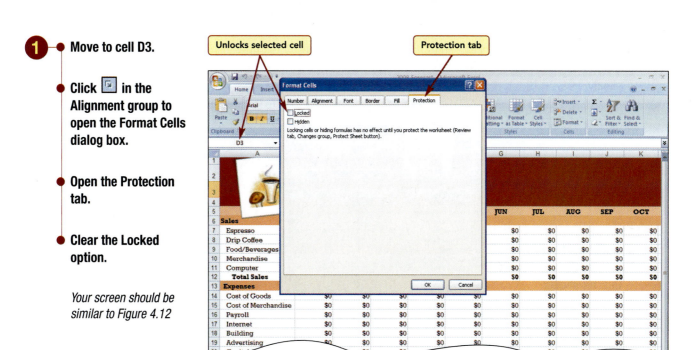

Unlocks selected cell

Protection tab

Figure 4.12

Once the cells you want to allow changes to in a worksheet are unlocked, you can add protection.

2 ● Click OK.

● Click ▦ Format ▾ in the Cells group and choose Protect Sheet.

Your screen should be similar to Figure 4.13

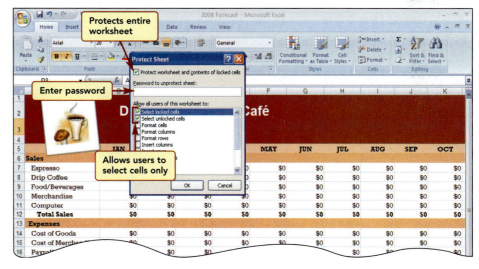

Protects entire worksheet

Enter password

Allows users to select cells only

Figure 4.13

In the Protect Sheet dialog box, you can enter a password to prevent unauthorized people from removing protection from the sheet and specify the options that you want to enable for all users of the template. The Select Locked Cells and Select Unlocked Cells options are enabled by default. Leaving these selected and the others unselected provides complete protection for the worksheet. You will complete the command to protect this sheet and then you will unlock the data entry areas of the four quarter sheets using another method.

3
- Enter your name as the password for the sheet.

- Click [OK].

- Reenter the password.

- Click [OK].

- Select the First Quarter through Fourth Quarter sheets.

- Select cells B7 through D11 and B16 through D21.

Having Trouble?
Hold down [Ctrl] to select nonadjacent ranges.

- Click  and choose Lock Cell to unlock all cells in the selection.

Your screen should be similar to Figure 4.14

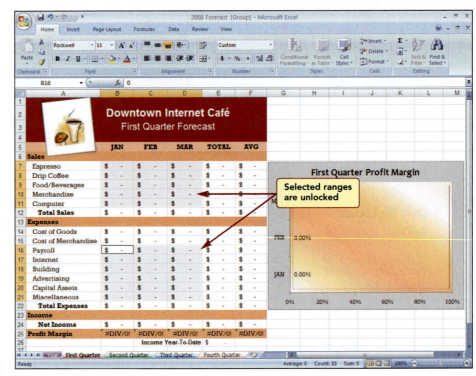

Figure 4.14

All selected cells in the four quarter sheets are unlocked. Next, you will protect the four quarter worksheets. When protecting worksheets, you must protect each sheet individually. You will ungroup the sheets and protect each sheet.

- Choose Ungroup Sheets from the sheet tab shortcut menu.

Another Method
You also can hold down ⇧Shift while clicking a sheet tab to ungroup sheets.

- If necessary, make the First Quarter sheet active.

- Click 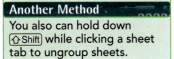 in the Cells group and choose Protect Sheet.

Another Method
You also can use 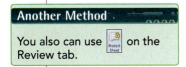 on the Review tab.

- Enter your password.

- Click OK.

- In a similar manner protect the other three quarter sheets.

Your screen should be similar to Figure 4.15

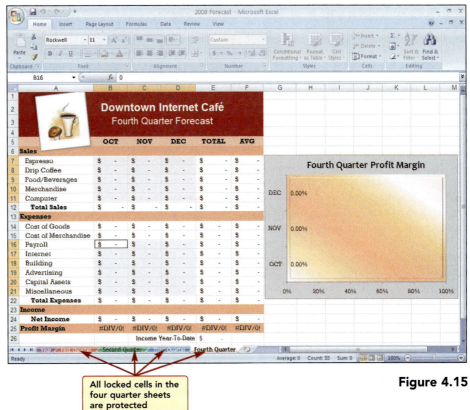

All locked cells in the four quarter sheets are protected

Figure 4.15

Now all locked cells in the four quarter sheets are protected. Only those cells you unlocked prior to turning on protection can be changed. To test this out, you will try to make an entry in a protected cell.

5
- Type any character in cell B5 of the Fourth Quarter sheet.

Your screen should be similar to Figure 4.16

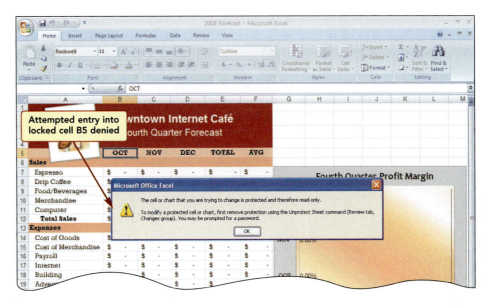

Attempted entry into locked cell B5 denied

Microsoft Office Excel

The cell or chart that you are trying to change is protected and therefore read-only.

To modify a protected cell or chart, first remove protection using the Unprotect Sheet command (Review tab, Changes group). You may be prompted for a password.

OK

Figure 4.16

The warning dialog box informs you that you cannot change entries in locked cells. Next, you will enter a value in an unlocked cell.

6 Click [OK] to clear the message.

- Type **1250** in cell B7 and press ↵Enter.

Your screen should be similar to Figure 4.17

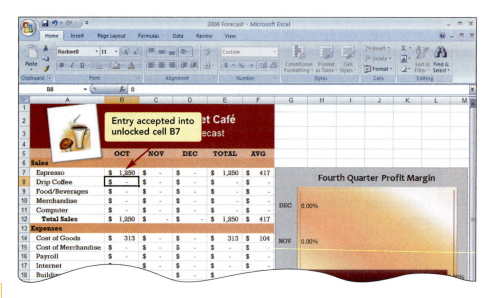

Figure 4.17

The entry is accepted because the cell was unlocked before protection was applied to the sheet.

Protecting the Workbook

In addition to protecting each worksheet, you can add protection to the workbook file. You will protect the structure of the file and include a password so that workbook protection cannot be changed by anyone who does not know the password.

1 Click [Protect Workbook] in the Changes group of the Review tab.

Your screen should be similar to Figure 4.18

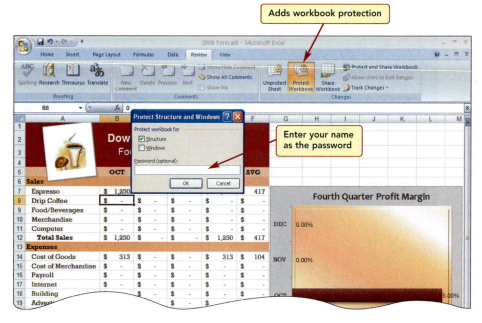

Figure 4.18

The default setting to protect the workbook structure is selected.

2 ● Enter your name as the password.

● Click [OK].

● Reenter the password.

● Click [OK].

Notice that [Unprotect Sheet] and [Unprotect Workbook] are now displayed in the Changes group. Protection can be turned off using these buttons and the appropriate passwords.

Saving the Template

Now that the sheets are protected, you will save this workbook as a template file. Excel saves a workbook template using a special file format with the file extension .xltx. Workbook templates are also stored in a special Templates folder.

First, you will clear the test entry and move the cell pointer to the location in the worksheet where you want it to appear when opened.

1 ● Click 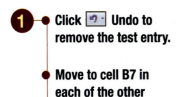 Undo to remove the test entry.

● Move to cell B7 in each of the other quarter sheets.

● Move to cell D3 in the Year sheet.

● Click 🅱 Office Button and choose Save As.

● Enter Forecast Template into the File Name text box.

● From the Save As Type list box, select Excel Template.

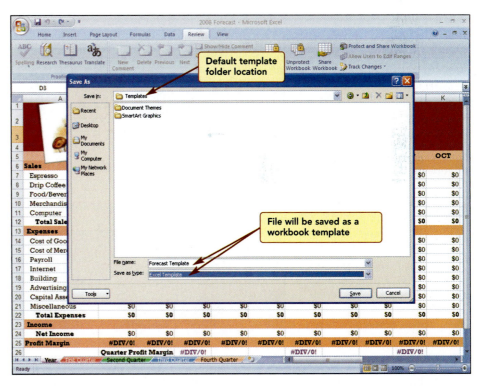

Figure 4.19

Your screen should be similar to Figure 4.19

Templates are saved by default to the Templates folder on your computer. You also can save templates to other locations just like any other workbook file.

2 ● **Click** [Save] **.**

Having Trouble?
If a file already exists with this name, click [Yes] to replace it.

● **Close the** Forecast Template **file.**

The Forecast Template workbook is now ready to use.

Using the Template

Now you will use the Forecast Template file to create a new forecast workbook for the following year, 2009. To use a workbook template, you select the template file name from the My Templates tab of the New Workbook dialog box. If it was recently used, the template also may appear in the Recently Used Templates section of the Blank and Recent tab.

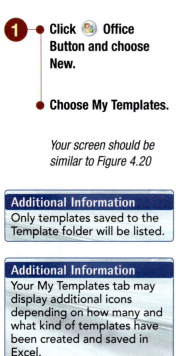

1 ● **Click** 🔘 **Office Button and choose New.**

● **Choose My Templates.**

Your screen should be similar to Figure 4.20

Additional Information
Only templates saved to the Template folder will be listed.

Additional Information
Your My Templates tab may display additional icons depending on how many and what kind of templates have been created and saved in Excel.

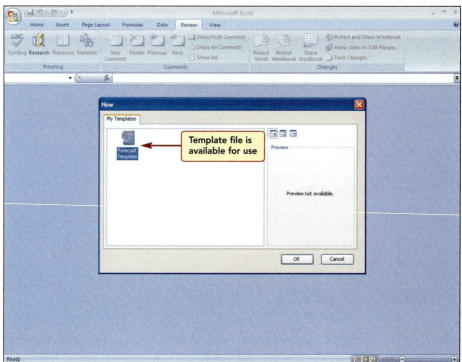

Template file is available for use

Figure 4.20

The Forecast Template file name appears in the My Templates dialog box. You will open the template and change the subtitle in the Year sheet to display the year 2009. Then you will try to move one of the sheets to verify that workbook protection is on.

2

- If necessary, select the Forecast Template file.

- Click [OK].

- Edit the subtitle in cell D3 of the Year sheet to 2009 Annual Forecast.

- Try to move the Year worksheet after the Fourth Quarter sheet.

Your screen should be similar to Figure 4.21

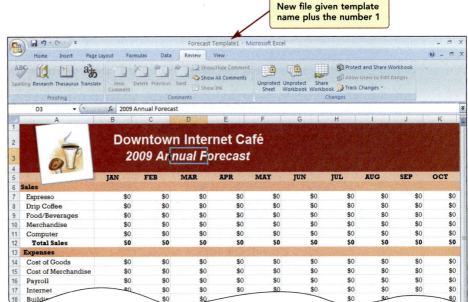

New file given template name plus the number 1

Figure 4.21

The subtitle was successfully changed to reflect the year; however, you were not able to move the sheet because that feature is restricted by workbook protection.

Before continuing, you want to save the revised template file as a new workbook file for use in entering the 2009 forecast data. Notice the file name in the title bar is Forecast Template1. Excel automatically adds a number to the file name when the template is opened to prevent you from accidentally overwriting the original template file when saving. Additionally, when using a template to create a new workbook file, even if you use the Save command, Excel automatically displays the Save As dialog box so that you can specify a new file name. It also changes the file type to an Excel workbook (.xlsx). This ensures that you do not unintentionally save over the template file.

3

- Click  in the Quick Access Toolbar.

- Enter the new name, 2009 Forecast, in the File Name text box.

- Change the Save In location to the appropriate location to save your files.

- Click [Save].

Your screen should be similar to Figure 4.22

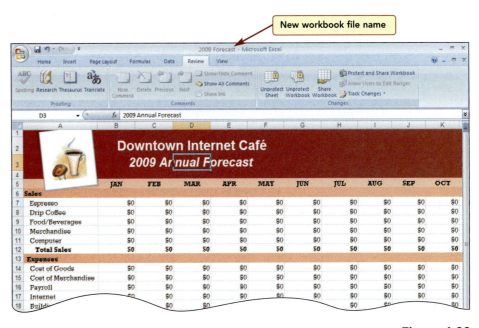

New workbook file name

Figure 4.22

Working with Multiple Workbooks

Evan wants you to focus on the 2009 first-quarter forecast. Because he expects all sales and expenses to remain the same as the December 2008 values, you can obtain this data from the 2008 Forecast workbook. To do this, you want to copy the data from one workbook to the other. In Excel, you can open multiple workbook files at the same time. Each workbook is opened in its own window. You also can open additional separate windows to display different parts of the active workbook. The open windows can be arranged so that you can see them simultaneously to make it easy to work with data in multiple workbooks at the same time.

Opening a Second Workbook File

You will open the workbook file containing the 2008 forecast data you saved earlier.

1 ● **Open the** 2008 Forecast **workbook file.**

Your screen should be similar to Figure 4.23

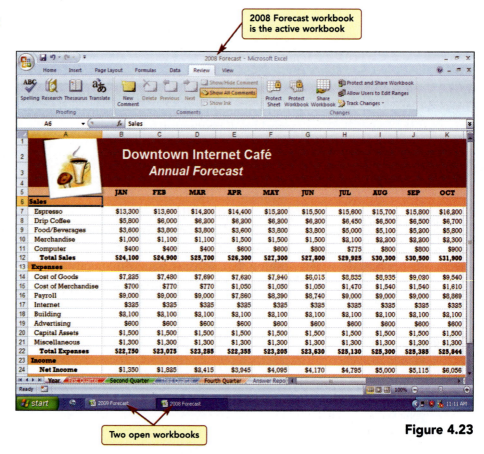

2008 Forecast workbook is the active workbook

Two open workbooks

Figure 4.23

Now there are two opened workbook files. The 2008 Forecast workbook file window is open on top of the 2009 Forecast workbook file window. The newly opened file is the **active workbook** file. It is the file that will be affected by changes and the file that contains the cell selector.

Lab 4: Using Solver, Creating Templates, and Evaluating Scenarios

www.mhhe.com/oleary

Arranging Workbook Windows

The way the workbooks are currently displayed makes it difficult to work with both files simultaneously. To make it easier to work with both files at the same time, you can change the arrangement of the windows.

Concept 4

Window Arrangement

4 The **window arrangement** feature displays all open workbook files in separate windows on the screen, making it easy to view and work with information in different workbooks. When new workbook windows are opened, they appear in the same size and on top of any other open windows. Open windows can be arranged in the following ways:

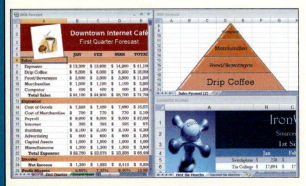

Tiled: The windows are displayed one after the other in succession, across and down the screen.

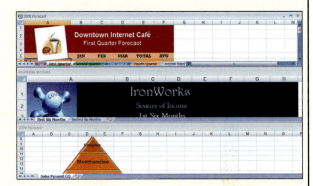

Horizontal: The windows are displayed one above the other.

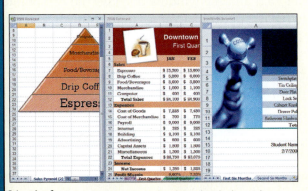

Vertical: The windows are displayed side by side.

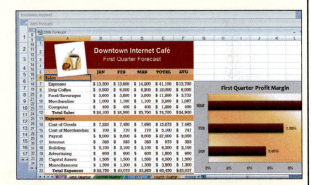

Cascade: The windows are displayed one on top of the other, cascading down from the top of the screen.

You decide that the easiest way to work with the two files is to tile them.

1 ● Open the View tab.

● Click 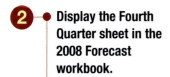 in the Window group.

Additional Information

The Windows of Active Workbook option arranges the windows of only the active workbook.

● If necessary, select Tiled.

● Click ☐ OK ☐.

Your screen should be similar to Figure 4.24

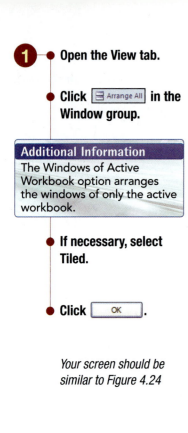

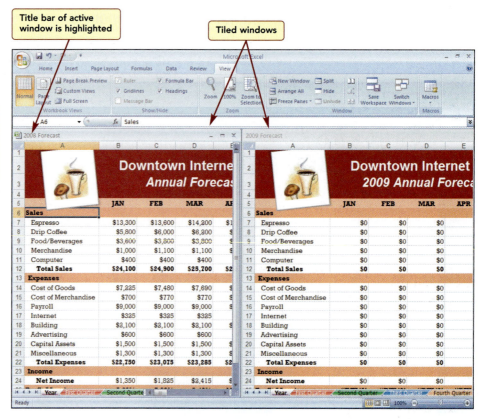

Figure 4.24

The two workbook windows appear side by side. The title bar of the active workbook file is highlighted and the window displays the cell pointer and scroll bar. You want to see the December values in the Fourth Quarter sheet of the 2008 Forecast and the First Quarter sheet from the 2009 Forecast.

2 ● Display the Fourth Quarter sheet in the 2008 Forecast workbook.

● Click in the 2009 Forecast workbook window to make it active.

● Display the First Quarter sheet.

Your screen should be similar to Figure 4.25

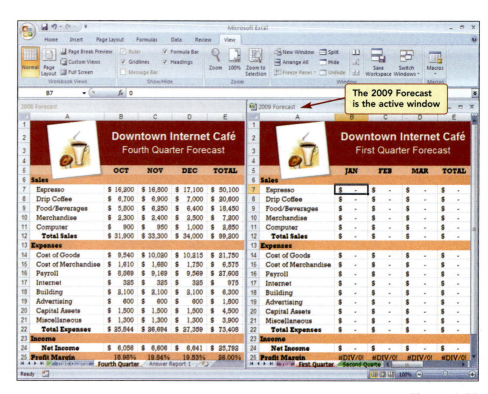

Figure 4.25

Linking Workbooks

You will use the December data from the 2008 Forecast workbook as the data for the first quarter of the 2009 Forecast workbook. Additionally, you want the data in the 2009 forecast to update automatically if the data in the 2008 forecast changes. To do this, you will create a link between the two workbook files.

Concept 5

Link

5 A **link**, also called an **external reference**, creates a connection between files that automatically updates the linked data in one file whenever the data in the other file changes. When data in a linked cell changes, the workbook that is affected by this change is automatically updated when it is opened.

   The link between the workbook files is formed by entering an **external reference formula** in one workbook that refers to a cell in another workbook. The formula is entered in the workbook that receives the data. This workbook file is called the **destination workbook**. The workbook that supplies the data is called the **source workbook**. The cell containing the external reference formula (the **destination cell**) refers to the cell (the **source cell**) in the source file that contains the data to be copied.

An external reference formula uses the following format:

$$= \text{[2008 Forecast]Fourth Quarter!\$D\$8}$$

[workbook file reference]sheet reference!cell reference

The file reference consists of the file name of the source workbook followed by the name of the worksheet. The cell reference of the cell or range of cells containing the number to be copied into the destination workbook follows the file reference. The two parts of the formula are separated by an exclamation point.

You will create a link between the two workbook files by entering external reference formulas in the 2009 First Quarter worksheet that reference the cells containing the values in the Fourth Quarter sheet of the 2008 Forecast workbook. The 2008 Forecast workbook is the source workbook, and the 2009 Forecast workbook is the destination workbook.

The first external reference formula you will enter will link the Espresso sales numbers. To create an external reference formula, you first select the cell or cells in which you want to create the link and begin by typing an = sign followed by an arithmetic operator if you want to perform a calculation using the linked data.

The source cell is cell D7 of the Fourth Quarter sheet in the 2008 Forecast workbook and the destination cell is cell B7 in the First Quarter sheet of the 2009 Forecast file.

1 ● **Select cell B7 in the First Quarter sheet of the 2009 Forecast workbook.**

● **Type =.**

● **Click on the Fourth Quarter sheet in the 2008 Forecast workbook to make it active and then click on cell D7.**

● **Press** ←Enter.

● **Move to cell B7.**

Your screen should be similar to Figure 4.26

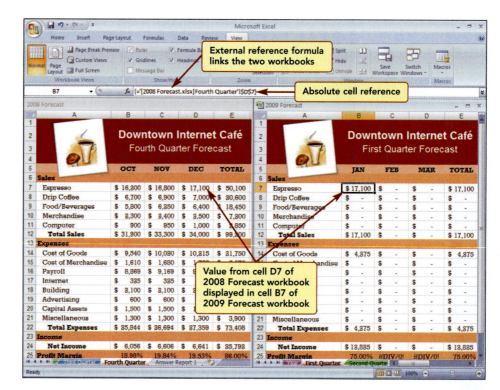

Figure 4.26

The link has been established and an external reference formula has been entered into the selected cell of the destination workbook. The formula is displayed in the formula bar, and the number in cell D7 of the source workbook is entered into the destination workbook and displayed in cell B7. Notice that Excel uses absolute references in the external reference formula.

Next, you want to create a link between the other December values in the source workbook. To do this quickly, you can copy the external reference formula down the column. However, you must first change the absolute cell reference, $D$7, in the external reference formula to a mixed reference of $D7 so that it will adjust appropriately as the formula is copied.

2 In cell B7 of the 2009 Forecast workbook, edit the absolute reference ($D$7) in the formula to $D7.

● Copy the external reference formula in cell B7 to cells B8 through B11 and B16 through B21.

● Click cell B21 to deselect the range.

Your screen should be similar to Figure 4.27

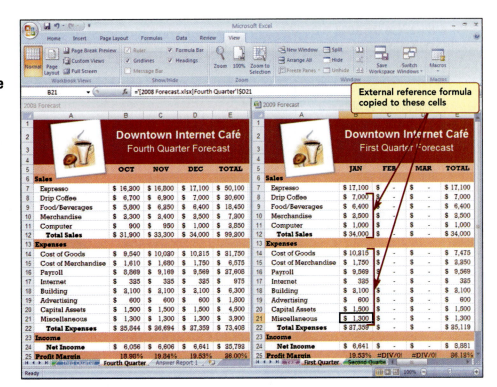

Figure 4.27

The data for January 2009 is now complete. It is the same as the December 2008 data. Because the data in the worksheets is linked, a change in the December 2008 worksheet values will automatically be reflected in the First Quarter 2009 worksheet.

Updating Linked Data

After reviewing your note regarding the unrealistic payroll values needed to achieve a 26 percent profit margin, Evan has decided to use the payroll values that were generated using Solver for the 25 percent profit margin. You will rerun Solver to quickly revise the figures in the Fourth Quarter worksheet.

1 Switch to the 2008 Forecast workbook window.

• Use Solver to obtain a 25 percent profit margin in the fourth quarter by adjusting the payroll values.

• Keep the Solver solution.

Your screen should be similar to Figure 4.28

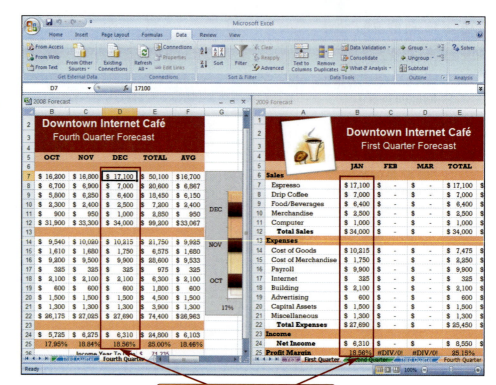

Values in linked cells are automatically updated to reflect change in data

Figure 4.28

All affected formulas are recalculated. Because the workbooks are linked, the change in the 2008 Forecast is automatically reflected in the 2009 Forecast. Once an external reference formula is entered in a worksheet, whenever the data in the cell referenced in the source file changes, the dependent file is automatically updated if it is open.

If the dependent file is not open, it is not updated. To ensure that a dependent file gets updated when you open the source file, Excel displays an alert message asking if you want to update references to unopened documents. If you respond Yes, Excel checks the source documents and updates all references to them so that you will have the latest values from the source worksheet.

You do not need to obtain any further data from the 2008 Forecast workbook at this time. You will save it and enlarge the 2009 Forecast window to make it easier to work with.

2
- Save the 2008 Forecast file.

- Maximize the 2009 Forecast window.

- Save the 2009 Forecast file.

Your screen should be similar to Figure 4.29

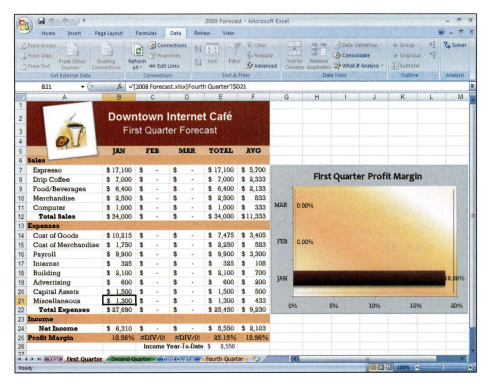

Figure 4.29

Hiding Workbooks and Worksheets

Evan has asked you to create a drawing to illustrate the relationship between the four sales categories. You decide to do this in the 2009 Forecast workbook. When you are working with two workbooks that have similar data in them, you might easily confuse them. To help in situations like this, Excel allows you to hide a workbook. By hiding a workbook, it stays in memory but is not visible to the user. To further simplify the display, you also can hide worksheets in a workbook file.

You will hide the 2008 Forecast file while you work with the 2009 Forecast. In addition, you want to hide all sheets except the First Quarter sheet in the 2009 Forecast workbook. To do this, you will first need to turn off workbook protection.

1 ● Make the 2008
Forecast window
active.

● Click [Hide] in the
Window group of the
View tab.

● Click [Unprotect Workbook] in the
Changes group of the
Review tab.

● Enter your password
and click [OK].

● Select the Year,
Second Quarter, Third
Quarter, and Fourth
Quarter sheets.

● Choose Hide from the
sheet tab shortcut
menu.

*Your screen should be
similar to Figure 4.30*

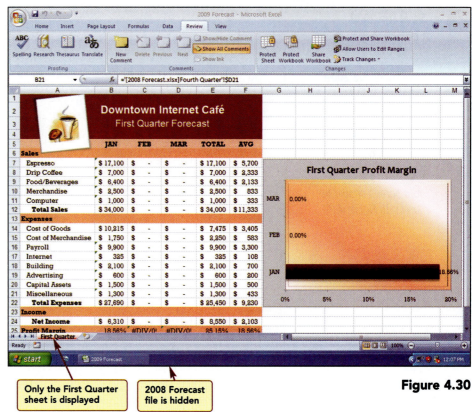

Only the First Quarter
sheet is displayed

2008 Forecast
file is hidden

Figure 4.30

The 2008 Forecast workbook file is no longer displayed. The only
worksheet that is displayed is the First Quarter sheet in the 2009 Forecast
workbook.

Inserting a Worksheet

You will create the drawing on a separate worksheet in the 2009 Forecast
workbook. To do this, you will insert a new worksheet in the workbook
and name it.

1 Click 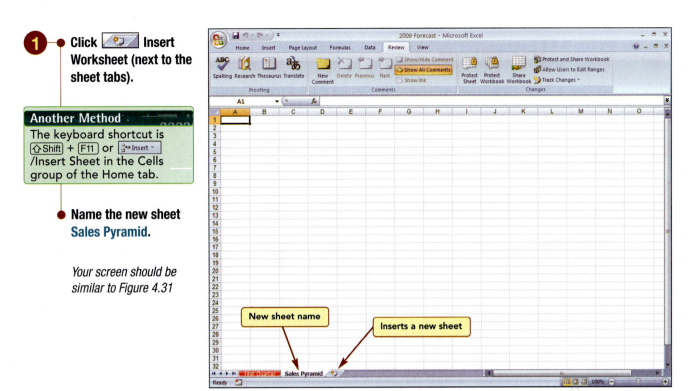 Insert Worksheet (next to the sheet tabs).

• **Name the new sheet Sales Pyramid.**

Your screen should be similar to Figure 4.31

New sheet name

Inserts a new sheet

Figure 4.31

A blank worksheet has been inserted into the workbook.

Arranging Worksheet Windows

You want to be able to see the data in the First Quarter worksheet while you create the graphic. Just like workbook windows, you can arrange displayed worksheets in the workspace. To do this, each worksheet you want to arrange must be open in a separate window. Then, you can specify the window arrangement.

1 Click New Window in the Window group of the View tab.

• Click Arrange All.

• **Choose Windows of Active Workbook.**

• Click OK.

Your screen should be similar to Figure 4.32

Opens a new window

Window number

Copy of 2009 Forecast workbook displayed in second window

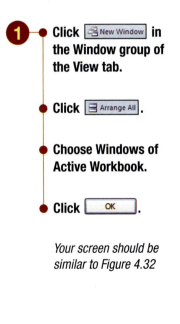
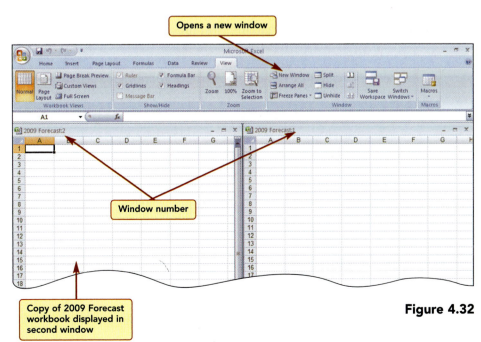

Figure 4.32

A copy of the 2009 Forecast workbook is displayed in the second window. The window title bar displays the file name followed by the window number to help you identify the windows.

Now you will display the First Quarter sheet in the right window (window 1).

2 ● **Click on the 2009 Forecast:1 window to make it active.**

● **Display the First Quarter sheet.**

Your screen should be similar to Figure 4.33

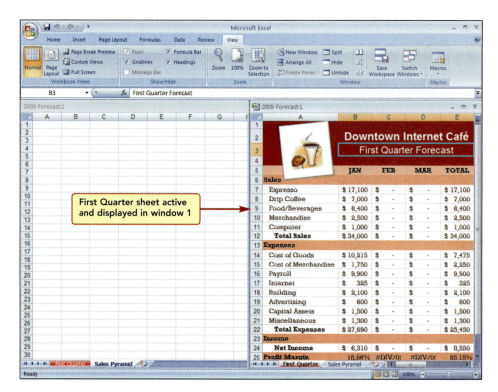

First Quarter sheet active and displayed in window 1

Figure 4.33

Creating SmartArt

You want to create a graphic that will display the importance of the four sales categories relative to each other. Excel includes several ready-made SmartArt graphics that help you quickly create a drawing to show this type of information.

Concept 6

6 A **SmartArt graphic** is used to create a visual representation of textual information. SmartArt graphics are based on text rather than numeric information. There are seven types of graphics you can use. The type of graphic you choose depends on the purpose of the graphic and the type of concept you want to illustrate. The table below describes the graphic types and uses.

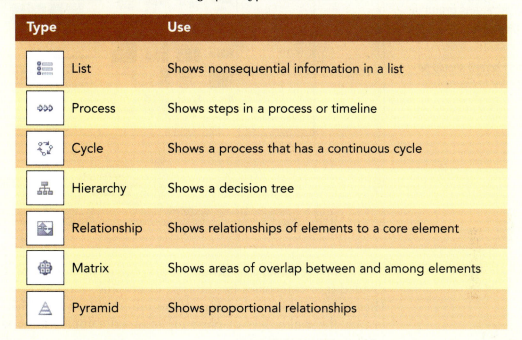

Type		Use
	List	Shows nonsequential information in a list
	Process	Shows steps in a process or timeline
	Cycle	Shows a process that has a continuous cycle
	Hierarchy	Shows a decision tree
	Relationship	Shows relationships of elements to a core element
	Matrix	Shows areas of overlap between and among elements
	Pyramid	Shows proportional relationships

Additionally, you can create flowcharts (or flow graphics) using a combination of shapes in the Drawing tools, including flowchart shapes and connectors. Flowcharts show a process that has a beginning and an end.

You will use the Pyramid SmartArt to illustrate how the four sales categories relate.

1 • **Click on the Sales Pyramid sheet in the 2009 Forecast:2 window to make it active.**

• **Click** [SmartArt] **in the Illustrations group of the Insert tab.**

Your screen should be similar to Figure 4.34

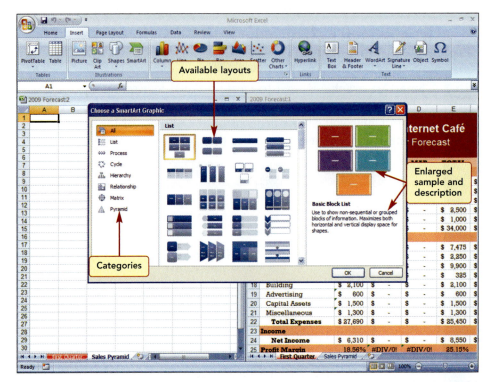

Figure 4.34

The complete gallery of SmartArt graphic designs is displayed. They are divided into categories by the type of graphic, such as Process, Cycle, or Hierarchy. Within each category are different layouts. When you select a layout, the dialog box displays an enlarged sample of the graphic and a brief description of its use.

2 • **Choose the Pyramid category.**

• **Click** ▲ .

• **Click** [OK] .

Your screen should be similar to Figure 4.35

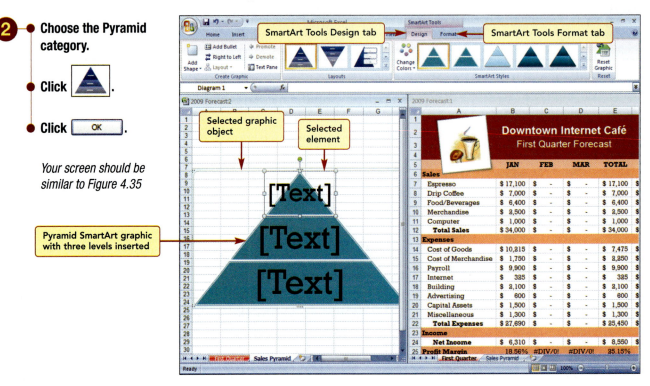

Figure 4.35

A pyramid graphic consisting of three levels is created by default. The pyramid graphic is the selected graphic object and is surrounded with a selection rectangle. The SmartArt Tools Design and Format tabs also are displayed and contain buttons to add shapes, modify the layout, and enhance the graphic. Each level is a separate element of the graphic that can be selected and modified independently. Currently, the top-level element of the pyramid is selected.

Adding Shapes to SmartArt

Because you want the graphic to represent the five sales categories, you first need to add two more levels to the pyramid for the fourth and fifth sales categories.

1 ● Click [Add Shape] twice in the Create Graphic group.

● Click [Text Pane] in the Create Graphic group of the SmartArt Tools Design tab.

● If necessary, move the Text pane so that you can see the five Sales categories.

Your screen should be similar to Figure 4.36

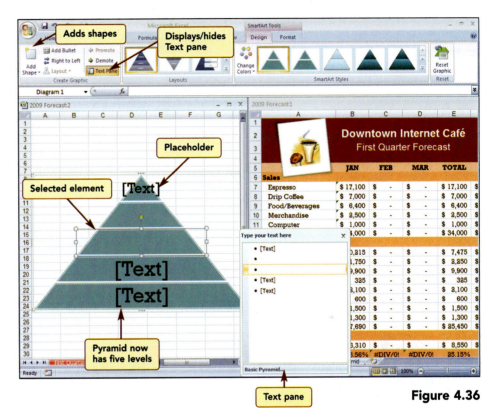

Text pane

Figure 4.36

The pyramid shape now consists of five levels and the Text pane is displayed.

Adding Text to a SmartArt Graphic

Next, you want to add text to each segment of the pyramid. To add text, you can type in the Text pane or you can select the [Text] placeholder and type in it.

When an element is selected, it is surrounded by a solid border and sizing handles that are used to decrease or enlarge the shape. While the element is selected like this, you can format the entire element. If you click the element again, the border changes to a dashed border and an insertion point appears. A dashed border indicates that you can enter, delete, select, and format text. If the element contains a [Text] placeholder, clicking directly on the placeholder displays a dashed border and insertion point, ready for entry of text.

First you will add text to the bottom element, which will represent the largest sales category. As you can see from the First Quarter worksheet, this category is Espresso. The next largest sales category will be represented in the next level, and so forth.

Additional Information

You also can copy text from another worksheet or program and paste it into the Text pane.

1 • **Click on [Text] in the bottom level.**

• **Type Espresso.**

Your screen should be similar to Figure 4.37

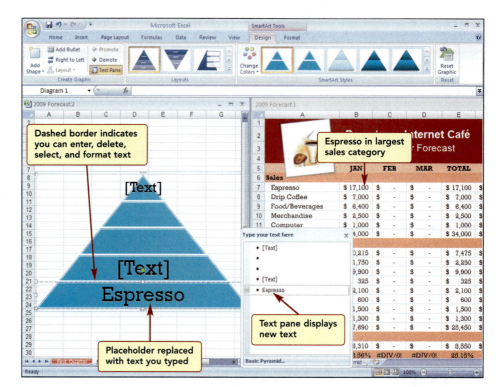

Dashed border indicates you can enter, delete, select, and format text

Espresso in largest sales category

[Text]

[Text]
Espresso

Placeholder replaced with text you typed

Text pane displays new text

Figure 4.37

The placeholder text has been replaced with the text you entered. It is centered both horizontally and vertically in the pyramid segment. The text also appears in the lowest bullet in the Text pane. Using the First Quarter sheet as a reference, you will enter the remaining sales category names into the pyramid using the Text pane.

2 • **Click on the second bullet from the bottom in the Text pane and type Drip Coffee.**

• **In a similar manner, add the text Food/Beverages, Merchandise, and Computer to the other levels.**

Your screen should be similar to Figure 4.38

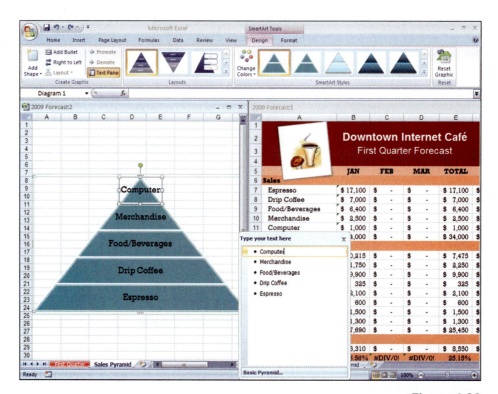

Computer

Merchandise

Food/Beverages

Drip Coffee

Espresso

Figure 4.38

Formatting the SmartArt Graphic

Notice that all the text has been sized to 14 points to match the Computer label. You want to customize the text size of each segment to more closely fit the size of the segment.

1
- **Double-click on the text in the top bullet of the Text pane to select it.**

- **Open the 14 Font Size list in the Mini toolbar and change the font size to 10.**

- **Select the Merchandise text in the second segment and decrease the font size to 14.**

- **Change the text size for the third segment to 16, the fourth to 24, and the bottom to 32.**

- **Click to the side of the pyramid to deselect the segment.**

Your screen should be similar to Figure 4.39

Additional Information

The Format tab contains options for changing the color of each shape individually.

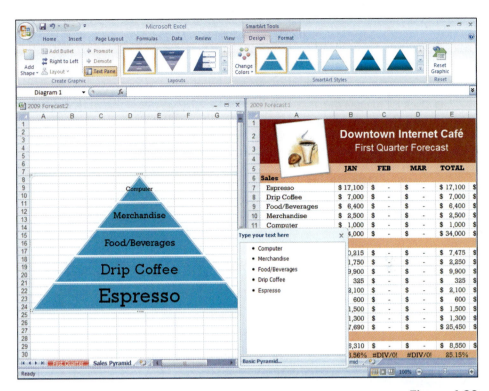

Figure 4.39

You also think the pyramid would look better if the segments were different colors that coordinate with the colors used in the worksheet. You could apply colors individually to each segment or you can use one of the preset color design schemes. You can then further enhance the appearance of the pyramid by applying a **SmartArt Style,** combinations of different formatting options such as edges, gradients, line styles, shadows, and three-dimensional effects. You can try different combinations of colors and styles until you find the one that suits you.

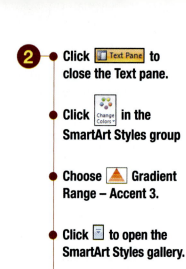

2 ● Click [Text Pane] to close the Text pane.

● Click [Change Colors] in the SmartArt Styles group

● Choose ▲ Gradient Range – Accent 3.

● Click ▼ to open the SmartArt Styles gallery.

● Point to several SmartArt Style designs to see the Live Preview.

● Choose Cartoon.

Your screen should be similar to Figure 4.40

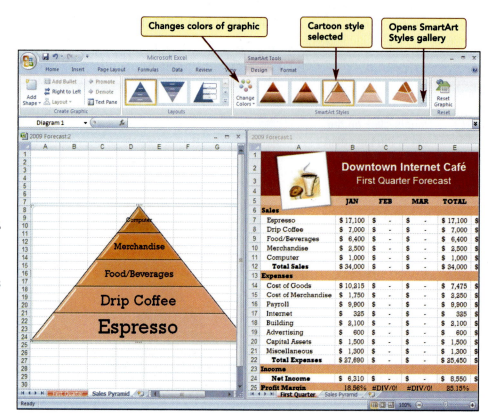

Changes colors of graphic

Cartoon style selected

Opens SmartArt Styles gallery

Figure 4.40

The selected colors and SmartArt Style greatly improve the appearance of the pyramid.

Unhiding Sheets and Workbooks

Now that you are finished working on the graphic, you will close the Forecast:2 window and maximize the remaining window. Then you will redisplay the other sheets in the workbook.

Additional Information

If, after making many formatting changes to a SmartArt graphic, you want to return to the original graphic design, use [Reset Graphic].

1

- Click ⊠ to close the Forecast:2 window.

- Maximize the 2009 Forecast window.

- Click 🗐 Format ▾ in the Cells group on the Home tab, select Hide & Unhide, and choose Unhide Sheet.

- Select the Year sheet from the Unhide dialog box and click OK.

- In a similar manner, unhide the three other sheets.

Your screen should be similar to Figure 4.41

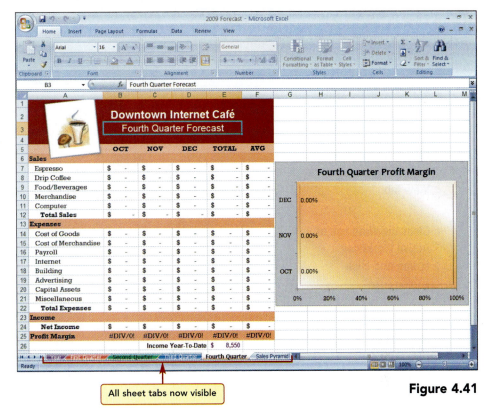

All sheet tabs now visible

Figure 4.41

Finally, you want to include a copy of the Sales Pyramid sheet in the 2008 workbook file. You will redisplay this file, tile the workbook windows, and copy the sheet.

2

- Click [□ Unhide] in the Window group of the View tab.

- Select 2008 Forecast and click [OK].

- Click [⊟ Arrange All] in the Window group on the View tab.

- Clear the Windows of Active Workbook option and click [OK].

- Display the Sales Pyramid sheet and choose Move or Copy from the sheet tab shortcut menu.

- From the To Book list, choose 2008 Forecast.xlsx.

- From the Before Sheet list, choose (move to end).

- Choose Create a copy.

- Click [OK].

Your screen should be similar to Figure 4.42

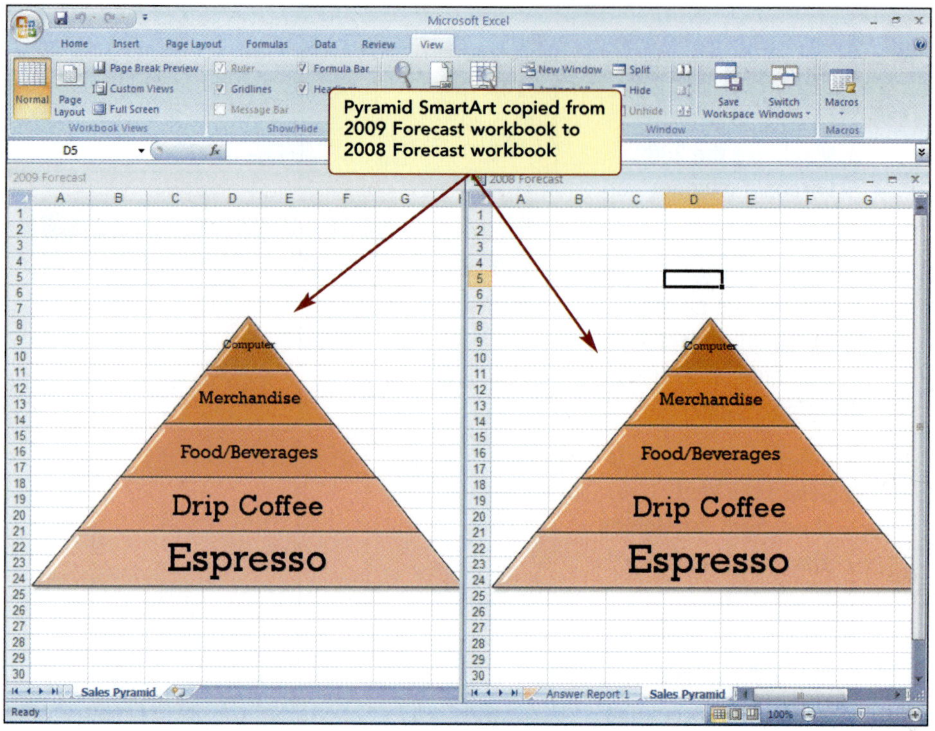

Figure 4.42

Now both workbooks include the pyramid graphic sheet.

3

- Save and close the 2008 Forecast workbook file.

- Maximize the 2009 Forecast workbook window.

- Preview the Sales Pyramid sheet.

- Add your name, left-aligned, and the current date, right-aligned, in the header.

- Center the pyramid horizontally on the page.

- Print the pyramid.

Lab 4: Using Solver, Creating Templates, and Evaluating Scenarios

Your printed output should be similar to that shown in the Case Study at the beginning of the lab.

Using Scenarios

Evan has reviewed the January 2009 values and is comfortable with them. He predicts, however, that post-holiday sales in February and March will decline. He has asked you to complete the First Quarter forecast with the following data:

	February	March
Espresso	16,800	16,200
Drip Coffee	6,900	6,700
Food/Beverages	6,250	5,800
Merchandise	2,200	2,000
Computer	950	900
Payroll	9,200	8,800
Internet	325	325
Building	2,100	2,100
Advertising	600	600
Capital Assets	1,500	1,500
Miscellaneous	1,300	1,300

1 ● **Display the First Quarter sheet.**

● **Enter the values shown in the table above to update the First Quarter forecast.**

Your screen should be similar to Figure 4.43

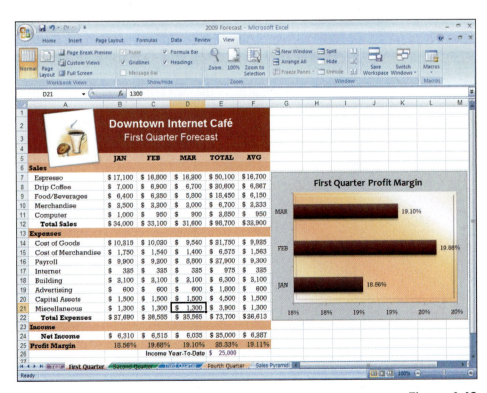

Figure 4.43

While he realizes that sales and costs may be higher or lower than those presented, Evan believes the most likely scenario, or set of values, is reflected in the First Quarter worksheet. He has asked you to evaluate a best-case scenario and a worst-case scenario.

Concept 7

Scenario

7 A **scenario** is a named set of input values that you can substitute in a worksheet to see the effects of a possible alternative course of action. Scenarios are designed to help forecast the outcome of various possible actions. You can create and save different groups of scenario values on a worksheet and then switch to any of these scenarios to view the results.

For example, if you want to create a budget forecast based on various revenue values, you could define the potential values and then switch between the scenarios to perform what-if analyses. You also can create reports in separate sheets that summarize the scenarios you create.

The current data in the First Quarter worksheet reflects the most likely scenario. Evan has identified the best-case scenario as one where Espresso sales increase 25 percent above the current estimate in February and March and all other values remain unchanged. His worst-case scenario is if Espresso sales decrease 10 percent below the current estimate for the entire quarter and the building expenses in March increase to $2,500.

Creating Scenarios

You will use the Scenario Manager tool to evaluate the alternative scenarios by changing the values for Espresso sales for January (cell B7), February (cell C7), and March (cell D7), and for March Building expense (cell D18). You could create separate worksheets to evaluate each scenario. However, using the Scenario Manager tool, you can create different scenarios and insert these scenarios directly into the workbook to see how each affects the worksheet.

1
- Open the Data tab.

- Click 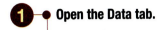 from the Data Tools group and choose Scenario Manager.

- Move the Scenario Manager dialog box to the right of column F.

Your screen should be similar to Figure 4.44

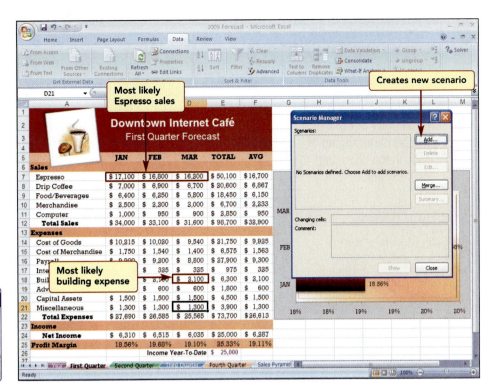

Figure 4.44

The Scenario Manager dialog box is used to add, delete, and edit scenarios. There are no scenarios named yet. First, you will define the most likely scenario.

2
- Click  .

Your screen should be similar to Figure 4.45

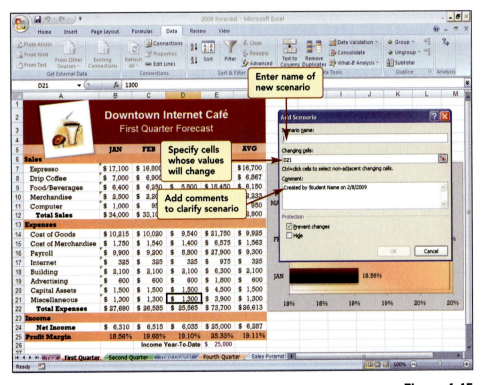

Figure 4.45

In the Add Scenario dialog box, you enter a name for the first scenario and the range of cells that will contain the changing values.

3 • Type **Most Likely** in the Scenario Name text box.

• Specify the range B7 through D7 and cell D18 as the changing cells in the Changing Cell text box.

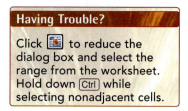

Having Trouble?

Click 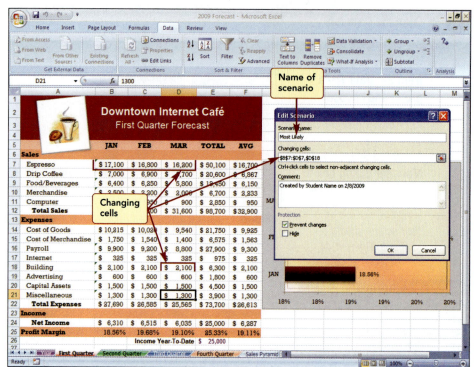 to reduce the dialog box and select the range from the worksheet. Hold down Ctrl while selecting nonadjacent cells.

Your screen should be similar to Figure 4.46

Figure 4.46

It is often helpful to add a comment to clarify the data included in the scenario. The default comment in the Comment text box is "Created by [name] on [date]." You will include additional information to clarify the meaning of the scenario.

4 • Click in the Comment text box.

• If necessary, replace the name with your name.

• Press ⏎Enter at the end of the date.

• Type **Expected first quarter sales and expenses.**

• Click [OK].

• Click [OK] to accept that formulas will be replaced by values.

Your screen should be similar to Figure 4.47

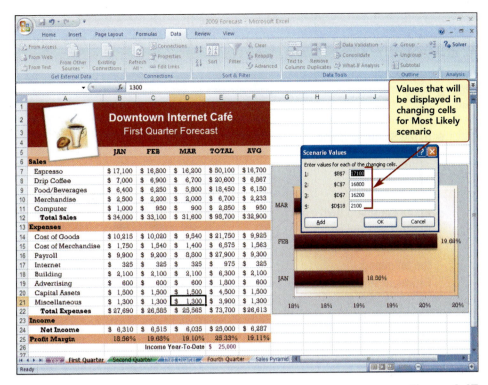

Figure 4.47

The Scenario Values dialog box is used to enter the values to be varied for the different scenarios. The current worksheet values are displayed. These are the values you want to use for the Most Likely scenario.

5 • Click [OK].

Your screen should be similar to Figure 4.48

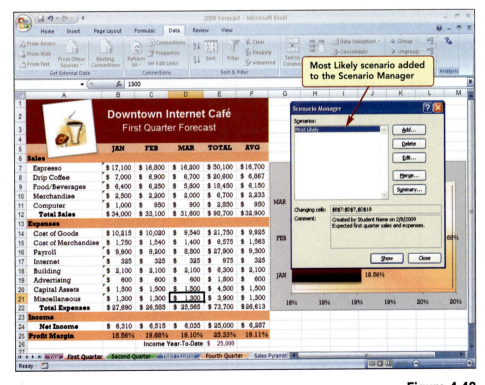

Figure 4.48

You are returned to the Scenario Manager dialog box and the name of the new scenario is displayed in the Scenarios list box.

Next, you will create the worst-case scenario. In this scenario, there would be a 10 percent decrease in Espresso sales and an increase in the Building expense.

6 ● Click [Add].

● In the Scenario Name text box, type **Worst Case**.

● In the Comment text box, change the name if necessary and enter the following: **Espresso sales are 10% less than the most likely values and March building expense increases to $2,500.**

● Click [OK] twice.

● Enter the following scenario values into the appropriate changing cells text boxes.

$B$7	15390
$C$7	15120
$D$7	14580
$D$18	2500

Your screen should be similar to Figure 4.49

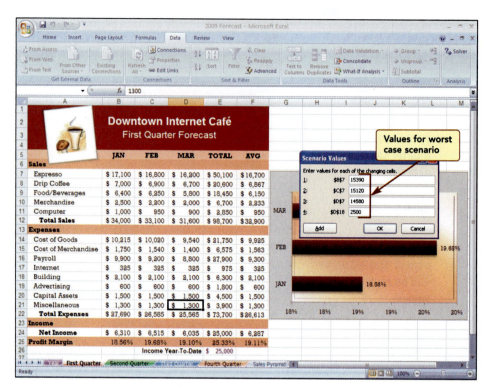

Figure 4.49

Next, you will create the best-case scenario. In this scenario, Evan anticipates that Espresso sales will increase 5 percent above the most-likely values and the March Building expense will remain the same. You could create the scenario in the same way by entering the new values in the changing cells. Another way is to use Solver to calculate the expected values for you and then create the scenario from the Solver result. You will need to provide the target cell value, 52650 for Solver, which reflects a 5 percent increase in total espresso sales for the quarter. You also will need to remove worksheet protection before using Solver.

7 • Click OK .

• Click Close .

• Save the workbook file.

• Click **Unprotect Sheet** in the Changes group of the Review tab, enter your password, and click OK .

• Click **Solver** Solver in the Analysis group on the Data tab.

• Set the target cell as E7, the value equal to 52650, and the changing cells as B7:D7.

• Click Solve .

Your screen should be similar to Figure 4.50

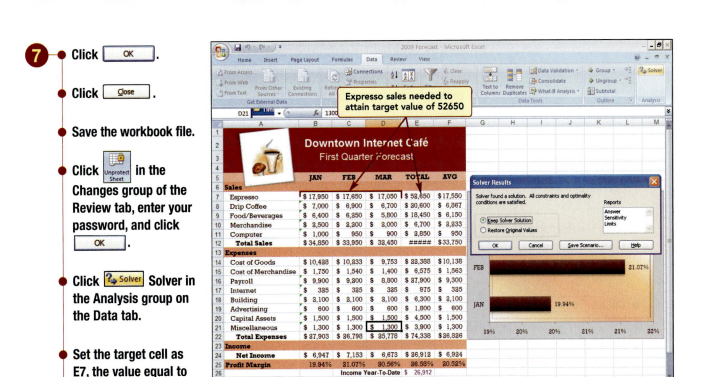

Figure 4.50

The Solver solution increases the Espresso sales for each month to attain the target value. You will create the scenario from these results. You will not keep the Solver solution, as you want the original values maintained in the worksheet.

8 • Click Save Scenario... .

• Enter the scenario name of Best Case.

• Click OK .

• Choose Restore Original Values.

• Click OK .

Your screen should be similar to Figure 4.51

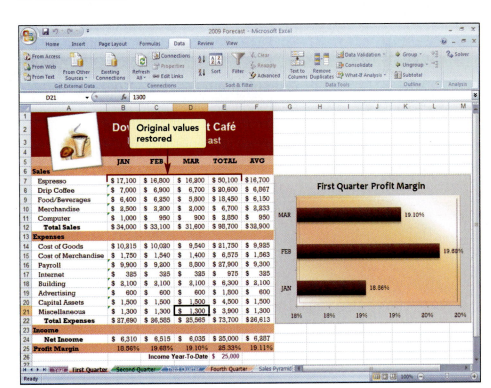

Figure 4.51

The original values are displayed in the worksheet again and the Solver results have been stored as a scenario.

Showing and Editing Scenarios

There are now three different scenarios in the worksheet. You want to see the effects of the worst-case and best-case scenarios.

1. • Click  in the Data Tools group and choose **Scenario Manager.**

   • From the Scenario Manager dialog box, select Worst Case.

   • Click [Show] .

   • Move the Scenario Manager dialog box so that you can see the chart.

   Your screen should be similar to Figure 4.52

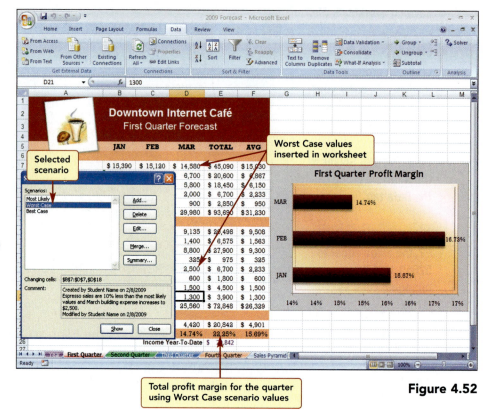

Figure 4.52

The worksheet displays the worst-case values. These values result in a total profit margin of 22.25 percent. The chart reflects the change in monthly profit margins.

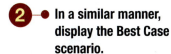

2 In a similar manner, display the Best Case scenario.

Having Trouble?
If Excel did not update the chart, move the Scenario Manager box slightly to refresh the window.

Your screen should be similar to Figure 4.53

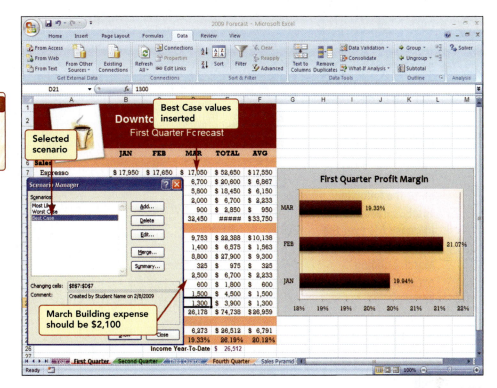

Figure 4.53

The best-case values are displayed in the worksheet. You notice, however, that the March Building expense value is the value that was last used in the Worst Case scenario. You need to edit the Best Case scenario to reset the March Building expense to $2,100. You also will add a comment to the scenario.

3 ● Click [Edit...].

● Specify the Changing Cells range as B7:D7 and cell D18.

● In the Comment text box, if necessary, change the name and enter the following: **Total Espresso sales increase 5% over the most likely values and March building expenses remain the same.**

● Click [OK].

● Enter **2100** as the value for D18.

● Click [OK].

● Click [Show].

Your screen should be similar to Figure 4.54

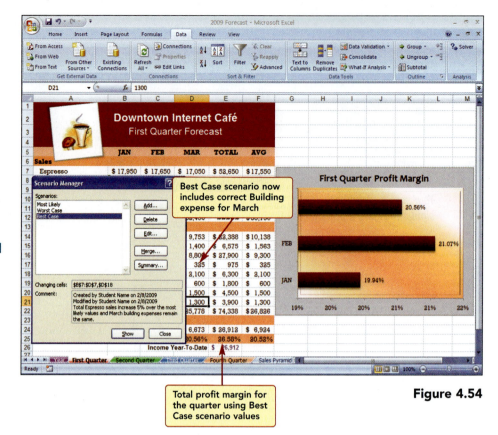

Figure 4.54

The Best Case scenario now shows a total profit margin of 26.58 percent.

Creating a Scenario Report

Another way to evaluate the scenarios is to create a summary report that will display the effect on the profit margins for each scenario.

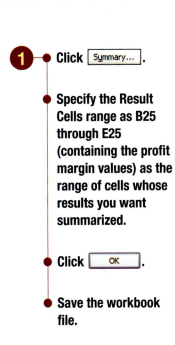

1 ● Click Summary... .

● Specify the Result Cells range as B25 through E25 (containing the profit margin values) as the range of cells whose results you want summarized.

● Click OK .

● Save the workbook file.

Your screen should be similar to Figure 4.55

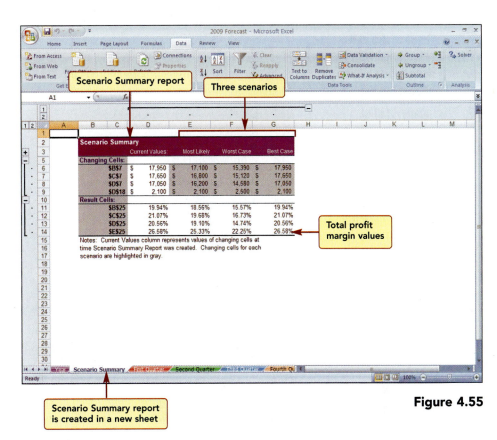

Figure 4.55

Scenario Summary report is created in a new sheet

The Scenario Summary report is created and displayed in a separate sheet. It displays the values for the three scenarios and the profit margin results for each scenario. As you can see from the summary, the Most Likely scenario shows a total profit margin of 25.33 percent. The Best Case scenario yields higher profit margins, with a total profit margin of 26.58 percent for the quarter. The Worst Case scenario yields lower profit margins, with a total profit margin of 22.25 percent.

The report, however, is hard to understand because it uses cell references as the labels. To clarify the meaning of the report, you will edit the row labels.

2 — **Replace the cell references with the descriptive labels shown below:**

Cell	Label	Cell	Label
C6	EspressoJAN	C11	ProfitMarginJAN
C7	EspressoFEB	C12	ProfitMarginFEB
C8	EspressoMAR	C13	ProfitMarginMAR
C9	BuildingMAR	C14	ProfitMarginTOTAL

● **AutoFit the width of column C to fit the column contents.**

Your screen should be similar to Figure 4.56

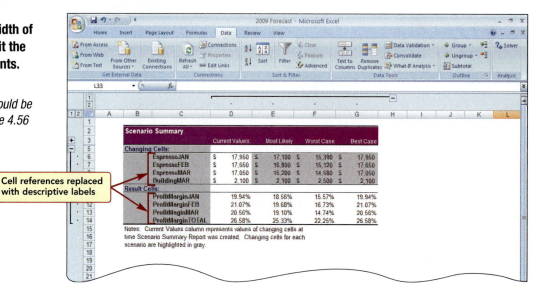

Cell references replaced with descriptive labels

Figure 4.56

You have now completed best- and worst-case scenarios for the first quarter of 2009, as Evan requested.

Inserting a Function

You would like to include a date and time stamp on the Scenario Summary worksheet to identify when the values were entered and the scenarios applied. You could just enter the current date and time on the worksheet, but you want to ensure that it reflects exactly when the most recent changes and analyses are done. To have the date and time automatically update whenever a worksheet is recalculated, the **NOW function** is used.

Using the Insert Function Feature

You will enter the function in cell B3. You could enter the function directly by typing it. However, another way is to use the Insert Function feature. This feature simplifies entering functions by prompting you to select a function from a list and then helps you enter the arguments correctly.

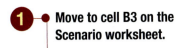

1 ● Move to cell B3 on the Scenario worksheet.

● Click [fx] Insert Function in the formula bar.

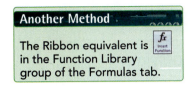

Another Method

The Ribbon equivalent is [fx Insert Function] in the Function Library group of the Formulas tab.

Your screen should be similar to Figure 4.57

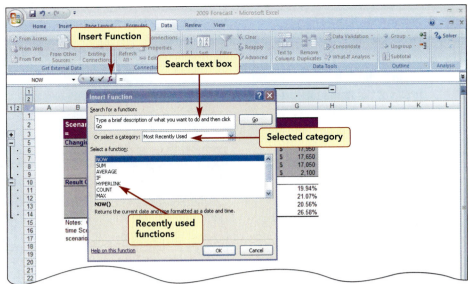

Figure 4.57

The NOW function may not be displayed in the most recently used category. You can locate a function by typing a description of what you want to do in the Search text box or by selecting a category. You will select a category.

2 ● From the Or select a Category drop-down list, choose Date & Time.

● Scroll the Select a function list and choose NOW.

● Click [OK].

● Click [OK] in response to the Function Arguments dialog box message.

Your screen should be similar to Figure 4.58

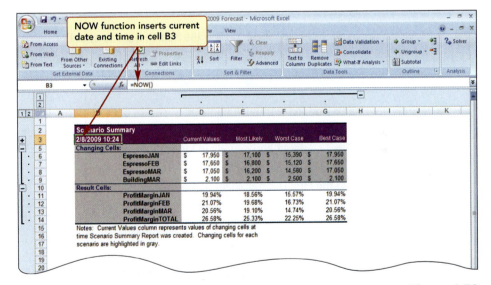

Figure 4.58

The current date and time are displayed in cell B3. If the function you were using required arguments, you would need to enter the function arguments in the Function Arguments dialog box to complete the function.

Shifting Cells

A final change you want to make is to move the note at the bottom of the Scenario Summary to the right. The text for this note was entered in three separate cells, B15:B17. Rather than cutting and pasting the cell contents, you will insert blank cells before the cells and shift the existing cells to the right.

Additional Information

You also can shift cells down the worksheet when inserting new cells.

1 • Select cells B15:B17.

• Open the `Insert` menu in the Cells group of the Home tab and choose Insert Cells from the drop-down menu.

• Choose Shift Cells Right.

• Click `OK`.

Your screen should be similar to Figure 4.59

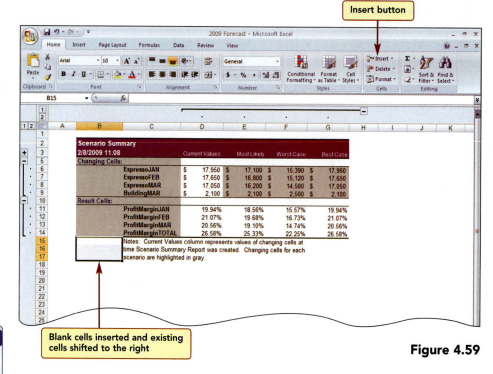

Insert button

Blank cells inserted and existing cells shifted to the right

Figure 4.59

Additional Information
You also can delete cells using `Delete`/Delete Cells and shift them to the left or up in the worksheet.

Three new cells have been inserted and the existing cells have shifted to the right. Now you are ready to print the worksheet.

2 • Move the Scenario Summary sheet to after the Fourth Quarter sheet.

• Display the Scenario Summary sheet in Page Layout view.

• Include your name and the workbook name on separate lines centered in a custom header.

• Print the worksheet centered horizontally in landscape orientation.

• Move to cell A6 in the First Quarter sheet and protect the sheet.

• Protect the workbook, save the workbook, and exit Excel.

Focus on Careers

EXPLORE YOUR CAREER OPTIONS

Cage Cashier
Do you like to count money? Have you ever wondered who handles the money in a casino behind the scenes? Cage cashiers manage the cash, chips, and all the paperwork needed to track the large amounts of money that change hands every day. Some cage cashiers work to verify guests' financial records so they can open house credit lines. Other cashiers are primarily responsible for using computer spreadsheet programs to access and reconcile the books. Cage cashiers must have good math skills and experience with accounting or bookkeeping. Salary is dependent on experience, and cage cashiers typically make tips in addition to an hourly wage. The demand for cage cashiers is expected to increase as gaming expands beyond the traditional centers in Nevada and New Jersey.

LAB 4

Using Solver, Creating Templates, and Evaluating Scenarios

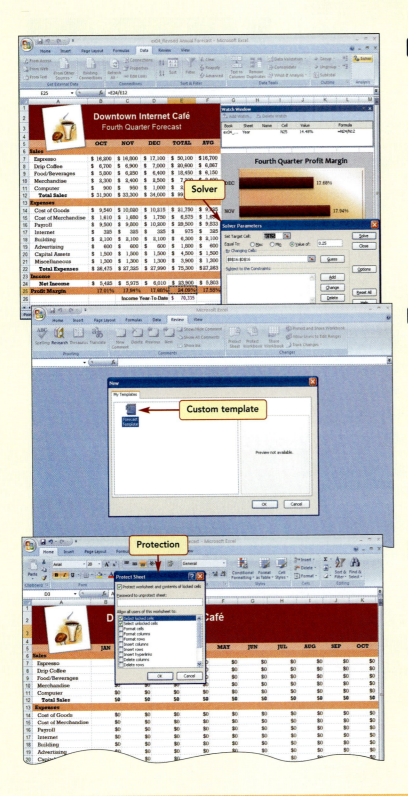

Solver (EX4.6)

Solver is a tool used to perform what-if analysis to determine the effect of changing values in two or more cells on another cell.

Custom Template (EX4.12)

Custom templates are specialized template files containing settings that are used as a pattern for creating similar worksheets in new workbooks.

Protection (EX4.14)

The protection feature controls what information can be changed in a workbook.

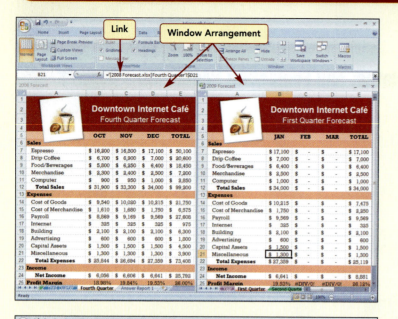

Window Arrangement (EX4.23)

The window arrangement feature displays all open workbook files in separate windows on the screen, making it easy to view and work with information in different workbooks.

Link (EX4.25)

A link creates a connection between files that automatically updates the data in one file whenever the data in the other file changes.

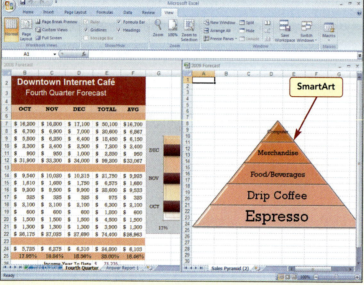

SmartArt (EX4.33)

SmartArt are graphic objects that can be used to illustrate concepts and to enhance your workbook.

Scenario (EX4.42)

A scenario is a named set of input values that you can substitute in a worksheet to see the effects of a possible alternative course of action.

Lab Review

Using Solver, Creating Templates, and Evaluating Scenarios

key terms

active workbook   EX4.22

adjustable cell   EX4.6

cascade   EX4.23

custom template   EX4.12

destination cell   EX4.25

destination workbook   EX4.25

external reference   EX4.25

external reference formula
EX4.25

horizontal   EX4.23

link   EX4.25

NOW function   EX4.52

password   EX4.14

protection   EX4.14

scenario   EX4.42

SmartArt graphic   EX4.33

SmartArt style   EX4.37

Solver   EX4.6

source cell   EX4.25

source workbook   EX4.25

target cell   EX4.6

tiled   EX4.23

vertical   EX4.23

window arrangement   EX4.23

MCAS skills

The Microsoft Certified Applications Specialist (MCAS) certification program is designed to measure your proficiency in performing basic tasks using the Office 2007 applications. Getting certified demonstrates that you have the skills and provides a valuable industry credential for employment. See Reference 2 Microsoft Certified Applications Specialist (MCAS) for a complete list of the skills that were covered in Lab 4.

Lab Review

command summary

Command	Shortcut	Action
🗔 Office Button		
`📄 Excel Options` /Add-Ins/Solver Add-In		Adds Solver tool to Ribbon
New/My Templates		Applies custom template to workbook
Home tab		
Alignment group		
`📑` Wrap Text		Makes all content visible in a cell by displaying it on multiple lines
Cells group		
`📑 Insert ▾` /Insert Cells/Shift Cells Right		Moves existing cells to right when new cells are inserted
`📑 Insert ▾` /Insert Sheet		Inserts a new worksheet into the workbook
`📑 Delete ▾` /Delete Cells/Shift Cells Left		Deletes selected cells and shifts remaining cells to left
`📑 Delete ▾` /Delete Cells/Shift Cells Up		Deletes selected cells and shifts remaining cells up
`📑 Format ▾` /Hide & Unhide/Hide Sheet		Hides selected sheets
`📑 Format ▾` /Hide & Unhide/Unhide Sheet		Redisplays hidden sheets
`📑 Format ▾` /Protect Sheet		Prevents unwanted changes to the data in a worksheet
`📑 Format ▾` /Unprotect Sheet		Removes worksheet protection and allows modification of contents
`📑 Format ▾` /Lock		Toggles between locking and unlocking a cell
Insert tab		
Illustrations group		
`📗 SmartArt`		Inserts a SmartArt graphic to visually communicate information
SmartArt Tools Design tab		
Create Graphics group		
`📄 Add Shape ▾`		Adds a shape to an existing SmartArt graphic shape
SmartArt Styles group		
`📄 Change Colors ▾`		Changes colors of selected SmartArt graphic

Lab 4: Using Solver, Creating Templates,
and Evaluating Scenarios

www.mhhe.com/oleary

command summary

Command	Shortcut	Action
⊡ More		Opens SmartArt Styles gallery to select over-all visual style for SmartArt graphic
Reset group		
Reset Graphic		Restores SmartArt graphic to original settings
Formulas tab		
Function Library group		
Insert Function		Prompts you to select a function from a list and helps you enter the arguments correctly
Data tab		
Data Tools group		
What-If Analysis ▼ /Scenario Manager		Starts Scenario Manager tool to create sets of data for what-if analysis
Analysis group		
?⇩ Solver		Starts Solver tool to perform what-if analysis
Review tab		
Changes group		
Protect Sheet		Prevents unwanted changes to the data in a worksheet
Unprotect Sheet		Removes worksheet protection
Protect Workbook		Prevents unwanted changes to the structure of the workbook
Unprotect Workbook		Removes workbook protection
View tab		
Window group		
New Window		Displays a new window
Arrange All		Arranges open windows vertically, horizontally, tiled, or cascaded
Hide		Hides current workbook
Unhide		Unhides selected workbook

Lab Exercises

matching

Match the lettered item on the right with the numbered list on the left.

1. cascade   _____   **a.** formula that links two workbooks

2. destination cell   _____   **b.** named set of input values that you can substitute in a worksheet to see the effects of a possible alternative course of action

3. external reference   _____   **c.** prevents changes to an entire workbook

4. password   _____   **d.** prevents any unauthorized person from either viewing or saving changes to a workbook

5. scenario   _____   **e.** windows that are displayed one on top of the other

6. Solver   _____   **f.** cell that contains data to be copied

7. source cell   _____   **g.** workbook that supplies data

8. source workbook   _____   **h.** cell affected by changes in other cells

9. target cell   _____   **i.** cell that contains the external reference formula

10. workbook protection   _____   **j.** tool used to perform what-if analysis

multiple choice

Circle the correct response to the questions below.

1. The workbook that receives the data is called the _____.
   a. source workbook
   b. destination workbook
   c. recipient workbook
   d. target workbook

2. _____ is a tool used for what-if analysis.
   a. Sheet Manager
   b. Solver
   c. Data tab
   d. Finder

3. _____ makes all content visible in a cell by displaying it on multiple lines.
   a. Merging
   b. Wrapping
   c. Hiding
   d. Splitting

4. In the external reference formula [Forecast.xls]Year!$N$8, Year is the _____.
   a. source file
   b. destination file
   c. active reference
   d. sheet reference

5. The _____ function automatically updates whenever a worksheet is recalculated.
   a. TODAY
   b. NOW
   c. DATE
   d. CURRENT

6. A(n) _____ is entered in one worksheet to create a link to another worksheet.
   a. dependent value
   b. linking formula
   c. internal reference formula
   d. external reference formula

7. _____ are designed to help forecast the outcome of various possible actions.
   a. Answer reports
   b. Scenarios
   c. Sensitivity reports
   d. Limit reports

8. _____ prevents users from changing the contents of a worksheet.
   a. Locking cells
   b. Protecting a worksheet
   c. Unlocking cells
   d. A password

9. _____ are objects that can be used to illustrate concepts and enhance the workbook.
   a. Clip Art graphics
   b. Pictures
   c. SmartArt graphics
   d. Shapes

10. A workbook _____ is a workbook file that contains predesigned worksheets that can be used as the basis for creating similar sheets in new workbooks.
    a. template
    b. model
    c. design
    d. pattern

Lab Exercises

true/false

Circle the correct answer to the following questions.

1. You can create a template file by typing the file extension .xltx when you save the file.   True   False

2. A scenario report shows the results of all scenarios created for a worksheet.   True   False

3. When the worksheet is protected, the contents of unlocked cells cannot be changed.   True   False

4. A worksheet that is protected requires a password.   True   False

5. Solver can produce a report about a solution.   True   False

6. SmartArt graphics are normally used to display numerical data.   True   False

7. Worksheet protection prevents unauthorized users from viewing or saving changes to a workbook.   True   False

8. Whenever data in an external reference formula is changed in the source workbook, data in the linked cell in the destination workbook is automatically changed as well.   True   False

9. Cells you select as variables in Solver must be related through formulas on a worksheet.   True   False

10. The vertical window arrangement displays windows side by side.   True   False

fill-in

Complete the following statements by filling in the blanks with the correct key terms.

1. The workbook that supplies data to another workbook is called the _____.

2. _____ is a tool used to perform what-if analyses to determine the effect of changing values in two or more cells.

3. The cell containing a formula you want to solve is called the _____.

4. The cells that contain the values to be changed when using Solver are called the _____.

5. To protect a worksheet from changes by an unauthorized person, you should include a _____.

6. To arrange displayed worksheets in the workspace, each worksheet you want to arrange must be open in a separate _____.

7. A _____ is a named set of input values used to help forecast the outcome of various possible actions.

8. Once a(n) _____ formula is entered in a worksheet, the _____ file is automatically updated if it is open.

9. The _____ is the workbook that the next action you take affects.

10. Windows are _____ when they are displayed one after the other in succession, across and down the screen.

Lab Exercises

Hands-on Exercises

step-by-step

IronWorks Income Analysis ★

1. IronWorks creates unique wrought iron home accents. The accounting manager uses a six-month income worksheet that tracks the amount of income from different sources. The company would like to create a template that it can use each year to track the information. Your completed worksheets will be similar to the one shown here.

   a. Open the file ex04_IronWorks Income.

   b. Make a copy of Sheet1. Rename Sheet1 **First Six Months** and Sheet 1(2) **Second Six Months**. Delete Sheet2 and Sheet3.

   c. Modify the month column labels in the Second Six Months sheet to reflect the last six months of the year. Change the title of the sheet in cell A3 to **2nd Six Months**.

   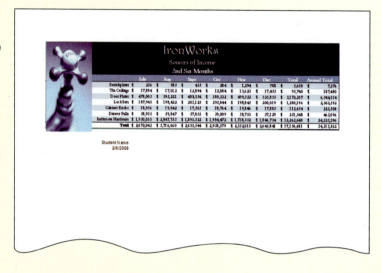

   d. Add the column label **Annual Total** in cell I4. Format this label to match the other column labels. AutoFit the column. Enter formulas in the Annual Total column to calculate the totals for the year.

   e. Extend the worksheet formatting to the new column. Recenter the worksheet titles.

   f. Enter your name and the current date using the NOW function in cells A15 and A16, respectively, in both sheets.

   g. Select both sheets. Select cell A3 and cells B5 through G11 and, if necessary, unlock the cells. Deselect the selection. Ungroup the worksheets. Protect both worksheets.

   h. Move to cell B5 of the First Six Months sheet.

   i. Preview the workbook. Change the orientation of both sheets to landscape. Center the worksheets horizontally. Print the Second Six Months worksheet.

   j. Save the workbook as IronWorks Income1.

   k. Delete the values in cells B5 through G11 on both worksheets. Save the workbook as a template with the name IronWorks Income Template to your solution file location. Close the workbook.

Doggie Fun Day Care Expense Projections ★★

2. The owners of Doggie Fun Day Care have two facilities, East Side and West Side. They have collected some data on the operational costs for each facility for the current year. The owners would like to remodel the East Side day care facility and to open a new facility to be known as North Side. They are concerned, however, about the rising costs of utilities. You will help them evaluate next year's costs by creating a scenario summary similar to the example shown.

a. Open the file ex04_Day Care.

b. The owners are particularly concerned about the cost for next year's electricity. They would like to evaluate a worst-case scenario in which electricity costs are 20 percent higher than the values in Sheet1. For example, the East Side's electricity would increase from $1,020 to $1,224. Use Solver to calculate the impact of this increase (keeping all other expenses unchanged) for each day care facility. Save the results as a scenario and restore the original values. (If Solver is not available to you, use Scenario Manager.)

c. The most-likely case would be for electricity to increase only 10 percent for each facility. Use Solver to determine the costs for each facility. Save the results as a scenario and restore the original values. (If Solver is not available to you, use Scenario Manager.)

d. Add a scenario using the original values as the best case. Save the workbook as Doggie Day Care to your solution file location.

e. Create a Scenario Summary for the electricity expenses. In cell A1, insert the title **Projected Expenses for Next Year**. Center this title over the table. In cell B3, use the NOW function to display the current date and time. Replace the cell references with the appropriate labels used in Sheet1. Size column C to fully display the labels. Replace the notes below the summary table with a short description of each scenario.

f. Delete Sheet2 and Sheet3. Rename Sheet1 **Budget**. Move the Scenario Summary sheet after the Budget sheet. Include your name in a custom header on both sheets.

g. Save the workbook and print the Scenario Summary centered horizontally in landscape orientation.

Lab Exercises

Adventure Travel Tours Income Analysis ★★

3. Adventure Travel Tours has begun a new marketing campaign that emphasizes their airline packages. You have been asked to create a Scenario Summary that analyzes quarterly income in three scenarios. The company also would like to create a template to allow easy analysis of next year's performance. Your completed worksheets should be similar to the one shown here.

   a. Open the file ex04_Travel Analysis.

   b. Make a copy of Sheet1. Rename Sheet1(2) **Current Income** and Sheet1 **Projected Income**. Delete the other sheets.

   c. Change the subtitle of the Projected Income sheet to **Projected Annual Sources of Income**. Change the subtitle of the Current Income Sheet to **Current Annual Sources of Income**.

   d. After lengthy discussion regarding projected Airlines income, it has been determined that the most-likely case is that Total Airlines income will be unchanged from the current year, or $917,287. Further, it has been determined that the worst case would be a 5 percent decrease, or $871,423, and the best case would be a 5 percent increase, or $963,151. Use the Projected Income sheet and Solver to calculate the quarterly income needed to achieve each of these Total Airlines income figures.

   e. Create a scenario for each case using the values you found with Solver. Keep the original values after using Solver. Create a Scenario Summary for the Total Airlines income with the results cell F6. Replace the cell references with the names of the quarters ($B$6=First Quarter). Increase column width as needed to fully display the labels. Delete the notes below the summary table.

   f. Add and format the worksheet title **Airlines Income Scenarios** in cell B1. Insert the current date in cell B3 using the NOW function.

   g. Display the Best Case scenario values in the Projected Income sheet. Move the Summary worksheet to the third tab position. Include your name and the date in a custom header on all sheets. Save the workbook as Airlines Income Analysis to your solution file location. Print the workbook with each sheet centered horizontally in landscape orientation.

   h. Delete the values in cells B5:E9 in the Current Income and Projected Income sheets. Unlock the appropriate cells and protect the worksheets. Delete the Scenario Summary sheet. Save the workbook as a template named Income Analysis Template to your solution file location.

Lab 4: Using Solver, Creating Templates,
and Evaluating Scenarios

www.mhhe.com/oleary

Cards & Gifts Financial Projections ★★★

4. Dennis Ma owns and operates Ma's Cards & Gifts. He is reviewing his quarterly sales and is preparing his projections for the fourth quarter. He will need to review the previous year's totals to make his projections. Your completed sheets and scenario summary should be similar to those shown here.

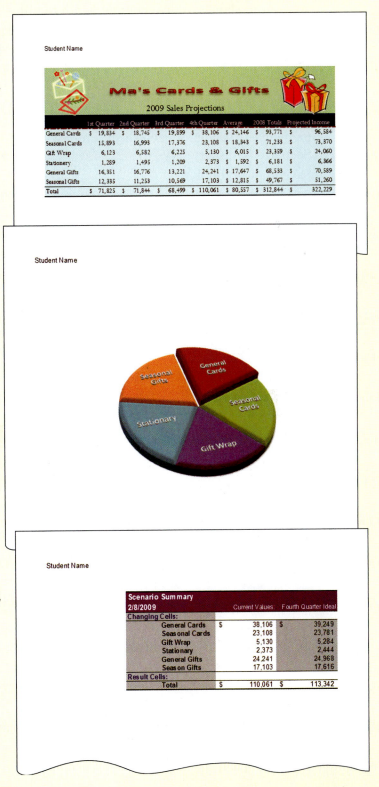

a. Open the file ex04_Cards and Gifts 2009. Change the name of Sheet1 to **2009**.

b. Insert formulas in columns F and H to calculate the average quarterly sales and the projected yearly totals.

c. Open the file ex04_Cards and Gifts 2008. In the ex04_Cards and Gifts 2009 file, paste links in column G to column G from the ex04_Cards and Gifts 2008 file. Save the workbook as Cards and Gifts 2009 to your solution file location. Save the ex04_Cards and Gifts 2008 file as Cards and Gifts 2008 to your solution file location.

d. Dennis hopes to achieve a 3 percent increase in total sales for each category. For each category of sales, use Solver to determine what level of sales is needed in the fourth quarter of 2009 to achieve projected yearly sales 103 percent higher than last year. For example, use Solver to determine the fourth-quarter sales level for General Cards in 2009 to achieve projected total sales equal to $96,584 (103 percent of 93,771). Use Solver in a similar manner for the other categories using total sales equal to $73,370, $24,060, $6,366, $70,589, and $51,260. Keep these solutions

e. Complete row 11 by entering the appropriate formulas in columns E through H.

f. Dennis is planning a new marketing campaign he hopes will increase fourth-quarter sales even more. Using the following fourth-quarter sales goals, create a scenario named **Fourth Quarter Ideal**.

General Cards	**$39,249**
Seasonal Cards	**$23,781**
Gift Wrap	**$ 5,284**

Stationery	$ 2,444
General Gifts	$24,968
Seasonal Gifts	$17,616

f. Create a Scenario Summary displaying the results for cell E11. Change the cell references to appropriate labels. Adjust column width to fully display labels. Delete the note below the summary report.

g. Insert the SmartArt Basic Pie from the Cycle category into Sheet2. Add two additional wedge shapes. For each wedge, enter the name of a sales category. Apply the SmartArt style Bird's Eye Scene and change the colors to Colorful – Accent Colors. Increase the size of the graphic.

h. Rename Sheet2 to **Sales Categories**. Delete Sheet3 and reorder the remaining sheets so that 2009 appears first, followed by Sales Categories, followed by Scenario Summary. Enter your name in the header of each sheet. Enter a function to display the current date in cell B3 of the Scenario Summary.

i. Save the workbook.

j. Print the workbook with each sheet centered horizontally in portrait orientation.

k. Delete the Sales Categories and Scenario Summary sheets. Delete the values in cells B5 through E10 and G5 through G10. Unlock the same cells. Protect the sheet. Save the workbook as a template named Cards and Gifts Analysis Template to your solution file location.

Animal Rescue Foundation Contributions ★★★

5. The Animal Rescue Foundation, a nonprofit animal rescue agency, relies on donations to cover all its expenses. You would like to analyze and project the amount that will be needed for next year based on various scenarios. Your completed analysis will be similar to that shown here.

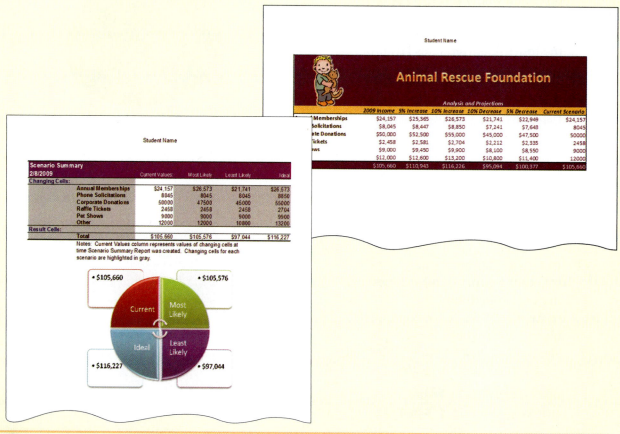

a. Open the file ex04_ARF Contributions to see last year's income. Save the file as ARF Contributions Reviewed.

b. Copy the Fall-Winter sheet to a new workbook. Rename the tab for the new sheet **Analysis**. Delete the extra sheets if necessary. Delete column H. Adjust the formatting as needed.

c. Insert a new row above row 5. In cell B5, enter the subtitle **Analysis and Projections**. Merge and center cells B5 through G5.

d. In cells B6 through G6, enter the labels **2009 Income**, **5% Increase**, **10% Increase**, **10% Decrease**, **5% Decrease**, and **Current Scenario**. Adjust the size of the columns to fully display the labels.

e. In cell B7, enter a link to cell H6 of the Fall-Winter sheet in the ARF Contributions Reviewed file. In a similar manner, enter links in cells B8 through B12 to cells H7 through H11 of the Fall-Winter sheet in the ARF Contributions Reviewed file. Close the ARF Contributions Reviewed workbook.

f. Delete the values in cells C7 through G12.

g. Use the number in cell B7 to calculate the values for cells C7 through F7. Copy the formulas down the columns to row 11. (Hint: Cell C7 should contain the formula = B7*1.05, cell F7 should contain the formula = B7*.95.) Then copy the formulas in cells C7 through F7 to cells C8 through F12.

h. Copy and paste just the values from column B to column G. Save the workbook as ARF Analysis.

i. Create three scenarios using cells G7 through G12 as the changing cells and the following scenario names and calculated values from the worksheet:

Scenario Name:	Most Likely	
Scenario Values:	Annual Memberships	10% increase
	Phone Solicitations	Current
	Corporate Donations	5% decrease
	Raffle Tickets	Current
	Pet Shows	Current
	Other	Current
Scenario Name:	Least Likely	
Scenario Values:	Annual Memberships	10% decrease
	Phone Solicitations	Current
	Corporate Donations	10% decrease
	Raffle Tickets	Current
	Pet Shows	Current
	Other	10% decrease
Scenario Name:	Ideal	
Scenario Values:	Annual Memberships	10% increase
	Phone Solicitations	10% increase
	Corporate Donations	10% increase
	Raffle Tickets	10% increase
	Pet Shows	10% increase
	Other	10% increase

j. Create a Scenario Summary displaying the results for cell G13. Change the cell references to appropriate labels and adjust the column width to fully display the labels. Shift the note at the bottom of the Scenario Summary to the right.

k. Insert the Cycle Matrix SmartArt graphic below the Scenario Summary. Adjust the size of the graphic as needed. Apply the SmartArt Polished style and change the colors to Colorful – Accent Colors. Starting with the upper-left segment of the graphic, enter the labels **Current**, **Most Likely**, **Least Likely**, and **Ideal**. In each segment's bullet, enter the total value for that segment. For example, the Current segment would have the bullet $105,660.

l. Enter your name in the header of the Scenario Summary and Analysis sheets. Enter a function to display the current date in cell B3 of the Scenario Summary.

m. Print the Analysis sheet centered horizontally in landscape orientation. Print the Scenario Summary sheet centered horizontally in portrait orientation.

n. Save the workbook.

o. Delete the Scenario Summary sheet. Delete the values in cells B7:B12 and G7:G12. Unlock the cells B6:B12 and G7:G12 and protect the sheet. Save the sheet as ARF Analysis Template.

on your own

Games Growth Projections ★

1. You have been hired as a consultant by a video game manufacturer to help the company project expected growth over the next five years based on its research. Assume that the company currently has 42 percent of the market. The current number of customers is 320,500. Available research estimates an increase of 2 percent in year 1; 3 percent in year 2; 5 percent in year 3; 8 percent in year 4; and 13 percent in year 5 over the previous year. Create a worksheet that shows the current number of customers and the estimated numbers for the next five years. Use these numbers to create revenue figures based on a yearly profit of $225 per customer. Create scenarios with the calculated values as the most-likely case, a 3 percent decrease per year in customers as the worst case, and an increase of 5 percent per year as the best case. Create a Scenario Summary report. Enter your name and the current date in all the worksheets. Save the file as Video Game Projections. Print the worksheets.

Spring Break Scenarios ★★

2. Now that your personal budget is complete, you have decided to do some analysis to determine whether a trip during spring semester break is possible. Use the budget you created in Lab 3, On Your Own exercise 1, and evaluate your yearly budget to determine whether you will have enough money to pay for a spring break trip next year. Use Solver to determine the number of hours you need to work to earn enough money for the trip in addition to the rest of your expenses. Create three scenarios: one showing the current values, a second showing a 7 percent decrease in entertainment expenses, and a third showing a decrease in one of your other expenses. Create a Scenario Summary. Enter your name and the current date in a header for all the worksheets. Save the file as Spring Break Analysis. Print the worksheets.

Small Business Expansion Projections ★★

3. You believe the small business you created in Lab 3, On Your Own exercise 5 could see greater profits with an additional location. Use the information you gathered in the previous workbook and Solver to determine what variables would increase profits by 30 percent. Create three scenarios to determine the effects of a 5 percent, 10 percent, and 15 percent increase in profits in each quarter on the total yearly profits. Create a Scenario Summary. Save your file as Expansion Projections. Print the summary.

Stock Portfolio Analysis ★★★

4. You have been studying the stock market in your economics class and would like to evaluate a portfolio of four different stocks. Using the Web or other news source, choose four stocks listed on the New York Stock Exchange and enter the following information about each stock in separate sheets of a workbook: stock exchange number, cost per share, brokerage fee, total cost per share, price/earnings ratio, dividend return percentage, and week-ending price. Enter data for each stock using the previous month's values. Create scenarios of good, bad, and expected market changes in the current month-ending price over the next month. Enter your name and the current date in headers in the worksheets. Save the file as Stock Analysis. Print the workbook.

Using Excel Templates ★★★

5. You would like to analyze the costs of a new car loan. Use the Excel Loan Amortization template and conduct research into new car prices and loan rates. Insert a new sheet and do a cost comparison of several cars you have analyzed. Add a picture of the cars you are researching. Create scenarios for different loan rates and create a Scenario Summary using the techniques you learned in the lab. Save the file as New Car Loan. Print the workbook. Save your sheet as a template named Loan Analysis Template, with the values removed.

Using Data Tables, Using Lookup and IF Functions, and Designing Forms

LAB 5

Objectives

After completing this lab, you will know how to:

1 Use the PMT function.

2 Research information on the Web.

3 Create a data table.

4 Create and modify shapes.

5 Use Lookup functions.

6 Create a form.

7 Name cell references.

8 Use the IF function.

9 Create a drop-down list.

10 Add cell comments.

11 Hide and unhide rows.

12 Prepare a workbook for distribution.

Case Study

Downtown Internet Café

Evan, the owner of the Downtown Internet Café, has been impressed with your use of Office Excel 2007 to forecast the café's future for the next two years. Now, he has two new projects that he wants you to complete.

First, he is considering the purchase of a new espresso machine to replace the current machine, which is leased. Evan plans to finance the purchase and would like you to evaluate several different loan options. You will create a loan analysis spreadsheet that incorporates Office Excel's PMT function and data table features.

Next, Evan would like you to develop a spreadsheet to calculate and record customer Bonus Dollars. Bonus Dollars are awarded to customers based on their monthly expenditures at the café and can be applied to their bill for any purchase. They are an incentive for customers to keep coming back to the café and, of course, spend more money while they're there. You will create a form to calculate and record customer Bonus Dollars. The completed loan analysis and Bonus Dollars form are shown on the opposite page.

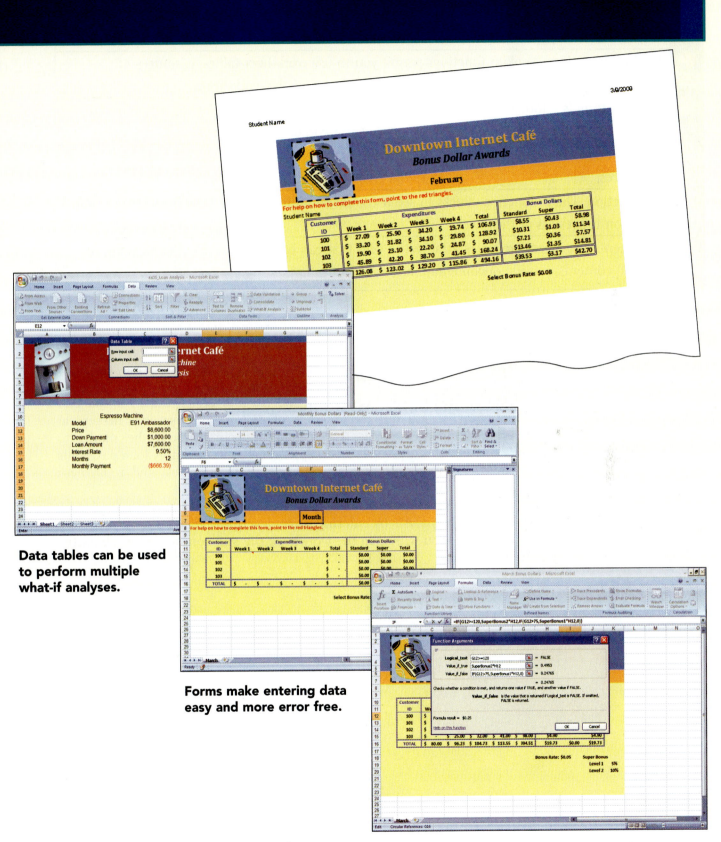

Data tables can be used to perform multiple what-if analyses.

Forms make entering data easy and more error free.

Using an IF function allows different calculations to be performed if certain conditions are met.

Concept Preview

① **Data Table** A data table is a range of cells that is used to quickly calculate multiple what-if versions in one operation and to show the results of all variations in the worksheet.

② **Lookup Functions** Lookup functions permit you to use worksheet tables as sources of information for formulas and calculations in other parts of the worksheet.

③ **Form** A form is a formatted worksheet with blank spaces that can be filled in online on an individual computer or on a network, or printed and completed on paper.

④ **Name** A name is a description of a cell or range of cells that can be used in place of cell references.

⑤ **IF Function** The IF function checks to see if certain conditions are met and then takes action based on the results of the check.

⑥ **Comment** Comments are notes attached to cells that can be used to clarify the meaning of the cell contents, provide documentation, or ask a question.

Calculating a Loan Payment

Evan has read several reviews in the *Tea and Coffee Trade Journal* and looked at several different models of commercial espresso makers at restaurant supply stores. He is still undecided about the model to purchase and wants to see an analysis of what the monthly loan payments would be for different down payments, interest rates, and repayment periods for each kind.

Based on the information Evan has given you, you started a workbook for the loan analysis by entering some descriptive labels and formats in a worksheet. You will open the workbook file and continue to work on the loan analysis.

1 ● **Start Office Excel 2007 and open the workbook file** ex05_Loan Analysis.

● **If necessary, maximize the application and worksheet windows.**

Your screen should be similar to Figure 5.1

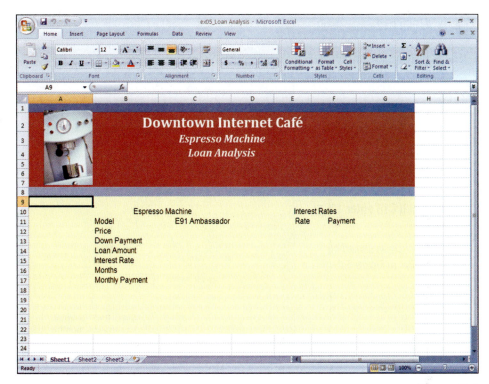

Figure 5.1

Much of the structure and formatting for the worksheet has already been completed. To continue to create the worksheet you will enter the price and down payment for the first espresso machine Evan is considering, the E91 Ambassador. Then, you need to enter a formula to calculate the loan amount. The amount of the loan is the price of the item minus the down payment. He wants to repay the loan in monthly payments over a one-year period.

First you will calculate loan payments using an 11.5 percent loan rate.

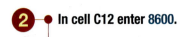

2 ● In cell C12 enter **8600.**

● In cell C13 enter **1000.**

● In cell C14 enter the formula =**C12-C13.**

● In cell C15 enter **11.5.**

● In cell C16 enter **12.**

Your screen should be similar to Figure 5.2

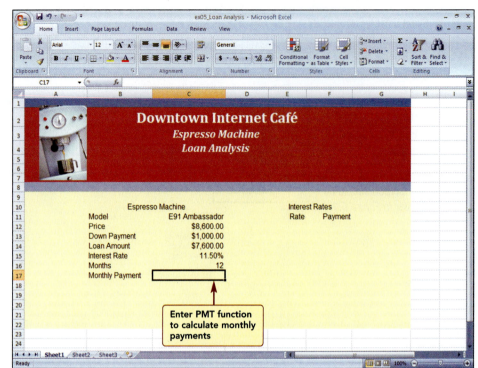

Figure 5.2

Using the PMT Function

Next you need to calculate the monthly payment using the PMT function. The **PMT function** calculates a periodic payment on a loan. The value returned includes the loan amount and interest but no taxes, reserve payments, or fees sometimes associated with loans. The PMT function uses the following syntax:

PMT(rate, nper, pv)

Additional Information

When using the PMT function, it is important to use consistent units for specifying rate and nper.

This function contains three arguments: rate, nper, and pv. The rate argument is the interest rate of the loan. The nper argument is the total number of payments for the loan. The pv argument is the amount of the loan, also referred to as the **principal** or preset value.

Additional Information

If the loan payment was in years, you would need to multiply the value by 12 to calculate the number of monthly payments.

The rate in the PMT function you will use to calculate the monthly loan payment for the espresso machine is the yearly interest rate (C15) divided by 12. This converts the yearly rate to a monthly rate. The nper argument is the length of the loan in months (C16). The pv argument is the loan amount in cell C14. You will use the Insert Function feature to help enter this function.

1 — If necessary, move to C17.

● Click ![fx] **Insert Function and choose PMT from the Financial category.**

● Click [OK].

● Enter **C15/12** as the Rate, **C16** as the Nper, and **C14** as the Pv.

● Click [OK].

Your screen should be similar to Figure 5.3

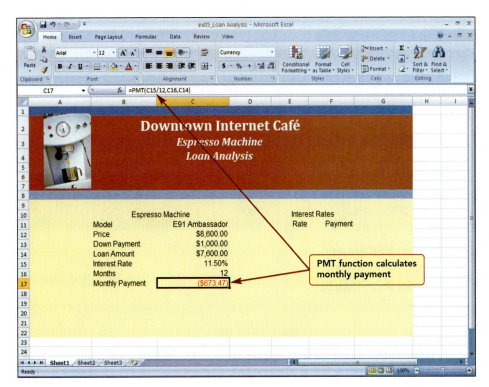

Figure 5.3

Excel calculates the monthly payment and displays it in cell C17 based on an 11.5 percent interest rate. Notice the payment value is displayed in red because a payment is a negative value.

Researching Information on the Web

Evan has checked with a local bank for information on short-term, small-business loan rates. He found that for loans less than $25,000, the maximum interest rate must not exceed the prime rate plus 4.25 percent when maturity is less than seven years. Prime rate is the lowest rate of interest on loans that is available from a bank set at a given time.

Before you can continue much further, you need to find out the current prime rate. You can do this quickly using the Research tool to search the Internet to find out the current prime rate as published by the *Wall Street Journal.*

Note: You need an Internet connection, and the Online Services feature must be activated. Click Research Options in the Research task pane and select the services you want to activate. If you do not have this feature available, skip to the next section, Creating a Data Table.

1 ● Open the Review tab.

● Click 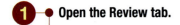 in the Proofing group.

● In the Search for text box of the Research pane, select any existing text and type **wsj prime rate**.

● Select MSN Search from the All Reference Books drop-down list box.

Your screen should be similar to Figure 5.4

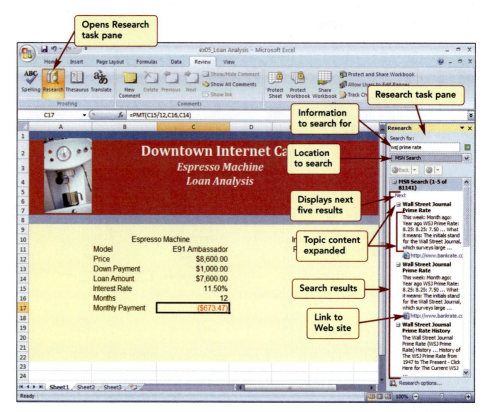

Figure 5.4

Additional Information

If a topic is not expanded, a ⊞ appears to the left of the topic heading. A ⊟ appears when the topic is expanded.

The Research task pane displays the search results for the first five Web sites that meet your search terms. A brief description of each located Web site is displayed along with a link to the site. You will use the information provided by the Bankrate.com Web site.

2 ● If necessary, scroll the Research pane or click Next to display the next five results until you locate a result with a link to the Bankrate.com Web site.

● Click the www.bankrate.com/ brm/ratewatch/wsj PrimeRate.asp link.

● If necessary, scroll down the Web page to locate the current WSJ Prime Rate.

Having Trouble?

If the Bankrate.com Web site is not available, select another of your choice. Your screen will display different information than in Figure 5.5, but it should include information about the current prime rate.

Your screen should be similar to Figure 5.5

Having Trouble?

Because the prime rate changes over time, the rate shown on your screen may be different than the rate shown in Figure 5.5.

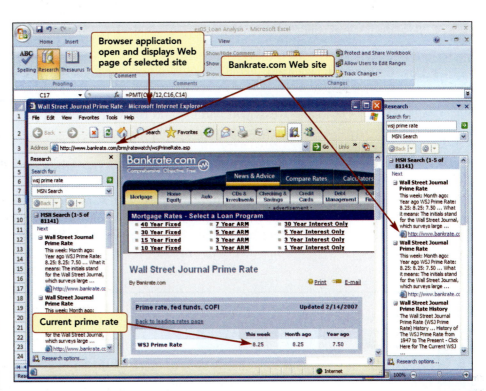

Figure 5.5

The browser program on your computer opens and displays the Web page for the selected site. The information for the last reported prime rate, 8.25%, is displayed. If your browser is Internet Explorer, the Research task pane is displayed along the left side of the screen to allow you to select and view other sites. Now that you know what the current prime rate is, you can continue to enter the information needed for the analysis.

3 ● **Close the browser window.**

● **Close the Research task pane.**

Next, you will expand the worksheet to evaluate the loan payments based on a range of possible loan rates.

Creating a Data Table

Because interest rates will vary depending on which loan institution finances the purchase and when the loan is obtained, you want to set up a data table that shows the effect of different interest rates on the monthly loan payment amount.

Concept 1

Data Table

1 A **data table** is a range of cells that is used to quickly calculate multiple what-if versions in one operation and to show the results of all variations in the worksheet. Data tables perform a type of what-if analysis in which one or more variables are changed to see the effect on the formulas that include these variables.

Espresso Machine		One-variable Table Varying Interest Rates Only		Two-variable table Varying Interest Rates and Length of Loan			
Model	ES1500 Royal	Rate		Rate	Months		
Price	$10,500.00		$559.67	$559.67	12	18	24
Down Payment	$1,000.00	6.25%	$554.28	6.25%	$818.72	$554.28	$422.12
Loan Amount	$9,500.00	6.50%	$555.35	6.50%	$819.82	$555.35	$423.19
Interest Rate	7.50%	6.75%	$556.43	6.75%	$820.91	$556.43	$424.26
Months	18.00	7.00%	$557.51	7.00%	$822.00	$557.51	$425.34
Monthly Payment	$559.67	7.25%	$558.59	7.25%	$823.10	$558.59	$426.42
		7.50%	$559.67	7.50%	$824.20	$559.67	$427.50
		7.75%	$560.75	7.75%	$825.29	$560.75	$428.58
		8.00%	$561.83	8.00%	$826.39	$561.83	$429.66
		8.25%	$562.92	8.25%	$827.49	$562.92	$430.74

A **one-variable data table** can contain one or more formulas, and each formula refers to one input cell. An **input cell** is a cell in which a list of values is substituted to see the resulting effect on the related formulas. Input values can be listed down a column (**column-oriented**) or across a row (**row-oriented**).

A **two-variable data table** uses only one formula that refers to two different input cells, one column-oriented and one row-oriented. The purpose of this table is to show the resulting effect on the formula when the values in both of these cells are changed.

Additional Information

The text will base the following loan analysis on a maximum loan rate of 12.5 percent (8.25 percent for prime plus a maximum of 4.25 percent).

Lab 5: Using Data Tables, Using Lookup and IF Functions, and Designing Forms

www.mhhe.com/oleary

Setting Up the Data Table

Since you are interested in seeing the effects of changing the interest rate only, you will create a one-variable data table. When designing a one-variable data table, the input values and formulas must be in adjacent rows or columns. The title and column headings have already been entered in cells E10 through F11 of the worksheet for the data table. To create the data table, you will begin by entering a series of interest rate percentages.

1 ● **In cell E13 enter 10.5%
and in cell E14 enter
10.75%.**

● **Select the range E13
through E14 and drag
the fill handle through
cell E21.**

*Your screen should be
similar to Figure 5.6*

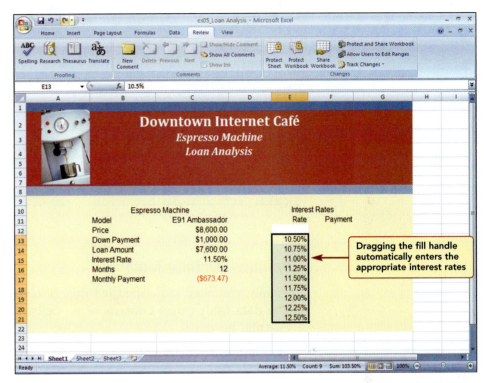

Figure 5.6

Dragging the fill handle filled column E with interest rates that range from 10.5 percent to 12.5 percent in 0.25 percent increments.

Next, you enter the monthly payment formula to be used in calculating the various payments. The formula is always entered in the row above the first input value and one cell to the right of the column of values. In this case, you will enter the formula in cell F12. You could copy this formula from the monthly payment cell in the loan analysis section of the worksheet. Instead, you will define the new formula as equal to that cell. This way, the data table formula will be automatically updated if the original formula (the one in the loan analysis section of the worksheet) changes.

Additional Information

If the input values are listed across the row, the formula is entered in the column to the left of the first value and one cell below the row of values.

2 **In cell F12 enter =C17.**

Your screen should be similar to Figure 5.7

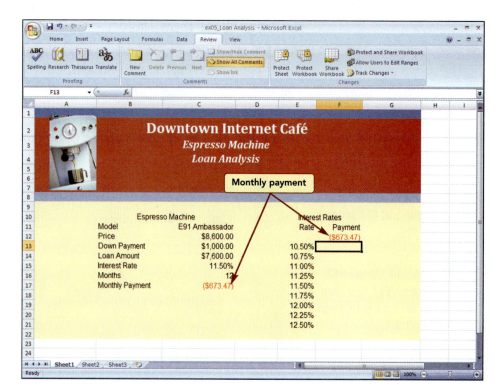

Figure 5.7

Defining the Data Table

Finally, you need to define the range of cells that comprise the data table. The data table range consists of all cells except the ones containing the title and headings.

1 **Select the range E12 through F21.**

Open the Data tab.

Click 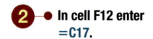 **in the Data Tools group and choose Data Table.**

Your screen should be similar to Figure 5.8

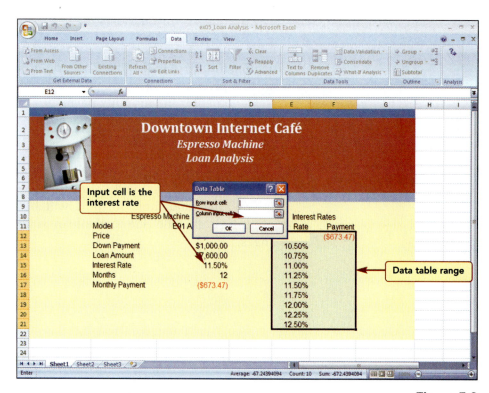

Figure 5.8

Lab 5: Using Data Tables, Using Lookup and IF Functions, and Designing Forms

www.mhhe.com/oleary

In the Data Table dialog box, you define the input cell in which values from the data table are substituted. Because the values in the data table are listed down a column, the input cell is entered as a Column Input Cell. In this case, the input cell is cell C15, the Interest Rate cell from the loan analysis section of the worksheet.

2 • Enter **C15** in the Column Input Cell text box.

Another Method
You also can define the input cell by reducing the dialog box and selecting the input cell in the worksheet.

• Click [OK].

• Deselect the table.

Your screen should be similar to Figure 5.9

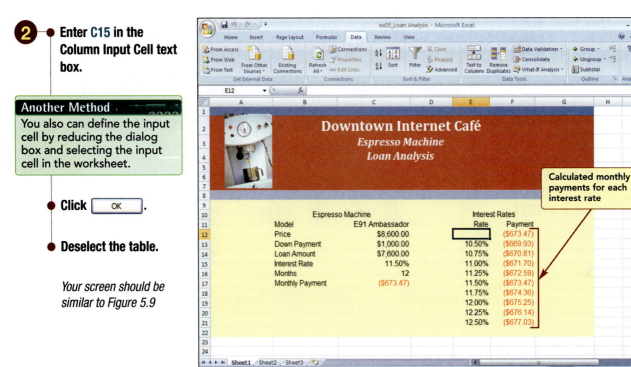

Figure 5.9

The data table shows the calculated monthly payments for each interest rate.

To quickly improve the appearance of the worksheet, you will format the data table and the loan analysis data.

3 ● Apply a Heading 1 cell style to the titles in cells B10 and E10.

● Apply a Heading 2 cell style to the four column headings in row 11.

● Apply the Accent 1 cell style to the range B12:C17.

● Apply the 40% – Accent 1 cell style to the range E12:F21.

Your screen should be similar to Figure 5.10

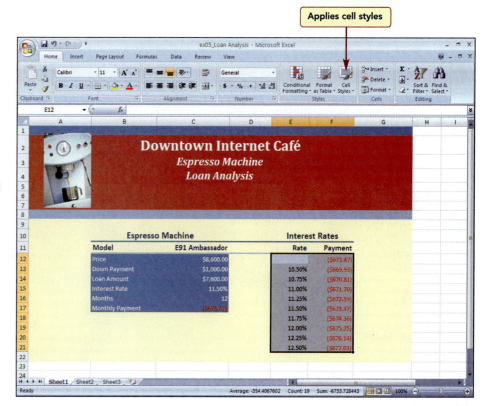

Figure 5.10

Adding Shapes

To clarify the meaning of the first payment value in the data table, you decide to add a descriptive note in a box with an arrow pointing to the value. To add these features to a worksheet, you first create the separate shape element and then add the descriptive text.

Creating a Text Box

The shape you will use to clarify the meaning of the first value in the data table is a text box shape. A **text box** is a graphic object that is a container for text or graphics. Because it is one of the most commonly used shapes, it has a separate button on the Ribbon.

1 • Open the Insert tab.

• Click 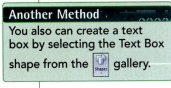 in the Text group.

Another Method
You also can create a text box by selecting the Text Box shape from the  gallery.

• Click in column G to the right of the data table.

• Type Calculated Loan Payment.

• Size the object to display the content on two lines.

Having Trouble?
Use the sizing handles to adjust the text box size.

Additional Information
To start a new line inside a text box, press ⏎Enter.

Your screen should be similar to Figure 5.11

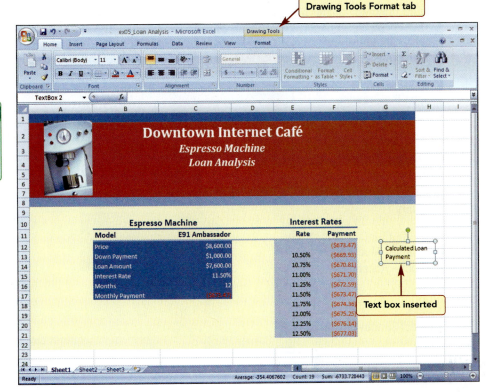

Figure 5.11

The content of the text box automatically wrapped to a second line as you reduced the width of the text box.

Adding a Shape Style

The text box can be enhanced using many of the Drawing Tools. You will add a background fill color, border line color, and text color. You could format each item individually, but using the Shape Styles feature provides a quick way to apply formatting.

1 ● If necessary, click on the text box border to select the entire text box object.

● Open the Drawing Tools Format tab.

● Click ⊟ More in the Shape Styles group to open the Shape Styles gallery.

● Click [Abc] Moderate Effect – Accent 2.

● Click [Shape Effects ▾] and select Shadow.

● Click ☐ Offset Diagonal Bottom Right .

● Size and position the text box as in Figure 5.12.

Having Trouble?
Drag the text box border when the mouse pointer shape is 🕂 to move the object.

● Click outside the text box to deselect it.

Your screen should be similar to Figure 5.12

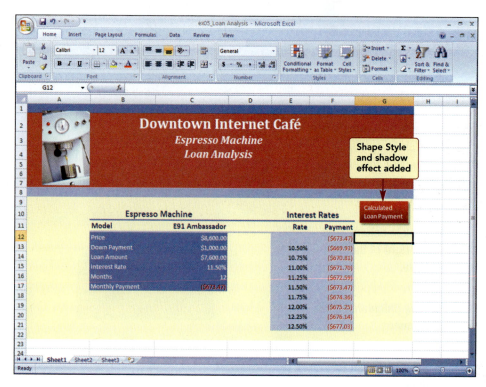

Figure 5.12

The selected Shape Style and shadow effects greatly improve the appearance of the text box.

Lab 5: Using Data Tables, Using Lookup and IF Functions, and Designing Forms

www.mhhe.com/oleary

Creating an Arrow Shape

Next, you will add an arrow from the text box to the value in cell F12.

1 ● Open the Insert tab and click [Shapes] in the Illustrations group.

● Click [↘] Arrow in the Lines category.

● Draw an arrow by clicking on the bottom edge of the text box and dragging from the text box to the right edge of cell F12.

● Click [▾] More in the Shape Styles group and click [—] Moderate Line – Accent 2 style.

Your screen should be similar to Figure 5.13

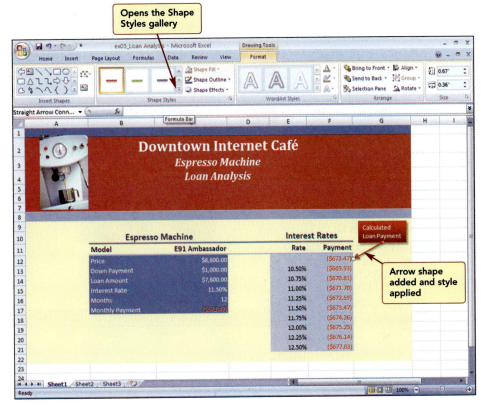

Opens the Shape Styles gallery

Calculated Loan Payment

Arrow shape added and style applied

Figure 5.13

Although you like how this combination of shapes looks, you decide to try another shape to see if you like it better. This shape will be a block arrow shape that contains text.

2 • Click ⏷ **More in the Insert Shapes group of the Drawing Tools Format tab and click** ⏴ **Left Arrow in the Block Arrows category.**

• **Click in column G below the text box to insert the shape.**

• **Type Calculated Loan Payment.**

• **Size the shape to display the text on two lines.**

Your screen should be similar to Figure 5.14

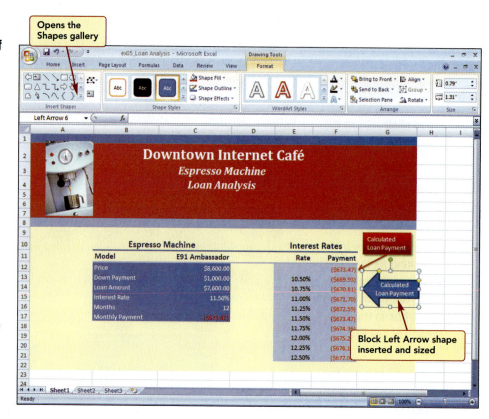

Figure 5.14

The block arrow shape already includes some basic style effects. You like how this shape looks, but it is too large. You will decrease the font size and then reduce the size of the shape.

3 • **Select the text in the shape and reduce the font size to 10 points using the Mini toolbar.**

• **Reduce the shape size to just fit the text on two lines.**

• **Open the Shape Style gallery and click** ▦ **Colored Fill – Accent 2.**

Your screen should be similar to Figure 5.15

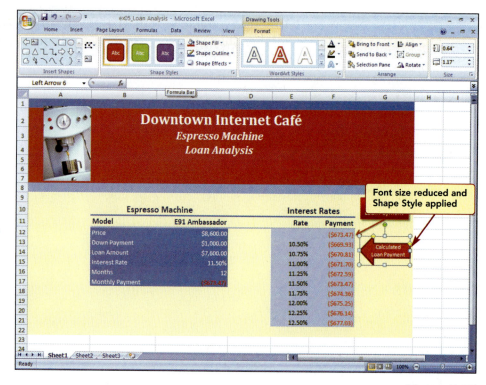

Figure 5.15

Lab 5: Using Data Tables, Using Lookup and IF Functions, and Designing Forms

www.mhhe.com/oleary

Deleting Shapes

You decide to use the block arrow shape and delete the text box and arrow.

1 ● **Select the line arrow shape and press** [Delete].

● **Delete the text box shape.**

● **Position the block arrow shape as in Figure 5.16.**

● **Click outside the shape to deselect it.**

Your screen should be similar to Figure 5.16

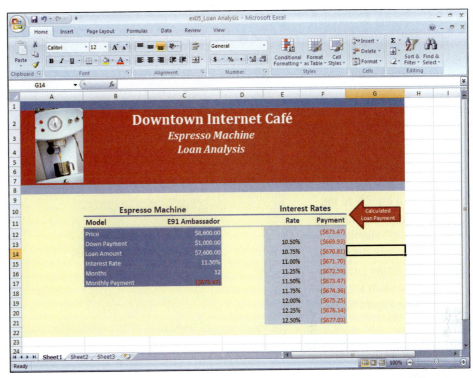

Figure 5.16

Rotating Objects and Sizing Elements

To add some more interest, you will rotate the shape so that it points to the value at an angle. Then you will make the arrow head element of the shape narrower. To rotate an object, click on the ● rotation handle at the top of the object and drag in the direction you want to rotate the object. To adjust the size of an element in an object, drag the ◇ located at the top of the object element.

1 ● Select the block arrow shape.

● Drag the ● rotation handle to the left to rotate the arrow as in Figure 5.17.

● Drag the ◇ at the head of the arrow to the left slightly to decrease the size of the arrow head and reposition the arrow as in Figure 5.17.

● Rename the Sheet1 tab **Analysis**.

● Move to cell A9 and save the workbook as Loan Analysis.

Your screen should be similar to Figure 5.17

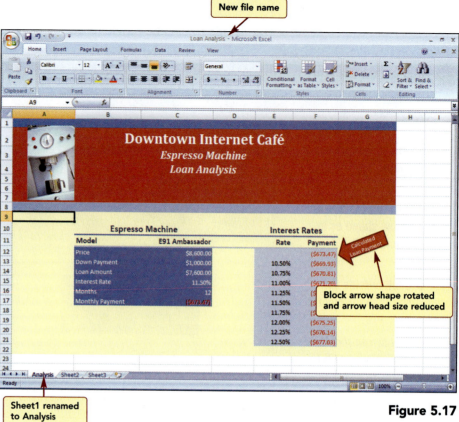

New file name

Sheet1 renamed to Analysis

Block arrow shape rotated and arrow head size reduced

Figure 5.17

You have completed the loan analysis for the E91 Ambassador model espresso machine that Evan requested. Evan can now easily see what the monthly payment would be for a range of possible interest rates.

Splitting Cell Content

Evan is pleased with the worksheet you created, and would like to see the same loan analysis applied to other espresso machines he is considering. He also wants to use the worksheet to evaluate other potential purchases.

Evan entered the product information for several espresso machines he is considering in a worksheet. You will copy this data into Sheet2 of the Loan Analysis workbook.

1 ● **Open the workbook file** ex05_Espresso Machines List**.**

● **Copy Sheet1 from the ex05_Espresso Machine List workbook to a new sheet positioned before Sheet2 in the Loan Analysis workbook.**

● **Rename the tab of this new sheet in the Loan Analysis workbook Models.**

Your screen should be similar to Figure 5.18

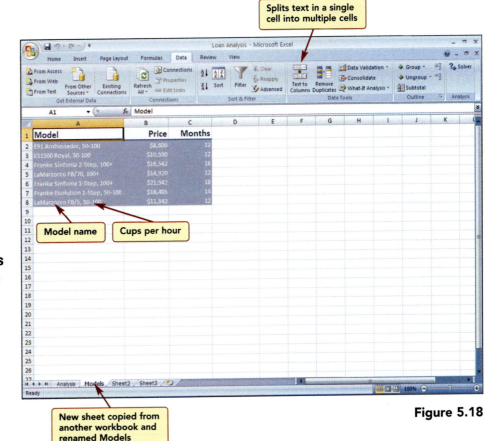

Splits text in a single cell into multiple cells

Model name

Cups per hour

New sheet copied from another workbook and renamed Models

Figure 5.18

You notice that Evan included the cups per hour that each machine can produce following the name and model information in column A. You want to separate this information into two columns, one for the model information and the other for the cups-per-hour information. You can quickly split text contained in a single cell into multiple cells using the Convert Text to Columns Wizard. When the cell content is split, the split content is entered in the column to the right of the existing column. To prevent the existing content in column B from being overwritten by the data that is distributed, you first need to insert a blank column following column A.

2 • Insert a blank column to the left of column B.

• Select A2:A8 to specify the range of cells containing the content to be split.

• Click  in the Data Tools group of the Data tab.

Your screen should be similar to Figure 5.19

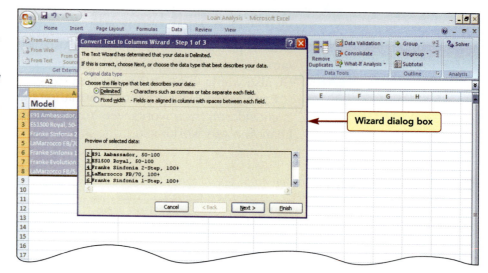

Wizard dialog box

Figure 5.19

The first wizard dialog box advises you that the wizard has determined that the data in the selected range is delimited. This is correct, as the cups-per-hour data is separated from the model information with a comma.

3 • Click [Next >] to continue.

Your screen should be similar to Figure 5.20

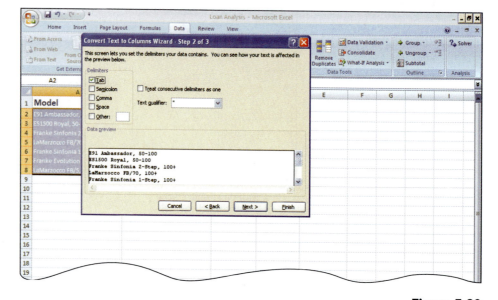

Figure 5.20

Next, you set the delimiters that are used. As you do, the preview area shows how the data will be divided into columns.

Lab 5: Using Data Tables, Using Lookup and IF Functions, and Designing Forms

www.mhhe.com/oleary

4 • **Choose Comma.**

• **Click** Next > .

Your screen should be similar to Figure 5.21

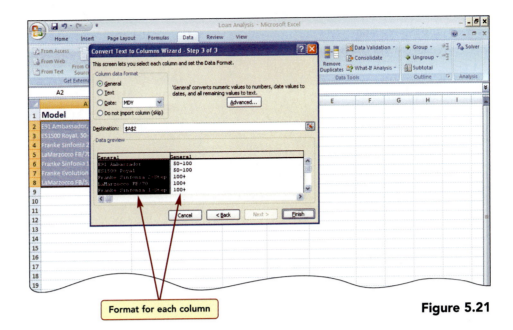

Format for each column

Figure 5.21

The final screen lets you set the format for each column. The General format is set appropriately for both columns.

5 • **Click** Finish .

• **Click** OK .

Your screen should be similar to Figure 5.22

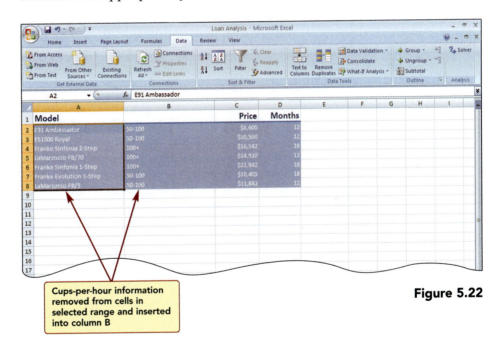

Cups-per-hour information removed from cells in selected range and inserted into column B

Figure 5.22

The cups-per-hour data has been removed from the cells in the selected range and inserted into adjacent cells in the column to the right.

6 ● Add the heading **Cups/Hour** in cell B1.

● AutoFit column B.

Your screen should be similar to Figure 5.23

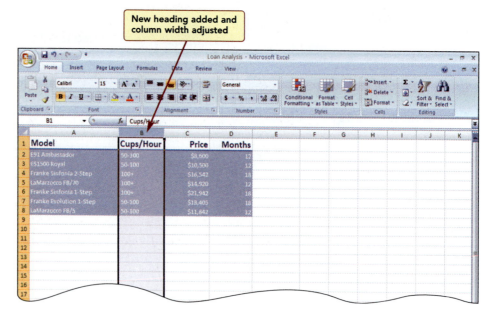

New heading added and column width adjusted

Figure 5.23

Now that you have information for several more espresso machines, you can use the loan analysis sheet to calculate the loan amounts for each. As you look at the information Evan has provided, you notice that he has changed the number of months for the loan to 18 months for the most expensive espresso machines. You also will need to reflect this change in the loan analysis for each machine.

Looking Up Values in a List

Each time you use the loan analysis worksheet, you need to enter the model data for each different espresso machine. Instead of entering the information each time, you will use a Lookup function to add the information from the list of data on the espresso machine models automatically for you. Then you can quickly generate the loan payment information for any model.

Concept 2

Lookup Functions

2 **Lookup functions** permit you to use worksheet tables as sources of information for formulas and calculations in other parts of the worksheet. There are two types of lookup functions: VLOOKUP is a vertical or columnar lookup and HLOOKUP is a horizontal or row-based lookup.

The **VLOOKUP function** searches for a value in the leftmost column of a table. It then returns a value in a cell you designate from the same row in a column you list in the table. The function is VLOOKUP(lookup_value, table_array, col_index_num, range_lookup).

The **HLOOKUP function** searches for a value in the top row of a table. It then returns a value in a cell you designate from the same column in a row that you list in the table. The function is HLOOKUP(lookup_value, table_array, row_index_um, range_lookup).

The arguments used in the lookup functions are explained in the following table.

Argument	Description
lookup_value	The value (number), reference, or text (in quotes) that you want to find
table_array	The range of cells to look in
col_index_num	The column of the table used to select the result
row_index_num	The row of the table used to select the result
range_lookup	A logical value that specifies whether you want the lookup function to find an exact match or an approximate match. TRUE returns the closest match and FALSE returns an exact match.

You will use the **VLOOKUP** function to add the model information to the loan analysis worksheet. To make it easier to see the model information as you enter and use the functions, you will copy the model data from the Models sheet to below the loan analysis data in the Analysis sheet.

1 ● **Copy A1:D8 from the Models sheet to cell B24 of the Analysis worksheet.**

Your screen should be similar to Figure 5.24

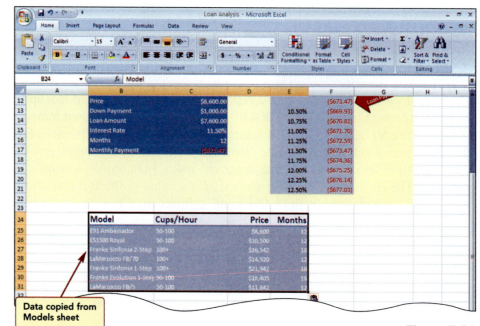

Data copied from Models sheet

Figure 5.24

You want to calculate the loan payment for the ES1500 Royal next. You will enter the model name in cell C11 and then a VLOOKUP function in cell C12 to display the price of the machine. The VLOOKUP function you will enter is =VLOOKUP(C11, B24:E31, 3, FALSE). This function will search the first column in the range B24:D31 for an exact match (FALSE) to the data in cell C11 and return the price data in column 3.

2 ● **Enter ES1500 Royal in cell C11.**

● **Enter =VLOOKUP(C11, B24:E31, 3, FALSE) in cell C12.**

● **Move to C12.**

Your screen should be similar to Figure 5.25

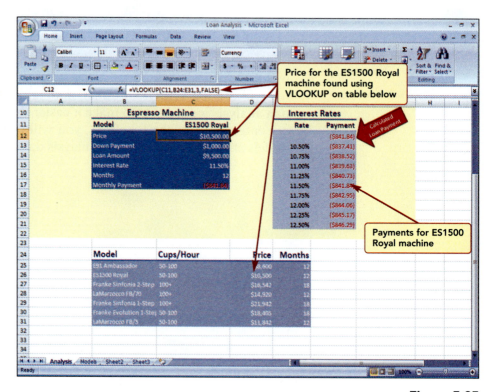

Price for the ES1500 Royal machine found using VLOOKUP on table below

Payments for ES1500 Royal machine

Figure 5.25

The price of the espresso machine, $10,500 from cell D26, is displayed in cell C12 and the new payments are displayed in cells F13 through F21.

Lab 5: Using Data Tables, Using Lookup and IF Functions, and Designing Forms

www.mhhe.com/oleary

Next, you will calculate the loan payment for the Franke Sinfonia 2-Step. Rather than typing the model name in cell C11, you will use a cell reference formula. Additionally, you notice that Evan wants to extend the term for this model to 18 months. Since this will occur with several models, you will enter a second VLOOKUP function to automatically add this data to the loan analysis.

3 ● Enter **=B27** in cell C11.

● Enter **=VLOOKUP(C11, B24:E31, 4, FALSE)** in cell **C16**.

Your screen should be similar to Figure 5.26

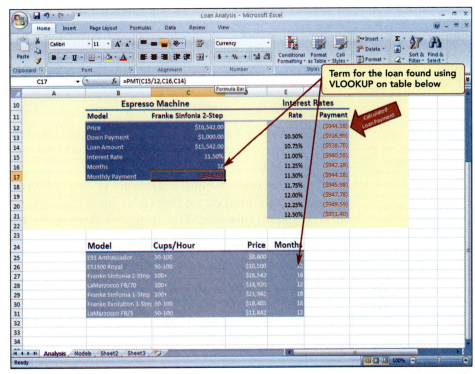

Figure 5.26

More About

For more information on VLOOKUP and HLOOKUP functions, see 3.5 Lookup Data Using a Formula in the More About appendix.

Using the cell reference to the model name in C11 ensures that the lookup function will find an exact match. Additionally, the second lookup function quickly enters the month information for each model.

4 ● Delete the Models sheet.

● Save and close the workbook.

● Close the ex05_Espresso Machines List workbook.

Creating a Form

The Downtown Internet Café recently started a Café Club that provides perks to members such as an e-mail newsletter, coupons, and Bonus Dollar awards. Your second project is to create a spreadsheet that calculates the Bonus Dollars earned by each customer. Bonus Dollars are awarded to customers who belong to the Café Club based on their monthly expenditures and can be applied toward any future purchases at the Café. You will create a form to record and calculate this information.

Concept 3

Form

3 A **form** is a formatted worksheet with blank spaces that can be filled in online on an individual computer or on a network, or printed and completed on paper. The steps in creating a form are the same for both purposes. However, certain elements are more appropriate for one than for the other. For example, color and shading are more effective on online forms, while simplicity of design and layout is very important in printed forms. In addition, online forms can contain formulas that immediately calculate results such as totals, whereas printed forms would need to include blank spaces where the calculations would be entered manually.

The first step when creating a form is to decide what should appear on the form and what information will be entered into the form. When customers make a purchase, the cashier swipes their Café Club card and the total purchase amount is then recorded as part of the transaction. Obtaining expenditures for each customer is just a matter of checking the computer file. The Bonus Dollars form needs to be designed to accept input of customer expenditures and to calculate Bonus Dollars earned. Although Evan wants the form to be electronic, he also wants to be able to print it out for reference.

You have already started designing the form by entering much of the text, many of the formulas, some formatting to improve the appearance, and some sample data.

1 ● **Open the workbook file ex05_Bonus Dollars.**

● **If necessary, maximize the worksheet.**

● **Move to H12.**

Your screen should be similar to Figure 5.27

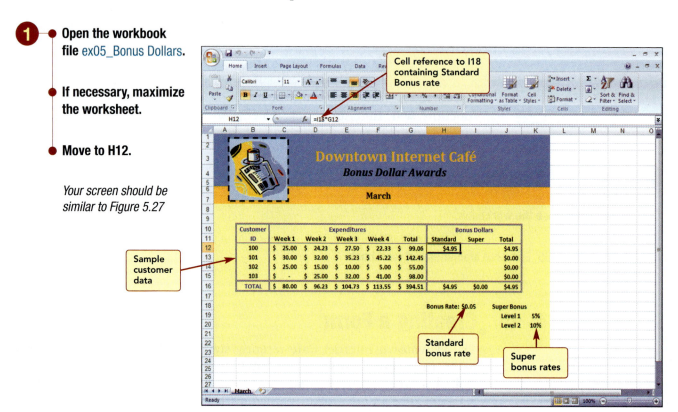

Figure 5.27

The worksheet displays identification numbers for four customers and their expenditures for each week in columns C through F.

The last three columns will be used to calculate and display customer Bonus Dollars. The Downtown Internet Café awards Bonus Dollars based on total monthly expenditures. A Standard Bonus is applied to every customer at a rate of $0.05 per dollar spent. An additional Super Bonus is awarded at two different levels for those customers who spend more. The bonus awards are explained in the following table.

Bonus	Award
Standard Bonus	All expenditures earn a standard bonus of $0.05 per dollar spent
Super Bonus Level 1	If total monthly expenditures are greater than $75 but less than $120, the Super Bonus is 5% of the Standard Bonus
Super Bonus Level 2	If total expenditures are greater than or equal to $120, the Super Bonus is 10% of the Standard Bonus.

Using Named Ranges

Many times, especially in a large worksheet, formulas are difficult to read and understand. This is because the cell references used in the formula do not identify the cell content. For example, the formula used in cell H12 references cell I18. To understand this formula, you would need to look at the worksheet to find out the content of cell I18. In this case, cell I18 contains the Standard Bonus rate amount of $0.05 per dollar.

To help clarify the meaning of a formula, you can name cells and ranges.

Concept 4

Name

4   A **name** is a description of a cell or range of cells that can be used in place of cell references. The name can be used any time a cell or range is requested as part of a command or in a formula or function. A name must begin with a letter, underscore (_), or backslash (\) and can be up to 255 characters long. It can include letters, numbers, underlines, periods, backslashes, and question marks. It cannot contain spaces. Names can contain upper- and lowercase characters. Excel displays the name as you enter it; however, it does not distinguish between names based on the case. Therefore, a cell name of Bonus is the same as bonus and Excel would prompt you to enter a unique name. A name that resembles a cell reference is not allowed.

There are two types of names that you can create: defined names and table names. A **defined name** represents a cell, range of cells, formula, or constant value. A **table name** represents the range of cells that stores an Excel data table. (You will learn about data tables in Lab 6.)

All names have a **scope**, or restriction to a location within which the name is recognized without qualification. A defined name scope can be limited to the worksheet in which it was created, called the **local worksheet level**, or to the entire workbook, or a **global workbook level**. The default scope is workbook level. This level is set by preceding the name with the worksheet name, similar to how you enter a formula that references data in another worksheet. A name must always be unique within its scope.

You will name several cells in this worksheet to make the formulas you will create easier to understand.

Naming Cell References

You will begin by naming cell I18, containing the Standard Bonus rate amount of $0.05 per dollar.

1 ● Move to I18.

● Open the Formulas tab.

● Click [📋 Define Name ▾] in the Defined Name group.

Your screen should be similar to Figure 5.28

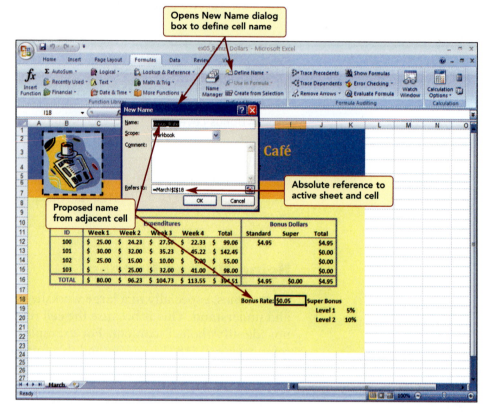

Figure 5.28

The New Name dialog box is used to name, modify, and delete cell names. In the Name text box, Excel has proposed the name Bonus_Rate. Excel automatically proposes a name for the cell or range using the contents of the active cell if it contains text, or the cell above or to the left of the active cell if the active cell does not contain text. If none of the proposed names is appropriate, you can type the name in the text box. In this case, the proposed name is the contents of the cell to the left of the active cell. Excel replaced the blank space between the words with an underscore character.

The Refers To text box displays the reference for the active cell. The reference includes the sheet name and cell reference. By default Excel makes named cell references absolute. In this case, both the name and the cell reference are acceptable.

Lab 5: Using Data Tables, Using Lookup and IF Functions, and Designing Forms

www.mhhe.com/oleary

2 • Click [OK].

Your screen should be similar to Figure 5.29

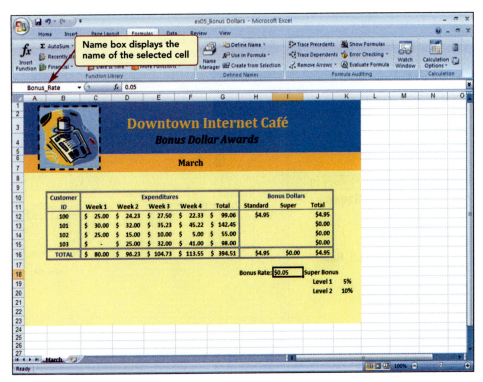

Figure 5.29

Another Method

You also could create a name by typing the name in the Name box in the formula bar.

Additional Information

You can toggle between temporarily displaying the cell reference and the name by holding down the mouse button on the cell to display the cell reference and releasing it to display the name.

In place of the cell reference in the Name box of the formula bar, the name is displayed.

Now you need to replace the cell reference in the formula in cell H11 with the name.

3
- Move to H12.

- Change to Edit mode.

- Select (highlight) the cell reference I18 in the formula.

- Click [Use in Formula ▾] in the Defined Names group.

- Choose Bonus_Rate.

- Click ✓ Enter.

Your screen should be similar to Figure 5.30

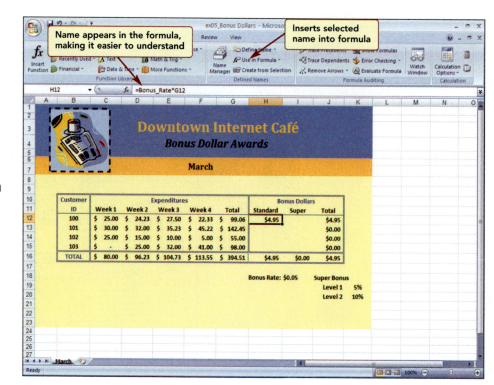

Name appears in the formula, making it easier to understand

Inserts selected name into formula

H12   =Bonus_Rate*G12

Figure 5.30

Additional Information

To quickly replace all cell references in formulas with a named range, click [Define Name ▾] and choose Apply Names.

The selected name has replaced the reference to cell I18 in the formula. Using a name makes the formula easier to understand.

Next, you will name the Super Bonus levels in cells K19 and K20 that will be used in the formula to calculate the Super Bonus. You will name both cells at the same time using the labels in J19 and J20 as the names.

4 • **Select J19 through K20.**

• **Click** [Create from Selection] **in the Defined Names group.**

Your screen should be similar to Figure 5.31

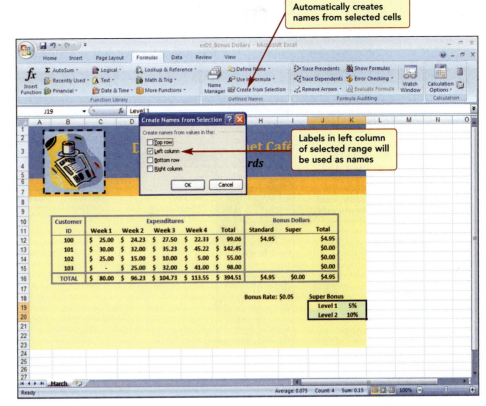

Automatically creates names from selected cells

Labels in left column of selected range will be used as names

Figure 5.31

In the Create Names from Selection dialog box, you specify the location of the labels you want to use for names in relation to the cells to be named. In this case, you want to use the labels in the column to the left (J), which is the default. You will accept the default and then move to the cells to verify that the names have been created.

5 • **Click** [OK].

• **Move to K19 and note that Level_1 is displayed in the Name box.**

• **Move to K20 and note that Level_2 is displayed in the Name box.**

• **Save the workbook as** March Bonus Dollars.

Using Name Manager

In a worksheet that has many named ranges, it is convenient to view and manage the named cells using the Name Manager feature.

1 ● Click 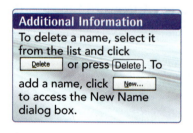 in the **Defined Names group.**

Your screen should be similar to Figure 5.32

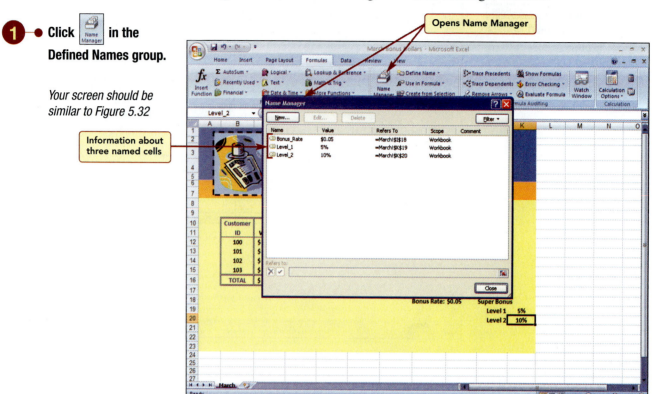

Figure 5.32

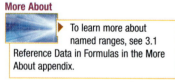
The Name Manager displays the name, values, and cell references for the three named cells. The scope of all three names is the current workbook. Using the Name Manager, you can create a new named range or edit or delete existing named ranges. You will edit the existing names.

2 ● Select the Bonus_Rate name from the list.

● Click [Edit...].

● Change the name to **BonusRate** and add the description **Standard Bonus** in the Comment box.

● Click [OK].

● In a similar manner, change Level_1 to **SuperBonus1** with a comment of **Level 1 Bonus** and Level_2 to **SuperBonus2** with a comment of **Level 2 Bonus**.

Your screen should be similar to Figure 5.33

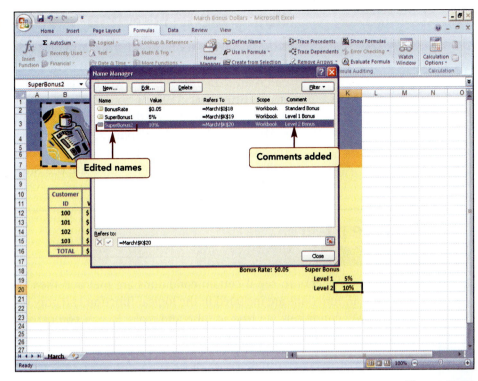

Figure 5.33

Next, you will copy the standard bonus formula down the column.

3 ● Click [Close].

● Move to cell H12.

● Use the fill handle to copy the formula to cells H13:H15.

● From the Auto Fill Options button menu, choose Fill Without Formatting.

● Click cell H15 to deselect the range.

● If necessary, Best Fit column H to fully display the cell borders.

Your screen should be similar to Figure 5.34

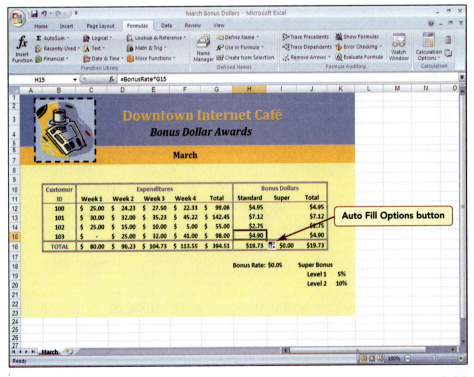

Figure 5.34

Using the IF Function

Now you want to enter a formula in cell I11 to calculate the Super Bonus. For any customer with more than $75 of expenditures, the Super Bonus is calculated using one of two levels. The highest level is for those with expenditures of $120 or more. Those customers receive a Super Bonus equal to 10 percent of their Standard Bonus. The other level is for those with expenditures less than $120 but more than $75. Those customers receive a Super Bonus equal to 5 percent of their Standard Bonus. You will use the IF function to calculate the Super Bonus.

Concept 5

IF Function

5 The **IF function** checks to see if certain conditions are met and then takes action based on the results of the check. IF functions are included in the logical function category because they use conditional logic to test whether conditions are true or false and make logical comparisons between expressions.

 The syntax for the IF function is

$$IF(logical\_test, value\_if\_true, value\_if\_false)$$

This function contains three arguments: logical_test, value_if_true, and value_if_false. The logical_test argument is an expression that makes a comparison using logical operators. **Logical operators** are symbols used in formulas that compare numbers in two or more cells or to a constant. The result of the comparison is either true (the conditions are met) or false (the conditions are not met). The logical operators are

Symbol	Meaning
=	Equal to
<	Less than
>	Greater than
<=	Less than or equal to
>=	Greater than or equal to
<>	Not equal to
NOT	Logical NOT
AND	Logical AND
OR	Logical OR

The logical_test argument asks the question, "Does the entry in this cell meet the stated conditions?" The answer is either True (Yes) or False (No). The second argument, value_if_true, provides directions for the function to follow if the logical test result is true. The third argument, value_if_false, provides directions for the function to follow if the logical test result is false.

Lab 5: Using Data Tables, Using Lookup and IF Functions, and Designing Forms

First you will enter the formula to calculate the bonus earned for monthly expenditures of $120 or more. Then you will modify the function to include the other conditions.

1 • **Move to cell I12.**

• **Click 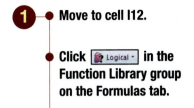 in the Function Library group on the Formulas tab.**

• **Choose IF.**

Your screen should be similar to Figure 5.35

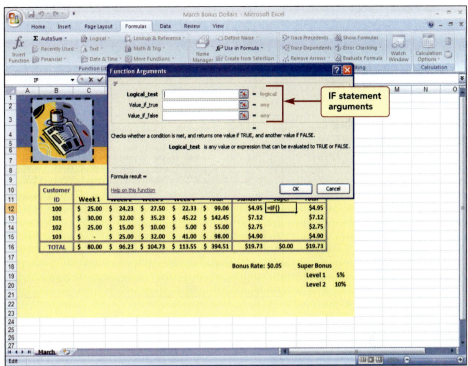

Figure 5.35

The Function Arguments dialog box is displayed to help you enter the parts of the function. The upper section of the dialog box contains three text boxes, one for each IF statement argument. The lower section provides information about the selected argument.

In this case, the logical test is whether the total expenditures for a customer are greater than or equal to $120. The value_if_true argument provides directions for what to do if the logical test is true. In this IF function, the value_if_true directions will be to multiply the value in cell H12 times the value in the cell named SuperBonus2.

2 ● In the **Logical_test** text
box, type **G12>=120.**

● Press **Tab**.

● In the **Value_if_true**
text box, type
SuperBonus2*H12.

*Your screen should be
similar to Figure 5.36*

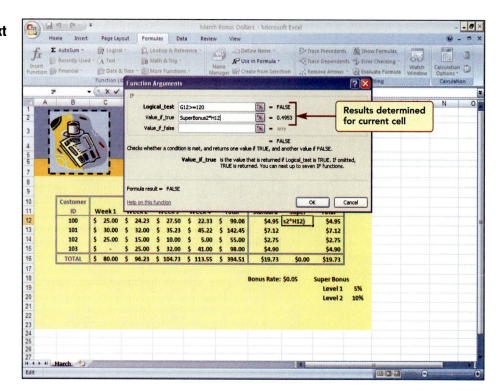

**Results determined
for current cell**

Figure 5.36

As you specify the arguments, to the right of the argument text box Excel has already determined whether the conditions are true or false for the current customer based on the values in the referenced cells. In this case, because the value in G12 is less than $120, the logical test result is False.

Next, you need to enter the value_if_false argument. It contains instructions that are executed if expenditures are less than $120. If the expenditures are greater than $75 but less than $120, then the Level_1 amount is used to calculate the Super Bonus. If the expenditures are less than or equal to $75 then the Super Bonus is 0. To enter this condition, you include a second IF statement that will apply the SuperBonus1 bonus. The arguments for the second IF statement are enclosed in their own set of parentheses. This is called a **nested function.**

3 • In the Value_if_false text box, type IF(G12>75,SuperBonus1 *H12,0).

Your screen should be similar to Figure 5.37

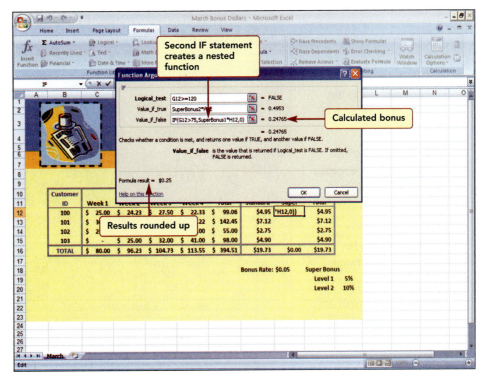

Figure 5.37

Now the calculated result is 0.24765 for the current customer. The formula result will be rounded up to $0.25.

4 • Click  OK.

Your screen should be similar to Figure 5.38

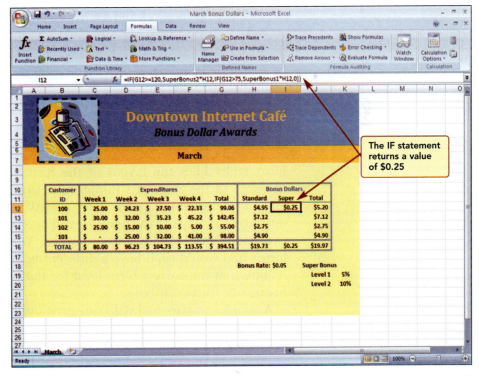

Figure 5.38

The Super Bonus for customer 100 is $0.25. The IF function determined that the number in cell G12 was less than 120 but greater than 75. Therefore, the bonus was calculated using SuperBonus1, or 5 percent.

Next, you will enter formulas to make these same calculations for the other three customers.

5 • Using the fill handle, copy cell I12 to the range I13 through I15.

• From the Auto Fill Options button menu, choose Fill Without Formatting.

• Click cell I15 to deselect the range.

Your screen should be similar to Figure 5.39

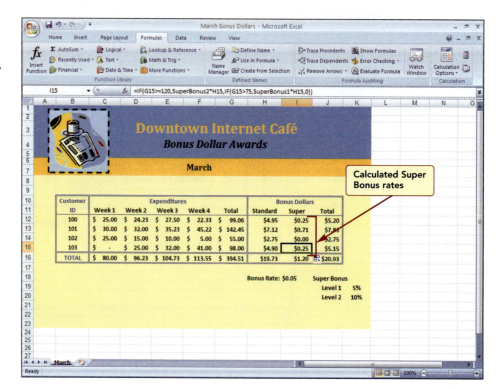

Figure 5.39

More About

➤ To learn about the AND, OR, NOT, and IFERROR logical functions, see 3.6 Use Conditional Logic in a Formula in the More About appendix.

Because the named references in the copied formulas are absolute, they copied correctly. Customer 101 earned a Super Bonus award of 10 percent because the value in cell G13 is greater than $120. Customer 102 did not earn a Super Bonus because the value in cell G14 is less than $75. Customer 103 earned a Super Bonus award of 5 percent because the value in cell G15 was greater than $75 but less than $120.

Using a Drop-Down List

Evan really likes the layout of the form. A change needs to be made, however, to the Standard Bonus rate. During the slowest months, Evan plans to increase the bonus rate to $0.08 or $0.10 per dollar spent. The formulas to calculate the bonuses will need to be adjusted to use the other two bonus rates during those months. You could create two additional forms that would each have a different bonus rate in cell I18. This would require that the correct form used for that month's input be based on the bonus rate for that month.

A simpler way to deal with this problem is to create a drop-down list of the bonus rates that can be selected to set the bonus rate for the month. The cell containing a drop-down list displays an arrow. Clicking on the arrow opens the list of the items that can be selected.

Creating a Drop-Down List

The first step in creating a drop-down list is to enter the items you want to appear in the drop-down list in a columnar range. You will enter the three bonus amounts as the items to appear in the list. Then you move to the cell where you want to create the drop-down list.

1 ● **In cells H19 through H21, enter .05, .08, and .10.**

Additional Information
Cells H19:H21 are preformatted to Currency.

● **Move to cell I18.**

● **Click** Data Validation **in the Data Tools group of the Data tab.**

● **If necessary, open the Settings tab.**

Your screen should be similar to Figure 5.40

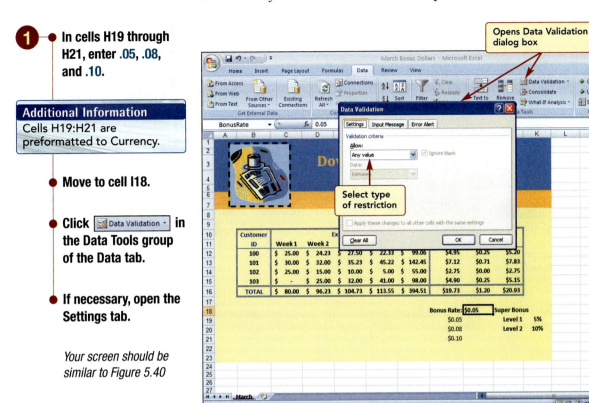

Figure 5.40

Additional Information
You will learn about other validation methods in Lab 6.

In the Settings tab, you specify the type of validation that you want to apply to the cell. **Validation** ensures that the data entered in a cell is acceptable or valid by placing restrictions on the data that can be entered. Initially, no restrictions are placed on entries that can be made in a cell. One way to restrict the data that can be entered is to limit the entries to those entries displayed in a drop-down list. Then you provide the location of the cells containing the list data.

2 ● Open the Allow drop-down list and choose List.

● Enter the range **H19:H21** as the Source.

● If necessary, make the source range an absolute reference.

Additional Information

If you select the range from the worksheet, it automatically will be entered as an absolute reference.

Your screen should be similar to Figure 5.41

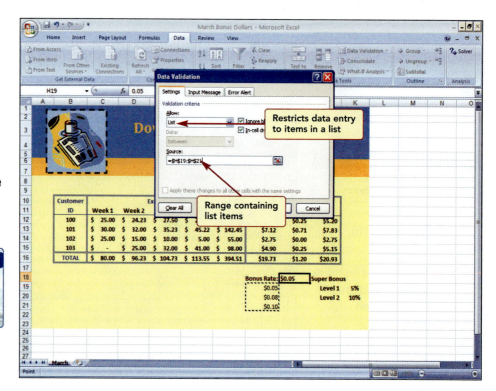

Figure 5.41

Next you want to add a message that will appear when the cell is selected to explain how to use the cell.

3 ● Open the Input Message tab.

● If necessary, choose Show input message when cell is selected.

● Type **Select the bonus rate for the month.** in the Input Message text box.

Additional Information

The title and text for the message can be up to 225 characters.

Your screen should be similar to Figure 5.42

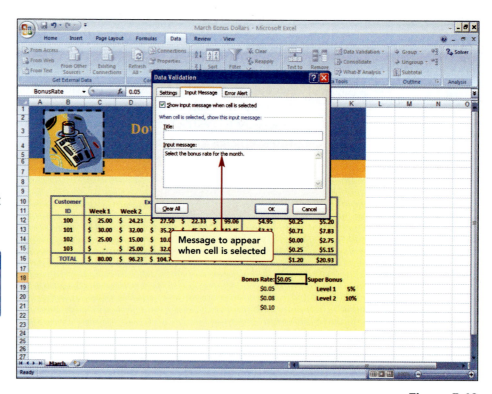

Figure 5.42

Lab 5: Using Data Tables, Using Lookup and IF Functions, and Designing Forms

www.mhhe.com/oleary

Finally, you want to include an error alert message that appears when an invalid entry is made in the cell. There are three error alert styles that can be selected: Stop, Warning, and Message. A Stop alert prevents entry of invalid data. Warning or Message alerts display a warning or information message but do not prevent entry of invalid data.

4 ● **Open the Error Alert tab.**

● **If necessary, choose Show error alert after invalid data is entered.**

● **If necessary, select the Stop style from the Style drop-down list.**

● **Type This entry is not allowed. Select an entry from the list. in the Error message text box.**

Additional Information

The title and text for the message can be up to 225 characters.

Your screen should be similar to Figure 5.43

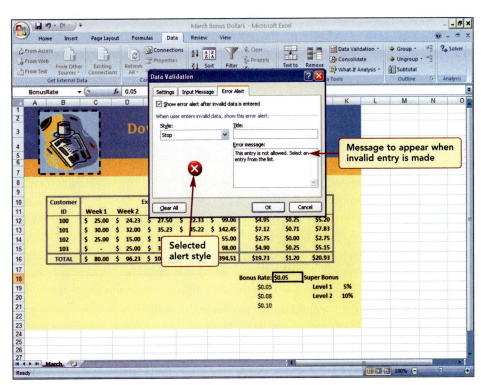

Figure 5.43

The error alert message will display the text you entered and the stop symbol in a dialog box if an invalid entry is made.

5 ● **Click** [OK].

Your screen should be similar to Figure 5.44

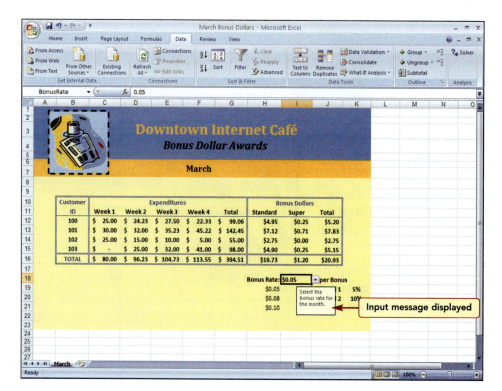

Input message displayed

Figure 5.44

The process of creating and defining the validation settings for the drop-down list are now complete. Because cell I18 is selected, the input message you entered is displayed, providing directions on how to use the cell.

Testing the Drop-Down List

The next step is to test the drop-down list cell to make sure the validation settings are working correctly. First you will select a bonus rate from the list.

1 Click ▼ next to cell I18 to display the list.

● Choose **$0.10**.

Your screen should be similar to Figure 5.45

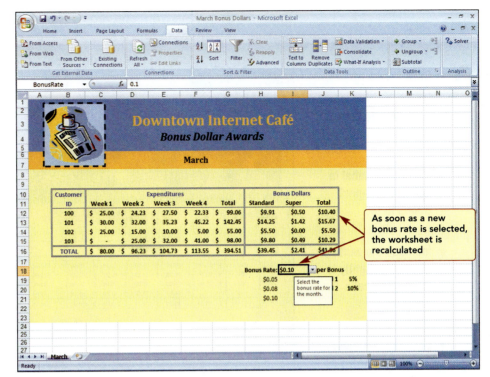

As soon as a new bonus rate is selected, the worksheet is recalculated

Figure 5.45

The selection you made from the drop-down list is entered in the Bonus Rate cell, I18, and the worksheet is recalculated using the new bonus rate.

Now you will test the data validation settings by entering an incorrect bonus amount.

2 Type **25** in cell I18 and press (←Enter).

Your screen should be similar to Figure 5.46

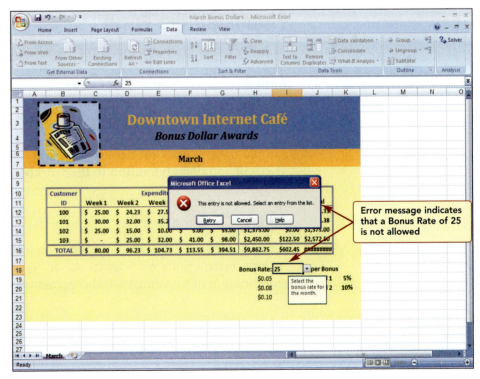

Error message indicates that a Bonus Rate of 25 is not allowed

Figure 5.46

Because the value you entered was not a value on the list, the error message is displayed. You will type in a correct entry next.

 ● Click **Retry**.

● Type **.08** and press **⏎Enter**.

● Change the label in cell H18 to Select Bonus Rate:.

● Increase the width of column H slightly to display the cell borders.

● Save the workbook.

Your screen should be similar to Figure 5.47

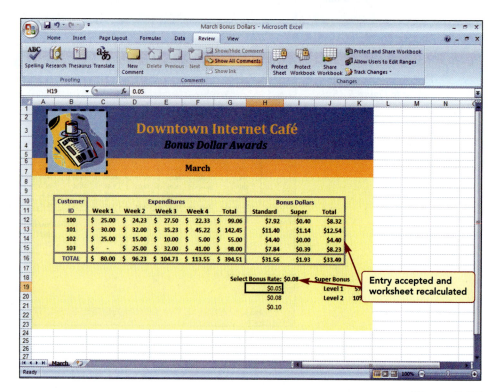

Figure 5.47

The entry is accepted because it is the same as one of the items in the list.

Finalizing the Form

Now you will prepare the form to be used for other months. A well-designed form is simple to use and uncluttered in design. To make the form easy to use, you will add comments and a command button to print the output. To simplify the design, you will hide nonessential items. Then you will prepare the workbook to be saved as a template to be used each month to record the customer's Bonus Dollar earnings. You will clear the sample data, unlock all data entry areas, and protect the worksheet. You also will add documentation to the workbook to clarify the purpose of the template.

Adding Comments

Since someone else will most likely use the form, it is a good idea to include instructions on how to use it. Typically, these instructions are a combination of text entries and comments.

6 A **comment** is a note attached to a cell that can be used to help clarify the meaning of the data, provide documentation, or ask a question. Using comments is a good method of adding instructions that do not interfere with the appearance of the worksheet.

A cell containing a comment displays a red indicator triangle in the upper-right corner. Pointing to a cell containing a comment displays the comment text in a comment box. You can move and resize a comment box just as you would any other type of graphic object. If you move the cell that contains a comment, the associated comment box moves with it.

You will add one text entry and three cell comments that will provide the instructions for this form.

1 ● Move to cell A8.

● Enter **For help on how to complete this form, point to the red triangles.**

● Format the entry in cell A8 using a font color of red and bold.

Your screen should be similar to Figure 5.48

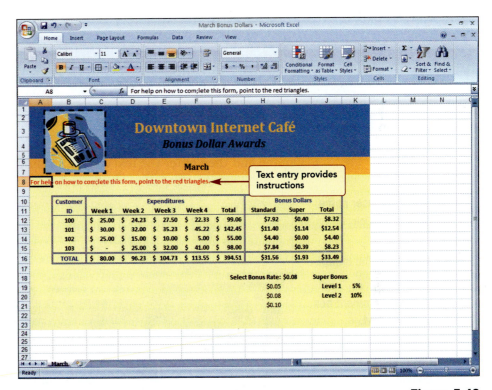

Figure 5.48

Next, you will add the cell comments using the Review tab. The first comment will appear in cell F6 and will direct users to update the month.

2
- Move to cell F6.
- Open the Review tab.
- Click 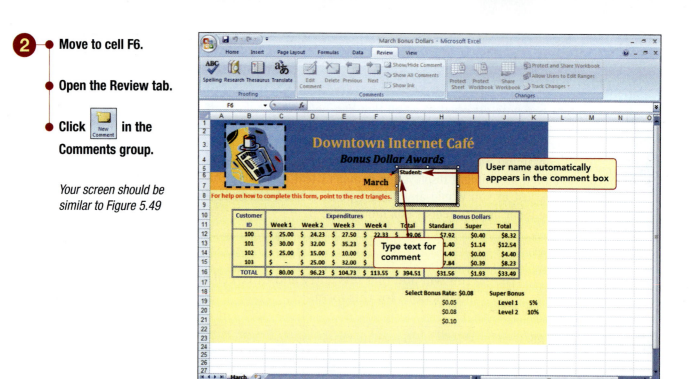 in the Comments group.

Your screen should be similar to Figure 5.49

Figure 5.49

By default, the comment box includes the user name. You will delete the name and then enter the text for the comment.

3
- Select the user name and press Delete.
- Type **Enter the month.**
- Size the comment box to fit the text.
- Click on any cell to complete the comment.

Having Trouble?

If the red triangle is not displayed, click 🔘 Office Button, click 🔲 Excel Options , and choose Indicators only, and comments on hover from the Display section of the Advanced category.

- Point to cell F6.

Your screen should be similar to Figure 5.50

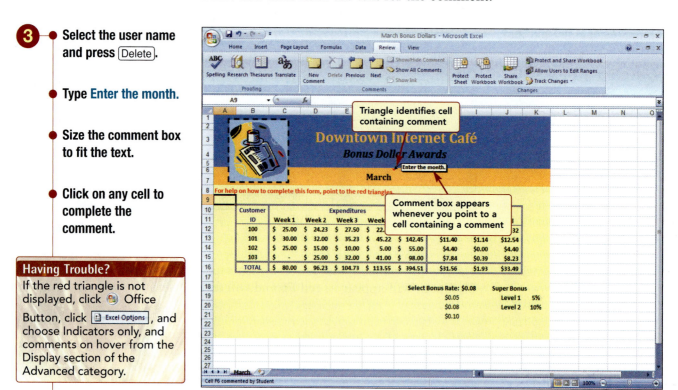

Figure 5.50

Lab 5: Using Data Tables, Using Lookup and IF Functions, and Designing Forms

www.mhhe.com/oleary

A red triangle appears in the upper-right corner of the cell containing the comment. When you point to a cell containing a comment, the comment text is displayed in a comment box. An arrow from the comment box points to the cell to which the comment is attached.

The second comment will be entered in cell C12.

4 ● Add a comment to C12 containing the text **Enter expenditures here.** and size the comment box to fit the text.

● Click on any cell to complete the comment.

● Point to cell C12 to display the comment.

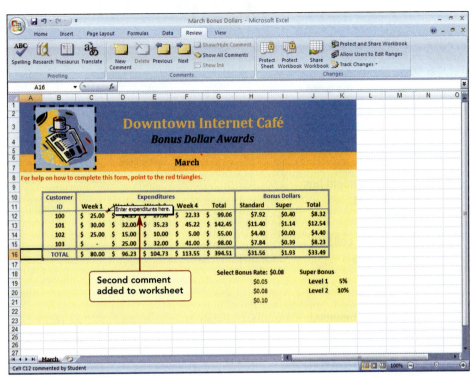

Figure 5.51

Another Method

You also can move to a cell containing a comment and click 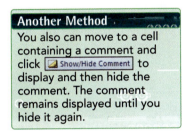 Show/Hide Comment to display and then hide the comment. The comment remains displayed until you hide it again.

Your screen should be similar to Figure 5.51

Editing Comments

You decide the comment is not descriptive enough and will edit the comment text.

1 ● **Move to cell C12 and click**  **.**

Another Method

You also can edit a comment using Edit Comment from the shortcut menu.

● **Move the insertion point before the word "expenditures" and type the word weekly followed by a space.**

● **Size the comment box to fit the text.**

● **Click on any cell to complete the comment.**

● **Display the comment.**

Your screen should be similar to Figure 5.52

Additional Information

You can delete a comment using Delete Comment from the shortcut menu or by clicking  in the Comments group.

More About

▶ See 5 Collaborating and Securing Data in the More About appendix to learn about deleting comments.

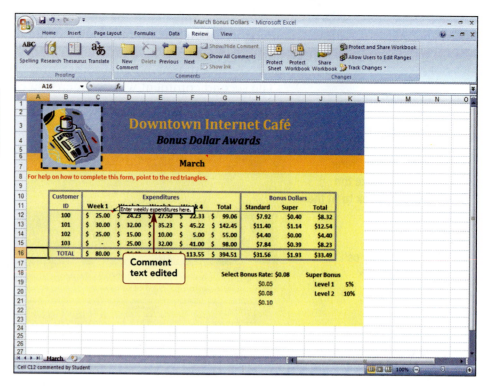

Figure 5.52

You have added two comments to the form to provide directions on how to use the form.

Viewing All Comments

To quickly check all comments, rather than displaying each comment individually, you can display all the comments at the same time.

1 ● Click  in the Comments group.

Your screen should be similar to Figure 5.53

 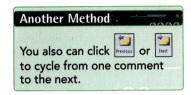
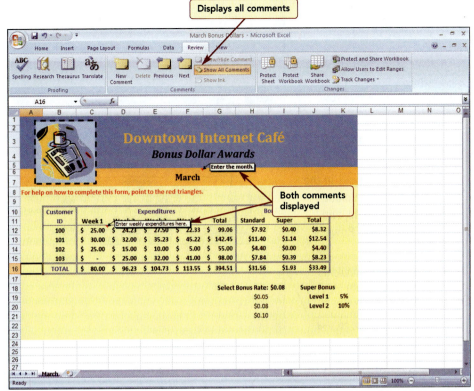

Figure 5.53

The two comments you entered are displayed. If comments overlay one another, you can move them around just like any other graphic object. However, when you hide and redisplay the comments, they return to their original location.

2 ● Click  to hide comments again.

Hiding and Unhiding Rows

Next, you will hide any nonessential information in the form to simplify its appearance.

Users of this form do not need to see the list of bonus rates and the two bonus levels. To simplify the form, you will hide this information.

1 ● Select rows 19
through 21.

Additional Information
Click the row number to
quickly select an entire row.

● Open the Home tab.

● Click [Format ▾] in the
Cells group, select
Hide & Unhide, and
choose Hide Rows.

*Your screen should be
similar to Figure 5.54*

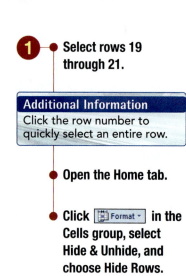

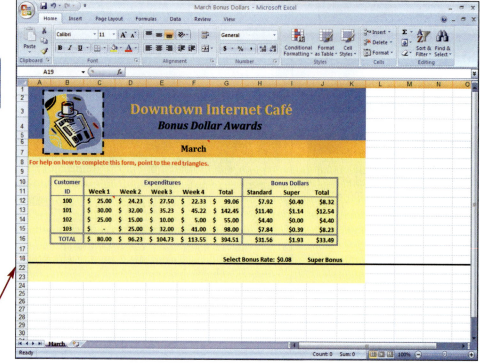

Rows 19, 20, and
21 hidden

Figure 5.54

The selected rows are hidden; however, the label for the Super Bonus
information is still visible in cell J18. You will unhide the rows and move
the Super Bonus information next to the bonus list of values. To redisplay
hidden rows, select the rows above and below the hidden rows and then
use the command to unhide rows.

2 ● Select rows 18
through 22.

● Click [Format ▾],
select Hide & Unhide,
and choose Unhide
Rows.

● Move the contents of
cells J18:K20 to J19.

● Reapply the fill color
to the vacated cell.

*Your screen should be
similar to Figure 5.55*

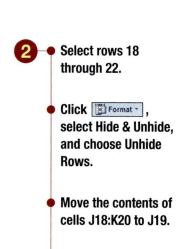

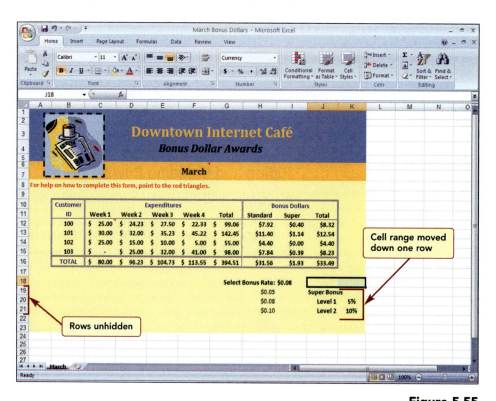

Cell range moved
down one row

Rows unhidden

Figure 5.55

Finally, you will hide the rows again.

3
- Select and hide rows 19 through 21.

- Move to cell I18.

- Save the workbook.

Your screen should be similar to Figure 5.56

Rows 19, 20, and 21 hidden

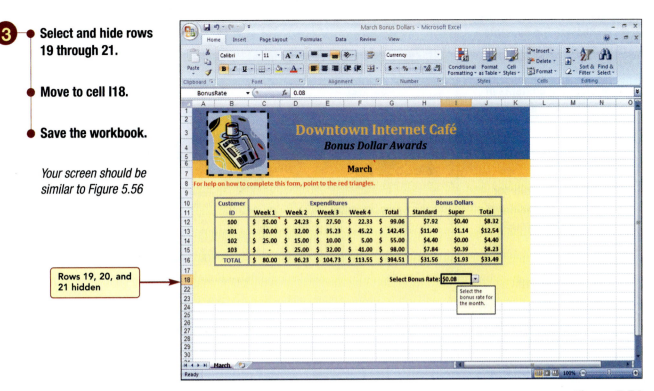

Figure 5.56

Now only the information that is necessary to complete the form is displayed.

Preparing the Workbook for Use

Each month, the form will be used to record the customer's Bonus Dollar earnings. Although the form needs to be expanded to include all the Club members, you will save the sample design as a template file for Evan to try out.

To prepare the form for use as a template, you need to first clear the sample data and unlock those cells for editing. Then you will include file documentation so that users of the template will understand the purpose of the file and perform several other steps to prepare the workbook for use by others. Finally, you will protect the worksheet.

Protecting Worksheet Elements

First, you will clear the contents of the entry areas and unlock these cells for editing.

1 Replace the contents of cell F6 with **Month**.

• Clear the contents of cells C12 through F15.

• Unlock cell F6.

• Unlock the cells for weekly expenditures (cells C12 through F15).

• Unlock cell I18.

Your screen should be similar to Figure 5.57

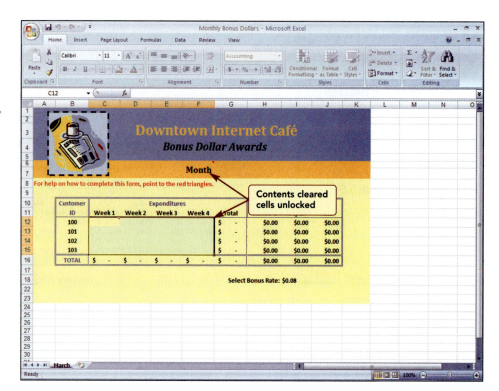

Figure 5.57

Next, you will enter basic documentation regarding the workbook file in the Document Information Panel.

2 Click 🔘 Office Button, select Prepare, and choose Properties.

• Enter your name in the Author text box.

• Enter **Monthly record of expenditures and bonuses** in the Subject text box.

• In the Comments text box, type **Point to the red triangles for instructions. Select the bonus amount for the month from the Bonus Rate drop-down list.**

Your screen should be similar to Figure 5.58

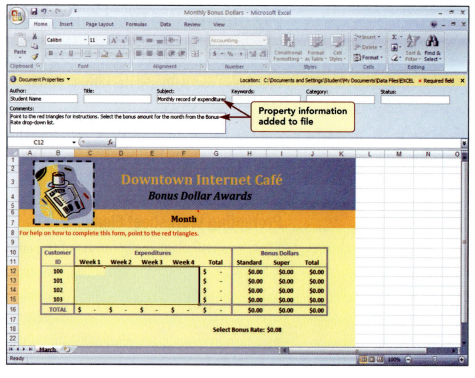

Figure 5.58

You are now ready to save this generalized workbook.

Lab 5: Using Data Tables, Using Lookup and IF Functions, and Designing Forms

www.mhhe.com/oleary

3 • Click [×] to close the Document Information Panel.

• Move to cell A9.

• Save the workbook as Monthly Bonus Dollars.

Checking for Private Information

Before you give a file to another user, it is a good idea to check the document for hidden data or personal information that may be stored in the computer itself or in the document's properties that you may not want to share. To help locate and remove this information, you can use the Document Inspector.

1 • Click 🗐 Office Button, select Prepare, and choose Inspect Document.

• If necessary, select [No] in response to the prompt to save the file since the file has been recently saved.

Your screen should be similar to Figure 5.59

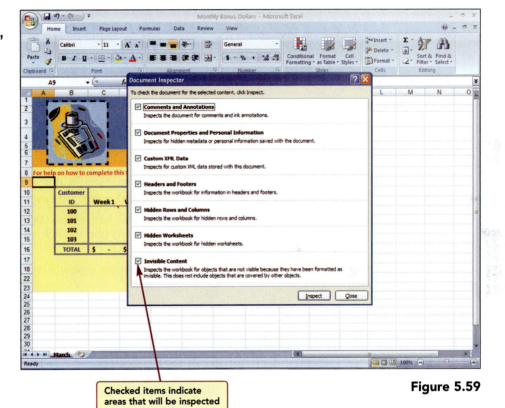

Checked items indicate areas that will be inspected

Figure 5.59

2 ● **Click** [Inspect] .

Your screen should be similar to Figure 5.60

Worksheet comments located

Document properties and named cell comments located

Hidden rows located

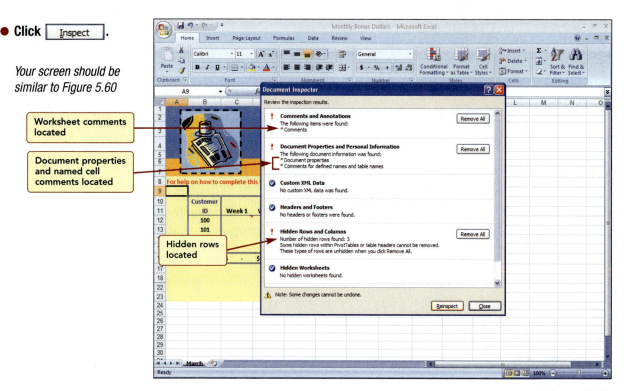

Figure 5.60

The inspector results identify three areas containing hidden data or personal information. These include comments and hidden rows as well as potentially private information in document properties. If you wanted to remove any of the located information, you would click [Remove All] next to each item in the list. In this case, you do not want to remove the comments or hidden rows, so you will close the inspector without making any changes.

3 ● **Click** [Close] .

● **Turn on worksheet protection.**

Marking a Workbook as Final

Another feature you can use when sharing a workbook with others is to mark it as final. This feature makes the document read-only and thereby prevents changes to the document. However, this feature is not a security feature, as anyone using the file can easily remove the Mark as Final status from the file. You will try out this feature to see how it works as it may be useful in other situations. Then you will turn the feature off.

1 **Click Office Button, select Prepare, and choose Mark as Final.**

- **Click OK to authorize saving the file.**
- **Click OK in response to the informational message about marking the document as final.**
- **Move to cell F6 and try to type the month.**

Your screen should be similar to Figure 5.61

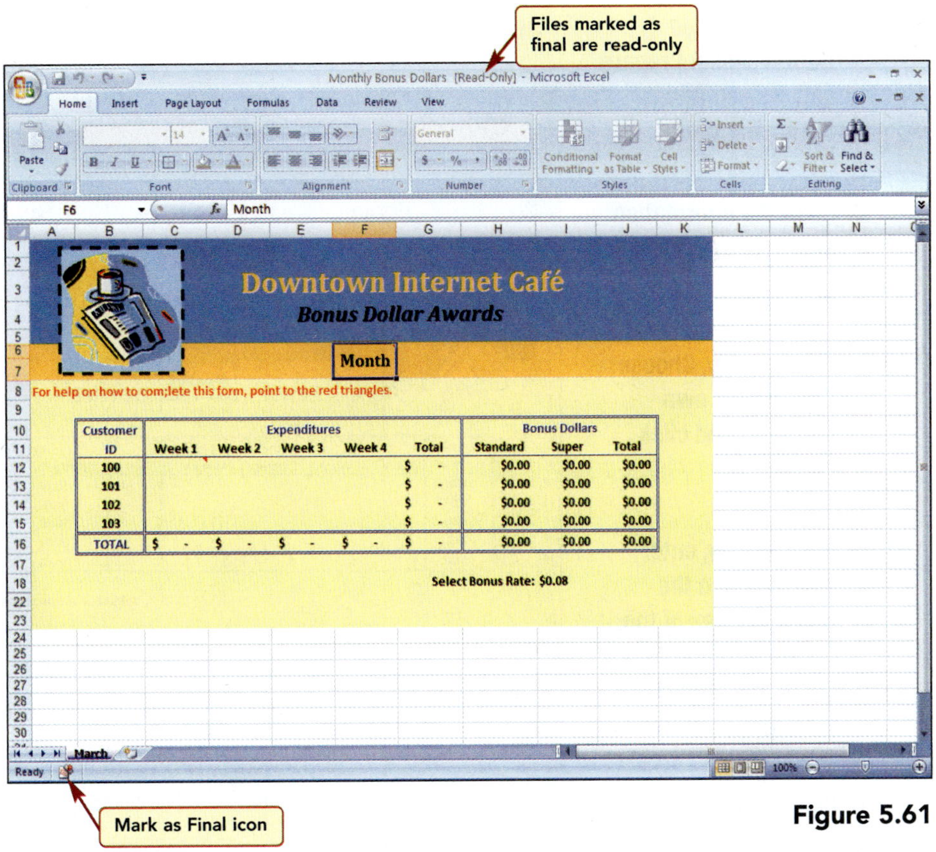

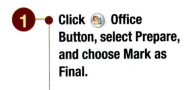

Figure 5.61

The Mark as Final icon appears in the status bar to show that this feature is on and any changes you try to make to the worksheet are prohibited. The title bar also displays [Read-Only] following the file name to show users that the file cannot be edited. Since you want Evan to be able to make changes to the worksheet, you will turn off this feature.

2 **Click Office Button, select Prepare, and choose Mark as Final.**

The read-only restriction is removed from the file and the Mark as Final icon is no longer displayed in the status bar.

Adding a Digital Signature

Another feature that can be used when giving someone else a file to look at is a digital signature. This feature authenticates that the people and products are who and what they claim to be through the use of a digital signature. A **digital signature** is an electronic encryption-based stamp of authentication that confirms the document originated from the signer and has not been changed. For the signature to be valid, it must by issued by a certificate authority (CA), a commercial organization that issues digital signatures.

Digital signatures can be visible in a document or invisible. A visible digital signature is displayed on a signature line in the document. An invisible signature is stored in the document file and recipients can verify that the document was digitally signed by viewing the document's digital signature or by looking at the Signatures icon in the status bar. You will add and then remove an invisible digital signature.

1 • Click 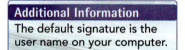 Office
Button, select Prepare,
and choose Add a
Digital Signature.

• Read the information
message and click
OK .

• If necessary, Choose
Create your own
digital ID and click
OK .

• If necessary, enter
your name in the
Name textbox of the
Create a Digital ID
dialog box and click
Create .

• Click Sign to
create your digital
signature.

Additional Information
The default signature is the
user name on your computer.

• Click OK in
response to the
Signature
Confirmation
message.

*Your screen should be
similar to Figure 5.62*

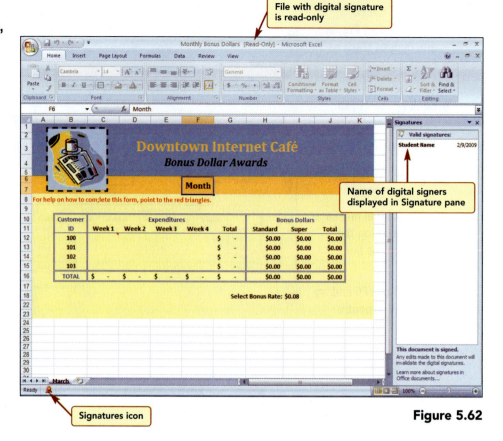

File with digital signature
is read-only

Name of digital signers
displayed in Signature pane

Signatures icon

Figure 5.62

The file is saved as a read-only file and the status bar displays the Signatures icon. Clicking on this button hides and displays the Signatures pane. The Signatures pane displays the names of the digital signers. Again, because you want Evan to be able to make changes to the worksheet, you will turn off this feature.

2 ● Point to the digital signature name in the Signatures pane and open the drop-down menu.

● Choose Remove Signature.

● Click [Yes] to permanently remove the signature.

● Click [OK] to acknowledge that the signature was removed.

● Close the Signatures pane.

The read-only restriction is removed and the 🔲 Signatures icon is no longer displayed in the status bar.

Protecting a Workbook File

To prevent any unauthorized users from opening the workbook file, you will add a password to the file. Using password protection enables only those users who know the password to access the file. This feature uses advanced encryption, a standard method used to help make files more secure. You will save the workbook as a template with a password.

1 ● Click 🔵 Office Button, select Save As, and choose Other Formats.

● Select Excel Template as the file type.

● Enter the file name Monthly Bonus Form.

● Change the location to the location where you save your solution files.

● Click [Tools] ▾ and choose General Options.

Your screen should be similar to Figure 5.63

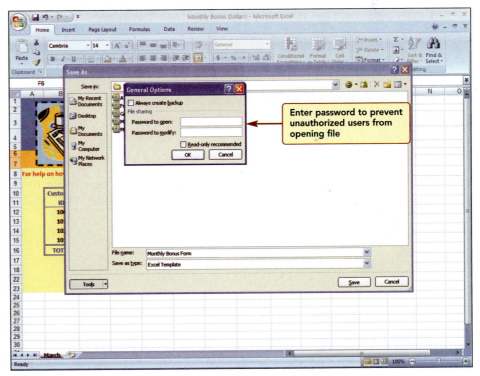

Figure 5.63

2 ● In the Password to open text box, enter your name and press `←Enter`.

● Reenter the password to confirm it.

● Click `Save`.

● Rename the folder tab **Month**.

● Close the workbook.

Now, when you reopen this workbook file, you will be prompted to enter the password exactly as you entered it when it was created.

3 ● Open Monthly Bonus Form using your password.

● Unprotect the worksheet and enter your name in cell A9.

● Protect the worksheet again.

● Enter the current month in cell F6 and enter some sample data.

● Save as an Excel Workbook with the file name Monthly Bonus Analysis to your solution file location.

● Print the worksheet in landscape orientation, centered horizontally with your name and date in the header.

● Exit Excel.

Your printed worksheet will be similar to that shown in the Case Study at the beginning of the lab.

Focus on Careers

EXPLORE YOUR CAREER OPTIONS

Payroll Clerk

Have you ever wondered who makes sure you get your paycheck? Have you ever had to address inaccuracies on your paycheck with someone in payroll? Payroll clerks track employee hours and compute employee pay after making subtractions for taxes and insurance. Payroll clerks also add new employees to the system and prepare earnings statements employees use for filing taxes. They must have excellent math skills and good communication skills. Some offices use automated payroll systems, but in these situations payroll clerks are typically responsible for doing analysis and looking at trends using spreadsheet programs. Salary range is typically between $30,000 and $40,000 depending on experience. The demand for payroll clerks is expected to decrease slightly as many companies move toward automation.

LAB 5

Using Data Tables, Using Lookup and IF Functions, and Designing Forms

Data Table (EX5.10)

A data table is a range of cells that is used to quickly calculate multiple what-if versions in one operation and to show the results of all variations in the worksheet.

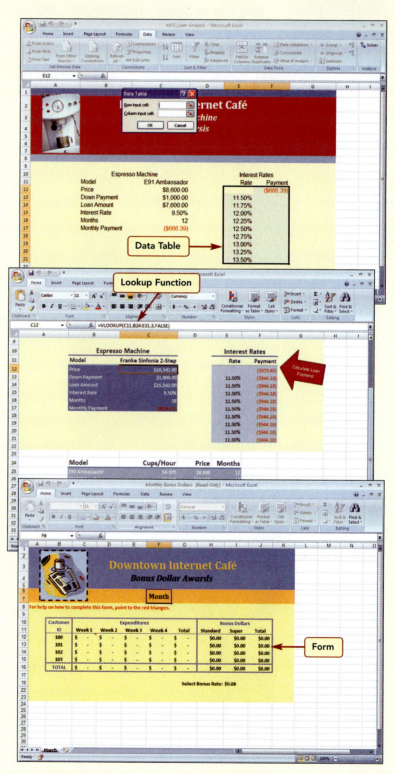

Lookup Functions (EX5.25)

Lookup functions permit you to use worksheet tables as sources of information for formulas and calculations in other parts of the worksheet.

Form (EX5.28)

A form is a formatted worksheet with blank spaces that can be filled in online on an individual computer or on a network, or printed and completed on paper.

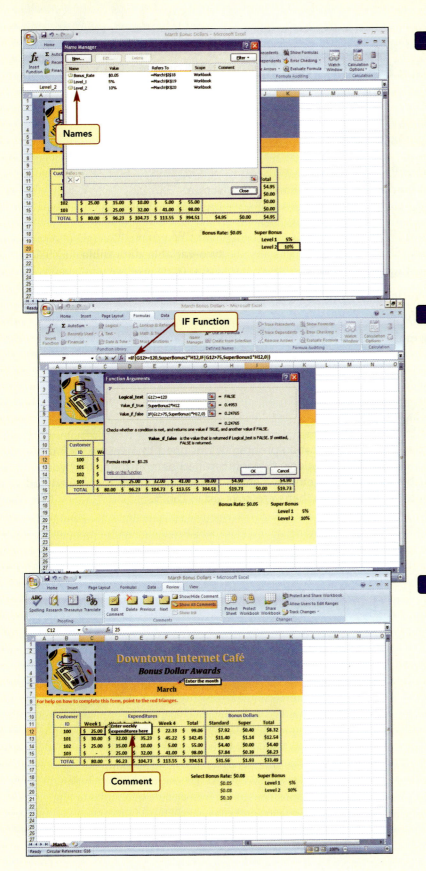

Name (EX5.29)

A name is a description of a cell or range of cells that can be used in place of cell references.

IF Function (EX5.36)

The IF function checks to see if certain conditions are met and then takes action based on the results of the check.

Comment (EX5.47)

A comment is a note attached to a cell that can be used to clarify the meaning of the cell contents, provide documentation, or ask a question.

key terms

column-oriented EX5.10	**input cell** EX5.10	**row-oriented** EX5.10
comment EX5.47	**local worksheet level** EX5.29	**scope** EX5.29
data table EX5.10	**logical operator** EX5.36	**table name** EX5.29
defined name EX5.29	**lookup function** EX5.25	**text box** EX5.14
digital signature EX5.57	**name** EX5.29	**two-variable data table** EX5.10
form EX5.28	**nested function** EX5.38	**validation** EX5.41
global workbook level EX5.29	**one-variable data table** EX5.10	**VLOOKUP function** EX5.25
HLOOKUP function EX5.25	**PMT function** EX5.6	
IF function EX5.36	**principal** EX5.6	

MCAS skills

The Microsoft Certified Applications Specialist (MCAS) certification program is designed to measure your proficiency in performing basic tasks using the Office 2007 applications. Getting certified demonstrates that you have the skills and provides a valuable industry credential for employment. See Reference 2 Microsoft Certified Applications Specialist (MCAS) for a complete list of the skills that were covered in Lab 5.

command summary

Command	Shortcut	Action
🔵 Office Button		
Prepare/Properties		Displays information about a file
Prepare/Inspect Document		Starts Document Inspector to locate and remove hidden and private information
Prepare/Mark as Final		Marks document as final and changes it to read-only
Prepare/Add a Digital Signature		Adds a digital signature to a document
Save As/Tools/General Options		Adds a password to the document
[🔲 Excel Options] /Advanced/Indicators only, and comments on hover		Displays comment indicators and comments when you point to a cell
Home tab		
Cells group		
[🔲 Format ▼] /Hide & Unhide/Hide Rows		Hides selected rows
[🔲 Format ▼] /Hide & Unhide/Unhide Rows		Displays rows that were previously hidden
Insert tab		
Illustrations group		
[Shapes]		Creates selected shape
Text group		
[Text Box]		Creates a text box
Formulas tab		
Function Library group		
[🔲 Logical ▼]		Creates a logical function
Defined Names group		
[Name Manager]		Creates, edits, and deletes cell and range names
[🔲 Define Name ▼]		Creates a range name using text in cells
[🔲 Use in Formula ▼]		Places selected range name in formula bar or lists names in worksheet
[🔲 Create from Selection]		Automatically generates name from selected cells

Lab Review

Command	Shortcut	Action
Data tab		
Data Tools group		
Data Validation /Settings/List		Creates a drop-down list
What-If Analysis /Data Table		Creates a data table based on specified input values and formulas
Text to Columns		Separates information contained in one cell into two columns
Review tab		
Proofing group		
Research		Searches through reference materials
Comments group		
New Comment		Inserts a new comment in selected cell
Edit Comment		Edits comment in selected cell
Delete		Deletes comment in selected cell
Show All Comments		Displays all comments
Drawing Tools Format tab		
Insert Shapes group		
More		Opens Shapes gallery to insert ready-made shapes
Shape Styles group		
More		Opens Shape Styles gallery to apply a visual style to a shape
Arrange group		
Rotate		Rotates selected shape

Lab Exercises

matching

Match the letter on the right to the item in the numbered list on the left.

1. comment   _____
2. data table   _____
3. digital signature   _____
4. form   _____

5. IF   _____

6. logical operators   _____
7. lookup   _____

8. name   _____
9. rotation handle   _____
10. validation   _____

a. changes the angle of the selected object

b. a note attached to a cell

c. a formatted worksheet with blank spaces to be filled in

d. a range of cells that is used to quickly calculate multiple what-if versions

e. a function that checks to see if a condition is met and takes action based on that condition

f. authentication that confirms the document's origination

g. a description of a cell or range that can be used in place of the cell or range reference

h. ensures that the data entered in a cell is acceptable

i. compares numbers in two or more cells or to a constant

j. functions that use worksheet tables as sources of information

multiple choice

Circle the correct response to the questions below.

1. The _____ function searches for a value in the top row of a table.
   a. HLOOKUP
   b. PMT
   c. VLOOKUP
   d. IF

2. A _____ data table can be row- or column-oriented.
   a. multivariable
   b. two-variable
   c. single-variable
   d. one-variable

3. A(n) _____ is a formatted worksheet with blank spaces to be filled.
   a. template
   b. form
   c. object
   d. cell

4. _____ locates hidden and private information in a document.
   a. Document Inspector
   b. Workbook Protector
   c. Private Investigator
   d. Finalizer

5. An Excel form can contain _____.
   a. text
   b. graphics
   c. cell comments
   d. all of the above

6. An IF statement is _____ if it contains one or more other IF statements as arguments.
   a. incomplete
   b. invalid
   c. nested
   d. circular

7. The _____ function calculates a periodic payment on a loan.
   a. PV
   b. RATE
   c. NPER
   d. PMT

8. _____ are used in formulas and functions that compare numbers in two or more cells.
   a. Logical operators
   b. Function arguments
   c. Relational operators
   d. Conditional arguments

9. A name assigned to a cell must start with _____.
   a. a letter
   b. an underscore
   c. a backslash
   d. any of the above

10. A(n) _____ argument is an expression that makes a comparison using logical operators.
   a. if_then
   b. logical_test
   c. and_or
   d. logical_if

true/false

Circle the correct answer to the following questions.

1. Dragging ◇ adjusts the size of an element in a shape.   True   False

2. The Stop warning does not prevent invalid entries.   True   False

3. The result of an IF argument is either true or false.   True   False

4. A comment cannot be attached to a formula.   True   False

5. The Lookup_value is the range of cells to look in.   True   False

6. A form created in Excel cannot be used online.   True   False

7. A digitally signed document is automatically read-only.   True   False

8. The IF function requires three arguments.   True   False

9. A range name can only include letters.   True   False

10. A text box can be used to display graphics.   True   False

fill-in

Complete the following statements by filling in the blanks with the correct key terms.

1. There are two types of lookup functions: VLOOKUP and _____.

2. A(n) _____ name represents a cell, range of cells, formula, or constant value.

3. All name have a(n) _____, or restriction to a location within which the name is recognized without qualification.

4. A(n) _____ name represents the range of cells that stores an Excel data table.

5. The _____ function checks to see if certain conditions are met and takes actions based on the results.

6. A cell containing a comment displays a(n) _____ in the upper-right corner.

7. A(n) _____ permits you to use worksheet tables as sources of information for formulas and calculations in other parts of the worksheet.

8. The PMT function contains three arguments: _____, nper, and pv.

9. A(n) _____ is a formatted worksheet that is intended to be filled in by the user.

10. In a one-variable data table, a(n) _____ is a cell in which a list of values is substituted to see the resulting effect on the related formulas.

Lab Exercises

Hands-On Exercises

step-by-step

Animal Rescue Foundation Volunteer Rewards ★

1. After viewing the revenue analysis you provided, Samuel Johnson and the other Animal Rescue Foundation board members have begun the budget planning for the next year. They have realized that daily operation of the agency depends on the volunteers. To repay them for their time, the board has decided to implement a rewards program with some of the budget surpluses you have anticipated. You have been asked to create a worksheet to track the number of hours people have worked and determine their award level. Your completed worksheets should be similar to the one shown here.

   a. Open the workbook file ex05_ARF Volunteers.

   b. Enter formulas to calculate the average and total hours for the year in columns F and G. Copy the formulas down the columns.

   c. Enter the labels **Award Level** in cell I40 and **Hours** in cell J40, right-aligned. Enter the labels **Star Level 1**, **Star Level 2**, and **Star Level 3** right-aligned in cells I41 through I43. In cells J41 through J43, enter **300, 200**, and **100** as the award levels.

   d. Apply formatting to enhance cells I40 through J43. Adjust the column widths and layout as necessary.

   e. Use the Create From Selection command to name the values for the three star levels.

   f. In cell H5 enter the following formula to calculate the award level for the volunteers: **=IF(G5>=Star_Level_1,1,IF(G5>=Star_Level_2,2,IF(G5>=Star_Level_3,3,0)))**.

Student Name — 3/9/2009

ANIMAL ANGELS VOLUNTEERS

	1st Qtr	2nd Qtr	3rd Qtr	4th Qtr	Average	Total	Level
Bell, Patricia	45	34	102	35	54	216	2
Carey, Ronnie	106	45	55	106	78	312	1
Carver, Kathi	30	83	3	3	29.75	119	3
Chorley, Besty	68	2	235	96	100.25	401	1
Clark, Jamel	51	30	28	58	41.75	167	3
Cody, Martin	28	66	6	45	36.25	145	3
Dickson, Diane	72	19	77	32	50	200	2
Edwards, Mike	12	20	61	28	30.25	121	3
Ferguson, Robby	99	12	0	43	38.5	154	3
Forester, Kimberly	32	66	34	30	40.5	162	3
Franklin, Stacey	57	98	93	80	82	328	1
Fulton, Anne	13	25	55	100	48.25	193	3
Garcia, Maria	5	23	61	36	31.25	125	3
Gatens, Chris	0	100	58	85	60.75	243	2
Henderson, James	9	76	51	60	49	196	3
Ingram, Helen	29	12	33	12	21.5	86	0
Isbell, Sonya	46	65	47	3	40.25	161	3
Johnson, Thaman	5	25	18	7	13.75	55	0
Jones, April	70	83	38	79	67.5	270	2
Kelly, William	13	78	52	88	57.75	231	2
Kettonhoeffer, Bill	4	59	57	8	32	128	3
Kullman, Rodney	28	30	35	16	27.25	109	3
La Paglia, Sally	39	10	12	134	48.75	195	3
Lee, Su	56	6	5	0	16.75	67	0
Legge, Cristan	3	81	73	34	47.75	191	3
Lopez, Andrew	83	3	165	0	62.75	251	2
Marcus, Danielle	3	19	24	2	12	48	0
Merwin, Michael	44	9	95	37	46.25	185	3
Nelson, Faith	10	115	8	0	33.25	133	3
Pennington, Neil	75	62	8	79	56	224	2
Peterson, Tracey	44	9	95	37	46.25	185	3
Pierce, Kai	6	98	4	75	45.75	183	3
Tranthorn, Ellie	27	35	19	12	23.25	93	0

EX5.70
Excel 2007
Lab 5: Using Data Tables, Using Lookup and IF Functions, and Designing Forms
www.mhhe.com/oleary

g. Change the value in cell B5 to **450** and then to **0** to check the formula. Return the value to **45**. Copy the formula down the column.

h. Add cell comments to the worksheet that explain the star system.

i. Select the entire worksheet excluding the star values. Print preview the selection. Enter **your name** and the **current date** in a header. Then center the worksheet horizontally.

j. Print the selection in portrait orientation. Save the workbook as Volunteers.

Analysis Tool to Project ATT Sales ★★

2. Your manager at Adventure Travel Tours is preparing for a corporate-level meeting to discuss next year's sales and marketing campaign. During past meetings, he has been asked to estimate the effect of increasing and decreasing sales. You have been directed to create a tool that your manager can use at the meeting in which he can input an overall percentage change in sales and display the quarterly impact.

a. Open the file ex05_ATT Sales. The Travel Packages sheet presents the actual sales of different package tours in 2009. You will modify this sheet to create an analysis tool for your manager.

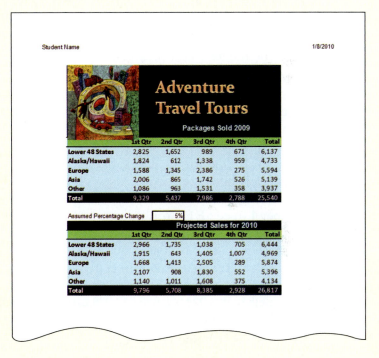

b. Enter functions to calculate the totals.

c. Starting in cell I5, enter the values **-5%** to **+10%**, incrementing by 1. Use these values to create a list box in cell C13 with the input message **Select the assumed percentage change from the current year's sales from the drop-down list.** and the error message **You must select one of the values in the drop-down list box.** Format cell C13 to display percentage with zero decimal places and surround the cell with a thick box border.

d. Enter the formula **=C13** in cell H5.

e. Enter the label **Assumed Percentage Change** in cell A13 and align the text to the right.

f. Copy cells A4 through F11 to cell A14. Change the title in cell A14 to **Projected Sales for 2010**.

g. In cell B16 enter the formula **=B6*(1+$H$5)**. Copy the formula through the cell range B16:E20.

h. Add a cell comment to cell C13 informing the user how to use the worksheet.

i. Hide columns H and I. Set the percentage change to 5%.

j. Enter your name and the current date in a header, center the worksheet horizontally, and print the worksheet range A1:F21 in portrait orientation.

k. Save the workbook as ATT Projected Sales.

l. Clear the values in cells B16 through E20 and save the workbook as a template named ATT Projected Sales Form.

Wilson Electronics Financial Analysis ★★

3. You have been hired as a salesperson for the Wilson Electronics Company. You want to be able to give your customers up-to-date and accurate information on the cost of high-end electronics you sell. To automate the process, you plan to use a data table containing the model information and a table to calculate the different payments at various loan interest rates. The completed worksheet will be similar to the one shown here.

a. Open the file ex05_Electronics Analyzer.

b. Instead of typing in the model and price of the item each time, you want to be able to enter a model number and choose it from a drop-down list that links to a data table. The information for the data table has already been created in cells D23 through E42. Enter the number **1** in cell B13. You will use the CHOOSE function to select the items in the data table based on the number entered in cell B13. In cell B12 enter

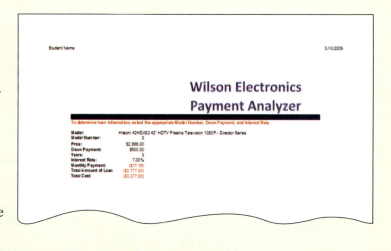

=CHOOSE(B13,D23,D24,D25,D26,D27,D28,D29,D30,D31,D32,D33,D34,D35,D36,D37,D38,D39,D40,D41,D42).

c. Create a similar CHOOSE function in cell B14 to display the price associated with each item. Format cells B14 and B15 as currency with two decimal places.

d. Enter the following sample data: **$500** for the down payment in cell B15, **2** for the years in cell B16, and **0.0725** for the interest rate in cell B17.

e. Enter the PMT function **=PMT(B17/12,B16*12,B14-B15)** in cell B18. To calculate the total amount of the loan, enter the formula **=B18*B16*12** in cell B19. To calculate the total cost, enter the formula **=-B15+B19** in cell B20.

Creating and Working with Tables

Objectives

After you have read this chapter, you should be able to:

1 Create a table.

2 Enter records in a table.

3 Format a table.

4 Ensure data integrity.

5 Sort data.

6 Filter data.

7 Summarize data.

8 Outline, group, and subtotal data.

9 Create a PivotTable Report

10 Create a PivotChart Report.

11 Create, edit, and use hyperlinks.

Case Study

Downtown Internet Café

The form you created to track the Downtown Internet Café's customer expenditures and Bonus Dollar awards is working quite well. Evan would now like to have a separate worksheet that contains the café customers' contact information so that he can use it to send out the Bonus Dollars discount coupons. This type of information can be entered into a worksheet as a table. While using Excel to create the table, you will learn about locating, modifying, sorting, and filtering records in the table. You also will learn how to analyze information in a table using totals and subtotals.

Now you have two workbooks containing data pertaining to the Downtown Internet Café customers. To make it easier to work with the two workbooks, you will create a hyperlink in one workbook to open the other workbook. A printout of a filtered table and a summary report are shown here.

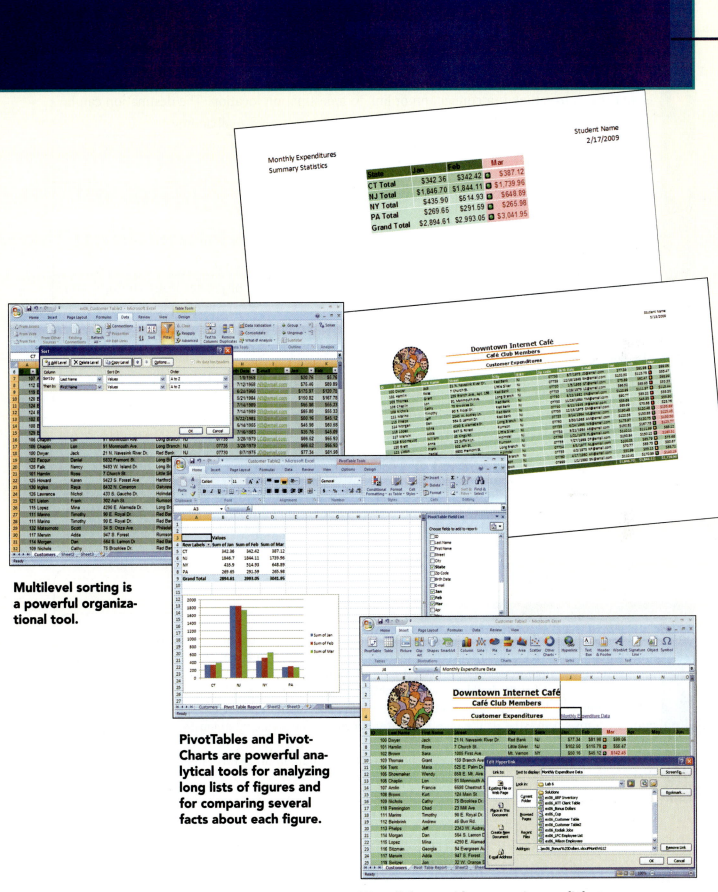

Multilevel sorting is a powerful organizational tool.

PivotTables and PivotCharts are powerful analytical tools for analyzing long lists of figures and for comparing several facts about each figure.

Hyperlinks provide connections or links to files, Web pages, E-mail addresses, and more.

Concept Preview

1 **Table** A table is an organized collection of related information that is entered into a series of worksheet rows and columns.

2 **Hyperlink** A hyperlink is a connection or link to a destination location. The destination can be a location in the current file or another file, a Web page, or an e-mail address.

3 **Sort** You can sort or arrange data in a specified sequence: alphabetically, numerically, or by date.

4 **Filter** A filter is a restriction you place on records in a table to quickly isolate and display a subset of records.

5 **Grouping and Outlining** Grouping and outlining data organizes data in a worksheet by showing and hiding different levels of detail for groups of related data.

6 **Subtotals** The Subtotal feature automatically takes data in a list, organizes it into groups, and includes subtotals for each group of data.

7 **PivotTable Report** A PivotTable report is an interactive table that can be used to summarize and manipulate worksheet data.

8 **PivotChart Report** A PivotChart report is an interactive chart that can be used to view and rearrange data.

Creating a Table

You want to create an Excel worksheet that will contain the café's customer contact information and monthly expenditures. So that you can manipulate the data the way you want, you decide to format this worksheet as a table.

Concept 1

Table

1 A **table** is an organized collection of related information that is entered into a series of worksheet rows and columns. Each row contains a **record,** which is all the information about one person, thing, or place. Each column is a **field,** which is the smallest unit of information about a record.

The first row, called the **header row,** in a table must contain column labels that serve as field names. A **field name** is a descriptive label used to identify the data stored in the field. Field names must be text entries. All rows below the field names contain the records. The area containing the records is called the **table range.**

The data in a table is managed independently from the data in other rows and columns of the worksheet. A worksheet also can contain more than one table.

You have already entered many of the field names to create the structure for the table and have saved it in a workbook file named Customer Table.

1 ● **Start Excel 2007 and open the workbook file ex06_Customer Table.**

Your screen should be similar to Figure 6.1

Field names in header row

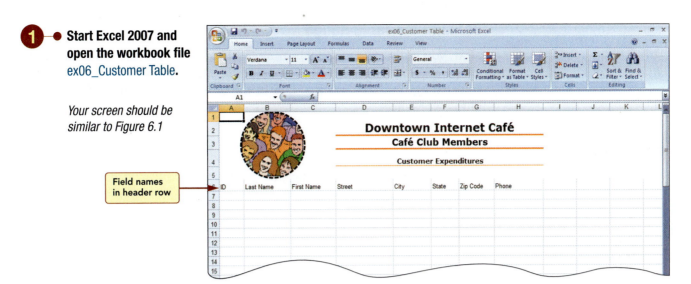

Figure 6.1

The worksheet titles are formatted using cell style headings associated with the current worksheet theme, Aspect. Row 6 contains the field names for the customer information that will be entered in the table.

Adding Field Names

You decide to change the phone field to a field for each customer's e-mail address. Additionally, you still need to add field names for the months, which will be used to record the monthly expenditures for each customer. You also will change the format of these cells to Currency.

1 ● **Replace the entry in H6 with E-mail.**

● **Enter Jan in cell I6.**

● **Drag the fill handle of cell I6 to extend the range through December (cell T6).**

● **Format cells I7 to T7 as currency with two decimals.**

● **Move to A6.**

● **Save the worksheet as Customer Table.**

Your screen should be similar to Figure 6.2

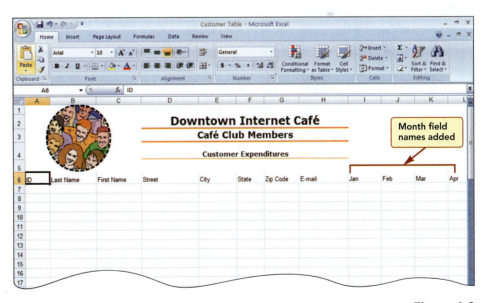

Month field names added

Figure 6.2

Defining the Table Range

Next, you define the row containing the field names as the table range, the area where the records will be entered. Designating a range as a table lets you manage and analyze the data in the table independently of other data in the worksheet.

1 • Select the range A6 through T6.

• Open the Insert tab.

• Click 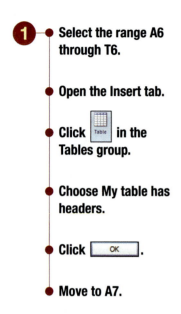 in the Tables group.

• Choose My table has headers.

• Click OK .

• Move to A7.

Your screen should be similar to Figure 6.3

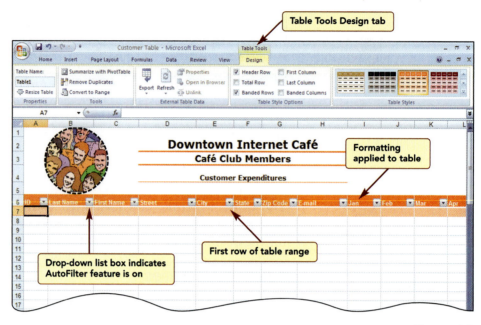

Figure 6.3

Additional Information
You also could define the table range after records have been entered by including the field name row and all rows containing records in the range.

The header row of the table is formatted with an orange fill color and white text color. This is the default formatting for a header row of a table that is associated with the Aspect worksheet theme. The first blank row below the header row is the first row of the table range. This area is formatted using the Input cell color associated with the Aspect theme. The first record of information will be entered in this row.

In addition, drop-down list buttons appear next to each field name in the header row. These buttons indicate the AutoFilter feature is on. The AutoFilter feature is used to filter and sort the data in the table. You will learn about these features shortly.

Also, when any cell in the table range is selected, the Table Tools Design tab is displayed. It is used to modify settings associated with the design of the table. When you select a cell outside the table, the table becomes inactive and the tab is not displayed.

You are now ready to begin entering the information for the first record.

Entering Records

You will use the Cafe Club membership sign-up sheets containing the information for each customer as the source of information for the table. In addition, you have a printout of the monthly expenditures for these customers for the first two months of the year. You want to enter this information into the table next.

When entering the data in a table, it is important that you enter it consistently. For example, if you abbreviate the word "Street" as "St.", it should be abbreviated in the same way for each record where it appears. Also, be careful not to include blank spaces before or after an entry as this can cause problems when trying to locate information in the table. The first record in the table must begin in the row immediately below the header row containing the field names.

1 • Enter the information shown here for the first record, using [Tab ⇆] to move from one field to the next.

ID	**100**
Last Name	**Dwyer**
First Name	**Jack**
Street	**21 N. Navesink River Dr.**
City	**Red Bank**
State	**NJ**
Zip	**07730**
E-mail	**JD@email.com**
Jan	**77.34**
Feb	**81.98**

Your screen should be similar to Figure 6.4

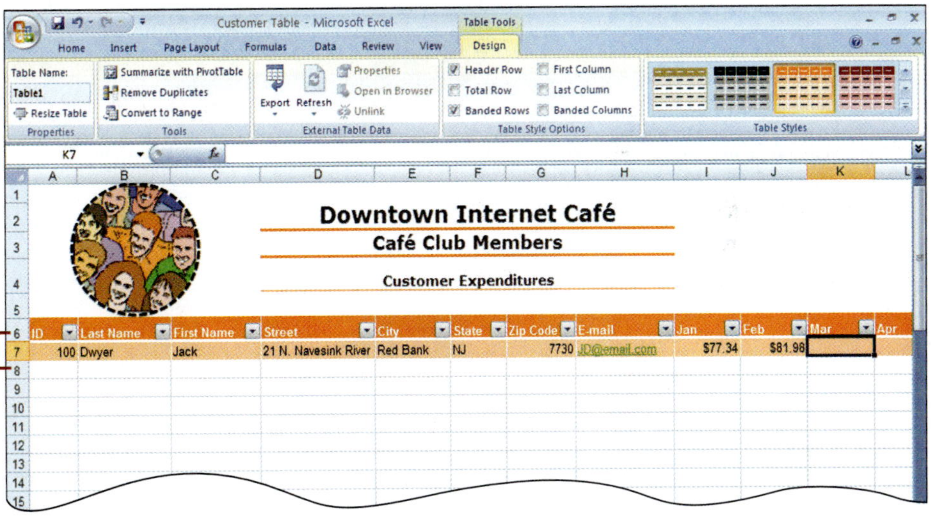

Figure 6.4

The data for the first record is complete.

Inserting Rows

You need to add another row to the table for the next record. If you are at the end of the table row and press [Tab ⇆], a new row is added to the table. Alternatively, entering new record data into the row just below the last record in a table automatically expands the table range to include that row.

1 ● **Press** ⏎Enter.

● **Press** Home.

● **Enter the information shown here for the second record.**

ID	**101**
Last Name	**Hamlin**
First Name	**Rose**
Street	**7 Church St.**
City	**Little Silver**
State	**NJ**
Zip	**07739**
E-mail	**RH@email.com**
Jan	**102.50**
Feb	**115.78**

Your screen should be similar to Figure 6.5

Second record added to table and table range expanded

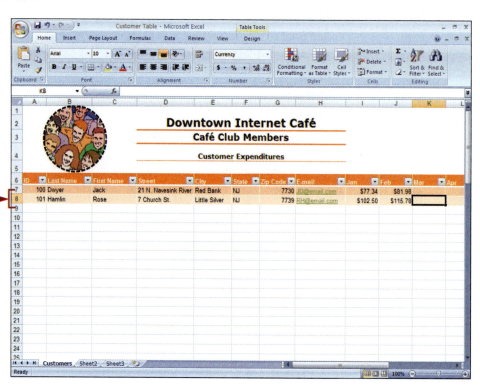

Figure 6.5

A new row was added to the table and the fill color from the selected table style is applied. The currency style is carried to the new row as well. Another way to add a row to the table is to insert a table row. This method can be used to insert records between existing records.

Additional Information

You can insert multiple rows by first selecting a range. The same number of rows as in the range are added to the table.

2 • Right-click in cell K8.

• Select Insert and choose Table Rows Above from the shortcut menu.

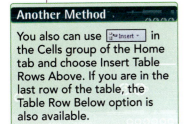

Another Method

You also can use  in the Cells group of the Home tab and choose Insert Table Rows Above. If you are in the last row of the table, the Table Row Below option is also available.

• Enter the following information in the newly created table row.

ID	**102**
Last Name	**Brown**
First Name	**Sara**
Street	**1005 First Ave.**
City	**Mt. Vernon**
State	**NY**
Zip	**10552**
E-mail	**SB@email.com**
Jan	**50.16**
Feb	**45.12**

Your screen should be similar to Figure 6.6

Figure 6.6

The record was inserted into the table between the existing records.

3 ● Finally, add the following information as the last record in the table.

ID	**103**
Last Name	**Thomas**
First Name	**Grant**
Street	**159 Branch Ave., Apt 15B**
City	**Red Bank**
State	**NJ**
Zip	**07730**
E-mail	**GT@email.com**
Jan	**75.89**
Feb	**62.47**

● AutoFit the Street column width so that the entries are fully displayed.

Your screen should be similar to Figure 6.7

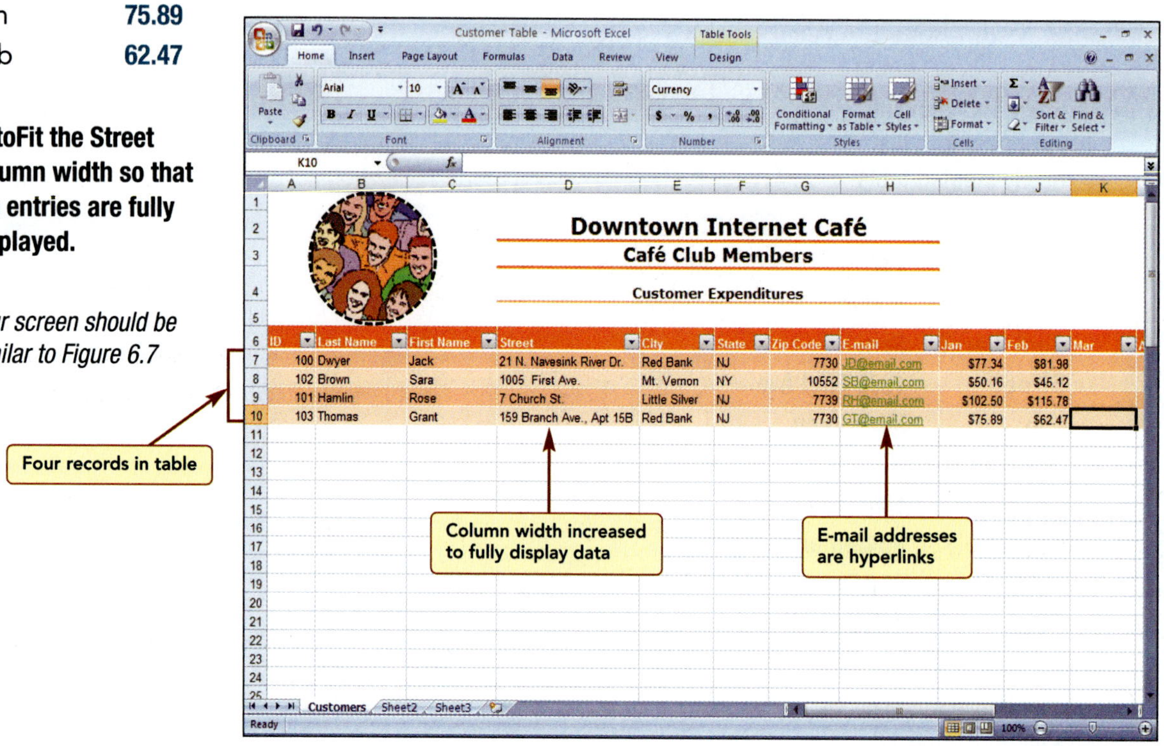

Four records in table

Column width increased to fully display data

E-mail addresses are hyperlinks

Figure 6.7

The field information for the first four records is displayed in the table range.

Using a Hyperlink

Notice the addresses in the E-mail column are underlined and in green. This is because they were automatically identified as an e-mail address and formatted as a hyperlink.

2 Point to several styles and look at the Live Preview.

Choose Table Style Medium 12.

Your screen should be similar to Figure 6.13

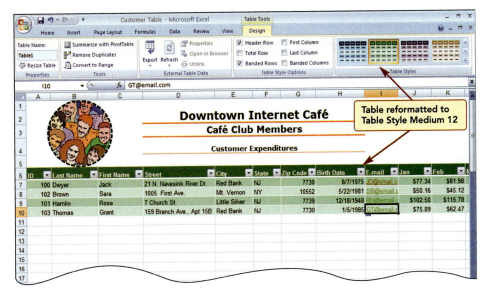

Figure 6.13

The table is reformatted to the new design. It includes a different color background for the heading row and banded shades of color for the table data. Using a table style was much faster than applying these features individually.

Even after applying a table style, you may want to make additional changes. For example, the selected table style applies special formatting to the header row and uses a banded row effect for the table data. If you do not want one or all of these features, you can turn them off using the Table Styles options. You would like to see how the table would look without some of these features.

3 Choose ☑ Header Row and ☑ Banded Rows in the Table Style Options group to turn off these features.

Choose ☐ First Column and ☐ Banded Columns to turn on these features.

Your screen should be similar to Figure 6.14

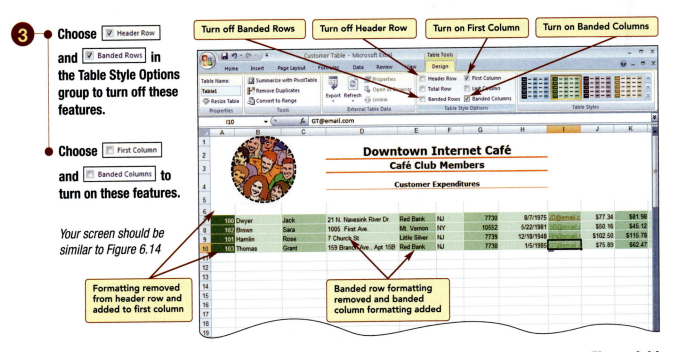

Figure 6.14

The dark green color background was removed from the table header row and because the text is white, the field names are not visible. A dark green background fill and white font color were added to the first column to emphasize the data. Finally, banded rows were removed and banded columns added. As you can see, the Table Style Options allow you to quickly emphasize different areas of the table. You prefer how the table looked before these changes and will restore these features.

4 ● **Choose** First Column **and** Banded Columns **to turn off these features.**

● **Choose** ✓ Header Row **and** ✓ Banded Rows **to restore these settings.**

Using Special Cell Formats

Notice that the ZIP codes for the several records do not display the leading zero (07730 and 07739). This is because Excel drops leading zeros for numeric data. Since this field will not be used in calculations, you will change the cell format so that numeric entries will appear as entered.

1 ● **Select the range G7 through G10.**

● **Click** 📉 **in the Number group of the Home tab to open the Format Cells dialog box.**

● **Select Special from the Category list of the Number tab.**

Your screen should be similar to Figure 6.15

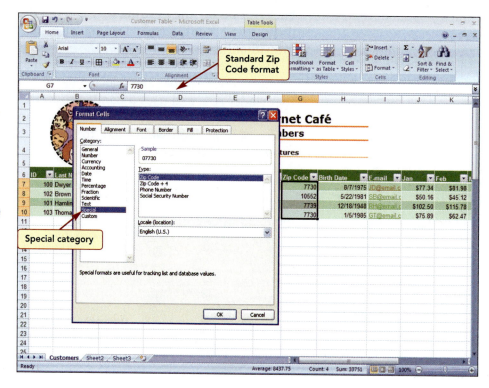

Figure 6.15

There are four special formats that are designed particularly for use in tables where numeric data is frequently entered but not used for calculations. You want to format the selection to the standard Zip Code format.

2 ● From the Type list box, select Zip Code.

● Click [OK].

Your screen should look similar to Figure 6.16

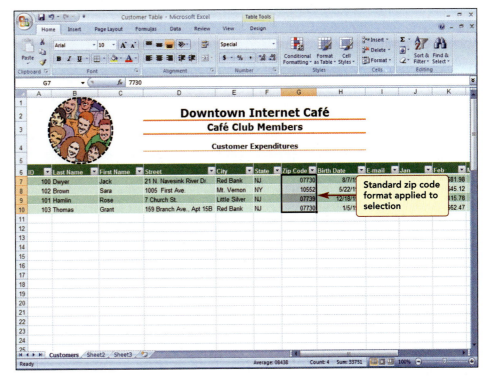

Figure 6.16

The number entries appear as they were entered because they are formatted as a special number entry. However, the entries are stored as numbers without the zero.

Ensuring Data Integrity

You asked one of your employees to add more records to the table including March expenditures. You will open the updated workbook file and continue working with the table.

1 • **Save and close the** Customer Table **workbook file.**

• **Open the workbook file** ex06_Customer Table2**.**

• **Move to row 39.**

• **Insert a new table row above row 39.**

• **Enter the following information using your first and last names into the newly created row.**

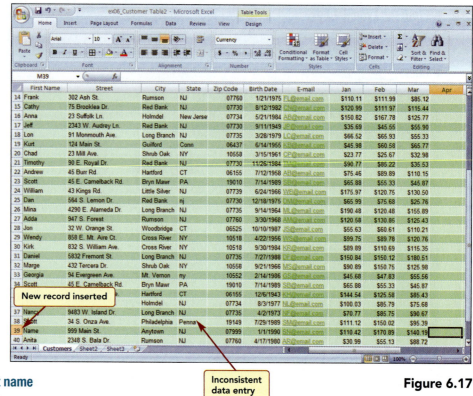

Figure 6.17

ID	999
Last Name	your last name
First Name	your first name
Street	999 Main St.
City	Anytown
State	NJ
Zip	07999
Birth Date	1/1/1990
E-mail	SN@email.com
Jan	110.42
Feb	170.89
Mar	140.19

Your screen should be similar to Figure 6.17

Unfortunately, as you review the records, you discover several errors. For example, in the ID column, there are blank entries as well as four-digit and two-digit entries. Additionally, several state entries are inconsistent, with some spelled out and others abbreviated differently.

Restricting Data Using Data Validation

The Café Club ID number is assigned to each member when his or her information is entered into the table. It is a number that uniquely identifies each member. As each member is added to the table, the next available sequential number is assigned. The first club member was assigned the number 100. To help ensure the validity of the data, you want to restrict the number of digits used in the ID field to three and to require that each new record include an ID number.

1

- Scroll to the top of the window.

- Point to the top edge of the ID column header and click when the mouse pointer changes to ↓ to select all the entries in the column.

Additional Information

If you click the top edge of the header twice, it selects the entire table column, including the header.

- Click [Data Validation ▾] in the Data Tools group of the Data tab.

- Choose **Whole Number** from the Allow drop-down list in the Settings tab.

- Select **"between"** from the Data drop-down list.

- Enter **100** as the minimum and **999** as the maximum.

- Choose **Ignore blank** to deselect this option.

- Add the Input Message Enter the three digit ID..

- Create a Stop style error alert with the error message of **Only three digit numbers are allowed.**.

- Click [OK].

Your screen should be similar to Figure 6.18

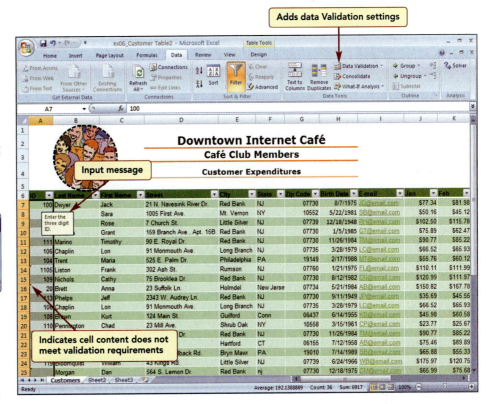

Figure 6.18

The process of creating and defining the validation settings for the text-length data restriction are now complete. Because the ID column is selected, the input message you entered is displayed, providing directions on how to use the cell. Also, any entries that do not meet the new restrictions, including blank cells, are identified with a green triangle in the upper-left cell corner, showing that the validation restriction is working correctly.

More About

> To learn more about other types of validation settings, see 1.2 Ensure Data Integrity in the More About appendix.

Testing Data Validation

Next, you will fix the identified errors and further test the data restriction to make sure it displays the error message and is working correctly.

1 ● Move to cell A14.

● Click ◇ ▾ and choose Display Type Information.

Your screen should be similar to Figure 6.19

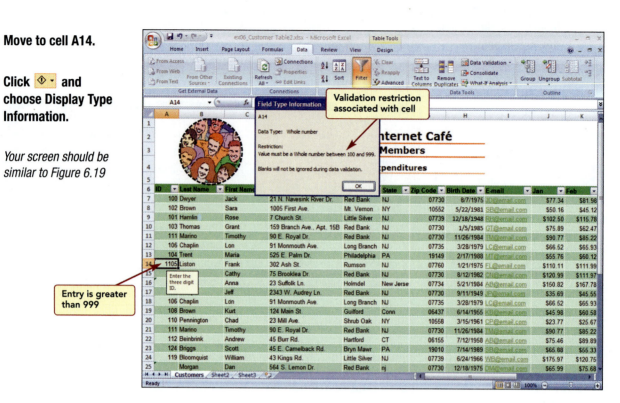

Figure 6.19

The Field Type Information dialog box describes the restrictions associated with this cell. First you will change the entry to another invalid entry to test the error message. Then you will enter valid ID numbers for the entries that contain invalid IDs.

EX6.20
Excel 2007
Lab 6: Creating and Working with Tables
www.mhhe.com/oleary

2 ● Click [OK] to close the dialog box.

● Attempt to change the entry in cell A14 to 10.

● Click [Retry].

● Attempt to change the entry to ten.

● Click [Retry].

● Change the entry in cell A14 to 121.

Your screen should be similar to Figure 6.20

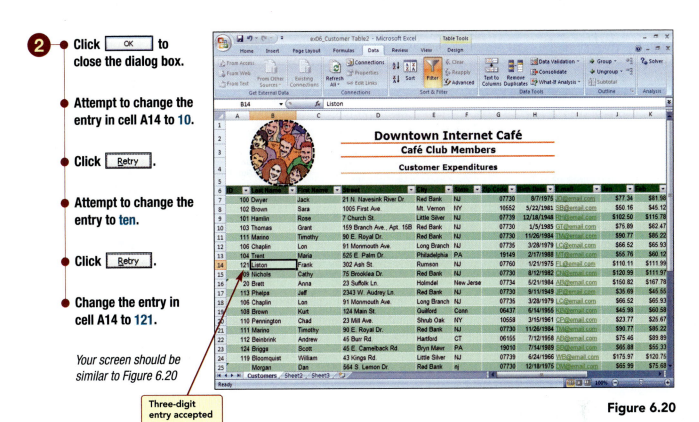

Three-digit entry accepted

Figure 6.20

The error alert message was displayed when you entered an invalid two-digit entry. The three-digit entry was accepted as valid. Now, you will correct the remaining errors in the ID column.

3 ● Enter the following correct ID numbers.

Cell	ID
A16	120
A25	114
A29	105
A43	107

Next, you want to restrict the data in the State column.

4 ● Select the State column of data and add the following validation restrictions:

- Allow only a text length of two.
- Include an input message of Enter 2-letter state abbreviation in uppercase..
- Include a Stop style error alert and error message of Only 2-letter entries are allowed..

● Fix all identified errors.

● Change any lowercase state abbreviations to uppercase.

Your screen should be similar to Figure 6.21

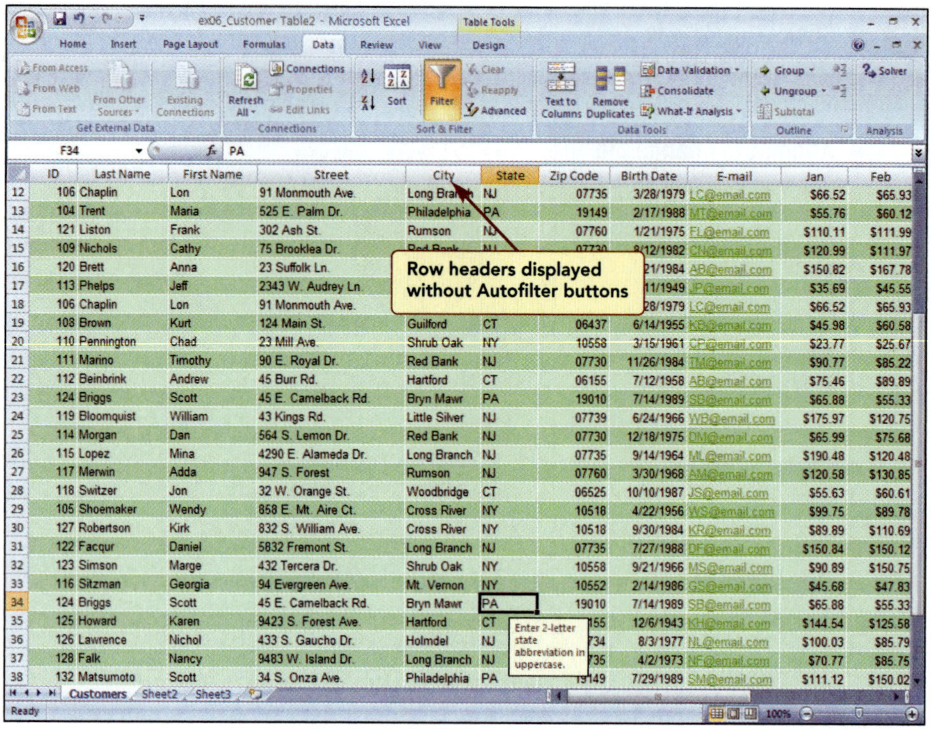

Figure 6.21

Although data validation helps ensure that only data meeting the restrictions is entered, it does not ensure that it is entered in the correct format. However, because the input message will always be visible to remind the user to enter uppercase letters only, fewer input errors should occur. Notice also that when you scroll the table, the worksheet column letters are hidden and the table row headers are displayed instead so that you can continue to identify the columns. However, the AutoFilter buttons are not displayed.

Sorting Data

Currently, the records in the table are in the order in which they were entered. However, you want the table to be in ascending ID number order when it is first opened. This way it is easier to see what the last-used ID number is when assigning a number to a new member. To do this, you can sort the records in the table.

Lab 6: Creating and Working with Tables

www.mhhe.com/oleary

Concept 3

Sort

3 You can **sort** or arrange data in a specified sequence: alphabetically, numerically, or by date. Sorting data often helps you find specific information quickly. The data in a worksheet can be sorted into ascending (A to Z, 1 to 9, earliest date to most recent date) or descending (Z to A, 9 to 1, most recent date to earliest date) order. When you sort, Excel rearranges the rows, columns, fields, or individual cells according to the sort order you specify.

You also can sort by cell attributes such as font or cell color, or on conditional formatting such as an icon set. Most sorts are performed on a selected range of cells or on a table column. However, you also can sort on rows.

A single sort operation can be based on up to three columns or fields of data. When a sort is done on more than one column or field, it is called a **multilevel sort**. For example, if you wanted to rearrange a table of employee data to begin with those who have worked for the company the longest, you could sort it in ascending order by date and then by name.

The settings, or criteria, you specify for a sort on a table are saved with the workbook file. This allows you to quickly reapply the sort when you open the workbook. Sort settings are not saved for sorts using a worksheet range. This feature is especially helpful when you have created a complicated multilevel sort.

Sorting on a Single Field

For the first sort, you want the records arranged in ascending order by ID. The cell selector needs to be in any cell in the table column to be sorted.

1 ● **Move to cell A7.**

● **Click** 🔼 **Sort A to Z in the Sort & Filter group.**

Another Method

You also can click 🔽 in the Editing group of the Home tab and choose Sort A to Z.

Your screen should be similar to Figure 6.22

All records in table rearranged in ascending numerical order

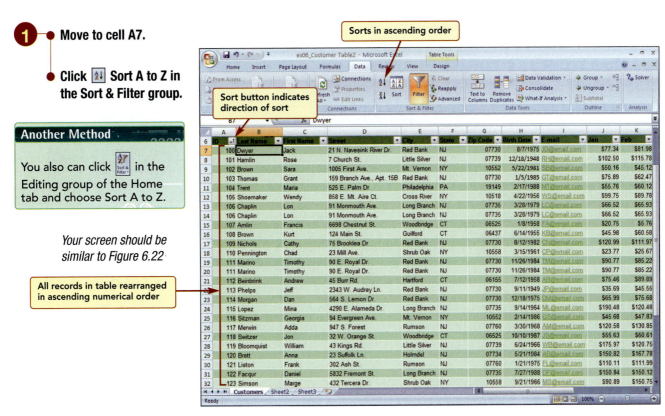

Figure 6.22

The records in the table range are rearranged to display in ascending numerical order. The AutoFilter button in the column header has changed to a ⬝↑ Sort button, which indicates the column is sorted and the direction of the sort.

This will make it easier to know the last-used ID number. When creating a table, if the order in which you enter records in a table is important, always include a field for a unique record number, such as the ID field in this table that identifies each customer. Then you can return to the entry order by sorting on the number field.

Sorting on Multiple Fields

Evan often asks for information in order by name. You will create this sort next.

1 ● **Open the AutoFilter menu for the Last Name column.**

● **Choose Sort A to Z.**

Your screen should be similar to Figure 6.23

All records in table rearranged in ascending alphabetized order by last name

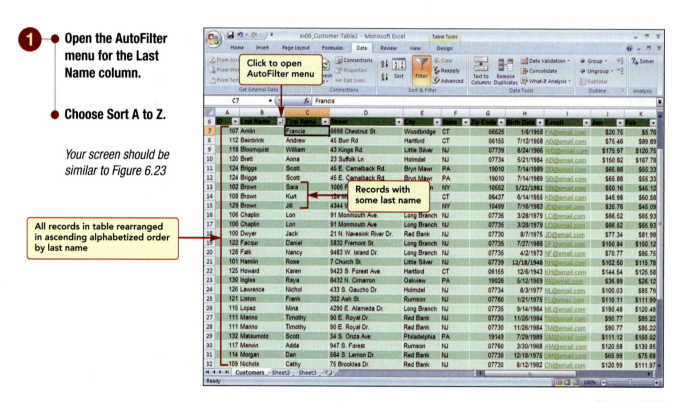

Figure 6.23

The records appear in ascending alphabetical order by last name. However, notice that although the records for Sara, Kurt, and Jill Brown are sorted correctly by last name, they are not sorted by first name. You want records that have the same last name to be further sorted by first name. To do this, you will perform a multilevel sort.

2 ● Click 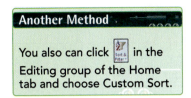 in the Sort & Filter group of the Data tab.

Your screen should be similar to Figure 6.24

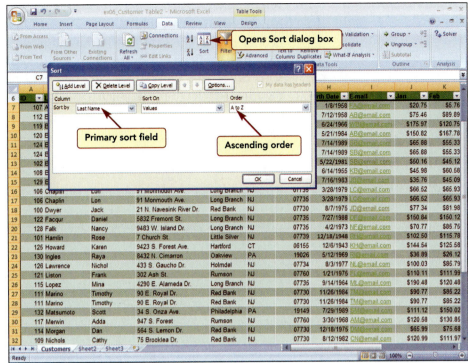

Figure 6.24

A multilevel sort uses the first field name selected in the Sort By section of the dialog box as the primary sort field; all other fields are sorted in order after the primary sort is performed. The Sort By text box correctly displays the name of the field on which the primary sort will be performed. Additionally, because the default setting is the A to Z sort order, this option does not need to be changed. You need to add the First Name field as the secondary sort.

3 ● Click .

● Select First Name from the first Then By drop-down list.

Your screen should be similar to Figure 6.25

Figure 6.25

When a sort is performed, Excel assumes that you want all data except the header row in the table range to be sorted. If your data did not include a header row as the first row in the range, you would need to choose the My data has headers option to change the setting to include this row in the sort. Since this worksheet includes field names in the first row, the My data has headers option is correctly specified already.

4 ● Click [OK].

● **Save the changes you have made to this workbook as** Customer Table2.

Your screen should be similar to Figure 6.26

All records with the same last name are further sorted alphabetically by first name

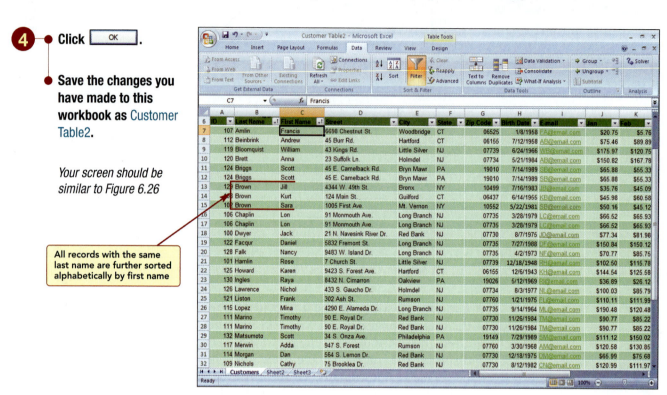

Figure 6.26

The records are now in sorted order first by last name and second by first name within the same last names. As you can see, sorting is a fast, useful tool. The sort order remains in effect until you replace it with a new sort order.

Sorting on Cell Attributes

Another way to perform a sort is to sort on a cell attribute such as a font color that was applied manually to specific cells or by using conditional formatting. To show Evan those club members who qualified for the Super Bonus Level 2 awards in March, you will first apply a highlight cells rule conditional formatting to the March column and then sort it in descending order.

1

- Select the Mar table column.

- Click [Conditional Formatting] in the Styles group of the Home tab.

- Select Highlight Cells Rules and choose Greater Than.

- Enter a value of 119.99 with Light Red Fill.

- Click [OK].

- Open the AutoFilter menu for the Mar column and select Sort by Color.

- Choose the Light Red Fill color option.

Your screen should be similar to Figure 6.27

Applies conditional formatting

All records rearranged by color of entries in the Mar column

Figure 6.27

Although all records that contain the selected cell format are sorted separately from the other data in the column, they are not in either ascending or descending sorted order. This is because there is no default cell color, font color, or icon sort order. The order must be specified for each sort using these criteria.

*Your screen should be
similar to Figure 6.28*

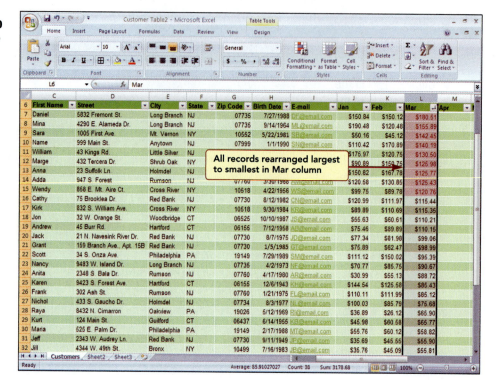

All records rearranged largest
to smallest in Mar column

Figure 6.28

This sort clearly identifies the Super Bonus Level 2 customers; however, the other two levels are not identified. You decide to use an icon set conditional format next to identify the three levels and display them in descending sort order.

3 ● Click [icon], select
Icon Sets, and choose
the Three Traffic
Lights (Rimmed)
icon set.

● Click [icon] and
choose Manage Rules.

● Edit the icon set to
identity Super Bonus
Level 2 (expenditures
> 119.99) with the
green light and to
identify Super Bonus
Level 1 (expenditures
> 74.99) with the
yellow light.

● Open the AutoFilter
menu for the Mar
column, select Sort by
Color, and choose the
green icon option.

● Open the AutoFilter
menu for the Mar
column, select Sort by
Color, and choose the
yellow icon option.

● Choose Sort Largest to
Smallest from the Mar
AutoFilter menu.

*Your screen should be
similar to Figure 6.29*

All records rearranged in
descending order within
each bonus level group

Figure 6.29

The records are now in descending sorted order by the March expenditure
values within each bonus level group. Sorting the table data helps you
better understand the table data by organizing it and helps you more
quickly find the data you want.

Filtering Data

When you sort data, it simply takes all the data in the table and reorganizes
it into the specified order. Consequently, there is often much more
information than you want included in the displayed data. To display only
those records that meet specific criteria, you can filter the table.

Concept 4

Filter

4 A **filter** is a restriction you place on records in the table to quickly isolate and display a subset of records. Filtering a table helps you quickly find and display only the information you want to see. A filter is created by specifying **criteria** that you want records to meet in order to be displayed. Unlike the Sort feature, the Filter feature does not rearrange a table but temporarily hides rows that do not meet the specified criteria. A filter is ideal when you want to display the subset for only a brief time and then return immediately to the full set of records. All records are redisplayed when you remove the filter.

You can work with the data in a filtered table much like any other table data. However, only the displayed subset of data is affected. You can find, edit, format, chart, and print the filtered records to help you analyze the data in a table. Filters are also additive, meaning that each additional filter you add to a filtered table further reduces the subset of data.

When you first create a table, filtering is on by default and AutoFilter buttons are displayed in the table header row. You can turn off filtering by clicking [Filter] in the Sort & Filter group of the Data tab. When filtering is off, AutoFilter buttons are not displayed in the header row and filtering cannot be used.

Filtering on a Single Criterion

The Café is located in New Jersey, and consequently the majority of club members are residents of that state. However, because the town attracts many summer visitors and college students, there are many club members from out of state. You decide to first filter the table to display only New Jersey residents first. To specify the criterion, you select the field value from the AutoFilter drop-down menu. This menu displays a list of the unique entries in the field.

Additional Information

Only the first 1,000 unique entries appear in the AutoFilter list.

1  **Open the State AutoFilter menu.**

Your screen should be similar to Figure 6.30

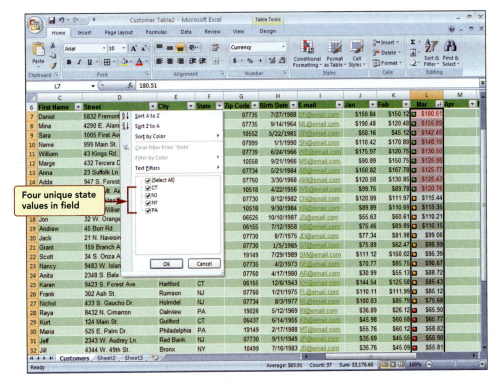

Figure 6.30

The drop-down list displays the four unique state values in the field. Because the filter list of values is derived from the content of the column, it is important that data in a table be entered consistently. It is also important that data not include leading spaces. However uniqueness is not affected by the case of the entry; for example, nj and NJ would not be considered unique entries. When there are different variations of the same information, the filter list displays each variation; for example, NJ and New Jersey would both appear on the list and both items would need to be selected to obtain the correct filter results.

All the values are selected; therefore, the table displays all records. The Select All option above the list of unique values is used to quickly select all values in the field or to deselect all the values.

Immediately above the list of values are three commands that are used to specify the filter criteria or to clear all filter settings. These options, described in the following table, vary depending upon the type of data contained in the column; for example, text, date, or numbers.

Option	Effect
Clear Filter	Removes the filter from the field
Filter by Color	Filters by fill or text color if applied
Text/Number/Date Filter	Applies custom filter based on the type of data

You want to set the filter criterion to display only records that have a state value of NJ.

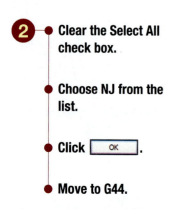

2 • Clear the Select All check box.

• Choose NJ from the list.

• Click [OK].

• Move to G44.

Your screen should be similar to Figure 6.31

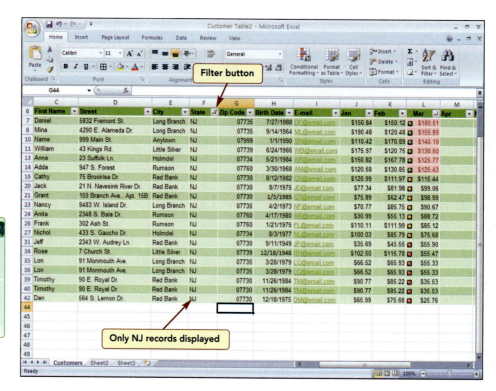

Figure 6.31

Only those records for customers whose state is NJ are displayed. The icon in the column heading displays a ⌄ Filter button, which shows that the table is filtered on data in that column. A ScreenTip displays the type of filter when you point to the Filter button.

Filtering on Multiple Criteria

Next, you decide to find out how many of the NJ customers are also in the Super Bonus Level 2 category for March.

1 • Open the Mar AutoFilter menu.

• Select Filter by Color and choose the green icon.

Your screen should be similar to Figure 6.32

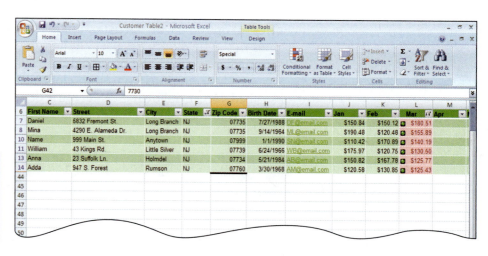

Figure 6.32

Only those NJ customers whose March expenditures meet the Super Bonus Level 2 criteria are displayed. Finally, you want to how many non–New Jersey customers met this expenditure level.

2 ● Open the State AutoFilter menu, select Select All, and clear the NJ selection.

● Click OK.

Your screen should be similar to Figure 6.33

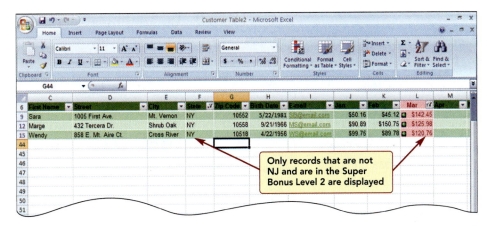

Figure 6.33

Now the filtered table displays only those records that have a March value over $119.99 and do not include a state of New Jersey. Each time you added a new filter criterion, fewer records were displayed in the subset. Next, you will remove the filters and redisplay all the records.

3 ● Open the Mar AutoFilter menu and choose Clear Filter from "Mar".

● Open the State AutoFilter menu and choose Clear Filter from "State".

Another Method

You also could click  in the Sort & Filter group of the Data tab to remove all filters from the table.

Your screen should be similar to Figure 6.34

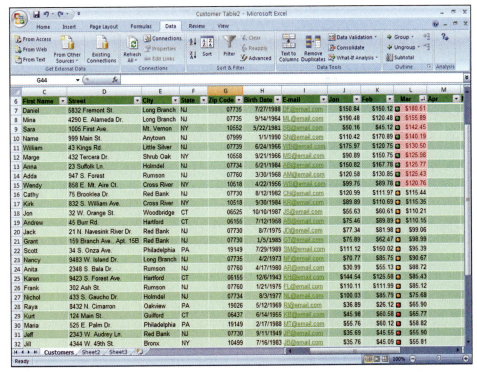

Figure 6.34

All filters are removed and all records are redisplayed.

Creating a Custom AutoFilter

Evan wants to send e-mails to all customers who have qualified for the Super Bonus Level awards for all three months, thanking them for their patronage and giving them a 50 percent off espresso drink coupon. To accomplish this, you want to specify further criteria to filter out values less than $75 in the month fields.

1
- Open the Mar AutoFilter menu.

- Select Number Filters and choose Greater Than Or Equal To.

Additional Information

You also can select Number Filters/Custom from the shortcut menu.

Your screen should be similar to Figure 6.35

Figure 6.35

The Custom AutoFilter dialog box is used to specify a filtering operation that makes comparisons between two values. The type of comparison to make is specified in the box on the left, and the value to compare to is specified in the box on the right. You can include a second set of criteria by selecting the And or Or option and specifying the settings in the lower row of boxes. The AND and OR operators are used to specify multiple conditions that must be met for the records to display in the filtered table. The AND operator narrows the search, because a record must meet both conditions to be included. The OR operator broadens the search, because any record meeting either condition is included in the output.

Because you selected "Is greater than or equal to" from the shortcut menu, that value is filled in. You just need to specify the value.

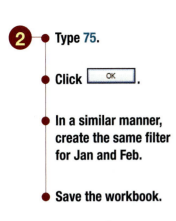

2
- Type **75**.
- Click [OK].

- In a similar manner, create the same filter for Jan and Feb.

- Save the workbook.

Your screen should be similar to Figure 6.36

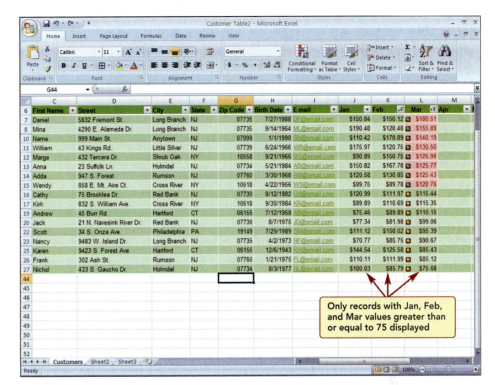

Only records with Jan, Feb, and Mar values greater than or equal to 75 displayed

Figure 6.36

Only the records that meet the specified criteria are displayed.

Filtering for Unique Values and Removing Duplicates

Sometimes, when data is entered in a table, the same data can be inadvertently entered more than once. To check the data in a table or worksheet range, you can identify unique data and then remove duplicate data. Duplicate data is one where all values in a row are an exact match of all values in another row. The duplicate data is determined by the displayed value, not the stored value, in the cell. For example, if the same values are stored in a cell, but formatted differently, they would be considered unique.

Before removing duplicate values, it is a good idea to filter to locate unique values first to confirm that the results are what you want before removing the duplicates.

- Click [Advanced] in the Sort & Filter group of the Data tab.

- If necessary, select Filter the list, in-place.

- Select Unique Records only.

The default range to filter is the entire table range.

- Click [OK].

Your screen should be similar to Figure 6.37

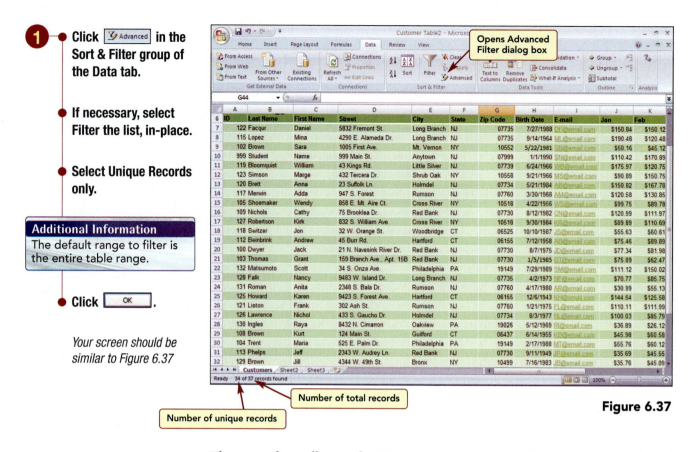

Number of total records

Number of unique records

Figure 6.37

The status bar tells you that 34 unique records were found from the 37 total records. This means that there are three duplicate records. Before removing the duplicate records, you will verify them by redisplaying all records and then sorting the ID column.

- Click [Clear] in the Sort & Filter group to remove the filter from the table.

You also can use [Sort & Filter] in the Editing group on the Home tab and choose Clear.

- Sort the ID column in ascending sort order.

Move to the ID column and click [↓]

- Move to B7.

Your screen should be similar to Figure 6.38

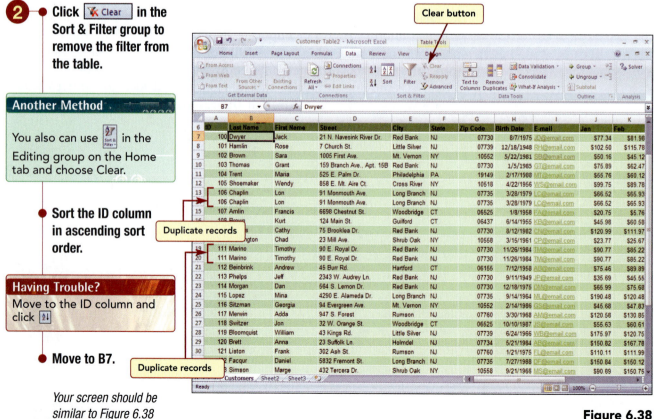

Clear button

Duplicate records

Duplicate records

Figure 6.38

After reviewing the records, you note that there are three duplicate records: 106, 111, and 124. To remove the duplicate records, you could select each record row and delete it individually or you can use the Remove Duplicates feature. You will use both methods.

3 **Right-click on any cell in row 14 of the table, select Delete, and choose Table Rows.**

Another Method

You also could use Delete in the Cells group of the Home tab and choose Delete Table Rows to delete the selected table row.

Your screen should be similar to Figure 6.39

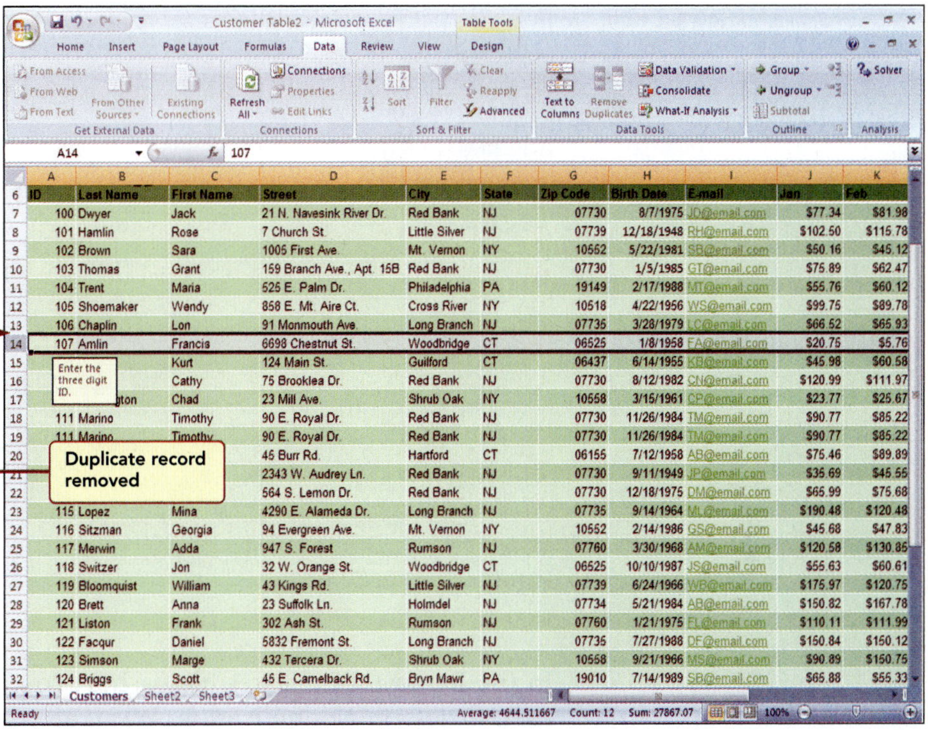

Figure 6.39

Additional Information:

Do not use the Delete Sheet Rows command to delete a table row, as this will delete the entire worksheet row and any data in that row that is not part of the table range.

The duplicate record for ID 106 has been deleted. To quickly remove the remaining duplicates, you will use the Remove Duplicates feature.

4 Click  in the Data Tools group.

Your screen should be similar to Figure 6.40

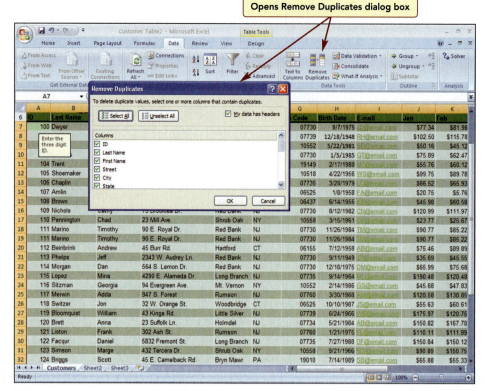

Opens Remove Duplicates dialog box

Figure 6.40

In the Remove Duplicates dialog box, you can specify the columns to be used to determine duplication. When all columns are selected, each entry in every column must exactly match those in another record. Selecting specific columns limits the match to data in those columns only. Because you want to find and remove records that contain duplicate information in all columns, you want to use all columns.

5 If necessary, click [Select All] to select all columns.

● Click [OK] to complete the command.

● Click [OK] in response to the informational message about the number of duplicates found and deleted.

Your screen should be similar to Figure 6.41

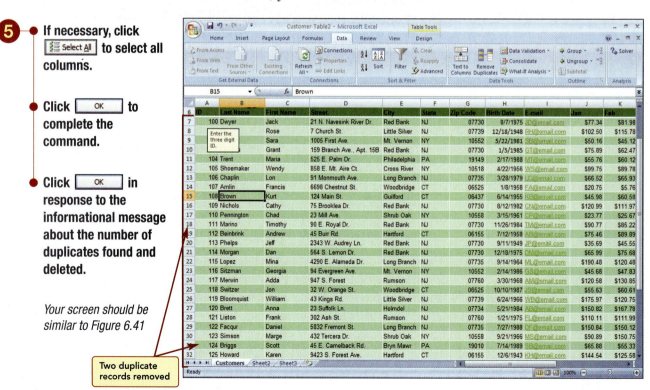

Two duplicate records removed

Figure 6.41

It is a good idea to check for duplicates before filtering data or analyzing the information in a table or worksheet to ensure that the results are as accurate as possible.

Summarizing Data

The next piece of information you want to gather from the table is a total amount for each state for the three months and a grand total of each month's expenditures. Additionally, you want to display a count of the number of records in the table. You can get this information easily by displaying a total row and inserting subtotals.

Displaying a Total Row

To calculate statistics for all records in the table, you can display a total row and select the type of calculation you want performed on the data in a field. You will first use this feature to display a count of records in the table.

1 ● **Open the Table Tools Design tab.**

● **Select** ☐ Total Row **in the Table Style Options group.**

Your screen should be similar to Figure 6.42

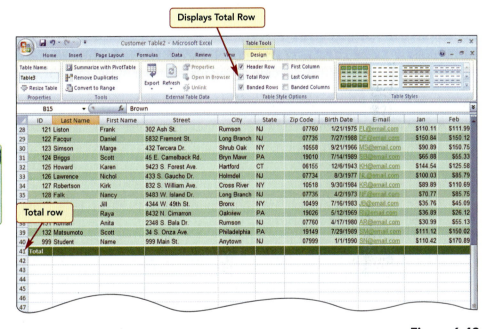

Figure 6.42

The worksheet window scrolls to display the bottom of the table where a Total row is displayed.

The word "Total" appears in the left-most cell of the totals row and an appropriate calculation is automatically entered in the right-most cell of the table. Selecting any cell in the totals row displays a ▼ drop-down list arrow that when clicked displays a list of function names from which you can select. You will use the Count function to display the number of records below the Last Name field column.

2 • Click in the totals row for the Last Name field.

• Click ▼ to open the drop-down list and choose Count.

Your screen should be similar to Figure 6.43

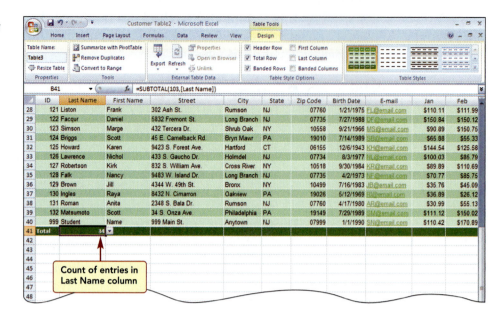

Figure 6.43

A count of all entries in the Last Name field column is displayed. You also decide to calculate a total of the monthly expenditures.

3 • Open the Jan Total drop-down list and choose Sum.

• In a similar manner, display the sum for Feb and Mar.

Your screen should be similar to Figure 6.44

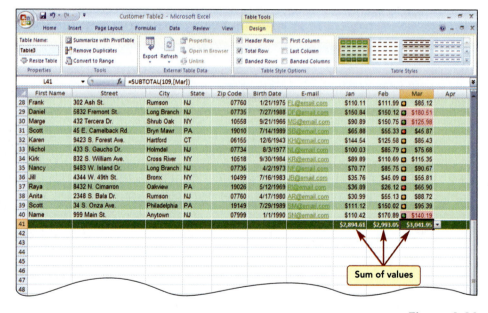

Figure 6.44

You also can enter formulas in the total row that are not included in the drop-down list or type a text entry in a cell of this row.

You will add a text entry in the E-mail column of the totals row to describe the values to the right and then change the entry in the ID row to Count.

4 • Type **TOTAL:** in cell I41.

• Change the text color to white and the alignment to right, and remove the underline.

• Replace the entry in A41 with **COUNT:**.

Your screen should be similar to Figure 6.45

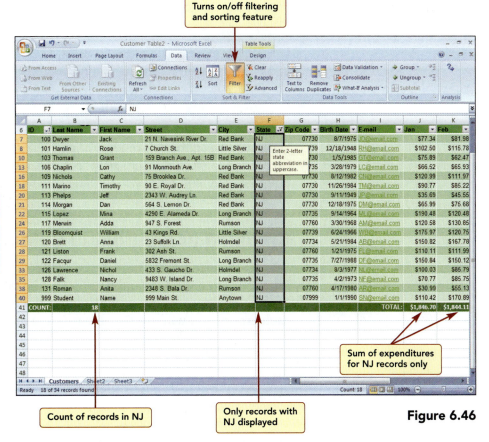

Descriptive text entry

Figure 6.45

Now, if you apply a filter to the table, the calculated values in the totals row change to reflect the amounts for the displayed records only.

5 • Click [Filter] in the Data tab to redisplay the AutoFilter buttons.

• Filter the table to display only those records whose State is NJ.

Having Trouble?
Scroll back to the top of the table to display the AutoFilter buttons in the header row.

• Print the range A1:L41 to fit in landscape orientation on one page with your Name and the current data in a header.

Your screen should be similar to Figure 6.46

Turns on/off filtering and sorting feature

Count of records in NJ

Only records with NJ displayed

Sum of expenditures for NJ records only

Figure 6.46

Now the totals row Count and Sum functions have been updated to calculate these values based on the displayed data in the table only.

Creating a Calculated Column

The last calculation you want to include is the average expenditures for each customer. You will enter a column label in cell V6 and the function to calculate the average in cell V7.

1 ● Type **AVG** in cell V6.

● Enter an AVG function in V7 to calculate the average of cells J7:U7.

● Save the workbook.

Your screen should be similar to Figure 6.47

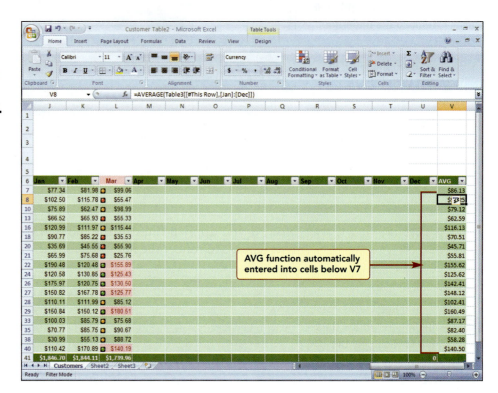

Figure 6.47

When you typed the column heading in cell V6, the table range automatically expanded to include the new column. Additionally, the formula was automatically copied down the column to calculate the average for each displayed record in the table.

Grouping and Outlining Data

You have sorted and filtered the table to organize the data and used functions to analyze the information in the table. Now you want to further analyze the data by grouping related data and displaying subtotals for each group. You will use Excel's grouping and outlining tools to do this.

Concept 5

Grouping and Outlining

5   **Grouping and outlining** data organizes data in a worksheet by showing and hiding different levels of detail for groups of related data. Grouping data has two functions: to collapse and expand rows or columns. Collapsing a group hides the rows within the group to display only the row with subtotals. After a group is collapsed, it can be expanded to redisplay the hidden rows. Worksheet data that is grouped also can be summarized using Summary functions.

Groups can be created for any level and location that you want on the worksheet. In contrast, outlines are based on a structured list or table. By sorting table data into categories first, you can then create groups that you can manipulate to show or hide rows within the group. For example, if you first sort the table by state, you can then create groups to manipulate the records within each state group.

Grouping Data

You decide grouping will be helpful in analyzing the data by state and city. First, you will create a group of the records with a state of CT. Before grouping data, you first need to sort the table so that the data you want grouped are together. You also will hide the totals row.

1 ● **Clear the filter from the State column.**

● **Clear the Total Row option in the Table Style Options group on the Table Tools Design tab.**

● **Do a multilevel sort on the table data by State and then by City.**

● **Select the range A7:A11, which contains the IDs of the five individuals living in CT.**

● **Click ⇒ Group ▾ in the Outline group of the Data tab.**

● **Choose Rows and click OK .**

Your screen should be similar to Figure 6.48

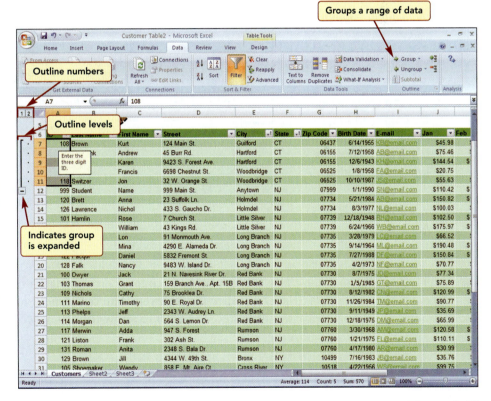

Figure 6.48

The outline levels are displayed in a column to the left of the table data. The numbers at the top of the column indicate the number of outline levels, with the higher number representing each inner level. The outline symbols are used to hide and show the detail information in a group.

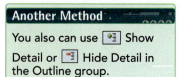
Because the CT group does not contain any sublevels, there are only two levels of data that can be displayed; level one hides the detail data and level two displays the detail data.

A level bar next to the group extends from the first row to the last row of data in the group and each bullet identifies a record in the group. The [+] and [−] outline symbols indicate if the group is expanded [−] and all levels are showing or collapsed [+] and all levels are hidden. Clicking on these buttons hides and displays the data in the associated group.

You will hide and display the data in the CT group and then you will define another level for the city of Woodbridge in the group.

2 ● Click [−] to hide the data in the CT group.

● Click [2] to display the data in the group again.

● Create a group using the range A10:A11, which contain the IDs of the two individuals living in Woodbridge.

Your screen should be similar to Figure 6.49

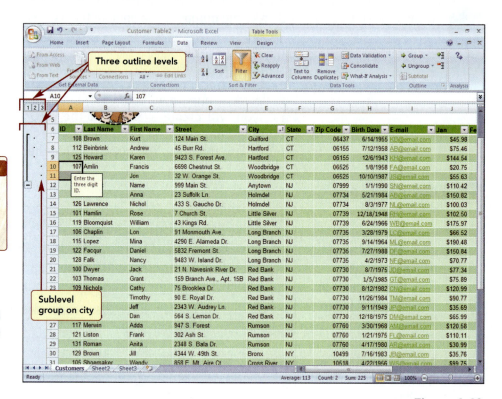

Figure 6.49

The City group is a sublevel group within the CT State group and a third level number is displayed. The bullet next to the two records in this group are indented one level to show that they are at a higher level.

3 • Click 2 to display only level-two records.

Your screen should be similar to Figure 6.50

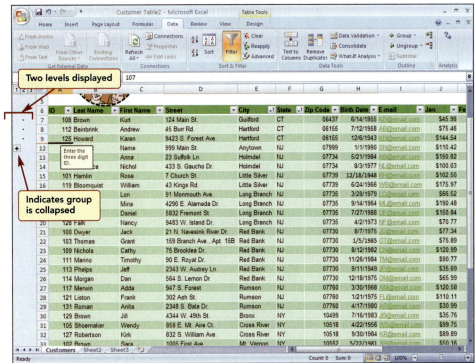

Figure 6.50

Now the Woodbridge records are hidden. When a group contains several levels, using the ➕ and ➖ symbols hides and displays all records within the group and the level buttons control the levels within the group.

You decide that creating the sublevel by city within the group is not necessary and will remove it.

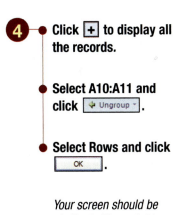

4 • Click ➕ to display all the records.

• Select A10:A11 and click ⬆ Ungroup ▾.

• Select Rows and click ▭ OK ▭.

Your screen should be similar to Figure 6.51

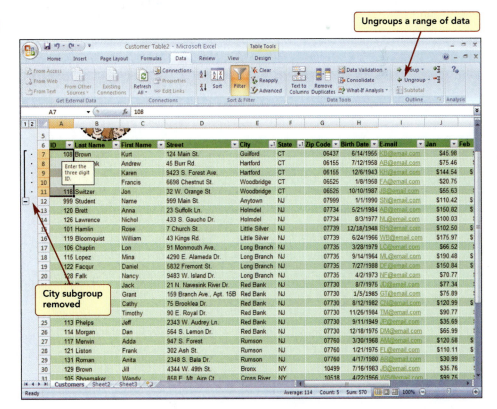

Figure 6.51

The subgroup has been removed.

In addition, you want to know how much money each group spends in each month. To do this, you need to add a summary row and the SUM Subtotal function to calculate a subtotal for the group.

Grouping Data and Calculating Subtotals

Although you could continue to define groups and add summary rows, a faster way is to use the automatic Subtotal feature.

Concept 6

Subtotal

6 The Subtotal feature automatically takes data in a list, organizes it into groups, and includes subtotals for each group of data. A **list** is a series of rows that contain related data but are not defined as a table. Subtotals can be calculated on any column or columns you select that contain numbers. The SUM subtotal is the default calculation; however, you can change it to subtotal using other functions such as COUNT, MAX and MIN. The SUBTOTAL function uses the syntax =SUBTOTAL(function_num, ref1, ref2 . . .) where the function_num tells the function the type of calculation to apply and ref refers to the range to subtotal.

When using the Subtotal feature, the data in the table needs to be in sorted order first so that the rows you want to subtotal are grouped together. The table data is already in sorted order as you want it. Additionally, because the Subtotal feature can only be used on a list of data, and not data defined as a table, you need to convert the table range to a normal range. You also will remove the current group from the table.

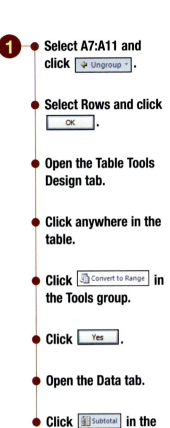

1
- Select A7:A11 and click ▣ Ungroup ▾.

- Select Rows and click OK.

- Open the Table Tools Design tab.

- Click anywhere in the table.

- Click ▣ Convert to Range in the Tools group.

- Click Yes.

- Open the Data tab.

- Click ▣ Subtotal in the Outline group.

Your screen should be similar to Figure 6.52

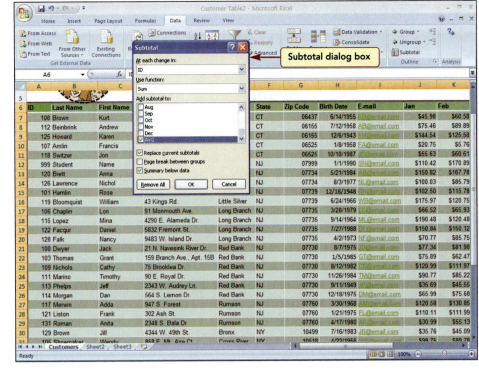

Figure 6.52

From the Subtotal dialog box, you first specify the field you want to display subtotals after each change in data. In this case, you want subtotals calculated after each change in State. Then you select the type of function you want to use to calculate the subtotals, such as Sum, Count, or Average. You want to calculate a sum. Finally, you select the fields that contain the values you want to subtotal. You will display subtotals for the three months of expenditures. You also can have an automatic page break after each subtotal and can have the subtotals displayed above the subtotaled rows instead of below.

2 • Choose State from the At Each Change In drop-down list.

• Click on AVG in the Add Subtotal To list to remove the checkmark.

• Select Jan, Feb, and Mar in the Add Subtotal To list.

• Click [OK].

• Scroll to see the bottom of the range and the monthly expenditure data.

Your screen should be similar to Figure 6.53

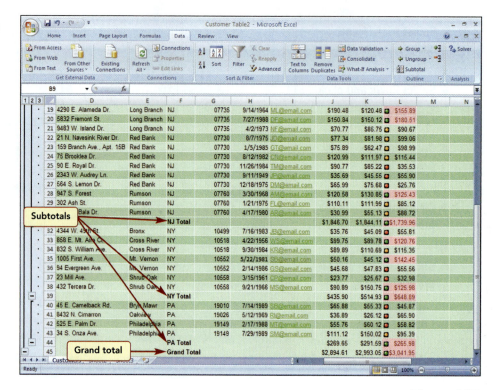

Figure 6.53

The worksheet now displays a subtotal for each change in state and a grand total for each month. Additionally, along the left side of the row numbers, the worksheet is outlined so you can see its structure.

You can create a summary report by clicking the numeric outline symbols 1, 2, 3 to display different levels of detail. Clicking 1 displays the grand total only, 2 the subtotals, and 3 all levels. You can also use + to display and − to hide the details within a group.

3 • Click 2.

Your screen should be similar to Figure 6.54

Additional Information
You also can create a chart of the visible data in a worksheet that contains subtotals.

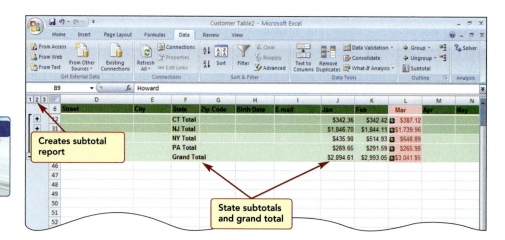

Figure 6.54

The worksheet displays the subtotals and grand total values only.

Printing a Summary Report

Next you will print the summary report for Evan showing the State and the three month columns only. To do this, you will hide the Zip Code, Birth Date, and E-mail columns. Then you will select the range of cells containing the data that you want printed.

1 ● Autofit columns F, J, K, and L.

● Hide columns G through I.

● Select the range containing the field names and summary statistics (F6:L45).

● Click 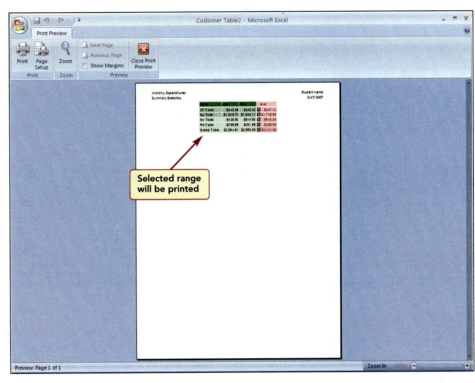 Office Button, select Print, and choose Print.

● Change the Print What setting in the Print dialog box to Selection.

● If necessary, select the printer.

● Click [Preview].

● Center the table horizontally on the page.

● In the left section of a custom header, enter **Monthly Expenditures** on the first line and **Summary Statistics** on the second.

● In the right section of a custom header, enter **your name** on the first line and the **current date** on the second.

Your screen should be similar to Figure 6.55

Figure 6.55

Only the selected range of the worksheet is displayed in the preview window. You will print the selection, unhide the columns, and then remove the subtotals.

2 • Click  to print the selection.

• Click **Format**, select Hide & Unhide, and choose Unhide Columns.

• Click **3** to show all details.

• Click anywhere in the list range.

• Click **Subtotal** in the Data tab and click **Remove All**.

• Sort the worksheet in ascending order by ID.

• Move to cell A5 and save the workbook.

Your screen should be similar to Figure 6.56

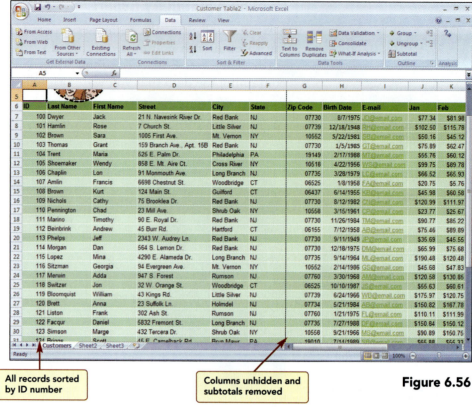

All records sorted by ID number

Columns unhidden and subtotals removed

Figure 6.56

The worksheet is in sorted order by ID number. Because the list has not been redefined as a table range, the AutoFilter buttons do not display in the header row.

Creating a PivotTable Report

Another way to analyze your worksheet data from different viewpoints is to create a PivotTable report.

Concept 7

PivotTable Report

7 A **PivotTable** report is an interactive, crosstabulated table that summarizes and analyzes worksheet data. When a PivotTable report is created, Excel automatically sorts, subtotals, and totals the data. You can then expand and collapse levels of data to focus your results as you want. You can move rows to columns or columns to rows (or pivot) to see different data summaries. You also can filter, sort, group, and conditionally format the data to create a concise, attractive, and informative report. A PivotTable is most useful for when you want to analyze a long list of figures and you want to compare several facts about each figure.

The criteria to create a PivotTable report are that the worksheet data must be a data table or list, the columns and rows must contain unique labels, and there cannot be any blank rows or columns. In a Pivot-Table report, each column or field from the source data becomes a PivotTable field that summarizes multiple rows of information. A numeric field provides the values to be summarized. After a PivotTable is created, it is interactive, meaning that you can rearrange the data in many ways by adding or removing fields.

A typical PivotTable report pivots one column against another, with the intersection of the two columns serving as the area for the summary data. A PivotTable report can calculate the sum, count, average, maximum, minimum, standard deviation, and variance without the need for entering formulas.

You will create a PivotTable report of the data in the list.

1 ● Move to cell A7.

● Click [PivotTable] in the Tables group of the Insert tab.

Your screen should be similar to Figure 6.57

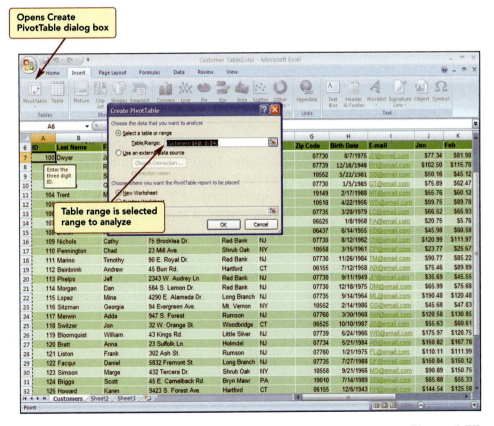

Figure 6.57

In the Create PivotTable dialog box, you specify the data to analyze and where to place the PivotTable. The default data selection is the current table, which is the one you want to analyze. The default location is a new worksheet, but you could specify a range of cells in which to place the PivotTable on the current worksheet. You decide to place the PivotTable on a separate worksheet.

2 ● **Click** OK .

Your screen should be similar to Figure 6.58

Blank PivotTable form

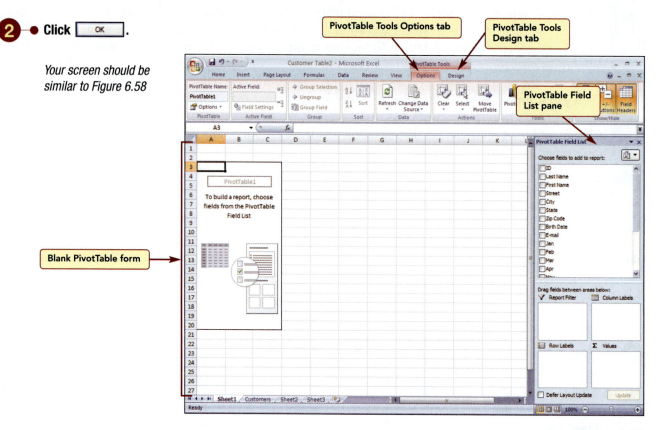

PivotTable Tools Options tab

PivotTable Tools Design tab

PivotTable Field List pane

Figure 6.58

A blank PivotTable form is displayed in a new sheet. In addition, the PivotTable Tools Options tab, the PivotTable Tools Design tab, and the PivotTable Field List pane are displayed. You would like this table to summarize monthly expenditures by city and state. To set up this table layout, you need to select the fields from the Field List pane to add them to the form.

3 In the Choose fields to add to report list, select City, State, Jan, Feb, and Mar.

Your screen should be similar to Figure 6.59

PivotTable report of monthly expenditures for each city

Selected fields appear in report

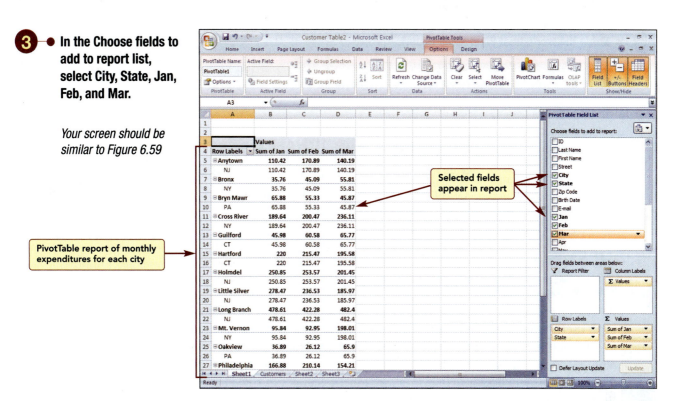

Figure 6.59

The PivotTable report displays a sum of the monthly expenditures in each month for each city within the state. Rows 5 through 37 of the table show the expenditures for each city in each month as well as the grand total of their expenditures.

You decide that the data would be more meaningful without the city breakdown.

4 Clear the City field.

Your screen should be similar to Figure 6.60

PivotTable report of monthly expenditures for each state

City field removed from report

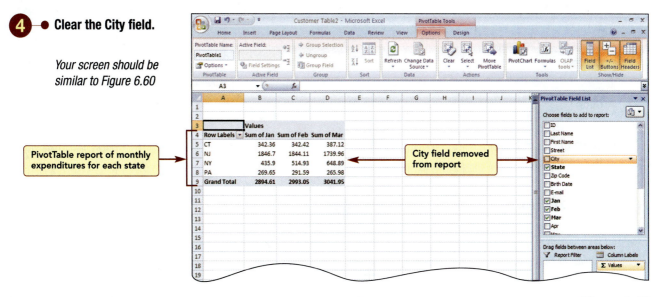

Figure 6.60

The table now simply shows a summary of expenditures for each month by state. You are satisfied with the PivotTable, so you are going to name and move the worksheet.

5 ● Name the worksheet **Pivot Table Report.**

● Move the Pivot Table Report worksheet so it follows the Customers worksheet.

Creating a PivotChart Report

Next, you want to see the state and monthly expenditure data graphed on a chart. To do this, you will create a PivotChart using the PivotTable you just created as the data source.

Concept 8

PivotChart Report

8 A **PivotChart** report is an interactive chart that can be used to view and rearrange data. A PivotChart is most useful when you need to quickly change data views to see comparisons and trends in different ways.

A PivotChart report must have an associated PivotTable report in the same workbook. Both of these reports contain the same source data and, as in the PivotTable report, you can rearrange the data to see different views and display details. When you make changes to a PivotTable (such as removing a field from it), the associated PivotChart also changes, and vice versa.

---

1 ● Open the PivotTable Tools Options tab.

● Click [PivotChart] in the Tools group.

● Choose ▮▮ Clustered Column.

● Click [OK].

● Move the chart below the PivotTable.

● Move to cell A3.

Your screen should be similar to Figure 6.61

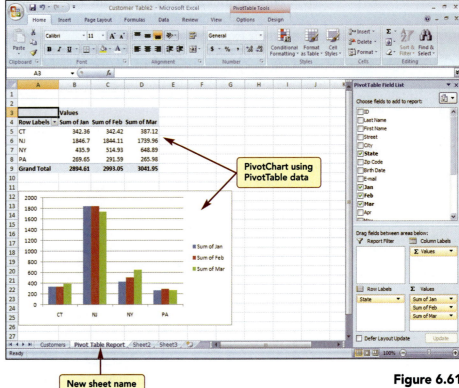

PivotChart using PivotTable data

New sheet name

Figure 6.61

The PivotChart has been automatically created using the PivotTable data. The row fields in the PivotTable become the category fields in the PivotChart, and the column fields in the PivotTable become the series fields in the PivotChart.

The PivotChart Filter pane can be used to apply filters to the data displayed in the fields. Any changes you make to the PivotChart are also reflected in the PivotTable report.

As with the PivotTable report, you can manipulate and reformat the PivotChart to view the data in different ways. But remember, anything you do to the PivotChart fields will affect the associated PivotTable report fields.

2 ● Print the Pivot Table Report worksheet with your name and the current date in the header.

● Save the workbook.

Working with Hyperlinks

Creating a Hyperlink between Workbooks

The last thing you want to do with this workbook is to create a hyperlink from the Customers worksheet to the Bonus Dollars workbook. Your plans are to include the Bonus Dollars worksheets for each month of the year in separate sheets of this workbook file. Adding a hyperlink to this workbook file will make it easy to switch to the appropriate sheet in the Bonus Dollars workbook and copy the customers' total monthly expenditures into the Customers table. You will link to the Bonus Dollars workbook file and will display the hyperlink in cell J4 above the expenditure columns of data.

1 ● Move to J4 of the Customers sheet.

● Click 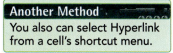 in the Links group of the Insert tab.

Another Method
You also can select Hyperlink from a cell's shortcut menu.

Your screen should be similar to Figure 6.62

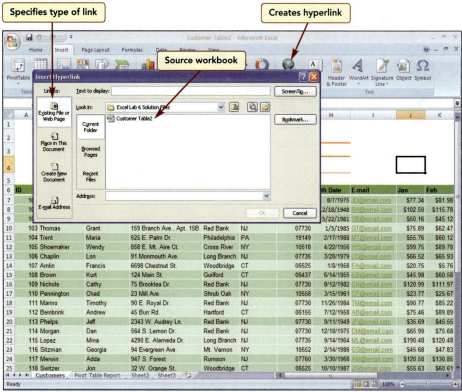

Figure 6.62

From the Insert Hyperlink dialog box, you first need to specify the type of link from the Link To bar. The four options are described below.

Option	Effect
Existing File or Web Page	Creates a link in an existing Web page or file
Place in This Document	Creates a link to a place in the active file
Create New Document	Creates a link to a file that you have not created yet.
E-mail Address	Creates a link that allows users to create an e-mail message with the correct address in the To line.

You want to create a link to a location in another workbook file. You also need to enter the text that the hyperlink will display in the worksheet. If you do not enter anything in the Text to Display box, the hyperlink automatically displays the path of the linked file. Finally, you will add instructions that will appear in the hyperlink ScreenTip.

2

- If necessary, select **Existing File or Web Page** from the Link To bar.

- If necessary, change to your Excel data files location and select ex06_Bonus Dollars from the file list.

- Replace the entry in the Text to Display text box with **Monthly Expenditure Data.**

- Click ScreenTip....

- Type **Click to open the worksheet.**

- Click OK.

Your screen should be similar to Figure 6.63

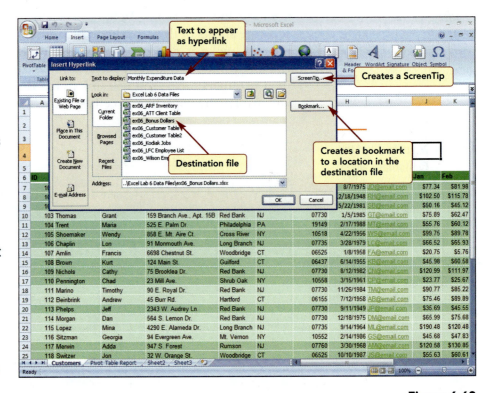

Figure 6.63

In the future, as you record each month's Bonus Dollar awards using the Monthly Bonus Form template, you plan to maintain the completed monthly worksheets in a single workbook file. When the workbook contains many worksheets, you will want to make sure that the user is taken directly to the worksheet containing the data for the appropriate month. To do this, you create a bookmark to that location in the linked workbook file. A **bookmark** establishes a link to a specific worksheet location.

3 • Click  .

Your screen should be similar to Figure 6.64

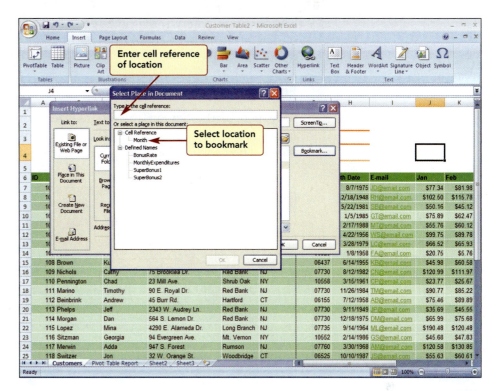

Figure 6.64

In the Select Place in Document dialog box, you select a specific location to which you want the user to be taken in the linked document. The list box displays a tree diagram showing the outline of the information in the workbook and named ranges. From the outline, you select the location to which you want to link. In this case, you want the cell pointer positioned on the first customer's total expenditures (G12).

4 • Select Month in the Cell Reference list.

• In the Type in the cell reference text box, enter **G12**.

• Click  to close the Select Place in Document dialog box.

• Click OK to close the Insert Hyperlink dialog box.

• Point to cell J4.

Your screen should be similar to Figure 6.65

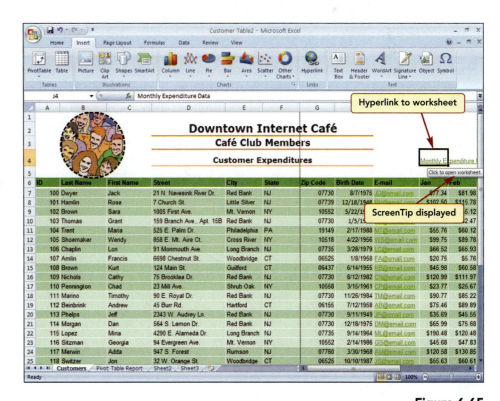

Figure 6.65

The text you entered for the hyperlink is displayed in the cell. It appears underlined and in the default hyperlink colors. The ScreenTip displays the text you entered.

Editing a Hyperlink

As you read the ScreenTip, you realize it does not provide enough information. You decide to change the ScreenTip text to include the worksheet name. Then you will use the hyperlink to open the worksheet.

1 • **Right-click cell J4.**

• **Choose Edit Hyperlink from the shortcut menu.**

Additional Information
You can edit the text of the hyperlink just like any other cell entry.

Another Method
When the cell containing a hyperlink is selected, you also can click  in the Links group on the Insert tab to edit the hyperlink.

Your screen should be similar to Figure 6.66

More About

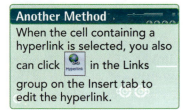

See 2.3 Format Cells and Content in the More About appendix to learn how to remove a hyperlink.

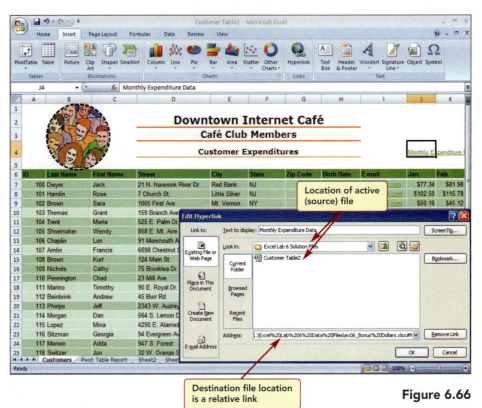

Location of active (source) file

Destination file location is a relative link

Figure 6.66

The Edit Hyperlink dialog box displays the hyperlink destination. The Look In location identifies the location of the active workbook file. The Address box displays the destination workbook file name and cell location the link will follow. Notice the Address box does not include the drive location of the destination workbook file as part of the address. This is because it is a **relative link,** which means it will locate the destination workbook file relative to the location of the current workbook file. If you move both files to the same location, the link will continue to operate correctly because the relative positions of the files remains unchanged. If you move one of the files to another location, the link would not work. You would then need to edit the address to include the complete destination path location, making the address an **absolute link.**

You will edit the ScreenTip text to include the destination workbook file name.

2
- Click [ScreenTip...].
- Add the text **Bonus Dollars** before the word "worksheet".
- Click [OK].
- Click [OK].
- Point to the hyperlink cell to see the ScreenTip.

Your screen should be similar to Figure 6.67

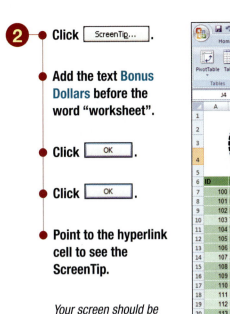

Figure 6.67

The revised ScreenTip is now much more descriptive of the purpose of the hyperlink. Now you will use the hyperlink.

3
- Click on the hyperlink.

Your screen should be similar to Figure 6.68

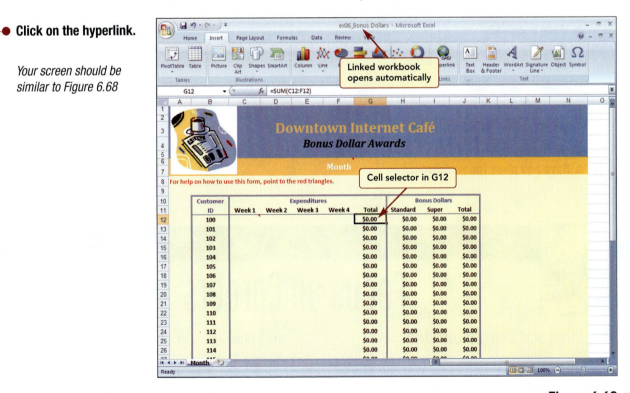

Figure 6.68

The Bonus Dollars workbook is open and the cell selector is in the location you specified as the bookmark. Now, assuming that the worksheet contained the data for the month, you could copy the customer monthly expenditure totals from the Bonus Dollars workbook to the Customers worksheet.

4 • Close the ac06_Bonus Dollars **workbook files.**

Restoring the Table

After converting the table to a normal range and using the Subtotal feature, the banded row alternating pattern is no longer correct. You will convert the range back to a table range and then fix the banded row pattern.

1 • Move to cell A6.

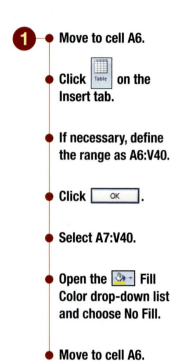

• Click on the Insert tab.

• If necessary, define the range as A6:V40.

• Click [OK].

• Select A7:V40.

• Open the Fill Color drop-down list and choose No Fill.

• Move to cell A6.

Your screen should be similar to Figure 6.69

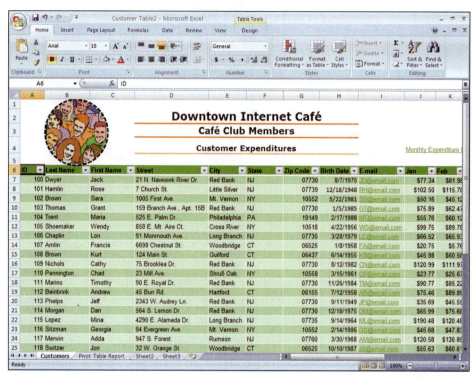

Figure 6.69

The range is now again recognized as a table and the alternating row pattern is correctly applied.

2 • Save and close the workbook.

Focus on Careers

EXPLORE YOUR CAREER OPTIONS

Lodging Manager

Have you ever wondered who ensures you get excellent customer service and enjoy your stay at a hotel? Have you ever attended a convention in a hotel and wondered who made sure the equipment and resources the group needed were attended to? Lodging managers are responsible for making sure customers are satisfied and the establishment is profitable. Managers must use guidelines to allocate and disperse funds for needed improvements and maintenance. They must track income and manage overhead. Many use spreadsheet programs to handle these tasks. The salary range for lodging managers is typically between $25,000 and $40,000. College graduates with experience in the lodging industry will have a competitive advantage in this industry.

LAB 6

Creating and Working with Tables

Table (EX6.4)

A table is an organized collection of related information entered in sequential rows and columns.

Table →

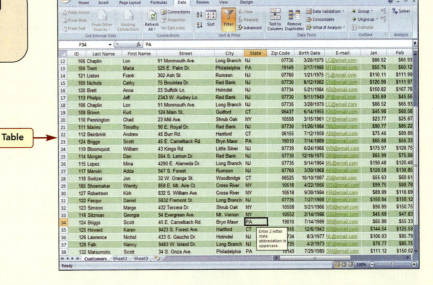

Hyperlink (EX6.11)

A hyperlink is a connection or link to a destination location. The destination can be a location in the current file or another file, a Web page, or an e-mail address.

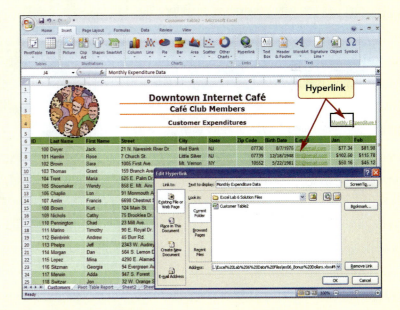

Concept Summary

Sort (EX6.23)

You can sort or arrange data in a specified sequence: alphabetically, numerically, or by date.

Filter (EX6.30)

A filter is a restriction you place on records in a table to quickly isolate and display a subset of records.

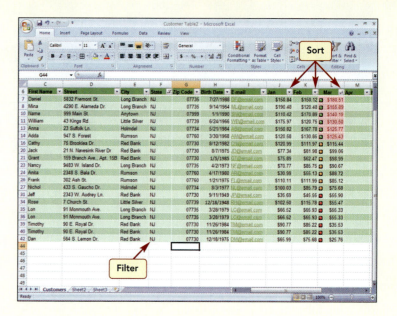

Grouping and Outlining (EX6.43)

Grouping and outlining data organizes data in a worksheet by showing and hiding different levels of detail for groups of related data.

Subtotal (EX6.46)

The Subtotal feature automatically takes data in a list, organizes it into groups, and includes subtotals for each group of data.

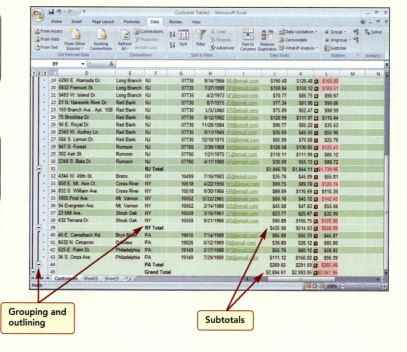

PivotTable Report (EX6.51)

A PivotTable report is an interactive table that can be used to summarize and manipulate worksheet data.

PivotChart Report (EX6.54)

A PivotChart report is an interactive chart that can be used to view and rearrange data.

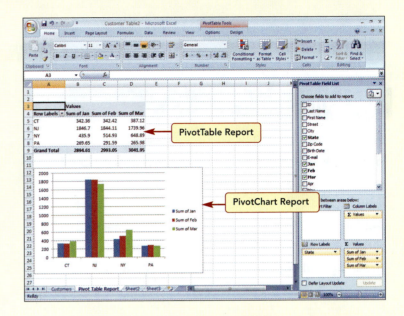

PivotTable Report

PivotChart Report

Lab Review

LAB 6
Creating and Working with Tables

key terms

absolute link   EX6.58

bookmark   EX6.56

criteria   EX6.30

field   EX6.4

field name   EX6.4

filter   EX6.30

grouping and outlining   EX6.43

header row   EX6.4

hyperlink   EX6.11

list   EX6.46

multilevel sort   EX6.23

PivotChart   EX6.54

PivotTable   EX6.51

record   EX6.4

relative link   EX6.58

sort   EX6.23

table   EX6.4

table range   EX6.4

Uniform Resource Locator (URL)   EX6.11

MCAS skills

The Microsoft Certified Applications Specialist (MCAS) certification program is designed to measure your proficiency in performing basic tasks using the Office 2007 applications. Getting certified demonstrates that you have the skills and provides a valuable industry credential for employment. See Reference 2 Microsoft Certified Applications Specialist (MCAS) for a complete list of the skills that were covered in Lab 6.

command summary

Command	Shortcut	Action
🏢 Office Button		
[Excel Options] /Proofing/ [AutoCorrect Options...] /AutoFormat As You Type/Internet and network paths with hyperlinks		Automatically formats a hyperlink
Home tab		
Number group		
[icon]		Formats cells
Styles group		
[Conditional Formatting]		Formats cells based on selected criteria
Cells group		
[Insert ▾] /Table Row Below	[Tab ⇥]	Adds a new row below the current row in a table
[Format ▾] /Format Cells/Number/Special		Applies selected special format to number entries
[Format ▾] /Hide & Unhide		Hides and unhides rows and/or columns
Editing group		
[Sort & Filter ▾] /Sort A to Z		Sorts the table column in ascending alphabetical order
[Sort & Filter ▾] /Custom Sort		Performs a multilevel sort on the table column
[Sort & Filter ▾] /Filter		Turns AutoFilter on or off
[Sort & Filter ▾] /Clear		Clears filters from a table
Insert tab		
Tables group		
[PivotTable ▾]		Inserts a PivotTable
[Table]		Converts a range of data into a table

Lab Review

Command	Shortcut	Action
Links group		
Hyperlink		Inserts a new hyperlink or modifies selected hyperlink
Data tab		
Sort & Filter group		
Sort Smallest to Largest		Sorts a column of data in ascending order
Sort		Arranges data alphabetically, numerically, or by date
Filter		Turns AutoFilter on or off
Clear		Redisplays all records
Advanced		Specifies complex criteria to limit records in a query result
Data Tools group		
Remove Duplicates		Deletes duplicate rows
Data Validation		Prevents invalid data from being entered into a cell
Outline group		
Group		Ties range of cells so they can be collapsed or expanded
Ungroup		Ungroups range of cells
Subtotal		Displays totals for each change in a category
Subtotal / Remove All		Removes subtotals from worksheet
Table Tools Design tab		
Tools group		
Convert to Range		Converts table to normal range

command summary

Command	Shortcut	Action
Table Style Options group		
☑ Banded Rows		Formats even rows differently from odd rows
☐ First Column		Displays formatting for first column of the table
☑ Header Row		Formats the top row of the table
☐ Total Row		Adds a totals row to the table
Table Styles group		
▾ More		Opens Table Styles gallery to apply a predefined format and colors to a table
PivotTable Tools Options tab		
Tools group		
PivotChart		Inserts a chart based on the PivotTable data

Lab Exercises

matching

Match the letter on the right to the item in the numbered list on the left.

1. multilevel _____   **a.** an organized collection of related information

2. Web page _____   **b.** a row of a table that contains a group of related fields

3. PivotTable _____   **c.** a connection to a location in another file

4. sort _____   **d.** Z to A order

5. filter _____   **e.** summarizes and manipulates worksheet data

6. field name _____   **f.** organizes data in a specified sequence

7. field _____   **g.** a sort on more than one column or field

8. descending _____   **h.** the smallest unit of information about a record

9. table _____   **i.** displays a subset of records according to specified criteria

10. record _____   **j.** the label used to identify the data stored in a field

multiple choice

Circle the correct response to the questions below.

1. A(n) _____ is a hyperlink to a specific location in a file.
   a. marker
   b. absolute link
   c. relative link
   d. bookmark

2. A _____ is one group of information in a table.
   a. field
   b. record
   c. sort
   d. database

3. _____ can be used to summarize numbers in a table.
   a. Filters
   b. Subtotals
   c. Graphics
   d. Sorts

4. When a hyperlink is created, it stores the information about the location of the destination as a _____.
   a. URL
   b. sort
   c. filter
   d. HTML

5. The single-level sort operation feature lets you sort on up to _____ column(s) or field(s) in a table at a time.
   a. 1
   b. 2
   c. 3
   d. 4

6. You can _____ or arrange data in a specified sequence: alphabetically, numerically, or by date.
   a. sum
   b. sort
   c. filter
   d. pivot

7. The _____ feature temporarily hides rows that do not meet the specified criteria.
   a. sum
   b. sort
   c. filter
   d. pivot

8. _____ data has two functions: to collapse and expand rows or columns.
   a. Sorting
   b. Filtering
   c. Analyzing
   d. Grouping

9. Use a _____ to quickly jump to another location in a file.
   a. Web page
   b. hyperlink
   c. browser
   d. filter

10. _____ a group hides the rows within the group to display only the row with subtotals.
    a. Sorting
    b. Expanding
    c. Collapsing
    d. Pivoting

Lab Exercises

true/false

Circle the correct answer to the following questions.

1. Subtotals can be added above each category in the worksheet.   True   False
2. A multilevel sort displays a subset of the records.   True   False
3. Changing the data in a PivotChart also changes the PivotTable.   True   False
4. Each column is a field, which is the smallest unit of information about a record.   True   False
5. Field names are entered in the first row of a table.   True   False
6. A hyperlink is a connection to a location in the current file or in another file, or to a Web site.   True   False
7. Changing data on a PivotChart does not affect the worksheet data.   True   False
8. A filter rearranges data according to the criteria you specify.   True   False
9. An absolute link includes the complete destination path location.   True   False
10. A bookmark establishes a link to a specific worksheet location.   True   False

fill-in

Complete the following statements by filling in the blanks with the correct key terms.

1. A(n) _____ is an interactive table that can be used to summarize and manipulate worksheet data.

2. _____ a table to display records in a specified order.

3. Apply a _____ to a table to display a subset of records.

4. A(n) _____ is a descriptive label used to identify the data stored in the field.

5. A(n) _____ jumps you to a new location in a worksheet, workbook, document, or Web page.

6. When a sort is done on more than one column or field, it is called a(n) _____ sort.

7. A filter is created by specifying _____ that you want records to meet in order to be displayed.

8. An organized collection of related information is called a(n) _____.

9. The group of related fields in a table is called a(n) _____.

10. A(n) _____ does not include the drive and folder location of the destination file as part of the address.

Hands-On Exercises

step-by-step

Lifestyle Fitness Club Employee Database ★

1. You work in human resources at the Lifestyle Fitness Club. One of your duties includes maintaining an Excel database of employee information. Your supervisor requested some payroll information that will be used to determine pay raises. You have been asked to provide an analysis of jobs and pay rates. Your completed analysis will be similar to the one shown here.

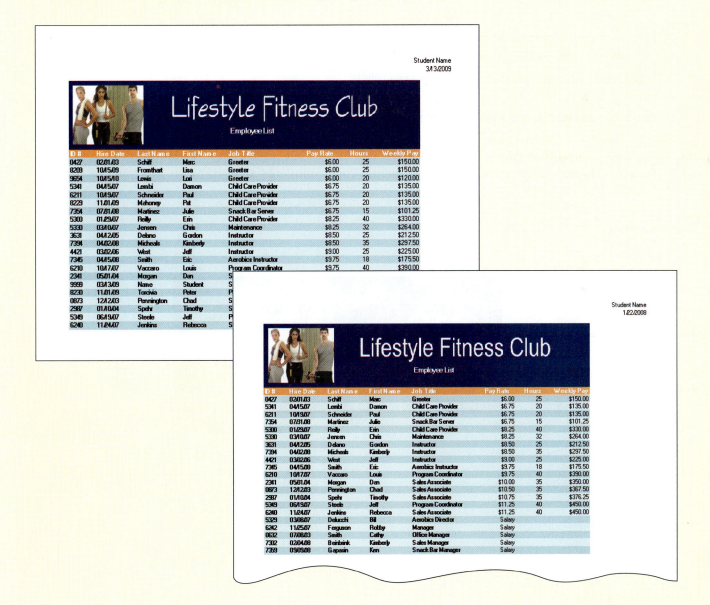

a. Open the file ex06_LFC Employee List.

b. Convert rows 6–32 to a table with headers. Apply a table style of your choice.

c. Enter a new record into the table. Use **your name** as the employee. Enter **9999** as your employee number, the **current date** as the hire date, **Sales Associate** as your job title, **10.00** as your pay rate, and **20** as your hours.

d. Edit the entry for Kimberly Kieken. Her last name is now **Beinbrink**.

e. Sort the table to display the records by pay rate first, job title second, and hire date third, all in ascending sort order.

f. Filter the table to exclude records with a pay rate of salary. Add your name and the current date to the header. Print the sorted table in landscape orientation, centered horizontally.

g. Remove the Pay Rate filter. Filter the complete table again to display only those records with a hire date before November 2008.

h. Print the filtered table in landscape orientation, centered horizontally with your name and the current date in the header.

i. Save your completed workbook as LFC Analysis.

Kodiak Construction Database ★★

2. The Kodiak Construction Company uses an Excel table to keep track of jobs for the year and the permit fees paid on them. They have asked you to do some analysis on the data so they can better see trends and make any needed adjustments. Your completed analysis of the table will be similar to the one shown here.

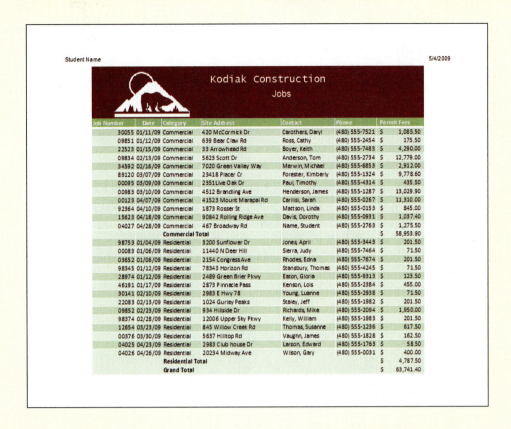

Kodiak Construction
Jobs

Job Number	Date	Category	Site Address	Contact	Phone	Permit Fees
30055	01/11/09	Commercial	420 McCormick Dr	Carothers, Daryl	(480) 555-7521	$ 1,085.50
09851	01/12/09	Commercial	639 Bear Claw Rd	Ross, Cathy	(480) 555-2454	$ 175.50
22523	01/15/09	Commercial	33 Arrowhead Rd	Boyer, Keith	(480) 555-7483	$ 4,290.00
09834	02/13/09	Commercial	5623 Scott Dr	Anderson, Tom	(480) 555-2734	$ 12,779.00
34592	02/16/09	Commercial	7020 Green Valley Way	Merwin, Michael	(480) 555-6853	$ 2,912.00
89120	03/07/09	Commercial	23418 Placer Cr	Forester, Kimberly	(480) 555-1324	$ 9,778.60
00095	03/09/09	Commercial	2351 Live Oak Dr	Paul, Timothy	(480) 555-4314	$ 435.50
00983	03/10/09	Commercial	4512 Brandling Ave	Henderson, James	(480) 555-1287	$ 13,029.90
00123	04/07/09	Commercial	41523 Mount Marapai Rd	Carilisi, Sarah	(480) 555-0267	$ 11,310.00
92364	04/10/09	Commercial	1873 Rosser St	Mattson, Linda	(480) 555-0153	$ 845.00
15623	04/18/09	Commercial	90842 Rolling Ridge Ave	Davis, Dorothy	(480) 555-0931	$ 1,037.40
04027	04/28/09	Commercial	467 Broadway Rd	Name, Student	(480) 555-2763	$ 1,275.50
		Commercial Total				$ 58,953.90
98753	01/04/09	Residential	3200 Sunflower Dr	Jones, April	(480) 555-3443	$ 201.50
00083	01/06/09	Residential	11440 N Deer Hill	Sierra, Judy	(480) 555-7464	$ 71.50
03652	01/06/09	Residential	2154 Congress Ave	Rhodes, Edna	(480) 555-7674	$ 201.50
98345	01/12/09	Residential	78343 Horizon Rd	Stansbury, Thomas	(480) 555-4245	$ 71.50
28974	01/12/09	Residential	2489 Green Brier Pkwy	Eaton, Gloria	(480) 555-9313	$ 123.50
46191	01/17/09	Residential	2873 Pinnacle Pass	Kenson, Lois	(480) 555-2384	$ 455.00
30141	02/10/09	Residential	2983 E Hwy 78	Young, Luanne	(480) 555-2938	$ 71.50
22083	02/13/09	Residential	1024 Gurley Peaks	Staley, Jeff	(480) 555-1982	$ 201.50
09852	02/23/09	Residential	934 Hillside Dr	Richards, Mike	(480) 555-2094	$ 1,950.00
98374	02/28/09	Residential	12006 Upper Sky Pkwy	Kelly, William	(480) 555-1983	$ 201.50
12654	03/23/09	Residential	845 Willow Creek Rd	Thomas, Susanne	(480) 555-1236	$ 617.50
00376	03/30/09	Residential	5637 Hilltop Rd	Vaughn, James	(480) 555-1828	$ 162.50
04025	04/23/09	Residential	2983 Club house Dr	Larson, Edward	(480) 555-1763	$ 58.50
04026	04/26/09	Residential	20234 Midway Ave	Wilson, Gary	(480) 555-0031	$ 400.00
		Residential Total				$ 4,787.50
		Grand Total				$ 63,741.40

a. Open the workbook file ex06_Kodiak Jobs.

b. Convert rows 5–28 to a table with headers. Apply a table style of your choice.

c. You have been given invoices for three new jobs. Enter the following three new records into the table.

Job Number	Date	Category	Site Address	Contact	Phone	Permit Fees
04025	04/23/09	Residential	2983 Club House Dr	Larson, Edward	(480) 555-1763	$58.50
04026	04/26/09	Residential	20234 Midway Ave	Wilson, Gary	(480) 555-0031	$400.00
04027	04/28/09	Commercial	467 Broadway Rd	enter your name	(480) 555-2763	$1,275.50

d. The Accounting department has requested a table of jobs whose permit fees were more than $1,000. Filter the table to display these records only.

e. Display a totals row that includes a count of the records in the category field and a sum of the Permit Fees.

f. Print the filtered table with your name and the date in the header, in landscape orientation, centered horizontally.

g. Remove the filter. Sort the table on Category. Use the Subtotal feature to group the data and calculate subtotals for the Permit Fees field.

h. Print all the fields of the table with your name and the current date in the header, in landscape orientation, centered horizontally on a single page. Adjust the top and bottom margins as needed.

i. Remove all subtotals. Convert the range back to a table. Save the workbook as Kodiak Jobs Update.

Wilson Electronics Employee Database ★★

3. Part of your job in the Personnel department at Wilson Electronics is to maintain the employee sales database. Recently, in order to boost sales, the company has been running a rewards program for the employees based on sales performance. In addition to the standard database maintenance, you have been asked to examine the employee database and determine the appropriate rewards. Your completed analysis and update of the database should be similar to that shown here.

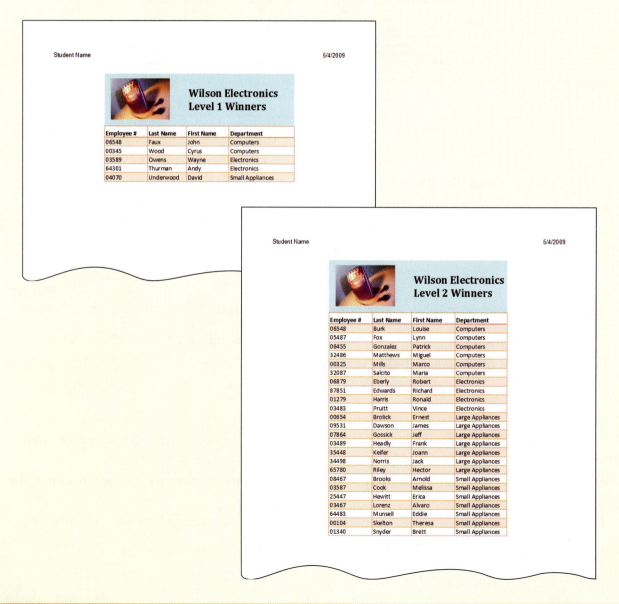

a. Open the file ex06_Wilson Employees.

b. Convert rows 5–44 to a table with headers. Apply a table style of your choice.

c. The employee data for several new employees has not been included in the database. Enter the records shown below.

Employee #	Last Name	First Name	Department	Total Sales
45925	Phillips	Jennifer	Audio	$752.98
08420	Schwartz	Grant	Small Appliances	$1,230.79
64301	Thurman	Andy	Electronics	$2,951.50
00345	Wood	Cyrus	Computers	$3,459.97

d. Sort the Last Name column alphabetically.

e. There have been some personnel changes since the last database update. Tony Patel and Eugene Radden are no longer with the company. Find and remove their records from the database. Joann Hancock recently got married. Find her record and change her last name to **Keifer**.

f. You have finished making the necessary changes to the database and can now begin your analysis. Use a multilevel sort to display the records first by department and then by last name.

g. Now that you have the data organized, you need to filter the records to determine which employees have earned rewards. There are two awards levels. Level 1 includes those who have sales from $2,000 up to sales less than $4,000. Use AutoFilter to determine these employees.

h. Copy this filtered sheet to a new sheet and name the new sheet **Bonus Level 1**. Replace the subtitle in cell C3 of this new sheet with **Level 1 Winners**.

i. Print this sheet without displaying the field Total Sales (adjust the width of column D as needed) with your name and the date in the header, in portrait orientation, centered horizontally.

j. Level 2 winners include those individuals with sales grater than or equal to $4,000. Create another sheet for these individuals. Name this sheet **Bonus Level 2** and edit the subtitle to **Level 2 Winners**.

k. Print this sheet without displaying the field Total Sales (adjust the width of column D as needed) with your name and the date in the header, in portrait orientation, centered horizontally.

l. Remove the filter from the Employee Sales sheet and save the workbook as Wilson Employee Rewards.

Adventure Travel Tours Clients ★ ★ ★

4. As a travel agent at Adventure Travel Tours, you maintain an Excel table of your clients. You have recently created several new tour packages and would like to inform your clients about them. Your table includes information about where customers have traveled in the six areas your new packages cover. You would like to target those who have already traveled in the new areas of your packages. You decide to create PivotTables to break down the volume of customers into more manageable segments. Some of your completed PivotTables will be similar to those shown here.

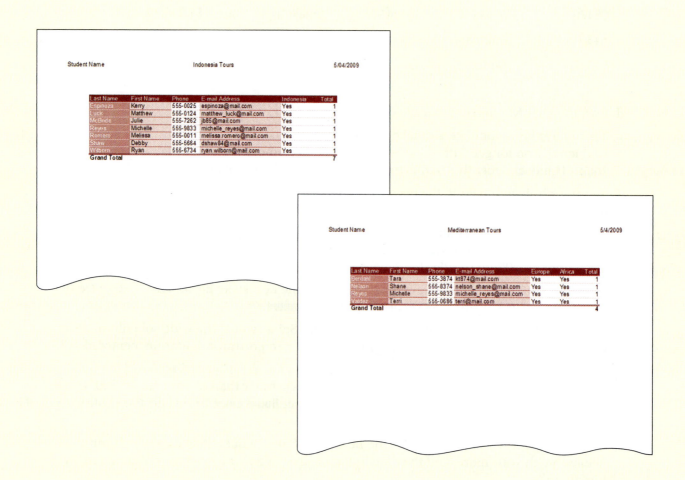

Student Name			Indonesia Tours		5/04/2009
Last Name	**First Name**	**Phone**	**E-mail Address**	**Indonesia**	**Total**
Espinoza	Kerry	555-0025	espinoza@mail.com	Yes	1
Luck	Matthew	555-0124	matthew_luck@mail.com	Yes	1
McBride	Julie	555-7262	jb85@mail.com	Yes	1
Reyes	Michelle	555-9833	michelle_reyes@mail.com	Yes	1
Romero	Melissa	555-0011	melissa.romero@mail.com	Yes	1
Shaw	Debby	555-5664	dshaw84@mail.com	Yes	1
Wilborn	Ryan	555-6734	ryan.wilborn@mail.com	Yes	1
Grand Total					7

Student Name			Mediterranean Tours			5/4/2009
Last Name	**First Name**	**Phone**	**E-mail Address**	**Europe**	**Africa**	**Total**
Berdahl	Tara	555-3874	kt874@mail.com	Yes	Yes	1
Nelson	Shane	555-8374	nelson_shane@mail.com	Yes	Yes	1
Reyes	Michelle	555-9833	michelle_reyes@mail.com	Yes	Yes	1
Valdez	Terri	555-0686	terri@mail.com	Yes	Yes	1
Grand Total						4

a. Open the file ex06_ATT Client Table.

b. Merge and center your name and the words **Client Table** under the company name at the top of the worksheet. Set the font to bold, size to 14, and color to light green.

c. One of your new packages is a tour of Indonesia. Insert a PivotTable in a new worksheet. Choose the Last Name, First Name, Phone, and E-mail Address fields for the report. Hide the plus/minus buttons. (Hint: Click [+/- Buttons] in the Show/Hide group on the PivotTable Tools Options tab.) Turn off subtotals. (Hint: Click [Subtotals] and then click [Do Not Show Subtotals] in the Layout group on the PivotTable Tools Design tab.)

d. Add the Indonesia field to the report and then drag it to the Report Filter box. Filter the PivotTable to display those clients who have traveled to Indonesia in the past. Add the Client Number field to the report. Change the field settings to Count. (Hint: Click [▾] in the values box and select value Field Settings from the drop-down list. Then select Count.)

e. Click [Report Layout] in the Layout group on the PivotTable Tools Design tab and choose Show in Tabular Form. Change the contents of cell F3 to **Total** and Autofit each of the columns.

f. Apply a PivotTable style of your choice. Insert your name, **Indonesia Tours**, and the current date in a header. Rename the sheet **Indonesia Tours** and move it to after the Client List sheet. Print the Indonesia Tours sheet in portrait orientation, centered horizontally.

g. You have another tour package that explores the Mediterranean and then ventures into Africa. Create a copy of the Indonesia sheet and move it to the end.

h. Change the title of this new sheet to **Mediterranean Tours**. Uncheck the Indonesia field and clear the filter. Choose the Europe and Africa fields. Filter the Europe and Africa fields to show those clients who traveled to Europe and Africa.

i. Change the title in the header to **Mediterranean Tours**. Print the Mediterranean Tour sheet in portrait orientation, centered horizontally. Save the workbook as ATT Client Table2.

Animal Rescue Foundation Donation Inventory ★ ★ ★

5. The Animal Rescue Foundation relies on donations to furnish foster homes with needed supplies. They have started to record the donation information in an Excel workbook so they can keep an inventory of goods. You have been asked to update and maintain this inventory and furnish the board of directors with an inventory status report identifying those items with dangerously low inventory levels. Your completed worksheets should be similar to those shown here.

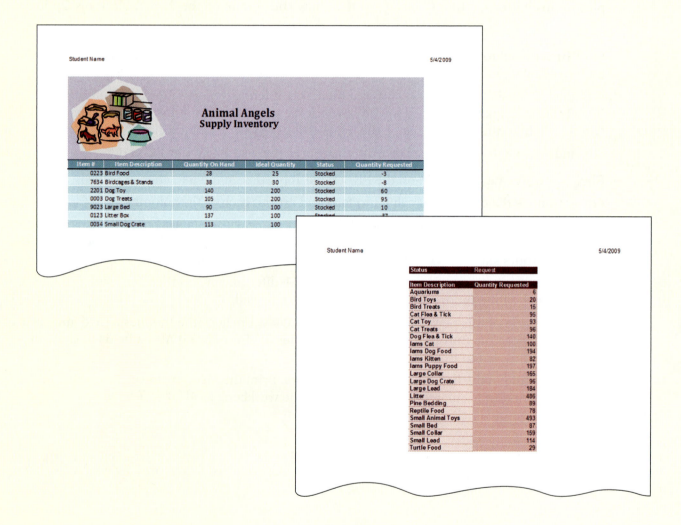

a. Open the file ex06_ARF Inventory.

b. The inventory consists of a table of items showing the quantity on hand and the desired quantity. You need to add a column that will identify whether a shortage or surplus exists for each item. Add a table column to the right of the Ideal Quantity column. Add the label **Status** in cell E9.

c. In order to indicate a need for an item, you will enter a formula that will calculate when an item's on-hand amount is less than half of the ideal amount, and display either "Stocked" or "Request" based on the determination. Enter the formula =**IF(C10<(D10/2), "Request", "Stocked")** in cell E10. If necessary, copy the formula to the rest of the cells in that column and center the text.

d. Add a table column to the right of the Status column and add the label **Quantity Requested** in cell F9. Adjust the formatting as needed. In cell F10, create a formula to calculate the difference between the Ideal Quantity and the Quantity On Hand.

e. Extend the background fill color in the title area to above the two new columns. Sort the table on Item Description.

f. You now have a table that displays which items need to be restocked and how many of each. Now you need to provide a table of low-stock items to the board. Create a PivotTable on a new worksheet that displays only the Item Description and Quantity Requested for those items with "Request" status. (Hint: Add the Item Description and Quantity Requested fields to the Row Labels box, add the Status field to the Report Filter box, and filter the list on "Request.") Hide the plus/minus buttons. (Hint: Click [Buttons] in the Show/Hide group on the PivotTable Tools Options tab.) Turn off subtotals. (Hint: Click [Subtotals] and then click [Do Not Show Subtotals] in the Layout group on the PivotTable Tools Design tab.) Turn off the grand total. (Hint: Click [Grand Totals] and then click [Off for Rows and Columns] in the Layout group on the PivotTable Tools Design tab.) Click [Report Layout] and choose Show in Tabular Form (in the Layout group on the PivotTable Tools Design tab.)

g. Apply a PivotTable style of your choice. Rename the sheet **Inventory Request** and move it after the Supply Inventory sheet. Add your name and the current date to a custom header and print the sheet in portrait orientation centered horizontally.

h. Save your completed workbook as **ARF Inventory**. Print the stocked items only of the supply inventory worksheet with your name and the date in the header, in landscape orientation, centered horizontally.

Lab Exercises

Bradford Suppliers Table ★

1. Bradford Building Supply needs you to create a table to hold supplier information such as company name, location, sales representative, and product category (such as wood, hardware, hand tools, electric tools, and so on). Enter at least 20 records in an Excel table with the appropriate fields. Format the table in an attractive manner. Sort the table by the supplier's state. Print the sorted table with your name and the date in the header, in portrait orientation, centered horizontally. Filter the table to display suppliers of the same category of product. Enter a total row to count the number of records. Print the filtered table with your name and the date in the header, in portrait orientation, centered horizontally. Save the workbook as Bradford Suppliers.

Kids Express Inventory Analysis ★★

2. The Kids Express Toy Company needs help with its inventory. Create a table that has 20 inventory records. The records should contain a product identification number, description, wholesale distributor, wholesale price, retail price, and quantity on hand. Format the table in an attractive manner. Sort the records by distributor. Print the sorted table with your name and the date in the header, in portrait orientation, centered horizontally. Filter the records to display a selected distributor and total the quantity on hand for that distributor. Print the filtered table with your name and the date in the header, in portrait orientation, centered horizontally. Filter the table next to find all items with a retail price higher than a selected value. Print the filtered table with your name and the date in the header, in portrait orientation, centered horizontally. Save the workbook as Toy Inventory.

Baseball League Roster ★★

3. You have a summer internship working in your town's community activities department. You have been asked to create a database of players enrolled in the summer baseball program in order to divide them into the various teams. Create a table that lists the players' names, addresses, phone numbers, ages, and positions. Format the table in an attractive manner. Enter 30 records in the table. Include your name as one of the records and a position of pitcher. Sort the database by player name, position, and age. Print the sorted table with your name and the date in the header, in portrait orientation, centered horizontally. Filter the table to show only pitchers. Print the filtered table with your name and the date in the header, in portrait orientation, centered horizontally. Save the workbook as Summer Baseball League.

Pet Sitting Customer Table ★★★

4. Wags and Purrs Pet Sitting wants to keep track of its customers with an Excel worksheet database. Create a table that includes customer ID number, home address with suite or apartment number, contact name, phone number, type of pet, and pet name. Format the table in an attractive manner.

Enter 15 records into the table. Enter your name as the contact for the first record. Sort the table by contact name. Create PivotTables for dogs and cats. Enter functions to display the count of pet type. Include appropriate labels. Print the PivotTables with your name and the date in the header, in portrait orientation, centered horizontally. Save the workbook as Pet Sitting Customers.

Changing Hands Inventory Planning ★★★

5. The Changing Hands Bookstore has a challenge keeping track of its book inventory. To demonstrate how they might use Excel to maintain their inventory records and how to use those records or analysis, you have agreed to develop a demonstration workbook. Create a table that includes at least 25 titles. Include an inventory number, title, author, ISBN number, number of copies on hand, ideal number of copies to have on hand, and status. Status will be either "order" or "hold." Whenever actual inventory is less than the ideal, the table will indicate "order." Otherwise, the table will indicate "hold." Name this sheet **Store Inventory**. Create a PivotTable on a new worksheet that displays only the title and ISBN number for those items with "order" status. Format this table appropriately and apply a PivotTable style of your choice. Name this sheet **Analysis**. Print the workbook with your name and the date in the header, in portrait orientation, centered horizontally. Save the Inventory worksheet as CHB Inventory.

Working Together 2: Importing Access Data, Sharing Workbooks, and Creating a Web Page

Case Study

Downtown Internet Café

On a weekly basis, you need to check the inventory on hand of certain items. If some items are over-stocked, such as a certain type of coffee beans, you run a special on them to lower inventory. On the other hand, if certain items are low, you reorder the item with the vendor. The inventory information is maintained in an Access database table. You plan to import the table into Office Excel 2007 to quickly analyze the inventory numbers. Then you will share the Excel workbook of this information with Evan so he can make changes directly in the worksheet.

The second project you are working on is to make the bonus dollar award information available to customers on the Café's Web site so they can check their award status. To do this, you will convert the monthly bonus awards worksheet to a Web page.

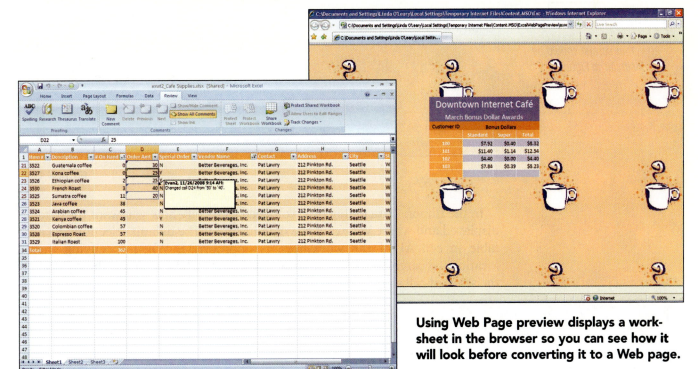

Using Web Page preview displays a worksheet in the browser so you can see how it will look before converting it to a Web page.

Importing data from Access allows you to analyze the table information using Excel.

Importing Data

The inventory information is maintained in an Access database table. You have found, however, that it is easier to use Excel to analyze the inventory numbers. To do this, you will import the information in the Access database table into Office Excel 2007. **Importing** converts external data that has been saved in another format into a format that can be used by the application. **External data** is data such as a database or text file that is stored outside the application, in this case Excel.

Importing Access Table Data to Excel

You want to import the data from the Vendors table of the Café Supplies Access database to an Excel workbook so you can more easily analyze the inventory-on-hand data.

1 ● Start Office Excel 2007.

● Open the Data tab.

● Click [From Access] in the Get External Data group.

● Select exwt2_Café Supplies.accdb from your data file location.

● Click [Open].

Your screen should be similar to Figure 1

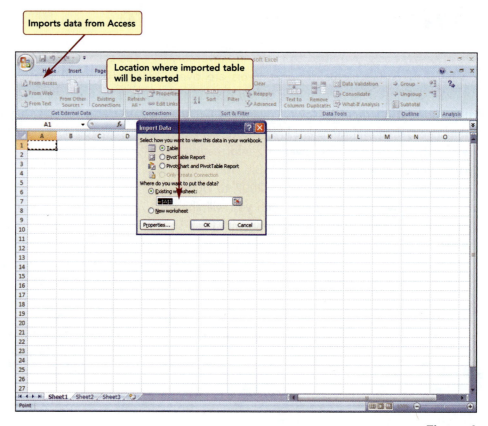

Imports data from Access

Location where imported table will be inserted

Figure 1

In the Import Data dialog box, you need to specify how you want the data displayed and where you want the data inserted. The default selections, as a table in cell A1 of the worksheet, is appropriate. When specifying the location, be careful to select an area that is empty below and to the right of the selected cell so that any existing data in the worksheet is not overwritten.

2 • If necessary, choose Table from the Import Data dialog box.

• Click **OK**.

Your screen should be similar to Figure 2

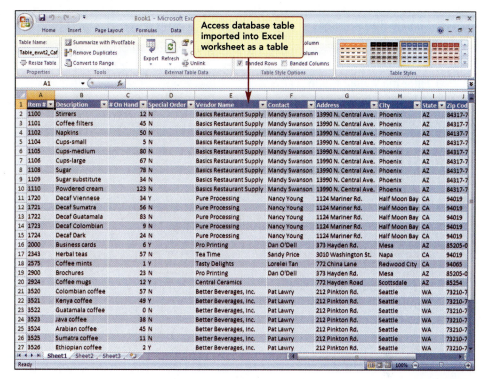

Access database table imported into Excel worksheet as a table

Figure 2

The database table is converted to an Excel table with the field names in the first row of the worksheet and the records beginning in row 2. The column heads and column widths are formatted as they appeared in the Access table.

Analyzing the Table

Now the data can be manipulated using Excel commands and features. You want to find out how much coffee is on hand to determine what coffee specials to offer next week. Because the data is set up as a table, you can filter the data and use Excel functions to calculate values.

1 ● **Change the table style to Medium 14.**

● **Filter the Vendor Name column to show only Better Beverages, Inc.**

● **Sort the # On Hand field in ascending sort order.**

● **Display a totals row and enter a SUM function to calculate the total coffee on hand.**

Your screen should be similar to Figure 3

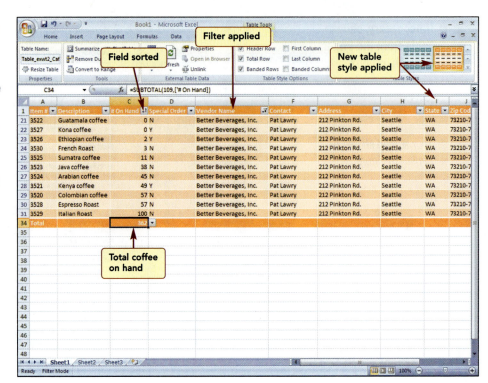

Figure 3

You can now easily see that the Italian Roast coffee quantity on hand is very high and decide to offer a special on that item. At the same time, you need to order several coffees whose quantity is very low.

Next, you will create a column to be used to specify the order amount so that Evan can confirm your ordering decisions.

2 ● **Right-click on any cell in the Special Order column.**

● **Choose Insert/Table Columns to the Left.**

● **Enter Order Amt as the new column label.**

● **Best fit all columns.**

Your screen should be similar to Figure 4

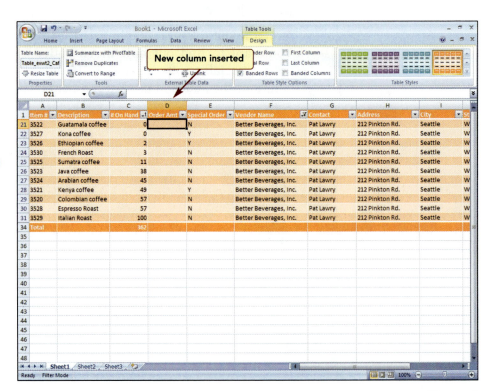

Figure 4

Working Together 2: Importing Access Data, Sharing Workbooks, and Creating a Web Page

www.mhhe.com/oleary

Collaborating on Workbook Data

Now you want to enter your suggested orders for Evan to review. Collaborating on documents, such as creating a travel brochure using Word 2007 or preparing a budget using Excel 2007, is frequently not a solo effort. One person is typically responsible for assembling the document, but several people may be involved in reviewing the content. Office 2007 includes many features that make it easy to collaborate or work with others to complete a project. These features include the capability to circulate documents for review; to insert, view, and edit comments; and to track and accept or reject proposed changes.

To make online reviewing of documents easier, you can track changes made to a document. **Tracked changes** identify any insertion, deletion, or formatting change that is made to the document. Typically a document is sent out for review by several people. When it is returned to the author, a document that has been edited using tracked changes can then be quickly reviewed to evaluate the suggested changes. As the author reviews tracked changes, each change can be accepted or rejected as appropriate.

To show Evan what order amounts you are suggesting, you will use the Track Changes feature. However, before you can turn on this feature, the table needs to be converted to a range.

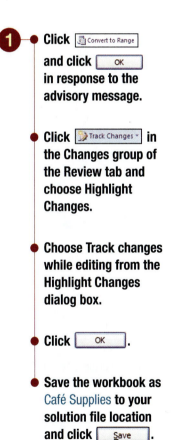

- **1** ● Click [Convert to Range] and click [OK] in response to the advisory message.

- ● Click [Track Changes ▾] in the Changes group of the Review tab and choose Highlight Changes.

- ● Choose Track changes while editing from the Highlight Changes dialog box.

- ● Click [OK].

- ● Save the workbook as Café Supplies to your solution file location and click [Save].

Your screen should be similar to Figure 5

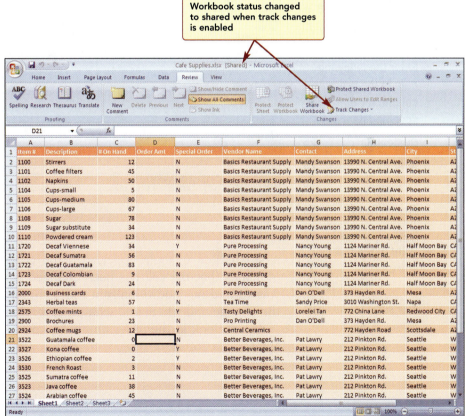

Workbook status changed to shared when track changes is enabled

Figure 5

When Track Changes is enabled, the workbook status is also changed to shared and [Shared] appears in the title bar. When a workbook status is shared, the workbook can be made available to others on a server and can be changed and manipulated simultaneously.

Now you want to enter the order amounts. As you do so, the worksheet will display markup of the tracked changes.

2 ● Click [Filter] in the Data tab to turn on filtering.

● Filter the Vendor Name column to show only Better Beverages, Inc.

● If necessary, sort the # On Hand field in ascending sort order.

● Enter the following data in the Order Amt column for the specified items:

Guatemala **25**

Kona **25**

Ethiopian **25**

French Roast **50**

● Point to the last cell entry.

Your screen should be similar to Figure 6

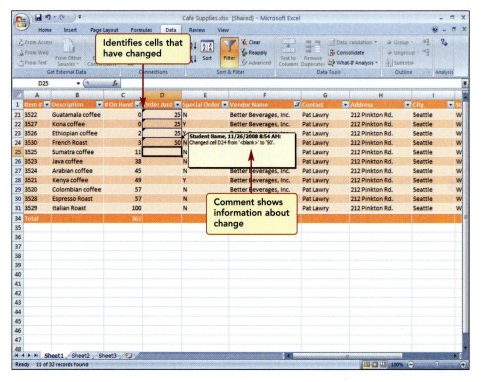

Identifies cells that have changed

Comment shows information about change

Figure 6

A small blue triangle appears in the corner of each changed cell that indicates that the cell has been changed since the Track Changes feature was turned on. Additionally, a cell comment appears showing who made the change and when, and what information was changed.

As you look at the order amounts, you decide to increase the order for Guatamala coffee.

3 ● **Change the Guatemala coffee order amount to 30.**

● **Click on the Guatemala order amount and point to the cell entry to see the updated comment.**

Your screen should be similar to Figure 7

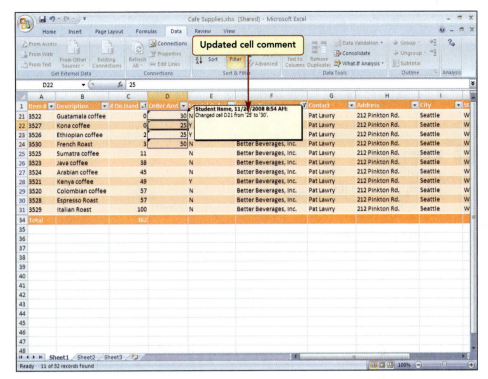

Figure 7

The comment displays updated information about the change made to the cell.

4 ● **Save and close the workbook.**

The workbook status is still saved with the shared workbook status enabled. Next, you will provide a copy of the workbook to Evan via e-mail containing your proposed orders for him to review.

Comparing and Merging Documents

While checking your e-mail for new messages, you see that Evan has returned the workbook file you sent to him to review. As you requested, he saved it using a new file name. When you receive changes from multiple reviewers for the same file, the easiest way to review them is to combine or merge the documents together. This way you can review the changes from a single document.

You will first open the original document you sent to Evan. Then you will merge the file containing his changes with the original. When merging workbook files, the files must be in the same folder and the shared workbook file name must be unique from the original file name. You may also need to add the Compare and Merge Workbooks command to the Quick Access Toolbar.

If the ⚪ Compare and Merge Workbooks icon is not displayed in the Quick Access Toolbar, follow step 1; otherwise, skip to step 2.

1 ● Open the Quick Access Toolbar menu and choose More Commands.

● Choose All Commands from the Choose commands from drop-down list.

● Select Compare and Merge Workbooks from the list, click [Add >>], and click [OK].

2 ● Open the file exwt2_Cafe Supplies from your data file location.

● If necessary, move the workbook file exwt2_Cafe Supplies Evan from your data file location to the same folder as the exwt2_Cafe Supplies workbook.

● Click [○] Compare and Merge Workbooks in the Quick Access Toolbar.

● If necessary, click [OK] to save the workbook.

● Select the file exwt2_Cafe Supplies Evan and click [OK].

● Click [Track Changes ▾] in the Review tab and choose Highlight changes.

● Open the When drop-down list, change the selection to All and click [OK].

● Point to the French Roast order amount to see the comment.

Your screen should be similar to Figure 8

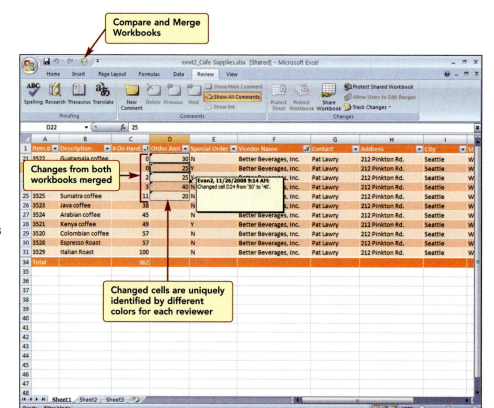

Figure 8

The changes from Evan's workbook have been combined with the original workbook. Excel automatically assigns unique colors to the tracked changes made by each reviewer. Evan made two changes to the worksheet: he revised the French Roast order amount and added an order for the Sumatra coffee.

Having Trouble?
The colors used to identify the tracked changes may be different on your screen.

Accepting and Rejecting Changes

Now you are ready to review the changes. In a document where many responses were received, it is helpful to use the Accept/Reject feature to quickly move from one tracked change to another and make a decision regarding whether to keep or reject the change.

1 ● Click **Track Changes ▾** and choose Accept/Reject Changes.

● Click **OK** to accept the default settings in the Select Changes to Accept or Reject dialog box.

● If necessary, move the dialog box to see the Order Amt column.

Your screen should be similar to Figure 9

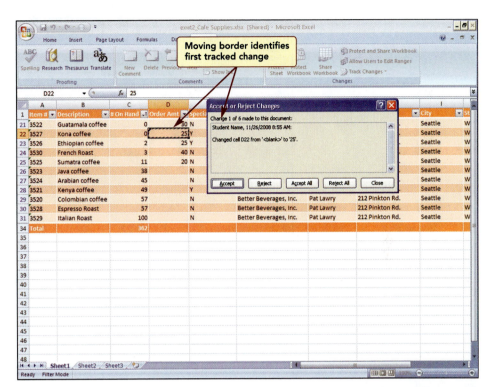

Figure 9

The first tracked change (based on the date and time associated with the change) made to the workbook is identified with a moving border. The dialog box displays the single change that was made in that cell. Since Evan did not change the Kona order, you will accept the change.

2  Click [Accept].

Your screen should be similar to Figure 10

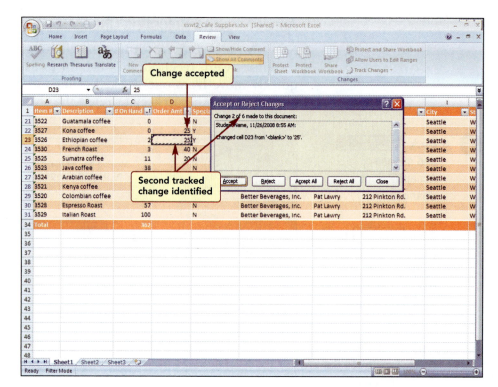

Figure 10

The number is accepted and the next tracked change is identified. If you do not want to accept a change, click [Reject] and the original value is reentered. You will try this feature by rejecting this change.

3 Click [Reject].

Your screen should be similar to Figure 11

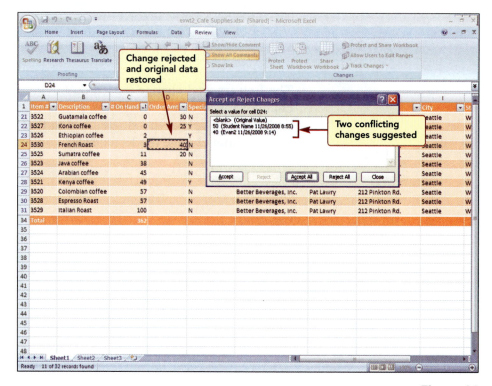

Figure 11

The order amount you entered is removed from the cell and the previous entry, a blank, is restored. The next tracked change shows both your order amount and Evan's. Frequently when reviewing tracked changes from multiple workbooks, there may be conflicting changes that need to be resolved. Selecting one of the suggested changes replaces the current entry in the worksheet. You need to select the change you want to use. In this case, you will accept Evan's change.

Select Evan's change from the list.

Click Accept.

Your screen should be similar to Figure 12

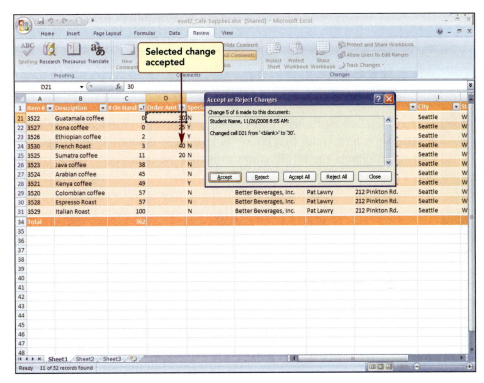

Figure 12

Because you know that all the remaining changes are correct, you will accept them all.

Click Accept All.

Enter 25 for the Ethiopian coffee order again.

Click Share Workbook **and clear the Allow changes option.**

Click OK **and then click** Yes.

Save the workbook as Coffee Orders.

Your screen should be similar to Figure 13

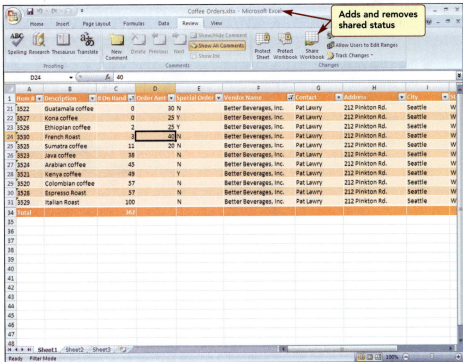

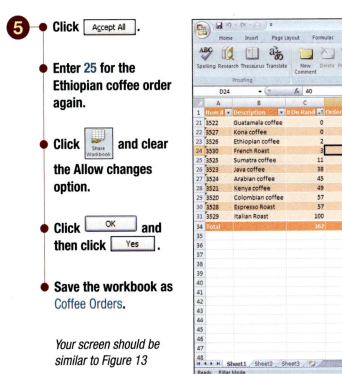

Figure 13

Creating a Web Page

The last project Evan has asked you to look into is to make the Bonus Dollar award information available to customers on the Café's Web site so they can check how much they earned each month. To do this, you will convert the Excel worksheet to a Web page.

Concept 1

Web Page

1 A **Web page** is a document that can be used on the World Wide Web (WWW) and displayed in a browser. A **browser** is a program that connects to remote computers and displays the Web pages you request. The browser interprets the HTML commands that are included in the Web page in order to know how to display the page contents. **HTML (Hypertext Markup Language)** is a programming language used to create Web pages. HTML commands control the display of information on a page, such as font colors and sizes, and how an item will be processed. HTML also allows users to click on hyperlinks and jump to other locations on the same page, other pages in the same site, or other sites and locations on the WWW.

Previewing the Web Page

Note: This section assumes that a Web browser is installed on your computer. The figures show the use of Microsoft Internet Explorer 7.

You made several changes to the worksheet that were needed before it could be used on the Web. First you converted all formulas to values and removed the weekly amounts and the Bonus Rate information. Then you removed the graphic and all cell comments. Finally, you removed and modified fill colors and text colors to match other pages on the Web site.

1 • **Close the Coffee Orders workbook.**

• **Open the workbook file** exwt2_March Bonus Dollars Web.

Your screen should be similar to Figure 14

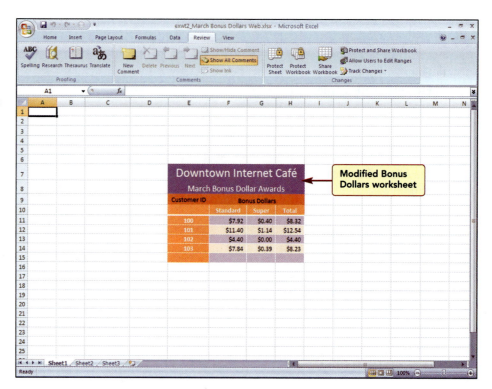

Figure 14

Working Together 2: Importing Access Data, Sharing Workbooks, and Creating a Web Page

www.mhhe.com/oleary

Now the only information that is included in the worksheet is the summary information for the month. Before you convert the worksheet to a Web page, you want to preview how it will look as a Web page first. To do this, you use the Web Page Preview command on the Quick Access Toolbar. If the [icon] Web Page Preview icon is not displayed in the Quick Access Toolbar, follow step 2; otherwise, skip to step 3.

2 ● Open the Quick Access Toolbar menu and choose More Commands.

● Choose All Commands from the Choose commands from drop-down list.

● Select Web Page Preview from the list, click [Add >>], and click [OK].

3 ● Click [icon] Web Page Preview in the Quick Access Toolbar.

● If necessary, maximize the browser window.

Your screen should be similar to Figure 15

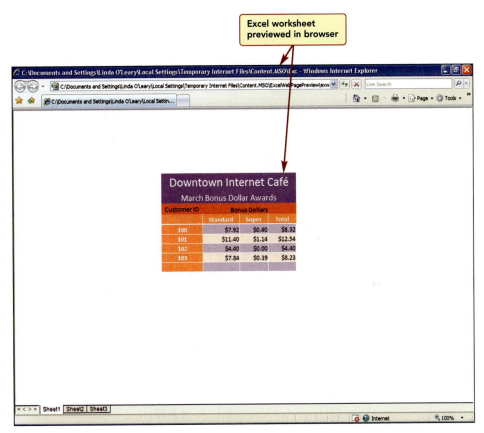

Excel worksheet previewed in browser

Figure 15

The browser on your system opens and displays the worksheet as it would appear when converted to a Web page. Although the information looks good, you decide to add a background image to make it more interesting.

Adding a Worksheet Background

A background is a graphic that is repeated to fill the viewing area of the sheet. You will add a graphic of a blue coffee cup with a yellow background behind the worksheet content. Adding a graphic to the background is similar to inserting a picture or clip art on the worksheet. Because background patterns are designed for viewing only, they do not print when you print the worksheet data.

1 • Close the browser application.

• Click 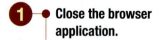 in the Page Setup group of the Page Layout tab.

• Select exwt2_Cup from your data file location.

• Click Insert.

• Preview the Web page in your browser.

Your screen should be similar to Figure 16

Background image added to worksheet makes Web page more interesting

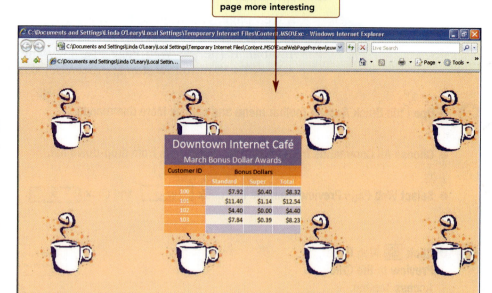

Figure 16

Additional Information

To remove a background, click  in the Page Setup group.

A repeated pattern of coffee cups appears behind the worksheet data.

Saving the Worksheet as a Web Page

You think the background makes the worksheet more interesting and decide to go ahead and save the worksheet as a Web page. You can save the entire workbook, a worksheet, or selected portions of a worksheet as a Web page. Additionally, the worksheet can be saved with or without interactivity. When it is saved with interactivity, users can manipulate data and formatting, switch between sheets, and change formulas while viewing the worksheet in the browser. When saved without interactivity, the data appears as it would in Excel, but users cannot change or interact with the data in the browser.

1 ● Close the browser.

● Click ⊞ Office Button and choose Save as.

● If necessary, select the location where you save your files.

● From the Save as Type list box, select Web Page (*.htm, *.html).

Your screen should be similar to Figure 17

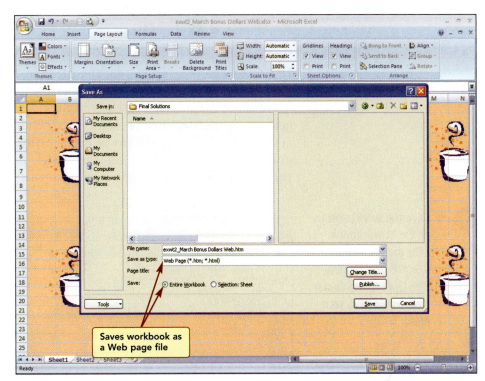

Figure 17

In the Save As dialog box, you enter a name for the Web page file and specify whether you want the entire workbook or the current selection saved as your Web page contents. To retain the background image, you need to save the entire workbook as a Web page. You also can add a title that will appear centered over the selection and add interactivity to your Web page. You will save the entire workbook without interactivity as the contents for the Web page. Because the worksheet already contains its own title, you will not add a title.

2 ● If necessary, choose Entire Workbook.

● Change the file name to March Bonus Dollars Web.

● Click [Save] and click [Yes] in response to the informational dialog box.

Making a Web Page Public

Now that you have created a Web page, in order for others to see it, you need to make it available on the Internet. The steps that you take to make your pages public depend on how you want to share them. There are two main avenues: on your local network or intranet for limited access by people within an organization or on the Internet for access by anyone using the WWW. To make pages available to other people on your network, save your Web pages to a network location. To make your Web pages available on the WWW, you need to either install Web server software on your computer or locate an Internet service provider that allocates space for Web pages.

Adding a Watermark

Finally, you want to save the workbook again as an Excel file and include a Draft watermark to show that the file is not final. A **watermark** is text or pictures that appear behind text in a document. Unlike Word 2007, where a watermark is inserted directly in the document page, in Excel 2007, the graphic is inserted in the worksheet header or footer area. It can then appear at the top or bottom of every printed page of the worksheet. The graphic can be sized to fill the entire page and appears behind the worksheet text, mimicking how a watermark appears in a text document.

1
- Save the workbook as an Excel workbook with the file name March Bonus Dollars Web Draft to the folder where you save your files.

- Click **Header & Footer** in the Text group of the Insert tab.

- Click **Picture** in the Header & Footer Elements group of the Header & Footer Tools Design tab.

- Select exwt2_Draft from your data file location and click **Insert**.

- Click **Format Picture** and increase the Height Scale to 200%.

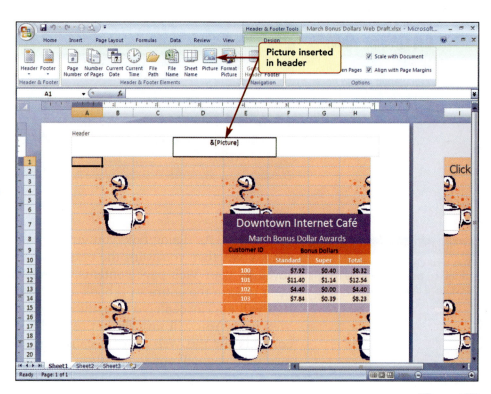

Figure 18

> **Additional Information**
> Both the height and width scales will change together because the Lock Aspect Ratio option is enabled.

- Click **OK**.

Your screen should be similar to Figure 18

A picture placeholder is displayed in the header until you make the worksheet area active again. You will add your name and date to the header and then preview and print the worksheet in landscape orientation.

2 ● Enter your name and the current date in the right header section.

● Click in the worksheet to make it the active area.

● Display the worksheet in Print Preview.

● Change the orientation to landscape.

Your screen should be similar to Figure 19

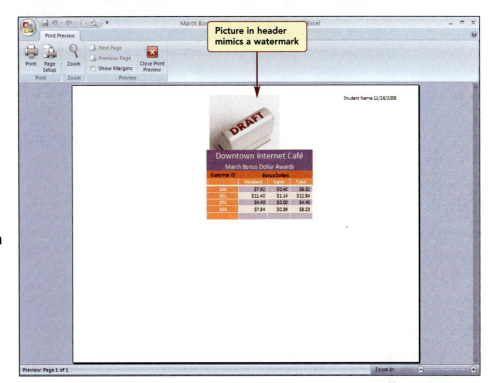

Picture in header mimics a watermark

Student Name 11/26/2008

Figure 19

Notice the preview of the March Bonus Dollars worksheet does not include the background image. This is because background images are designed for viewing only and will not print.

3 ● Print the worksheet.

● Save the workbook.

● Open the Quick Access Toolbar menu and choose More Commands.

● Click [Reset] to restore the Quick Access Toolbar to the default settings.

● Click [Yes] and then click [OK].

● Exit Excel.

Additional Information

You also can individually remove commands from the Quick Access Toolbar by selecting them and clicking [Remove].

WORKING TOGETHER 2

Importing Access Data, Sharing Workbooks, and Creating a Web Page

key terms

browser EXWT2.12	**HTML** EXWT2.12	**watermark** EXWT2.16
export EXWT2.2	**import** EXWT2.2	**Web page** EXWT2.12
external data EXWT2.2	**tracked changes** EXWT2.5	

MCAS skills

The Microsoft Certified Applications Specialist (MCAS) certification program is designed to measure your proficiency in performing basic tasks using the Office 2007 applications. Getting certified demonstrates that you have the skills and provides a valuable industry credential for employment. See Reference 2 Microsoft Certified Applications Specialist (MCAS) for a complete list of the skills that were covered in the Excel Working Together 2 lab.

command summary

Command	Shortcut	Action
Quick Access Toolbar		
Compare and Merge Workbooks		Merges multiple shared workbook changes
Web Page Preview		Displays the worksheet in the browser
Page Layout tab		
Page Setup group		
Background		Displays an image as the background on a worksheet
Delete Background		Removes the background image from the worksheet
Data tab		
Get External Data group		
From Access		Imports data from Access into a worksheet
Review tab		
Changes group		
Share Workbook		Changes workbook status to shared to allow multiple people to work on it at the same time
Track Changes /Highlight		Identifies all changes made to the worksheet, including insertions, deletions, and formatting changes
Track Changes /Accept/Reject Changes		Cycles through all tracked changes and allows you to make a decision regarding whether to keep or reject the change

Hands-On Exercises

step-by-step

Decorator's Resource Gallery ★

1. Alice works at the Decorator's Resource Gallery. An invoice for a garden-themed office has arrived. The decorator has requested that the prints all be by the same artist. Alice believes Bassett's prints will be ideal. She needs to find out the number of prints by Bassett in stock. To do this, she plans to use the information in the Access Gallery database file and analyze it using Excel.

   a. Open a blank workbook in Excel.

   b. Import the Vendor table from the exwt2_Decorator's Resource Gallery Access database file.

   c. Add the title **Decorator's Resource Gallery** on the first row and **Artist Inventory** on the next row above the table. Apply formatting of your choice.

   d. Filter the list to display the artist Bassett only.

   e. Appropriately size the columns.

   f. Add a totals row and total the Stock column.

   g. Save the workbook as Artist Inventory.

   h. Include your name and the date in a header. Print the filtered list.

   i. Remove the filter and close the file.

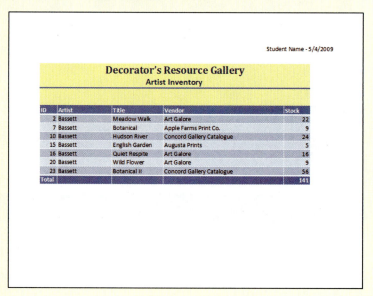

Employee Rewards Web Page ★★

2. The Wilson Electronics employee rewards program is running well now that you are tracking employee sales using the Excel table you recently set up. However, employees are always asking you for their latest sales information. Rather than have to look it up for each employee, you decide to share the information on the company's Web site. To do this, you will create a Web page using the information in the Wilson Employee Rewards workbook.

a. Open the workbook Wilson Employee Rewards (Lab 6, Step-by-Step exercise 3).

b. Sort the table by Employee Number.

c. Convert the table to a range.

d. Delete the graphic. Move the worksheet titles to the left into column A.

e. Delete the last name and first name columns.

f. Save the workbook as Employee Rewards Web Page.

g. Preview the worksheet as a Web page.

h. Add a page background using the exwt2_Awards image.

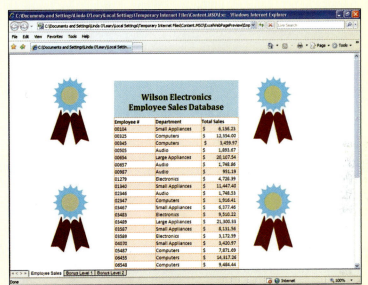

i. Make any improvements to the layout and design as you like.

j. Save the worksheet changes you have made both as an Excel workbook and with the same name as a Web page.

Command	Shortcut	Action
[Sort & Filter] /Custom Sort		Performs a multilevel sort on the selection
[Sort & Filter] /Filter		Turns AutoFilter on or off
[Sort & Filter] /Clear		Clears filters and sort from a range

Insert tab

Tables group

Command	Shortcut	Action
[PivotTable]		Inserts a PivotTable
[Table]		Converts a range of data into a table

Illustrations group

Command	Shortcut	Action
[Picture]		Inserts a picture from a file
[Clip Art]		Inserts selected graphic from Clip Organizer and Microsoft Clip Art and Media Web site
[SmartArt]		Inserts a SmartArt graphic to visually communicate information
[Shapes]		Creates selected shape

Charts group

Command	Shortcut	Action
[Column]		Inserts a column chart
[Pie]		Inserts a pie chart

Links group

Command	Shortcut	Action
[Hyperlink]		Inserts a new hyperlink or modifies selected hyperlink

Text group

Command	Shortcut	Action
[Text Box]		Creates a text box
[Header & Footer]		Edit the header or footer

Page Layout tab

Themes group

Command	Shortcut	Action
[Themes]		Applies selected theme to worksheet
[Themes] /Save Current Theme		Saves modified theme settings as a custom theme

Command	Shortcut	Action
Page Setup group		
Margins /Narrow		Changes margin settings
Margins /Custom Margins/Horizontally		Centers worksheet horizontally on page
Margins /Custom Margins/Vertically		Centers worksheet vertically on page
Orientation /Landscape		Changes page orientation to landscape
Orientation /Portrait		Changes page orientation to portrait
Print Area /Set Print Area		Sets print area to selected range
Breaks /Insert Page Break		Inserts a page break at cell pointer location
Breaks /Remove Page Break		Removes page break at cell pointer location
Breaks /Reset All Page Breaks		Restores automatic page break locations
Background		Displays an image as the background on a worksheet
Delete Background		Removes the background image from the worksheet
Scale to Fit group		
Width:		Scales worksheet horizontally to specified number of pages
Height:		Scales worksheet vertically to specified number of pages
Scale:		Scales worksheet both horizontally and vertically by entering a percentage
Sheet Options group Gridlines/Print		Displays/hides gridlines for printing
Formulas tab		
Function Library group		
fx Insert Function		Prompts you to select a function from a list and helps you enter the arguments correctly
Σ AutoSum ▾		Enters Sum, Average, Count, Minimum, or Maximum functions
Logical ▾		Create a logical function

Command	Shortcut	Action
Defined Names group		
Name Manager		Creates, edits, and deletes cell and range names
Define Name ▾		Creates a range name using text in cells
Use in Formula ▾		Places selected range name in formula bar or lists names in worksheet
Create from Selection		Automatically generates name from selected cells
Formula Auditing group		
Error Checking ▾		Checks worksheet for formula errors
Watch Window		Opens Watch Window toolbar
Show Formulas	Ctrl + `	Displays and hides worksheet formulas

Data tab

Command	Shortcut	Action
Get External Data group		
From Access		Imports data from Access into a worksheet
Sort & Filter group		
Sort Smallest to Largest		Sorts a column of data in ascending order
Sort		Sorts on multiple criteria
Filter		Turns AutoFilter on or off
Clear		Redisplays all records
Advanced		Specifies complex criteria to limit records in a query result
Data Tools group		
Text to Columns		Separates information contained in one cell into multiple columns
Remove Duplicates		Deletes duplicate rows
Data Validation ▾		Prevents invalid data from being entered into a cell
Data Validation ▾ /Settings/List		Creates a drop-down list
What-If Analysis ▾ /Scenario Manager		Starts Scenario Manager tool to create sets of data for what-if analysis
What-If Analysis ▾ /Goal Seek		Adjusts value in specified cell until a formula dependent on that cell reaches specified result
What-If Analysis ▾ /Data Table		Creates a data table based on specified input values and formulas

Command	Shortcut	Action
Outline group		
→ Group ▾		Ties range of cells so they can be collapsed or expanded
↓ Ungroup ▾		Ungroups range of cells
Subtotal		Displays totals for each change in category
Subtotal /Remove all		Removes subtotals from worksheet
Analysis group		
?→ Solver		Starts Solver tool to perform what-if analysis
Review tab		
Proofing group		
ABC Spelling	F7	Spell-checks worksheet
Research		Searches through reference materials
Thesaurus		Opens the thesaurus for the selected word in the Research task pane
Comments group		
New Comment		Inserts a new comment in selected cell
Edit Comment		Edits comment in selected cell
Delete		Deletes comment in selected cell
Show All Comments		Displays all comments
Changes group		
Protect Sheet		Prevents unwanted changes to the data in a worksheet
Unprotect Sheet		Removes worksheet protection
Protect Workbook		Prevents unwanted changes to the structure of the workbook
Unprotect Workbook		Removes workbook protection
Share Workbook		Changes workbook status to shared to allow multiple people to work on it at the same time
Track Changes ▾ /Highlight		Identifies all changes made to the worksheet, including insertions, deletions, and formatting changes

Command	Shortcut	Action
Track Changes ▾ /Accept/Reject Changes		Cycles through all tracked changes and allows you to make a decision regarding whether to keep or reject the change

View tab

Workbook Views group

Command	Shortcut	Action
Normal	▦	Changes worksheet view to Normal view
Page Layout	▣	Displays worksheet as it will appear when printed
Page Break Preview	▥	Displays where pages will break when a worksheet is printed

Show/Hide group

Command	Shortcut	Action
☑ Gridlines		Turns on/off display of gridlines
☑ Headings		Turns on/off display of row and column headings

Zoom group

Command	Shortcut	Action
Zoom		Changes magnification of window

Window group

Command	Shortcut	Action
New Window		Displays a new window
Arrange All		Arranges open windows vertically, horizontally, tiled, or cascaded
Freeze Panes ▾ /Freeze Panes		Keeps rows and columns visible while the rest of the worksheet scrolls
Freeze Panes ▾ /Unfreeze Panes		Unfreezes window panes
Split		Divides window into multiple resizeable panes at active cell or removes split
Hide		Hides current workbook
Unhide		Unhides selected workbook

Picture Tools Format tab

Picture Styles group

Command	Shortcut	Action
▾ More		Opens the Picture Styles gallery to apply a combination of shapes, borders, and effects to picture
Picture Shape ▾		Changes shape of drawing, preserving all formatting
Picture Border ▾		Specifies color, width, and line style for outline of shape
Picture Effects ▾		Adds glow, shadow, and other effects to pictures

Command	Shortcut	Action
Chart Tools Design tab		
Type group		
Change Chart Type		Changes selected chart to a different type of chart
Data group		
Switch Row/Column		Swaps the data over the axis
Select Data		Changes the data range included in chart
Chart Layouts group		
More		Opens the Chart Layouts gallery to apply selected combination of titles, data labels, and legends to a chart
Chart Styles group		
More		Opens the Chart Styles gallery to apply selected combination of colors, backgrounds, and outlines to chart
Location group		
Move Chart		Moves chart to another sheet in the workbook
Chart Tools Layout tab		
Labels group		
Chart Title		Adds, removes, or positions the chart title
Axis Titles		Adds, removes, or positions the axis titles
Legend		Adds, removes, or positions the chart legend
Data Labels		Adds, removes, or positions the data labels
Background group		
Chart Wall		Formats chart walls
Chart Tools Format tab		
Current Selection group		
Chart Area /Chart Elements		Selects an element on the chart
Format Selection		Opens Format dialog box for selected element
Shape Styles group		
More		Opens Shape Styles gallery to apply selected combination of shape outline, fill, and effects
Shape Fill		Adds selected fill to shape
Shape Outline		Specified color, weight, and type of outline
Shape Effects		Adds selected effect to shape

Command	Shortcut	Action
Print Preview tab		
Print group		
Print	Ctrl + P	Prints selection, worksheets, or workbook
Page Setup		Opens the Page Setup dialog box
Page Setup /Landscape		Changes page orientation to landscape
Page Setup /Fit To		Scales the worksheet to fit specified number of pages
Page Setup /Header/Footer tab		Adds header or footer to worksheet
Page Setup /Margins tab/Horizontally		Horizontally aligns worksheet between margins
Zoom group		
Zoom		Magnifies worksheet
Preview group		
Next Page		Displays next page
Previous Page		Displays previous page
Close Print Preview		Closes Print Preview and returns to editing document
SmartArt Tools Design tab		
Create Graphics group		
Add Shape		Adds a shape to an existing SmartArt graphic shape
SmartArt Styles group		
Change Colors		Changes colors of selected SmartArt graphic
More		Opens SmartArt Styles gallery to select overall visual style for SmartArt graphic
Reset group		
Reset Graphic		Restores SmartArt graphic to original settings
Drawing Tools Format tab		
Insert Shapes group		
More		Opens Shapes gallery to insert ready-made shapes

Command	Shortcut	Action
Shape Styles group		
⬚ More		Opens Shapes Styles gallery to apply a visual style to a shape or line
Arrange group		
Rotate ▾		Rotates selected shape

Table Tools Design tab

Command	Shortcut	Action
Tools group		
Convert to Range		Converts table to normal range
Table Style Options group		
☑ Banded Rows		Formats even rows differently from odd rows
☐ First Column		Displays formatting for first column of the table
☑ Header Row		Formats the top row of the table
☐ Total Row		Adds a totals row below the last row of table data
Table Styles group		
⬚ More		Opens Table Styles gallery to apply a predefined format and colors to a table

PivotTable Tools Options tab

Command	Shortcut	Action
Tools group		
PivotChart		Inserts a chart based on the PivotTable data

Glossary of Key Terms

3-D reference   A reference to the same cell or range on multiple sheets in the same workbook.

absolute link   An address with the complete destination path location.

absolute reference   A cell or range reference in a formula whose location remains the same (absolute) when copied. Indicated by a $ character entered before the column letter and row number.

active cell   The cell displaying the cell selector that will be affected by the next entry or procedure.

active sheet   A sheet that contains the cell selector and that will be affected by the next action.

active workbook   The workbook that contains the cell selector and that will be affected by the next action.

adjacent range   A rectangular block of adjoining cells.

adjustable cell   In Solver, the cell or cells whose values will be changed in order to attain the value set in the target cell.

alignment   The vertical or horizontal placement and orientation of an entry in a cell.

antonym   Words with opposite meaning, such as "cheerful" and "sad."

area chart   A chart that shows trends by emphasizing the area under the curve.

argument   The data used in a function on which the calculation is performed.

AutoCorrect   Makes some basic assumptions about the text you are typing and, based on these assumptions, automatically corrects the entry.

AutoFill   Feature that logically repeats and extends a series.

AutoFit   Feature that automatically adjusts the column width or row height to fit the contents.

AutoRecover   Feature that periodically saves your open files to a temporary recovery file as a protection against accidental loss of work.

bar chart   Displays data as evenly spaced bars.

bookmark   Establishes a link to a specific worksheet location.

browser   A program that connects to remote computers and displays Web pages.

bubble chart   A chart that compares sets of three values, similar to a scatter chart. The third value determines the size of bubble markers.

cascade   The window arrangement that displays one workbook window on top of another, cascading down from the top of the screen.

category axis   Another name for the X axis of a chart.

category-axis title   A label that describes the X axis.

cell   The space created by the intersection of a vertical column and a horizontal row.

cell reference   The column letter and row number of a cell.

cell selector   The heavy border surrounding a cell in the worksheet that identifies the active cell.

cell style   A named combination of formats that can be applied to a selection.

character effect   A modification to the characters, such as bold or italics, that enhances the appearance of text.

chart   A visual representation of data in a worksheet.

chart gridlines   Lines extending from the axis lines across the plot area that make it easier to read and evaluate the chart data.

chart layout   A predefined set of chart elements that can be quickly applied to a chart.

chart object   One type of graphic object that is created using charting features included in Excel 2003. A chart object can be inserted into a worksheet or into a special chart sheet.

chart style   A predefined set of chart formats that can be quickly applied to a chart.

chart title   Appears at the top of a chart and is used to describe the contents of the chart.

clip art   A collection of graphics that is usually bundled with a software application.

column   A vertical block of cells one cell wide in the worksheet.

column chart   A chart that represents data as evenly spaced bars.

column letter   The border of letters across the top of the worksheet that identifies the columns in the worksheet.

column-oriented   In a data table, the orientation of the data down a column as opposed to across a row (row-oriented).

comment   Notes attached to cells that can be used to clarify cell meaning, provide documentation, or ask a question.

conditional formatting   Formatting that changes the appearance of a range based on a condition that you specify.

constant   A value that does not change unless you change it directly by typing in another entry.

copy area   The cell or cells containing the data to be copied; also called the source.

criteria   A set of limiting conditions that you want records to meet in order to be displayed.

custom dictionary   An additional dictionary you create to supplement the main dictionary.

custom templates   Specialized templates designed for very specific applications.

data label   A label for a data point or bar that shows the values being plotted on a chart.

data marker   Represents a data series on a chart. It can be a symbol, color, or pattern, depending upon the type of chart.

data series   The numbers to be charted.

data table   A range of cells that is used to quickly calculate multiple what-if versions in one operation and to show the results of all variations together in the worksheet.

default   Initial program settings.

defined name   A defined name represents a cell, range of cells, formula, or constant value.

destination   The cell or range of cells that receives the data from the copy area or source; also called the paste area.

destination cell   The cell that receives the linked data.

destination file   A document in which a linked object is inserted.

destination workbook   The linked workbook that receives the data.

digital signature   A digital signature is an electronic encryption–based stamp of authentication that confirms the document originated from the signer and has not been changed.

doughnut chart   Like a pie chart, this chart shows the relationship of each value in a data series to the series as a whole. Each data series is displayed as a segment of a ring. It can contain more than one data series.

drawing object   An object consisting of shapes such as lines and boxes that can be created using features on the Drawing toolbar.

embedded chart   A chart that is inserted into another file.

embedded object   Information inserted into a destination file of another application that becomes part of this file but can be edited within the destination file using the server application.

explode   To separate a slice of a pie chart slightly from the other slices in the pie.

export   Save data in another format so that it can be used in an application other than the application in which it was created.

external data   Data stored outside the application in which it was created.

external reference   A connection between the information in the destination file and the source file in a linked object. Also called a link. The external reference contains references to the location of the source file and the selection within the document that is linked to the destination file.

external reference formula   A formula that creates a link between workbooks.

field   A single category of data in a list, the values of which appear in a column of a worksheet.

field name   A label used to identify the data stored in a field.

file property   A setting that is associated with a file, such as the date or author.

fill handle   A small black square located in the lower-right corner of the selection that is used to create a series or copy to adjacent cells with a mouse.

filter   A restriction placed on records in a list to temporarily isolate a subset of records.

Find and Replace   Feature that quickly finds and automatically replaces specific information with new information.

font   A set of characters with a specific design; also called a typeface.

footer   A line (or several lines) of text that appears at the bottom of each page just above the bottom margin.

form   A formatted worksheet that is designed to be completed by filling in data in the blank spaces.

format   Settings such as font, color, patterns, and so forth, that affect the display of entries in a worksheet.

Format Painter   A feature that applies the formats associated with the current selection to new selections.

formula   An entry that performs a calculation.

formula bar   The bar near the top of the Excel window that displays the cell contents.

freeze panes   To fix in place on the screen specified rows or columns or both when scrolling.

function   A prewritten formula that performs certain types of calculations automatically.

global workbook level   A defined name scope can be limited to the worksheet in which it was created, called the local worksheet level, or to the entire workbook, or a global workbook level. The default scope is workbook level.

Goal Seek   Tool used to find the value needed in one cell to attain a result you want in another cell.

gradient   A gradual progression of colors and shades that can be from one color to another or from one shade to another of the same color.

graphic   A nontext element or object such as a drawing or picture that can be added to a document.

group   Two or more objects that behave as a single object when moved or sized.

grouping and outlining   Organizes data in a worksheet by showing and hiding different levels of detail for groups of related data. Grouping data has two functions: to collapse and expand rows or columns.

header   A line (or several lines) of text that appears at the top of each page just below the top margin.

header row   The first row in a table containing the field names.

heading   Row and column entries that are used to create the structure of the worksheet and describe other worksheet entries.

HLOOKUP function   A horizontal or row-based lookup function.

horizontal   The window arrangement that displays one open workbook window above the other.

HTML (Hypertext Markup Language)   A programming language whose commands are interpreted by the browser software you are using and that controls how the information on a Web page is displayed.

hyperlink   A special type of link that provides a shortcut or jump to another location in the same or a different workbook, to a document in a different application, to a Web site, or to an e-mail address.

IF function   A function that checks that certain conditions are met and takes action based on the check.

import   Convert external data that has been saved in another format into a format that can be used by the application.

input cell   A cell in which a list of values is substituted to see the resulting effect on the related formulas. Input values can be listed down a row or across a column.

keyword   A word or phrase descriptive of a type of graphic.

landscape   The orientation of the printed document so that it prints sideways across the length of the page.

legend   A brief description of the symbols that represent the data ranges in a chart.

line chart   A chart that represents data as a set of points along a line.

link   A connection between the information in the destination file and the source file in a linked object. Also called an external reference.

The link contains references to the location of the source file and the selection within the document that is linked to the destination file.

linked object   Information created in a source file from one application and inserted into a destination file of another application while maintaining a link between files.

list   A list is a series of rows that contain related data but are not defined as a table.

live link   A linked object that automatically reflects in the destination document any changes made in the source document when the destination document is opened.

Live Preview   An Office 2007 feature that shows how a selected formatting effect will appear in the document if it is chosen.

local workbook level   A defined name scope can be limited to the worksheet in which it was created, called the local worksheet level.

logical operator   A symbol used in formulas that compares values in two or more cells.

lookup function   Lookup functions permit you to use worksheet tables as sources of information for formulas and calculations in other parts of the worksheet.

main dictionary   The dictionary included with Office 2007.

margin   The blank space around the edge of the paper.

merged cell   A cell made up of several selected cells combined into one.

mixed reference   A cell address that is part absolute and part relative.

multilevel sort   A sort on more than one column or field.

name   A description of a cell or range that can be used in place of cell or range references.

Name box   The area located on the left side of the formula bar that provides information about the selected item such as the reference of the active cell.

nested function   A second argument in a function that is enclosed within its own set of parentheses.

nonadjacent range   Cells or ranges that are not adjacent but are included in the same selection.

NOW function   A function that displays the current date and time and automatically updates the date and time when the workbook is opened.

number   A cell entry that contains any of the digits 0 to 9 and any of the special characters + = ( ) , . / $ % ? =.

number format   Affects how numbers look onscreen and when printed.

object   An element that can be added to a workbook and that can be selected, sized, and moved.

one-variable data table   A data table that contains one or more formulas, with each formula referring to one input cell.

operand   A value on which a numeric formula performs a calculation.

operator   Specifies the type of calculation to be performed.

order of precedence   Order in which calculations are performed; can be overridden by the use of parentheses.

orientation   The direction the output is printed on a page; portrait or landscape.

page break   The location where one printed page ends and another starts.

pane   A division of the worksheet window, either horizontal or vertical, through which different areas of the worksheet can be viewed at the same time.

password   A secret code that prevents unauthorized users from turning off protection in a workbook or opening a workbook.

paste area   The cells or range of cells that receive the data from the copy area or source; also called the destination.

picture   An illustration such as a scanned photograph.

pie chart   A chart that compares parts of the whole. Each value in the data range is a slice of the pie (circle).

PivotChart   An interactive chart that can be used to view and rearrange data in a PivotTable.

PivotTable   An interactive, crosstabulated table that summarizes and analyzes worksheet data.

placeholder   A graphic element that is designed to contain specific types of information.

plot area   The area of the chart bounded by the axes.

PMT function   Calculates a periodic payment on a loan.

point   Measure used for height of type; one point equals 1/72 inch.

portrait   The orientation of the printed document so that it prints across the width of the page.

principal   The amount of the loan.

print area   The area that is highlighted and where a page break shows where the selected range will print on a page.

protection   A feature that prevents users from making changes to data and formats.

radar chart   A chart that compares the aggregate values of a number of data series. It displays changes in values relative to a center point.

range   A selection consisting of two or more cells in a worksheet.

range reference   Identifies the cells in a range.

recalculation   A feature that, when a number in a referenced cell in a formula changes, automatically recomputes all formulas that are dependent on the changed value.

record   A row of a table that contains all the information about one person, thing, or place.

relative link   Workbook link that will locate the destination workbook file relative to the location of the current workbook file.

relative reference   A cell or range reference that automatically adjusts to the new location in the worksheet when the formula is copied.

row   A horizontal block of cells one cell high in the worksheet.

row number   The border of numbers along the left side of the worksheet that identifies the rows in the worksheet.

row-oriented   In a data table, the orientation of the data across a row as opposed to down a column (column-oriented).

sans serif   A font, such as Arial or Helvetica, that does not have a flair at the base of each letter.

scenario   A named set of input values that you can substitute in a worksheet to see the effects of a possible alternative course of action.

scope   All cell or range names have a scope, or restriction to a location within which the name is recognized without qualification: local worksheet level or global workbook level.

selection rectangle   An outline border that surrounds an object when it is selected.

serial value   The way Excel stores dates, with each day numbered from the beginning of the 20th century.

series formula   A formula that links a chart object to the source worksheet.

serif   A font, such as Times New Roman, that has a flair at the base of each letter.

sheet   Used to display different types of information in Excel, including charts. The primary sheets are worksheets and chart sheets.

sheet name   A descriptive name that you create to help identify the contents of the sheet.

sheet reference   Used in references to other worksheets. Consists of the name of the sheet enclosed in quotes and separated from the cell reference by an exclamation point.

sheet tab   On the bottom of the workbook window, the tabs where the sheet names appear.

size   The height and width of a character in a font, commonly measured in points, abbreviated pt.

sizing handle   Box used to size a selected object.

SmartArt graphic   SmartArt graphics are used to create a visual representation of textual information.

SmartArt style   Combinations of different formatting options such as edges, gradients, line styles, shadows, and three-dimensional effects that can be applied to a SmartArt graphic.

Solver   A tool that is used to perform what-if analysis to determine the effects of changing values in two or more cells, called the adjustable cells, on another cell, called the target cell.

sort   To arrange data in a specified sequence: alphabetically, numerically, or by date.

source   The cell or range of cells containing the data to be copied.

source cell   In Solver, the cell or range of cells containing the data you want to copy.

source file   The document that stores the data for the linked object.

source program   The program in which an object was created.

source workbook   The workbook file that supplies the linked data.

spelling checker   Feature that locates misspelled words and proposes corrections.

split window   A feature that allows you to divide a worksheet window into sections.

spreadsheet   A rectangular grid of rows and columns used to enter data.

stack   The order in which objects are added in layers to the worksheet.

stacked-column chart   A chart that displays the data values as columns stacked upon each other.

stock chart   A chart that shows fluctuations in values, such as stock prices and temperature.

surface chart   A chart that shows trends in values across two dimensions in a continuous curve.

synonym   Words with similar meanings, such as "cheerful" and "happy."

syntax   Rules of structure for entering functions.

tab scroll buttons   Located to the left of the sheet tabs, they are used to scroll sheet tabs right or left.

table   An organized collection of related information that is entered into a series of worksheet rows and columns.

table name   A table name represents the range of cells that stores an Excel data table.

table range   The area containing the records in a table is the table range.

target cell   In Solver, the cell you set to the value that you want to attain.

template   A file that contains settings that are used as the basis for a new file you are creating.

text   A cell entry that contains text, numbers, or any other special characters.

text box   A graphic object that is a container for text or graphics.

theme   A predefined set of formatting choices, consisting of different combinations of colors, fonts, and effects, that can be applied to an entire workbook in one step.

thesaurus   A reference tool that provides synonyms, antonyms, and related words for a selected word or phrase.

tiled   A window arrangement in which open workbook windows are displayed one after the other in succession, across and down the screen.

Track Changes   A feature that identifies any insertion, deletion, or formatting change that is made to the document. Typically, a document is sent out for review by several people.

two-variable data table   A data table that uses only one formula that refers to two different input cells, one column-oriented and one row-oriented. The purpose of this table is to show the resulting effect on the formula when the values in both of these cells are changed.

typeface   A set of characters with a specific design; also called a font.

Uniform Resource Locator (URL)   An address that specifies the location of the destination document.

validation   Validation ensures that the data entered in a cell is acceptable or valid by placing restrictions on the data that can be entered.

value axis   Y axis of a chart that usually contains numerical values.

value-axis title   A label that describes the values on the Y axis.

variable   The resulting value of a formula that changes if the data it depends on changes.

vertical   The window arrangement in which open workbook windows are displayed side by side.

VLOOKUP function   A vertical or columnar lookup function.

watermark   Text or pictures that appear behind text in a document.

Web page   A document that can be used on the World Wide Web (WWW) and displayed in a browser.

what-if analysis   A technique used to evaluate what effect changing one or more values in formulas has on other values in the worksheet.

window arrangement   A feature that displays open workbooks in separate windows on the screen, making it easy to view and work with information in different workbooks.

workbook   The file in which you work and store sheets created in Excel 2007.

workbook window   A window that displays an open workbook file.

worksheet   Similar to a financial spreadsheet in that it is a rectangular grid of rows and columns used to enter data.

X axis   The bottom boundary line of a chart.

XY (scatter) chart   A chart that shows the relationship among the numeric values in several data series, or plots two groups of numbers as one series of XY coordinates.

Y axis   The left boundary line of a chart.

Z axis   The left boundary line of a 3-D chart.

Appendix

1. CREATING AND MANIPULATING DATA

1.2 ENSURE DATA INTEGRITY

Data integrity can be ensured by adding restrictions that are applied to cell entries. These restrictions can be to limit the entry to entries from a list, dates and times within a timeframe, text length, whole numbers within limits, decimal values within limits, and calculations based on values in another cell. These restrictions are all entered using the [Data Validation] command.

One of the most common data restrictions is to limit whole numbers that can be entered in a cell to a range of values, to values less than, greater than, and equal to a specified value. To restrict whole numbers to specified values, follow these steps:

- Click [Data Validation] in the Data Tools group of the Data tab.
- Choose Data Validation and, if necessary, open the Settings tab.
- Choose Whole Number from the Allow drop-down list.
- In the Data box, select the type of restriction that you want.
- Enter the minimum, maximum, or specific value to allow.
- Click [OK].

Additional Information
For example, to specify that values less than x can be entered, select less than.

Additional Information
You also can enter a formula that returns a number value.

1.3 MODIFY CELL CONTENTS AND FORMATS

MORE PASTE SPECIAL OPTIONS

While copying or cutting data, you can further specify how the data is pasted into a worksheet using features in the [Paste] drop-down menu or the Paste Special dialog box. Two convenient features are Transpose and Paste Values.

The Transpose option changes columns of copied data to rows, and vice versa when you select this check box. Follow these steps to transpose data:

- Copy or cut the rows and columns of data you want transposed.
- Move to the location in the worksheet where you want the data pasted.
- Open the [Paste] drop-down menu in the Home tab and choose Transpose.

The Paste Values option pastes only the values of the copied data as displayed in the cells, without the underlying formulas. Follow these steps to copy values only:

- Copy or cut the rows and columns of data whose values you want copied.
- Move to the location in the worksheet where you want the data pasted.
- Open the [Paste] drop-down menu in the Home tab and choose Paste Values.

Another Method
You also can choose Transpose from the Paste Special dialog box.

Another Method
You also can choose Values or Values and number formats from the Paste Special dialog box.

1.5 MANAGE WORKSHEETS

COPY WORKSHEETS BETWEEN WORKBOOKS

Sometimes you will want to copy (or move) an entire worksheet to another workbook. The process is similar to copying between sheets in the same workbook. To copy (or move) worksheets between workbooks, follow these steps:

Another Method

You also could click [Format] in the Cells group of the Home tab and choose Move or Copy Sheet.

- Open the workbook file you want to copy to.
- In the workbook that contains the sheets that you want to move or copy, select the sheets.
- Right-click the selected sheet tab and choose Move or Copy on the shortcut menu.
- In the To book list of the Move or Copy dialog box, select the workbook to which you want to move or copy the selected sheets or select New book to move or copy the selected sheets to a new workbook.
- In the Before sheet list, select the sheet before which you want to insert the moved or copied sheets.
- Select the Create a copy check box. (Do not select this box if you want to move the sheet).

The entire sheet is copied (or moved) to the specified location in the selected workbook.

2. FORMATTING DATA AND CONTENT

2.2 INSERT AND MODIFY ROWS AND COLUMNS

INSERT MULTIPLE ROWS OR COLUMNS SIMULTANEOUSLY

You also can insert multiple rows or multiple columns simultaneously by selecting the same number of rows or columns as you want to insert before using the command. For example, to insert three new rows, you need to select three rows. To insert three columns, select three columns. You also can insert nonadjacent rows and columns by holding down Ctrl while you make your selections.

To insert multiple rows simultaneously, follow these steps:

- Select the same number of rows as you want to insert above the row where you want them inserted.
- Open the [Insert ▾] drop-down menu in the Cells group of the Home tab.
- Choose Insert Sheet Rows.

All rows below the selection are shifted down and the number of rows you specified in the selection are inserted.

To insert multiple columns simultaneously, follow these steps:

- Select the same number of columns as you want to insert immediately to the right of where you want to insert columns.
- Open the [Insert ▾] drop-down menu in the Cells group of the Home tab.
- Choose Insert Sheet Columns.

The specified number of columns are inserted and all columns to the right of the selection are shifted to the right.

2.3 FORMAT CELLS AND CELL CONTENT

CREATE CUSTOM CELL FORMATS

You also can create a custom cell format by following these steps:

- Choose Custom from the Category list in the Number tab of the Format Cells dialog box.
- Select the format code that you want to customize from the list.
- Edit the number format code using the existing code as a starting point.

Once a custom format is created, you can apply the custom format by selecting it from the Custom list.

MERGE AND SPLIT CELLS

If needed, you can split a merged cell back into individual cells. To do this, follow these steps:

- Select the merged cell.
- Click [icon] Merge in the Alignment group of the Home tab.
- Choose Unmerge Cells.

The contents of the merged cell are displayed in the upper-leftmost cell of the unmerged cells.

REMOVE HYPERLINKS

Many times, you will not want a Web address to be formatted as a hyperlink. There are several ways to remove hyperlinks. These methods are demonstrated below.

- Right-click on the hyperlink and choose Remove Hyperlink on the shortcut menu.

or

- Select the cell containing the hyperlink and click [Hyperlink icon] in the Insert tab.
- Click [Remove Link] in the Edit Hyperlink dialog box.

3. CREATING AND MODIFYING FORMULAS

3.1 REFERENCE DATA IN FORMULAS

MIXED CELL REFERENCES

A mixed cell reference stops the adjustment of only that part of the cell reference that is absolute when the formula is copied.

To create a mixed cell reference, follow these steps:

- Move to the cell containing the formula with the cell reference you want to change.
- Change to Edit mode.
- Type a $ in front of the column letter or row number of the cell reference that you want to stop adjusting.
- Press [←Enter].

NAMED RANGES

Modify a Named Range

You can easily modify the range of an existing named range by adding or deleting cells, rows, or columns. To add a column to an existing named range, follow these steps:

- Click [Name Manager icon] in the Defined Names group of the Formulas tab.
- Select the name you want to modify in the Name Manager dialog box.
- Click [Edit...] and click in the Refers to box to see the existing range.
- Type in the new range or drag in the worksheet to specify the new range.
- Click [OK].

> **Another Method**
> You also could select the new range in the worksheet and enter the existing name in the Name box. The new range replaces the previously defined range.

Delete a Named Range

If you no longer need a named range in a worksheet, it can be easily removed following these steps:

- Click [Name Manager] in the Defined Names group of the Formulas tab.
- Select the name (or names) you want to delete in the Name Manager dialog box.
- Click [Delete ▾] or press [Delete].
- Click [OK] to confirm the deletion.

Additional Information

To select more than one name in a contiguous group, click and drag the names, or hold down [⇧Shift] while selecting each name in the group. For noncontiguous names, press [Ctrl] while selecting each name.

3.2 SUMMARIZE DATA USING A FORMULA

The COUNT and COUNTA functions are entered just like the Sum, Average, Min, and Max functions. The COUNT function returns the number of cells in a range that contain numbers and the COUNTA function counts the number of cells in a range that are not empty. For complete information about the range and criteria arguments, refer to the Office Help.

Follow these steps to use the COUNT function with the sample data shown here:

	A
1	CONTAINER
2	10
3	12
4	X
5	15
6	18
7	22
8	23

- Enter **=COUNT(A1:A8)**.

The calculated count is 6. The number of cells containing a numeric entry is displayed in the cell.

Follow these steps to use the COUNTA function with the sample data shown here:

	A
1	CONTAINER
2	10
3	12
4	X
5	
6	
7	22
8	23

- Enter **=COUNTA(A1:A8)**.

The calculated count is 6. The number of cells containing any type of entry is displayed in the cell.

3.4 CONDITIONALLY SUMMARIZE DATA USING A FORMULA

The SUMIF, SUMIFS, COUNTIF, COUNTIFS, AVERAGEIFS, and AVERAGEIF functions all perform calculations on cells within a range that meet multiple criteria. For complete information about the range and criteria arguments, refer to the Office Help.

SUMIF AND SUMIFS

SUMIF adds the cells specified by a given criterion.

> **Syntax:** SUMIF(range,criteria,sum_range)

Using the data shown below to find the sum of oranges whose container value is greater than 15, follow these steps:

	A CONTAINER	B ORANGES	C PEACHES
1			
2	10	220	420
3	12	235	435
4	14	250	450
5	15	275	475
6	18	300	500
7	22	325	525
8	23	335	535

- Enter **=SUMIF(A2:A8,">=15")**.
The calculated sum is 78.
- Enter **=SUMIF(A2:A8,">=15",B2:C8)**.
The calculated sum is 1235.

SUMIFS adds the cells in a range that meet multiple criteria.

> **Syntax:** SUMIFS(sum_range,criteria_range1,criteria1,criteria_range2, criteria2 . . .)

Note: The order of arguments is different between SUMIFS and SUMIF. In particular, the sum_range argument is the first argument in SUMIFS, but it is the third argument in SUMIF.

Using the data shown below to find the sum of oranges whose container value is greater than 15, follow these steps:

	A CONTAINER	B ORANGES	C PEACHES
1			
2	10	220	420
3	12	235	435
4	14	250	450
5	15	275	475
6	18	300	500
7	22	325	525
8	23	335	535

- Enter **=SUMIFS(A2:A8,">=15")**.
The calculated sum is 78.
- Enter **=SUMIFS(A2:A8,">=15",B2:C8)**.
The calculated sum is 1235.

COUNTIF AND COUNTIFS

COUNTIF counts the number of cells within a range that meet multiple criteria.

Syntax: COUNTIF(range1,criteria1,range2,criteria2 . . .)

Using the data shown below to find the count of container items whose value is greater than 15, follow these steps:

	A	B
1	**CONTAINER**	**ORANGES**
2	10	220
3	12	235
4	14	250
5	15	275
6	18	300
7	22	325
8	23	335

- Enter **=COUNTIF(A2:A8,">=15")**.

The calculated count is 4.

Note: Each cell in a range is counted only if all of the corresponding criteria specified are true for that cell. If the criterion is an empty cell, COUNTIFS treats it as a 0 value.

COUNTIFS counts the number of cells within a range that meet multiple criteria.

Syntax: COUNTIFS(range1,criteria1,range2,criteria2 . . .)

Using the data shown below to find the count of container items whose value is greater than 15 and oranges whose value is greater than 300, follow these steps:

	A	B
1	**CONTAINER**	**ORANGES**
2	10	220
3	12	235
4	14	250
5	15	275
6	18	300
7	22	325
8	23	335

- Enter **=COUNTIFS(A11:A17,">=15", B11:B17,">=300")**.

The calculated count is 3.

AVERAGEIF AND AVERAGEIFS

AVERAGEIF returns the average (arithmetic mean) of all the cells in a range that meet a given criterion.

Syntax: AVERAGEIF(range,criteria,average_range)

Note: Average_range is the actual set of cells to average. If omitted, range is used.

Using the data shown below to find the average of container items whose value is greater than 15 and the average of oranges whose container value is greater than 15, follow these steps:

	A	B	C
1	CONTAINER	ORANGES	PEACHES
2	10	220	420
3	12	235	435
4	14	250	450
5	15	275	475
6	18	300	500
7	22	325	525
8	23	335	535

- Enter **=AVERAGEIF(A11:A17,">=15")**.
The average is 19.5.
- Enter **=AVERAGEIF(A11:A17,">=15", B11:C17)**.
The average is 308.75.

AVERAGEIFS returns the average (arithmetic mean) of all cells that meet multiple criteria.

Syntax: AVERAGEIFS(average_range,criteria_range1,criteria1,criteria_range2,criteria2 . . .)

Using the data shown below to find the average of oranges whose container value is greater than 15 and oranges whose value is greater than 300, follow these steps:

	A	B
1	CONTAINER	ORANGES
2	10	220
3	12	235
4	14	250
5	15	275
6	18	300
7	22	325
8	23	335

- Enter **=AVERAGEIFS(B2:B8,A2:A8,">=15", B2:B8,">=300")**.
The average is 320.

3.5 LOOKUP DATA USING A FORMULA

VLOOKUP

In Lab 5, you used a VLOOKUP (false) function. A VLOOKUP (true) function is entered in the same manner, except the range_lookup values in the first column of table_array must be placed in ascending order. The default range_lookup is TRUE, which returns the closest match. If TRUE is omitted, an approximate match is returned if an exact match is not found (the next largest value that is less than lookup_value is returned. If FALSE, HLOOKUP will find an exact match. If one is not found, the error value #N/A is returned.

VLOOKUP (true)

Using the data shown below to find the result for the sample value closest to 19, follow these steps:

1	A SAMPLE	B RESULT
2	10	220
3	12	235
4	14	250
5	15	275
6	18	300
7	22	325
8	23	335

- Set up a table that contains the values in the first column with the values in ascending order.
- Enter the function =VLOOKUP(19,A2:B8,2,TRUE) in any cell.

The value 300 is returned.

HLOOKUP

The HLOOKUP function is used when your comparison values are located in a row across the top of a table of data, and you want to look down a specified number of rows. The HLOOKUP function searches for a value in the top row of a table. It then returns a value in a cell you designate from the same column in a row that you list in the table.

Syntax: HLOOKUP(lookup_value,table_array,row_index_num,range_lookup)

If range_lookup is TRUE, the values in the first row of table_array must be placed in ascending order. The default range_lookup is TRUE, which returns the closest match. To obtain an exact match, use FALSE.

Using the data shown below, follow these steps:

	A	B	C
1	CONTAINER	ORANGES	PEACHES
2	10	220	420
3	12	235	435
4	14	250	450
5	15	275	475
6	18	300	500
7	22	325	525
8	23	335	535

HLOOKUP (true)

- Set up a table that contains the values in a row across the top of a table that you want to look up in ascending order.
- Enter the function =HLOOKUP("P",A1:C8,3,TRUE) in any cell.

The function looks up P in row 1 and because there is no exact match finds the next-closest value (O) and returns the value of 250 from row 3 of column B.

HLOOKUP (false)

Using the data shown above, follow these steps:

- Set up a table that contains the values in a row across the top of a table that you want to look up in ascending order.
- Enter the function =HLOOKUP("Oranges",A1:C8,3,FALSE) in any cell.

The function looks up Oranges in row 1 and returns the value of 250 from row 3 of the same column.

- Enter the function =HLOOKUP("O",A1:C8,3,FALSE) in any cell.

The function looks up O in row 1, and because there is no exact match, returns N/A.

3.6 USE CONDITIONAL LOGIC IN A FORMULA

In addition to the IF logical function used in Lab 5, you also can create conditional formulas using AND, OR, and NOT. In addition, the IFERROR function returns a value you specify if a formula evaluates to an error; otherwise, it returns the result of the formula. Several examples of conditioned formulas that use the data shown below are provided on the next page.

	A
1	DATA
2	10
3	12
4	14
5	15
6	18
7	22
8	23

FUNCTION	RETURNS	DESCRIPTION
=AND(A3>A4,A3<A2)	False	Is 12 greater than 14 and less than 10
=OR(A5>A4,A5<A3)	True	Is 15 greater than 14 or less than 12
=NOT(A5+A2=25)	False	Is 15 plus 10 not equal to 25
=IFERROR(A5+A2,"Error")	25	Returns value of formula
=IFERROR(A5+A1,"Error")	Error	Displays error because cell A1 contains a text entry that cannot be used in a formula

FORMAT OR MODIFY TEXT USING FORMULAS

Excel includes a category of functions that perform operations on text rather than values. Three functions from this category will change the case of characters. A fourth will replace text with other text.

PROPER capitalizes the first letter in a text string and any other letters in text that follow any character other than a letter. It converts all other letters to lowercase letters.

Syntax: =PROPER(text)

Note: Text is text enclosed in quotation marks, a formula that returns text, or a reference to a cell containing the text you want to partially capitalize.

UPPER converts text to uppercase.

Syntax: =UPPER(text)

Note: Text is the text you want converted to uppercase. Text can be a reference or text string.

LOWER converts all uppercase letters in a text string to lowercase.

Syntax: =LOWER(text)

Note: Text is the text you want to convert to lowercase. LOWER does not change characters in text that are not letters.

SUBSTITUTE substitutes new_text for old_text in a text string. Use SUBSTITUTE when you want to replace specific text in a text string.

Syntax: =SUBSTITUTE(text,old_text,new_text,instance_num)

Note: Text is the text or the reference to a cell containing text for which you want to substitute characters. Old_text is the text you want to replace. New_text is the text you want to replace old_text with. Instance_num specifies which occurrence of old_text you want to replace with new_text. If you specify instance_num, only that instance of old_text is replaced. Otherwise, every occurrence of old_text in text is changed to new_text.

Note: Use the REPLACE function when you want to replace any text that occurs in a specific location in a text string.

These functions are demonstrated using the following data:

	A
1	FRUIT
2	apples
3	Bananas
4	ORANGES
5	peaches

FUNCTION	RETURNS
=PROPER(A2)	Apples
=UPPER(A2)	APPLES
=LOWER(A4)	oranges
=SUBSTITITE(A5,"peaches","Grapes")	Grapes

4. PRESENTING DATA VISUALLY

4.3 APPLY CONDITIONAL FORMATTING

ALLOW MORE THAN ONE RULE TO BE TRUE

Sometimes you may want to apply several conditional formatting cell rules to the same range of cells. When this occurs, the rules are evaluated in order of precedence by how they are listed in the Rules Manager dialog box. A rule higher in the list has greater precedence than a rule lower in the list. By default, new rules are always added to the top of the list and therefore have a higher precedence, but you can change the order of precedence by using the Move Up and Move Down arrows in the dialog box.

Sometimes when multiple rules are applied to the same range, a conflict can occur if more than one conditional formatting rule evaluates to true. For example, if one rule formats a cell with a bold font and another rule formats the same cell with a red color, the cell is formatted with both a bold font and a red color. Because there is no conflict between the two formats, both rules are applied. In contrast, if one rule sets a cell font color to red and another rule sets a cell font color to green, a conflict occurs and only one can apply. The rule that is applied is the one that is higher in precedence.

To change the order of precedence of cell rules, follow these steps:

- Click [Conditional Formatting] in the Styles group of the Home tab and choose Manage Rules.

- Choose This Worksheet from the Show formatting rules for list.

- Select the rule that you want to move up or down in the list.

- Use the [↓] Move Up and [↑] Move Down arrows to move the selected rule above or below the rule in the list that you want to have a lower or higher precedence.

- Click [Apply].

APPLY TOP AND BOTTOM RULES, COLOR SCALES, AND ICON SETS CONDITIONAL FORMATS

Top and Bottom Rules

You can find the highest and lowest values in a range of cells based on a cutoff value that you specify. For example, you can find the top five highest values or the bottom 10 percent.

To apply a Top and Bottom cell rule, follow these steps:

- Select a range of cells.

- Click [Conditional Formatting] in the Styles group of the Home tab and choose Top/Bottom Rules.

- Select the command that you want, such as Top 10 items or Bottom 10%.

- Enter the values that you want to use for the rules.

- Select a format you want to apply.

- Click [OK].

The cells in the range meeting the conditions are formatted using the selected format.

Color Scales

Color scales apply a gradation of two colors to cells in a range to help you understand data distribution and variation. The shade of the color represents higher or lower values. For example, in a green and red color scale, you can specify higher-value cells have a more green color and lower-value cells have a more red color.

To apply a color scale, follow these steps:

- Select a range of cells.
- Click [Conditional Formatting] in the Styles group of the Home tab and choose Color Scales.
- Select a two-color scale format.

A two-color gradient color scale is applied to all cells in the range.

Icon Sets

Icon sets are used to annotate and classify data into three to five categories separated by a threshold value. Each icon represents a range of values. For example, in the 3 Arrows icon set, the red up arrow represents higher values, the yellow sideways arrow represents middle values, and the green down arrow represents lower values.

To apply an icon set to a range of cells, follow these steps:

- Select a range of cells.
- Click [Conditional Formatting] in the Styles group of the Home tab and choose Icon Sets.
- Select the icon set you want to use.

The icon set you selected is applied to the range of cells.

5. COLLABORATING AND SECURING DATA

5.1 MANAGE CHANGES TO WORKBOOKS

DELETE COMMENTS

Comments can be quickly removed from a worksheet in several ways.

- Click the cell that contains the comment that you want to delete.
- Click [Delete] in the Comments group of the Review tab.

or

- Click [Show/Hide Comment] in the Comments group of the Review tab.
- Double-click the comment text box, and then press Delete.

or

- Right-click on the comment and choose Delete Comment from the shortcut menu.

5.2 PROTECT AND SHARE WORKBOOKS

ALLOW USERS TO EDIT RANGES

In addition to unlocking cells in a protected worksheet, you can allow users to edit specific ranges. You also can restrict permission to edit ranges to specific users in a protected worksheet.

Follow these steps to use these features:

- Select the worksheet that you want to protect.
- Click [Allow Users to Edit Ranges] in the Changes group of the Review tab.

- Click [New...] to add a new editable range.
- In the Title box, type the name for the range that you want to unlock.
- In the Refers to cells box, type an equal sign (=), and then type the reference of the range that you want to unlock.
- Type a password in the Range password box.

Restricting permission to edit the ranges requires that your computer must be running Microsoft Windows XP or later, and your computer must be on a domain.

- To add access permissions, click [Permissions...] and then click [Add >>].
- Type the names of the users that you want to be able to edit the ranges in the Enter the object names to select (examples) box.
- Click [OK].
- To specify the type of permission for the user that you selected, in the Permissions box, select or clear the Allow or Deny check boxes, and then click Apply.
- Click [OK] two times.
- If necessary, type the password that you specified.
- In the Allow Users to Edit Ranges dialog box, click [Protect Sheet...].

- In the Password to unprotect sheet box, type a password, click [OK], and then retype the password to confirm it.

5.4 SAVE WORKBOOKS

SAVE WORKBOOKS FOR USE IN A PREVIOUS VERSION OF EXCEL

In Excel 2007, you can open files created in previous versions of Excel, from Excel 95 to Excel 2007. You also can create a file in Excel 2007 format and then save it as the previous version (.xls). If any 2007 features are not compatible with the previous version, the Compatibility Checker tells you so and any new features will not work. The Compatibility Checker runs automatically; however, you can run it manually if you want to find out what features in a workbook you are creating will be incompatible. The Compatibility Checker identifies those features that are incompatible and the number of occurrences in the workbook.

Follow these steps to run the Compatibility Checker:

- Click 🔵 Office Button and select Prepare.
- Choose Run Compatibility Checker.
- Click [OK] after looking at the features that were identified and the number of occurrences.

Once you have identified those features that are incompatible, you may want to save the workbook in the format of a previous version of Excel. To do this, follow these steps:

- Click 🔵 Office Button and select Save As.
- Enter the location and file name in the Save As dialog box.
- Select Excel 97-2003 workbook (*.xls) from the Save as Type drop-down menu.
- Click [Save].

If you open a file in Excel 2007 that was created in an earlier version, the automatic option in the Save As dialog box is to save it as the previous version type (.xls).

SAVE A WORKBOOK USING THE CORRECT FORMAT

Excel 2007 uses a new file format based on the Office Open XML formats (XML is short for Extensible Markup Language). This new format makes your workbooks safer by separating files that contain scripts or macros, which makes it easier to identify and block unwanted code or macros that could be dangerous to your computer. It also makes file sizes smaller and makes files less susceptible to damage. The file extensions shown in the table below are used to identify the different types of Excel workbook files.

FILE EXTENSION	DESCRIPTION
.xlsx	Excel 2007 workbook without macros or code
.xlsm	Excel 2007 workbook that could contain macros or code
.xltx	Excel 2007 template without macros or code
.xltm	Excel 2007 template that could contain macros or code
.xps	Excel 2007 shared workbook (see note below)
.xls	Excel 97-2003 workbook

SAVE A WORKBOOK IN OTHER FORMATS

There are also many other formats in which a workbook file can be saved. For example, there are many situations where it is useful to save your file in a fixed-layout format that is easy to share and print and hard to modify. Two common types of file that do this are Portable Document Format (PDF) file format and XML Paper Specification (XPS) file types.

To save a workbook as either a PDF or XPS file, you must have first installed the free add-in to save or export this type of file. Then, to view a PDF file, you must have a PDF reader installed on your computer. One reader is the Acrobat Reader, available from Adobe Systems. To view a file in XPS format, you need a viewer. You or the recipient of your file can download a free viewer from Downloads on Microsoft Office Online.

Follow these steps to learn several different ways to save an Excel workbook as any of these types:

- Click 🖭 Office Button and select Save As.
- Choose Excel workbook or Other Formats to open the Save As dialog box.
- Open the Save As Types drop-down list and select the file type.
- Specify a name for the file and location to save it.
- Click [Save].

or

- Click 🖭 Office Button and select Save As.
- Select Excel Workbook, Excel Template, PDF or XPS, or Excel 97-2003 Workbook. (The default file type in the Save As Type drop-down list will reflect the file type of your selection. You could still change it to any other type.)
- Specify a name for the file and location to save it.
- If necessary select the file type from the Save As Type list.
- Click [Save].

Workbooks also can be saved as macro-enabled. The purpose of a macro is to automate frequently used tasks. Although some macros are simply a recording of your keystrokes or mouse clicks, more powerful Visual Basic for Applications (VBA) macros are written by developers who use code that can run many commands on your computer. For this reason, VBA macros pose a potential security risk. A hacker can introduce a malicious macro through a document that, if opened, allows the macro to run and potentially spread a virus (virus: A computer program or macro that "infects" computer files by inserting copies of itself into those files. When the infected file is loaded into memory, the virus can infect other files. Viruses often have harmful side effects.) on your computer. See Excel Office Help for complete information about macro security.

If your workbook includes macros, it can be saved as macro-enabled following these steps:

- Click 🔘 Office Button and select Save As.
- Choose Excel Macro-Enabled Workbook to open the Save As dialog box.
- Open the Save As Type drop-down list and if necessary select the Excel Macro-Enabled Workbook file type.
- Specify a name for the file and location to save it.
- Click [Save] .

The workbook is saved with an .xlsm file extension.

Reference 1

Data File List

Open	Create/Save As
Lab 1	
ex01_Cafe Forecast1	Café Forecast
	Café Forecast1
Step-by-Step	
1. ex01_Animal Housing	Animal Housing Analysis
2. ex01_US Hurricanes	US Hurricanes Analysis
3. ex01_Family Income	Family Income
4. ex01_Publishing Salaries	Publishing Salaries2
5. ex01_Pecan Groves Budget	Pecan Groves Budget2
On Your Own	
1.	Calorie Tracking
2.	Personal Budget
3.	Project Hours
4.	Music Analysis
5.	Home Electronics Analysis
Lab 2	
Ex02_Cafe Sales	
Ex02_Internet Café.wmf	Café Sales Forecast
Step-by-Step	
1. ex02_Credit Data	Teens and Credit
ex02_Credit Card.bmp	
2. ex02_Music Download Analysis	Music Download Analysis
ex02_mp3 player.bmp	
3. ex02_Adoptions	Adoption Tracking
ex02_Pets.bmp	
4. ex02_Basketball.bmp	Youth Sports Data
ex02_Volleyball.bmp	
5. ex02_Computer Girl.bmp	Teen Online Activities
ex02_Computer Boy.bmp	
On Your Own	
1. ex02_Job Market	Seminar
2.	Grades
3.	Mutual Funds

Open	Create/Save As
4. ex02_Graduate School	Graduate School2
5.	Insurance

Lab 3

Open	Create/Save As
ex03_First Quarter Forecast	Forecast3
ex03_Annual Forecast	Café Forecast/Annual Forecast

Step-by-Step

Open	Create/Save As
1. ex03_Juice Bar	Juice Bar
2. ex03_Cookie Time	Cookie Time
3. ex03_Paris Tour	Tour Analysis/Paris Tour
4. ex03_Grade Report	Grade Analysis/Grade Report
5. ex03_Doggie Day Care	Doggie Day Care

On Your Own

Open	Create/Save As
1. Personal Budget (from Lab 1)	Personal Budget2
2.	Business/Company Expenses
3.	Housing/House Analysis
4.	Inventory Tracking
5.	My Business

Working Together 1

Open	Create/Save As
exwt1_Sales Forecast Memo.docx	Sales Forecast Memo.docx
exwt1_Sales Charts	Sales Forecast Linked
exwt1_Second Quarter Memo.docx	Second Quarter Memo.docx
exwt1_Second Quarter	

Step-by-Step

Open	Create/Save As
1. exwt1_Rescue Memo.docx	Rescue Memo Linked.docx
exwt1_Contributions	Contributions
2. exwt1_Tour Status Report.docx	March Status Report.docx
exwt1_Adventure Travel Status	Adventure Travel Status
3. exwt1_Home Price Memo.docx	Home Price Memo.docx
exwt1_Real Estate Prices	

Lab 4

Open	Create/Save As
ex04_Revised Annual Forecast	2008 Forecast
	Forecast Template
	2009 Forecast

Step-by-Step

Open	Create/Save As
1. ex04_IronWorks Income	IronWorks Income1
	IronWorks Income Template
2. ex04_Day Care	Doggie Day Care
3. ex04_Travel Analysis	Airlines Income Analysis
	Income Analysis Template
4. ex04_Cards and Gifts 2008	Cards and Gifts 2009
ex04_Cards and Gifts 2009	Cards and Gifts Analysis Template
5. ex04_ARF Contributions	ARF Contributions Reviewed
	ARF Analysis
	ARF Analysis Template

Open	Create/Save As
On Your Own	
1.	Video Game Projections
2.	Spring Break Analysis
3.	Expansion Projections
4.	Stock Analysis
5.	New Car Loan Loan Analysis Template

Lab 5

Open	Create/Save As
ex05_Loan Analysis ex05_Espresso Machines List ex05_Bonus Dollars	Loan Analysis March Bonus Dollars Monthly Bonus Dollars Monthly Bonus Form Monthly Bonus Analysis
Step-by-Step	
1. ex05_ARF Volunteers	Volunteers
2. ex05_ATT Sales	ATT Projected Sales ATT Projected Sales Form
3. ex05_Electronics Analyzer	Electronics Analyzer
4. ex05_Furniture Sales	Furniture Delivery Furniture Delivery Form
5. ex05_Grades	Gradebook Gradebook Form
On Your Own	
1.	Car Purchase Analysis Car Payment Analysis Template
2.	My 401K
3.	Furniture Loan Analysis Furniture Loan Analysis Template
4.	Speeding Fines Speeding Fines Template
5.	Laptop Computers Laptop Computer Template

Lab 6

Open	Create/Save As
ex06_Customer Table ex06_Customer Table2 ex06_Bonus Dollars	Customer Table Customer Table2
Step-by-Step	
1. ex06_LFC Employee List	LFC Analysis
2. ex06_Kodiak Jobs	Kodiak Jobs Update
3. ex06_Wilson Employees	Wilson Employee Rewards
4. ex06_ATT Client Table	ATT Client Table2
5. ex06_ARF Inventory	ARF Inventory

	Create/Save As
On Your Own	
1.	Bradford Suppliers
2.	Inventory
3.	Summer Baseball League
4.	Pet Sitting Customers
5.	CHB Inventory
Working Together 2	
exwt2_Cafe Supplies.accdb	Café Supplies
exwt2_Cafe Supplies	Coffee Orders
exwt2_Cafe Supplies Evan	March Bonus Dollars Web.html
exwt2_Cup	March Bonus Dollars Draft
exwt2_Draft	
exwt2_March Bonus Dollars Web	
Step-by-Step	
1. exwt2_Decorator's Resource Gallery	Artists Inventory
2. Wilson Employee Rewards (from Lab 6)	Wilson Employee Rewards.html
exwt2_Award	Wilson Employee Rewards

Reference 2

Microsoft Certified Applications Specialist (MCAS)

Microsoft Office Excel 2007

The Microsoft Certified Applications Specialist (MCAS) certification program is designed to measure your proficiency in performing basic tasks using the Office 2007 applications. Getting certified demonstrates that you have the skills and provides a valuable industry credential for employment.

After completing the labs in the Microsoft Office Excel 2007 Introductory edition, you have learned the following MCAS skills:

Skill/Description	Lab
1. Creating and Manipulating Data	
1.1 Insert data using AutoFill	Labs 1, 2, 3, 5
1.2 Ensure data integrity	Labs 5, 6
1.3 Modify cell contents and formats	Labs 1, 2, 3, More About
1.4 Change worksheet views	Labs 1, 2, 3, 4, Common Features
1.5 Manage worksheets	Labs 3, 4, More About
2. Formatting Data and Content	
2.1 Format worksheets	Labs 2, 3, Working Together 2
2.2 Insert and modify rows and columns	Labs 1, 4, 5, More About
2.3 Format cells and cell content	Labs 1, 2, 4, 5, 6, More About
2.4 Format data as a table	Lab 6
3. Creating and Modifying Formulas	
3.1 Reference data in formulas	Labs 1, 3, 4, 5, More About
3.2 Summarize data using a formula	Labs 1, 3, 5, More About
3.3 Summarize data using subtotals	Lab 6
3.4 Conditionally summarize data using a formula	Lab 5, More About
3.5 Look up data using a formula	Lab 5, More About
3.6 Use conditional logic in a formula	Lab 5, More About
3.7 Format or modify text using formulas	Lab 5, More About
3.8 Display and print formulas	Lab 1

ill/Description	Lab
4. Presenting Data Visually	
4.1 Create and format charts	Lab 2
4.2 Modify charts	Lab 2
4.3 Apply conditional formatting	Lab 3, More About
4.4 Insert and modify illustrations	Labs 2, 4, 5
4.5 Outline data	Lab 6
4.6 Sort and filter data	Lab 6
5. Collaborating and Securing Data	
5.1 Manage changes to workbooks	Labs 5, Working Together 2, More About
5.2 Protect and share workbooks	Lab 4
5.3 Prepare workbooks for distribution	Labs 2, 5
5.4 Save workbooks	Labs 1, 4, Working Together 2, More About
5.5 Set print options for printing data, worksheets, and workbooks	Labs 1, 2, 3

Reference 2: Microsoft Certified Applications Specialist (MCAS)

www.mhhe.com/oleary

Index

Q

Quick Access toolbar, EX1.5, EX1.87, EX3.73, I.11

R

Radar chart, EX2.19
Range, EX1.37
Range reference, EX1.37
Ready mode, EX1.6
Recalculation, EX1.54–EX1.55, EX2.49
Record, EX6.4
Redo, EX1.66
#REF!, EX3.6
Reference
    absolute, EX3.11–EX3.15
    external, EXWT1.4
    mixed, EX3.13
    range, EX1.37
    relative, EX1.46
    sheet, EX3.23
    3-D, EX3.23
Referencing multiple sheets, EX3.21–EX3.24
Relationship graphic, EX4.33
Relative link, EX6.58
Relative reference, EX1.46
Remove Duplicates dialog box, EX6.38
Renaming sheets, EX3.17–EX3.18
Replacing information, EX3.32–EX3.34
Report
    PivotChart, EX6.54–EX6.55
    PivotTable, EX6.50–EX6.54
    scenario, EX4.50–EX4.52
    Solver, EX4.9–EX4.10
    summary, EX6.49–EX6.50
Research information on Web, EX5.7–EX5.9
Research task pane, EX5.8
Research tool, EX5.7
Review tab, EX1.89
Ribbon, EX1.5, I.11, I.16–I.22
Rotate objects, EX5.19
Row, EX1.7
    insert, EX1.56–EX1.57
Row numbers, EX1.7
Row-oriented, EX5.10
Rules Manager, EX3.52–EX3.55

S

Sans serif fonts, EX1.62
Save
    template, EX4.19
    theme, EX2.13–EX2.14
    workbook, EX1.24–EX1.27
    workbook for use in previous edition of Excel, EXA.13
    workbook in other formats, EXA.14–EXA.15
    workbook using correct format, EXA.14
    worksheet as Web page, EXWT2.14–EXWT2.15
Save As command, EX1.24
Save As dialog box, EX1.25
Save-In drop-down list box, EX1.25
Scale to Fit group, EX3.74

Scale to fit group, EX2.74
Scaling, EX1.81
Scatter (XY) chart, EX2.19
Scenario, EX4.41–EX4.52
    create, EX4.42–EX4.48
    defined, EX4.42
    report, EX4.50–EX4.52
    show/edit, EX4.48–EX4.50
Scenario Manager dialog box, EX4.43
Scenario report, EX4.50–EX4.52
Scenario Summary report, EX4.51
Scenario Values dialog box, EX4.45
Scope, EX5.29
ScreenTip, I.13
Scroll bar, I.11
Select
    chart type, EX2.22–EX2.23
    data to chart, EX2.21–EX2.22
    range, EX1.36–EX1.38
Select Data Source dialog box, EX2.35
Select Place in Document dialog box, EX6.57
Selection cursor, I.12
Selection rectangle, EX2.7
Sensitivity report, EX4.10
Serial values, EX1.75
Series, filling a, EX3.19–EX3.21
Series formula, EX2.54
Serif fonts, EX1.62
Shape
    arrow, EX5.16–EX5.18
    delete, EX5.19
    rotate objects, EX5.19
    sizing elements, EX5.19
    SmartArt, EX4.34–EX4.35
    style, EX5.15
    text box, EX5.14
Shape style, EX2.57
Shape Styles feature, EX5.15
Shape Styles group, EX2.76
Share workbooks, EXA.12–EXA.13
Sheet. See also Worksheet
    active, EX1.8
    copying between sheets, EX3.16–EX3.17
    defined, EX1.7
    delete, EX3.28
    move, EX3.26–EX3.27
    multiple sheets, EX3.21–EX3.24
    rename, EX3.17–EX3.18
Sheet Options group, EX3.74
Sheet reference, EX3.23
Sheet tab scroll buttons, EX3.27
Sheet tabs, EX1.7, EX1.8
=Sheet1!A1 + Sheet2!B2, EX3.23
=Sheet2!B17, EX3.23
Shifting cells, EX4.53–EX4.54
Shortcut keys. See Command summary
Show/Hide group, EX3.75
Side handle, EX2.7
Signatures pane, EX5.58
Single data series chart, EX2.20
Size, EX1.62
Sizing
    chart, EX2.24
    elements, EX5.19
    graphic, EX2.7–EX2.8
Sizing handles, EX2.7

SmartArt graphic, EX4.32–EX4.41
    add shapes, EX4.34–EX4.35
    add text, EX4.35–EX4.36
    formatting, EX4.37–EX4.38
    graphic types, EX4.32
    unhide sheets/workbooks, EX4.38–EX4.41
SmartArt Style, EX4.37
Solver, EX4.5–EX4.9
Solver Parameters dialog box, EX4.7
Solver Results dialog box, EX4.9
Sort, EX6.22–EX6.29
    cell attributes, EX6.26–EX6.29
    multiple fields, EX6.24–EX6.26
    single field, EX6.23–EX6.24
Source, EX1.33
Source cell, EX4.25
Source file, EXWT1.4
Source program, EX2.5
Source workbook, EX4.25
Special cell formats, EX6.16–EX6.17
Spelling checker, EX1.28–EX1.31
Split cells, EXA.3
Split command, EX3.39
Split window, EX3.37–EX3.41
Splitting cell content, EX5.20–EX5.24
Spreadsheet. See Worksheet
Stack, EX2.24
Stacked-column chart, EX2.39
Standard Colors bar, EX1.71
Starting up, I.10–I.11
Statistics tab, EX2.61
Status bar, EX1.6, I.11
Stock chart, EX2.19
Stop alert, EX5.43
Strikethrough, EX1.64
Style
    cell, EX2.14–EX2.18
    chart, EX2.26–EX2.27
    shape, EX2.57
Styles group, EX2.74, EX3.73
Subscript, EX1.64
SUBSTITUTE, EX1.48, EXA.10
Subtotal, EX6.46–EX6.48
Subtotal dialog box, EX6.47
SUM, EX1.47
Sum button, EX1.50
=SUM(Sheet1!H6:K6), EX3.23
=SUM(Sheet1:Sheet4!H6:), EX3.23
=SUM(Sheet1:Sheet4!H6:K6), EX3.23
SUMIF, EXA.5
SUMIFS, EX4.5–EXA.6
Summarizing data, EX6.39–EX6.42
Summary report, EX6.49–EX6.50
Summary tab, EX2.61
Super tooltips, I.18
Superscript, EX1.64
Surface chart, EX2.19
Synonym, EX1.31
Syntax, EX1.47
System clipboard, EX1.33

T

Tab, I.11, I.17–I.18
Tab Color, EX3.19
Tab scroll buttons, EX1.8

Credits

ExcelLab1	Jules Frazier/Getty Images
ExcelLab2	RF/Corbis
ExcelLab3	Photomondo/Getty Images
ExcelLab4	Jack Star/PhotoLink/Getty Images
ExcelLab5	Getty Images
ExcelLab6	Steve Mason/Getty Images